Using SAS for Econometrics

Using SAS for Econometrics

R. CARTER HILL
Louisiana State University

RANDALL C. CAMPBELL
Mississippi State University

JOHN WILEY & SONS, INC
New York / Chichester / Weinheim / Brisbane / Singapore / Toronto

Carter Hill dedicates this work to Melissa Waters, his loving and very patient wife.

Randy Campbell dedicates this work to his wonderful wife Angie.

VICE PRESIDENT AND EXECUTIVE PUBLISHER	George Hoffman
PROJECT EDITOR	Jennifer Manias
ASSISTANT EDITOR	Emily McGee
PRODUCTION MANAGER	Micheline Frederick

This book was set in Times New Roman by the authors.

This book is printed on acid-free paper. ∞

The paper in this book was manufactured by a mill whose forest management programs include sustained yield harvesting of its timberlands. Sustained yield harvesting principles ensure that the numbers of trees cut each year does not exceed the amount of new growth.

ISBN 978-111-803209-1

10 9 8 7 6 5 4 3 2 1

PREFACE

SAS (www.sas.com) describes itself as "...the leader in business intelligence and predictive analytics software." Its users

- Include 96 of the top 100 companies on the 2006 Fortune Global 500 List.
- More than 43,000 business, government and university sites rely on SAS.
- Organizations in 113 different countries use SAS.

The wide use of SAS in business, government and education means that by learning to use SAS for econometrics, you will be adding a valuable skill whether your goal is a graduate degree or work in the private or public sector.

From the point of view of learning econometrics, SAS is very useful as it has powerful built-in commands for many types of analyses, superb graphics, and is a language in which users can construct specialized programs of their own.

Our goal is to provide the basics of using SAS for standard econometric analyses. *Using SAS for Econometrics* provides a relatively concise and easy to use reference. We provide clear and commented code, with the SAS output, which we have edited to as leave it recognizable, but including less spacing few headers than the actual output. The SAS data sets and complete program files used in this book can be found at

http://www.principlesofeconometrics.com/poe4/usingsas.htm

The programs in this book assume that the default SAS directory contains all the SAS files for data in *Principles of Econometrics, 4e* (Hill, Griffiths and Lim, 2011, John Wiley and Sons, Inc.)

There are a tremendous number of other resources available for learning SAS. Google "Learning SAS" and you will find more than one-half million hits. Appendix 1A is "A Guide to Using SAS Help and Online Documentation," which gives perspectives on SAS Help systems.

A supplement such as this is actually quite essential for use in a classroom environment, for those attempting to learn SAS, and for quick and useful reference. The SAS documentation comes in many volumes, and several are thousands of pages long. This makes for a very difficult challenge when getting started with SAS. The previously published *Learning SAS: A Computer Handbook for Econometrics* (Hill, John Wiley & Sons, 1993) is now difficult to obtain, and out of date.

The design of the book will be such that it is not tied exclusively to *Principles of Econometrics, 4e* (Hill, Griffiths and Lim, 2011, John Wiley and Sons, Inc.). It will follow the outline of *Principles of Econometrics, 4e*, and will use *Principles of Econometrics, 4e* data and empirical examples from the book, but we have included enough background material on econometrics so that instructors using other texts could easily use this manual as a supplement.

The volume spans several levels of econometrics. It will be suitable for undergraduate students who will use "canned" SAS statistical procedures, and for graduate students who will use advanced procedures as well as direct programming in SAS's matrix language, discussed in chapter appendices. Our general strategy has been to include material within the chapters that is accessible to undergraduate and or Masters students, with appendices to chapters devoted to more advanced materials and matrix programming.

Chapter 1 introduces elements of SAS. Chapters 2-4 discuss estimation and use of the simple linear regression model. Chapter 3's appendix introduces the concept of Monte Carlo experiments, and Monte Carlo experiments are used to study the properties of the least squares estimators and tests based on them in data generation processes with both normal and non-normal errors.

Chapters 5 and 6 discuss the multiple linear regression model: the estimators, tests and predictions. Chapter 5 appendices cover (A) a Monte Carlo experiment demonstrating the properties of the delta method; (B) an introduction to matrix and vector operations using SAS/IML and (C) SAS/IML code for the linear regression model and hypothesis testing. Chapter 7 deals with indicator variables, introduces the Chow test, the idea of a fixed effect and also treatment effect models.

Chapter 8 discusses heteroskedasticity, its effects on the least squares estimator, robust estimation of standard errors, testing for heteroskedasticity, modeling heteroskedasticity and the implementation of generalized least squares. There are four appendices to Chapter 8: (A) Monte Carlo experiments with heteroskedastic data, (B) two-step feasible GLS, (C) multiplicative heteroskedasticity and (D) maximum likelihood estimation of the multiplicative heteroskedasticity model. The last appendix covers aspects of numerical optimization calls from PROC IML.

Chapter 9 discusses dynamic models including finite distributed lags, autocorrelation and autoregressive distributed lag models. This is the introduction to time-series data and the focus is on stationary series, with an emphasis on testing, estimating and forecasting. Appendices to Chapter 9 include estimation using PROC ARIMA in 9A. Appendix 9B includes PROC IML code for generalized least squares estimation of an AR(1) error model.

Chapters 10 and 11 deal with random regressors and the failure of least squares estimation. Chapter 10 first introduces the use of instrumental variables with simulated data. The method for simulating the data is explained in Appendix 10A. The first section of Chapter 10 discusses tests of endogeneity and the validity of over identifying restrictions and the consequences of weak instruments. A second example uses Mroz's wage data for married women. Appendix 10B includes SAS/IML code for 2SLS including the Cragg-Donald statistic used for testing weak instruments, Appendix 10C uses a Monte Carlo experiment to examine the consequences of weak instruments, and Appendix 10D introduces robust 2SLS and the generalized method of moments. Chapter 11 introduces 2SLS and LIML estimation of simultaneous equations models, and only briefly mentions systems estimation methods. The appendix to Chapter 11 uses Monte Carlo experiments to study the properties of LIML and Fuller's modifications. SAS/IML code for the LIML estimator are included in this appendix.

Chapters 12-14 cover several topics involving time-series estimation with nonstationary data. Chapter 12 focuses on testing for unit roots and cointegration using Dickey-Fuller tests. Chapter 13 discusses estimation of vector error correction and vector autoregressive models. Chapter 14 focuses on macroeconomic and financial models with time varying volatility or conditional heteroskedasticity. This chapter introduces the ARCH and GARCH models as well as several extensions of these models.

Chapter 15 treats panel data models, including the pooled least squares estimator with cluster corrected standard errors, the fixed and random effects estimators, with some detailed explanation of the within transformation. The Breusch-Pagan test for random effects and the Hausman test for endogeneity are covered. Seemingly unrelated regressions are discussed and an example given. Chapter 15 appendices include SAS/IML code for pooled regression, the estimation details of variance components, robust fixed effects estimation and the Hausman-Taylor model. Chapter 16 covers the array of qualitative and limited dependent variable models, probit, logit, multinomial and conditional logit, ordered choice, count data models, tobit models and selectivity models. The appendix to Chapter 16 again takes the opportunity to cover maximum likelihood estimation, this time in the context of probit.

Following the book Chapters are two short Appendices, A and B, that serve as a reference for commonly used functions in SAS and probability distributions and random number generation. Appendix C is a pedagogic coverage of the estimation and hypothesis testing in the context of the model of the mean. Several sections outline the maximum likelihood estimation and inference methods in one parameter and two parameter models. Bill Greene kindly allowed us the use of his exponential and gamma distribution example for which we provide SAS/IML code.

The authors would like to especially thank Michelle Savolainen for careful comments, as well as Michael Rabbitt, Lee Adkins, Genevieve Briand and the LSU SAS workshop participants. A reader from the SAS Institute provided useful guidance on an early draft. Of course we could not have done this without the support of Bill Griffiths and Guay Lim, co-authors of *Principles of Econometrics, 4th Edition*.

R. Carter Hill
eohill@lsu.edu

Randall C. Campbell
rcampbell@cobilan.msstate.edu

September 1, 2011

BRIEF CONTENTS

CONTENTS

CHAPTER 1

Introducing SAS

1.1 THE SAS SYSTEM

Our goal is to provide the basics of using SAS for standard econometric analyses. *Using SAS for Econometrics* provides a relatively concise and easy to use reference. There are a tremendous number of other resources available for learning SAS. Google "Learning SAS" and you will find more than one-half million hits. Appendix 1A to this chapter is "A Guide to Using SAS Help and Online Documentation," which gives perspectives on SAS Help systems.

1.2 STARTING SAS

SAS can be started several ways. First, there may be shortcut on the desktop that you can double-click. For the SAS Version 9.2 it will look like

Earlier versions of SAS have a similar looking Icon. Alternatively, using the Windows menu, click the **Start > All Programs > SAS > SAS 9.2**.

1.3 THE OPENING DISPLAY

Once SAS is started a display will appear that contains windows titled

    Editor—this is where SAS commands are typed. There are actually two editors: an Enhanced Editor (automatically opened when SAS begins) and a Program Editor. Both serve the same purpose, but the Enhanced Editor offers automatic color coding and other nice features. In this book we **always** use the **Enhanced Editor**, so in any reference to Editor that is what we mean. To open one, or the other, click **View** on **menu bar**.

Log—record of commands, and error messages, appear here

Output—where SAS output will appear

Explorer & Results—sidebar tabs.

It should look something like Figure 1.1 on the following page. Across the top are SAS **pull-down menus**. We will explore the use of some of these. In the lower right-hand corner is the **current path** to a working directory where SAS saves graphs, data files, etc. We will change this in a moment.

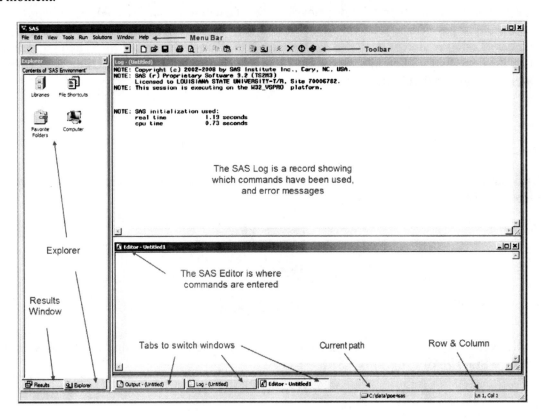

Figure 1.1 SAS 9.2 Opening Display

1.4 EXITING SAS

To end a SAS session click on **File**

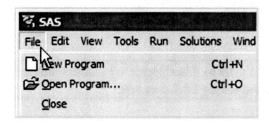

Select **Exit**

We will denote sequential clicking commands like this as **File > Exit**. Alternatively, simply click the "X" in the upper right-hand corner

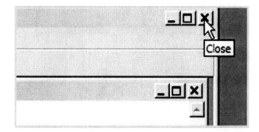

You will be asked if you are sure. Click **OK**.

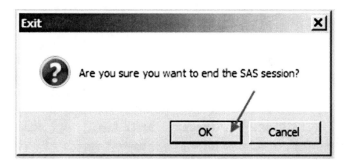

1.5 *USING PRINCIPLESOF ECONOMETRICS, 4E* DATA FILES

All of the data used in the book are provided as SAS data files, or **data sets**, for your use. These files are at http://www.principlesofeconometrics.com/poe4/poe4sas.htm, the website for the textbook *Principles of Econometrics, 4th Edition* (2011) by Hill, Griffiths and Lim, New York: John Wiley and Sons, Inc.

You can download individual data files, or the entire collection of SAS data files, to your computer or a "memory stick" with adequate storage. In this Windows-based book we will use the subdirectory **c:\data\poe4sas** for all our data and result files. **All of our programs assume that the *POE4* data are in the default directory.**

SAS data files have the extension ***.sas7bdat**. These files should not be opened with any program but SAS.

> **Remark:** In Appendix 1B to this Chapter we discuss methods of importing data into SAS, creating and saving SAS data sets.

1.5.1 Data definition files

Accompanying each SAS dataset is a **data definition file** with variable definitions and sources: http://www.principlesofeconometrics.com/poe4/poe4def.htm. These files have extension ***.def** and are simple **text files**. They can be opened using a utility like **Notepad**, or word processing software or a SAS Editor. For example, we will soon open the data file *food*. Open *food.def*.

There are 40 observations on individuals in this sample. It is **cross-sectional** data. The definition file includes:

1. the file name

2. the list of variables in the data file [food_exp, income, etc.]

3. the number of observations

4. a brief description of the variables

5. data summary statistics

```
food.def

food_exp income

  Obs:   40

  1. food_exp (y)              weekly food expenditure in $
  2. income   (x)              weekly income in $100

    Variable |     Obs      Mean    Std. Dev.      Min       Max
 ------------+-------------------------------------------------------
    food_exp |      40   283.5735   112.6752     109.71    587.66
      income |      40   19.60475   6.847773       3.69      33.4
```

1.6 A WORKING ENVIRONMENT

To change the working directory, or **current folder**, double-click the directory icon and use the resulting **Change Folder** window to select your directory.

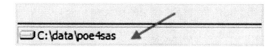

If you are working in a computer laboratory, you may want to have a storage device such as a "flash" or "travel" drive. These are large enough to hold the SAS data files, definition files and your class work. Make a subdirectory on the device. Calling it **x:\data\sas**, where **x:** is the path to your device, would be convenient.

Also, at this time
- Close the **Explorer** and the **Results** tabs. This is optional, but it reduces the clutter.

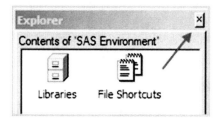

- Click inside the **Editor** window to make it active. The blue bar across the top should darken.
- Fully open the editor window by clicking the "maximize window" button

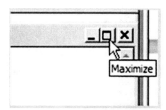

Your screen should now look like this.

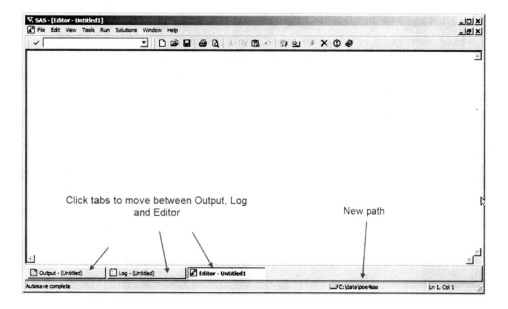

The new path is indicated at the bottom right of the screen.

1.7 SAS PROGRAM STRUCTURE

SAS programs are written in the **Editor** window. SAS programs consist of a set of **SAS statements**. There should be a beginning, the middle, and an end.

1. Beginning: Open (or create) a SAS data set and perhaps modify it, i.e., create new variables or data subsets.
2. Middle: Analyze the data using SAS procedures, or PROCs.
3. End: Save the output in a usable way. Save the SAS program code.

1.7.1 SAS comment statements

When writing a SAS program it is good practice to put **comments** in the program. This is very useful so that you can remember what you were doing, and it also helps others who are looking at your code. In SAS there are two types of comments. The first is a **comment statement**, which begins with an asterisk and ends with a semi-colon ";". Examples of comment statements (which show up in green in the SAS editor) are:

```
* this is a legal comment statement;

* a comment statement can stretch over one
  or more lines as long as it ends in a semi-colon;
```

A second type of comment statement begins with "/*" and ends with "*/".

```
/* the second type of comment looks like this */

/* this type of comment can also stretch over more
   than one line. It can be used to COMMENT OUT
   portions of code that you do not wish executed. */
```

Any commands that appear within this type of comment will not execute. Thus, including the following line in a SAS program will not cause anything to be executed.

```
/* proc print; run; */
```

Comment statements of the first type can be "nested" inside comments of the second type, but not vice versa.

```
/* this type of comment can include
   a *commment statement; */
```

We will make great use of comments in all of our programming examples.

1.7.2 Creating a SAS program

We will begin with a very simple example of a SAS program. In it we will read some data, and print the data. In this initial example we type data lines directly into the SAS program. Into the **Editor** window type the following lines:

```
data htwt;                               * name data set;
input name $ sex $ age height weight;    * specify variables;
x = height + weight;                     * define variable;
datalines;
alfred     M 14 69 112
alice      F 13 56  84
barbara    F 14 62 102
henry      M 15 67 135
john       M 16 70 165
sally      F 16 63 120
;
run;
```

In this book we have altered the SAS defaults so that SAS code and output appears in black & white. If using SAS with the default settings color is very important. For example, in the SAS **Editor** SAS commands appear dark blue, with other recognized terms in a lighter blue. [We have these in **bold**.] Data lines are shaded yellow. In the SAS **Log** "blue" generally means no errors have been identified, but "red" indicates that SAS has found a problem.

Let us examine these lines one by one. In each line, note that the following rule is obeyed.

All SAS statements, except data lines, end in a semi-colon ";" SAS statements can be written over several lines. The SAS statement does not end until a semi-colon is reached.

---

1. In the first line the keywords **data** *datasetname* tell SAS to construct an internal array, named *datasetname*, that will hold data lines on one or more variables. The array will have rows (different data lines) and columns (for variables). In this example we have named the data set "**HTWT**" because the entries will be heights and weights of individual teenagers. The *datasetname* should be short, with no spaces, and informative.

   ```
   data htwt;
   ```

2. In the second line **input** provides a list of names for the variables we will enter. The first two variables, **name** and **sex**, are in SAS terminology "Character" data. That is they consist of alphanumeric data instead of numeric data. The $ following these two names indicate this fact to SAS. The next 3 variables, **age**, **height** and **weight** are numeric.

   ```
   input name $ sex $ age height weight;
   ```

3. In the third line we define a new variable called **x**. When directly entering data as we are in this example, new variables are created just after the **input** statement. SAS has many mathematical and statistical functions that can be used in the variable creation process.

```
x = height + weight;
```

4. The fourth line **datalines** informs SAS that the following lines are data and not SAS statements.

```
datalines;
```

5. The next block of lines contains the data for this example. The first variable is the teen's name, then their sex indicated by **M** or **F**. Then follows their age (years), weight (pounds), and height (inches). These lines **do not** end with a semi-colon. However, at the end of the data lines there is a separate line with a semi-colon that serves to terminate the block of data lines.

```
alfred      M 14 69 112
alice       F 13 56  84
barbara     F 14 62 102
henry       M 15 67 135
john        M 16 70 165
sally       F 16 63 120
;
```

6. The **run** statement indicates the end of a set of program lines that will be executed at the same time.

```
run;
```

1.7.3 Saving a SAS program

Having entered the SAS code it is prudent to save it. Click **File/Save As** on the SAS menu.

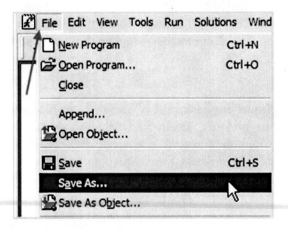

Enter a **File name** that will help you later recall its contents. The **Type** is ***.sas**.

Having saved it once, the key stroke **Ctrl + S** will re-save it after alterations are made, or select **File/Save** on the SAS menu. The file name now shows up in the Editor header.

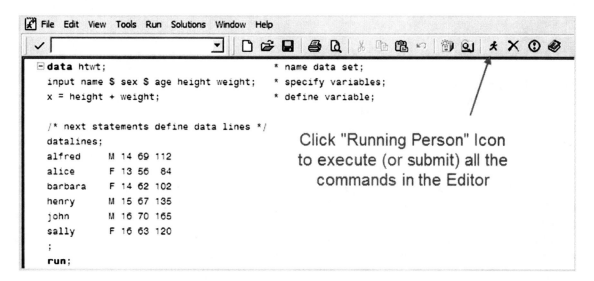

1.7.4 Running a SAS program

To **execute** (or **run**) all the commands in the Editor window click the **Running Person** on the toolbar.

Now examine the SAS **Log**. Check it first each time you execute some commands. Click the **Log** tab

The SAS **Log** shows the commands that have been executed and **Notes** about the execution. Here again the color of the messages is a good indicator. Comments that are **blue** are **good!**

In this case we have created a SAS data set called **WORK.HTWT**. In this two level name only the second part **HTWT** is relevant. The first part **WORK** refers to an organizational device that SAS calls a **Library**, which we are skipping for now. So, for practical purposes the name of the data set created is **HTWT**.

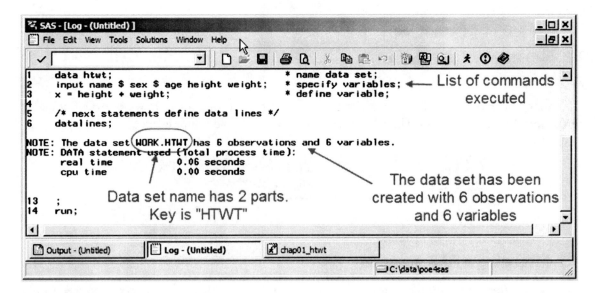

There is no **Output** created so far, but we will now **Print** the data set using the SAS **Print Procedure**.

1.7.5 Printing data with PROC PRINT

The SAS **Print Procedure** (known generally as **PROC PRINT**) writes a data file to the **Output** window. To our SAS program add the lines

```
proc print data=htwt;
run;
```

The statements will cause the data set **HTWT** to be written to the **Output** window. Note that altering the program file in the **Editor** changes the file name to **chap01_htwt.sas***. The asterisk reminds you that the file has not yet been saved.

In the SAS editor portions of code can be executed. This is very handy when building a SAS program. Each "block" of instructions can be tested without executing all the commands in the Editor window.

Highlight the two new lines, click **Submit**.

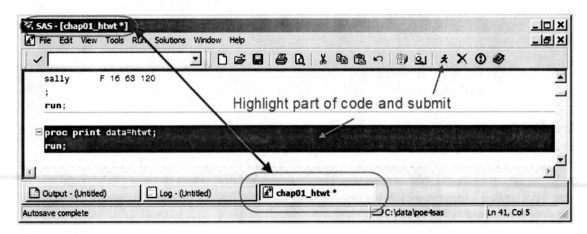

First we examine the SAS **Log**—click on the **Log** tab—and see that the **Print** procedure executed. No signs of an error, which is good.

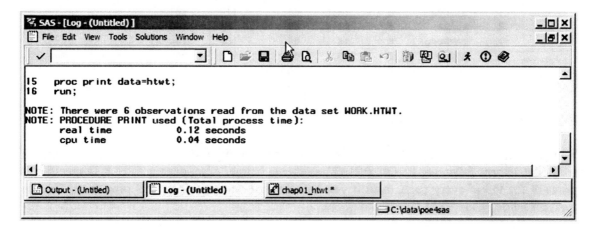

SAS automatically opens the **Output** window. Resist examining the output too closely until the **Log** is examined. The **Output** window shows the 6 observations on the original variables plus the variable **x** that we created.

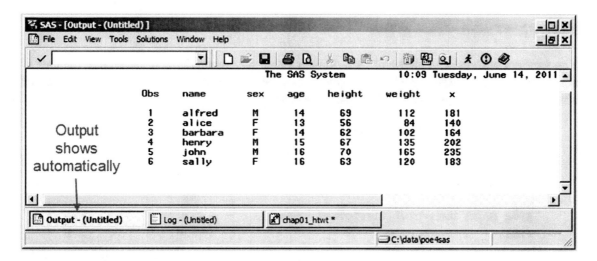

PROC PRINT data default

When the data set name is omitted in a SAS procedure command, then the **most recently created** data set is used. Thus to print the SAS data set **HTWT** (since it was created most recently) we could have used the command statement **PROC PRINT;** Also, we can add a title to the output by using a **TITLE** statement with the descriptive title in quotes. Execute the commands

```
proc print;
title 'Height-Weight Data';          * add title;
run;
```

Now we find the data array printed with a title.

```
                        Height-Weight Data

        Obs    name     sex    age    height    weight    x
         1     alfred    M      14      69       112      181
         2     alice     F      13      56        84      140
         3     barbara   F      14      62       102      164
         4     henry     M      15      67       135      202
         5     john      M      16      70       165      235
         6     sally     F      16      63       120      183
```

PROC PRINT selected variables

You may not wish to print all the variables in a data set. Specify the variables you wish to print in a **VAR** statement following **PROC PRINT**, as shown below. Also, once a **TITLE** is specified it prints at the top of every page, even if you have moved on to another SAS procedure. Thus to **turn off** a title, insert **TITLE;** with no quote.

```
proc print data=htwt;
var name sex age;                  * specify variable to print;
title;                             * turn title off;
run;
```

PROC PRINT selected observations

You may not wish to print all the observations in a data set, especially if it has a large number of observations. The **PROC PRINT** statement can be altered to print a specific number of observations. To print just the first 3 observations use

```
proc print data=htwt(obs=3);
run;
```

To print observations 2 to 4 use

```
proc print data=htwt(firstobs=2 obs=4);
run;
```

Now that we have output, what shall we do with it?

1.7.6 Saving SAS output

SAS allows output to be erased, saved, printed, copied and pasted. In the **Output** window these options are available with a few clicks.

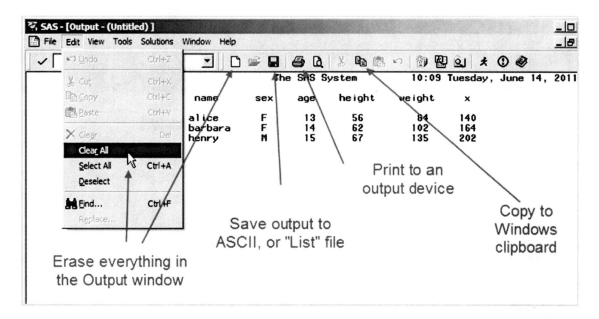

Clear all

The SAS **Output** window is "cumulative." It saves all the output from any and all procedures that have been submitted. This is good when creating a program and you are engaged in some trial and error. At the end of the process, however, we want the SAS program to have clean, clear, concise output. This can be accomplished by selecting **Clear All,** and then "running" the SAS program a final time. Instead of Clear All, click the **Blank Sheet** icon gives a new and empty window.

Save output contents to a file

When the contents of the **Output** window are to your liking, click the usual Windows "disk" icon.

This opens a dialog box so that you can save the output as a file. The SAS default is a **List File** which is a simple text file.

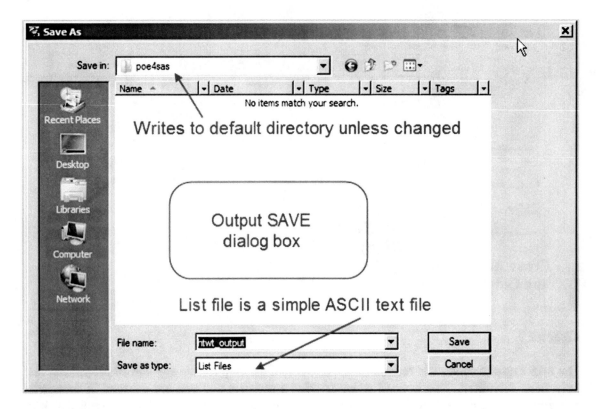

Print

Click on the Windows "printer" icon to obtain a hardcopy. **We recommend that you <u>never</u> do this.** The reason for this recommendation is that SAS includes many **page breaks** in the output, so that printing will use many sheets of paper. You should always edit the output before printing a hardcopy or for final presentation.

Copy and paste

To preserve important output import it into a word processor for further editing and simplification. This can be accomplished by saving the output contents to a **List** file and then opening it in your word processor, or by a **Copy/Paste** operation. On the **Output** window menu select **Edit > Select All** to highlight all the output. This can also be achieved using the key stroke **"Ctrl + A"**. This means press the "A" key while holding down the "**Ctrl**" key.

To choose just a portion of the output, highlight it (hold down left mouse button and drag), then press the Windows "copy" icon. This can also be achieved by using the keystroke **"Ctrl + C"**. Then switch to the word processor and in an open document paste the result using **"Ctrl + V"** or by clicking the "paste" icon, such as for Microsoft Word,

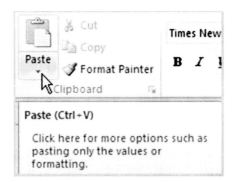

When you paste SAS output (or program code) into a document it may become ragged and messy. This results when your word processor assigns its default font (often Times New Roman) to your SAS code. To straighten everything up, highlight the SAS output or code, and change the font to "**Courier**" or "**SAS monospace**". You may have to reduce the font size and/or alter the margins it to fit neatly.

1.7.7 Opening SAS programs

In example above we entered the program directly into the Enhanced Editor. Previously saved programs can be open using **File > Open (Ctrl + O)**

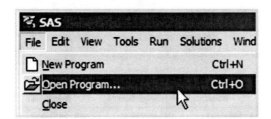

It is also very handy to note that SAS code from another source (a saved program, a sample program from SAS Help, or from an online sample) can be **copied and pasted** into the Editor.

1.8 SUMMARY STATISTICS USING PROC MEANS

In addition to examining the data using **PROC PRINT**, when beginning a new analysis it is always a good idea to obtain some simple summary statistics, to see if they make sense. When using large data sets, with thousands of lines, you will not inspect every single number. Summary statistics serve as a check. Finding that the minimum height of a teenager in a sample is 7.2 inches would lead you to suspect a typographical error (since the number is probably 72).

In the SAS program **chap01_htwt.sas** add the two lines

```
proc means data=htwt;
run;
```

PROC MEANS reports summary statistics for the data set **HTWT**. Highlight these two commands and click the **Submit** icon.

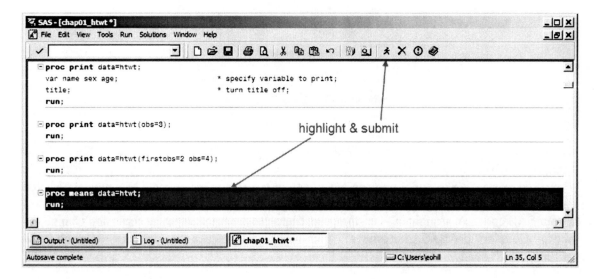

The SAS Display Manager switches to the **Output** window and shows the basic summary statistics provided by **PROC MEANS**: the number of sample observations "**N**", the sample mean (**Mean**), the sample standard deviation (**Std Dev**), the minimum value and the maximum value for the variable in question.[1]

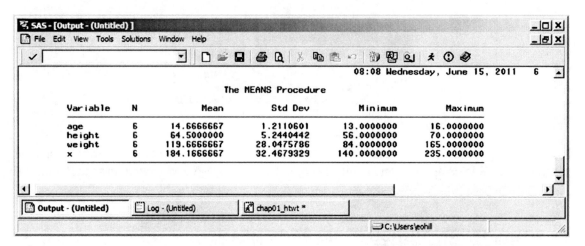

The variables "**name**" or "**sex**" have no summary statistics because they are alphanumeric, rather than numerical, variables. Also, SAS has reported a large number of decimal places for the summary statistics, which we may want to modify. All SAS procedures have many "options" for controlling what is reported and how it is reported.

Checking the SAS **Log** we find no errors.

---

[1] If you are rusty on the interpretation of mean and standard deviation, see Appendix B of this manual.

You may not want **PROC MEANS** to compute summary statistics for all variables in the data set. Use the **VAR option** after **PROC MEANS** to select variables. Also, **PROC MEANS** follows the rule that if no data set is specified, it operates on the most recently created SAS data set.

```
proc means;                           * on most recent data set;
var age height weight;                * specify variables;
run;
```

You also may not wish to report as many decimals as SAS does by default. Add the option **MAXDEC** to the **PROC MEANS** statement.

```
proc means data=htwt maxdec=3;        * set maximum decimals;
var age height weight;                * specify variables;
run;
```

The SAS output is now

```
                       The MEANS Procedure

    Variable    N        Mean      Std Dev     Minimum      Maximum
    ------------------------------------------------------------------
    age         6      14.667        1.211      13.000       16.000
    height      6      64.500        5.244      56.000       70.000
    weight      6     119.667       28.048      84.000      165.000
    ------------------------------------------------------------------
```

1.9 MAKING ERRORS IN SAS PROGRAMS

Errors in SAS programming are inevitable. SAS will not work as expected when there is an error and it is sometimes good at providing clues about the location of the error. Return to **chap01_htwt.sas** and **Save** what you have done so far.

1.9.1 Typing errors

Add the following two commands:

```
proc means data=hwtt;
run;
```

The name of the SAS data set has been misspelled. Highlight and submit these two commands. The first indication that something is wrong is that SAS does not immediately switch to the **Output** window. If you switch to the **Output** window you will find nothing new has been added. Examining the SAS **Log** we find **ERROR** (in **red** letters with default colors) which is never good. The error says **File WORK.HWTT.DATA does not exist.** The "**WORK**" identifies a SAS Library, a feature we have not discussed. The key is that **HWTT.DATA** does not exist.

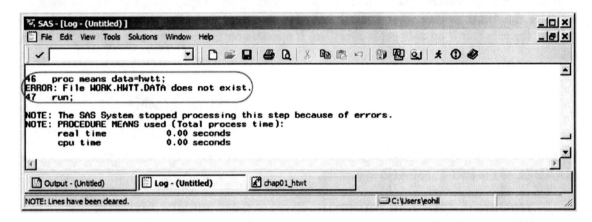

Typing errors are perhaps the most common type of error. Incorrect commands such as **PORC PRINT** or **PROC MEENS** will always "spell" disaster.

1.9.2 The SAS semi-colon ";"

The semi-colons in SAS statements are critical as they indicate that one command ends so that another can begin. We have been placing each SAS command on a separate line for easy reading, but as long as semi-colons are in the correct places, putting several commands on one line is OK.

```
proc means data=htwt; run;
```

It is also OK to put one command on several lines, which is handy for long commands.

```
proc means
data=htwt; run;
```

Execute following command, omitting the semi-colon after **htwt**

```
proc means data=htwt run;
```

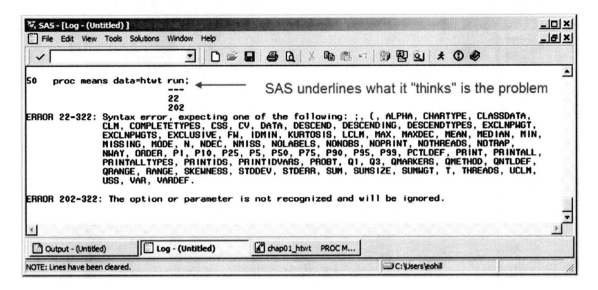

Examining the SAS **Log** you can judge that SAS is unhappy by the amount of **red** ink. It thinks that you think that "**run**" is an option of the **PROC MEANS** statement. Based on these clues you must find the error and correct it. This is not easy and it requires experience.

1.10 SAS GRAPHICS: A SCATTER DIAGRAM

SAS can produce brilliant graphics. Having "pictures" is very useful when analyzing data, because "a picture is worth a thousand words." Sayings such as this endure the ages because they are so true.

The first type of graphic tool we introduce is a **scatter diagram**. This is a plot in the "x-y" plane with the values of one variable on one axis and the values of another variable on the other axis. To illustrate we create a scatter diagram with "height" on the horizontal axis and "weight" on the vertical axis.

1.10.1 PROC PLOT

Computing graphics go back to the days when a computer filled a room, programs were on punch cards, and printers were gigantic machines that printed dots on accordion paper. For a crude plot, enter the commands

```
proc plot data=htwt;
plot weight*height;
run;
```

In the **Output** window you will find a rough diagram showing the plot.

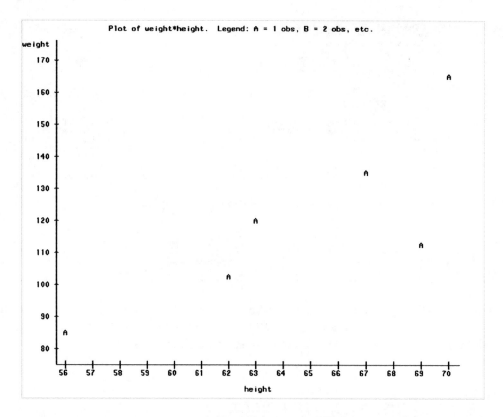

The second line of the command **plot weight*height;** identifies the order of the variables in the plot, with weight on the **vertical** (*Y*) **axis** and height on the **horizontal** (*X*) **axis**. While this plot is simple, it is in the **Output** window and thus part of a simple text file, which can sometimes be useful.

1.10.2 PROC GPLOT

A "publication quality" scatter plot is produced by the **GPLOT** procedure. Enter and submit the commands

```
symbol1 value=dot;
proc gplot data=htwt;
plot weight*height;
run;
```

PROC GPLOT produces output in a new window. To alter the appearance of the "dots" in the graph we used a **symbol** statement <u>prior</u> to issuing the **PROC GPLOT** command. The statement actually is **symboln** where **n** is a number from 1 to 255. When graphs have several plots each can have its own symbols. The resulting plot will now have "dots" that are filled circles, and we can clearly see that larger weights are associated with greater heights.

The difference between this graph and the previous graph is that this is a **graphics** image.

In this Graphics window, select **File > Export as Image** (or right-click on the graph).

This will open a dialog box from which you can choose a number of formats. The various export formats include:

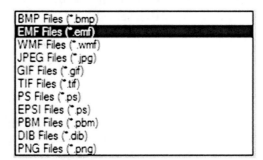

Click on your favorite **File type** and assign a **File name**, then click **Save** to save the image.

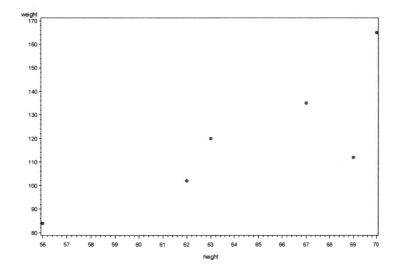

Alternatively, while in the **Graphics** window, simply click the "copy" icon and paste the figure into your document.

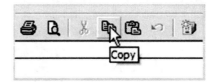

PROC GPLOT has many wonderful options. We demonstrate some as we proceed through the book.

1.11 CREATING OR MODIFYING DATA SETS

1.11.1 The SET statement

To create a new SAS data set from an existing one, or to modify an existing data set, use the **SET** statement. **SET** begins adding the content of an existing data set to a new one. Assume that the data set **HTWT** exists. Then to create a new data set called **HTWT2** use

```
data htwt2;                              * creates a new data set;
set htwt;                                * read HTWT;
/* more statements can go here */
run;
```

> **Remark:** SAS's **Memory** retains all data sets created during a SAS "session". The session lasts as long as SAS remains open. After you close a SAS session, everything stored in memory is deleted. The commands listed above assume that data set **HTWT** is in SAS's memory. If you closed SAS, and you are now coming back to it, re-run **chap01_htwt.sas** so that the data set will be recognized. Otherwise you will get an error message saying **ERROR: File WORK.HTWT.DATA does not exist.**

The data set **HTWT2** will contain all the variables that existed in **HTWT**.
To modify an existing data use

```
data htwt;                               * open HTWT;
set htwt;                                * read HTWT;
/* more statements can go here */
run;
```

1.11.2 Using DROP and KEEP

When creating a new data set using **SET** all the variables from the existing data set are included in the new one, plus any new variables you might create. If you do not want to keep all these variables you can use a **DROP** or **KEEP** statement.

For example, suppose you wish to create a new data set from **HTWT** including only **name** and **sex**. Then it would be convenient to use **KEEP**.

```
data htwt2;
set htwt;
keep name sex;                       * KEEP statement;
proc print data=htwt2;
run;
```

On the other hand, if you wished to delete **x**, **height** and **weight** (keeping only **name**, **sex** and **age**) you would use **DROP**.

```
data htwt2;
set htwt;
drop x height weight;                * DROP statement;
proc print data=htwt2;
run;
```

1.12 CREATING NEW VARIABLES

1.12.1 Arithmetic operators

The basic arithmetic operators are

Operator	Function	Priority
**	Exponentiation	1
-	Negation	2
*	Multiplication	3
/	Division	3
+	Addition	4
-	Subtraction	4

If there are several operations in one statement the order of operations is by their priority. Operations with equal priority are evaluated from left to right. It is best to control the order of operations using parentheses if there is any question. Items in parentheses are computed first, with innermost created before outermost.

To illustrate create a new data set called **ARITH** from **HTWT** and carry out some operations.

```
data arith;                          * new data set;
set htwt;                            * read HTWT;
sum = height + weight;               * sum;
diff = height - weight;              * difference;
prod = height * weight;              * product;
div = height / weight;               * division;
power = age**2;                      * age squared;
```

```
sqrt = age**.5;                    * power 1/2;
recip = age**-1;                   * power -1;
negage = -age;                     * minus age;
negage2 = -age*2;                  * minus age times 2;
```

When computing complicated expressions it is best to use **parentheses** to **control** the **order** of operation. Expressions in parentheses are evaluated first. If parentheses are nested then the innermost are computed first, then the outer ones. This is illustrated in the following statement, in which height and weight are summed, then the sum divided by age, with the result squared.

```
complex = ((height + weight)/age)**2;   * inner paren first;
run;

proc print data=arith;
var name age height weight sum diff prod div power sqrt recip
        negage negage2 complex;
run;
```

1.12.2 Comparison operators

Comparison operators evaluate expressions and return a one if it is true, but return a zero if it is false. The operator can be represented by a symbol or letter equivalent.

Symbol	Definition
= or EQ	Equal to
^= or NE	Not equal to
< or LT	Less than
> or GT	Greater than
>= or GE	Greater than or equal to
<= or LE	Less than or equal to

Create a new data set **COMPARE** from **HTWT**.

```
data compare;                      * new data set;
set htwt;                          * set HTWT;
female = (sex='F');                * equal;
```

The above definition makes **female** = 1 for females and **female** = 0 for males. Having numeric values for discrete variables is often more convenient than letters.

```
sixteen = (age=16);                * equal;
male = (female ^= 1);              * not equal;
older = (age >=16);                * greater than or equal;

proc print data=compare;
var name age female sixteen male older;
run;
```

1.12.3 Logical operators

The logical operator **AND** returns a 1 if two expressions linked together are both true and it returns a 0 if either statement is false. The logical operator **OR** returns a 1 either of the linked statements are true or if both are true, and it returns a 0 if both statements are false.

Create a new data set called **LOGICAL** from **COMPARE**.

```
data logical;                         * new data set;
set compare;                          * open COMPARE;
oldermale = (sex='M' and age>=16);    * use of AND;
oldrfem = (female=1 or older=1);      * use of OR;

proc print data=logical;
var name age oldermale oldrfem;
run;
```

1.12.4 Using SAS functions

SAS has many built in mathematical and statistical functions. We illustrate a few common ones here. Create a SAS data set **FUNCTION** from **ARITH**.

```
data function;                        * new data set;
set arith;                            * read ARITH;
lage = log(age);                      * natural log;
```

In statistics and econometrics any time a logarithm is used it is the **natural logarithm**. See Appendix A for a further discussion of the properties of the natural logarithm. In textbooks the natural log may be referred to as either $y = \log(x)$ or $y = \ln(x)$.

```
rootage = sqrt(age);                  * square root;
expage = exp(age/10);                 * exponential function;
```

The exponential function **exp** computes e^a which is sometimes denoted $\exp(a)$. If a is large the the value of the exponential function can get large, so in this illustration we scaled age by 10 before computing the exponential.

```
roundx = round(complex);              * round to nearest integer;
floorx = floor(complex);              * round down to integer;
ceilx = ceil(complex);                * round up to integer;
absx = abs(complex);                  * absolute value;

proc print data=function;
var name age complex lage rootage expage roundx floorx ceilx absx;
run;
```

1.12.5 Missing values

If you perform an illegal operation then SAS will return a missing value. This is denoted by a period "." in SAS. For example, let's take the logarithm of **female** which takes the values 1 and 0. the log(1) = 0, but the log(0) is undefined, so we will get a missing value.

```
data missing;                        * new data set;
set htwt;                            * read HTWT;
female = (sex = 'F');                * female;
lsex = log(female);                  * log female;
run;

proc print data=missing;
var name female lsex;
run;
```

The SAS **Log** tells us there is a problem, and even tells us the line and column where the problem might be. The notation **_N_=1** indicates that that this error is in the first observation or data line. The variable **_N_** is the observation number. This variable is always created by SAS when a data set is formed, and having it is very handy.

```
150   female = (sex = 'F');           * female;
151   lsex = log(female);             * log(0) is illegal;
152   run;

NOTE: Invalid argument to function LOG at line 151 column 8.
name=alfred sex=M age=14 height=69 weight=112 x=181 female=0 lsex=.
_ERROR_=1 _N_=1
```

The result of **PROC PRINT** is

Obs	name	female	lsex
1	alfred	0	.
2	alice	1	0
3	barbara	1	0
4	henry	0	.
5	john	0	.
6	sally	1	0

1.12.6 Using IF-THEN to recode variables

IF-THEN statements check a condition, and if it is true, then they do something else. If the statement is not true, then the statement is skipped. For example, we wish to create a new variable called **wtgrp** [values 1, 2, and 3] that indicates if **weight** is in a certain range [less than 110, 110 up to, but not including 130, and greater than or equal to 130]. When the **IF** part of the statement is true, the **THEN** part of the statement is executed.

```
data htwt2;
set htwt;
if weight < 110 then wtgrp = 1;
```

```
if 110 <= weight < 130 then wtgrp = 2;
if weight >= 130 then wtgrp = 3;

proc print data=htwt2;
var name weight wtgrp;
run;
```

The output shows the assignment of individuals to a group.

```
Obs     name      weight    wtgrp
 1      alfred      112        2
 2      alice        84        1
 3      barbara     102        1
 4      henry       135        3
 5      john        165        3
 6      sally       120        2
```

1.12.7 Creating a data subset

If you want to create a new data set containing just a subgroup of the original data use what SAS calls a **SUBSETTING IF** statement. This is really nothing more than using an **IF** statement with a **SET** statement. The **SET** statement starts reading the existing data set one observation at a time. When the **IF** statement is true, it retains the observation, otherwise the observation is discarded. Create a data set containing just males from **HTWT**.

```
data male;                          * new data set;
set htwt;                           * read HTWT;
if sex = 'M';                       * subsetting IF;

proc print data=male;
run;
```

```
Obs     name     sex    age    height    weight    x
 1      alfred    M      14       69        112     181
 2      henry     M      15       67        135     202
 3      john      M      16       70        165     235
```

1.12.8 Using SET to combine data sets

If two data sets have the same variables but different observations, they can be combined using a **SET** statement. Think of this as stacking one data set on top of another to create a new larger one.
Create a data set for females.

```
data female;
set htwt;
if sex = 'F';
```

Now combine the data sets **MALE** and **FEMALE** into a new data set including all the observations on both.

```
data all;
set male female;                        * Use SET to combine;

proc print data=all;
run;
```

1.13 USING SET TO OPEN SAS DATA SETS

Using SAS for Econometrics uses data from *Principles of Econometrics, 4th Edition,* by Hill, Griffiths and Lim (2011). The book data have been converted into permanent SAS data sets by the book authors. The website is http://principlesofeconometrics.com/poe4/poe4.htm. Use the link for **SAS data sets**. There you can download individual files, or all the book data files in ZIP format. These permanent SAS data sets carry the extension ***.sas7bdat**. The beauty of using these data sets is that they include variable names, and labels for the variables. Such data files are easily opened using a **SET** statement. All we must do is put the **path** to the new data set in single or double quotations in the **SET** statement. To open the SAS data set **food.sas7bdat**, assuming your default SAS directory points to location of the SAS data sets, use

```
data food;                              * new data set;
set "food";                             * read sas dataset;
```

Then, to view all sorts of information about this data set use **PROC CONTENTS**. In the command below we specify that we wish to see the contents of the data set **FOOD** and use the option **POSITION** which will show us the order of the variables in the original data set, as well as in alphabetical order.

```
proc contents data=food position;       * examine contents;
```

The output includes much technical information, but also the following:

```
                    The CONTENTS Procedure
```

Data Set Name	WORK.FOOD	Observations	40
Member Type	DATA	Variables	2

[some items deleted]

```
             Alphabetic List of Variables and Attributes
```

#	Variable	Type	Len	Label
1	food_exp	Num	8	household food expenditure per week
2	income	Num	8	weekly household income

```
                 Variables in Creation Order
```

#	Variable	Type	Len	Label
1	food_exp	Num	8	household food expenditure per week
2	income	Num	8	weekly household income

In this case the alphabetical listing of the variables is the same as the creation order. We find that there are two variables, 40 observations, and the variables are weekly food expenditure and weekly income. The labels are nice to have for some presentations when data are unfamiliar.

Use **PROC MEANS** to obtain the summary statistics

```
proc means data=food;                    * summary statistics;
run;
```

The output is

```
                    The MEANS Procedure

Variable  Label                              N         Mean       Std Dev
──────────────────────────────────────────────────────────────────────────
food_exp  household food expenditure per week 40  283.5735000   112.6751810
income    weekly household income             40   19.6047500     6.8477726


   Variable  Label                               Minimum       Maximum
──────────────────────────────────────────────────────────────────────────
   food_exp  household food expenditure per week 109.7100000   587.6600000
   income    weekly household income               3.6900000    33.4000000
```

SAS had to wrap the output onto a second tier to fit because the labels take up room.

1.13.1 Using SAS system options

The labels can be turned off and on using an **OPTIONS** statement. To suppress the labels in printed output use

```
options nolabel;                         * turn labels off;
proc means data=food;                    * summary stats nolabels;
run;
```

The **options** stay in effect until changed, or until SAS is restarted. The output with no labels is

```
                    The MEANS Procedure

   Variable    N         Mean       Std Dev      Minimum       Maximum
──────────────────────────────────────────────────────────────────────────
   food_exp   40   283.5735000   112.6751810   109.7100000   587.6600000
   income     40    19.6047500     6.8477726     3.6900000    33.4000000
```

To turn the labels back on use

```
options label;                           * turn labels on;
proc means data=food;                    * summary stats & labels;
run;
```

Examine the first line of the program **chap01.sas**[2] listed at the end of the chapter. This is a list of all the commands used in this chapter. Our first line is

```
options nodate nonumber linesize=78;
```

These options tell SAS not to print the date at the top of each page, not to print a page number at the top of each page, and to use a line size of 78 characters when printing.

1.13.2 Adding labels

The data set **HTWT** we have created does not include labels, however they are easily added in a DATA STEP. Open the data set **HTWT**

```
data htwt2;
set htwt;
```

The label statement assigns a label to each variable in one long SAS statement. Note that the labels do NOT have semi-colons after each, only at the end of the statement.

```
label name = 'teenager name'
      sex = 'teen gender'
      age = 'age in years'
      height = 'height in inches'
      weight = 'weight in pounds';
```

Rather than labeling **x**, we drop it, and then compute summary statistic using the **MAXDEC** option.

```
drop x;                          * drop x from data set;
proc means data=htwt2 maxdec=3;  * summary stats with labels;
run;
```

The labels now appear in **PROC MEANS** output.

Variable	Label	N	Mean	Std Dev	Minimum
age	age in years	6	14.667	1.211	13.000
height	height in inches	6	64.500	5.244	56.000
weight	weight in pounds	6	119.667	28.048	84.000

Variable	Label	Maximum
age	age in years	16.000
height	height in inches	70.000
weight	weight in pounds	165.000

---

[2] SAS files for each chapter can be found at www.principlesofeconometrics.com/UsingSAS.htm.

1.14 USING PROC SORT

Sorting data means to arrange the observations in either **ascending** or **descending** order, according to the magnitude of one or more variables. For example, sort the data according to sex. The sorting variable is indicted using a **BY** statement. Here "F" is lower in the alphabet than "M", and **PROC SORT** carries out the sorting in **ascending order by default**, so we find the data for females listed first, then males.

```
proc sort data=htwt;              * sorted data;
by sex;                           * sorting variable;

proc print data=htwt;
run;
```

```
Obs     name     sex     age    height    weight     x
 1      alice     F       13      56        84       140
 2      barbara   F       14      62       102       164
 3      sally     F       16      63       120       183
 4      alfred    M       14      69       112       181
 5      henry     M       15      67       135       202
 6      john      M       16      70       165       235
```

1.14.1 PROC PRINT with BY

Once the data are sorted, it is possible to use **PROC PRINT** and **PROC MEANS** with a **BY SEX** statement to have reports separately for males and females. Execute the following code.

```
proc print data=htwt;
by sex;
run;
```

The output is now organized by **F** and **M**.

```
-------------------------------- sex=F --------------------------------------

        Obs     name     age    height    weight     x
         1      alice     13      56        84       140
         2      barbara   14      62       102       164
         3      sally     16      63       120       183


-------------------------------- sex=M --------------------------------------

        Obs     name     age    height    weight     x
         4      alfred    14      69       112       181
         5      henry     15      67       135       202
         6      john      16      70       165       235
```

1.14.2 PROC MEANS with BY

PROC MEANS can also be used with the **BY** statement.

```
proc means data=htwt;
by sex;
run;
```

```
------------------------------- sex=F -----------------------------------
```

The MEANS Procedure

Variable	N	Mean	Std Dev	Minimum	Maximum
age	3	14.3333333	1.5275252	13.0000000	16.0000000
height	3	60.3333333	3.7859389	56.0000000	63.0000000
weight	3	102.0000000	18.0000000	84.0000000	120.0000000
x	3	162.3333333	21.5483951	140.0000000	183.0000000

```
------------------------------- sex=M -----------------------------------
```

Variable	N	Mean	Std Dev	Minimum	Maximum
age	3	15.0000000	1.0000000	14.0000000	16.0000000
height	3	68.6666667	1.5275252	67.0000000	70.0000000
weight	3	137.3333333	26.5769324	112.0000000	165.0000000
x	3	206.0000000	27.2213152	181.0000000	235.0000000

1.14.3 PROC SORT on two variables

Data can then be sorted on a secondary factor with an expanded **BY** statement. Here we sort first on **sex** and then on **height**. Females will be listed first, in order of their height, then males, according to their height.

```
proc sort data=htwt;
by sex height;                          * sorting variables;

proc print data=htwt;
run;
```

Obs	name	sex	age	height	weight	x
1	alice	F	13	56	84	140
2	barbara	F	14	62	102	164
3	sally	F	16	63	120	183
4	henry	M	15	67	135	202
5	alfred	M	14	69	112	181
6	john	M	16	70	165	235

1.14.4 Sort in descending order

If we wished to first sort on **sex** and then on **height**, but in **descending** order of **height**, add the option **descending** before **height**.

```
proc sort data=htwt;
by sex descending height;

proc print data=htwt;
run;
```

1.15 MERGING DATA SETS

In Section 1.12.8 we used the **SET** statement to combine two data sets with the same variables, but with different observations. We described that action as "stacking" one data set on top of another. Now we will **MERGE** two (or more) data sets with different variables. This is more or less like stacking the data sets side-by-side.

Let us put the data set **HTWT** back into its original alphabetical order, using **PROC SORT** and sorting by **name**.

```
proc sort data=htwt;              * put into original order;
by name;                          * sort by name;
run;
```

When merging data sets it is a very good idea to have one variable in each data set that serves as a **matching** variable. Create a data set from **HTWT** and create a new variable **ID** that is equal to the observation number. In this case the **ID** will represent alphabetical order.

```
data htwt2;                       * new data set;
set htwt;                         * read HTWT;
id = _N_;                         * create id variable;
proc print data=htwt2;
run;
```

Obs	name	sex	age	height	weight	x	id
1	alfred	M	14	69	112	181	1
2	alice	F	13	56	84	140	2
3	barbara	F	14	62	102	164	3
4	henry	M	15	67	135	202	4
5	john	M	16	70	165	235	5
6	sally	F	16	63	120	183	6

Assume we have given the students a test and recorded their **ID** number and test score. Create a data set with these two variables.

```
data test;                        * data sorted on score;
input id score;                   * input id and score;
datalines;
```

```
6 99
4 92
5 88
3 82
1 72
2 69
;
```

Before merging this new data set with **HTWT** we must sort it according to the **matching** variable, in this case **ID**.

```
proc sort data=test;                    * sort data ascending order;
by id;                                  * sort on variable id;
proc print data=test;
run;
```

```
Obs     id     score
 1       1       72
 2       2       69
 3       3       82
 4       4       92
 5       5       88
 6       6       99
```

Now create a new data set, or modify an existing one, by merging the two data sets using the **BY** statement to identify the matching variable.

```
data test;
merge test htwt2;                        * merge combines data sets;
by id;                                   * BY indicates match variable;
proc print data=test;
run;
```

The students and their scores are now correctly matched.

Obs	id	score	name	sex	age	height	weight	x
1	1	72	alfred	M	14	69	112	181
2	2	69	alice	F	13	56	84	140
3	3	82	barbara	F	14	62	102	164
4	4	92	henry	M	15	67	135	202
5	5	88	john	M	16	70	165	235
6	6	99	sally	F	16	63	120	183

APPENDIX 1A A GUIDE TO SAS HELP AND ONLINE DOCUMENTATION

There is no better documentation for software than that provided by SAS. It is vast, detailed and readily available. In this appendix we provide an overview of Help resources.

1A.1 SAS command line

The SAS command line is below the **Menu Bar**. Here you can enter a request for help on a particular keyword.

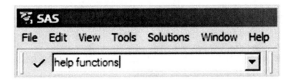

This opens SAS help and displays topics found. Select one and click **Display**.

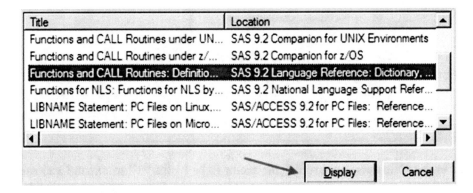

As you become more familiar with SAS the search can be made more efficient by seeking help on a particular item, like the SAS function "RAND," which is used to generate random numbers.

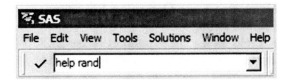

1A.2 SAS help

Using this window

While SAS is running, help is but a click away. On the **Menu Bar** select **Help**.

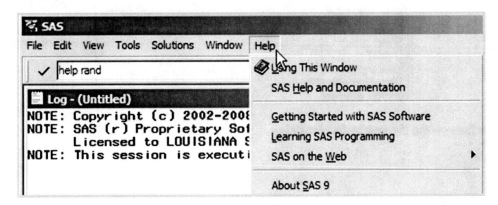

The first item **Using this Window** has help on the SAS Editor, SAS Log or Output, depending on which window you are currently in. If the SAS Editor window is selected, then **Help** displays on the right links to tips on using the Enhanced Editor.

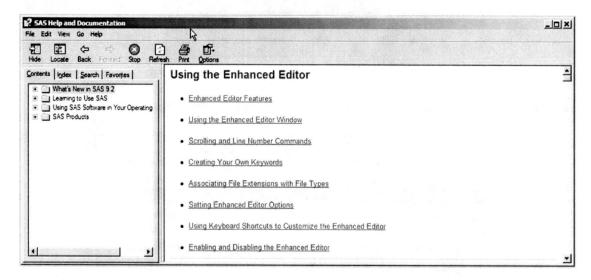

On the left, under **Contents**, are expandable menu links (plus "+" to expand and minus "−" to reduce) to

- **What's New in SAS 9.2**. See what additions have been made in Version 9.2.
- **Learning to Use SAS**. See Sample SAS programs, the SAS e-Learning programs, a SAS tutorial and Accessing Help from a Command Line.
- **Using SAS Software in Your Operating Environment**. Tips on using SAS under Windows, UNIX, and so on.
- **SAS Products**. Links to the SAS products (Base SAS, SAS/ETS, etc.) and to each Procedure. These help files are comparable to the HTML link in Figure 1A.1.

Select the **Index** tab. Type a **keyword** to find potential sources of help

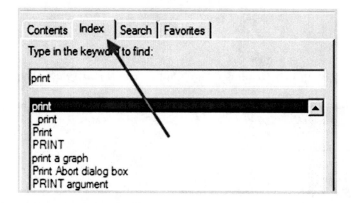

Select an item on the list that looks promising

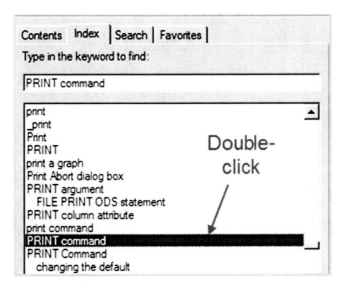

Double click on a heading. This may produce a dialog box from which you can choose again. Highlight and select **Display**.

Getting started with SAS software

Under **Help** select the item **Getting Started with SAS Software**.

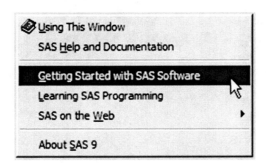

Select **New SAS Programmer (quick start guide)**, then **Go**. There you will find slide show presentations. Spend some time on **Getting to Know SAS** to learn about SAS data sets and libraries.

1A.3 SAS online documentation

The SAS support website provides extensive documentation

http://support.sas.com/documentation/index.html

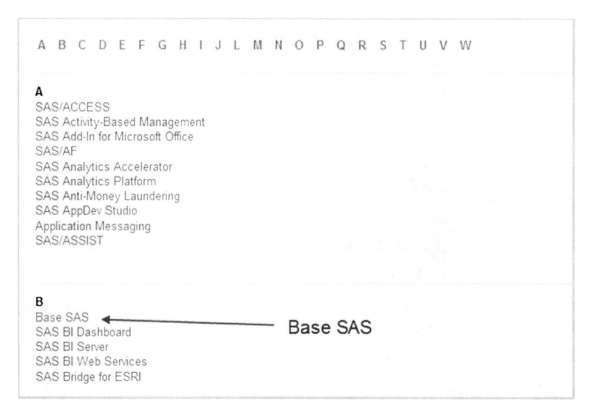

Select **Base SAS**. Here you will find a convenient layout. You can download a large PDF file with the complete set of Base SAS Procedures (PROCs). The HTML link is

http://support.sas.com/documentation/cdl/en/proc/61895/PDF/default/proc.pdf

Figure 1A.1

Select the **HTML** link.

Expand the **Procedures** link. Base SAS includes **many** procedures. Scroll down to **The MEANS Procedure**.

You will find links for various syntax elements and examples. The code in the examples can be copied and pasted into the SAS Editor so that you can run them yourself, and later perhaps make use of the code.

Return to the Base SAS home as shown in Figure 1A.1. Select **SAS 9.2 Procedures by Name and Product**.

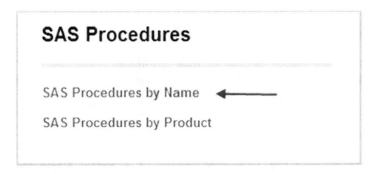

Select **SAS Procedures by Name**. The procedures used in this book include:

Procedure Name	Location of Procedure Documentation
ARIMA	SAS/ETS User's Guide
AUTOREG	SAS/ETS User's Guide
CONTENTS	Base SAS Procedures Guide
CORR	Base SAS Procedures Guide: Statistical Procedures
FORECAST	SAS/ETS User's Guide
IML	SAS/IML User's Guide
MDC	SAS/ETS User's Guide
MEANS	Base SAS Procedures Guide
MODEL	SAS/ETS User's Guide
PANEL	SAS/ETS User's Guide

PRINT	Base SAS Procedures Guide
PROBIT	SAS/STAT User's Guide
QLIM	SAS/ETS User's Guide
REG	SAS/STAT User's Guide
SGPLOT	SAS/GRAPH: Statistical Graphics Procedures Guide
SORT	Base SAS Procedures Guide
SYSLIN	SAS/ETS User's Guide
TIMESERIES	SAS/ETS User's Guide
TTEST	SAS/STAT User's Guide
UNIVARIATE	Base SAS Procedures Guide: Statistical Procedures
VARMAX	SAS/ETS User's Guide

Each of these SAS procedures has a home page like that for Base SAS in Figure 1A.1.

1A.4 SAS online examples

The SAS website

http://support.sas.com/documentation/onlinedoc/code.samples.html

lists sample code and data from books published by the SAS Press and in SAS Documentation. Select one. The text content can be copied and pasted into the SAS Editor and executed. The examples are from a variety of different academic fields and there is code for both SAS beginners and experts.

1A.5 Other resources

Use your favorite internet search engine to seek additional resources. The usual disclaimers should apply about "whom to trust." One excellent learning site is provided by the Statistical Consulting Group, UCLA Academic Technology Services.

http://www.ats.ucla.edu/stat/sas/

Begin with the **SAS Starter Kit**, shown in Figure 1A.2. Select **Class Notes with Movies**. Explore the **Learning Modules** for practical examples of basic tasks.

Figure 1A.2 SAS at UCLA Academic Technology Services

APPENDIX 1B IMPORTING DATA INTO SAS

In this appendix we illustrate reading external data files, saving SAS data sets, and importing data from a spreadsheet or other data format. Begin a new SAS session for this appendix.

1B.1 Reading ASCII data

As illustrated in Chapter 1.7.2 data can be embedded into the SAS program. This is a useful way to provide examples, and much sample SAS code is structured this way. The data can be arranged in many different ways and yet be successfully read by SAS. In particular, the sample data do not require strict column alignment.

```
data htwt;
input name $ sex $ age height weight;
datalines;
alfred M 14 69 112
alice F 13 56  84
barbara F 14 62 102
henry M 15 67 135
john M 16 70 165
sally F 16 63 120
```

```
;
run;
```

To learn about various data input options, and see examples, enter into the command line **help input**.

1B.2 Reading an external ASCII file

If the amount of data is too large to include into the program, data can be read from an external ASCII file. As an example, we use the data file *brumm.dat* from

http://www.principlesofeconometrics.com/poe4/poe4dat.htm

Corresponding to each data file is a "definition" file containing information about the data. The definition file *brumm.def* can be found at

http://www.principlesofeconometrics.com/poe4/poe4def.htm

The (edited) definition file is a text file with the contents shown below.

```
brumm.def

money inflat output initial poprate inv school

  Obs:   76 countries

  1. money = growth rate of money supply = change ln(m)
  2. inflat = growth rate of prices = change ln(p)
  3. output = growth rate of output = change ln(q)
  4. initial = initial level of GDP per capita
  5. poprate = average population growth rate
  6. inv = average investment share of GDP
  7. school = a measure of the population's educational attainment
```

The second line contains the order of the variables in the data file. This is essential information when reading an external ASCII data file. In the code below
- The first line creates a new working SAS dataset called BRUMM.
- The second line, the **INFILE** statement, identifies the location of the file on your computer or storage device. The path name is enclosed in quotes.
- The **INPUT** statement names the variables, and we have provided more informative identifiers for these variables.
- Use the **LABEL** statement to attach variable descriptions.

```
data brumm;
infile 'brumm.dat';
input money inflation growth initial poprate inv school;
```

```
label money = 'growth rate of money supply'
      inflation = 'growth rate of prices'
      growth = 'growth rate of output'
      initial = 'initial level of GDP per capita'
      poprate = 'average population growth rate'
      inv = 'average investment share of GDP'
      school = 'educational attainment';
run;
```

The SAS Log shows

```
NOTE: The infile 'c:\data\poe4\ascii\brumm.dat' is:
      Filename=c:\data\poe4\ascii\brumm.dat,
      RECFM=V,LRECL=256,File Size (bytes)=6004,
      Last Modified=01Jul2010:12:10:22,
      Create Time=07Oct2010:12:23:06

NOTE: 76 records were read from the infile 'c:\data\poe4\ascii\brumm.dat'.
      The minimum record length was 77.
      The maximum record length was 77.
NOTE: The data set WORK.BRUMM has 76 observations and 7 variables.
```

There is some technical information about the file *brumm.dat*. The final line identifies the data set WORK.BRUMM. The WORK designation identifies the SAS Library containing the data. We will explore this further in the next section.

> **Remark:** The default **infile** record length is 256 characters. If you are working with a wide ASCII data file the maximum record length can be specified using the additional option **LRECL=** . To read an ascii file called *gpa.raw* with 270 characters per line of data, use
>
> ```
> infile 'gpa.raw' lrecl=270;
> ```

Use **PROC CONTENTS** to examine the contents of the SAS data set BRUMM. If the labels do not appear remember to have them turned on with **options label;**

```
proc contents data=brumm position;
run;
```

Examining the SAS data set

SAS data sets are automatically placed in the WORK Library when first created. Enter **help library** into the command line,

From the topics returned choose **SAS Libraries**.

Title	Location
Invoking SAS/INSIGHT Software	SAS Documentation
Opening a Data Window	SAS Documentation
Reading and Writing Data: Using the G...	SAS Stat Studio for SAS/STAT Users
Reading and Writing Data: Using the G...	SAS/IML Studio for SAS/STAT Users
SAS Libraries	Base SAS Help

To examine the WORK Library, use SAS Explorer. In Figure 1.1 Explorer is indicated by a tab in the left-hand panel. If the Explorer tab is not shown (you may have closed it), on the **Menu Bar** select **View**, then select **Explorer**.

Using the Explorer tab, we see several "file cabinet" icons, which represent SAS Active Libraries. Double-click the **Libraries** icon.

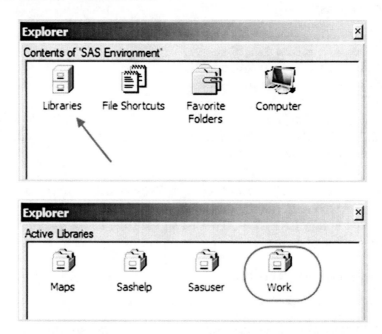

Double click on **Work**. The Work Library contents from the current session are

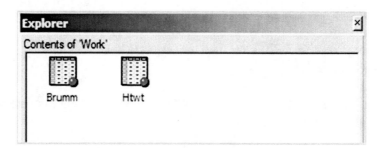

The icons represent SAS datasets named BRUMM and HTWT.

Double click on the BRUMM icon. A spreadsheet is shown with the data and variable names and labels. A portion is shown below.

	growth rate of money supply	growth rate of prices	growth rate of output	initial level of GDP per capita	average population growth rate	average investment share of GDP	educational attainment
1	356.7	374.3	0.8	3.091	1.4	0.1819	1.06
2	11.5	6.1	3.1	5.182	1.5	0.2447	0.98
3	7.3	3.6	2.3	3.908	0.3	0.2563	1.04
4	18	8.6	4.2	0.444	2.1	0.1199	0.61
5	6.3	1.4	2.7	0.595	3	0.1814	0.4
6	207.1	187.1	1.1	0.882	2.1	0.1708	0.68
7	25.2	12.3	9.6	0.493	3.4	0.3738	0.65

In this format the contents of WORK.BRUMM is displayed. Scroll across the **Menu Bar** to identify the options.

Select the **Help** icon to read more about VIEWTABLE. Click **x** in the upper right-hand corner of VIEWTABLE to close it.

Saving the SAS data set

Once the working dataset has been modified and judged correct, it can be saved as a permanent SAS dataset. In the lines below the **DATA** statement defines the path to the new SAS dataset BRUMMDATA. The **SET** statement, described in Chapter 1.11.1, is used to read the data line by line into the new data set BRUMM.

```
data 'brummdata';
set brumm;
run;
```

After these statements are run, we find BRUMMDATA.SAS7BDAT, which is a SAS data set, in the subdirectory we have specified.

Creating a SAS library

When SAS is closed the contents of the Library WORK are lost. It is convenient to have your SAS datasets available to SAS Explorer. To do this, create a Library linked to the subdirectory c:\data\poe4sas. Click inside the SAS Explorer window. Navigate up one directory level.

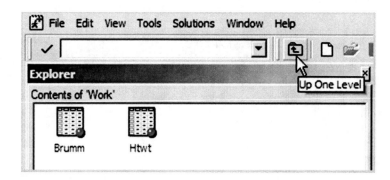

In the Explorer window, select the "NEW" icon.

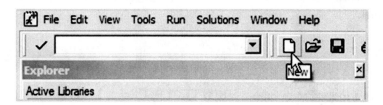

In the dialog box for a New Library fill in the **Name:** and **Path:** and check the box to **Enable at startup**. By doing so the Library will open when SAS is started. Then select **OK**.

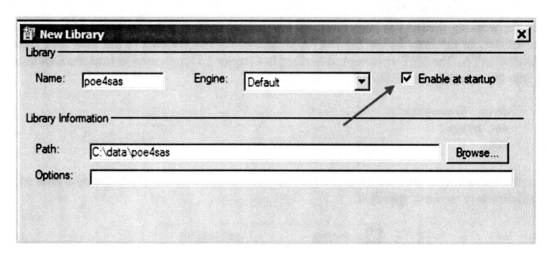

The new Library POE4SAS appears in SAS Explorer.

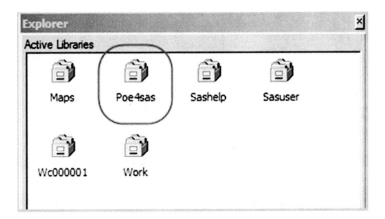

Double-click on **Poe4sas** in Explorer to find the SAS dataset BRUMMDATA you have just created.

Reading an existing SAS data set

Existing SAS datasets can be read into SAS using a **SET** statement. To read the SAS dataset **c:\data\sas\cps.sas7bdat** use the lines

```
data cps;
set 'cps';
run;
```

The SAS Log shows that 4733 observations have been read into WORK.CPS.

```
NOTE: There were 4733 observations read from the data set c:\data\poe4sas\cps.
NOTE: The data set WORK.CPS has 4733 observations and 15 variables.
```

1B.3 Importing data in Excel format

Data on web sites is often available in an Excel spreadsheet, or some other format. SAS has a powerful IMPORT WIZARD that easily reads alternative data formats. On the **Menu Bar** select **File**. On the pull-down menu select **Import Data**.

In the resulting dialog box choose the type of data file you wish to import. Select **Next**.

What type of data do you wish to import?

☑ Standard data source

Select a data source from the list below.

Microsoft Excel Workbook(*.xls *.xlsb *.xlsm *.xlsx)

The next screen allows you to browse to the Excel file that you want to import. Then select **OK**.

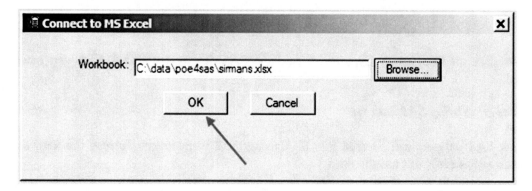

If the Excel Workbook has more than one "sheet" you will be asked to identify which one you want. Select **Next**.

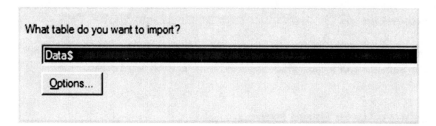

Choose the Library and a data set name of your choice. Select **Next**.

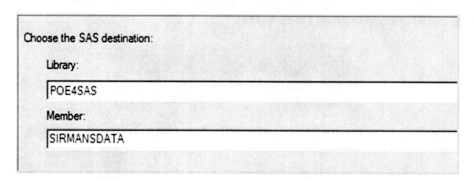

The Wizard will actually create the SAS statements for reading the data directly. Enter a file name for saving those statements. Select **Finish**.

> The Import Wizard can create a file containing PROC IMPORT statements that can be used in SAS programs to import this data again.
>
> If you want these statements to be generated, enter the filename where they should be saved:
>
> | read_sirmans |
>
> ☑ Replace file if it exists.

In the SAS Log we see

```
NOTE: POE4SAS.SIRMANSDATA data set was successfully created.
```

Using SAS Explorer, within the Library **Poe4sas**, we find the new SAS data set.

Sirmansdata

Opening the automatically created SAS file **READ_SIRMANS** we find the code for reading in such an Excel file.

```
PROC IMPORT OUT= POE4SAS.SIRMANSDATA
        DATAFILE= "C:\data\poe4sas\sirmans.xlsx"
        DBMS=EXCEL REPLACE;
    RANGE="Data$";
    GETNAMES=YES;
    MIXED=NO;
    SCANTEXT=YES;
    USEDATE=YES;
    SCANTIME=YES;
RUN;
```

CHAPTER **2**

The Simple Linear Regression Model

2.1 ECONOMETRIC MODEL AND ESTIMATORS

The simple linear regression model relates the values of a dependent variable y to an explanatory (regressor) variable x. Specifically, the value of y, for each value of x, is

$$y_i = \beta_1 + \beta_2 x_i + e_i \tag{2.1}$$

The regression parameters are the y-intercept β_1 and the slope β_2. The term e is a random error. This relation is assumed to hold for each observation in a data sample, $i = 1,\ldots,N$. The standard assumption is that the expected value of the random error e is zero, or

$$E(e_i) = 0$$

which is equivalent to assuming that

$$E(y_i) = \beta_1 + \beta_2 x_i$$

The variance of the random error e is

$$\mathrm{var}(e_i) = \sigma^2 = \mathrm{var}(y_i)$$

The random variables y and e have the same variance because they differ only by a constant. We also assume that the covariance between any pair of random errors, e_i and e_j is zero,

$$\mathrm{cov}(e_i, e_j) = \mathrm{cov}(y_i, y_j) = 0$$

The stronger version of this assumption is that the random errors e are statistically independent, in which case the values of the dependent variable y are also statistically independent. Initially assume that x is not random, and must take at least two different values. The values of e may be normally distributed about their mean

$$e \sim N(0, \sigma^2)$$

if the values of y are normally distributed, and *vice versa.*

To estimate β_1 and β_2 we will use the **least squares principle**. This principle asserts that to fit a line to the data values we should make the sum of the squares of the vertical distances from each point to the line as small as possible. The intercept and slope of this line, the line that best fits the data using the least squares principle, are b_1 and b_2, the least squares estimates of β_1 and β_2. The fitted line itself is then

$$\hat{y}_i = b_1 + b_2 x_i \tag{2.2}$$

The vertical distances from each point to the fitted line are the **least squares residuals**. They are given by

$$\hat{e}_i = y_i - \hat{y}_i = y_i - b_1 - b_2 x_i \tag{2.3}$$

The sum of the least squares residuals is

$$SSE = \sum_{i=1}^{N} \hat{e}_i^2 = \sum_{i=1}^{N} (y_i - \hat{y}_i)^2 = \sum_{i=1}^{N} (y_i - b_1 - b_2 x_i)^2 \tag{2.4}$$

The formulas for the least squares estimators are

$$b_2 = \frac{N \sum x_i y_i - \sum x_i \sum y_i}{N \sum x_i^2 - (\sum x_i)^2} \tag{2.5a}$$

$$b_2 = \frac{\sum (x_i - \bar{x})(y_i - \bar{y})}{\sum (x_i - \bar{x})^2} \tag{2.5b}$$

$$b_1 = \bar{y} - b_2 \bar{x} \tag{2.6}$$

where $\bar{x} = \sum x_i / N$ and $\bar{y} = \sum y_i / N$ are the sample means of x and y.

Because the sample data are randomly collected, the least squares estimators are random, meaning that they have probability distributions, with means, variances and covariances. Under standard assumptions the least squares estimators are unbiased. If the errors are normal then the least squares estimators are normal. If the errors are not normal, then the least squares estimators are approximately normal in large samples. The estimated variances and covariance of the least squares estimators are

$$\widehat{var(b_1)} = \hat{\sigma}^2 \left[\frac{\sum x_i^2}{N \sum (x_i - \bar{x})^2} \right], \quad \widehat{var(b_2)} = \frac{\hat{\sigma}^2}{\sum (x_i - \bar{x})^2} \tag{2.7a}$$

$$\widehat{cov(b_1, b_2)} = \hat{\sigma}^2 \left[\frac{-\bar{x}}{\sum (x_i - \bar{x})^2} \right] \tag{2.7b}$$

where

$$\hat{\sigma}^2 = \frac{\sum \hat{e}_i^2}{N - 2} \tag{2.8}$$

is an unbiased estimator of the variance of the error term σ^2.

The square roots of the estimated variances are called the **standard errors** of b_1 and b_2 and are denoted

$$\operatorname{se}(b_1) = \sqrt{\widehat{\operatorname{var}(b_1)}}, \quad \operatorname{se}(b_2) = \sqrt{\widehat{\operatorname{var}(b_2)}} \tag{2.9}$$

2.2 EXAMPLE: THE FOOD EXPENDITURE DATA

For illustration we examine typical data on household food expenditure (y) and weekly income (x) from a random sample of $N = 40$ households. We control for household size by only considering three-person households. The values of y are weekly food expenditures for a three-person household, in dollars. Instead of measuring income in dollars, we measure it in units of $100, because a $1 increase in income has a numerically small effect on food expenditure. The data are in the SAS data set *food*, introduced in Section 1.13 of this manual.

To open the SAS data set use the **SET** statement and then **PROC CONTENTS**. We assume that the SAS path is set to the directory containing the SAS data files for *Principles of Econometrics, 4th Edition*.

```
data food;
set 'food';

proc contents data=food position;
run;
```

The contents are shown in Section 1.13. It is also useful to look at the data to check magnitudes. Print the first 10 observations using **PROC PRINT** with the option **(obs=10)**.

```
proc print data=food(obs=10);
run;
```

Recall that in this example y = *FOOD_EXP* (food expenditure in $) and x = *INCOME* (income in $100).

Obs	FOOD_EXP	INCOME
1	115.220	3.6900
2	135.980	4.3900
3	119.340	4.7500

Another initial step is to obtain summary statistics. Use the option **nolabel** since we know the variable definitions.

```
options nolabel;
proc means data=food;
run;
```

The MEANS Procedure

Variable	N	Mean	Std Dev	Minimum	Maximum
FOOD_EXP	40	283.5734993	112.6751802	109.7099991	587.6599731
INCOME	40	19.6047501	6.8477728	3.6900001	33.4000015

2.3 SCATTER DIAGRAM USING PROC GPLOT

A scatter diagram should have axes that span the range of the data, plus a little more. The useful range is determined by looking at the summary statistics from **PROC MEANS**, along with some thought and "trial and error." In simple regression it is often useful to include the origin (0,0). Controlling the axes is accomplished using an **axis** statement. We define two **axis** statements, one for the vertical and one for the horizontal. The **order=()** option is used to specify the range (**0 to 600**) and the points at which "tick-marks" will be located (**by 100**). The **label=()** puts a label on the axis. We use the **symbol** statement to obtain nice dots in the diagram.

```
symbol1 value=dot color=blue;
axis1 order=(0 to 600 by 100) label=("Food Expenditure");
axis2 order=(0 to 40 by 10) label=("Income");
```

The axis options are specified in the **PLOT** statement following "/", which denotes options. The vertical axis is **vaxis** and the horizontal axis is **haxis**.

```
proc gplot data=food;
plot food_exp*income / vaxis=axis1 haxis=axis2;
title 'Food Expenditure data';
run;
```

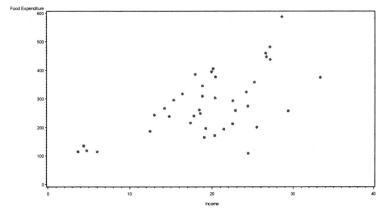

Food Expenditure data

2.4 USING PROC REG FOR SIMPLE REGRESSION

Many different procedures in SAS carry out regression analysis. We begin with **PROC REG**, where **REG** is short for **REGRESSION**. SAS Help is obtained by entering **help reg** into the SAS command line.

The command for carrying out a regression of *FOOD_EXP* on *INCOME*, which are the variable names in the *food* data set, is

```
proc reg data=food;
model food_exp = income;
title 'food expenditure regression';
run;
```

We call on **PROC REG** and specify **data=food** so that we are sure the analysis is carried out on the correct data set.

The regression is specified in the **model** statement. The standard format of the **model** statement is

```
model dependent = regressor;
```

The most common error is probably omitting the "=" sign. The dependent variable is the *y*-variable and the regressor is the independent or explanatory variable *x*. The **title** statement is optional, and to clear previous titles use **title;**

The output of **PROC REG** is divided into several blocks, which we will examine one by one. The first part might be called the "header". It shows the **title** specified, if there is one. It shows that this is **The REG Procedure**. The **Model: MODEL1** is a generic label for the model, since we did not provide one. The **Number of Observations Read** and the **Number of Observations Used** should be equal if there are no missing values. The number used is $N = 40$.

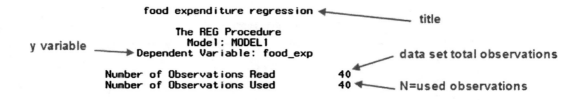

2.4.1 Analysis of variance table

The second part of the output is called an **Analysis of Variance**. It contains several components that we will not explain until later chapters.

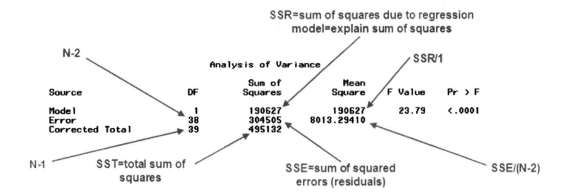

The **Source** of variation is attributed to the
- **Model** denotes the variation in y due to (explained by) the regression model
- **Error** denotes the least squares residual, which is the variation in y not explained by the regression
- **Corrected Total** represents the total variation in y about its mean

The **DF** column denotes **degrees of freedom**
- **Model** degrees of freedom = number of explanatory variables = 1
- **Error** degrees of freedom = $N - 2 = N -$ the number of model **parameters**
- **Corrected Total** degrees of freedom = $N - 1$

The **Sum of Squares** are
- **Model:** $SSR = \sum(\hat{y}_i - \bar{y})^2$ = explained sum of squares (due to regression model)
- **Error:** $SSE = \sum_{i=1}^{N}\hat{e}_i^2 = \sum_{i=1}^{N}(y_i - \hat{y}_i)^2$ = sum of squared errors (residuals)
- **Total:** $SST = \sum(y_i - \bar{y})^2$ = total sum of squares = corrected sum of squares

Note that the sum of squared residuals $\sum\hat{e}_i^2 = 304505$ for the food expenditure data. The total sum of squares is the total variation in the y-variable about its mean. The term "corrected" sum of squares denotes "about its mean". You will note that $SST = SSR + SSE$.

The **Mean Square** is the **Sum of Squares** divided by its corresponding degrees of freedom **DF**
- **Model Mean Square** = $SSR = SSR/1 = \sum(\hat{y}_i - \bar{y})^2/1$
- **Error Mean Square** = $SSE/(N-2) = \sum_{i=1}^{N}\hat{e}_i^2 / (N-2) = \sum_{i=1}^{N}(y_i - \hat{y}_i)^2 / (N-2) = \hat{\sigma}^2$

The entry for **Error Mean Square** (or **Mean Square Error = MSE**) is the estimated variance of the error term, in this case

$$\hat{\sigma}^2 = \sum_{i=1}^{N}\hat{e}_i^2 / (N-2) = 304505/38 = 8013.29403$$

The column labeled **F-Value** and **Pr > F** will be explained in Chapter 6.

2.4.2 ANOVA auxiliary information

Below the **Analysis of Variance** table is some auxiliary information.

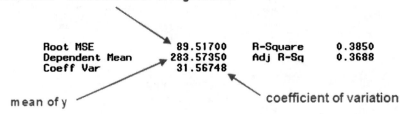

The **Root MSE** is the square root of the **Mean Square Error** from the analysis of variance table

$$\hat{\sigma} = \sqrt{\hat{\sigma}^2} = \sqrt{8013.29403} = 89.51700$$

The **Dependent Mean** is the sample mean of y

$$\bar{y} = \frac{\sum y_i}{N} = 283.57350$$

The **Coeff Var** is the coefficient of variation based on the regression model.

$$CV = \frac{\hat{\sigma}}{\bar{y}} \times 100$$

The values **R-Square** and **Adj R-Sq** are discussed in Chapter 6.

2.4.3 PROC MEANS options

Some of the information in the ANOVA table is produced by **PROC MEANS** when some options are specified.

```
proc means data=food n mean css var std cv;
var food_exp;
run;
```

Here we apply **PROC MEANS** to **data=food** and then list some **statistical keywords** denoting other sample statistics. They are

n	sample size
mean	sample mean $\bar{y}$
css	corrected sum of squares = $\sum(y_i - \bar{y})^2$
var	sample variance $s_y^2 = \sum(y_i - \bar{y})^2 / (N-1)$

std	sample standard deviation $= \sqrt{s_y^2} = s_y$
cv	sample coefficient of variation $= 100\left(s_y/\overline{y}\right)$

The output, for the variable *FOOD_EXP = y* is

```
                 The MEANS Procedure
              Analysis Variable : FOOD_EXP
                                                    Coeff of
  N        Mean    Corrected SS     Variance    Std Dev    Variation

  40   283.5734993     495132.15     12695.70   112.6751802   39.7340303
```

Note that these quantities relate just to the sample data:
- the sample size *N*, the sample mean (**Mean Dependent**), and corrected sum of squares (**SST**) are the same as the values reported by **PROC REG**.
- the **Std Dev** is **<u>NOT</u>** the **Root MSE**
- the **Coeff of Variation** is **<u>NOT</u>** the same as that reported by **PROC REG**.

Other statistical keywords that can be requested with **PROC MEANS** are

min	minimum
max	maximum
range	max – min
sum	sum
uss	uncorrected sum of squares $= \sum y_i^2$

2.5 PROC REG OPTIONS

2.5.1 Covariance matrix

It is customary to arrange the variances and covariances of the least squares estimators into an array called the **covariance matrix**, with variances on the diagonal and covariances in the "off-diagonal" positions.

$$\begin{bmatrix} \widehat{\text{var}(b_1)} & \widehat{\text{cov}(b_1,b_2)} \\ \widehat{\text{cov}(b_1,b_2)} & \widehat{\text{var}(b_2)} \end{bmatrix}$$

In order to view this matrix we must request the option **covb** on the **Model** statement in **PROC REG**.

```
proc reg data=food;
model food_exp = income / covb;
title 'regression with covariance options';
run;
```

In the output, following the regression results, we find

Covariance of Estimates

Variable	Intercept	INCOME
Intercept	1884.4421918	-85.9031527
INCOME	-85.9031527	4.3817519872

Using the estimated variances on the diagonal we can compute the **Standard Error** reported in the regression output. For example

$$se(b_2) = \sqrt{\widehat{\text{var}(b_2)}} = \sqrt{4.3817519872} = 2.09326$$

2.5.2 The least squares residuals

Analyzing the least squares residuals following a regression is an important diagnostic. The least squares residuals are our proxies for the true random errors e_i which we never observe. The model assumptions make assertions about the random errors that we should check, because the good properties of the least squares estimators do not hold if the assumptions are violated.

The least squares residuals are obtained by using the option "**r**" [for **residual**] on the **Model** statement in **PROC REG**.

```
proc reg data=food;
model food_exp = income / r;
```

In the output we find a listing (we show a partial list) that includes the value of the **Dependent Variable** (y), the **Predicted Value** ($\hat{y}_i = b_1 + b_2 x_i$) and the **Residual** ($\hat{e}_i = y_i - \hat{y}_i = y_i - b_1 - b_2 x_i$).

Output Statistics

Obs	Dependent Variable	Predicted Value	Std Error Mean Predict	Residual	Std Error Residual	Student Residual
1	115.2200	121.0896	36.1958	-5.8696	81.873	-0.0717
2	135.9800	128.2363	34.8519	7.7437	82.454	0.0939
3	119.3400	131.9118	34.1647	-12.5718	82.741	-0.152
4	114.9600	144.9802	31.7455	-30.0202	83.699	-0.359
5	187.0500	210.7303	20.5763	-23.6803	87.120	-0.272

Other statistics are reported, and you may not know what they mean. One of the skills required when using a statistical package is to locate what you are interested in, and not worry about the rest. The other quantities will be explained in Chapter 6.

2.5.3 Output residuals

After a regression you may wish to save certain calculations to a data set for further analysis. SAS offers a variety of tools like this. To output the least squares residuals to a data set use an **output**

statement following the **Model** statement. You must provide a name for the new SAS data set (*foodout*) and a name for the least squares residual (**ehat**). We add a **title** and **run**.

```
output out=foodout r=ehat;
title 'regression with residual option';
run;
```

The SAS **Log** shows

```
NOTE: The data set WORK.FOODOUT has 40 observations and 3 variables.
```

The output data set contains 3 variables, the least squares residuals AND the original variables in the *food* data set.

2.5.4 PROC UNIVARIATE analysis of residuals

When detailed summary statistics are required, use **PROC UNIVARIATE**. For more help see Base SAS 9.2: Statistical Procedures. Not only will this procedure provide detailed statistics, it will create some useful graphs.

To analyze the least squares residuals submit the following commands. The command **histogram/normal;** produces a histogram with a superimposed normal distribution. See Appendix C for more on **histograms.**

```
proc univariate data=foodout;
var ehat;
histogram / normal;
run;
```

There is a great deal of output. Most of these are explained in Appendix C. However for the moment focus on the top portion

```
              The UNIVARIATE Procedure
                 Variable:  ehat

                      Moments
```

N	40	Sum Weights	40
Mean	0	Sum Observations	0
Std Deviation	88.361898	Variance	7807.82502
Skewness	-0.1011522	Kurtosis	0.15395803
Uncorrected SS	304505.176	Corrected SS	304505.176
Coeff Variation	.	Std Error Mean	13.9712428

The analysis shows that the sum of the least squares residuals is **ZERO!** Can this be true? The answer is yes, it is always true that $\sum \hat{e}_i = 0$ as long as the model contains an intercept, which is 99.999% of the time.[1] Since the sum of the residuals is zero so is the sample mean of the residuals.

---

[1] In the rare case in which you wish to omit the intercept add the option **NOINT** to the **Model** statement.

The histogram of the least squares residuals, with a normal distribution curve superimposed on it, is

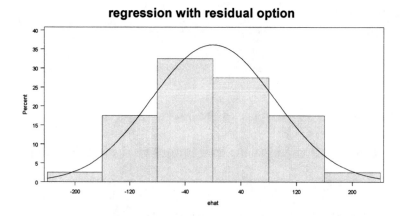

It is important to construct this figure each time a regression is carried out. What you do want to see is a nice "bell-shaped" curve similar to the normal distribution. The food expenditure data only uses 40 observations, which is a bit on the small side for a histogram. What you do not want to see is a very tall center and/or fat or skinny tails, relative to the normal, or any other "abnormality." The distribution of the least squares estimators is normal in large samples even if the true disturbances are not normal, but of course things work better in smaller samples if the true disturbances (and thus the residuals) are normally, or close to normally, distributed.

2.6 PREDICTION WITH PROC REG

For any value of x we can obtain a predicted value of y using the fitted equation $\hat{y} = b_1 + b_2 x$. Given the least squares estimates you can carry out the calculation. However, it is nice to have SAS carry out the calculation because (1) it prevents calculation errors (2) it facilitates making several (or many) predictions. To use **PROC REG** for prediction we will create a pseudo-data set containing the "x" values, combine this data set with the *food* data, then estimate the regression on the new data set, with an option to produce the predictions. Execute the following commands:

```
data morefood;
input food_exp income;
datalines;
. 10
. 20
. 30
;
run;
```

These commands create a new SAS data set called *morefood*. It contains two variables, *FOOD_EXP* and *INCOME*. The tricky bit is that for *FOOD_EXP* we enter **missing values** indicated by a period (.). For *INCOME* we enter values for which we wish predictions. Recall that income is measured in $100, so *INCOME* = 10 implies an income of $1000 per month, and so on.

The new data set is combined with the 40 observations the data set *food* using a **SET** statement. We can do this because *food* and *morefood* contain the same variables. Print out the combined data set just to be sure that it worked.

```
data morefood;
set food morefood;
run;

proc print data=morefood;
title 'Augmented food data';
run;
```

The augmented food data set has 43 observations, but with the last 3 observations on *FOOD_EXP* missing.

```
            Augmented food data

        Obs    FOOD_EXP    INCOME
         1      115.220     3.6900
```

[some observations omitted here]

```
        40     375.730    33.4000
        41        .       10.0000
        42        .       20.0000
        43        .       30.0000
```

Now estimate the regression model with the new data set

```
proc reg data=morefood;
model food_exp=income / p;
title 'regression with predict option';
output out=foodpred p=yhat;
run;
```

Note that
- we specify that the regression uses the data set *morefood*, and we add the option "**p**" [for **predict**] to the **model** statement.
- we have added an **output** statement following the **model** statement, which will output a new variable **yhat** containing the predicted values, using **p = yhat** and **p** stands for predicted values. The name of the new data set is specified in **out = foodpred**.

The regression results are identical to earlier ones, but note that in the header information we see that 43 observations were **read**, but only 40 **used** in the regression.

```
            regression with predict option

              The REG Procedure
               Model: MODEL1
          Dependent Variable: FOOD_EXP
```

```
Number of Observations Read                        43
Number of Observations Used                        40
Number of Observations with Missing Values          3
```

The prediction option on the **model** statement yields

```
          Dependent    Predicted
   Obs     Variable        Value       Residual
     1     115.2200     121.0896        -5.8696
     2     135.9800     128.2363         7.7437
```

[some observations deleted]

```
    40     375.7300     424.4181       -48.6881
    41            .     185.5124              .
    42            .     287.6089              .
    43            .     389.7053              .
```

Despite the fact that only 40 observations were used in the regression calculations SAS will create predicted values for all observations where x has a value. Thus we predict that a household with \$2000/month income will spend \$287.61 on food.

The SAS **Log** shows that the **output** statement created data set *foodpred* with 43 observations on 3 variables, **yhat** plus *FOOD_EXP* and *INCOME*.

NOTE: The data set WORK.FOODPRED has 43 observations and 3 variables.

We can conveniently examine just the predicted values using

```
proc print data=foodpred(firstobs=41 obs=43);
var income food_exp yhat;
run;
```

```
            regression with predict option

       Obs     income     food_exp        yhat
        41         10            .     185.512
        42         20            .     287.609
        43         30            .     389.705
```

2.6.1 Deleting missing values from data set

Before plotting the fitted regression line we will edit the data set *foodpred* to eliminate the missing values. This step is an optional one. We will open *foodpred*, use the **SET** statement to read in the observations, and then using an **IF** condition to discard observations with missing values.

```
data foodpred;
set foodpred;
if food_exp ^= .;
run;
```

In the **IF** statement the symbol "^=" is shorthand for "not equal". Thus the **IF** statement retains an observation only if *FOOD_EXP* is **not** missing.

2.6.2 Plotting a fitted line using PROC GPLOT

We will produce a plot with the regression line superimposed over the data scatter. Just as we had a **symbol1** statement for the "dots" used in the scatter diagram in Section 2.3, we now will create a **symbol2** statement for the fitted regression line. The key new feature in **symbol2** is the **interpol** option, which is short for "interpolation." To interpolate means to construct new data points between known points, or, to "connect the dots." By specifying **value = none** we are eliminating the dots themselves, so we will have just a line.

```
symbol2 color=black interpol=join value=none;
```

The form of the **plot** statement shows that we want two plots, the first *FOOD_EXP* plotted against *INCOME* using **symbol1**, which is indicated by the "=1", and the predicted value **yhat** also plotted against *INCOME* using **symbol2**. The overlay option after the slash "/" indicates that the two plots are to appear in the sample plot. The **vaxis** and **haxis** are explained in Section 2.3.

```
proc gplot data=foodpred;
plot food_exp*income=1 yhat*income=2 /overlay vaxis=axis1 haxis=axis2;
run;
```

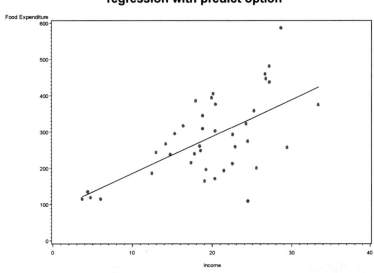

2.7 CREATING PLOTS USING PROC REG

It is possible to obtain some useful plots from within **PROC REG**. Execute the following commands. The first **plot** statement plots the least squares residuals against income. The random errors are supposed to be truly random, which means no patterns in the least squares residuals no matter how you examine them. The second **plot** statement replicates the **scatter diagram** constructed in Section 2.3, but with the addition of the fitted regression line. Note that the **axis** control has to be incorporated directly here.

```
proc reg data=food;
model food_exp = income;
plot residual.*income;
plot food_exp*income/vaxis=(0 to 600 by 100)
                     haxis=(0 to 40 by 10);
title 'regression with plot options';
run;
```

The plot of the residuals against income has the estimated regression across the top and some summary statistics on the right. The "funnel shape" in the residuals is something we will consider in Chapter 8. The scatter diagram shows the data points with the fitted regression line superimposed, similar to the plot above.

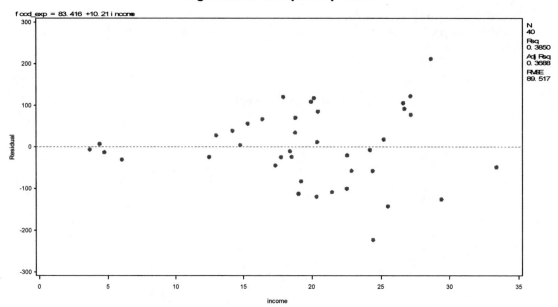

2.8 SAS ODS GRAPHICS

SAS has introduced a new type of graphics capability in Version 9.2. It is called **ODS Graphics**, where **ODS** stands for **Output Delivery System**. For documentation enter **help ods** into the SAS command line.

To initiate the **ODS graphics** it must be turned on, and then off. The usual **PROC REG** statement is augmented with **plots = ( )** and two of many possible options. These choices will plot the residuals and create a nice residual histogram. Note that after running this portion of code we turn the **ODS** graphics off.

```
ods graphics on;
proc reg data=food plots=(ResidualPlot ResidualHistogram);
model food_exp = income;
title 'regression with ods graphs';
run;
ods graphics off;
```

Implementing the code above produces the usual regression output, but nothing else happens. The **ODS** graphs do not show up in the usual **Graphics** window. Instead, after a few seconds, they are output as graphics files to your default directory, which we have called **c:\data\poe4sas**.

There are 4 new PNG files: **ResidualPlot.png** and **ResidualHistogram.png** are the ones we specified in the **plots** statement. The other two, **FitPlot.png** and **DiagnosticsPanel.png**, are automatically created by the **ODS** graphics. If you double-click the file name the image will appear in whatever viewer your computer has. Alternatively, in **Microsoft Word** select **Insert > Picture** and use the dialog box to select the one you want. If you wish to edit the photo within SAS select **Tools > Image Editor** on the SAS pull-down menu. Or use Photoshop, etc.

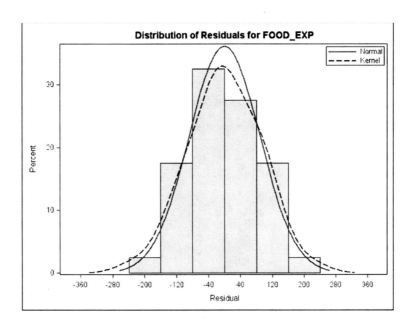

The histogram produced by the **ODS graphics** is nice, superimposing a **Normal** distribution and also fitting a **Kernel** distribution. The **Kernel** distribution is an approximation to the distribution, whatever it might be, and not requiring it follow a **Normal** distribution.[2]

---

[2] The procedure for creating the kernel density can be found in the Statistical Graphics Procedures Guide, page 43. This is advanced material.

2.9 FITTING NONLINEAR RELATIONSHIPS

In this chapter we consider only "simple" regression models that include a single explanatory variable. It is still possible to account for nonlinear relationships by including explanatory variables raised to a power, or by taking logarithms of the dependent and/or independent variables. To illustrate we use real estate data. Open the data set *br* and examine its contents.

```
options label;
data br;
set 'br';
proc contents data=br;
run;
options nolabel;
```

The key variables for the present are *PRICE* and *SQFT*. Plot *PRICE* against *SQFT*. For completeness we include the **SYMBOL** statements again.

```
symbol1 value=dot color=blue;
symbol2 color=black interpol=join value=none;
proc gplot data=br;
plot price*sqft=1;
title 'price versus sqft';
run;
```

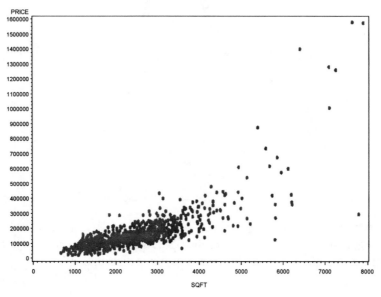

There is in the data scatter an indication that the center of the data curves, so that the marginal effect of additional house size has a greater impact on price for large houses than small houses. Choosing a functional form that is capable of fitting the data is one model specification problem that is faced each time a model is specified. If we choose an incorrect functional form then one or more of the least squares assumptions will be violated, and the good properties of the least squares estimators will not follow.

One way to capture this curvilinear relationship is to include *SQFT* squared, so that the model becomes

$$PRICE = \alpha_1 + \alpha_2 SQFT^2 + e \tag{2.10}$$

Equation (2.10) is not a complete quadratic equation because it does not include *SQFT*. The reason for this omission is that we are now only considering simple regression models. We have given the parameters alternative symbols because their interpretation is not the same as in the linear model (2.1). The fitted function is $\widehat{PRICE} = \hat{\alpha}_1 + \hat{\alpha}_2 SQFT^2$, where $\hat{\alpha}_k$ denotes the least squares estimates. The slope of the fitted function is

$$\frac{d\left(\widehat{PRICE}\right)}{dSQFT} = 2\hat{\alpha}_2 SQFT \tag{2.11}$$

Another alternative is to use a log-linear relationship, in which the dependent variable is in logarithmic form

$$\ln\left(PRICE\right) = \gamma_1 + \gamma_2 SQFT + e \tag{2.12}$$

For this model the fitted function is $\widehat{\ln\left(PRICE\right)} = \hat{\gamma}_1 + \hat{\gamma}_2 SQFT$. Solving for $\widehat{PRICE}$ we have

$$\widehat{PRICE} = \exp\left(\widehat{\ln\left(PRICE\right)}\right) = \exp\left(\hat{\gamma}_1 + \hat{\gamma}_2 SQFT\right) \tag{2.13}$$

The slope is

$$\frac{d\widehat{PRICE}}{dSQFT} = \exp\left(\hat{\gamma}_1 + \hat{\gamma}_2 SQFT\right)\hat{\gamma}_2 = \widehat{PRICE} \times \hat{\gamma}_2 \tag{2.14}$$

See Chapter 2.8 in *Principles of Econometrics, 4th Edition* for discussion of interpretation issues related to these two functional forms.

To fit these two functional forms in SAS we first create the transformed variables.

```
data br;
set br;
sqft2 = sqft**2;                    * square-feet squared;
lprice = log(price);                * ln(price);
run;
```

For future purposes we sort the data according to the magnitude of *SQFT*.

```
proc sort data=br;
by sqft;
run;
```

Estimate the quadratic model

```
proc reg data=br;
quad:model price = sqft2;
output out=quadout p=pricehat;
title 'quadratic relationship';
run;
```

The parameter estimates are

Variable	DF	Parameter Estimate	Standard Error	t Value	Pr > |t|
Intercept	1	55777	2890.44121	19.30	<.0001
sqft2	1	0.01542	0.00031310	49.25	<.0001

We included the **Output** command in the code. With this statement we create a new SAS dataset called *quadout*. It contains the variables from *br* plus the fitted value from the estimation which we call *PRICEHAT*. Plot the fitted curve along with the data by specifying **data=quadout** with **proc gplot**.

```
proc gplot data=quadout;
plot price*sqft=1 pricehat*sqft=2 /overlay;
run;
```

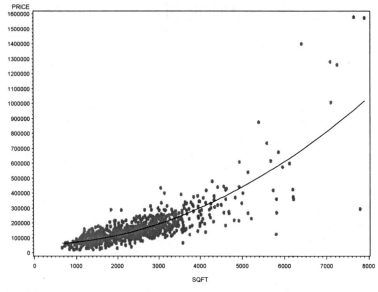

quadratic relationship

To estimate the log-linear model use

```
proc reg data=br;
loglin:model lprice = sqft;
output out=loglinout p=lpricehat;
title 'log-linear relationship';
run;
```

Variable	DF	Parameter Estimate	Standard Error	t Value	Pr > |t|
Intercept	1	10.83860	0.02461	440.46	<.0001
SQFT	1	0.00041127	0.00000971	42.36	<.0001

Again we will output the predicted values and then obtain the fitted value of *PRICE*.

```
data loglinout;
set loglinout;
phat = exp(lpricehat);              * exp is exponential fn;
run;
```

Merge the two output data sets into one called *both*. This is facilitated by the fact that we previously sorted the data on *SQFT*.

```
data both;
merge quadout loglinout;
run;
```

Plot both fitted curves and the data values in the same graph using

```
symbol3 color=black interpol=join value=none line=2;
proc gplot data=both;
plot price*sqft=1 phat*sqft=2 pricehat*sqft=3/overlay;
title 'quadratic and log-linear fitted curves';
run;
```

The additional **symbol** statement creates a line that is dashed (**line=2**). For complete documentation enter **help symbol** in the SAS command line, and then choose **SAS/GRAPH Statements: SYMBOL**.

Both of the estimated models "fit" the data. Which should we choose? This problem is considered more fully in Chapter 4 of this manual.

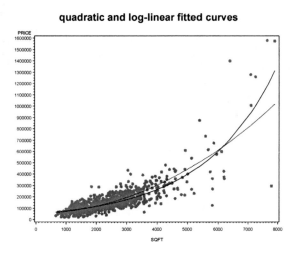

quadratic and log-linear fitted curves

2.10 USING INDICATOR VARIABLES

Regression analysis is not restricted to using only continuous variables. One the variables included in the data set *br* is *WATERFRONT*. This variable is 1 if the home is on the waterfront and is 0 otherwise, for homes not on a waterfront. Thus *WATERFRONT* is a binary variable and often called an indicator variable, or a dummy variable. Use this variable as the regression explanatory variable.

$$PRICE = \delta_1 + \delta_2 WATERFRONT + e \qquad (2.15)$$

```
proc reg data=br;
indicator:model price = waterfront;
title 'indicator function regression'; run;
```

Variable	DF	Parameter Estimate	Standard Error	t Value	Pr > |t|
Intercept	1	144239	3693.46299	39.05	<.0001
WATERFRONT	1	147101	13744	10.70	<.0001

The regression function we have specified is

$$E(PRICE) = \begin{cases} \delta_1 & \text{if } WATERFRONT = 0 \\ \delta_1 + \delta_2 & \text{if } WATERFRONT = 1 \end{cases} \qquad (2.16)$$

We see that δ_2 is the difference in expected price between homes on the waterfront and those that are not. We estimate this value to be \$147,101. This interpretation is confirmed by calculating the sample means of the two types of houses. First, sort the data according to the values of *WATERFRONT*, then compute the summary statistics **by** this variable.

```
proc sort data=br;
by waterfront;
run;

proc means data=br;
var price;
by waterfront;
title 'average price by waterfront';
run;
```

```
                    average price by waterfront

------------------------------ WATERFRONT=0 ------------------------------

                        The MEANS Procedure

                     Analysis Variable : PRICE
```

N	Mean	Std Dev	Minimum	Maximum
1002	144239.20	88046.43	22000.00	1260000.00

```
----------------------------------- WATERFRONT=1 -----------------------------------

                          Analysis Variable : PRICE

      N          Mean        Std Dev       Minimum       Maximum
     ─────────────────────────────────────────────────────────────
     78      291340.38      300976.85      34000.00    1580000.00
     ─────────────────────────────────────────────────────────────
```

We see that the average price for properties on the waterfront is \$291,340.38. The average price for houses not on the waterfront is \$144,239, which is the same value as the estimated intercept parameter in the regression. The difference between these average prices is \$147,101.

APPENDIX 2A CALCULATION OF LEAST SQUARES ESTIMATES: DETAILS

The calculations in **PROC REG** are not magic. The SAS procedures implement the formulas in Section 2.1. To see that this is true, we will use **PROC MEANS** to make the calculations of the least squares estimates in (2.5) and (2.6). Also, we demonstrate that SAS can serve as a wonderful "calculator."

First, note that the computation

$$b_2 = \frac{N \sum x_i y_i - \sum x_i \sum y_i}{N \sum x_i^2 - \left(\sum x_i\right)^2}$$

uses the sum of the x variable, the sum of the y variable, the sum of the x variable squared, and the sum of the product of x and y. The estimated intercept uses b_2 and the sample means

$$b_1 = \bar{y} - b_2 \bar{x}$$

Use a **data step** to create the variables and then **PROC MEANS** to compute the sums and the sample means.

```
data foodreg;                          * new data set;
set food;                              * read food;
y = food_exp;                          * rename food_exp;
x = income;                            * rename income;
xy = x*y;                              * x-y crossproduct;
x2 = x**2;                             * x squared;
run;

proc means data=foodreg n sum mean;    * summary stats;
var y x xy x2;                         * selected variables;
title 'summary calculations for equation (2.5) and (2.6)';
run;
```

The output is

```
        summary calculations for equation (2.5) and (2.6)

                      The MEANS Procedure

        Variable    N            Sum              Mean
        ─────────────────────────────────────────────────
        y          40        11342.94        283.5734993
        x          40       784.1900039       19.6047501
        xy         40       241046.77           6026.17
        x2         40        17202.64         430.0659182
        ─────────────────────────────────────────────────
```

Now create a new data set, but enter no data, and use SAS as calculator. The numbers entered below come from the above summary calculations.

```
data foodreg;                              * new data set;
n = 40;                                    * sample size;
sumxy = 241046.77;                         * sum(x*y);
sumx = 784.1900;                           * sum(x);
sumy = 11342.94;                           * sum(y);
sumx2 = 17202.64;                          * sum(x**2);
* estimate slope;
b2 =  (n*sumxy - sumx*sumy)/(n*sumx2 - sumx**2);
ybar = 283.5734993;                        * sample mean y;
xbar = 19.604750;                          * sample mean x;
b1 =  ybar - b2*xbar;                       * estimate intercept;
run;

proc print data=foodreg;                   * print;
title 'using simple calculations for LS estimates';
run;
```

The results show the sums and means, as well as the calculated values of b_1 and b_2.

```
              using simple calculations for LS estimates

Obs  n    sumxy     sumx     sumy     sumx2     b2      ybar     xbar      b1
 1   40 241046.77 784.19 11342.94 17202.64 10.2096 283.573 19.6048 83.4164
```

The estimate of the slope can also be obtained using the "deviation about the mean" formula (2.5b)

$$b_2 = \frac{\sum (x_i - \bar{x})(y_i - \bar{y})}{\sum (x_i - \bar{x})^2}$$

Once again we use a **data step** to create the variables required, and then **PROC MEANS** to compute the sums and means;

```
data foodreg;                              * new data set;
set food;                                  * read food;
y = food_exp;                              * rename food_exp;
```

```
x = income;                          * rename income;
xbar = 19.604750;                    * sample mean x;
ybar = 283.5734993;                  * sample mean y;
xd = x - xbar;                       * deviation about mean;
xd2 = xd**2;                         * deviation about mean sq;
yd = y - ybar;                       * deviation about mean;
xdyd = xd*yd;                        * deviations cross product;
run;

proc means data=foodreg sum mean;    * summary stats;
var xd  yd xd2 xdyd;                  * selected variables;
title 'calculations for deviations about mean formula (2.5b)';
run;
```

The results are

```
        calculations for deviations about mean formula (2.5b)

                        The MEANS Procedure

            Variable          Sum              Mean

            xd         3.8719179E-6       9.6797947E-8
            yd        -7.617098E-8       -1.904274E-9
            xd2           1828.79         45.7196919
            xdyd         18671.27        466.7817149
```

The SAS notation **9.6797947E-8** is scientific notation. It means multiply the number, 9.6797947, by 10^{-8}, moving the decimal 8 places to the left. Note that the sum of the deviations about the means variables XD and YD is zero. This will always be true. Take these values and calculate b_2.

```
data foodreg;                        * new data set;
xdyd = 18671.27;                     * sum(xd*yd);
xd2 = 1828.79;                       * sum(xd**2);
b2 = xdyd/xd2;                       * slope estimate;
run;
proc print data=foodreg;             * print;
title 'slope estimate uisng (2.5b)';
run;
```

The result is the same as that given by **PROC REG**.

```
              slope estimate uisng (2.5b)

        Obs      xdyd       xd2        b2
         1     18671.27   1828.79   10.2096
```

We can compute the least squares predicted values and residuals in a similar way.

```
data foodreg;                          * new data set;
set food;                              * read food;
b2 = 10.2096;                          * slope estimate;
b1 = 83.4164;                          * intercept estimate;
y = food_exp;                          * rename food_exp;
x = income;                            * rename income;
yhat = b1 + b2*x;                      * yhat = predicted value;
ehat = y - yhat;                       * ehat = ls residual;
ehat2 = ehat**2;                       * squared residuals;
run;

proc print data=foodreg(obs=10);       * print 10 observations;
var x y yhat ehat;                     * selected variables;
title 'LS predicted values and residuals (some rounding error)';
run;
```

The result is identical to what we have shown in Section 2.5.2 with a <u>slight</u> bit of rounding error. When SAS computes the predicted values and residuals it uses many more decimal places for the least squares estimates than we have used above.

```
LS predicted values and residuals (some rounding error)

Obs       x          y         yhat        ehat
 1      3.6900    115.220    121.090     -5.8698
 2      4.3900    135.980    128.237      7.7435
 3      4.7500    119.340    131.912    -12.5720
 4      6.0300    114.960    144.980    -30.0203
 5     12.4700    187.050    210.730    -23.6801
 6     12.9800    243.920    215.937     27.9830
 7     14.2000    267.430    228.393     39.0373
 8     14.7600    238.710    234.110      4.5999
 9     15.3200    295.940    239.827     56.1125
10     16.3900    317.780    250.752     67.0283
```

Use **PROC MEANS** to compute the sum of squared residuals *SSE*.

```
proc means data=foodreg n sum;         * summary stats;
var ehat2;                             * selected variable;
title 'sum squared LS residuals';
run;
```

The value we obtain is the same as that given in the **ANOVA**

```
sum squared LS residuals

Analysis Variable : ehat2

     N              Sum
    _____

    40          304505.17
    _____
```

APPENDIX 2B MONTE CARLO SIMULATION

The statistical properties of the least squares estimators are well known if the assumptions in Section 2.1 hold. In fact we know that the least squares estimators are the best linear unbiased estimators of the regression parameters under these assumptions. And if the random errors are normal, then we know that the estimators themselves have normal distributions and that t-tests and confidence intervals work the way they are supposed to in **repeated experimental trials**. It is the meaning of "repeated trials" that is difficult to grasp. Simulation experiments, which have become commonly known as **Monte Carlo** experiments, use random number generators to replicate the random way that data are obtained.

In a simulation we specify a **data generation process**, create some artificial data, and then "try out" estimation methods and test procedures on the data we have created. In this way we can study how statistical procedures behave under ideal, and not so ideal, conditions. This is important because economic, business and social science data are not always (indeed, not usually) as nice as the assumptions we make.

The data generation process for the simple linear regression model is given by equation (2.1) with specific values given for the unknown parameters

$$y_i = \beta_1 + \beta_2 x_i + e_i = 100 + 10 x_i + e_i$$

We take the slope and intercept parameters to take the value 100 and 10, respectively. The term e is a random error, which we assume to be normally and independently distributed with mean zero and variance 2500, $e \sim N(0, \sigma^2 = 50^2)$. All that remains is to choose the sample size and values for x. In this example we will choose $N=40$ and choose x values to be 10 for the first 20 observations, and 20 for the second 20 observations. For each value of x, we randomly choose, or draw, a random error, then combine the elements to create an artificial value of y. This process is repeated N times.

How is this done in SAS? Examine the code below.

```
data normal;                          * data set;
call streaminit(1234567);             * set random number stream;
      do n = 1 to 40;                 * do loop 40 times;
      if n < 21 then x = 10;          * x = 10 for n<=20;
      else x = 20;                    * x = 20 for n>20;
      e = rand('normal',0,50);        * e is N(0,2500);
      y = 100 + 10*x + e;             * DGP=data generating process;
      output;                         * observation to data set;
      end;                            * end do loop;
run;
```

Creating random numbers is a science, and random numbers are actually not totally random. See Appendix B4 in *Principles of Econometrics, 4th Edition* for a discussion of random numbers. We create them using a function, and so that we can replicate our results during a SAS session we set the starting value, called a **seed**, to be some value. This starting value can be anything, but we tend to use 7-9 digit odd numbers. The **RAND** random number seeds require **call streaminit(*positivenumber*)**.[3]

---

[3] The older style random number generators, such as rannor and ranuni use a seed=1234567; statement to initialize the random number stream. RAND is a newer function.

To create a sample of size 40 we use a **do loop**, which is a way to replicate a command, or a set of commands. These loops start with the word **do** and stop with the command **end**. The command **do n = 1 to 40;** replicates a block of commands 40 times, while the **index variable** (here called **n**) automatically iterates from 1 to 40.

As **n** goes from 1 to 40 the variable **x** is assigned the value 10 for the first 20 observations using an **IF-THEN** statement. When the **IF** part is not true, then **ELSE** defines the value of **x**. The value y is $100 + 10x$ plus a random number from a normal distribution with mean zero and standard deviation 50. The SAS function **RAND** will create a random number from the distribution indicated by the keyword, here **'normal'**. For documentation enter **help rand** into the SAS command line.

2B.1 The true estimator variance

The SAS data set *normal* will have an observation added each time the **output** statement is encountered. Print observations 15-25.

```
proc print data=normal(firstobs=15 obs=25);
var x y;
title 'Observations from normal DGP';
run;
```

Observations from normal DGP

Obs	x	y
15	10	256.393
16	10	102.068
17	10	189.704
18	10	245.316
19	10	172.645
20	10	192.968
21	20	253.793
22	20	234.539
23	20	285.468
24	20	227.729
25	20	276.873

Because we know the true slope parameters, and the true variance of the error term, σ^2, we can calculate the true variance of b_2 the least squares slope estimator. It is $\mathrm{var}(b_2) = \sigma^2 / \sum(x_i - \bar{x})^2$. The corrected sum of squares for x is obtained using the commands

```
proc means data=normal css;          * summary stats;
var x;                                * specify variable;
title 'corrected ss for x';
run;
```

Analysis Variable : x
Corrected SS

———————

1000.00

———————

Then $\text{var}(b_2) = \sigma^2/\sum(x_i - \bar{x})^2 = 2500/1000 = 2.50$. Compute this value using SAS. The true standard error of b_2 is the square root of this quantity, so we can calculate it as well.

```
data truevar;                          * data set;
sig2 = 2500;                           * true variance e;
ssx =  1000;                           * sum(x-xbar)**2;
truevar = sig2/ssx;                    * true var(b2);
truese = sqrt(truevar);                * true se(b2);
run;
proc print data=truevar;               * print;
var truevar truese;                    * true var & se;
title 'true var(b2) and se(b2)';
run;
```

```
              true var(b2) and se(b2)

        Obs     truevar      truese
         1        2.5       1.58114
```

In a simulation experiment, we can compare the estimated values of the variance and standard error to the true values, which is something we cannot do in the real world.

2B.2 Regression on artificial data

Estimate the simple linear model $y = \beta_1 + \beta_2 x + e$ using the artificial data.

```
proc reg data=normal outest=est tableout mse;
model y = x;
title 'regression with normal data';
title2 'true intercept = 100 & slope = 10';
run;
```

The **PROC REG** statement has the options **outest=est**. The **outest=** option results in estimates being written to a SAS data set, here "**est**". The option **tableout** results in additional regression statistics being added to the output data set **est**. The option **MSE** results in the estimate of σ^2 being added to the outset data set. The **model** statement specifies the model. A portion of the output is

```
                   Analysis of Variance

                          Sum of        Mean
Source            DF      Squares       Square     F Value    Pr > F

Model              1       79366        79366       28.31     <.0001
Error             38      106517     2803.08893
Corrected Total   39      185883
```

```
        Root MSE              52.94421   R-Square    0.4270
        Dependent Mean       246.04475   Adj R-Sq    0.4119
        Coeff Var             21.51812

                      Parameter      Standard
   Variable    DF     Estimate         Error    t Value   Pr > |t|
   Intercept    1     112.41359      26.47210      4.25     0.0001
   x            1       8.90874       1.67424      5.32     <.0001
```

In this one sample of data the estimated variance of the error term is $\hat{\sigma}^2 = 2803.09$, compared to the true value of 2500. The estimated intercept and slope are 112.41 and 8.91 compared to the true values of 100 and 10, respectively. Seeing how our estimators perform in data, when we know what the values should be, is very informative.

2B.3 OUTEST from PROC REG

In the Monte Carlo experiment the **outest=est** and **tableout** and **MSE** options will result in a recording of regression output in a convenient form. Examine the contents of the data set **est**.

```
proc print data=est;                    * example of outest;
title 'OUTEST data';
run;
```

```
                          OUTEST data

                          I
                          n
                 _        t
            _    D        e
            M    E   _    r
            O T  P   R    c               _  E  M   _
            D Y  V   M    e            _  I _ D   S   R
         O  E P  A   S    e       x  y I N P F   E   S
         b  L E  R   E    p          _ N P F   E   S Q
         s  _ _  _   _    t    x   y  _ _ _   _   _   _

      1 MODEL1 PARMS  y 52.9442 112.414  8.9087 -1 1 2 38 2803.09 0.42697
      2 MODEL1 STDERR y 52.9442  26.472  1.6742  . .  .       .       .
      3 MODEL1 T      y 52.9442   4.246  5.3211  . .  .       .       .
      4 MODEL1 PVALUE y 52.9442   0.000  0.0000  . .  .       .       .
      5 MODEL1 L95B   y 52.9442  58.824  5.5194  . .  .       .       .
      6 MODEL1 U95B   y 52.9442 166.004 12.2981  . .  .       .       .
```

The variable _TYPE_ shows which statistic is recorded, and the column INTERCEPT and X are for the two regression parameters. The _TYPE_ = PARMS is the parameter estimate. The column labeled Y has -1 to indicate that it is the dependent variable.

2B.4 Simulating samples using do-loops

In the Monte Carlo experiment we will repeat the above steps many times to replicate the process of repeated sampling. We will use 10,000 Monte Carlo samples.[4] This amounts to putting another **do-loop** around our previous loop.

```
data normal;                        * data set;
call streaminit(1234567);           * set random number stream;
do sample = 1 to 10000;             * outer loop repeat samples;
      do n = 1 to 40;               * start inner loop;
      if n < 21 then x = 10;        * x = 10 for n<=20;
      else x = 20;                  * x = 20 for n>20;
      e = rand('normal',0,50);      * e is N(0,2500);
      y = 100 + 10*x + e;           * DGP;
      output;                       * output to data set;
      end;                          * end inner loop;
end;                                * end outer loop;
run;
```

The SAS data set *normal* will contain 400,000 observations in total; 10,000 samples of size $N = 40$. We will recover the estimates, standard errors and so on from 10,000 regressions.

The addition we make to the **PROC REG** statement is the all important **noprint** option. We do not want to see the regression output 10,000 times. Also, we have added the statement **by sample;** In the **do-loop** the index variable **sample** keeps track of which sample we are creating. Each sample has a unique value of **sample** from 1 to 10,000. The **BY** statement says that **PROC REG** is to be repeated for each value of **sample**.

```
proc reg noprint data=normal outest=est tableout MSE;
model y = x;
by sample;                          * repeat for each sample;
run;
```

2B.5 Summarizing parameter estimates

What about the parameter estimates themselves? Extract them to a SAS data set, and use **PROC UNIVARIATE** to obtain details, and a histogram.

```
data parm;                          * data set;
set est;                            * read est;
if _type_='PARMS';                  * keep if PARMS;
b1 = intercept;                     * b1 est intercept;
b2 = x;                             * b2 est slope;
sig2 = _MSE_;                       * sig2 est variance;
keep sample b1 b2 sig2;             * keep 4 variables;
run;
```

---

[4] The value 10,000 is chosen with care. See A. Colin Cameron and Pravin K. Trivedi (2005) *Microeconometrics: Methods and Applications*, Cambridge University Press, page 252.

```
proc means data=parm mean var std min max p1 p99;
var b1 b2 sig2;
title 'Monte Carlo summary statistics';
run;
```

We find that (partial output shown) the average of the 10,000 estimates of the slope is 10.01 (compared to the true value of 10), demonstrating the unbiasedness of the least squares estimator when the usual model assumptions hold. We also see that the sample variance of the 10,000 estimates is 2.56. The true variance of b_2 is 2.50, which illustrates what variance of b_2 actually measures—the sampling variation of the least squares estimates in repeated (many) samples. The average estimate of the error variance is 2493.29 compared to the true value of 2500.

Monte Carlo summary statistics

The MEANS Procedure

Variable	Mean	Variance	Std Dev	Minimum	Maximum
b1	99.7424750	634.2905778	25.1851261	1.5730896	192.6158233
b2	10.0176981	2.5582152	1.5994421	3.3165349	16.0624534
sig2	2493.29	325056.30	570.1370907	930.2318606	5472.07

For more detailed summary statistics for the slope use **PROC UNIVARIATE**.

```
proc univariate data = parm;
var b2;
histogram/normal;
title 'Sampling distribution of b2';
title2 'Errors Normal';
run;
```

The histogram shows a symmetrical "bell shape" which is what we expected. If the model errors are normally distributed then the least squares estimator is normally distributed.

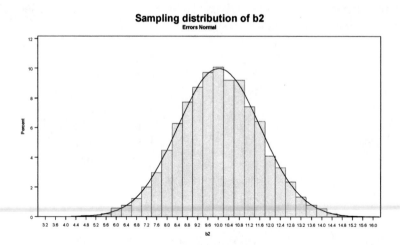

Sampling distribution of b2
Errors Normal

One final item worth checking is the estimator of the variance of b_2. In the **OUTEST** data set **EST** we have the estimated standard errors of the estimates. Using these values we can recover the variance estimates.

```
data se;                              * data set;
set est;                              * read est;
if _type_='STDERR';                   * keep if STDERR;
se = x;                               * rename std error;
varb2 = se**2;                        * var(b2);
keep sample varb2 se;                 * keep 3 variables;
run;

proc means data=se mean;
var varb2;                            * true var(b2) = 2.50;
title 'average value estimated var(b2):normal data';
title2 'true var(b2)= 2.50';
run;
```

```
                Analysis Variable : varb2

                          Mean
                     _____

                      2.4932851
                     _____
```

This simulation exercise will be continued and extended in Chapter 3.

CHAPTER 3

Interval Estimation and Hypothesis Testing

3.1 INTERVAL ESTIMATION

Assume that the assumptions in Chapter 2.1 of this manual hold, including the assumption that the random errors are normally distributed. In this case we know that the least squares estimators b_1 and b_2 have normal distributions. The least squares residuals are $\hat{e}_i = y_i - b_1 - b_2 x_i$ and our estimator of σ^2 is $\hat{\sigma}^2 = \sum \hat{e}_i^2 / (N-2)$. An important statistic for interval estimation is

$$t = \frac{b_2 - \beta_2}{\sqrt{\hat{\sigma}^2 / \sum (x_i - \bar{x})^2}} = \frac{b_2 - \beta_2}{\sqrt{\widehat{\operatorname{var}(b_2)}}} = \frac{b_2 - \beta_2}{\operatorname{se}(b_2)} \sim t_{(N-2)}$$

The ratio $t = (b_2 - \beta_2)/\operatorname{se}(b_2)$ has a t-distribution with $(N-2)$ degrees of freedom, which we denote as $t \sim t_{(N-2)}$. A similar result holds for b_1, so in general we can say, if all the assumptions of the simple linear regression model hold then

$$t = \frac{b_k - \beta_k}{\operatorname{se}(b_k)} \sim t_{(N-2)} \text{ for } k = 1,2$$

The t-distribution is a bell shaped curve centered at zero. It looks like the standard normal distribution, except it is more spread out, with a larger variance and thicker tails. The shape of the t-distribution is controlled by a single parameter called the **degrees of freedom**, often abbreviated as df. We use the notation $t_{(m)}$ to specify a t-distribution with m degrees of freedom. For m degrees of freedom the 95th percentile of the t-distribution is denoted $t_{(.95,m)}$. This value has the property that 0.95 of the probability falls to its left, so $P(t_{(m)} \le t_{(0.95,m)}) = 0.95$.

We can find a "critical value" t_c from a t-distribution such that $P(t \geq t_c) = P(t \leq -t_c) = \alpha/2$, where α is a probability often taken to be $\alpha = 0.01$ or $\alpha = 0.05$. The critical value t_c for degrees of freedom m is the percentile value $t_{(1-\alpha/2,m)}$ depicted below.

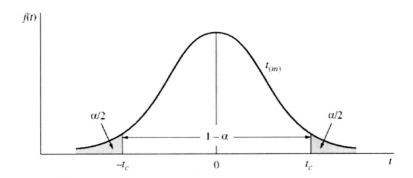

The values $b_k - t_c \text{se}(b_k)$ and $b_k + t_c \text{se}(b_k)$ are the endpoints of an **interval estimator** for β_k, also known as a confidence interval.

Using **PROC REG** we can obtain confidence intervals for the regression coefficients with a simple option. First, read in the food expenditure data, and turn off the labels.

```
data food;                          * open data set;
set 'food';                         * read food default path;
options nolabel;                    * turn off labels;
run;
```

Estimate the food expenditure regression using a new option for the **model** statement

label:model dependent = independent / options;

Note that in the **PROC REG** statement below we have added the option **outset=est tableout**. This will save the parameter estimates to a SAS data set called "**EST**". Before **model** we place a label (**conf_int_95**) that will appear in the regression output. We add two options to the model statement:

- **alpha = .05** controls the confidence interval probability.
- **clb** requests that confidence limits for the regression coefficients be printed.

```
proc reg data=food outest=est tableout;
conf_int_95:model food_exp = income/ alpha=.05 clb;
title '95% confidence interval estimates';
run;
```

Partial output is

```
            95% confidence interval estimates


                  The REG Procedure
                  Model: conf_int_95
              Dependent Variable: food_exp
```

```
Variable       DF       95% Confidence Limits
Intercept      1        -4.46328      171.29528
income         1         5.97205       14.44723
```

Note that the Model is now called **conf_int_95**. And below the parameter estimates are the 95% confidence intervals for each parameter.

3.1.1 Interval estimation details

The option **outset=est tableout** used with **PROC REG** creates a SAS data set of estimation results. To see the contents we print it.

```
proc print data=est;
title 'OUTEST data';
run;
```

                                    OUTEST data

```
Obs    _MODEL_      _TYPE_    _DEPVAR_    _RMSE_    Intercept    income    food_exp
 1    conf_int_95   PARMS     food_exp    89.5170     83.416    10.2096      -1
 2    conf_int_95   STDERR    food_exp    89.5170     43.410     2.0933       .
 3    conf_int_95   T         food_exp    89.5170      1.922     4.8774       .
 4    conf_int_95   PVALUE    food_exp    89.5170      0.062     0.0000       .
 5    conf_int_95   L95B      food_exp    89.5170     -4.463     5.9721       .
 6    conf_int_95   U95B      food_exp    89.5170    171.295    14.4472       .
```

This data set contains the estimated parameters in the PARMS row, the standard errors in the STDERR row, and so on. The column labeled **income** identifies the slope coefficient. Under **food_exp** the value -1 indicates that it is the dependent variable. To ensure our understanding of interval estimates we can re-create the values reported by SAS.

First, we will create a data set containing only the parameter estimates, then another containing the standard errors.

```
data parms;                         * new data set;
set est;                            * read est;
if _TYPE_='PARMS';                  * select _TYPE_;
b2 = income;                        * rename slope;
b1 = intercept;                     * rename intercept;
keep b1 b2;                         * keep two values;
run;

data se;                            * new data set;
set est;                            * read est;
if _TYPE_='STDERR';                 * select _TYPE_;
se2 = income;                       * rename se(b2);
se1 = intercept;                    * rename se(b1);
keep se1 se2;                       * keep two values;
run;
```

A new command of importance is **TINV(p,df)**. The **TINV** function returns the **p**[th] quantile (percentile) from the Student's t distribution with degrees of freedom **df**. The interval estimates can be constructed using the commands

```
data interval;
merge parms se;                     * merge data sets;
tc = tinv(.975,38);                 * 97.5 percentile t(38);
lb2 = b2 - tc*se2;                  * lower bound beta 2;
ub2 = b2 + tc*se2;                  * upper bound beta 2;
run;


proc print data=interval;
var b2 se2 tc lb2 ub2;
title '95% interval estimate';
run;
```

```
                  95% interval estimate

   Obs      b2        se2        tc        lb2       ub2
    1     10.2096   2.09326   2.02439   5.97205   14.4472
```

To fully appreciate the meaning of confidence intervals the repeated sampling context of classical statistics must be understood. In Appendix 3A we carry out a simulation, or **Monte Carlo**, experiment illustrating the concepts.

3.2 HYPOTHESIS TESTING THEORY

The null hypothesis, which is denoted H_0 (*H-naught*), specifies a value for a regression parameter, which for generality we denote as β_k, for $k = 1$ or 2. The null hypothesis is stated $H_0 : \beta_k = c$, where c is a constant, and is an important value in the context of a specific regression model. A null hypothesis is the belief we will maintain until we are convinced by the sample evidence that it is not true, in which case we *reject* the null hypothesis. For the null hypothesis H_0: $\beta_k = c$ the three possible alternative hypotheses are:

- $H_1 : \beta_k > c$ leads to a right tail test.
- $H_1 : \beta_k < c$ leads to a left tail test
- $H_1 : \beta_k \neq c$ leads to a two tail test.

The test statistic starts with the key result $t = (b_k - \beta_k)/\text{se}(b_k) \sim t_{(N-2)}$. *If* the null hypothesis $H_0 : \beta_k = c$ is *true*, *then* we can substitute c for β_k and it follows that

$$t = \frac{b_k - c}{\text{se}(b_k)} \sim t_{(N-2)} \qquad (3.1)$$

The null hypothesis is rejected in favor of the alternative if the *t*-statistic value falls in the **rejection region.**

3.2.1 Right tail t-tests

We reject the null hypothesis if the test statistic is larger than the critical value for the level of significance α. The critical value that leaves probability α in the right tail is the (1−α)-percentile $t_{(1-\alpha, N-2)}$, as shown below.

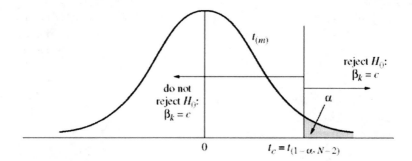

3.2.2 Left tail t-tests

We reject the null hypothesis if the test statistic is smaller than the critical value for the level of significance α. The critical value that leaves probability α in the left tail is the α-percentile $t_{(\alpha, N-2)}$ as shown below.

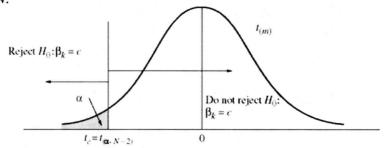

3.2.3 Two-tail t-tests

We reject the null hypothesis that $H_0 : \beta_k = c$ in favor of the alternative that $H_1 : \beta_k \neq c$ if the test statistic $t \leq t_{(\alpha/2, N-2)}$ or $t \geq t_{(1-\alpha/2, N-2)}$, as shown below.

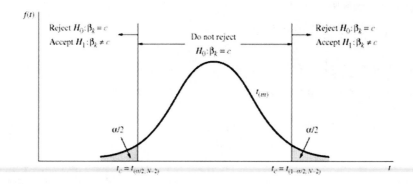

3.2.4 The *p*-value for t-tests

When reporting the outcome of statistical hypothesis tests, it has become standard practice to report the *p*-value (an abbreviation for **probability value**) of the test.

> *p*-**value rule**: Reject the null hypothesis when the *p*-value is less than, or equal to, the level of significance α. That is, if $p \le \alpha$ then reject H_0. If $p > \alpha$ then do not reject H_0.

How the *p*-value is computed depends on the alternative. If t is the calculated value of the *t*-statistic, then:

if $H_1 : \beta_k > c$, p = probability to the right of t

if $H_1 : \beta_k < c$, p = probability to the left of t

if $H_1 : \beta_k \ne c$, p = <u>sum</u> of probabilities to the right of $|t|$ <u>and</u> to the left of $-|t|$

3.3 HYPOTHESIS TESTING EXAMPLES

3.3.1 Right tail test of significance

The null hypothesis is $H_0 : \beta_2 = 0$. The alternative hypothesis is $H_1 : \beta_2 > 0$. The test statistic is (3.1). In this case $c = 0$, so $t = b_2 / \text{se}(b_2) \sim t_{(N-2)}$ if the null hypothesis is true. Let us select $\alpha = 0.05$. The critical value for the right-tail rejection region is the 95th percentile of the *t*-distribution with $N - 2 = 38$ degrees of freedom, $t_{(0.95,38)} = 1.686$. Thus we will reject the null hypothesis if the calculated value of $t \ge 1.686$. If $t < 1.686$, we will not reject the null hypothesis. Using the food expenditure data, we found that $b_2 = 10.21$ with standard error $\text{se}(b_2) = 2.09$. The value of the test statistic is

$$t = \frac{b_2}{\text{se}(b_2)} = \frac{10.21}{2.09} = 4.88$$

Since $t = 4.88 > 1.686$, we reject the null hypothesis that $\beta_2 = 0$ and accept the alternative that $\beta_2 > 0$. That is, we reject the hypothesis that there is no relationship between income and food expenditure, and conclude that there is a *statistically significant* positive relationship between household income and food expenditure.

We will use the **outset=est tableout** results shown above, in Section 3.1.1 of this manual, to implement this test in SAS[1]. We need a new function **PROBT(x,df)**. The **PROBT** function returns the cumulative probability that an observation from a Student's t distribution, with degrees of freedom **df**, is less than or equal to **x**. The area in the right tail is then **1 − PROBT(x,df)**.

---

[1] SAS PROC REG has "automatic" commands for hypothesis testing. These are introduced in Chapter 6.

```
data ttest;
merge parms se;
tstat = b2/se2;
tc = tinv(.95,38);                    * 95th percentile t(38);
pval = 1 - probt(tstat,38);           * right tail p value;
run;

proc print data=ttest;
var b2 se2 tstat tc pval;
title 'right tail test beta2=0 alpha=.05';
run;
```

In the above code **tc** is the 0.05 critical value for the right tail test, and **pval** is the right tail p-value.

```
                right tail test beta2=0 alpha=.05

    Obs      b2        se2       tstat       tc         pval
     1     10.2096   2.09326   4.87738    1.68595    .000009729
```

3.3.2 Right tail test for an economic hypothesis

Consider the null hypothesis $H_0 : \beta_2 \leq 5.5$. This test is carried out exactly as if $H_0 : \beta_2 = 5.5$. The alternative hypothesis is $H_1 : \beta_2 > 5.5$. The test statistic $t = (b_2 - 5.5)/\text{se}(b_2) \sim t_{(N-2)}$ if the null hypothesis is true. Let us select $\alpha = 0.01$. The critical value for the right-tail rejection region is the 99th percentile of the t-distribution with $N - 2 = 38$ degrees of freedom, $t_{(0.99,38)} = 2.429$. We will reject the null hypothesis if the calculated value of $t \geq 2.429$. If $t < 2.429$ we will not reject the null hypothesis. Using the food expenditure data, $b_2 = 10.21$ with standard error $\text{se}(b_2) = 2.09$. The value of the test statistic is

$$t = \frac{b_2 - 5.5}{\text{se}(b_2)} = \frac{10.21 - 5.5}{2.09} = 2.25$$

Since $t = 2.25 < 2.429$ we do not reject the null hypothesis that $\beta_2 \leq 5.5$.

The SAS commands are

```
data ttest;
merge parms se;
tstat = (b2-5.5)/se2;
tc = tinv(.99,38);                    * 99th percentile t(38);
pval = 1 - probt(tstat,38);           * right tail p value;
run;

proc print data=ttest;
var b2 se2 tstat tc pval;
title 'right tail test beta2=5.5 alpha=.01';
run;
```

In the above code **tc** is the 0.01 critical value for the right tail test, and **pval** is the right tail p-value.

```
              right tail test beta2=5.5 alpha=.01

     Obs      b2        se2       tstat       tc        pval
      1     10.2096   2.09326   2.24990    2.42857   0.015163
```

The p-value is shown in the figure below.

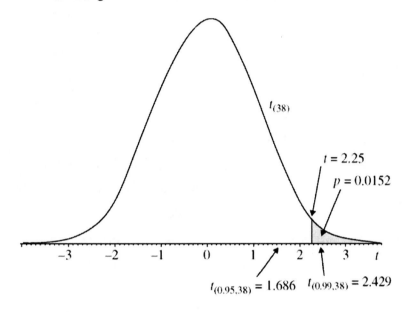

3.3.3 Left tail test of an economic hypothesis

Consider the null hypothesis $H_0 : \beta_2 \geq 15$. The alternative hypothesis is $H_1 : \beta_2 < 15$. The test statistic $t = (b_2 - 15)/\text{se}(b_2) \sim t_{(N-2)}$ if the null hypothesis is true. Let us select $\alpha = 0.05$. The critical value for the left-tail rejection region is the 5th percentile of the t-distribution with $N - 2 = 38$ degrees of freedom, $t_{(.05,38)} = -1.686$. We will reject the null hypothesis if the calculated value of $t \leq -1.686$. If $t > -1.686$ we will not reject the null hypothesis. Using the food expenditure data, $b_2 = 10.21$ with standard error $\text{se}(b_2) = 2.09$. The value of the test statistic is

$$t = \frac{b_2 - 15}{\text{se}(b_2)} = \frac{10.21 - 15}{2.09} = -2.29$$

Since $t = -2.29 < -1.686$ we reject the null hypothesis that $\beta_2 \geq 15$ and accept the alternative that $\beta_2 < 15$.

```
    data ttest;
    merge parms se;
    tstat = (b2-15)/se2;
    tc = tinv(.05,38);                   * 5th percentile t(38);
```

```
pval = probt(tstat,38);                      * left tail p value;
run;

proc print data=ttest;
var b2 se2 tstat tc pval;
title 'left tail test beta2=15 alpha=.05';
run;
```

For the left tail test **TINV(.05,38)** gives the left tail critical value, and **PROBT(t,38)** is the left tail p-value.

```
                left tail test beta2=15 alpha=.05

    Obs        b2        se2        tstat        tc        pval
     1      10.2096    2.09326    -2.28846    -1.68595    0.013881
```

3.3.4 Two tail test of an economic hypothesis

Consider the null hypothesis $H_0 : \beta_2 = 7.5$. The alternative hypothesis is $H_1 : \beta_2 \neq 7.5$. The test statistic $t = (b_2 - 7.5)/\mathrm{se}(b_2) \sim t_{(N-2)}$ if the null hypothesis is true. Let us select $\alpha = .05$. The critical values for this two-tail test are the 2.5-percentile $t_{(0.025,38)} = -2.024$ and the 97.5-percentile $t_{(0.975,38)} = 2.024$. Thus we will reject the null hypothesis if the calculated value of $t \geq 2.024$ **or** if $t \leq -2.024$. If $-2.024 < t < 2.024$ we will not reject the null hypothesis. For the food expenditure data the value of the test statistic is

$$t = \frac{b_2 - 7.5}{\mathrm{se}(b_2)} = \frac{10.21 - 7.5}{2.09} = 1.29$$

Since $-2.204 < t = 1.29 < 2.204$ we do not reject the null hypothesis that $\beta_2 = 7.5$.

```
data ttest;
merge parms se;
tstat = (b2-7.5)/se2;
tc = tinv(.975,38);                  * 97.5 percentile t(38);
pval = 2*(1-probt(abs(tstat),38));   * two tail p value;
run;

proc print data=ttest;
var b2 se2 tstat tc pval;
title 'two tail test beta2=7.5 alpha=.05';
run;
```

For this two tail test **TINV(.975,38)** gives the 97.5 percentile of the t-distribution. The p-value must be computed as the <u>sum</u> of probabilities to the right of $|t|$ <u>and</u> to the left of $-|t|$. The area to the right of $|t|$ is **1-probt(abs(t),38)**. Then twice that is the area in the two tails.

```
                  two tail test beta2=7.5 alpha=.05

     Obs        b2       se2      tstat        tc        pval
      1     10.2096   2.09326   1.29446   2.02439    0.20332
```

3.3.5 Two tail test of significance

The null hypothesis is $H_0 : \beta_2 = 0$. The alternative hypothesis is $H_1 : \beta_2 \neq 0$. The test statistic $t = b_2 / \text{se}(b_2) \sim t_{(N-2)}$ *if the null hypothesis is true.* Let us select $\alpha = .05$. The critical values for this two-tail test are the 2.5-percentile $t_{(.025,38)} = -2.024$ and the 97.5-percentile $t_{(.975,38)} = 2.024$. We will reject the null hypothesis if the calculated value of $t \geq 2.024$ *or* if $t \leq -2.024$. If $-2.024 < t < 2.024$, we will not reject the null hypothesis. Using the food expenditure data, the value of the test statistic is $t = b_2 / \text{se}(b_2) = 10.21/2.09 = 4.88$. Since $t = 4.88 > 2.024$ we reject the null hypothesis that $\beta_2 = 0$ and conclude that there is a statistically significant relationship between income and food expenditure. The SAS code is identical to that above, in Section 3.3.4, except that now the *t*-statistic is **t = b/se**.

The two tail test of significance is carried out automatically by **PROC REG** and the other regression procedures we will use. Examine the food regression output. The column labeled **t Value** is the *t*-statistic for a test of significance. The column labeled **Pr > |t|** is the two-tail *p*-value. For the slope parameter it is reported as "less than .0001" because tests of significance are rarely carried out at significance levels below $\alpha = .01$, thus the additional decimal places are not needed in practice.

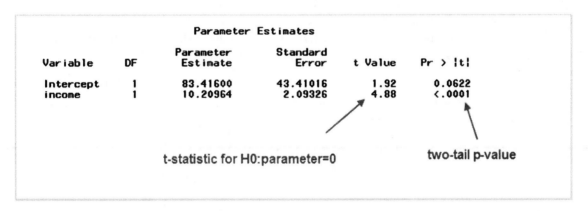

3.4 TESTING AND ESTIMATING LINEAR COMBINATIONS

So far we have discussed statistical inference (point estimation, interval estimation and hypothesis testing) for a single parameter, β_1 or β_2. More generally we may wish to estimate and test hypotheses about a **linear combination of parameters** $\lambda = c_1\beta_1 + c_2\beta_2$, where c_1 and c_2 are constants that we specify. The estimator $\hat{\lambda} = c_1 b_1 + c_2 b_2$ is the best linear unbiased estimator of $\lambda = c_1\beta_1 + c_2\beta_2$, with estimated variance

$$\widehat{\text{var}\left(\hat{\lambda}\right)} = \overline{\text{var}\left(c_1 b_1 + c_2 b_2\right)} = c_1^2 \widehat{\text{var}(b_1)} + c_2^2 \widehat{\text{var}(b_2)} + 2c_1 c_2 \widehat{\text{cov}(b_1, b_2)}$$

The standard error of $\hat{\lambda} = c_1 b_1 + c_2 b_2$ is the square root of the estimated variance,

$$\text{se}\left(\hat{\lambda}\right) = \text{se}\left(c_1 b_1 + c_2 b_2\right) = \sqrt{\widehat{\text{var}\left(c_1 b_1 + c_2 b_2\right)}}$$

Thus a $100(1-\alpha)\%$ interval estimate for $c_1 \beta_1 + c_2 \beta_2$ is

$$\left(c_1 b_1 + c_2 b_2\right) \pm t_c \, \text{se}\left(c_1 b_1 + c_2 b_2\right)$$

A more **general linear hypothesis** involves both parameters and may be stated as

$$H_0 : c_1 \beta_1 + c_2 \beta_2 = c_0$$

where c_0, c_1 and c_2 are specified constants, with c_0 being the hypothesized value. Despite the fact that the null hypothesis involves both coefficients, it still represents a single hypothesis to be tested using a t-statistic. Sometimes it is written equivalently in implicit form as

$$H_0 : \left(c_1 \beta_1 + c_2 \beta_2\right) - c_0 = 0$$

The alternative hypothesis might be two-tail or one-tail. The test statistic is the t-statistic

$$t = \frac{\left(c_1 b_1 + c_2 b_2\right) - c_0}{\text{se}\left(c_1 b_1 + c_2 b_2\right)} \sim t_{(N-2)} \text{ if the null hypothesis is true}$$

The rejection regions for the one- and two-tail alternatives are the same as those described in Section 3.3, and conclusions are interpreted the same way as well.

To implement the interval estimate or hypothesis test the estimated covariance matrix is required. It is obtained using an option on the **model** statement in **PROC REG**.

```
proc reg data=food;
model food_exp = income / covb;
run;
```

At the bottom of the regression output we find

```
                 Covariance of Estimates

    Variable        Intercept            income
    Intercept      1884.4422634      -85.90315668
    income         -85.90315668       4.381752212
```

It is more convenient to use PROC MODEL's built in command for estimating linear combinations.

3.4.1 PROC MODEL

Another procedure in SAS is **PROC MODEL**, which is found under the SAS/ETS set of procedures. Enter **help model** in the SAS command line and select **MODEL: SAS/ETS 9.2 User's Guide.**

PROC MODEL is a powerful, powerful procedure that we will use in many ways. It is designed to handle systems of linear and nonlinear equations. For now we are only considering a single linear equation but PROC MODEL still applies. The notation is a bit different, and the output is arranged differently. It has many different capabilities than PROC REG.

In order to "automatically" estimate and test linear combinations we can use

```
proc model data=food;
label b1 = 'intercept'
      b2 = 'income';
food_exp = b1 + b2*income;              * equation;
fit food_exp;
estimate 'lincom' b1+20*b2, 'test1' b1+20*b2-250;
title 'proc model for linear combinations';
run;
```

The LABEL statement is optional but helps when viewing the output. The equation to estimate is specified in algebraic form, food_exp = b1 + b2*income. We have called the parameters b1 and b2. The command that tells PROC MODEL to estimate the equation is fit food_exp. SAS then recognizes that it is to estimate (or fit to the data) the equation with food_exp on the left-hand side. Following the fit statement comes estimate statement, which will estimate and test linear and nonlinear combinations of the parameters. Here we have shown two items for estimate to work on, separated by a comma. The part in single quotes is a label. The output covers 3 pages. However the first two contain model and technical information, so we skip them. In the regression results, first comes some of the elements of the usual ANOVA table, then the parameter estimates. PROC MODEL calls the estimates "Nonlinear" which you can ignore— these are the usual least squares estimates. Following are the estimates of the linear combinations and their standard errors, t-values and two tail p-values.

```
                    proc model for linear combinations

                         The MODEL Procedure

                  Nonlinear OLS Summary of Residual Errors

                  DF      DF                                              Adj
Equation       Model   Error       SSE        MSE    Root MSE   R-Square   R-Sq

food_exp          2      38      304505     8013.3    89.5170    0.3850   0.3688


                   Nonlinear (OLS Parameter Estimates)

                              Approx            Approx
Parameter      Estimate     Std Err   t Value   Pr > |t|   Label

b1              83.416      43.4102     1.92     0.0622    intercept
b2             10.20964      2.0933     4.88     <.0001    income


                   Nonlinear (OLS  Estimates)    of linear combinations

                              Approx            Approx
Term           Estimate     Std Err   t Value   Pr > |t|   Label

lincom         287.6089     14.1780    20.29     <.0001    b1+20*b2
test1          37.60886     14.1780     2.65     0.0116    b1+20*b2-250
```

We find that the estimate of $\beta_1 + \beta_2 20$ is 287.6089 with standard error 14.178. Using this value, and a t-critical value, an interval estimate can be created. The estimated value of $\beta_1 + \beta_2 20 - 250$

is 37.60886. The t-value is for the null hypothesis $\beta_1 + \beta_2 20 - 250 = 0$, or $\beta_1 + \beta_2 20 = 250$. Using the p-value we reject this hypothesis at the 5% level of significance. The importance of these particular linear combinations is discussed in Chapter 3.6 of *Principles of Econometrics, 4th Edition*.

APPENDIX 3A MONTE CARLO SIMULATION

We continue the simulation experiment begun in Appendix 2A of this manual. Now we add summary measures for success of interval estimation and hypothesis tests. The first part of the code is the same as in Appendix 2A.

```
data normal;                       * data set;
call streaminit(1234567);          * set random number stream;
do sample = 1 to 10000;            * outer loop repeat samples;
      do n = 1 to 40;              * start inner loop;
      if n < 21 then x = 10;       * x = 10 for n<=20;
      else x = 20;                 * x = 20 for n>20;
      e = rand('normal',0,50);     * e is N(0,2500);
      y = 100 + 10*x + e;          * DGP;
      output;                      * output to data set;
      end;                         * end inner loop;
end;                               * end outer loop;
run;
```

To the **PROC REG** statement we include the option for computation of a 95% interval estimate.

```
proc reg noprint data=normal outest=est tableout;
model y = x/ alpha=.05 clb;
by sample;
run;
```

3A.1 Summarizing interval estimates

Now, we must extract the pieces from the SAS data set **est** that we wish to study. First, we examine the interval estimate for the slope. Consider the following statements:

```
data lb;                           * data set for lower bound;
set est;                           * read est;
if _type_='L95B';                  * keep if L95B;
lb = x;                            * rename lower bound;
keep sample lb;                    * keep only 2 var;
run;
```

The data set **lb** keeps the lower bound of the 95% interval estimate for the slope. We repeat this for the upper bound, and merge the two data sets into one.

```
data ub;                             * data set for upper bound;
set est;                             * read est;
if _type_='U95B';                    * keep if U95B;
ub = x;                              * rename upper bound;
keep sample ub;                      * keep 2 var;
run;

data bound;                          * data set;
merge lb ub;                         * merge data sets;
by sample;                           * control merge by sample;
cover = (lb <= 10 <= ub);            * cover = 1 or 0;
run;
```

The variable **cover** is 1 if the true slope value (10) is in the interval and it is zero otherwise. Print 10 observations from the data set *bound.*

```
proc print data=bound(obs=10);          * print 10 obs;
title '10 samples interval estimates: normal data';
run;
```

```
            10 samples interval estimates: normal data

      Obs     sample       lb         ub       cover
       1         1       5.51942    12.2981      1
       2         2       7.29521    14.2545      1
       3         3       7.31734    12.6362      1
       4         4       9.76215    14.7366      1
       5         5       7.52624    13.3568      1
       6         6       9.11726    14.3455      1
       7         7       9.89270    15.2301      1
       8         8       6.44272    12.8077      1
       9         9       6.88669    13.6123      1
      10        10       5.34435    11.4173      1
```

We see that for each of the first 10 samples the true value is contained within the 95% interval estimate. To see what happens in all 10,000 samples use **PROC MEANS** and choose the option **mean** so that only the average is computed.

```
proc means data=bound mean;             * compute only mean;
var cover;
title 'average values interval estimates:normal data';
run;
```

```
              Analysis Variable : cover

                      Mean
                 _____

                  0.9454000
                 _____
```

We see that 94.54% of the intervals we have created cover, or contain, the true parameter value. That is what a **confidence interval estimate** is supposed to do.

3A.2 Summarizing t-tests

How do the *t*-tests of significance perform? Extract the slope estimates and the standard error of the slope from the SAS data set **est**.

```
data parm;                          * data set;
set est;                            * read est;
if _type_='PARMS';                  * keep if PARMS;
b2 = x;                             * rename slope;
keep sample b2;                     * keep 2 variables;
run;

data se;                            * data set;
set est;                            * read est;
if _type_='STDERR';                 * keep if STDERR;
se = x;                             * rename std error;
keep sample se;                     * keep 2 variables;
run;
```

Construct two *t*-statistics, one testing the true null hypothesis that $\beta_2 = 10$ and then another testing the false null hypothesis that $\beta_2 = 12$. Using the calculated *t*-statistics, carry out a two-tail test at the 5% level of significance. The rejection rule for a two tail test can be restated as rejecting the null hypothesis when the absolute value of the *t*-statistic is greater than or equal to the critical value. The variables **reject0** and **reject1** are 0/1 variables indicating whether the null hypothesis is rejected, or not.

```
data ttest;                         * data set;
merge parm se;                      * merge statement;
by sample;                          * control merge by sample;
tstat0 = (b2 - 10)/se;              * test true Ho:beta2=10;
tstat1 = (b2 - 12)/se;              * test false Ho:beta2=12;
tc = tinv(.975,38);                 * alpha=.05 critical value;
reject0 = (abs(tstat0) >= tc);      * record rejection;
reject1 = (abs(tstat1) >= tc);      * record rejection;
run;
```

Print the first 10 observations of this data set.

```
proc print data=ttest(obs=10);      * print 10 obs;
title 't-test values:normal data';
run;
```

Note that we do not reject any of the "true" null hypotheses, but we reject one of the false null hypotheses. This is what we want in a test.

```
                        t-test values:normal data
```

Obs	sample	b2	se	tstat0	tstat1	tc	reject0	reject1
1	1	8.9087	1.67424	-0.65179	-1.84636	2.02439	0	0
2	2	10.7749	1.71886	0.45080	-0.71276	2.02439	0	0

3	3	9.9768	1.31369	-0.01769	-1.54013	2.02439	0	0
4	4	12.2494	1.22863	1.83080	0.20297	2.02439	0	0
5	5	10.4415	1.44009	0.30661	-1.08220	2.02439	0	0
6	6	11.7314	1.29132	1.34080	-0.20800	2.02439	0	0
7	7	12.5614	1.31827	1.94300	0.42586	2.02439	0	0
8	8	9.6252	1.57208	-0.23839	-1.51059	2.02439	0	0
9	9	10.2495	1.66114	0.15019	-1.05380	2.02439	0	0
10	10	8.3808	1.49995	-1.07949	-2.41287	2.02439	0	1

Compute the averages of the 10,000 values.

```
proc means data=ttest mean;          * compute only mean;
var tstat0 reject0 tstat1 reject1;
title 'average values & pct rejections';
title2 'normally distributed errors';
run;
```

These averages (partial output) show that the *t*-test of the true null hypothesis is rejected 5.4% of the time, which is close to the 5% nominal value (level of significance) of the test. The false null hypothesis is rejected 23.5% of the time. This is called the **power** of the test, and power is good. It is the probability of rejecting a false null hypothesis.

```
average values & pct rejections
   normally distributed errors

     The MEANS Procedure
```

Variable	Mean
tstat0	0.0087930
reject0	0.0546000
tstat1	-1.2836140
reject1	0.2351000

3A.3 Illustrating the central limit theorem

What if not all of the assumptions hold? In particular, what if the random errors do not have a normal distribution? We will carry out the same experiment but with random errors that follow a **triangular** distribution. Let the continuous random variable v have the probability density function $f(v) = 2v, \quad 0 < v < 1$. If you sketch this density you will find that it is a triangle. The expected value of this random variable is $E(v) = 2/3$ and the variance is $\mathrm{var}(v) = 1/18$. To adjust the mean and variance to zero and one, respectively, compute

$$e = \frac{v - 2/3}{\sqrt{1/18}}$$

To implement this idea consider the following commands. The triangular random values are created using the SAS function **rand('triangle',1);** The keyword **triangle** indicates the type of random numbers. The value "1" is the upper bound of the random values we create. Just for illustration create 10,000 values and summarize them using **PROC UNIVARIATE**.

```
data triangle;
call streaminit(1234567);          * set random number stream;
nobs = 10000;                      * number observations;
     do n = 1 to nobs;             * do NOBS times;
     tri = rand('triangle',1);     * triangle in (0,1);
     tri = (tri-2/3)/sqrt(1/18);   * mean=0 and std=1;
     output;                       * output to data set;
     end;                          * end loop;
run;

proc univariate data=triangle;     * summarize;
var tri;                           * variable;
histogram;                         * histogram plot;
title 'triangle distribution mean=0 std=1';
run;
```

The summary statistics show that these 10,000 random numbers have mean 0.005 (close to desired value of zero) and standard deviation 1.00.

```
                The UNIVARIATE Procedure
                     Variable:  tri

                          Moments

N                       10000   Sum Weights             10000
Mean                0.0054417   Sum Observations   54.4169747
Std Deviation      1.00055623   Variance           1.00111277
```

The histogram shows the shape of the distribution

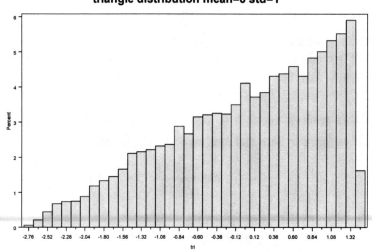

triangle distribution mean=0 std=1

3A.4 Monte Carlo experiment with triangular errors

Now carry through the same Monte Carlo experiment with triangle random errors, with the variance adjusted to 2500.

```
data triangle;
call streaminit(1234567);          * set random number stream;
nobs = 40;                         * number sample observations;
do sample = 1 to 10000;            * outer loop repeat samples;
      do n = 1 to nobs;            * loop NOBS times;
      if n < (nobs/2)+1 then x = 10;   * x = 10 for first half;
      else x = 20;                 * x = 20 for second half;
      tri = rand('triangle',1);    * triangle in (0,1);
      tri = (tri-2/3)/sqrt(1/18);  * mean=0 and std=1;
      e = 50*tri;                  * std = 50;
      y = 100 + 10*x + e;          * y = 100 + 10*x + e;
      output;                      * output to data set;
      end;                         * end inner loop;
end;                               * end outer loop;
run;

proc reg noprint data=triangle outest=est2 tableout;
model y = x/ alpha=.05 clb;
by sample;                         * repeat for each sample;
run;
```

Summarize interval estimates

```
data lb;                  * data set for lower bound;
set est2;                 * read est2;
if _type_='L95B';         * keep if L95B;
lb = x;                   * rename lower bound;
keep sample lb;           * keep only 2 var;
run;

data ub;                  * data set for upper bound;
set est2;                 * read est2;
if _type_='U95B';         * keep if U95B;
ub = x;                   * rename upper bound;
keep sample ub;           * keep 2 var;
run;

data bound2;              * data set;
merge lb ub;             * merge data sets;
by sample;               * control merge by sample;
cover = (lb <= 10 <= ub);  * cover = 1 or 0;
run;

proc print data=bound2(obs=10);    * print 10 obs;
title '10 samples interval estimates: triangle errors';
```

```
run;

proc means data=bound2 mean;          * compute only mean;
var cover;
title 'average values interval estimates: triangle errors';
run;
```

For this very nonnormal data the interval estimates coverage is

```
                     Analysis Variable : cover


                                 Mean
                             _____

                              0.9499000
                             _____
```

Summarize parameter estimates

What about the properties of the estimators?

```
data parm2;                       * data set;
set est2;                         * read est2;
if _type_='PARMS';                * keep if PARMS;
b2 = x;                           * rename slope;
keep sample b2;                   * keep 2 variables;
run;

proc univariate data = parm2;
var b2;
histogram/normal;
title 'Sampling distribution of b2';
title2 'Errors Triangular N=40';
run;
```

The summary statistics show that the average value of the least squares estimates is 9.99, compared to the true parameter value 10. The variance of the estimates is 2.509 compared to the true variance of 2.50. These properties do not depend on the distribution of the errors.

```
                    The UNIVARIATE Procedure

                            Moments

    N                  10000    Sum Weights            10000
    Mean          9.99187078    Sum Observations  99918.7078
    Std Deviation 1.58411753    Variance          2.50942834
    Skewness      0.00626361    Kurtosis          -0.0186471
```

The surprising feature of the Monte Carlo simulation is the distribution of the parameter estimates. The histogram shows that even with seriously non-normal errors, the distribution of the parameter estimates is the beautiful bell shaped curve. This is the consequence of the **central limit theorem**, one of the most remarkable results in all of statistics.

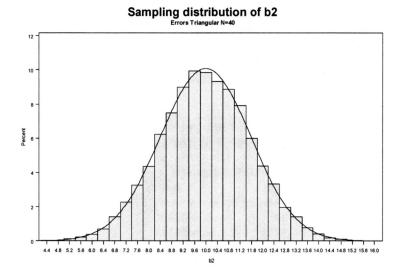

The approximate normality of the parameter estimates means that interval estimates and hypothesis tests should work as planned.

Summarizing t-tests

Repeat the code that computes the *t*-statistics and records their performance.

```
data se2;                              * data set;
set est2;                              * read est;
if _type_='STDERR';                    * keep if STDERR;
se = x;                                * rename std error;
varb2 = se**2;                         * estimated var(b2);
keep sample varb2 se;                  * keep 3 variables;

proc means data=se2 mean;              * sample mean;
var varb2;                             * true var(b2) = 2.50;
title 'average value estimated var(b2): triangle errors';
title2 'true var(b2)= 2.50';
run;

data ttest2;                           * data set;
merge parm2 se2;                       * merge statement;
by sample;                             * control merge by sample;
tstat0 = (b2 - 10)/se;                 * test true Ho:beta2=10;
tstat1 = (b2 - 12)/se;                 * test false Ho:beta2=12;
tc = tinv(.975,38);                    * alpha=.05 critical value;
reject0 = (abs(tstat0) >= tc);         * record rejection;
reject1 = (abs(tstat1) >= tc);         * record rejection;
run;

proc print data=ttest2(obs=10);        * print 10 obs;
title 't-test values: triangle errors';
```

```
run;

proc means data=ttest2 mean;                    * compute only mean;
title 'average values & pct rejections';
var tstat0 reject0 tstat1 reject1;
title2 'triangle error distribution';
run;
```

```
               average values & pct rejections
                  triangle error distribution

                    The MEANS Procedure
                    Variable          Mean
                   _____

                    tstat0      -0.0057851
                    reject0      0.0501000
                    tstat1      -1.2877200
                    reject1      0.2348000
                   _____
```

CHAPTER 4

Prediction, Goodness-of-Fit, and Modeling Issues

4.1 LEAST SQUARES PREDICTION THEORY

Given the simple linear regression model and standard assumptions, let x_0 be a value of the explanatory variable. We want to predict the corresponding value of y, which we call y_0. In order to use regression analysis as a basis for prediction we must assume that y_0 and x_0 are related to one another by the same regression model that describes our sample of data, so that, in particular,

$$y_0 = \beta_1 + \beta_2 x_0 + e_0 \tag{4.1}$$

where e_0 is a random error. We assume that $E(y_0) = \beta_1 + \beta_2 x_0$ and that $E(e_0) = 0$. We also assume that e_0 has the same variance as the regression errors, $\text{var}(e_0) = \sigma^2$, and e_0 is uncorrelated with the random errors that are part of the sample data, so that $\text{cov}(e_0, e_i) = 0$ $i = 1, 2, \ldots, N$. The **least squares predictor** of y_0 comes from the fitted regression line

$$\hat{y}_0 = b_1 + b_2 x_0 \tag{4.2}$$

That is, the predicted value $\hat{y}_0$ is given by the point on the least squares fitted line where $x = x_0$.

How good is this prediction procedure? The least squares estimators b_1 and b_2 are random variables—their values vary from one sample to another. It follows that the least squares predictor $\hat{y}_0 = b_1 + b_2 x_0$ must also be random. To evaluate how well this predictor performs we define the **forecast error**, which is analogous to the least squares residual,

$$f = y_0 - \hat{y}_0 = (\beta_1 + \beta_2 x_0 + e_0) - (b_1 + b_2 x_0) \tag{4.3}$$

Taking the expected value we find $E(f) = 0$, which means, on average, the forecast error is zero, and $\hat{y}_0$ is an **unbiased predictor** of y_0.

Using (4.3) and what we know about the variances and covariance of the least squares estimators, we can show that the variance of the forecast error is

$$\text{var}(f) = \sigma^2 \left[1 + \frac{1}{N} + \frac{(x_0 - \bar{x})^2}{\sum (x_i - \bar{x})^2} \right] \tag{4.4}$$

In practice we replace σ^2 in (4.4) by its estimator $\hat{\sigma}^2$ to obtain

$$\widehat{\text{var}(f)} = \hat{\sigma}^2 \left[1 + \frac{1}{N} + \frac{(x_0 - \bar{x})^2}{\sum (x_i - \bar{x})^2} \right]$$

The square root of this estimated variance is the **standard error of the forecast**

$$\text{se}(f) = \sqrt{\widehat{\text{var}(f)}} \tag{4.5}$$

Defining the critical value t_c to be the $100(1-\alpha/2)$-percentile from the t-distribution, we can obtain a $100(1-\alpha)\%$ **prediction interval** as

$$\hat{y}_0 \pm t_c \text{se}(f) \tag{4.6}$$

4.2 LEAST SQUARES PREDICTION EXAMPLE

In Chapter 2 we predicted that a household with $x_0 = \$2000$ weekly income would spend \$287.61 on food using the calculation

$$\hat{y}_0 = b_1 + b_2 x_0 = 83.4160 + 10.2096(20) = 287.6089$$

Now we are able to attach a "confidence interval" to this prediction. The standard error of the forecast is

$$\text{se}(f) = \sqrt{\widehat{\text{var}(f)}} = \sqrt{8214.31} = 90.6328$$

If we select $1-\alpha = 0.95$, then $t_c = t_{(0.975,38)} = 2.0244$ and the 95% prediction interval for y_0 is

$$\hat{y}_0 \pm t_c \text{se}(f) = 287.6069 \pm 2.0244(90.6328) = [104.1323, 471.0854]$$

To compute these values we first read the food expenditure data.

```
data food;            * open data set;
set 'food';           * read food;
options nolabel;      * turn off labels;
run;
```

Add an additional observation with $x_0 = 20$ and y_0 being a missing value (denoted by a period ".").

```
data morefood;        * added observations;
input food_exp income; * input var;
datalines;
```

```
. 20
;
run;
```

Combine the two data sets and estimate the food expenditure model, with some options. On the model statement we add the option "**p**" that causes predictions to be printed. The option **cli** causes 95% prediction intervals to be printed.

```
data morefood;                          * open morefood;
set food morefood;                      * combine food & morefood;
run;

proc reg data=morefood;
model food_exp=income/p cli;            * p & cli options;
output out=foodpred p=yhat stdi=sef lcl=lcl ucl=ucl;
title 'food regression with prediction';
run;
```

The **output** statement creates a new SAS data set *foodpred* containing the contents of *morefood* and in addition four new variables

Option	content	variable name
p	predicted value	yhat
stdi	standard error of forecast	sef
lcl	95% prediction interval lower bound	lcl
ucl	95% prediction interval upper bound	ucl

The regression output is the same as in other cases, but we note the additional header information that 41 observations were read but only 40 used in estimation.

```
Number of Observations Read                 41
Number of Observations Used                 40
Number of Observations with Missing Values   1
```

Even though only 40 observations are used in the estimation, all 41 observations will be used for prediction. The **p** and **cli** options produce the predicted values and interval predictions for all 41 observations. Observation 41 contains the predictions for $x = 20$.

```
        Dependent  Predicted    Std Error
  Obs    Variable      Value  Mean Predict    95% CL Predict      Residual
    1    115.2200   121.0896       36.1958  -74.3817   316.5609    -5.8696
    2    135.9800   128.2363       34.8519  -66.2315   322.7042     7.7437

                    Some observations omitted

   40    375.7300   424.4181       32.1593  231.8609   616.9752   -48.6881
   41           .   287.6089       14.1780  104.1323   471.0854          .
```

We should note that the variable SAS reports as **Std Error Mean Predict** in the above is not the standard error of the forecast, but rather the square root of

$$\widehat{\operatorname{var}}(b_1 + b_2 x_0) = \hat{\sigma}^2 \left(\frac{1}{N} + \frac{(x_0 - \bar{x})^2}{\sum(x_i - \bar{x})^2} \right)$$

Using these values we can build the prediction intervals ourselves to verify the calculations. We use the data set *foodpred* that contains the output data but also the original observations.

```
data foodpred;                          * open data set;
set foodpred;                           * read data;
tc = tinv(.975,38);                     * 97.5 percentile t(38);
lb = yhat-tc*sef;                       * prediction lower bound;
ub = yhat+tc*sef;                       * prediction upper bound;
run;
```

Print for observations 40 and 41 the upper and lower bounds (**lb** and **ub**) we have created along with the "automatic" values (**lcl** and **ucl**) created in the previous step to see that they are the same.

```
proc print data=foodpred(firstobs=40 obs=41);
var income sef tc lcl lb yhat ub ucl;
title 'predicted values';
run;
```

Obs	income	sef	tc	lcl	lb	yhat	ub	ucl
40	33.4	95.1184	2.02439	231.861	231.861	424.418	616.975	616.975
41	20.0	90.6328	2.02439	104.132	104.132	287.609	471.085	471.085

To produce a plot of the prediction interval, and the data, we take two approaches: first, using **PROC GPLOT**, and second using a **PLOT** statement within **PROC REG**.

In order to use **PROC GPLOT** we first sort the data according to the magnitude of the variable **income**.

```
proc sort data=foodpred;
by income;
run;
```

Then we define symbol statements and overlay plots of the data, predicted values, and lower and upper prediction intervals.

```
symbol1 value=dot color=blue;
symbol2 value=none interpol=join color=black;
symbol3 value=none interpol=join color=black line=2;
proc gplot data=foodpred;
plot food_exp*income=1 yhat*income=2 lcl*income=3 ucl*income=3 / overlay;
title 'food regression 95% prediction interval';
run;
```

The resulting plot is

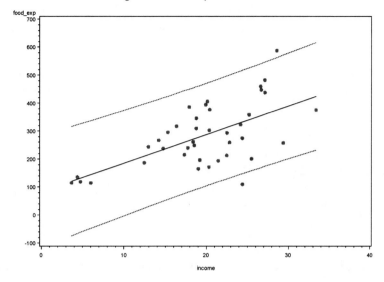

A similar plot, with some enhancements, is produced automatically using

```
proc reg data=food;
model food_exp = income;
plot food_exp*income / pred;          * plot & prediction interval;
title 'food regression & automatic 95% prediction interval';
run;
```

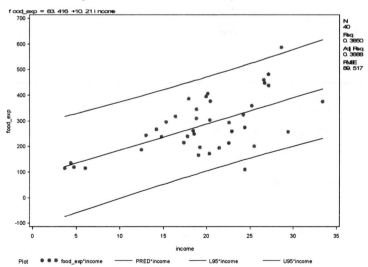

4.3 MEASURING GOODNESS-OF-FIT

To develop a measure of the variation in y that is explained by the model, we begin by separating y into its explainable and unexplainable components. We have assumed that $y = E(y) + e$ where $E(y) = \beta_1 + \beta_2 x$ is the explainable, "systematic" component of y, and e is the random, unsystematic and unexplainable component of y. While both of these parts are unobservable to us, we can estimate the unknown parameters β_1 and β_2. Decompose the value of y_i into

$$y_i = \hat{y}_i + \hat{e}_i$$

where $\hat{y}_i = b_1 + b_2 x_i$ and $\hat{e}_i = y_i - \hat{y}_i$.

The "point of the means" $(\bar{x}, \bar{y})$ falls on the least squares fitted line. This is a characteristic of the least squares fitted line whenever the regression model includes an intercept term. Subtract the sample mean $\bar{y}$ from both sides of the equation to obtain

$$y_i - \bar{y} = (\hat{y}_i - \bar{y}) + \hat{e}_i$$

The difference between y_i and its mean value $\bar{y}$ consists of a part that is "explained" by the regression model, $\hat{y}_i - \bar{y}$, and a part that is unexplained, $\hat{e}_i$. This breakdown leads to a decomposition of the total sample variability in y into explained and unexplained parts.

$$\sum (y_i - \bar{y})^2 = \sum (\hat{y}_i - \bar{y})^2 + \sum \hat{e}_i^2$$

This is a decomposition of the "total sample variation" in y into explained and unexplained components. Specifically, these "sums of squares" are:

1. $\sum (y_i - \bar{y})^2$ = total sum of squares = SST: a measure of total variation in y about the sample mean.

2. $\sum (\hat{y}_i - \bar{y})^2$ = sum of squares due to the regression = SSR: that part of total variation in y, about the sample mean, that is explained by, or due to, the regression. Also known as the "explained sum of squares."

3. $\sum \hat{e}_i^2$ = sum of squares due to error = SSE: that part of total variation in y about its mean that is not explained by the regression. Also known as the unexplained sum of squares, the residual sum of squares, or the sum of squared errors.

Using these abbreviations the decomposition becomes

$$SST = SSR + SSE$$

This decomposition of the total variation in y into a part that is explained by the regression model and a part that is unexplained allows us to define a measure, called the **coefficient of determination**, or R^2, that is the proportion of variation in y explained by x within the regression model.

$$R^2 = \frac{SSR}{SST} = 1 - \frac{SSE}{SST}$$

This decomposition, along with R^2 is shown when **PROC REG** is used for regression in the Analysis of Variance Table.

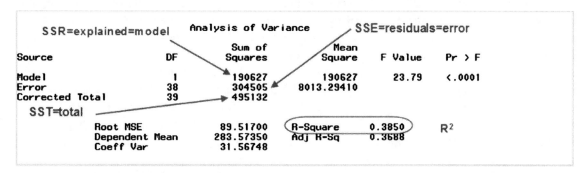

It is also worth noting that the R^2 measure is the <u>squared</u> simple correlation between the fitted value $\hat{y}$ and data values y. To compute a simple correlation in SAS use **PROC CORR**. We add a **var** statement to choose the variables

```
proc corr data=foodpred;              * simple correlations;
var food_exp yhat;                    * variables;
title 'correlation between fitted value and dependent variable';
run;
```

The output shows the correlation, called the **Pearson Correlation Coefficients**, the number of observations for each variable, and the p value of a test of whether the correlation is zero.

```
          Pearson Correlation Coefficients
             Prob > |r| under HO: Rho=0
               Number of Observations

                        food_exp            yhat
        food_exp         1.00000         0.62049
                                         <.0001
                              40              40


        yhat             0.62049         1.00000
                         <.0001
                              40              41
```

Note that the correlation squared $(0.62049)^2$ is $R^2 = 0.385$.

4.4 RESIDUAL ANALYSIS

The assumptions of the linear regression model state that the random errors are uncorrelated, with constant variance. A key component to any regression model evaluation is analysis of the residuals, which are the empirical counterparts of the true random errors. With every regression the residuals should be examined several ways. The residuals should be plotted against the x-variable, against the y-variable, and against the predicted y. If any patterns are detected it may indicate that the regression assumptions do not hold. Some of these graphs are produced automatically by SAS as we will examine in the next section on ODS graphics.

Recall that hypothesis tests and interval estimates for the coefficients rely on the assumption that the errors, and hence the dependent variable y, are normally distributed. While our tests and confidence intervals are valid in large samples whether the data are normally distributed or not, it is nevertheless desirable to have a model in which the regression errors are normally distributed, so that we do not have to rely on large sample approximations. If the errors are not normally distributed we might be able to improve our model by considering an alternative functional form or transforming the dependent variable. When choosing a functional form one criteria we might examine is whether a model specification satisfies regression assumptions, and in particular whether it leads to errors that are normally distributed. How do we check out the assumption of normally distributed errors?

We cannot observe the true random errors, so we must base our analysis of their normality on the least squares residuals, $\hat{e}_i = y_i - \hat{y}_i$. To construct a histogram we output the residuals to a data set and apply **PROC UNIVARIATE** with the **histogram** option. We also add "**normal**" to the **PROC UNIVARIATE** statement. This will produce a variety of tests for normality.

```
proc reg data=food;
model food_exp=income;
output out=foodresid r=ehat;          * output residuals;
title 'food regression with residual option';
run;

proc univariate data=foodresid normal;  * stats & normality tests;
var ehat;                                * variable;
histogram / normal;                      * histogram & normal;
title 'default analysis of food regression residuals';
run;
```

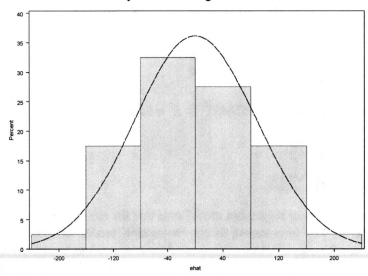

default analysis of food regression residuals

What does this histogram tell us? First, notice that it is centered at zero. This is not surprising because the mean of the least squares residuals is always zero if the model contains an intercept. Second, it seems symmetrical, however just checking the shape of the histogram is not a statistical "test."

There are many tests for normality. **PROC UNIVARIATE** produces

```
                       Tests for Normality

Test                  --Statistic---     -----p Value------
Shapiro-Wilk          W    0.988383      Pr < W      0.9493
Kolmogorov-Smirnov    D    0.067026      Pr > D     >0.1500
Cramer-von Mises      W-Sq 0.02788       Pr > W-Sq  >0.2500
Anderson-Darling      A-Sq 0.201366      Pr > A-Sq  >0.2500
```

We will not explain the workings of these tests, but note that the test p values are all above .05 so we fail to reject the null hypothesis of normality.

The **Jarque-Bera test** for normality is based on two measures, skewness and kurtosis. In the present context, **skewness** refers to how symmetric the residuals are around zero. Perfectly symmetric residuals will have a skewness of zero. **Kurtosis** refers to the "peakedness" of the distribution. For a normal distribution the kurtosis value is 3. For more on skewness and kurtosis see Appendix B and Appendix C. The Jarque-Bera statistic is given by

$$JB = \frac{N}{6}\left(S^2 + \frac{(K-3)^2}{4} \right)$$

where N is the sample size, S is skewness and K is kurtosis. Thus, large values of the skewness, and/or values of kurtosis quite different from 3, will lead to a large value of the Jarque-Bera statistic. When the residuals are normally distributed, the Jarque-Bera statistic has a chi-squared distribution with 2 degrees of freedom. We reject the hypothesis of normally distributed errors if a calculated value of the statistic exceeds a critical value selected from the chi-squared distribution with 2 degrees of freedom. The 5% critical value from a χ^2-distribution with 2 degrees of freedom is 5.99, and the 1% critical value is 9.21.

PROC UNIVARIATE reports skewness and kurtosis measures

```
N                     40      Sum Weights              40
Mean                   0      Sum Observations          0
Std Deviation  88.3618976     Variance          7807.82495
Skewness       -0.1011523     Kurtosis          0.15395753
```

These however are not <u>exactly</u> the ones used in the calculation of the Jarque-Bera test. The reason is that by default SAS constructs sample variances, etc. with the divisor $N-1$ rather than just N, which is what we want for Jarque-Bera. To obtain the proper skewness and kurtosis measures for this calculation we add the **vardef=n** option to **PROC UNIVARIATE**.

```
proc univariate data=foodresid vardef=n normal;
var ehat;
title 'analysis of food regression residuals with vardef=n';
run;
```

SAS now reports

```
Skewness          -0.0973189    Kurtosis          -0.0109667
```

But wait!! Now the skewness value is correct, but we note that SAS also reports kurtosis relative to the normal, so it is actually "excess kurtosis", the kurtosis value − 3. To obtain the calculated kurtosis K, the way we have defined it, add 3.

Applying these ideas to the food expenditure example, we have

$$JB = \frac{40}{6}\left(-.097^2 + \frac{(2.99-3)^2}{4}\right) = .063$$

Because .063 < 5.99 there is insufficient evidence from the residuals too conclude that the normal distribution assumption is unreasonable at the 5% level of significance.

4.4.1 Using PROC AUTOREG

There is another SAS procedure that will estimate a regression called **PROC AUTOREG**. It is found among the collection of procedures within **SAS/ETS**. See the documentation at http://support.sas.com/documentation/onlinedoc/ets/index.html. **PROC AUTOREG** is designed for regression analysis with economic, financial and time series data. The commands are similar to **PROC REG**, but with some other options. Below we invoke the **normal** option on the **model** statement.

```
proc autoreg data=food;               * autoreg;
model food_exp = income / normal;     * Jarque-Bera option;
title 'Jarque-Bera test in proc autoreg';
run;
```

The output of **PROC AUTOREG** is different than that of **PROC REG**. First, there is no ANOVA table, but the **SSE, MSE, root MSE** and **Regress R-Square** are present and the same as reported by **PROC REG**. The **DFE** reported is $N − 2$. Most other items will be explained later. The regression estimates are the same as using **PROC REG**. In the center we see the item under **Miscellaneous Statistics** called **Normal Test** which is the Jarque-Bera statistic, and a p-value upon which the test outcome can be based. We also fail to reject the null hypothesis on the grounds that 0.9688 > 0.05.

```
              Miscellaneous Statistics

     Statistic        Value      Prob        Label
     Normal Test     0.0633     0.9688    Pr > ChiSq
```

4.5 SAS ODS GRAPHICS

SAS has introduced a new type of graphics capability in Version 9.2. It is called **ODS Graphics**, where **ODS** stands for **Output Delivery System**.[1] It is very useful for us because it prints a variety of diagnostic graphs with little effort, and with no formatting worries. For more documentation enter **help ods** into the SAS command line, and select **Understanding and Customizing SAS Output: The Output Delivery System (ODS)**. In addition, visit http://support.sas.com/documentation/onlinedoc/stat/index.html and then locate

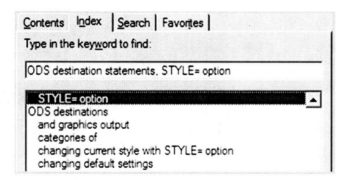

To initiate the **ODS graphics** it must be turned on, and then off. Also, the ODS graphs are sent to the default directory unless told otherwise. This is somewhat clumsy because then we have figures mixed among data sets and programs. We create a new subdirectory **c:\figures** and change the path where graphs are sent. We have specified **style=journal**. For a list of ODS options, on the SAS menu, select **Help** and then enter **ODS** in the **Index**.

There you will find descriptions of the various styles. Once changed this path is in effect until the SAS session ends, or until you change it.

```
ods listing gpath='c:\figures' style=journal;  * change path;
ods graphics on;                                * must turn ODS on;
proc reg data=food  plots=(residualhistogram);
model food_exp = income;
title 'food regression with ods graphics';
run;
ods graphics off;                               * must turn ODS off;
```

Implementing the code above produces the usual regression output, although it takes a few seconds longer. The **ODS** graphs do not show up in the usual **Graphics** window. Instead, after a few seconds, they are output as graphics files in **c:\figures**.

---

[1] The ODS system is vast. One reference, in addition to SAS documentation is Haworth, Lauren E., Zender, Cynthia, L., and Burlew, Michele M. (2009) *Output Delivery System: The Basics and Beyond*, Cary, N.C.: SAS Institute Inc.

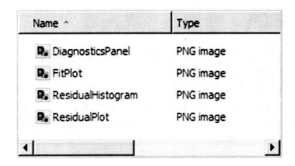

There are 4 new PNG (image) files: **DiagnosticsPanel.png, FitPlot.png, ResidualHistogram.png** and **ResidualPlot.png**. If you double-click the file name the image will appear in whatever viewer your computer has. Alternatively, in **Microsoft Word** select **Insert > Picture** and use the dialog box to select the one you want. If you wish to edit the photo within SAS select **Tools > Image Editor** on the SAS pull-down menu. Or use Photoshop, etc.

4.5.1 The SAS Image Editor

To use the SAS Image Editor, click on **Tools** on the **Menu** and select **Image Editor**.

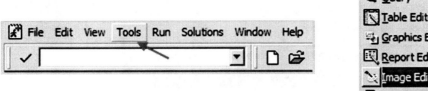
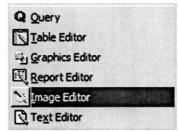

The Image Editor window has the usual Windows appearance. To open a file, select **File/Open** or click **Open**.

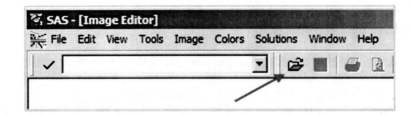

The ODS Graphics create ***.png** files by default. And we have changed the path for the ODS graphics to **c:\figures**. In the dialog box that opens choose *.png from the **Files of Type** list. Then choose the figure you wish to examine, and open it. Once the figure is open, you can copy, paste or print the figure. There are editing tools that can be used to enhance the figure.

4.5.2 ODS plots

The **DiagnosticsPanel.png** image shows 9 panels. A few are
- upper left corner: plot of residuals vs. predicted value. This should show no pattern if model assumptions hold.
- top row, center: plot of **studentized residual** vs. predicted value. The studentized residuals are "standardized" by dividing by the standard deviation of the least squares residual so that they have variance 1. Thus the ±2 reference lines are often added to help identify "significant" residuals.[2]
- middle row, center: plot of FOOD_EXP vs. predicted value. Values falling along 45-degree line indicate good fit, with no patterns evident.
- lower left panel: residual histogram.

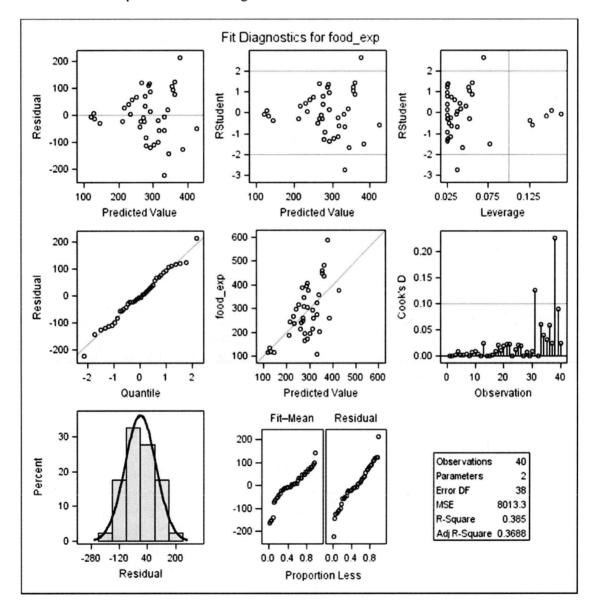

---

[2] The exact definition and calculation is given in the SAS/STAT User's Guide in Table 73.9. This material is advanced.

The **FitPlot.png** shows the scatter diagram with the fitted line, and 95% prediction interval (dotted lines), as well as a 95% confidence interval for $E(y)$ (shaded). When estimating $E(y_0)$ the best linear unbiased estimator is $b_1 + b_2 x_0$. The expected value and variance are

$$E(b_1 + b_2 x_0) = E(b_1) + E(b_2) x_0 = \beta_1 + \beta_2 x_0$$

$$\text{var}(b_1 + b_2 x_0) = \sigma^2 \left(\frac{1}{N} + \frac{(x_0 - \bar{x})^2}{\sum (x_i - \bar{x})^2} \right)$$

The variance of this estimator is smaller than the variance of a prediction, and its confidence interval is narrower.

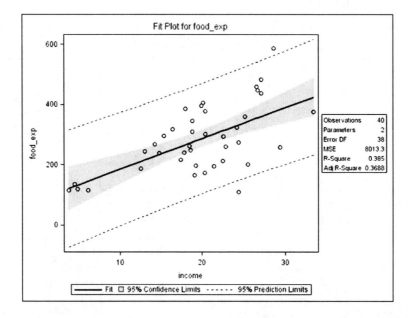

The **ResidualHistogram.png** produced by the **ODS graphics** is nice, superimposing a **Normal** distribution and also fitting a **Kernel** distribution. The **Kernel** distribution is an approximation to the distribution, whatever it might be, and not requiring it follow a **Normal** distribution.[3]

---

[3] The procedure for creating the kernel density can be found in the Statistical Graphics Procedures Guide, page 43. This is advanced material.

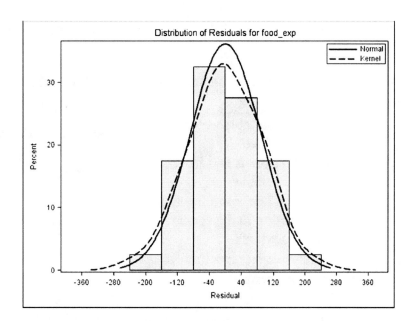

The **ResidualPlot.png** shows the least squares residuals plotted against the explanatory variable *INCOME*. Again, if the model assumptions hold we should see no patterns.

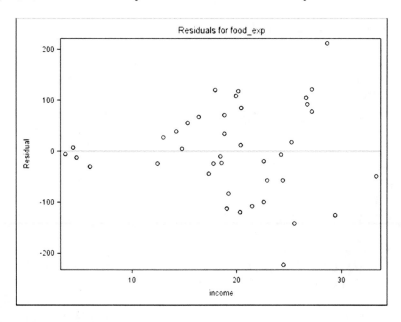

The **ODS Graph** possibilities are different for each **PROC**, such as **PROC REG, PROC AUTOREG**, etc. To see the list for **PROC REG**, enter **help reg** into the SAS command line. Scroll down to **ODS Graphics** and select this entry.

- Computer Resources in Regression Analysis
- Displayed Output
- ODS Table Names
- ODS Graphics ⬅

A portion of Table 74.11 shows lots of options. These can be selected in the space where we have **plots=(residualhistogram)**.

Table 74.11 ODS Graphical Displays Produced by PROC REG

ODS Graph Name	Plot Description	PLOTS Option
ObservedByPredicted	Dependent variable versus predicted values	OBSERVEDBYPREDICTED
PredictionPanel	Panel of residuals and fit versus specified variable	PREDICTIONS
PredictionPlot	Regression line, confidence limits, and prediction limits versus specified variable	PREDICTIONS(UNPACK)
PredictionResidualPlot	Residuals versus specified variable	PREDICTIONS(UNPACK)
ResidualByPredicted	Residuals versus predicted values	RESIDUALBYPREDICTED
ResidualHistogram	Histogram of fit residuals	RESIDUALHISTOGRAM
ResidualPlot	Plot of residuals versus regressor	RESIDUALS

4.6 NONLINEAR RELATIONSHIPS

Using the least squares estimation procedure we can estimate straight line relationships, and we can also estimate nonlinear relationships. See the variety of nonlinear functions in *Principles of Econometrics, 4th Edition*, page 142.

Open the SAS data set *wa_wheat*, and view its contents. As usual we compute the summary statistics and examine a few observations. Call the production in Greenough Shire *YIELD*.

```
data wheat;                          * open data set;
set 'wa_wheat';                      * read wa_wheat;
yield = greenough;                   * name yield;
label yield='wheat yield Greenough Shire';
run;
options label;
proc contents data=wheat;            * examine contents;
title 'wheat production data';
run;
options nolabel;                     * turn off label;
```

Recall that the data definitions are in the file *wa_wheat.def* that can be found at http://principlesofeconometrics.com/poe4/poe4.htm. We will explore the relationship between yield and time for Greenough Shire. The observations are for the period 1950-1997, and time is measured using the values 1,2,...,48.

Estimate a simple regression with dependent variable *YIELD* and independent variable *TIME*. First we change the ODS path, and turn on ODS graphics.

```
ods listing gpath='c:\figures' style=journal; * change path;
ods graphics on;                               * graphics on;
```

These are time series data. The most common error violation is correlated random errors. To help detect this problem we add an option **residuals(smooth)** in the **plots=()** statement.

```
proc reg data=wheat plots=(residuals(smooth) residualhistogram);
model yield = time;
title 'linear wheat production model';
run;
ods graphics off;
```

The regression output shows

Variable	DF	Parameter Estimate	Standard Error	t Value	Pr > |t|
Intercept	1	0.63778	0.06413	9.94	<.0001
TIME	1	0.02103	0.00228	9.23	<.0001

The **ODS FitPlot** shows the data scatter and fitted line. It takes some practice and experience, but notice the pattern in the residuals. First they are mostly positive, then mostly negative, and finally mostly positive again. This pattern indicates serial correlation which we discuss further in Chapter 9.

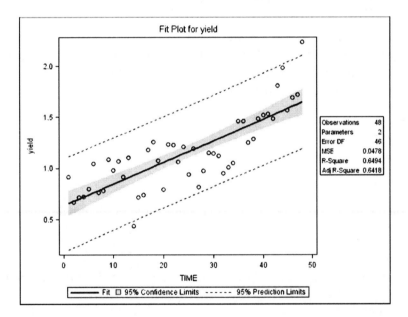

It is somewhat easier to detect his phenomenon by examining the ODS graphic plot **ResidualPlot.png** produced by the **plots=(residuals(smooth)** addition to the **PROC REG** statement. The "smooth" option results in a line being fit through the residuals to show the general trend. This is a good option to use when examining time series data.

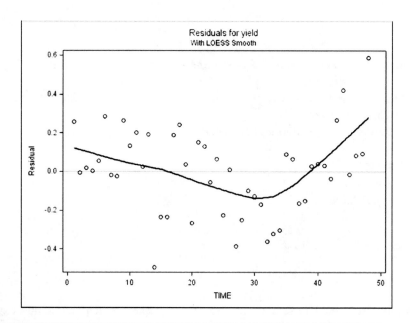

Remark: When ODS graphics are produced several times, the figure names have a post-script value 2, 3, etc to differentiate them. This will be true even when the **c:\figures** subdirectory is emptied between uses.

The problem with the model is that we are trying to capture a nonlinear relationship, clearly shown by the data scatter, with a straight line. One solution is to modify the model so that it will capture the curve in the data. A cubic equation is a possibility. The variable $TIME^3$ contains some large values, so we scale $TIME$ before cubing it.

```
data wheat;                        * open data set;
set wheat;                         * read wheat;
timecube = (time/100)**3;          * new variable;
run;
```

In the regression we use $TIMECUBE$ as the explanatory variable. Output the predicted values and residuals for later plots.

```
ods graphics on;
proc reg data=wheat plots=(residuals(smooth) residualhistogram);
model yield = timecube;
output out=wheatout p=yhat r=ehat;
title 'cubic wheat production model';
run;
ods graphics off;
```

The parameter estimates are

Variable	DF	Parameter Estimate	Standard Error	t Value	Pr > |t|
Intercept	1	0.87412	0.03563	24.53	<.0001
timecube	1	9.68152	0.82235	11.77	<.0001

The **ResidualPlot.png** image shows that relative to *TIMECUBE* there is much less of a "sine curve" shape.

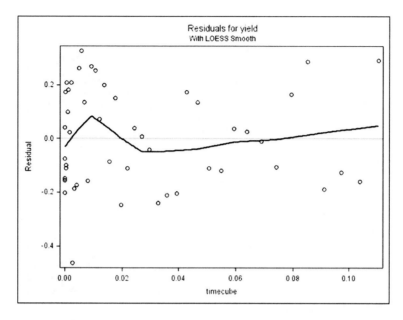

When using time series data it is always of interest to examine what happens relative to *TIME*, not a transformation of time. Using the output data set *wheatout* and **PROC GPLOT** we can construct a fitted line.

```
goptions reset=all;                        * reset graph options;
symbol1 value=dot color=blue;
symbol2 value=none interpol=join color=black;
symbol3 value=dot interpol=join color=black;
```

In the plot statements we use **symbol1** and **symbol2** for the scatter diagram with fitted line. The residual plot uses **symbol3**, a connected black line with dots.

```
proc gplot data=wheatout;
plot yield*time=1 yhat*time=2 / overlay;
plot ehat*time=3 / vref=0;                 * VREF adds ZERO line;
title 'cubic wheat production model';
run;
```

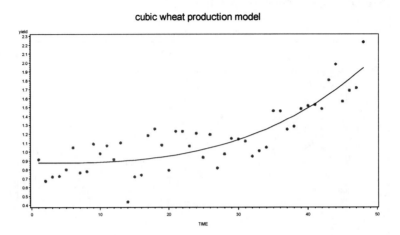

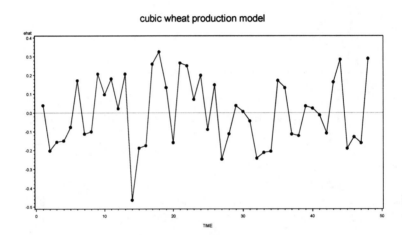

This scatter diagram clearly shows that the cubic equation fits the curved data better than a straight line. The plot of the residuals against time shows no particular pattern, which is good.

4.7 LOG-LINEAR MODELS

An alternative to the cubic model in the previous section is to use a logarithmic variable transformation.

4.7.1 A growth model

Specifically, suppose that the yield in year t is $YIELD_t = (1+g)YIELD_{t-1}$, with g being the fixed growth rate in one year. By substituting repeatedly we obtain $YIELD_t = YIELD_0 (1+g)^t$. Here $YIELD_0$ is the yield in year "0", the year before the sample begins, so it is probably unknown. Taking logarithms we obtain

$$\ln\left(YIELD_{t}\right) = \ln\left(YIELD_{0}\right) + \ln\left(1+g\right)t = \beta_{1} + \beta_{2}t$$

This is simply a log-linear model with dependent variable $\ln\left(YIELD_{t}\right)$ and explanatory variable t, or time. We expect growth to be positive, so that $\beta_{2} > 0$.

```
data wheat;                                      * open data set;
set wheat;                                       * read data set;
lyield = log(yield);                             * create variable;
run;

ods graphics on;
proc reg data=wheat plots=(residuals(smooth) residualhistogram);
model lyield = time;
title 'log-linear wheat production model';
run;
ods graphics off;
```

The parameter estimates are

Variable	DF	Parameter Estimate	Standard Error	t Value	Pr > |t|
Intercept	1	-0.34337	0.05840	-5.88	<.0001
TIME	1	0.01784	0.00208	8.60	<.0001

The **FitPlot.png** image shows that ln(*YIELD*) fits the data well.

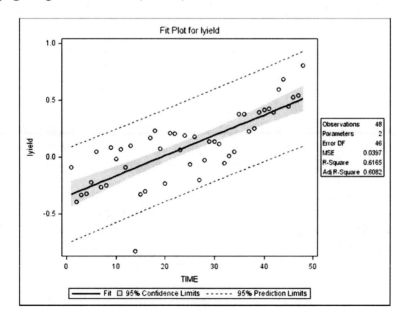

The residual plot shows only a small dip

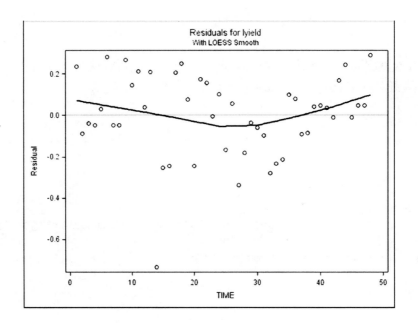

4.7.2 A wage equation

A key relationship in labor economics (and no doubt in your mind) is the relationship between wages and education. Suppose that the rate of return to an extra year of education is a constant r. That is, in the first year after an additional year of education your wage rate rises from an initial value $WAGE_0$ to $WAGE_1 = (1+r)WAGE_0$. For an extra two years of education this becomes $WAGE_2 = (1+r)^2 WAGE_0$, and so on. Taking logarithms we have a relationship between $\ln(WAGE)$ and years of education ($EDUC$)

$$\ln(WAGE) = \ln(WAGE_0) + \ln(1+r)EDUC$$

$$= \beta_1 + \beta_2 EDUC$$

An additional year of education leads to an approximate $100\beta_2 \%$ increase in wages.

Data on hourly wages, years of education and other variables are in the file *cps4_small*. These data consist of 1000 observations from the 2008 Current Population Survey (CPS).

```
data cps4_small;                     * new data set;
set 'cps4_small';                    * read data;
proc contents data=cps4_small;       * examine contents;
title 'cps data';
run;
```

PROC CONTENTS shows us that there are a number of variables in this data set.

```
         Alphabetic List of Variables and Attributes

    #    Variable    Type    Len    Label
   12    asian       Num      8     = 1 if asian
   11    black       Num      8     = 1 if black
    2    educ        Num      8     years of education
```

```
3    exper      Num    8    post education years experience
6    female     Num    8    = 1 if female
4    hrswk      Num    8    usual hours worked per week
5    married    Num    8    = 1 if married
7    metro      Num    8    = 1 if lives in metropolitan area
8    midwest    Num    8    = 1 if lives in midwest
9    south      Num    8    = 1 if lives in south
1    wage       Num    8    earnings per hour
10   west       Num    8    = 1 if lives in west
```

The two key variables are *WAGE* (dollars per hour) and *EDUC* (years).Now, reduce the data set to the two key variables using a **keep** statement, and examine the summary statistics.

```
data wage;
set cps4_small;
keep wage educ;
run;

options nolabel;                        * turn off labels;
proc means;
title 'wage data';
run;
```

Variable	N	Mean	Std Dev	Minimum	Maximum
wage	1000	20.6156600	12.8347247	1.9700000	76.3900000
educ	1000	13.7990000	2.7110789	0	21.0000000

Add one observation for a prediction exercise (*EDUC* = 12 and *WAGE* = missing). Combine the data sets using **set** and create ln(*WAGE*)

```
data morewage;
input wage educ;
datalines;
. 12
;

/* combine data sets */
data wage;                              * open data;
set wage morewage;                      * combine data sets;
lwage = log(wage);                      * create log wage;
run;
proc print data=wage(obs=5);            * print some obs;
run;
```

A few of the observations are

```
Obs     wage    educ    lwage
 1     18.70    16     2.92852
 2     11.50    12     2.44235
 3     15.04    16     2.71071
 4     25.95    14     3.25617
 5     24.03    12     3.17930
```

In the pre-regression phase let us set up the ODS graphics path.

```
ods listing gpath='c:\figures' style=journal;
ods graphics on;
```

Carry out a regression of ln(*WAGE*) on *EDUC* and output some results.

```
proc reg data=wage;                    * regression;
model lwage = educ;                    * log(wage) model;
title 'log-linear wage equation';
output out=wageout p=yhat lcl=lcl ucl=ucl;
run;
ods graphics off;
```

The parameter estimates and fit plot are

Variable	DF	Parameter Estimate	Standard Error	t Value	Pr > |t|
Intercept	1	1.60944	0.08642	18.62	<.0001
educ	1	0.09041	0.00615	14.71	<.0001

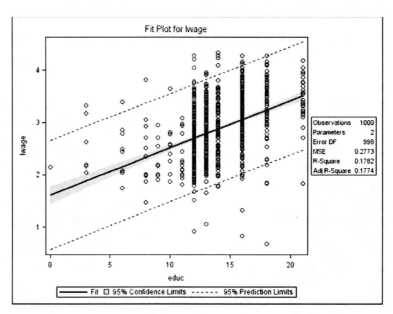

The fit plot shows that the data are "fan shaped" which will produce a corresponding set of "fan shaped" residuals, which may indicate a violation of the homoskedasticity (constant σ^2) assumption. This issue will be addressed in Chapter 8.

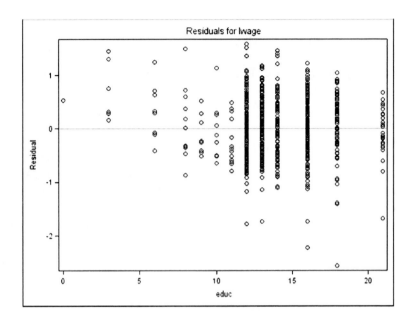

4.7.3 Prediction in the log-linear model

How shall we obtain the predicted value of y? A first inclination might be to take the anti-log of $\widehat{\ln(y)} = b_1 + b_2 x$. For the natural logarithm the anti-log is the exponential function, so that a natural choice for prediction is

$$\hat{y}_n = \exp\left(\widehat{\ln(y)}\right) = \exp(b_1 + b_2 x)$$

In the log-linear model this is not necessarily the best we can do. Using properties of the log-normal distribution it can be shown that an alternative predictor is

$$\hat{y}_c = \widehat{E(y)} = \exp\left(b_1 + b_2 x + \hat{\sigma}^2/2\right) = \hat{y}_n e^{\hat{\sigma}^2/2}$$

If the sample size is large, the "corrected" predictor $\hat{y}_c$ is, on average, closer to the actual value of y and should be used. In small samples (less than 30) the "natural" predictor may actually be a better choice. The reason for this incongruous result is that the estimated value of the error variance, $\hat{\sigma}^2$, adds a certain amount of "noise" when using $\hat{y}_c$, leading it to have increased variability relative to $\hat{y}_n$ that can outweigh the benefit of the correction in small samples.

We have a corrected predictor $\hat{y}_c$ for y in the log-linear model. It is the "point" predictor, or point forecast, that is relevant if we seek the single number that is our best prediction of y. If we prefer a prediction or forecast interval for y, then we must rely on the natural predictor $\hat{y}_n$[4]. Specifically we follow the procedure outlined in Section 1 of this chapter, and then take anti-logs. That is, compute $\widehat{\ln(y)} = b_1 + b_2 x$ and then $\widehat{\ln(y)} \pm t_c \text{se}(f)$, where the critical value t_c is the $100(1-\alpha/2)$-percentile from the t-distribution and $\text{se}(f)$ is the standard error of forecast. Then a $100(1-\alpha)\%$ prediction interval for y is

---

[4] The corrected predictor includes the estimated error variance, making the t-distribution no longer relevant.

$$\left[\exp\left(\widehat{\ln(y)} - t_c \mathrm{se}(f) \right), \exp\left(\widehat{\ln(y)} + t_c \mathrm{se}(f) \right) \right]$$

To implement these steps in SAS, we must use a number from the regression ANOVA table. Recall that $\hat{\sigma}^2 = MSE = 0.27732$.

```
data predict;                    * new data set;
set wageout;                     * merge;
yn = exp(yhat);                  * natural predictor;
sig2 =  0.27732;                 * sig2 = MSE from ANOVA;
yc = yn*exp(sig2/2);             * corrected predictor;
yn_lb = exp(lcl);                * prediction lower bound;
yn_ub = exp(ucl);                * prediction upper bound;
run;
```

Now print a few observations, including 1001 that we added to the data set.

```
proc print data=predict(firstobs=999 obs=1001);
var educ wage sig2 yn_lb yn yn_ub yc;
title 'log-linear predictions';
run;
```

```
                        log-linear predictions

Obs    educ    wage      sig2      yn_lb       yn      yn_ub      yc
999      8     7.50     0.27732    3.65625   10.3058   29.0489   11.8387
1000    13     8.50     0.27732    5.75919   16.1958   45.5452   18.6047
1001    12      .       0.27732    5.26040   14.7958   41.6158   16.9964
```

We predict that the wage for a worker with 12 years of education will be \$14.80 per hour if we use the natural predictor, and \$17.00 if we use the corrected predictor. In this case the sample is large ($N = 1000$) so we would use the corrected predictor. For the wage data, a 95% prediction interval for the wage of a worker with 12 years of education is \$5.26 to \$41.62.

For a graph, we first delete the observation with missing data, and then sort the data on the values of *EDUC*.

```
data predict;
set predict;
if wage ne .;
run;
proc sort data=predict;
by educ;
run;
symbol1 value=dot color=blue;
symbol2 color=black interpol=join value=none;
symbol3 color=black interpol=join value=none line=2;
proc gplot;
plot wage*educ=1 yn*educ=3 yn_lb*educ=3 yn_ub*educ=3 yc*educ=2/ overlay;
title 'log-linear predictions';
run;
```

log-linear predictions

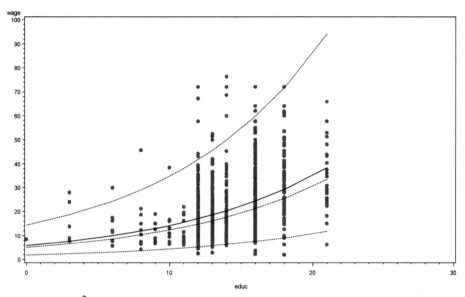

Finally, what about R^2? In the regression output the value **R-Square 0.1782** gives the percent of $\ln(WAGE)$ explained by the model. But we are interested in explaining *WAGE*. It is a general rule that the squared simple correlation between y and its fitted value $\hat{y}$, where $\hat{y}$ is the "best" prediction one can obtain, is a valid measure of goodness-of-fit that we can use as an R^2 in many contexts. As we have seen, what we may consider the "best" predictor can change depending upon the model under consideration. That is, a general goodness-of-fit measure, or general R^2 is

$$R_g^2 = \left[\text{corr}(y, \hat{y})\right]^2 = r_{y,\hat{y}}^2$$

In the wage equation $R_g^2 = \left[\text{corr}(y, \hat{y}_c)\right]^2 = 0.4312^2 = 0.1859$. The correlation 0.4312 is obtained using **PROC CORR**.

```
proc corr data=predict;
var wage yn yc;
title 'generalized r2 = corr**2';
run;
```

```
        Pearson Correlation Coefficients, N = 1000
              Prob > |r| under HO: Rho=0


                    wage            yn            yc
      wage       1.00000       0.43120       0.43120
                               <.0001        <.0001


      yn         0.43120       1.00000       1.00000
                 <.0001                      <.0001
```

CHAPTER **5**

The Multiple Regression Model

5.1 MULTIPLE REGRESSION THEORY AND METHODS

In a general multiple regression model a dependent variable y is related to a number of **explanatory variables** $x_2, x_3, \ldots, x_K$ through a linear equation that can be written as

$$y_i = \beta_1 + \beta_2 x_{i2} + \beta_3 x_{i3} + \cdots + \beta_K x_{iK} + e_i \tag{5.1}$$

The coefficients $\beta_2, \beta_3, \ldots, \beta_K$ are unknown coefficients corresponding to the explanatory variables $x_2, x_3, \ldots, x_K$. A single parameter, call it β_k, measures the effect of a change in the variable x_k upon the expected value of y, all other variables held constant. In terms of partial derivatives,

$$\beta_k = \frac{\Delta E(y)}{\Delta x_k}\bigg|_{\text{other } x\text{'s held constant}} = \frac{\partial E(y)}{\partial x_k}$$

The parameter β_1 is the intercept term. We can think of it as being attached to a variable x_1 that is always equal to 1. That is, $x_{i1} = 1$. We use K to denote the number of unknown parameters in (5.1).

The error assumptions in the multiple regression model are the same as in the simple regression model:

- $E(e_i) = 0$. Each random error has a probability distribution with zero mean. Some errors will be positive, some will be negative; over a large number of observations they will average out to zero.

- $\text{var}(e_i) = \sigma^2$. Each random error has a probability distribution with variance σ^2. The variance σ^2 is an unknown parameter and it measures the uncertainty in the statistical model. It is the same for each observation, so that for no observations will the model uncertainty be more, or less, nor is it directly related to any economic variable. Errors with this property are said to be homoskedastic.

- $\text{cov}(e_i, e_j) = 0$. The covariance between the two random errors corresponding to any two different observations is zero. The size of an error for one observation has no bearing on the likely size of an error for another observation. Thus, any pair of errors is uncorrelated.
- We will sometimes further assume that the random errors e_i have normal probability distributions. That is, $e_i \sim N\left(0, \sigma^2\right)$.

In addition to the error assumptions we assume that the values of the explanatory variables x_{ik} are not random. This assumption will be relaxed in Chapter 10. A second assumption is that any one of the explanatory variables is not an exact linear function of the others. This assumption is equivalent to assuming that no variable is redundant. As we will see, if this assumption is violated, a condition called **exact collinearity**, the least squares procedure fails.

The sum of squared errors depends on the K regression parameter values.

$$S\left(\beta_1, \beta_2, \ldots, \beta_K\right) = \sum_{i=1}^{N}\left(y_i - E(y_i)\right)^2 = \sum_{i=1}^{N}\left(y_i - \beta_1 - \beta_2 x_{i2} \cdots - \beta_K x_{iK}\right)^2$$

The least squares estimates minimize the sum of squared errors. Unlike the simple regression case there are no easy formulas for the least squares estimates unless matrix algebra is used, as in the appendix to this chapter.

Define the least squares residuals as

$$\hat{e}_i = y_i - \hat{y}_i = y_i - \left(b_1 + b_2 x_{i2} + \cdots + b_K x_{iK}\right)$$

An unbiased estimator for σ^2 that uses $\hat{e}_i^2$ is

$$\hat{\sigma}^2 = \frac{\sum_{i=1}^{N} \hat{e}_i^2}{N - K}$$

where K is the number of β_k parameters being estimated in the multiple regression model.

The least squares estimators are the Best Linear Unbiased Estimators (BLUE). Furthermore, if the regression errors are normal then $b_k \sim N\left[\beta_k, \text{var}(b_k)\right]$. The expression for the estimated variance of the least squares estimator can be shown to be[1]

$$\widehat{\text{var}}\left(b_k\right) = \frac{\hat{\sigma}^2}{\left(1 - R_{k.}^2\right)\sum\left(x_{ik} - \bar{x}_k\right)^2}$$

where $R_{k.}^2$ is the usual R^2 from an "auxiliary" regression of x_k on all <u>other</u> explanatory variables (including the intercept)[2].

If the regression errors are not normal then the least squares estimators have approximate normal distributions in large samples. It follows that we can construct a t-random variable, for hypothesis testing and interval estimation, as

$$t = \frac{b_k - \beta_k}{\sqrt{\widehat{\text{var}}\left(b_k\right)}} = \frac{b_k - \beta_k}{\text{se}(b_k)} \sim t_{(N-K)}$$

---

[1] See William Greene (2012) *Econometric Analysis*, 7th *Edition*, Pearson-Prentice Hall, page 90.
[2] Exact collinearity occurs if the denominator is zero.

Define $t_c = t_{(.975, N-K)}$ to be the 97.5 percentile of the $t_{(N-K)}$-distribution (the area or probability to the left of t_c is 0.975). Then a 95% interval estimate of β_k is $b_k \pm t_c \text{se}(b_k)$. Similarly, hypothesis tests about individual parameters are carried out using the same procedures as in Chapter 3, with the only difference being that the t-distribution critical values come from the $t_{(N-K)}$-distribution.

If $y_0 = \beta_1 + \beta_2 x_{02} + \beta_3 x_{03} + \cdots + \beta_K x_{0K} + e_0$ then a predicted value of y_0 is

$$\hat{y}_0 = b_1 + b_2 x_{02} + b_3 x_{03} + \cdots + b_K x_{0K}$$

A 95% prediction interval is $\hat{y}_0 \pm t_c \text{se}(f)$. The standard error of the forecast se(f) does not have the simple form from Chapter 3.

The goodness-of-fit measure R^2 is computed just as in the simple regression model, as

$$R^2 = \frac{SSR}{SST} = \frac{\sum_{i=1}^{N}(\hat{y}_i - \bar{y})^2}{\sum_{i=1}^{N}(y_i - \bar{y})^2} = 1 - \frac{SSE}{SST} = 1 - \frac{\sum_{i=1}^{N}\hat{e}_i^2}{\sum_{i=1}^{N}(y_i - \bar{y})^2}$$

An alternative measure of goodness of fit called the adjusted-R^2, and often symbolized as $\bar{R}^2$, is usually reported by regression programs; it is computed as

$$\bar{R}^2 = 1 - \frac{SSE/(N-K)}{SST/(N-1)}$$

This measure does not always go up when a variable is added, because of the degrees of freedom term $N - K$ in the numerator. As the number of variables K increases, SSE goes down, but so does $N - K$. The effect on $\bar{R}^2$ depends on the amount by which SSE falls. While solving one problem, this corrected measure of goodness of fit unfortunately introduces another one. It loses its interpretation; $\bar{R}^2$ is no longer the percent of variation explained. This modified $\bar{R}^2$ is sometimes used and misused as a device for selecting the appropriate set of explanatory variables. This practice should be avoided. We prefer to concentrate on the unadjusted R^2 and think of it as a descriptive device for telling us about the "fit" of the model; it describes the proportion of variation in the dependent variable explained by the explanatory variables, and the predictive ability of the model over the sample period.

5.2 MULTIPLE REGRESSION EXAMPLE

We will set up an economic model for monthly sales of a hamburger chain that we call Big Andy's Burger Barn. We initially hypothesize that sales revenue is linearly related to price and advertising expenditure. The economic model is:

$$SALES = \beta_1 + \beta_2 PRICE + \beta_3 ADVERT + e$$

where $SALES$ represents monthly sales revenue in a given city, $PRICE$ represents price (a price index for all products sold) in that city and $ADVERT$ is monthly advertising expenditure in that city. Both $SALES$ and $ADVERT$ are measured in terms of thousands of dollars. The data are contained in the SAS data set $andy$. Load the data set, examine its contents and summary statistics.

```
data andy;                          * open data set;
set 'andy';                         * read andy;
run;
proc contents data=andy;            * examine contents;
run;
title 'andy fast food data';
options nolabel;                    * turn off labels;
proc means data=andy;               * summary stats;
title 'andy summary stats';
run;
```

PROC CONTENTS shows three variables.

```
#   Variable   Type   Len   Label
3   ADVERT     Num     8    Expenditure on advertising ($1000s)
2   PRICE      Num     8    Price index for all products sold in a given month
1   SALES      Num     8    Monthly sales revenue ($1000s)
```

PROC MEANS gives the summary statistics

```
                    The MEANS Procedure

Variable    N        Mean        Std Dev      Minimum        Maximum

SALES       75    77.3746658    6.4885367    62.4000015    91.1999969
PRICE       75     5.6871999    0.5184320     4.8299999     6.4899998
ADVERT      75     1.8440000    0.8316769     0.5000000     3.0999999
```

5.2.1 Using PROC REG

As a first step, prior to the regression estimation, turn on ODS graphics and change the path.

```
ods listing gpath='c:\figures' style=journal; * change path;
ods graphics on;                               * must turn ODS on;
```

The actual regression estimation is different from earlier Chapters in that additional variables are listed on the right hand side.

```
proc reg data=andy plots(unpack)=(residuals(smooth) residualhistogram);
model sales = price advert/covb clb;
title 'regression with covb & clb options';
run;
ods graphics off;
```

In these statements
- the **plots(unpack)=(residuals(smooth) residualhistogram)** produces the ODS plot of the least squares residuals against each explanatory variable, with a fitted smooth curve, and a histogram of the residuals;

- the option **covb** on the **model** statement prints the estimated variances and covariances of the least squares estimators; and
- the option **clb** on the **model** statement produces 95% interval estimates of the parameters.

In the ANOVA table, the **Sum of Squares Error** is $\sum \hat{e}_i^2 = 1718.94281$. The **Mean Square Error** is $\hat{\sigma}^2 = 23.87421$. The **Degrees of Freedom (DF) Error** is $N - K = 75 - 3 = 72$.

```
                    Analysis of Variance

                       Sum of        Mean
Source          DF     Squares       Square    F Value   Pr > F
Model            2    1396.53921    698.26960    29.25    <.0001
Error           72    1718.94281     23.87421
Corrected Total 74    3115.48202
```

Below the ANOVA table we find the R^2 and the "Adjusted R^2"

```
Root MSE           4.88612    R-Square    0.4483
Dependent Mean    77.37467    Adj R-Sq    0.4329
Coeff Var          6.31489
```

The parameter estimates are arrayed as usual, with the parameter estimate, its standard error, the *t*-statistic for the null hypothesis that the corresponding parameter is zero, and the *p*-value for the two-tail test of significance.

```
Variable     DF    Estimate      Error    t Value   Pr > |t|
Intercept     1    118.91361    6.35164     18.72    <.0001
price         1     -7.90785    1.09599     -7.22    <.0001
advert        1      1.86258    0.68320      2.73    0.0080
```

The **clb** option on the model statement produces 95% interval estimates.

```
Variable     DF     95% Confidence Limits
Intercept     1    106.25185    131.57537
price         1    -10.09268     -5.72303
advert        1      0.50066      3.22451
```

A covariance matrix is a square array containing the variances and covariances of the least squares estimator, in the form

$$\text{cov}(b_1, b_2, b_3) = \begin{bmatrix} \text{var}(b_1) & \text{cov}(b_1, b_2) & \text{cov}(b_1, b_3) \\ \text{cov}(b_1, b_2) & \text{var}(b_2) & \text{cov}(b_2, b_3) \\ \text{cov}(b_1, b_3) & \text{cov}(b_2, b_3) & \text{var}(b_3) \end{bmatrix}$$

The **covb** option on the model statement prints the estimates of these values.

```
                    Covariance of Estimates
Variable       Intercept          price           advert
Intercept    40.343299011    -6.795064119    -0.748420602
price        -6.795064119     1.2012007044   -0.019742152
advert       -0.748420602    -0.019742152     0.4667560554
```

The square roots of the diagonal elements are the standard errors $se(b_k)$ that appear in the regression output.

The output of the ODS graphics includes a diagnostic panel, and also the **ResidualPlot.png** which shows the least squares residuals plotted against each of the explanatory variables. Our assumptions imply that the residuals should show no patterns when plotted. Do you see anything suspicious in the plot of residuals against *ADVERT*?

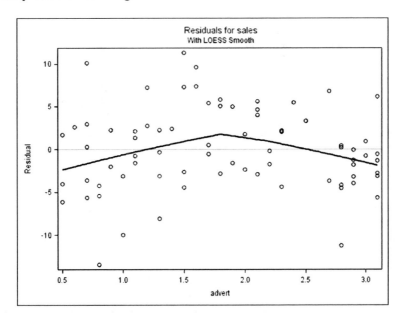

The **ResidualHistogram.png** shows the residuals with the superimposed normal distribution and the kernel distribution. The fitted and normal curves are reasonably similar suggesting that we will not reject a test of normality. In fact the Jarque-Bera test *p*-value (from **PROC AUTOREG**) is 0.92.

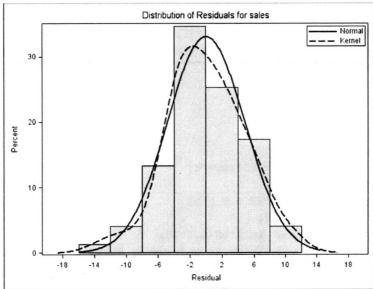

Test of hypotheses concerning individual parameters are carried out as in Chapter 3.

5.2.2 Using PROC AUTOREG

Using PROC AUTOREG produces the same output in a slightly different arrangement.

```
proc autoreg data=andy;
model sales = price advert / normal;    * prints Jarque-Bera;
title 'regression with proc autoreg';
run;
```

Ordinary Least Squares Estimates

SSE	1718.94294	DFE	72
MSE	23.87421	Root MSE	4.88612
SBC	460.691497	AIC	453.739032
MAE	3.80892555	AICC	454.07706
MAPE	4.98038748	HQC	456.515075
Durbin-Watson	2.1830	Regress R-Square	0.4483
		Total R-Square	0.4483

Miscellaneous Statistics

Statistic	Value	Prob	Label
Normal Test	0.1590	0.9236	Pr > ChiSq

Parameter Estimates

Variable	DF	Estimate	Standard Error	t Value	Approx Pr > |t|
Intercept	1	118.9136	6.3516	18.72	<.0001
price	1	-7.9079	1.0960	-7.22	<.0001
advert	1	1.8626	0.6832	2.73	0.0080

5.2.3 Using PROC MODEL

When there are linear combinations of parameters to estimate or test then PROC MODEL has some advantages over PROC REG and PROC AUTOREG. To illustrate we use some calculations from *Principles of Econometrics, 4th Edition*, Chapters 5.6.2 and 5.6.3. We present the code and then explain the parts.

```
proc model data=andy;
label b1='intercept'
      b2='price'
      b3='advert';
sales = b1 + b2*price + b3*advert;
fit sales / normal;
estimate 'lincom' -0.4*b2 + 0.8*b3,
         'ttest' b3 - 1,
         'test_lincom' -0.2*b2-0.5*b3;
title 'regression and estimates using proc model';
run;
```

- The **label** statement is a convenience.
- The model to estimate is specified by the **sales** expression.

- The model is estimated, and tests for normality of the errors, are provided by the **fit** statement.
- The **estimate** statement has 3 parts, each representing a different linear combination of parameters that is of interest:
  - **lincom**: Increasing advertising expenditure by $800 and dropping the price by 40 cents. If the current price is $PRICE_0$ and the current advertising level is $ADVERT_0$, then the change in expected sales is $-0.4\beta_2 + 0.8\beta_3$.
  - **ttest**: Advertising is effective if $\beta_3 > 1$
  - **test_lincom**: Is dropping the price by 20 cents more effective for increasing sales revenue than increasing advertising expenditure by $500? In other words, is $-0.2\beta_2 > 0.5\beta_3$, or is $-0.2\beta_2 - 0.5\beta_3 > 0$?

The regression results are identical to earlier ones. However now we obtain

```
                    Nonlinear OLS  Estimates

                         Approx              Approx
Term          Estimate   Std Err   t Value   Pr > |t|   Label
lincom        4.653209   0.7096      6.56     <.0001    -0.4*b2 + 0.8*b3
ttest         0.862584   0.6832      1.26     0.2108    b3 - 1
test_lincom   0.650279   0.4010      1.62     0.1092    -0.2*b2-0.5*b3
```

- The **lincom** estimate for the increase in revenue is $4653. Using the standard error we can compute an interval estimate.
- The **ttest** estimate gives a 2-tail test for the hypothesis $\beta_3 > 1$. Using the t-value and a one-tail critical value the one tail test can be carried out.
- Using the **test_lincom** t-value with a one-tail critical value the one tail test can be carried out.
- The normality tests are below. We fail to reject normality of errors in each case.

```
                       Normality Test
Equation      Test Statistic        Value      Prob
sales         Shapiro-Wilk W         0.98      0.7944
System        Mardia Skewness        0.07      0.7924
              Mardia Kurtosis        0.31      0.7579
              Henze-Zirkler T        0.01      0.9944
```

5.3 POLYNOMIAL MODELS

To capture the anticipated diminishing marginal benefit of additional advertising we might use the quadratic model

$$SALES = \beta_1 + \beta_2 PRICE + \beta_3 ADVERT + \beta_4 ADVERT^2 + e$$

In this model the marginal effect of advertising is

$$\frac{\Delta E(SALES)}{\Delta ADVERT}\bigg|_{(PRICE \text{ held constant})} = \frac{\partial E(SALES)}{\partial ADVERT} = \beta_3 + 2\beta_4 ADVERT$$

The profit maximizing level of advertising, where marginal revenue equals marginal cost is obtained by solving $\beta_3 + 2\beta_4 ADVERT = 1$, or $ADVERT_o = (1-\beta_3)/2\beta_4$ The *SALES* maximizing value of advertising is the solution of $\beta_3 + 2\beta_4 ADVERT = 0$, or $ADVERT_m = -\beta_3/2\beta_4$. These are **nonlinear functions** of the parameters. Their estimates have standard errors given by the **delta method**. See *Principles of Econometrics, 4th Edition*, Appendix 5B.4 and 5B.5.

5.3.1 Using PROC REG

To estimate a polynomial model using **PROC REG** we must first create the squared variable and then include it in the model.

```
data andy2;
set andy;
advert2 = advert**2;
run;
proc reg data=andy2;
model sales = price advert advert2;
title 'polynomial model using proc reg';
run;
```

5.3.2 Using PROC MODEL

The use of **PROC MODEL** has some advantages. The quadratic variable can be created within the equation, and the marginal effects, optimal advertising and turning point can be calculated with the **estimate** statement, which also automatically applies the **delta method** for nonlinear functions of the parameters.

```
proc model data=andy;
label b1='intercept'
      b2='price'
      b3='advert'
      b4='advertsq';
sales = b1 + b2*price + b3*advert + b4*advert**2;
fit sales;
advert1 = .5;
advert2 = 2;
estimate 'me_advert1' b3 + 2*b4*advert1,
         'me_advert2' b3 + 2*b4*advert2,
         'opt_advert' (1-b3)/(2*b4),
         'turning point' -b3/(2*b4);
title 'polynomial model and estimates in proc model';
run;
```

In the above
- **advert1** and **advert2** are values of advertising for which we desire marginal effects **me_advert1** and **me_advert2**
- **opt_advert** is the estimated optimal value of advertising

- **turning point** is the estimated value of advertising yielding maximum value of sales.

```
               Nonlinear OLS Summary of Residual Errors

                 DF      DF                                             Adj
Equation      Model   Error      SSE      MSE   Root MSE  R-Square     R-Sq
sales             4      71    1532.1  21.5787    4.6453    0.5082   0.4875

               Nonlinear OLS Parameter Estimates

                         Approx            Approx
Parameter    Estimate   Std Err  t Value  Pr > |t|   Label
b1            109.719    6.7990    16.14    <.0001    intercept
b2             -7.64     1.0459    -7.30    <.0001    price
b3           12.15124    3.5562     3.42    0.0011    advert
b4           -2.76796    0.9406    -2.94    0.0044    advertsq

                  Nonlinear OLS   Estimates

                         Approx            Approx
Term         Estimate   Std Err  t Value  Pr > |t|   Label
me_advert1   9.383273    2.6370     3.56    0.0007    b3 + 2*b4*advert1
me_advert2   1.079383    0.7019     1.54    0.1286    b3 + 2*b4*advert2
opt_advert    2.01434    0.1287    15.65    <.0001    (1-b3)/(2*b4)
turning point 2.194978   0.1638    13.40    <.0001    -b3/(2*b4)
```

- The marginal effect of advertising when advertising is \$500 is \$9,383. It is \$1,079 when advertising is currently \$2000.
- The optimal level of advertising is estimated to be 2.014 (\$2014), with standard error 0.1287.
- The sales maximizing level of advertising is estimated to be 2.195 (\$2,195) with standard error 0.1638.

5.4 LOG-LINEAR MODELS

Log-linear models, with dependent variable in logarithmic form, are common in economics. To illustrate we use Current Population Survey data, *cps4_small*.

```
data cps4_small;
set 'cps4_small';
run;

options label;
proc contents data=cps4_small;
run;
options nolabel;
```

The included variables are

#	Variable	Type	Len	Label
12	asian	Num	8	1 if asian
11	black	Num	8	1 if black
2	educ	Num	8	years of education
3	exper	Num	8	post education years experience
6	female	Num	8	1 if female
4	hrswk	Num	8	usual hours worked per week
5	married	Num	8	1 if married
7	metro	Num	8	1 if lives in metropolitan area
8	midwest	Num	8	1 if lives in midwest
9	south	Num	8	1 if lives in south
1	wage	Num	8	earnings per hour
10	west	Num	8	1 if lives in west

Models of interest include

1. $\ln(WAGE) = \beta_1 + \beta_2 EDUC + \beta_3 EXPER + e$. The approximate percentage change in *WAGE* for an extra year of experience, with education held constant, is $100\beta_3\%$.

2. $\ln(WAGE) = \beta_1 + \beta_2 EDUC + \beta_3 EXPER + \beta_4 (EDUC \times EXPER) + e$. Here the approximate percentage change in wage given a one year increase in experience is $100(\beta_3 + \beta_4 EDUC)\%$.

3. $\ln(WAGE) = \beta_1 + \beta_2 EDUC + \beta_3 EXPER + \beta_4 (EDUC \times EXPER) + \beta_5 EXPER^2 + e$. Then a one year increase in experience leads to an approximate percentage wage change of $\%\Delta WAGE \cong 100(\beta_3 + \beta_4 EDUC + 2\beta_5 EXPER)\%$.

5.4.1 Using PROC REG

With **PROC REG** we must create variable transformations prior to estimation.

```
data cps4_small;
set cps4_small;
lwage = log(wage);
educ_exper = educ*exper;
exper2 = exper**2;
run;

proc reg data=cps4_small;
linear:model lwage = educ exper;
interact:model lwage = educ exper educ_exper;
quad:model lwage = educ exper educ_exper exper2;
title 'log-linear models using proc reg';
run;
```

5.4.2 Using PROC MODEL

With **PROC MODEL** we can form the variable transformations within the equation. To illustrate, estimate the log-linear model (3) from the previous section with both a quadratic and interaction term.

```
proc model data=cps4_small;
label b1='intercept'
      b2='educ'
      b3='exper'
      b4='educ*exper'
      b5='exper**2';
log(wage) = b1 + b2*educ + b3*exper + b4*(educ*exper) + b5*exper**2;
fit 'log(wage)';
educ0 = 16;
exper0 = 10;
estimate 'me_exper' 100*(b3 + b4*educ0 + 2*b5*exper0);
title 'log-linear model using proc model';
run;
```

Note that in the **fit** statement we enclose **log(wage)** in quotes. The approximate marginal effect is evaluated for a person with 16 years of education and 10 years of experience.

Nonlinear OLS Summary of Residual Errors

Equation	DF Model	DF Error	SSE	MSE	Root MSE	R-Square	Adj R-Sq
log(wage)	5	995	254.4	0.2557	0.5057		

Nonlinear OLS Parameter Estimates

Parameter	Estimate	Approx Std Err	t Value	Approx Pr > |t|	Label
b1	0.529677	0.2267	2.34	0.0197	intercept
b2	0.127195	0.0147	8.64	<.0001	educ
b3	0.062981	0.00954	6.60	<.0001	exper
b4	-0.00132	0.000495	-2.67	0.0077	educ*exper
b5	-0.00071	0.000088	-8.11	<.0001	exper**2

Nonlinear OLS Estimates

Term	Estimate	Approx Std Err	t Value	Approx Pr > |t|	Label
me_exper	2.754372	0.3175	8.67	<.0001	100*(b3 + b4*educ0 + 2*b5*exper0)

Note that **PROC MODEL** quite rightly does not report R^2 or adjusted-R^2 for this model since the dependent variable is in logarithmic form. The generalized R^2 can be computed if desired.

APPENDIX 5A THE DELTA METHOD IN PROC MODEL

Suppose we are interested in **nonlinear functions** of regression parameters. Nonlinear functions of the least squares estimators are not normally distributed in finite samples, and usual variance formulas do not apply. If the functions are continuous and continuously differentiable then the **delta method** can be applied.[3] For single functions this result is discussed in Appendices 5B.4 and 5B.5 in *Principles of Econometrics, 4th Edition*. For the function $g_1(\beta_2)$ the estimator $g_1(b_2)$ is consistent and asymptotically normal with approximate distribution

$$g_1(b_2) \overset{a}{\sim} N\left[g_1(\beta_2), \left[g_1'(\beta_2) \right]^2 \operatorname{var}(b_2) \right]$$

where $g_1'(\beta_2)$ denotes the first derivative. For the function $g_2(\beta_1,\beta_2)$ the estimator $g_2(b_1,b_2)$ is consistent and has an approximate normal distribution in large samples

$$g_2(b_1,b_2) \overset{a}{\sim} N\left(g_2(\beta_1,\beta_2), \operatorname{var}\left[g_2(b_1,b_2) \right] \right)$$

where

$$\operatorname{var}\left[g_2(b_1,b_2) \right] \cong \left[\frac{\partial g_2(\beta_1,\beta_2)}{\partial \beta_1} \right]^2 \operatorname{var}(b_1) + \left[\frac{\partial g_2(\beta_1,\beta_2)}{\partial \beta_2} \right]^2 \operatorname{var}(b_2)$$

$$+ 2\left[\frac{\partial g_2(\beta_1,\beta_2)}{\partial \beta_1} \right]\left[\frac{\partial g_2(\beta_1,\beta_2)}{\partial \beta_2} \right] \operatorname{cov}(b_1,b_2)$$

PROC MODEL will calculate the nonlinear estimates and compute their standard errors automatically. To illustrate we use the SAS data set *mc2* which contains one sample (x, y) with $N = 20$ observations from the same data generation process as in Appendix 3A of this manual. The nonlinear functions we consider are $g_1(\beta_2) = \exp(\beta_2/10)$ and $g_2(\beta_1,\beta_2) = \beta_1/\beta_2$. In the simulation the true parameter values are $\beta_1 = 100$ and $\beta_2 = 10$ so that $g_1(\beta_2) = 2.71828$ and $g_2(\beta_1,\beta_2) = 10$. The SAS code and output are

```
data mc2;
set 'mc2';
run;

proc model data=mc2;
y = b1+b2*x;
fit y;
estimate 'g1' exp(b2/10),
         'g2' b1/b2, / outest=gest outcov;
title 'estimate model for data mc2';
run;
```

---

[3] For general discussion see Appendix D.2.7 in William Greene (2012) *Econometric Analysis, Seventh Edition*, Prentice-Hall.

```
                Nonlinear OLS Parameter Estimates

                            Approx              Approx
        Parameter    Estimate   Std Err   t Value   Pr > |t|
        b1            87.4431   33.8764      2.58     0.0188
        b2           10.68456    2.1425      4.99    <.0001


                  Nonlinear OLS  Estimates

                        Approx             Approx
      Term      Estimate  Std Err  t Value  Pr > |t|  Label
      g1        2.910882   0.6237     4.67    0.0002  exp(b2/10)
      g2         8.18406   4.7559     1.72    0.1024  b1/b2
```

The estimates **g1** and **g2** with their standard errors can be used to test hypotheses and construct interval estimates. The **outset=gest outcov** options on the fit statement create the data set *gest*.

```
proc print data=gest;
title 'saved estimates';
run;
```

```
                              saved estimates

  Obs   _NAME_    _TYPE_     _STATUS_      _NUSED_       g1        g2
   1               OLS      0 Converged       20      2.91088    8.1841
   2     g1        OLS      0 Converged       20      0.38896   -2.8994
   3     g2        OLS      0 Converged       20     -2.89943   22.6186
```

The first observation contains the estimates. The second and third rows contain the 2×2 covariance matrix of the estimates, in the columns labeled **g1** and **g2**.

5A.1 Monte Carlo study of delta method

A Monte Carlo study, following the same design as in Appendix 3A of this manual, is executed below to illustrate the properties of the delta method. The random errors are independently distributed but with normalized chi-square distributions. We will use the $\chi^2_{(4)}$ in this simulation, which is skewed with a long tail to the right. Let $v_i \sim \chi^2_{(4)}$. The expected value and variance of this random variable are $E(v_i) = 4$ and $\text{var}(v_i) = 8$, respectively, so that $z_i = (v_i - 4)/\sqrt{8}$ has mean 0 and variance 1. The random errors we employ are $e_i = 50z_i$ so that $\text{var}(e_i \mid x_i) = \sigma^2 = 2500$, as in earlier appendices.

We use $M = 10,000$ Monte Carlo simulations with sample size $N = 40$. Our objectives are to illustrate that the delta method produces interval estimates and tests with the claimed sampling properties. The code is very much the same as in Appendix 3A, but using PROC MODEL and the chi-square distribution for errors.

```
data chisq;                          * data set;
nobs=40;
call streaminit(1234567);            * set random number stream;
```

```
        do sample = 1 to 10000;            * start outer loop;
        do n = 1 to nobs;                  * start inner loop;
        if n < (nobs/2)+1 then x = 10;     * x = 10 for first half;
        else x = 20;                       * x = 20 for second half;
        v = rand('chisquare',4);           * v is chi-square with 4 df;
        e = 50*(v-4)/sqrt(8);              * E(e)=0, var(e)=2500;
        y = 100 + 10*x + e;                * DGP;
        output;                            * output to data set;
        end;                               * end inner loop;
        end;                               * end outer loop;
run;

proc model noprint data=chisq;
by sample;
y = b1+b2*x;
fit y;
estimate 'g1' exp(b2/10),
         'g2' b1/b2, / outest=gest outcov;
run;

data g12;
set gest;
if _name_= ' ';
n = _nused_;
keep sample n g1 g2;
run;

data vg1;
set gest;
if _name_= 'g1' ;
vg1 = g1;
seg1 = sqrt(vg1);
keep sample vg1 seg1;
run;

data vg2;
set gest;
if _name_='g2';
vg2 = g2;
seg2 = sqrt(vg2);
keep sample vg2 seg2;
run;
data delta;
merge g12 vg1 vg2;
by sample;
tc = tinv(.975,n-2);
lbg1 = g1 - tc*seg1;
ubg1 = g1 + tc*seg1;
trueg1 = exp(1);
cover1 = (lbg1 <= trueg1 <= ubg1);
```

```
lbg2 = g2 - tc*seg2;
ubg2 = g2 + tc*seg2;
cover2 = (lbg2 <= 10 <= ubg2);
run;
```

For 3 samples the estimates are:

```
proc print data=delta;
var n tc g1 vg1 seg1 lbg1 ubg1 cover1;
where sample <= 3;
title 'g1 estimates & intervals for 3 samples';
run;
```

```
              g1 estimates & intervals for 3 samples

  Obs   n     tc       g1      vg1      seg1     lbg1     ubg1   cover1
   1   40  2.02439  3.13717  0.13723  0.37044  2.38726  3.88709    1
   2   40  2.02439  2.02088  0.06628  0.25746  1.49968  2.54207    0
   3   40  2.02439  2.77044  0.25311  0.50310  1.75197  3.78890    1
```

```
proc print data=delta;
var n tc g2 vg2 seg2 lbg2 ubg2 cover2;
where sample <= 3;
title 'g2 estimates and intervals for 3 samples';
run;
```

```
              g2 estimates and intervals for 3 samples

  Obs   n     tc       g2       vg2      seg2     lbg2     ubg2    cover2
   1   40  2.02439   6.2320   5.0751   2.25280  1.67149  10.7926     1
   2   40  2.02439  18.7102  38.0837   6.17120  6.21730  31.2032     1
   3   40  2.02439   9.7436  20.2377   4.49863  0.63656  18.8506     1
```

The coverage rates of the interval estimates are very close to their nominal 95% values.

```
proc means data=delta mean;              * compute only mean;
var cover1 cover2;
title 'coverage of interval estimates';
run;
```

```
                    The MEANS Procedure
                 Variable         Mean
                 ─────────────────────────
                 cover1        0.9457000
                 cover2        0.9400000
                 ─────────────────────────
```

The distribution of **g1** is very much bell-shaped.

```
proc univariate data = delta;
var g1;
histogram/normal;
```

```
title 'Sampling distribution of g1';
title2 'Errors Chi-square N=40';
run;
```

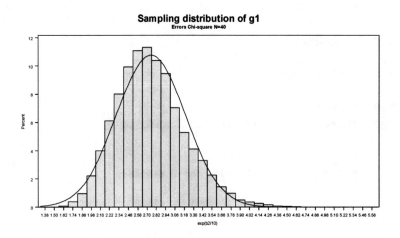

The distribution of **g2** estimates has a slight skew.

```
proc univariate data = delta;
var g2;
histogram/normal;
title 'Sampling distribution of g2';
title2 'Errors Chi-square N=40';
run;
```

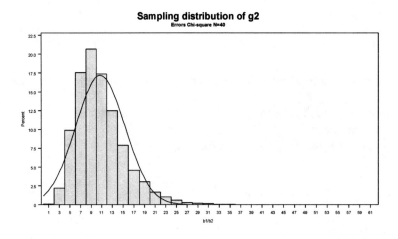

Experiment using samples of larger size to see for yourself how quickly the normality approximation improves.

APPENDIX 5B MATRIX OPERATIONS

SAS/IML is a matrix language, where "IML" stands for interactive matrix language. We will introduce **SAS/IML** for two reasons. First, by learning the matrix commands for regression you will learn to write programs that will replicate results obtained from PROCs, such as **PROC REG**, enhancing your understanding of the methods of econometrics. Second, if you know how to use **PROC IML** you will be able to write procedures that are not included in SAS as PROC whatever. For those of you in graduate school, or planning to attend graduate school, this is an important tool. Documentation, including tutorials, can be found at

http://support.sas.com/documentation/onlinedoc/iml/index.html.

As usual, you do not really want to print this documentation. It is over 1000 pages long.

The general form of an IML program is

```
proc iml;
IML statements
quit;
```

The IML statements are arranged in groups called **modules**. Modules are begun with **start** and ended with **finish** statements, and then executed using a **run** statement. The general form of an IML module is

```
start modulename;
IML statements
finish;
run modulename;
```

The IML statements within a module define various matrix operations.

5B.1 Vector concepts

While we cannot present all matrix algebra concepts, we will present some essentials[4]. A column vector is an $n \times 1$ array and is denoted by a bold letter or symbol. Two vectors are equal if they are equal element by element. For example, the two (3×1) vectors $\mathbf{v}$ and $\mathbf{w}$

$$\mathbf{v} = \begin{bmatrix} v_1 \\ v_2 \\ v_3 \end{bmatrix} \qquad \mathbf{w} = \begin{bmatrix} w_1 \\ w_2 \\ w_3 \end{bmatrix}$$

are equal if and only if $v_1 = w_1$, $v_2 = w_2$, and $v_3 = w_3$. Then we can write $\mathbf{v} = \mathbf{w}$.

To add two vectors, $\mathbf{v}$ and $\mathbf{w}$, they must be of the same dimensions. The sum is a new vector $\mathbf{c}$ whose elements are the sums of the corresponding elements of $\mathbf{v}$ and $\mathbf{w}$. If

$$\mathbf{v} = \begin{bmatrix} 2 \\ -1 \\ 3 \end{bmatrix} \qquad \mathbf{w} = \begin{bmatrix} 8 \\ 9 \\ 5 \end{bmatrix} \rightarrow \mathbf{c} = \mathbf{v} + \mathbf{w} = \begin{bmatrix} 10 \\ 8 \\ 8 \end{bmatrix}$$

The usual laws of addition hold, so if $\mathbf{v}$, $\mathbf{w}$ and $\mathbf{c}$ are vectors of the same dimension, then

$$\mathbf{v} + \mathbf{w} = \mathbf{w} + \mathbf{v}$$
$$(\mathbf{v} + \mathbf{w}) + \mathbf{c} = \mathbf{v} + (\mathbf{w} + \mathbf{c})$$

If a is a number, or **scalar**, and if $\mathbf{v}$ is column vector, then the product of a times $\mathbf{v}$ is called **scalar multiplication**. The product is a new column vector that is a times each element of $\mathbf{v}$. For example, if $a = 2$, then

$$\mathbf{c} = a\mathbf{v} = \mathbf{v}a = 2\begin{bmatrix} 2 \\ -1 \\ 3 \end{bmatrix} = \begin{bmatrix} 4 \\ -2 \\ 6 \end{bmatrix}$$

Similar definitions hold for **row vectors** which have 1 row and n columns.

SAS/IML statements illustrating these operations are

```
proc iml;                              * invoke iml;

/* --- Illustrating vector operations --- */
start vectors;                         * begin module;
print / "---vectors module---",,;      * print message;

/* working with column vectors */
```

---

[4] A complete but advanced presentation of matrix algebra used in econometrics can be found in William Greene (2012) *Econometric Analysis, 7th Edition*, Pearson/ Prentice Hall, Appendix A.

```
v = {2, -1, 3};                          * define column v;
w = {8, 9, 5};                           * define column w;
c = v + w;                               * sum column vectors;
print , "c = v + w" c;                   * print vectors;

/* scalar multiplication */
c = 2#v;                                 * scalar multiplication;
d = v#2;                                 * scalar multiplication;
print , "c=2#v" c,,  "d=v#2" d;          * print c & d;

/* working with row vectors */
v = {2 -1 3};                            * define row v;
w = {8 9 5};                             * define row w;
c = v + w;                               * sum row vectors;
print , "c = v + w" c;                   * print vectors;

/* end and run module */
finish;                                  * end module;
run vectors;                             * run module;
quit;
```

The edited output [we have used **options nocenter;**] is

```
---vectors module---

c = v + w          10
                    8
                    8

c=2#v           4
               -2
                6

d=v#2           4
               -2
                6

c = v + w          10        8        8
```

In this module observe that:
- the **print** statement can be used to print one or more vectors, or matrices; " / " denotes skip to a new page of SAS output, and " , " denote skip to a new line.
- Braces " { ... } " are used to define rows of a matrix or a vector, with " , " separates rows.
- Vector or matrix addition is denoted by " + ", and scalar multiplication by " # ".

5B.2 Matrix concepts

A matrix is a rectangular array. The matrix **A** below has m rows and n columns and is said to be of **dimension** $m \times n$, with the ij'th element denoted a_{ij}. Matrices are denoted by bold upper case letters. A matrix with a single column is a column vector. A matrix with a single row is a row vector.

$$A = \begin{bmatrix} a_{11} & a_{12} & \cdots & a_{1n} \\ a_{21} & a_{22} & & a_{2n} \\ \vdots & & \ddots & \\ a_{m1} & a_{m2} & \cdots & a_{mn} \end{bmatrix}$$

Matrix definitions of equality, addition and scalar multiplication are similar to the vector definitions.

The sum of two matrices **A** and **B** requires that they be of the same dimensions and is a new matrix **C** such that $c_{ij} = a_{ij} + b_{ij}$. Thus for example if

$$A = \begin{bmatrix} 2 & 3 \\ -1 & 7 \end{bmatrix}, \qquad B = \begin{bmatrix} 8 & 1 \\ 9 & 6 \end{bmatrix}$$

then

$$C = A + B = \begin{bmatrix} 10 & 4 \\ 8 & 13 \end{bmatrix}$$

It is also true that $A + B = B + A$, and $(A + B) + C = A + (B + C)$.

If λ is a number (or scalar) and **A** is a matrix, then the product of λ times **A** is called scalar multiplication. The product is a new matrix **C** that is λ times each element of **A**, so $c_{ij} = \lambda a_{ij}$. For example, if $\lambda = 2$, then

$$C = \lambda A = A\lambda = 2\begin{bmatrix} 2 & 3 \\ -1 & 7 \end{bmatrix} = \begin{bmatrix} 4 & 6 \\ -2 & 14 \end{bmatrix}$$

The **transpose** of a matrix, denoted by a prime is a matrix or vector obtained by interchanging the rows and columns. The transpose of an $m \times n$ matrix is an $n \times m$ matrix. That is, if

$$A = \begin{bmatrix} a_{11} & a_{12} & a_{13} \\ a_{21} & a_{22} & a_{23} \end{bmatrix}$$

then, **A** transpose, denoted A', is

$$A' = \begin{bmatrix} a_{11} & a_{21} \\ a_{12} & a_{22} \\ a_{13} & a_{23} \end{bmatrix}$$

Some useful properties of transposes are $(A')' = A$ and $(A + B)' = A' + B'$.

If **A** is a matrix of dimension $m \times n$ and **B** is a matrix of dimension $n \times p$ then the **product** **AB** is an $m \times p$ matrix whose ij'th element is formed by multiplying corresponding elements in the i'th row of **A** and the j'th column of **B**, and summing the resulting products. Let **A** and **B** be

$$\mathbf{A} = \begin{bmatrix} a_{11} & a_{12} & a_{13} \\ a_{21} & a_{22} & a_{23} \end{bmatrix}, \qquad \mathbf{B} = \begin{bmatrix} b_{11} & b_{12} \\ b_{21} & b_{22} \\ b_{31} & b_{32} \end{bmatrix}$$
$$ (2 \times 3) (3 \times 2)$$

The product **C** will be a 2×2 matrix

$$\mathbf{AB} = \mathbf{C} = \begin{bmatrix} c_{11} & c_{12} \\ c_{21} & c_{22} \end{bmatrix}$$

The element c_{11} is formed by taking the first row of **A** and the first column of **B** to obtain

$$c_{11} = a_{11}b_{11} + a_{12}b_{21} + a_{13}b_{31}$$

In general

$$c_{ij} = \sum_{k=1}^{n} a_{ik}b_{kj}$$

In order for matrix multiplication to be possible the number of columns of the first matrix (n) must be same as the number of rows in the second matrix. Such matrices are said to be **conformable** for multiplication.

To illustrate matrix multiplication, let

$$\mathbf{A} = \begin{bmatrix} 2 & 3 & -1 \\ -1 & 7 & 0 \end{bmatrix}, \qquad \mathbf{B} = \begin{bmatrix} 6 & 1 \\ -2 & 9 \\ 3 & -4 \end{bmatrix}$$

then

$$\mathbf{AB} = \begin{bmatrix} (2)(6)+(3)(-2)+(-1)(3) & (2)(1)+(3)(9)+(-1)(-4) \\ (-1)(6)+(7)(-2)+(0)(3) & (-1)(1)+(7)(9)+(0)(-4) \end{bmatrix}$$
$$= \begin{bmatrix} 12-6-3 & 2+27+4 \\ -6-14+0 & -1+63+0 \end{bmatrix}$$
$$= \begin{bmatrix} 3 & 33 \\ -20 & 62 \end{bmatrix} = \mathbf{C}$$

Matrix multiplication is unlike algebraic multiplication because, in general, $\mathbf{AB} \neq \mathbf{BA}$. But it is true that $\mathbf{A(BC)} = \mathbf{(AB)C}$ and $\mathbf{A(B+C)} = \mathbf{AB} + \mathbf{AC}$. Also $\mathbf{(AB)'} = \mathbf{B'A'}$. The matrix equivalent of the number 1 is called an identity matrix. It is a square matrix with 1's on the diagonal and zeros elsewhere.

$$\mathbf{I}_3 = \begin{bmatrix} 1 & 0 & 0 \\ 0 & 1 & 0 \\ 0 & 0 & 1 \end{bmatrix}$$

The identity matrix has the property that **AI = IA=A**.

Examples of these operations are given in the following SAS/IML code.

```
proc iml;                               * invoke iml;
/* --- Illustrating matrix operations --- */
start matrices;                         * begin module;
print /   "---matrices module---",,;    * print message;

/* adding matrices */
a = {2 3,-1 7};                         * define matrix a;
b = {8 1,9 6};                          * define matrix b;
c = a + b;                              * sum matrices;
print , "c = a + b" c;                  * print matrices;

/* scalar multiplication */
d = 2#a;                                * scalar multiplication;
print , "scalar product d = 2#a" d;     * print d;

/* matrix transpose */
a = {2 3 -1,-1 7 0};                    * define matrix a;
at = a`;                                * define a transpose;
print , "a transpose " at;              * print a, a`;

/* column transpose */
v = {1,2,3};                            * define column v;
vt = v`;                                * v transpose;
print , "column transpose" vt;          * print v, v`;

/* matrix multiplication */
b = {6 1,-2 9,3 -4};                    * define matrix b;
c = a*b;                                * multiply matrices;
print , "c = a*b" c;                    * print a, b, c;

/* matrix inner and outer products */
a1 = a`*a;                              * a transpose times a;
a2 = a*a`;                              * a times a transpose;
v1 = v`*v;                              * v transpose times v;
v2 = v*v`;                              * v times v transpose;
print , "a`*a " a1,,
        "a*a` " a2,,
        "v`*v " v1,,
        "v*v` " v2;                     * print products;

/* identity matrices */
imat = i(3);                            * identity matrix;
```

```
ai = a*imat;                        * a times the identity;
print ,"a*I " ai;                   * print a*I;
finish;                             * end module;
run matrices;                       * run module;
quit;
```

In the above code note that:
- The transpose of a matrix is denoted with a back-quote " ` "
- Matrix multiplication is denoted by " * "
- If $\mathbf{v}$ is a column vector, then the product $\mathbf{v}'\mathbf{v} = \sum v_i^2$ is the sum of squares.
- An $(n \times n)$ identity matrix is formed by the command " **i(n)** "

The edited output is (using **options nocenter;**)

```
---matrices module---

c = a + b          10          4
                    8         13

scalar product d = 2#a          4          6
                               -2         14

a transpose             2         -1
                        3          7
                       -1          0

column transpose            1          2          3

c = a*b          3         33
               -20         62

a`*a          5         -1         -2
             -1         58         -3
             -2         -3          1


a*a`          14         19
              19         50

v`*v          14

v*v`           1          2          3
               2          4          6
               3          6          9

a*I            2          3         -1
              -1          7          0
```

APPENDIX 5C REGRESSION CALCULATIONS IN MATRIX NOTATION

The multiple regression model is

$$y_i = \beta_1 + \beta_2 x_{i2} + \cdots + \beta_K x_{iK} + e_i \quad i = 1, \ldots, N$$

We can use vector notation for the x-values for observation i, as the $1 \times K$ vector

$$\mathbf{x}_i = \begin{bmatrix} 1 & x_{i2} & \cdots & x_{iK} \end{bmatrix}$$

The parameters $\beta_1, \ldots, \beta_K$ are stacked into a $K \times 1$ vector

$$\boldsymbol{\beta} = \begin{bmatrix} \beta_1 \\ \beta_2 \\ \vdots \\ \beta_K \end{bmatrix}$$

then

$$y_i = \beta_1 + \beta_2 x_{i2} + \cdots + \beta_K x_{iK} + e_i = \mathbf{x}_i \boldsymbol{\beta} + e_i$$

A matrix containing all the x values is formed by stacking these vectors one on top of the other, to form the $N \times K$ matrix

$$\mathbf{X} = \begin{bmatrix} \mathbf{x}_1 \\ \mathbf{x}_2 \\ \vdots \\ \mathbf{x}_N \end{bmatrix}$$

Then, all the observations on a regression are written in matrix notation as

$$\mathbf{y} = \mathbf{X}\boldsymbol{\beta} + \mathbf{e}$$

where

$$\mathbf{y} = \begin{bmatrix} y_1 \\ y_2 \\ \vdots \\ y_N \end{bmatrix} \quad \mathbf{X} = \begin{bmatrix} 1 & x_{12} & \cdots & x_{1K} \\ 1 & x_{22} & \cdots & x_{2K} \\ \vdots & \vdots & & \vdots \\ 1 & x_{N2} & \cdots & x_{NK} \end{bmatrix} \quad \boldsymbol{\beta} = \begin{bmatrix} \beta_1 \\ \beta_2 \\ \vdots \\ \beta_K \end{bmatrix} \quad \mathbf{e} = \begin{bmatrix} e_1 \\ e_2 \\ \vdots \\ e_N \end{bmatrix}$$

The least squares estimator of $\boldsymbol{\beta}$ is

$$\mathbf{b} = \begin{bmatrix} b_1 \\ b_2 \\ \vdots \\ b_K \end{bmatrix} = \left(\mathbf{X}'\mathbf{X} \right)^{-1} \mathbf{X}'\mathbf{y}$$

A square matrix $\mathbf{A}$ has an inverse, denoted $\mathbf{A}^{-1}$ if $\mathbf{A}\mathbf{A}^{-1} = \mathbf{A}^{-1}\mathbf{A} = \mathbf{I}$. The matrix $\mathbf{X}'\mathbf{X}$ is $K \times K$, square and symmetric ($\mathbf{A}$ is symmetric if $\mathbf{A}' = \mathbf{A}$). It has an inverse $\left(\mathbf{X}'\mathbf{X} \right)^{-1}$ as long as none of the explanatory variables is an exact linear function of the others, meaning that there is no exact collinearity.

The least squares residuals are

$$\hat{\mathbf{e}} = \begin{bmatrix} \hat{e}_1 \\ \hat{e}_2 \\ \vdots \\ \hat{e}_N \end{bmatrix} = \mathbf{y} - \hat{\mathbf{y}} = \mathbf{y} - \mathbf{Xb}$$

The sum of squared least squares residuals is

$$SSE = \sum \hat{e}_i^2 = \hat{\mathbf{e}}'\hat{\mathbf{e}} = (\mathbf{y} - \mathbf{Xb})'(\mathbf{y} - \mathbf{Xb})$$

The estimator of the error variance σ^2 is

$$\hat{\sigma}^2 = \frac{\hat{\mathbf{e}}'\hat{\mathbf{e}}}{N - K} = \frac{(\mathbf{y} - \mathbf{Xb})'(\mathbf{y} - \mathbf{Xb})}{N - K}$$

The unbiased estimator of the covariance matrix for **b** is

$$\widehat{\text{cov}}(\mathbf{b}) = \begin{bmatrix} \widehat{\text{var}}(b_1) & \widehat{\text{cov}}(b_1,b_2) & \cdots & \widehat{\text{cov}}(b_1,b_K) \\ \widehat{\text{cov}}(b_2,b_1) & \widehat{\text{var}}(b_2) & \cdots & \widehat{\text{cov}}(b_2,b_K) \\ \vdots & \vdots & \ddots & \vdots \\ \widehat{\text{cov}}(b_K,b_1) & \widehat{\text{cov}}(b_K,b_2) & \cdots & \widehat{\text{var}}(b_K) \end{bmatrix} = \hat{\sigma}^2 (\mathbf{X'X})^{-1}$$

5C.1 SAS/IML module for multiple regression

We will write a regression module that **assumes**
- the data on the dependent variable is contained in a vector **y**
- that all the explanatory variables except the intercept are contained in a matrix called **X**
- that the names of the variables are in a vector called **parm**

We will show how to carry out these preliminary steps below. The model we estimate is the quadratic sales model

$$SALES = \beta_1 + \beta_2 PRICE + \beta_3 ADVERT + \beta_4 ADVERT^2 + e$$

First, make sure the data *andy* is open in SAS.

```
data andy;                           * open data set;
set 'andy';                          * read andy;
advert2 = advert**2;                 * advert squared;
run;
```

Open IML and print opening

```
proc iml;                            * invoke iml;
start ols;                           * begin module;
print / "---ols module---",,;        * print message;
```

Add an intercept column of ones to the existing **X** matrix.

```
n = nrow(y);                    * n = number rows in y;
x1 = j(n,1,1);                  * x1 is column of ones;
x = x1||x;                      * X is horizontal concant;
```

> **Remark**: When typing SAS/IML or other SAS programs we refrain from using "upper case" letters, for ease of keyboarding. Also, when writing these programs use names for variables, and matrices, that correspond to algebraic names, so that when you look at it next time, or if someone else looks at it, the meaning of the names will be clear.

In these statements
- **nrow(A)** counts the number of rows in the matrix **A**.
- **j**(a, b, c) creates a matrix of dimension $a \times b$ all of whose elements are the value c.
- || stacks two matrices horizontally (horizontal concatenation).

Count the number of columns of **X** and create the degrees of freedom.

```
k = ncol(x);                    * k = number of parms;
df = n - k;                     * degrees of freedom;
```

Form **X'X** and create its inverse using the SAS function **inv**, and use these to construct the least squares estimates.

```
xtx = x`*x;                     * X transpose times X;
xtxi = inv(xtx);                * inverse of X'X;
b = inv(x`*x)*x`*y;             * ols estimator;
```

The estimated covariance matrix is

```
sse = ssq(y - x*b);            * sum of squared errors;
sig2 = sse/df;                 * variance estimate;
covb = sig2#xtxi;              * ols covariance estimate;
```

In these statements
- **ssq(a)** computes the sum of squares of the elements of **a**. Using the IML function **ssq** is one option for this calculation. Another option would have been to use the fact that the inner product of two vectors is a sum of squares, so **sse=(y - x*b)`(y - x*b);** would have worked fine. Or we could have defined the residual vector **e=(y - x*b);** and then **sse=e`e;** In any programming task there are always several equally good approaches.
- " / " denotes elementwise division, here one scalar by another
- " # " denotes elementwise multiplication, here a scalar times a matrix

The standard errors are the diagonal elements of the covariance matrix, and the t-statistics are the ratios of the estimates to the standard errors.

```
stderr = sqrt(vecdiag(covb));           * standard errors;
tstat = b/stderr;                       * t-statistics;
pval = 2*(1-probt(abs(tstat),df));      * p-values;
```

In the above statements
- **sqrt(A)** is the SAS function that takes the square root of each element of **A**.
- **vecdiag(A)** extracts the diagonal elements of the matrix **A** into a vector.
- **probt(t,df)** is the cumulative distribution function of the *t*- distribution with **df** degrees of freedom. That is, it returns a matrix of probabilities if **t** is a matrix.
- **abs(A)** computes the absolute value of each element of **A**.
- scalars can be multiplied times matrices using " * " or " # "

Stack the results next to each other and print.

```
result = b||stderr||tstat||pval;        * result table;
cols = {est se tstat pval};             * result column names;
                                        * print estimation results;
print result [rowname=parm colname=cols format=12.4];
```

In the above statements

- || denotes horizontal concatenation (stacking).
- the vectors **cols** has names for table columns.
- the print statement assigns row names contained in **parm** and column names assigned in **col**.
- the **format** statement allows 12 spaces per number with 4 spaces after the decimal.

To compute the R^2 we use the *SST* calculation $\sum (y_i - \bar{y})^2 = \sum y_i^2 - N\bar{y}^2$

```
ybar = sum(y)/n;                        * mean of y;
sst = y`*y - n#ybar##2;                 * total sum of squares;
r2 = 1 - sse/sst;                       * R-squared;
print,,"Summary statistics",
        "sse =" sse
        "sst =" sst
        "r-squared =" r2;
finish;                                 * end module;
```

In the above statements

- **sum(A)** computes the sum of all elements of **A**.
- ## computes the elementwise square. That is, **A##2** contains the squares of each element of **A**.
- **finish** ends the module.

5C.2 Estimating a linear combination of parameters

To estimate a linear combination of parameters, we take the linear combination of the least squares estimates. That is, suppose we wish to estimate $a_1\beta_1 + a_2\beta_2 + \cdots + a_K\beta_K$. The a_k are constants. To use vector and matrix notation let $\mathbf{R} = \begin{bmatrix} a_1 & a_2 & \ldots & a_K \end{bmatrix}$, so $\mathbf{R\beta} = a_1\beta_1 + a_2\beta_2 + \cdots + a_K\beta_K$. The best linear unbiased estimator of this linear combination of parameters is $\mathbf{Rb} = a_1b_1 + a_2b_2 + \cdots + a_Kb_K$. The estimated variance of the estimator is $\widehat{\text{var}}(\mathbf{Rb}) = \mathbf{R}\widehat{\text{cov}}(\mathbf{b})\mathbf{R'} = \hat{\sigma}^2\mathbf{R}(\mathbf{X'X})^{-1}\mathbf{R'}$. Given the estimate an interval estimate is $\mathbf{Rb} \pm t_c\text{se}(\mathbf{Rb})$.

In order to use the following module first run the OLS module, and specify the vector $\mathbf{R}$.

```
start linest;                              * start module;
est = r*b;                                 * estimate;
v = r*covb*r`;                             * variance;
se = sqrt(v);                              * std error;
tc = tinv(.975,df);                        * t critical;
lb = est - tc*se;                          * lower bound;
ub = est + tc*se;                          * upper bound;
print   "r vector               " r,,
        "estimate               " est,,
        "95% interval estimate  " lb ub;
finish;
```

5C.3 Testing a single linear hypothesis

Consider a single linear hypothesis about the parameters $H_0 : a_1\beta_1 + a_2\beta_2 + \cdots + a_K\beta_K = r$. The a_k are constants. To use vector and matrix notation let $\mathbf{R} = \begin{bmatrix} a_1 & a_2 & \ldots & a_K \end{bmatrix}$, so $H_0 : \mathbf{R\beta} = a_1\beta_1 + a_2\beta_2 + \cdots + a_K\beta_K = r$. The best linear unbiased estimator of this linear combination of parameters is $\mathbf{Rb} = a_1b_1 + a_2b_2 + \cdots + a_Kb_K$. The estimated variance is $\widehat{\text{var}}(\mathbf{Rb}) = \mathbf{R}\widehat{\text{cov}}(\mathbf{b})\mathbf{R'} = \hat{\sigma}^2\mathbf{R}(\mathbf{X'X})^{-1}\mathbf{R'}$. Given the estimate a t-statistic is

$$t = \frac{\mathbf{Rb} - r}{\text{se}(\mathbf{Rb})} \sim t_{(N-K)}$$

Left, right and two-tail p-values are computed as usual. In order to use the following module first run the OLS module, and specify the vector $\mathbf{R}$ and r (which is denoted lr in the module).

```
start lintest;                             * start module;
est = r*b;                                 * estimate;
v = r*covb*r`;                             * variance;
se = sqrt(v);                              * standard error;
tc = tinv(.975,df);                        * t critical;
tstat = (est-lr)/se;                       * t stat h0:r*beta=lr;
pleft = probt(tstat,df);                   * left tail p-value;
pright= 1- pleft;                          * right tail p-value;
ptwo = 2*(1-probt(abs(tstat),df));         * two tail p-value;
```

```
print   "r vector                        " r,,
        "lr value                        " lr,,
        "estimate  r*b                   " est,,
        "standard error                  " se,,
        "t stat                          " tstat,,
        "p-value left tail               " pleft,,
        "p-value right tail              " pright,,
        "p-value two tail                " ptwo;
finish;
```

5C.4 Illustrating computations

The above statements are a complete regression program. Before we can use the module we must read the data into SAS/IML. The general form for reading data into SAS/IML is

> use *sasdatasetname*;
> read *range* var{*list*} into *matrixname*;

In the **use** statement the SAS data set from which the observations are to be read is named. In the **read** statement *range* refers to the observations that are to be read; and the *matrixname* is the name of the matrix into which the specified observations on the named variables (*list*) are to be read. Read in the variables into **y** and **X**. Create variable names, which will be *const* and then the variable names in most cases.

```
use andy;                              * open data set;
read all var{sales} into y;            * read y;
read all var{price advert advert2} into x;     * read x;
parm = {const price advert advert2};   * estimates names;
run ols;                               * run module;
```

Run the module OLS. The output matches that from **PROC REG**.

```
---ols module---

                    result
            EST        SE       TSTAT       PVAL

CONST    109.7190    6.7990    16.1374     0.0000
PRICE     -7.6400    1.0459    -7.3044     0.0000
ADVERT    12.1512    3.5562     3.4170     0.0011
ADVERT2   -2.7680    0.9406    -2.9427     0.0044

Summary statistics
            sse           sst              r2

sse = 1532.0845 sst = 3115.4819 r-squared = 0.5082352
```

To illustrate the module **linest**, estimate the linear combination $\beta_3 + 3.8\beta_4 = \mathbf{R}\boldsymbol{\beta} = \begin{bmatrix} 0 & 0 & 1 & 3.8 \end{bmatrix}\boldsymbol{\beta}$. Specify the **R** vector and run the module

```
r = {0 0 1 3.8};
print / "Estimate linear combination";
run linest;
```

```
Estimate linear combination [edited output]
```

```
r vector                          0        0        1        3.8
estimate                    1.6329759
95% interval estimate       0.3285579   2.937394
```

To illustrate the module **lintest** consider the null hypothesis

$$H_0 : \beta_3 + 3.8\beta_4 = \mathbf{R}\beta = \begin{bmatrix} 0 & 0 & 1 & 3.8 \end{bmatrix}\beta = r = 1$$

Specify the vector **R** and the scalar r, which is called lr (little r) in the code.

```
r = {0 0 1 3.8};
lr = 1;
print / "Test linear hypothesis";
run lintest;
```

Note that the module computes the p-values for left, right and two-tail tests.

```
Test linear hypothesis [Edited output]
```

```
r vector                          0        0        1        3.8
lr value                          1
estimate   r*b              1.6329759
standard error             0.6541901
t stat                     0.9675719
p-value left tail          0.8317287
p-value right tail         0.1682713
p-value two tail           0.3365427
```

5C.5 Delta method

Consider the function $g(\mathbf{b}) = (1 - b_3)/(2b_4)$. SAS/IML will compute the function and calculate its numerical derivative, which is required for the delta method, using **call nlpfdd**. See the SAS/IML User's Guide for details. To use this function we first create a module defining the function.

```
start g(b);
    g = (1-b[3])/(2*b[4]);
    return(g);
finish;
```

In the above **g(b)** denotes the name of the module with **b** denoting an argument that must be provided. The module calculates **g** and **return(g)** outputs the value to IML. The calculations are made using

```
call nlpfdd(est,grad,hess,"g",b);
```

In this statement **est** is the returned value of the function, **grad** is the first derivative and **hess** is the second derivative of the function evaluated at the given point. The name of the module is given in quotes **"g"** and the point at which the function is evaluated is **b** which in our case contains the vector of least squares estimates.

The vector **grad** is

$$\mathbf{grad} = \left[\frac{\partial g(\mathbf{b})}{\partial b_1} \quad \frac{\partial g(\mathbf{b})}{\partial b_2} \quad \frac{\partial g(\mathbf{b})}{\partial b_3} \quad \frac{\partial g(\mathbf{b})}{\partial b_4} \right] = \frac{\partial g(\mathbf{b})}{\partial \mathbf{b}'}$$

The variance of the estimator $g(\mathbf{b}) = (1 - b_3)/(2b_4)$ is $\mathrm{var}\left[g(\mathbf{b})\right] = \mathbf{grad}\,\mathbf{V}\,\mathbf{grad}'$ where $\mathbf{V}$ is the estimated covariance matrix of the least squares estimator.

```
call nlpfdd(est,grad,hess,"g",b);
varg = grad*covb*grad`;
seg = sqrt(varg);
lb = est - tc*seg;                              * lower bound;
ub = est + tc*seg;                              * upper bound;
print   "delta method estimate" ,,
        "estimate                    " est,,
        "95% interval estimate       " lb ub;
```

The output is

```
estimate                2.0143397
95% interval estimate   1.7576732 2.2710061
```

To exit IML use

```
quit;
```

CHAPTER **6**

Further Inference in the Multiple Regression Model

6.1 JOINT HYPOTHESIS TESTS

A joint null hypothesis is tested via an *F*-test. The *F*-test for a joint null hypothesis is based on a comparison of the sum of squared errors from the original, unrestricted multiple regression model with the sum of squared errors from a regression model in which the null hypothesis is assumed to be true.

The imposition of the parameter constraints means the sum of squared errors will increase; a constrained minimum is larger than an unconstrained minimum. The sum of squared errors in a model that assumes a null hypothesis is true is called the **restricted sum of squared errors** or SSE_R; the subscript *R* indicates that the parameters have been restricted or constrained. To make a clear distinction between the restricted sum of squared errors and the sum of squared errors from the original, unrestricted model, the sum of squared errors from the original model is called the **unrestricted sum of squared errors** or SSE_U. It is *always* true that $SSE_R - SSE_U \geq 0$. The null hypothesis can be a single null hypothesis or a joint null hypothesis. Let *J* be the number of restrictions in the null hypothesis. The general *F*-statistic is given by

$$F = \frac{\left(SSE_R - SSE_U\right)/J}{SSE_U/\left(N - K\right)}$$

If the null hypothesis is true, then the statistic *F* has what is called an *F*-distribution with *J* numerator degrees of freedom and $N - K$ denominator degrees of freedom. We *reject* the null hypothesis if the value of the *F*-test statistic becomes too large. What is too large is decided by comparing the value of *F* to a critical value F_c, which leaves a probability α in the upper tail of the *F*-distribution with *J* and $N - K$ degrees of freedom.

A related test is based on the chi-square distribution. It is called a Wald test, and for the linear regression model the Wald test statistic is $W = J \times F$. *If the null hypothesis is true*, then the statistic *W* has a chi-square distribution with *J* degrees of freedom. We *reject* the null hypothesis if the value of the Wald test statistic becomes too large. What is too large is decided by comparing the value of W to a critical value χ_c^2 which leaves a probability α in the upper tail of the chi-square distribution with J degrees of freedom.

Further discussion of the relation between these two test statistics is provided in Appendix 6A of *Principles of Econometrics, 4th Edition*.[1] You may be wondering why we need two tests for the same thing. The Wald test is the basic test for joint hypotheses once we leave the world of the linear regression model and linear hypotheses. That is, starting in about Chapter 8 of this manual, and *POE4*, we will see the Wald test much more frequently.

6.1.1 An example

To illustrate what is meant by an unrestricted multiple regression model and a model which is restricted by the null hypothesis, consider the Big Andy's Burger Barn example where sales (*SALES*) are a function of a price index of all products sold (*PRICE*) and expenditure on advertising (*ADVERT*) and its square.

$$\text{Unrestricted model:} \quad SALES = \beta_1 + \beta_2 PRICE + \beta_3 ADVERT + \beta_2 ADVERT^2 + e$$

Suppose that we wish to test the hypothesis that advertising has no effect on sales revenue against the alternative that advertising does have an effect. The null and alternative hypotheses are: $H_0 : \beta_3 = 0, \beta_4 = 0$ and $H_1 : \beta_3 \neq 0$ or $H_1 : \beta_4 \neq 0$. The restricted model, that assumes the null hypothesis is true, is

$$\text{Restricted model:} \quad SALES = \beta_1 + \beta_2 PRICE + e$$

To illustrate we use the data set *andy*. Estimate the unrestricted and restricted models using **PROC REG**, and then compute the F-statistic value.

```
data andy;                              * open data set;
set 'andy';                             * read andy;
advert2 = advert**2;                    * advert**2;
run;


proc reg data=andy;                     * regression;
unrest:model sales = price advert advert2;   * unrestricted model;
rest:model sales = price;               * restricted model;
title 'andy unrestricted and restricted';
run;
```

From the two regression outputs we obtain the sums of squared residuals (*SSE*).

```
data ftest;                             * new data set;
sseu = 1532.08446;                      * unrestricted sse;
sser = 1896.39084;                      * restricted sse;
```

The number of hypotheses, sample size and number of explanatory variables in the unrestricted model are

---

[1] At a more advanced level, see Chapter 5.4 in William Greene (2012) *Econometric Analysis, Seventh Edition*, Prentice-Hall.

```
j = 2;                              * number hypotheses;
n = 75;                             * sample size;
k = 4;                              * number parameters;
df = n-k;                           * degrees of freedom;
```

The F-statistic is somewhat easier to compute if it is slightly rewritten, recognizing that $SSE_U/(N-K)$ is the unbiased estimator of σ^2 in the unrestricted model,

$$F = \frac{(SSE_R - SSE_U)/J}{SSE_U/(N-K)} = \frac{SSE_R - SSE_U}{J\hat{\sigma}_U^2}$$

```
sig2 = sseu/df;                     * sigma-hat squared;
fstat = (sser - sseu)/(j*sig2);     * f-test stat;
```

The F-critical value is obtained using the SAS function **FINV**,

FINV(*p, df1, df2*)

where

p = percentile value, such as .95 or .99
df1 = numerator degrees of freedom = J for a joint hypothesis test
df2 = denominator degrees of freedom = $N - K$ for hypothesis test

The p–value for an F-test is the area in the right tail of the F-distribution greater than the calculated value of F. The *cdf* of the F-distribution is computed using the SAS function **PROBF**,

PROBF(*F value, df1, df2*)

where

F value = value of the F statistic
df1 = numerator degrees of freedom = J for a joint hypothesis test
df2 = denominator degrees of freedom = $N - K$ for a joint hypothesis test

```
fc = finv(.95,j,df);                * f-critical value;
pval_f = 1-probf(fstat,j,df);       * f-test pval;
```

The Wald test statistic critical value comes from the chi-square distribution and in SAS the function is **CINV**.

CINV(*p, df*)

where

p = percentile value, such as 0.95 or 0.99
df = degrees of freedom = J for a joint hypothesis test

The *p*–value for a chi-square test is the area in the right tail of the chi-square distribution greater than the calculated value of the Wald test statistic. The *cdf* of the chi-square distribution is computed using the SAS function **PROBCHI**,

PROBCHI(*chi-square value, df*)

where

chi-square value = value of the Wald statistic
df = degrees of freedom = *J* for a joint hypothesis test

For our example the SAS commands are

```
waldstat = j*fstat;                    * wald test stat;
chic = cinv(.95,j);                    * chi-square crit val;
pval_w = 1-probchi(waldstat,j);        * wald p-val;
run;
```

First, print the *F*-test results.

```
proc print data=ftest;
var fstat fc pval_f;                   * variable list;
title 'f-test';
run;
```

```
                    f-test

         Obs     fstat      fc      pval_f
          1     8.44136   3.12576   .000514159
```

Then print the Wald test results.

```
proc print data=ftest;
var waldstat chic pval_w;              * variable list;
title 'Wald test';
run;
```

```
                   Wald test

         Obs    waldstat    chic      pval_w
          1     16.8827    5.99146   .000215757
```

6.1.2 PROC REG Test statement

In the sales revenue model there are several tests of interest.

1. Is advertising significant? $H_0 : \beta_3 = 0, \beta_4 = 0$
2. Are any of the model variables significant? $H_0 : \beta_2 = 0, \beta_3 = 0, \beta_4 = 0$

3. Is the optimal level of advertising (where marginal revenue = marginal cost = 1, or $\beta_3 + 2\beta_4 A_o = 1$) $ADVERT$ = 1.9 ($1900)? $H_0 : \beta_3 + 2 \times \beta_4 \times 1.9 = 1$

4. If $ADVERT$ = 1.9 and $PRICE$ = 6 will sales revenue = 80 ($80,000)? In addition to $H_0 : \beta_3 + 2 \times \beta_4 \times 1.9 = 1$ we test

$$E(SALES) = \beta_1 + \beta_2 PRICE + \beta_3 ADVERT + \beta_4 ADVERT^2 = \beta_1 + 6\beta_2 + 1.9\beta_3 + 1.9^2 \beta_4 = 80$$

Using **PROC REG** these tests are carried out with **TEST** statements. We have used labels for each for easy identification.

```
proc reg data=andy;
model sales = price advert advert2;
testad:test advert=0, advert2=0;              * test ads;
testmodel:test price=0, advert=0, advert2=0;  * overall f-test;
opt:test advert + 3.8*advert2 = 1;            * optimal advert = 1900;
opt2:test advert + 3.8*advert2 = 1,
          intercept + 6*price + 1.9*advert + 3.61*advert2 = 80;
title 'testing andy in proc reg';
run;
```

The test results are:

1. Is advertising significant? $H_0 : \beta_3 = 0, \beta_4 = 0$

Source	DF	Mean Square	F Value	Pr > F
Numerator	2	182.15319	8.44	0.0005
Denominator	71	21.57865		

2. Are any of the model variables significant? $H_0 : \beta_2 = 0, \beta_3 = 0, \beta_4 = 0$

Source	DF	Mean Square	F Value	Pr > F
Numerator	3	527.79914	24.46	<.0001
Denominator	71	21.57865		

3. Is the optimal level of advertising $ADVERT$ = 1.9 ($1900)? $H_0 : \beta_3 + 2 \times \beta_4 \times 1.9 = 1$

Source	DF	Mean Square	F Value	Pr > F
Numerator	1	20.20183	0.94	0.3365
Denominator	71	21.57865		

4. If $ADVERT$ = 1.9 and $PRICE$ = 6 will sales revenue = 80 ($80,000)?

Source	DF	Mean Square	F Value	Pr > F
Numerator	2	123.88800	5.74	0.0049
Denominator	71	21.57865		

6.1.3 F-Test of model significance

The second test we report above is a very important one. The general multiple regression model with $(K-1)$ explanatory variables and K unknown coefficients

$$y_i = \beta_1 + x_{i2}\beta_2 + x_{i3}\beta_3 + \cdots + x_{iK}\beta_K + e_i$$

To examine whether we have a viable explanatory model, we set up the following null and alternative hypotheses

$$H_0 : \beta_2 = 0,\ \beta_3 = 0,\ \cdots,\ \beta_K = 0$$

$$H_1 : \textit{At least one} \text{ of the } \beta_k \text{ is nonzero for } k = 2,3,\dots K$$

The restricted model, obtained assuming the null hypothesis is true is,

$$y_i = \beta_1 + e_i$$

The least squares estimator of β_1 in this restricted model is $b_1^* = \sum_{i=1}^{N} y_i / N = \overline{y}$, which is the sample mean of the observations on the dependent variable. The *restricted* sum of squared errors is

$$SSE_R = \sum_{i=1}^{N}(y_i - b_1^*)^2 = \sum_{i=1}^{N}(y_i - \overline{y})^2 = SST$$

The unrestricted sum of squared errors is the sum of squared errors from the unconstrained model. That is, $SSE_U = SSE$. The number of restrictions is $J = K - 1$. Thus, to test the overall significance of a model, *but not in general*, the F-test statistic can be modified and written as

$$F = \frac{(SST - SSE)/(K-1)}{SSE/(N-K)}$$

This test is automatically reported by **PROC REG** as part of the ANOVA table.

Analysis of Variance

Source	DF	Sum of Squares	Mean Square	F Value	Pr > F
Model	3	1583.39741	527.79914	24.46	<.0001
Error	71	1532.08446	21.57865		
Corrected Total	74	3115.48187			

6.1.4 Testing in PROC AUTOREG

The default test in **PROC AUTOREG** is also the F-test, but it has an option for a Wald test. To illustrate we use the null hypothesis $H_0 : \beta_3 = 0, \beta_4 = 0$. As you can see the results match our calculation in Section 6.1.1 above.

```
proc autoreg data=andy;
model sales = price advert advert2;
testad:test advert=0, advert2=0;
testad_w:test advert=0, advert2=0 / type=wald;
```

```
title 'testing advertising in proc autoreg';
run;
```

Test TESTAD

Source	DF	Mean Square	F Value	Pr > F
Numerator	2	182.153189	8.44	0.0005
Denominator	71	21.578654		

Test Results

Test	Type	Statistic	Pr > ChiSq	Label
TESTAD_W	Wald	16.88	0.0002	advert=0,advert2=0

6.1.5 PROC AUTOREG fit statistics

PROC AUTOREG presents the ANOVA material in a different format.

Ordinary Least Squares Estimates

SSE	1532.08446	DFE	71
MSE	21.57865	Root MSE	4.64528
SBC	456.37796	AIC	447.108007
MAE	3.59181126	AICC	447.679436
MAPE	4.71058737	HQC	450.809398
Durbin-Watson	2.0431	Regress R-Square	0.5082
		Total R-Square	0.5082

SAS documentation is obtained by entering **help autoreg** into the SAS command line, and selecting *Goodness-of-fit Measures and Information Criteria*. Two information measures are discussed in *Principles of Econometrics, 4th Edition*, on page 238. There

$$AIC = \ln\left(\frac{SSE}{N}\right) + \frac{2K}{N}, \quad SC = \ln\left(\frac{SSE}{N}\right) + \frac{K\ln(N)}{N}$$

The SAS documentation defines their information criteria *SBC* and *AIC* in slightly different ways.

$$AIC = -2\ln(L) + 2k, \quad SBC = -2\ln(L) + \ln(N)k$$

The notation $\ln(L)$ stands for log-likelihood. If the regression errors are normally distributed, then the least squares estimates b_k are maximum likelihood estimates as well.[2] It can be shown that in the normal linear regression model the log-likelihood, evaluated at the maximum likelihood estimates for β and σ^2 is

$$\ln(L) = -\frac{N}{2}\left(\ln(2\pi) + 1\right) - \frac{N}{2}\ln\left(\frac{SSE}{N}\right)$$

Therefore SAS's *AIC* is

---

[2] See Greene (2012), op. cit., Chapter 14.9.1.

$$AIC = N\left(\ln(2\pi) + 1\right) + N\ln\left(\frac{SSE}{N}\right) + 2K$$

Thus the *AIC* SAS uses is *N* times the *AIC* in *POE4* plus the extra additive constant $\ln(2\pi) + 1$ which does not affect model comparisons. Smaller *AIC* values are preferred.

To illustrate, execute the following and match the results to PROC AUTOREG.

```
data fitstat;
n = 75;
k = 4;
sse = 1532.08446;
aic1 = log(sse/n) + 2*k/n;
aic2 = (log(2*3.14159)+1) + log(sse/n) + 2*k/n;
naic = n*(aic2);
lnl = -(n/2)*(log(2*3.14159)+1) -(n/2)*log(sse/n);
aic_sas = -2*lnl + 2*k;
sbc_sas = -2*lnl + log(n)*k;
run;

proc print data=fitstat;
var aic1 aic2 naic aic_sas sbc_sas;
title 'fit statistics in proc autoreg';
run;
```

```
              fit statistics in proc autoreg

  Obs      aic1      aic2      naic     aic_sas    sbc_sas
   1      3.12356   5.96144   447.108   447.108    456.378
```

6.1.6 Testing in PROC MODEL

In **PROC MODEL** the default test is the Wald statistic.

```
proc model data=andy;
label b1 = 'const'
      b2 = 'price'
      b3 = 'advert'
      b4 = 'advert**2';
sales = b1 + b2*price + b3*advert + b4*advert**2;
fit sales;
test 'testad' b3 = 0, b4=0;
title 'testing advertising in proc model';
run;
```

```
                      Test Results

Test          Type         Statistic   Pr > ChiSq   Label
testad        Wald           16.88        0.0002     b3 = 0, b4=0
```

6.2 RESTRICTED ESTIMATION

When economic theory suggests relations between parameters, these relations can be tested (using a *t*-test or *F*-test). If we are sure that the theory is solid we may impose them upon the estimation. Consider the demand for beer. Relate the quantity demanded (Q) to the price of beer (PB), the price of liquor (PL), the price of all other remaining goods and services (PR), and income (I). Assume the log-log functional form is appropriate

$$\ln(Q) = \beta_1 + \beta_2 \ln(PB) + \beta_3 \ln(PL) + \beta_4 \ln(PR) + \beta_5 \ln(I)$$

A key economic assumption is that economic agents do not suffer from 'money illusion'. If λ is a constant

$$\ln(Q) = \beta_1 + \beta_2 \ln(\lambda PB) + \beta_3 \ln(\lambda PL) + \beta_4 \ln(\lambda PR) + \beta_5 \ln(\lambda I)$$

$$= \beta_1 + \beta_2 \ln(PB) + \beta_3 \ln(PL) + \beta_4 \ln(PR) + \beta_5 \ln(I) + (\beta_2 + \beta_3 + \beta_4 + \beta_5)\ln(\lambda)$$

It must be true that $\beta_2 + \beta_3 + \beta_4 + \beta_5 = 0$. Solve for β_4: $\beta_4 = -\beta_2 - \beta_3 - \beta_5$ and substitute into the original model to obtain, after simplifying,

$$\ln(Q_t) = \beta_1 + \beta_2 \ln\left(\frac{PB_t}{PR_t}\right) + \beta_3 \ln\left(\frac{PL_t}{PR_t}\right) + \beta_5 \ln\left(\frac{I_t}{PR_t}\right) + e_t$$

To get least squares estimates that satisfy the parameter restriction, called **restricted least squares estimates**, we apply the least squares estimation procedure directly to the restricted model.

To illustrate we use the data set *beer*. Create a data set, open the data file, and examine its contents.

```
data beer;                              * new data set;
set 'beer';                             * read beer data;
proc contents data=beer;                * examine contents;
options nolabel;                        * turn off label;
title 'beer expenditure data';
run;
```

Now open the data set and add the natural logs of the variables, and the real price (price divided by price index) variables.

```
data beer;                              * open beer data;
set beer;                               * read beer data;
lq = log(q);                            * ln(quantity);
lpb = log(pb);                          * ln(price beer);
lpl = log(pl);                          * ln(price liquor);
lpr = log(pr);                          * ln(price remaining goods);
li = log(i);                            * ln(income);
lpbr = log(pb/pr);                      * ln(real price beer);
lplr = log(pl/pr);                      * ln(real price liquor);
lpir = log(i/pr);                       * ln(real price income);
run;
```

Estimate the unrestricted model and test the restriction.

```
proc reg data=beer;                  * regression;
unrest:model lq = lpb lpl lpr li;    * unresticted model;
test lpb + lpl + lpr + li = 0;       * test restriction;
title 'beer expenditure test money illustion';
run;
```

The test indicates that we do not reject the hypothesis.

Source	DF	Mean Square	F Value	Pr > F
Numerator	1	0.00898	2.50	0.1266
Denominator	25	0.00360		

Estimate the restricted model

```
proc reg data=beer;                  * regression;
rest:model lq = lpbr lplr lpir;      * restricted model;
title 'beer expenditure under no money illustion';
run;
```

The restricted model estimates are

Parameter Estimates

Variable	DF	Parameter Estimate	Standard Error	t Value	Pr > |t|
Intercept	1	-4.79780	3.71390	-1.29	0.2078
lpbr	1	-1.29939	0.16574	-7.84	<.0001
lplr	1	0.18682	0.28438	0.66	0.5170
lpir	1	0.94583	0.42705	2.21	0.0357

Let the restricted least squares estimates be denoted by $b_1^*, b_2^*, b_3^*, b_5^*$. To obtain an estimate for β_4 we use the restriction

$$b_4^* = -b_2^* - b_3^* - b_5^* = -(-1.2994) - 0.1868 - 0.9458 = 0.1668$$

SAS makes imposing parameter restrictions easy with a **RESTRICT** statement that has the same style as a **TEST** statement.

```
proc reg data=beer;                  * regression;
unrest:model lq = lpb lpl lpr li;    * unrestricted model;
restrict lpb + lpl + lpr + li = 0;   * parameter restriction;
title 'beer expenditure under no money illustion';
title2 'RLS estimation';
run;
```

The restricted estimates are

```
                     Parameter Estimates

                     Parameter      Standard
   Variable    DF     Estimate        Error     t Value    Pr > |t|
   Intercept    1     -4.79780       3.71390      -1.29      0.2078
   lpb          1     -1.29939       0.16574      -7.84     <.0001
   lpl          1      0.18682       0.28438       0.66      0.5170
   lpr          1      0.16674       0.07708       2.16      0.0399
   li           1      0.94583       0.42705       2.21      0.0357
   RESTRICT    -1     -0.01907       0.01241      -1.54      0.1266*
```

Probability computed using beta distribution.

The last line, labeled **RESTRICT** is a test associated with the validity of the restrictions. It is not a standard test and we will not explain it here. However, the *p*-value suggests we cannot reject the validity of the restriction being imposed.

In **PROC AUTOREG** the restrict statement is similar. In **PROC MODEL** the restrictions are written in terms of the model parameters, and can be of more general forms.

6.3 MODEL SPECIFICATION ISSUES

A most difficult problem when estimating regression models is to include all the relevant variables, but only the relevant variables. To introduce the **omitted variable problem**, we consider a sample of married couples where both husbands and wives work. This sample was used by labor economist Tom Mroz in a classic paper on female labor force participation. The variables from this sample that we use in our illustration are stored in the data set *edu_inc*.

```
options label;                    * turn labels on;
data edu_inc;                     * new data set;
set 'edu_inc';                    * read data;
run;
proc contents data=edu_inc;       * examine contents;
title 'Mroz data';
run;
options nolabel;                  * turn labels off;
```

Correlations are obtained using

```
proc corr data=edu_inc;           * summary stats & corr;
var faminc he we kl6;             * variable list;
title 'correlations';
run;
```

Note that husband's and wife's education is positively correlated with family income, and with each other.

```
          Pearson Correlation Coefficients, N = 428
                Prob > |r| under HO: Rho=0


              FAMINC          HE          WE         KL6
FAMINC       1.00000     0.35468     0.36233    -0.07196
                         <.0001      <.0001      0.1372
HE           0.35468     1.00000     0.59434     0.10488
             <.0001                  <.0001      0.0301
WE           0.36233     0.59434     1.00000     0.12934
             <.0001      <.0001                  0.0074
KL6         -0.07196     0.10488     0.12934     1.00000
             0.1372      0.0301      0.0074
```

Estimate a base model regression using husband's and wife's education as explanatory variables.

```
    proc reg data=edu_inc;                * regression;
    base:model faminc = he we;            * base model;


                 Parameter      Standard
Variable    DF    Estimate         Error    t Value    Pr > |t|
Intercept    1  -5533.63070         11230     -0.49      0.6224
HE           1   3131.50931     802.90799      3.90      0.0001
WE           1   4522.64120    1066.32665      4.24      <.0001
```

Omit wife's education and note the increase in the magnitude of the coefficient of husband's education. This is a consequence of omitted variables bias.

```
    omit:model faminc = he;               * omit we;


                 Parameter      Standard
Variable    DF    Estimate         Error    t Value    Pr > |t|
Intercept    1        26191    8541.10836      3.07      0.0023
HE           1   5155.48358     658.45735      7.83      <.0001
```

Include another plausible variable affecting family income, the number of young children.

```
    kids:model faminc = he we kl6;        * add kl6;
```

Adding it alters the base model coefficients little since the number of children is only weakly correlated with husband's and wife's income.

```
                 Parameter      Standard
Variable    DF    Estimate         Error    t Value    Pr > |t|
Intercept    1  -7755.33133         11163     -0.69      0.4876
HE           1   3211.52568     796.70264      4.03      <.0001
WE           1   4776.90749    1061.16372      4.50      <.0001
KL6          1       -14311    5003.92837     -2.86      0.0044
```

Add two irrelevant (artificial, made up) variables.

```
irrel:model faminc = he we kl6 xtra_x5 xtra_x6; * add irrelevant var;
title 'Mroz specification comparisons';
run;
```

Variable	DF	Parameter Estimate	Standard Error	t Value	Pr > |t|
Intercept	1	-7558.61308	11195	-0.68	0.4999
he	1	3339.79210	1250.03934	2.67	0.0078
we	1	5868.67716	2278.06723	2.58	0.0103
kl6	1	-14200	5043.71964	-2.82	0.0051
xtra_x5	1	888.84261	2242.49096	0.40	0.6920
xtra_x6	1	-1067.18560	1981.68531	-0.54	0.5905

The artificial variables are insignificant, but the standard errors of other coefficients increase.

6.3.1 The RESET test

The RESET test (Regression Specification Error Test) is designed to detect omitted variables and incorrect functional form. Suppose that we have specified and estimated the regression model

$$y_i = \beta_1 + \beta_2 x_{i2} + \beta_3 x_{i3} + e_i$$

Let (b_1, b_2, b_3) be the least squares estimates and let

$$\hat{y}_i = b_1 + b_2 x_{i2} + b_3 x_{i3}$$

be the predicted values of the y_i. Consider the following two artificial models

$$y_i = \beta_1 + \beta_2 x_{i2} + \beta_3 x_{i3} + \gamma_1 \hat{y}_i^2 + e_i$$

A test for misspecification is a test of $H_0 : \gamma_1 = 0$ against the alternative $H_1 : \gamma_1 \neq 0$.

$$y_i = \beta_1 + \beta_2 x_{i2} + \beta_3 x_{i3} + \gamma_1 \hat{y}_i^2 + \gamma_2 \hat{y}_i^3 + e_i$$

Testing $H_0 : \gamma_1 = \gamma_2 = 0$ against $H_1 : \gamma_1 \neq 0$ and/or $\gamma_2 \neq 0$ is a test for misspecification.

This test is automated in **PROC AUTOREG** with a **reset** option added to the **model** statement.

```
proc autoreg data=edu_inc;              * proc autoreg;
model faminc = he we kl6/reset;         * reset tests;
title 'Mroz reset test';
run;
```

Ramsey's RESET Test

Power	RESET	Pr > F
2	5.9840	0.0148
3	3.1226	0.0451
4	2.1523	0.0931

Based on the test outcome (using powers 2 & 3) we suspect that the model could be improved by adding some variable (such as *AGE*) or choosing an alternative functional form. Sadly, the test does not tell us what to do.

6.4 COLLINEARITY

One of the most discussed but most poorly understood concepts in econometrics is **collinearity**. Recall from Chapter 5 that the variance of the least squares estimator is

$$\widehat{\operatorname{var}}(b_k) = \frac{\hat{\sigma}^2}{\left(1 - R_{k\cdot}^2\right)\sum(x_{ik} - \bar{x}_k)^2}$$

Where $R_{k\cdot}^2$ is the R^2 from the auxiliary regression of x_k on all the other x variables (including an intercept), excluding x_k. As $R_{k\cdot}^2$ increases the variance of the least squares estimator b_k increases when the variable x_k is linearly related to the other explanatory variables. There is said to be a collinear relationship among the x-variables. Note that if the variation in x_k about its mean is small, then the variance of b_k is also increased. These two problems combined are generally described under the generic term **collinearity**.

The problem with collinear data is that standard errors may be large, meaning potentially wide interval estimates and insignificant *t*- tests for important variables. The data set *cars* contains observations on the following variables for 392 cars:

> *MPG* = miles per gallon
> *CYL* = number of cylinders
> *ENG* = engine displacement in cubic inches
> *WGT* = vehicle weight in pounds

Suppose we are interested in estimating the effect of *CYL, ENG* and *WGT* on *MPG*. All the explanatory variables are related to the power and size of the car. Although there are exceptions, overall we would expect the values for *CYL, ENG* and *WGT* to be large for large cars and small for small cars. They are variables that are likely to be highly correlated and whose separate effect on *MPG* may be difficult to estimate.

Open the data set and examine its contents.

```
options label;              * turn labels on;
data cars;                  * new data set;
set 'cars';                 * read data;
run;


proc contents data=cars;    * examine contents;
title 'car data';
run;
options nolabel;            * turn off labels;
```

6.4.1 Consequences of collinearity

Using collinear data can cause estimates to be statistically insignificant even when the variables should be important. To illustrate, first estimate the *MPG* model using only *CYL* as an explanatory variable.

```
proc reg data=cars;              * regression;
rest:model mpg = cyl;            * one variable;
```

Variable	DF	Parameter Estimate	Standard Error	t Value	Pr > |t|
Intercept	1	42.91551	0.83487	51.40	<.0001
CYL	1	-3.55808	0.14568	-24.42	<.0001

Adding the other two variables, we see that *CYL* and *ENG* are statistically insignificant, despite the fact that they are jointly significant.

```
unrest:model mpg = cyl eng wgt;  * add variables;
test cyl=0,eng=0;                * joint tests;
title 'collinearity consequences';
run;
```

Variable	DF	Parameter Estimate	Standard Error	t Value	Pr > |t|
Intercept	1	44.37096	1.48069	29.97	<.0001
CYL	1	-0.26780	0.41307	-0.65	0.5172
ENG	1	-0.01267	0.00825	-1.54	0.1253
WGT	1	-0.00571	0.00071392	-8.00	<.0001

Test 1 Results for Dependent Variable MPG

Source	DF	Mean Square	F Value	Pr > F
Numerator	2	79.34228	4.30	0.0142
Denominator	388	18.46018		

6.4.2 Diagnosing collinearity

A simple first check for collinearity is to compute the simple correlations between the explanatory variables.

```
proc corr data=cars;             * simple correlations;
var cyl eng wgt;                 * variable list;
title 'car correlations';
run;
```

Pearson Correlation Coefficients, N = 392
Prob > \|r\| under H0: Rho=0

	CYL	ENG	WGT
CYL	1.00000	0.95082	0.89753
		<.0001	<.0001
ENG	0.95082	1.00000	0.93299
	<.0001		<.0001
WGT	0.89753	0.93299	1.00000
	<.0001	<.0001	

High correlations such as these between variables are an indicator that collinearity may cause problems for the usefulness of the regression model.

Collinearity can be more than a pairwise relationship between variables. More complicated relationships can be detected using an auxiliary regression, of one explanatory variable upon the rest. A high R^2 indicates a strong linear relationship among the variables. For example

```
proc reg data=cars;                    * regression;
aux:model eng = cyl wgt;               * one auxiliary reg;
title 'auxiliary regression';
run;
```

Dependent Variable: ENG
Analysis of Variance

Source	DF	Sum of Squares	Mean Square	F Value	Pr > F
Model	2	4010374	2005187	2875.97	<.0001
Error	389	271219	697.22223		
Corrected Total	391	4281594			

Root MSE	26.40497	R-Square	0.9367
Dependent Mean	194.41199	Adj R-Sq	0.9363
Coeff Var	13.58196		

Variable	DF	Parameter Estimate	Standard Error	t Value	Pr > |t|
Intercept	1	-151.59817	4.87094	-31.12	<.0001
CYL	1	35.78844	1.77531	20.16	<.0001
WGT	1	0.05044	0.00357	14.15	<.0001

The high *F*-value, the high R^2 and *t*-values indicate strong relationships between *ENG*, *CYL*, and *WGT*.

SAS will automatically print out a **variance inflation factor**, or **VIF**. This is computed as

$$VIF = \frac{1}{\left(1 - R_{k\bullet}^2\right)}$$

An auxiliary regression $R_{k\bullet}^2 = .90$ leads to $VIF = 10$, and this value is sometimes used as a benchmark.

```
proc reg data=cars;
model mpg = cyl eng wgt/vif;           * variance inflation factors;
title 'vif'; run;
```

The **vif** option on the **model** statements leads to these being added to the regression output, in the last column.

Variable	DF	Parameter Estimate	Standard Error	t Value	Pr > |t|	Variance Inflation
Intercept	1	44.37096	1.48069	29.97	<.0001	0
CYL	1	-0.26780	0.41307	-0.65	0.5172	10.51551
ENG	1	-0.01267	0.00825	-1.54	0.1253	15.78646
WGT	1	-0.00571	0.00071392	-8.00	<.0001	7.78872

6.4.3 Condition indexes

SAS will also print out some advanced collinearity diagnostics.

```
proc reg data=cars;
model mpg = cyl eng wgt/collin;         * condition indexes;
title 'Belsley-Kuh-Welsch diagnostics';
run;
```

A condition index is an indicator of the severity of collinearity. Common rules of thumb are that collinearity is not severe if the index is less than 10, it is moderately severe if the index is between 10 and 30, and is severe if it is greater than 30.[3] More will be said about these index values in the appendix to this chapter, but the material is advanced and requires knowledge of matrix algebra.

Collinearity Diagnostics

Number	Eigenvalue	Condition Index
1	3.86663	1.00000
2	0.12033	5.66860
3	0.00829	21.60042
4	0.00475	28.52804

This same analysis will be produced in **PROC MODEL** using

```
proc model data=cars;
mpg = b1 + b2*cyl + b3*eng + b4*wgt;
fit mpg / collin;
title 'Belsley-Kuh-Welsch diagnostics in proc model';
run;
```

---

[3] See Hill, R. Carter and Lee C. Adkins (2003) "Collinearity," in *A Companion to Theoretical Econometrics*, ed. Badi H. Baltagi, Blackwell Publishing, 256-278. This is advanced material. Some exposition is given in the appendix to this chapter.

6.5 PREDICTION IN MULTIPLE REGRESSION

The prediction problem for a linear model with one explanatory variable extends naturally to the more general model that has more than one explanatory variable. Consider a model with an intercept term and two explanatory variables x_2, x_3. That is

$$y_i = \beta_1 + x_{i2}\beta_2 + x_{i3}\beta_3 + e_i$$

Given a set of values for the explanatory variables, say $(1, x_{02}, x_{03})$, the prediction problem is to predict the value of the dependent variable y_0, which is given by

$$y_0 = \beta_1 + x_{02}\beta_2 + x_{03}\beta_3 + e_0$$

Under standard assumptions the best linear unbiased predictor of y_0 is given by

$$\hat{y}_0 = b_1 + x_{02}b_2 + x_{03}b_3$$

If $f = (y_0 - \hat{y}_0)$ is the forecast error, then we can compute the standard error of the forecast $se(f)$. A $100(1-\alpha)\%$ interval predictor for y_0 is $\hat{y}_0 \pm t_c se(f)$, where t_c is a critical value from the $t_{(N-K)}$-distribution.

SAS will obtain predicted values and interval predictions following a regression for all the data, plus extra observations with just the missing value of the dependent variable. Let's predict the *MPG* of an 8 cylinder car, with a 400 cc engine, and that weighs 4000 pounds. Create a data set with these values, and *MPG* missing.

```
data car2;                          * new data;
input mpg cyl eng wgt;              * input statement;
datalines;
. 8 400 4000
;
run;
```

Combine these observations with the original data set using a **set** statement.

```
data car2;                          * open data set;
set cars car2;                      * combine data sets;
run;
```

Estimate the regression with options **p**, for the predictions, and **cli** for 95% interval predictions.

```
proc reg data=car2;                 * regression with new data;
model mpg = cyl eng wgt/p cli;      * predict and 95% interval;
title 'predictions and prediction interval';
run;
```

Obs	Dependent Variable	Predicted Value	Std Error Mean Predict	95% CL Predict		Residual
393	.	14.3275	0.6554	5.7824	22.8726	.

APPENDIX 6A EXTENDING THE MATRIX APPROACH

6A.1 ANOVA for ols module

In this appendix we will add some additional components and modules to the SAS/IML program begun in the Appendix to Chapter 5

First, estimate the quadratic sales model introduced in Chapter 6.1.4 of this manual

$$SALES = \beta_1 + \beta_2 PRICE + \beta_3 ADVERT + \beta_4 ADVERT^2 + e$$

```
data andy;                              * open data set;
set 'andy';                             * read andy;
advert2 = advert**2;                    * advert squared;
run;

options nolabel;                        * turn off label;
```

Add a single observation representing a price index of *PRICE* = 5.5 and advertising *ADVERT* = 2.

```
data andy2;                                 * new data set;
input sales price advert;               * input data;
advert2 = advert**2;                        * create square;
datalines;
. 5.5 2
;
run;
```

Combine the data sets.

```
data andy2;
set andy andy2;
run;
```

Estimate the model with options **covb** (print covariance matrix), **collin** (carry out advanced collinearity diagnostics), **p** (predict), and **cli** (prediction intervals), and test two hypotheses.

```
proc reg data=andy2;
model sales = price advert advert2/covb collin p cli;
ads:test advert=0,advert2=0;
opt2:test advert + 3.8*advert2 = 1,
          intercept + 6*price + 1.9*advert + 3.61*advert2 = 80;
run;
```

The SAS output (edited) is

The REG Procedure
Dependent Variable: sales

Analysis of Variance

Source	DF	Sum of Squares	Mean Square	F Value	Pr > F
Model	3	1583.39741	527.79914	24.46	<.0001
Error	71	1532.08446	21.57865		
Corrected Total	74	3115.48187			

Root MSE	4.64528	R-Square	0.5082	
Dependent Mean	77.37467	Adj R-Sq	0.4875	
Coeff Var	6.00362			

Variable	DF	Parameter Estimate	Standard Error	t Value	Pr > |t|
Intercept	1	109.71904	6.79905	16.14	<.0001
price	1	-7.64000	1.04594	-7.30	<.0001
advert	1	12.15124	3.55616	3.42	0.0011
advert2	1	-2.76796	0.94062	-2.94	0.0044

Covariance of Estimates

Variable	Intercept	price	advert	advert2
Intercept	46.227019103	-6.426113014	-11.60096014	2.9390263355
price	-6.426113014	1.0939881487	0.3004062437	-0.08561906
advert	-11.60096014	0.3004062437	12.646301979	-3.288745738
advert2	2.9390263355	-0.08561906	-3.288745738	0.8847735678

Collinearity Diagnostics

Number	Eigenvalue	Condition Index
1	3.68927	1.00000
2	0.30262	3.49160
3	0.00527	26.45914
4	0.00284	36.03995

	----------------Proportion of Variation----------------			
Number	Intercept	price	advert	advert2
1	0.00042577	0.00055060	0.00039867	0.00077297
2	0.00456	0.00602	0.00144	0.01929
3	0.18442	0.57176	0.34254	0.34157
4	0.81059	0.42167	0.65562	0.63837

Obs	Dependent Variable	Predicted Value	Std Error Mean Predict	95% CL Predict		Residual
75	75.0000	76.8328	0.8940	67.4004	86.2652	-1.8328
76	.	80.9297	0.8394	71.5172	90.3421	.

Now we will invoke IML and add an ANOVA table to the OLS module from Chapter 5.

```
proc iml;                                    * invoke iml;

/*------------------------------------------------------------*/
/* Matrix model for linear regression                         */
/* This assumes that y & x (without intercept) are in memory  */
/*------------------------------------------------------------*/
```

```
start ols;                              * begin module;
print / "---ols module---",,;           * print message;
n = nrow(y);                            * n = number rows in y;
x1 = j(n,1,1);                          * x1 is column of ones;
x = x1||x;                              * X is horizontal concant;
k = ncol(x);                            * k = number of parms;
df = n - k;                             * degrees of freedom;

xtx = x`*x;                             * X transpose times X;
xtxi = inv(xtx);                        * inverse of X'X;
b = inv(x`*x)*x`*y;                     * ols estimator;
sse = ssq(y - x*b);                     * sum of squared errors;
sig2 = sse/df;                          * variance estimate;
covb = sig2#xtxi;                       * ols covariance estimate;
stderr = sqrt(vecdiag(covb));           * standard errors;
tstat = b/stderr;                       * t-statistics;
pval = 2*(1-probt(abs(tstat),df));      * p-values;
result = b||stderr||tstat||pval;        * result table;
cols = {est se tstat pval};             * result column names;

print result [rowname=parm colname=cols format=12.4];
ybar = sum(y)/n;                        * mean of y;
sst = y`*y - n#ybar##2;                 * total sum of squares;
r2 = 1 - sse/sst;                       * R-squared;
print,,"Summary statistics",
        "sse =" sse
        "sst =" sst
        "r-squared =" r2;

ssr = sst - sse;                        * explained sum of squares ;
msr = ssr/(k-1);                        * explained mean square;
mse = sse/(n-k);                        * unexplained mean square;
mst = sst/(n-1);                        * total mean square;
                                        * construct ANOVA table;
anova = (ssr||(k-1)||msr||(msr/mse))//
        (sse||(n-k)||mse||0)//
        (sst||(n-1)||mst||0);

rnames = {model error total};           * ANOVA row names;
cnames = {source df meansq F_ratio};    * ANOVA column names;

print , "ANOVA TABLE",, anova [rowname=rnames colname=cnames];

finish;                                 * end module;
```

Now, import the data into SAS/IML and run the OLS module.

```
use andy;                               * open data set;
read all var{sales} into y;             * read y;
```

```
read all var{price advert advert2} into x;     * read x;
parm = {const price advert advert2};    * estimates names;

run ols;                               * run module;
```

We now see that the ANOVA table has been added, and the results match those from **PROC REG** above.

```
                      result
              EST         SE       TSTAT       PVAL
CONST     109.7190     6.7990     16.1374     0.0000
PRICE      -7.6400     1.0459     -7.3044     0.0000
ADVERT     12.1512     3.5562      3.4169     0.0011
ADVERT2    -2.7680     0.9406     -2.9427     0.0044


Summary statistics
              sse            sst                   r2
sse = 1532.0844 sst =  3115.482 r-squared = 0.5082352


                   anova
           SOURCE      DF    MEANSQ    F_RATIO
MODEL 1583.3976        3 527.79921 24.459321
ERROR 1532.0844       71 21.578653          0
TOTAL  3115.482       74 42.101108          0
```

6A.2 Prediction and prediction interval

Let $y_0 = \beta_1 + x_{02}\beta_2 + \cdots + x_{0K}\beta_K + e_0 = \mathbf{x}_0\boldsymbol{\beta} + e_0$ where $\mathbf{x}_0$ contains values of the explanatory variables. The best linear unbiased predictor is $\hat{y}_0 = \mathbf{x}_0\mathbf{b}$. The forecast error is $f = y_0 - \hat{y}_0 = \mathbf{x}_0\boldsymbol{\beta} + e_0 - \mathbf{x}_0\mathbf{b}$. The variance of the forecast error, assuming e_0 is uncorrelated with the sample observations, is $\text{var}(f) = \sigma^2 + \sigma^2\mathbf{x}_0(\mathbf{X'X})^{-1}\mathbf{x}_0'$. Then the usual prediction interval is $\mathbf{x}_0\mathbf{b} \pm t_c \text{se}(f)$.

In order to use this module, first run the OLS module, and specify the vector $\mathbf{x}_0$.

```
start predict;                          * start module;
y0 = x0*b;                              * estimate;
v = sig2*(1 + x0*xtxi*x0`);             * variance;
se = sqrt(v);                           * std error;
tc = tinv(.975,df);                     * t critical;
lb = y0 - tc*se;                        * lower bound;
ub = y0 + tc*se;                        * upper bound;
print   "x0                        " x0,,
        "prediction                " y0,,
        "std error forecast        " se,,
        "95% interval prediction   " lb ub;
finish;
```

To illustrate predict the value of *SALES* when *PRICE* = 5.5 and *ADVERT* = 2. Create the $\mathbf{x}_0$ vector and run the module.

```
       x0 = {1 5.5 2 4};                              * x0 values;
       print / "prediction of y0";
       run predict;
```

```
prediction of y0 [edited output]
```

```
x0                          1       5.5       2        4
prediction              80.929654
std error forecast       4.7205183
95% interval prediction 71.517207  90.3421
```

These values match those from **PROC REG** above. The only difference is that we have computed the actual standard error of the prediction in the IML module, while **PROC REG** reports the standard error of the estimated mean function, $\widehat{E(y)} = \mathbf{x_0 b}$

6A.3 Tests of a joint hypothesis

Consider several linear hypotheses, such as

$$H_0 : a_{11}\beta_1 + a_{12}\beta_2 + \cdots + a_{1K}\beta_K = r_1, a_{21}\beta_1 + a_{22}\beta_2 + \cdots + a_{2K}\beta_K = r_2$$

Specify a matrix $\mathbf{R}$ that is $J \times K$, where J is the number of hypotheses, containing the constants a_{ij}. Specify a vector $\mathbf{r}$ that contains the right-hand-side constants r_1 and r_2.

$$\mathbf{R} = \begin{bmatrix} a_{11} & a_{12} & \cdots & a_{1K} \\ a_{21} & a_{22} & \cdots & a_{2K} \end{bmatrix} \qquad \mathbf{r} = \begin{bmatrix} r_1 \\ r_2 \end{bmatrix}$$

The F-statistic is

$$F = \frac{(SSE_R - SSE_U)/J}{SSE_U/(N-K)} = \frac{SSE_R - SSE_U}{J\hat{\sigma}_U^2}$$

An equivalent algebraic form is

$$F = \frac{SSE_R - SSE_U}{J\hat{\sigma}_U^2} = \frac{(\mathbf{Rb} - \mathbf{r})'\left[\mathbf{R}(\mathbf{X'X})^{-1}\mathbf{R'}\right]^{-1}(\mathbf{Rb} - \mathbf{r})}{J\hat{\sigma}_U^2}$$

The Wald test statistic is

$$WALD = \frac{(\mathbf{Rb} - \mathbf{r})'\left[\mathbf{R}(\mathbf{X'X})^{-1}\mathbf{R'}\right]^{-1}(\mathbf{Rb} - \mathbf{r})}{\hat{\sigma}_U^2} = (\mathbf{Rb} - \mathbf{r})'\left[\mathbf{R}\widehat{cov}(\mathbf{b})\mathbf{R'}\right]^{-1}(\mathbf{Rb} - \mathbf{r})$$

In order to use the following module, first run the OLS module, specify $\mathbf{R}$ and $\mathbf{r}$ (called *lr* in module).

```
    start ftest;                          * start module;
    j = nrow(r);                          * number hypotheses;
    fstat = (r*b - lr)`*inv(r*xtxi*r`)*(r*b - lr)/(j*sig2);   * f-stat;
    pval = 1 - probf(fstat,j,df);         * F-statistic p-value;
```

```
        fc95 = finv(.95,j,df);                    * 95% critical value;
        fc99 = finv(.99,j,df);                    * 99% critical value;
        print   "R matrix               " r,,
                "r vector              " lr,,
                "95% critical value " fc95,,
                "99% critical value " fc99,,
                "fstat               " fstat,,
                "p value             " pval;
        finish;
```

The Wald statistic module is

```
        start waldtest;                           * start module;
        j = nrow(r);                              * number hypotheses;
        waldstat = (r*b - lr)`*inv(r*covb*r`)*(r*b - lr);   * Wald-stat;
        pval = 1 - probchi(waldstat,j);           * F-statistic p-value;
        waldc95 = cinv(.95,j);                    * 95% critical value;
        waldc99 = cinv(.99,j);                    * 99% critical value;
        print   "R matrix               " r,,
                "r vector              " lr,,
                "95% critical value " waldc95,,
                "99% critical value " waldc99,,
                "Wald stat           " waldstat,,
                "p value             " pval;
        finish;
```

Let us use the modules to carry out two tests. First, we test the null hypothesis that advertising has no effect on sales, $H_0 : \beta_3 = 0, \beta_4 = 0$. In matrix terms, this is written

$$\mathbf{R\beta} = \begin{bmatrix} 0 & 0 & 1 & 0 \\ 0 & 0 & 0 & 1 \end{bmatrix} \mathbf{\beta} = \mathbf{r} = \begin{bmatrix} 0 \\ 0 \end{bmatrix}$$

Create **R** and **r** in IML as

```
        r = {0 0 1 0, 0 0 0 1};                   * R matrix;
        lr = {0,0};                               * r vector;
        print / "Test of advertising significance ";
        run ftest;
```

```
Test of advertising significance [edited output]

R matrix                    0        0        1        0
                            0        0        0        1

r vector                    0
                            0

95% critical value  3.1257642
99% critical value  4.9172147
fstat               8.4413577
p value             0.0005142
```

Note that in the module we create the 5% and 1% critical values for the test. Repeat this test using the Wald statistic.

```
run waldtest;
```

```
95% critical value  5.9914645
99% critical value  9.2103404
Wald stat             16.88272
p value             0.0002158
```

As a second example we test jointly the two hypotheses

$$H_0 : \beta_3 + 3.8\beta_4 = 1, \beta_1 + 6\beta_2 + 1.9\beta_3 + 1.9^2 \beta_4 = 80$$

In matrix terms these are written

$$\mathbf{R\beta} = \begin{bmatrix} 0 & 0 & 1 & 3.8 \\ 1 & 6 & 1.9 & 3.61 \end{bmatrix} \beta = \mathbf{r} = \begin{bmatrix} 1 \\ 80 \end{bmatrix}$$

Set this up in IML as

```
r = {0 0 1 3.8, 1 6 1.9 3.61};
lr = {1, 80};
print / "Test optimal advertising & sales";
run ftest;
```

```
Test optimal advertising & sales [edited output]

R matrix                  0       0       1      3.8
                          1       6     1.9     3.61

r vector                  1
                         80

95% critical value  3.1257642
99% critical value  4.9172147
fstat               5.7412359
p value             0.0048846
```

```
run waldtest;
```

```
95% critical value  5.9914645
99% critical value  9.2103404
Wald stat            11.482458
p value             0.0032108
```

6A.4 Collinearity diagnostics

The collinearity diagnostics require some matrix background. Let $\mathbf{A}$ be a square $n \times n$ matrix. Suppose $\mathbf{p}$ is a column vector such that $\mathbf{Ap} = \lambda\mathbf{p}$. Then $\mathbf{p}$ is called an **eigenvector** (or characteristic vector) of $\mathbf{A}$ and λ is called an **eigenvalue** (or characteristic root) of $\mathbf{A}$. There are n eigenvectors and eigenvalues. The eigenvectors have the property that $\mathbf{p}'_i\mathbf{p}_i = 1$ and $\mathbf{p}'_i\mathbf{p}_j = 0$ Let the matrix of interest be $\mathbf{X'X}$. Then $(\mathbf{X'X})\mathbf{p}_i = \lambda_i\mathbf{p}_i$ and $\mathbf{p}'_i(\mathbf{X'X})\mathbf{p}_i = \lambda_i\mathbf{p}'_i\mathbf{p}_i = \lambda_i$. If $\lambda_i = 0$ then it must be true that $\mathbf{Xp}_i = \mathbf{0}$ and we have located a linear combination of the columns of $\mathbf{X}$ that is zero. This is exact collinearity. If $\lambda_i \cong 0$ then $\mathbf{Xp}_i \cong \mathbf{0}$ and we have located a nearly exact collinearity. It is customary to order the eigenvalues such that $\lambda_1 \geq \lambda_2 \geq \cdots \geq \lambda_K$. Thus the smallest eigenvalue is λ_K.

The square root of the ratio of the largest eigenvalue to the i'th is called a condition index or condition number.

$$CONDNO_i = (\lambda_1/\lambda_i)^{1/2}$$

PROC REG with the **COLLIN** option prints these. To remove scaling issues the condition index is computed after the $\mathbf{X}$ matrix variables have been scaled by their standard deviations. With such scaling the rules of thumb are that if the largest condition index is less than 10, then collinearity is mild, if it is between 10 and 30 the collinearity is moderate, and over 30 it is severe[4].

```
        Collinearity Diagnostics
                            Condition
Number     Eigenvalue        Index
   1        3.68927        1.00000
   2        0.30262        3.49160
   3        0.00527       26.45914
   4        0.00284       36.03996
```

Using the properties of eigenvectors and eigenvalues we can show that

$$\text{cov}(\mathbf{b}) = \sigma^2(\mathbf{X'X})^{-1} = \sigma^2\mathbf{P\Lambda^{-1}P'} = \sigma^2\sum_{i=1}^{K}\frac{1}{\lambda_i}\mathbf{p}_i\mathbf{p}'_i$$

For a single parameter b_j,

$$\text{var}(b_j) = \sigma^2\sum_{i=1}^{K}\frac{p_{ji}^2}{\lambda_i}$$

The proportion of the variance associated with the i'th eigenvalue is

$$PROP_{ij} = \frac{p_{ji}^2}{\lambda_i}\bigg/\sum_{i=1}^{K}\frac{p_{ji}^2}{\lambda_i}$$

When these values are arranged in a table, again for the $\mathbf{X}$ matrix that has been standardized, as does **PROC REG** with the **COLLIN** option we have

---

[4] These guidelines are suggested in Belsley, D.A., E. Kuh and R.E. Welsch (1980) *Regression Diagnostics*, Wiley.

```
                 ----------------Proportion of Variation----------------
    Number     Intercept        PRICE          ADVERT         advert2
       1      0.00042577     0.00055060     0.00039867     0.00077297
       2        0.00456        0.00602        0.00144        0.01929
       3        0.18442        0.57176        0.34254        0.34157
       4        0.81059        0.42167        0.65562        0.63837
```

The columns sum to 1. The last row corresponds to the smallest eigenvalue and the most severe collinearity. If two or more values are large (some say above 50%) then it is an indication that the corresponding values are involved in the collinearity relationship.

For completeness we have provided a module called COLLIN for IML that reproduces these values.

```
start collin;                          * start module;
ssq = vecdiag(xtx);                    * X sums of squares;
d = diag(1/sqrt(xtx));                 * normalizing matrix;
xn = x*d;                              * normalized X;
xtxn = xn`*xn;                         * cross product matrix;
call eigen(lam,p,xtxn);                * compute eigenval & vec;
ratio = lam[1]/lam;                    * ratio of eigenvalues;
condno = sqrt(ratio);                  * condition numbers;

print, "ratio of eigenvalues and condition numbers",,ratio condno;
p2 = (p##2)#(j(k,1,1)*(1/lam`));       * eigen vec**2 / eigen val;
sumr = p2[,+];                         * row sums;
prop = (diag(1/sumr)*p2)`;             * proportions table;
print, " proportions of coeff. variance ", prop [colname=parm];
finish;
```

Run the OLS module prior to using the module.

```
print / "Collinearity diagnostics";
run collin;
quit;
```

The IML output matches that from **PROC REG**. Note that we leave IML with **quit;**

```
Collinearity diagnostics

ratio of eigenvalues and condition numbers

    ratio     condno

        1          1
12.191263  3.4915989
700.08604  26.459139
1298.8784  36.039956
```

```
proportions of coeff. variance
                     prop
     CONST      PRICE     ADVERT    ADVERT2

0.0004258 0.0005506 0.0003987  0.000773
0.0045568 0.0060242 0.0014351 0.0192877
0.1844229 0.5717584 0.3425446 0.3415732
0.8105946 0.4216668 0.6556217 0.6383661
```

CHAPTER 7

Using Indicator Variables

7.1 INDICATOR VARIABLES

Indicator variables are used to account for qualitative factors in econometric models. They are often called **binary** or **dichotomous** variables, or **dummy** variables, as they take just two values, usually 1 or 0, to indicate the presence or absence of a characteristic. This choice of values is arbitrary but very convenient as we will see. Generally we define an indicator variable D as

$$D = \begin{cases} 1 & \text{if characteristic is present} \\ 0 & \text{if characteristic is not present} \end{cases}$$

Dummy variables are used to indicate gender, race, location, employment status and so on. Computationally the use of these variables is no different from other variables in a regression model. We must, however, take care with their interpretation.

7.1.1 Slope and intercept effects

A major use of indicator variables is to build flexibility into a regression model, allowing some subsets of observations to have different intercepts and slopes. Consider the relationship between house price and the size of the house. The nature of this relationship, either the slope or the intercept or both, may change depending on neighborhood amenities. For example, neighborhoods near universities are considered desirable by many. Open the SAS data set *utown*.

```
options label;
data utown;
set 'utown';
run;
```

Examine the contents.

```
proc contents data=utown position;
title 'utown data';
run;
```

```
#   Variable   Type   Len   Label
1   PRICE      Num    8     house price, in $1000
2   SQFT       Num    8     square feet of living area, in 100's
3   AGE        Num    3     house age, in years
4   UTOWN      Num    3     =1 if close to university
5   POOL       Num    3     =1 if house has pool
6   FPLACE     Num    3     =1 if house has fireplace
```

The variable labels for *UTOWN, POOL* and *FPLACE* are meant to show that they are indicator variables, indicating the presence or absence of these features. Examine a few observations.

```
options nolabel;
proc print data=utown (obs=5);
title 'utown observations';
run;
```

```
Obs    PRICE     SQFT      AGE    UTOWN    POOL    FPLACE
 1    205.452   23.4600    6      0        0       1
 2    185.328   20.0300    5      0        0       1
 3    248.422   27.7700    6      0        0       0
 4    154.690   20.1700    1      0        0       0
 5    221.801   26.4500    0      0        0       1
```

Note that the values of variables *UTOWN, POOL*, and *FPLACE* are zeros and ones.

```
proc means data=utown;
title 'utown means';
run;
```

Variable	N	Mean	Std Dev	Minimum	Maximum
PRICE	1000	247.6557211	42.1927288	134.3159943	345.1969910
SQFT	1000	25.2096500	2.9184799	20.0300007	30.0000000
AGE	1000	9.3920000	9.4267279	0	60.0000000
UTOWN	1000	0.5190000	0.4998889	0	1.0000000
POOL	1000	0.2040000	0.4031706	0	1.0000000
FPLACE	1000	0.5180000	0.4999259	0	1.0000000

The summary statistics show that 51.9% of the houses in this sample have *UTOWN* = 1, indicating that the house is near a university. Similarly 20.4% have a pool and 51.8% have a fireplace. Note that *PRICE* is measured in $1000s of dollars, and *SQFT* is measured in 100s.

Estimate the model

$$PRICE = \beta_1 + \delta_1 UTOWN + \beta_2 SQFT + \gamma \left(SQFT \times UTOWN \right) + \beta_3 AGE + \delta_2 POOL + \delta_3 FPLACE + e$$

The regression functions of interest show that the inclusion of the indicator variable *UTOWN* permits the intercept to change, and the **interaction variable** $SQFT \times UTOWN$ allows the slope to differ between neighborhoods.

$$E(PRICE) = \begin{cases} \beta_1 + \beta_2 SQFT + \beta_3 AGE + \delta_2 POOL + \delta_3 FPLACE & UTOWN = 0 \\ (\beta_1 + \delta_1) + (\beta_2 + \gamma)SQFT + \beta_3 AGE + \delta_2 POOL + \delta_3 FPLACE & UTOWN = 1 \end{cases}$$

Create the interaction variable and use **PROC REG** to estimate the relationship. Test the joint significance of δ_1 and γ using an *F*-test. Rejecting the null hypothesis $H_0 : \delta_1 = 0, \gamma = 0$ will reveal to us that there are statistically significant differences in the house price relationship between the two neighborhoods.

```
data utown2;
set utown;
sqft_utown=sqft*utown;
run;

proc reg data=utown2;
model price = utown sqft sqft_utown age pool fplace;
test utown=0,sqft_utown=0;
title 'utown regression';
run;
```

Variable	DF	Parameter Estimate	Standard Error	t Value	Pr > |t|
Intercept	1	24.49998	6.19172	3.96	<.0001
UTOWN	1	27.45295	8.42258	3.26	0.0012
SQFT	1	7.61218	0.24518	31.05	<.0001
sqft_utown	1	1.29940	0.33205	3.91	<.0001
AGE	1	-0.19009	0.05120	-3.71	0.0002
POOL	1	4.37716	1.19669	3.66	0.0003
FPLACE	1	1.64918	0.97196	1.70	0.0901

Test 1 Results for Dependent Variable PRICE

Source	DF	Mean Square	F Value	Pr > F
Numerator	2	453143	1954.83	<.0001
Denominator	993	231.80706		

The statistical significance of *UTOWN* and the interaction variable $SQFT \times UTOWN$, and the large *F*-statistic value indicate that there are significant neighborhood effects.

7.1.2 The Chow test

Indicator variables and their interactions can be used to test the equivalence of regression functions across sample partitions. Consider the wage equation

$$WAGE = \beta_1 + \beta_2 EDUC + \delta_1 BLACK + \delta_2 FEMALE + \gamma(BLACK \times FEMALE) + e$$

The variables *BLACK* and *FEMALE* are indicator variables, as is their interaction. Using U.S. data, is this relation different in the southern states from the remainder of the country? To answer this question build a **fully interacted model**, interacting *SOUTH* with all other variables.

$$WAGE = \beta_1 + \beta_2 EDUC + \delta_1 BLACK + \delta_2 FEMALE + \gamma\left(BLACK \times FEMALE\right) +$$

$$\theta_1 SOUTH + \theta_2\left(EDUC \times SOUTH\right) + \theta_3\left(BLACK \times SOUTH\right) +$$

$$\theta_4\left(FEMALE \times SOUTH\right) + \theta_5\left(BLACK \times FEMALE \times SOUTH\right) + e$$

This yields the regression functions

$$E\left(WAGE\right) = \begin{cases} \beta_1 + \beta_2 EDUC + \delta_1 BLACK + \delta_2 FEMALE + \\ \gamma\left(BLACK \times FEMALE\right) & SOUTH = 0 \\ \\ (\beta_1 + \theta_1) + (\beta_2 + \theta_2)EDUC + (\delta_1 + \theta_3)BLACK + & SOUTH = 1 \\ (\delta_2 + \theta_4)FEMALE + (\gamma + \theta_5)\left(BLACK \times FEMALE\right) \end{cases}$$

The null hypothesis $H_0 : \theta_1 = \theta_2 = \theta_3 = \theta_4 = \theta_5 = 0$ is that there is no difference in the regressions between regions. The test statistic is

$$F = \frac{(SSE_R - SSE_U)/J}{SSE_U/(N-K)}$$

Where SSE_R comes from the original specification and results from imposing the null hypothesis on the fully interacted model, and SSE_U comes from the fully interacted model.

This test is implemented in SAS by first creating the interaction variables and then using **PROC REG** with a **test** statement. Open the SAS data set *cps4*. We create the SAS data set *cps4* containing the data plus interaction variables. This is a larger data set than the previously used *cps4_small*.

```
data cps4;
set 'cps4';
black_fem = black*female;
educ_south = educ*south;
black_south = black*south;
fem_south = female*south;
black_fem_south = black*female*south;
run;
```

Estimate a base model,

```
proc reg data=cps4;
base:model wage = educ black female black_fem;
title 'base wage equation';
run;
```

The ANOVA table is

```
                        Model: base
                   Analysis of Variance

                              Sum of         Mean
Source               DF      Squares       Square    F Value   Pr > F
Model                 4       179330        44833     373.23   <.0001
Error              4833       580544    120.12093
Corrected Total    4837       759875
```

The Sum of Squares Error will be a key component in the F-test below.

Estimate the fully interacted model and test the interaction variables.

```
proc reg data=cps4;
full:model wage = educ black female black_fem
                  south educ_south black_south fem_south black_fem_south;
test south=0,educ_south=0,black_south=0,fem_south=0,black_fem_south=0;
title 'wage equation with interactions';
run;
```

The ANOVA table is

```
                        Model: full
                   Analysis of Variance

                              Sum of         Mean
Source               DF      Squares       Square    F Value   Pr > F
Model                 9       180085        20009     166.62   <.0001
Error              4828       579790    120.08903
Corrected Total    4837       759875
```

The SSE_U for the F-statistic is 579790. The result of the **test** statement gives

```
          Test 1 Results for Dependent Variable wage

                                  Mean
      Source         DF         Square    F Value   Pr > F
      Numerator       5      150.92792       1.26   0.2798
      Denominator  4828      120.08903
```

Note that the **Denominator** is the Mean Square Error from the "full" model, $\hat{\sigma}^2 = 120.08903$.

The SSE_R is obtained from the base regression above. In the ANOVA table from the "base" model find $SSE_R = 580544$. The **Numerator** of the F-statistic is

$$(SSE_R - SSE_U)/J = (580544 - 579790)/5 = 150.8 \cong 150.93$$

Our computation has some rounding error (in the SSE). The value calculated by SAS includes more decimals.

The SSE_U value is obtained by estimating the fully interacted model. You can verify that it can be obtained by estimating separate equations for the south and non-south and summing the SSEs.

$$SSE_U = SSE_{non-south} + SSE_{south}$$

```
proc reg data=cps4;
south:model wage = educ black female black_fem;
where south=1;
title 'wage regression in south';
run;

proc reg data=cps4;
nonsouth:model wage = educ black female black_fem;
where south=0;
title 'wage regression outside south';
run;
```

Model: south

Source	DF	Sum of Squares	Mean Square	F Value	Pr > F
Model	4	50918	12730	108.98	<.0001
Error	1425	166453	116.80911		
Corrected Total	1429	217371			

Model: nonsouth

Source	DF	Sum of Squares	Mean Square	F Value	Pr > F
Model	4	128683	32171	264.86	<.0001
Error	3403	413337	121.46249		
Corrected Total	3407	542020			

Combine these two "Sum of Squares" to obtain

$$SSE_U = SSE_{non-south} + SSE_{south} = 413337 + 166453 = 579790$$

7.2 USING PROC MODEL FOR LOG-LINEAR REGRESSION

PROC MODEL is useful for nonlinear models. In a log-linear regression the estimated coefficients have a modified interpretation. Consider the log-linear model

$$\ln(WAGE) = \beta_1 + \beta_2 EDUC + \delta FEMALE$$

A one year increase in education increases wages by approximately $100\beta_2\%$.

What is the interpretation of the parameter δ? *FEMALE* is an intercept dummy variable, creating a parallel shift of the log-linear relationship when *FEMALE* = 1. The wage difference is

$$\ln(WAGE)_{FEMALES} - \ln(WAGE)_{MALES} = \ln\left(\frac{WAGE_{FEMALES}}{WAGE_{MALES}}\right) = \delta$$

These are natural logarithms, and the anti-log is the exponential function,

$$\frac{WAGE_{FEMALES}}{WAGE_{MALES}} = e^\delta$$

Subtract one from each side to obtain

$$\frac{WAGE_{FEMALES}}{WAGE_{MALES}} - \frac{WAGE_{MALES}}{WAGE_{MALES}} = \frac{WAGE_{FEMALES} - WAGE_{MALES}}{WAGE_{MALES}} = e^{\delta} - 1$$

The percentage difference between wages of females and males is $100\left(e^{\delta} - 1\right)\%$.

Continue to use the *cps4* data set from the previous section. Use PROC MODEL to estimate the relationship and compute the exact "gender effect." Note that we can create **log(wage)** inside **PROC MODEL**

```
proc model data=cps4;
label b1='intercept'
      b2='educ'
      delta='female';
log(wage) = b1 + b2*educ + delta*female;
fit "log(wage)";
estimate 'gender effect' 100*(exp(delta)-1);
title 'log-linear dummy variable';
run;
```

Parameter	Estimate	Std Err	t Value	Pr > |t|	Label
b1	1.626193	0.0375	43.38	<.0001	intercept
b2	0.096151	0.00264	36.47	<.0001	educ
delta	-0.23984	0.0144	-16.64	<.0001	female

Term	Estimate	Approx Std Err	t Value	Approx Pr > |t|	Label
gender effect	-21.3244	1.1342	-18.80	<.0001	100*(exp(delta)-1)

If the log-linear model contains an interaction variable the calculation is again facilitated by using **PROC MODEL**. Consider the wage equation

$$\ln(WAGE) = \beta_1 + \beta_2 EDUC + \beta_3 EXPER + \gamma(EDUC \times EXPER)$$

What is the effect of another year of experience, holding education constant? Roughly,

$$\left.\frac{\Delta \ln(WAGE)}{\Delta EXPER}\right|_{EDUC\ fixed} = \beta_3 + \gamma EDUC$$

The approximate percentage change in wage given a one year increase in experience is $100\left(\beta_3 + \gamma EDUC\right)\%$. Compute this effect when $EDUC = 16$.

```
proc model data=cps4;
label b1='intercept'
      b2='educ'
      b3='exper'
      gamma='educ*exper';
log(wage) = b1 + b2*educ +b3*exper + gamma*(educ*exper);
fit "log(wage)";
educ0 = 16;
estimate 'marg effect exper' 100*(b3 + gamma*educ0);
```

```
    title 'log-linear interaction variables';
  run;
```

Parameter	Estimate	Std Err	t Value	Pr > |t|	Label
b1	1.347744	0.0899	14.99	<.0001	intercept
b2	0.096191	0.00632	15.22	<.0001	educ
b3	0.005436	0.00290	1.87	0.0610	exper
gamma	0.000045	0.000208	0.22	0.8279	educ*exper

		Approx		Approx	
Term	Estimate	Std Err	t Value	Pr > |t|	Label
marg effect exper	0.616035	0.0761	8.09	<.0001	100*(b3 + gamma*educ0)

Note that this is 0.616% since we have already multiplied by 100.

7.3 THE LINEAR PROBABILITY MODEL

When modeling choice between two alternatives, an indicator variable will be the **dependent** variable rather than an independent variable in a regression model. Suppose

$$y = \begin{cases} 1 & \text{if first alternative is chosen} \\ 0 & \text{if second alternative is chosen} \end{cases}$$

If p is the probability that the first alternative is chosen, then $P[y=1]=p$, then the expected value of y is $E(y)=p$ and its variance is $\text{var}(y)=p(1-p)$.

We are interested in identifying factors that might affect the probability p using a linear regression function, or in this context a **linear probability model**,

$$E(y) = p = \beta_1 + \beta_2 x_2 + \cdots + \beta_K x_K$$

The linear probability regression model is

$$y = \beta_1 + \beta_2 x_2 + \cdots + \beta_K x_K + e$$

The variance of the error term e is

$$\text{var}(e) = (\beta_1 + \beta_2 x_2 + \cdots + \beta_K x_K)(1 - \beta_1 - \beta_2 x_2 - \cdots - \beta_K x_K)$$

This error is not homoskedastic and will be treated in Chapter 8.

As an illustration consider the choice between Coke and Pepsi. Open *coke* and check its contents.

```
    options label;
    data coke;
    set 'coke';
    run;
    proc contents data=coke;
    title 'coke data';
    run;
    options nolabel;
```

To estimate the linear probability model for choosing Coke using the least squares regression.

```
proc reg data=coke;
ols:model coke = pratio disp_coke disp_pepsi;
output out=cokeout p=phat;
title 'coke regression';
run;
```

The least squares results are

Variable	DF	Parameter Estimate	Standard Error	t Value	Pr > |t|
Intercept	1	0.89022	0.06548	13.59	<.0001
pratio	1	-0.40086	0.06135	-6.53	<.0001
disp_coke	1	0.07717	0.03439	2.24	0.0250
disp_pepsi	1	-0.16566	0.03560	-4.65	<.0001

A concern with the linear regression approach is that the predicted probabilities can be outside the interval [0, 1]. For the OLS estimates we obtain the predicted values and then count the number outside the [0,1] interval.

```
data cokeout;
set cokeout;
badprob = phat > 1 or phat < 0;
keep badprob;
run;

proc means data=cokeout sum;
run;
```

Sum
16.0000000

We see that 16 of the 1140 observations have predicted values that cannot be probabilities.

7.4 TREATMENT EFFECTS

In order to understand the measurement of treatment effects, consider a simple regression model in which the explanatory variable is a dummy variable, indicating whether a particular individual is in the treatment or control group. Let y be the outcome variable, the measured characteristic the treatment is designed to affect. Define the indicator variable d as

$$d_i = \begin{cases} 1 & \text{individual in treatment group} \\ 0 & \text{individual in control group} \end{cases}$$

The effect of the treatment on the outcome can be modeled as

$$y_i = \beta_1 + \beta_2 d_i + e_i, \quad i = 1, \ldots, N$$

where e_i represents the collection of other factors affecting the outcome. The regression functions for the treatment and control groups are

$$E(y_i) = \begin{cases} \beta_1 + \beta_2 & \text{if in treatment group, } d_i = 1 \\ \beta_1 & \text{if in control group, } d_i = 0 \end{cases}$$

The **treatment effect** that we wish to measure is β_2. The least squares estimator of β_2 is

$$b_2 = \frac{\sum_{i=1}^{N}(d_i - \bar{d})(y_i - \bar{y})}{\sum_{i=1}^{N}(d_i - \bar{d})^2} = \bar{y}_1 - \bar{y}_0$$

where $\bar{y}_1 = \sum_{i=1}^{N_1} y_i / N_1$ is the sample mean of the N_1 observations on y for the treatment group (d = 1) and $\bar{y}_0 = \sum_{i=1}^{N_0} y_i / N_0$ is the sample mean of the N_0 observations on y for the control group (d = 0). In this treatment/control framework the estimator b_2 is called the **difference estimator** because it is the difference between the sample means of the treatment and control groups.

To illustrate, we use the data from project STAR described in *Principles of Econometrics, 4th Edition*, Chapter 7.5.3.

```
options label;
data star;
set 'star';
run;

proc contents data=star;
title 'star data';
run;
options nolabel;
```

To examine the effect of small versus regular size classes drop the observations for classes of regular size with a teacher aide.

```
data star;
set star;
if aide=0;
run;
```

We find that 3743 observations remain.

```
proc means data=star;
var totalscore small tchexper boy freelunch white_asian tchwhite
    tchmasters schurban schrural;
title 'summary stats for regular sized class';
where regular=1;
run;
```

```
proc means data=star;
var totalscore small tchexper boy freelunch white_asian tchwhite
    tchmasters schurban schrural;
where small=1;
title 'summary stats for small sized class';
run;
```

Partial output is

summary stats for regular sized class

Variable	N	Mean	Std Dev	Minimum	Maximum
totalscore	2005	918.0428928	73.1379917	635.0000000	1229.00

summary stats for small sized class

Variable	N	Mean	Std Dev	Minimum	Maximum
totalscore	1738	931.9418872	76.3586330	747.0000000	1253.00

We observe that the average test score for students in small classes is higher.

The core model of interest is

$$TOTALSCORE = \beta_1 + \beta_2 SMALL + e$$

Which we may augment with additional control variables such as

$$TOTALSCORE = \beta_1 + \beta_2 SMALL + \beta_3 TCHEXPER + e$$

```
proc reg data=star;
base:model totalscore = small;
ctrl:model totalscore = small tchexper;
title 'treatment effects';
run;
```

treatment effects

Model: base

Variable	DF	Parameter Estimate	Standard Error	t Value	Pr > |t|
Intercept	1	918.04289	1.66716	550.66	<.0001
small	1	13.89899	2.44659	5.68	<.0001

Model: ctrl

Variable	DF	Parameter Estimate	Standard Error	t Value	Pr > |t|
Intercept	1	907.56434	2.54241	356.97	<.0001
small	1	13.98327	2.43733	5.74	<.0001
tchexper	1	1.15551	0.21228	5.44	<.0001

The model including indicator variables for each school is

$$TOTALSCORE = \beta_1 + \beta_2 SMALL + \beta_3 TCHEXPER + \sum\nolimits_{j=2}^{79} \delta_j SCHOOL\_j_i + e$$

We can estimate this model in several ways in SAS. First, **PROC AUTOREG** supports a **CLASS** statement. The CLASS statement names the classification variables to be used in the analysis. Classification variables can be either character or numeric.

```
proc autoreg data=star;
class schid;
base:model totalscore = small schid / noint;
ctrl:model totalscore = small tchexper schid / noint;
title 'treatment effects with school fixed effects';
run;
```

PROC AUTOREG with the **CLASS** statement includes an indicator variable for each value of the variable *SCHID*. To avoid the "dummy variable trap" we use the option **NOINT**, which suppresses the overall intercept. The output is edited, showing only a few school fixed effects.

treatment effects with school fixed effects

Model				base	
Variable	DF	Estimate	Standard Error	t Value	Approx Pr > |t|
small	1	15.9978	2.2228	7.20	<.0001
schid 112038	1	838.7586	11.5596	72.56	<.0001
schid 123056	1	894.2657	11.3870	78.53	<.0001
schid 128068	1	887.0332	11.9175	74.43	<.0001

Model				ctrl	
Variable	DF	Estimate	Standard Error	t Value	Approx Pr > |t|
small	1	16.0656	2.2183	7.24	<.0001
tchexper	1	0.9132	0.2256	4.05	<.0001
schid 112038	1	830.7579	11.7036	70.98	<.0001
schid 123056	1	883.6532	11.6618	75.77	<.0001
schid 128068	1	881.8790	11.9606	73.73	<.0001

Using this approach we obtain the estimated coefficients of indicator variables for all 79 schools. That may be what is desired. If, however, the individual coefficients are not of interest, an alternative approach is to use **PROC GLM**. Using this procedure the individual school coefficients are "absorbed" into the regression prior to estimation. The meaning of this term will be explained in Chapter 15. Look for a discussion there of the "within" transformation. Before using this technique we must first sort the data according to the class variable.

```
proc sort data=star out=star2;
by schid;
run;
```

```
proc glm data=star2;
absorb schid;
model totalscore = small;
title 'treatment effects with absorbed school fixed effects';
run;
```

The output includes the parameter estimate of interest.

```
                                  Standard
Parameter        Estimate           Error     t Value    Pr > |t|
small          15.99777661      2.22284636        7.20      <.0001
```

The class sizes were assigned randomly within schools. It is important to check for associations between small and other variables using a linear probability model, with and without school fixed effects.

```
proc reg data=star;
ols:model small = boy white_asian tchexper freelunch;
title 'random assignment regression checks';
run;
```

Variable	DF	Parameter Estimate	Standard Error	t Value	Pr > |t|
Intercept	1	0.46646	0.02516	18.54	<.0001
boy	1	0.00141	0.01634	0.09	0.9312
white_asian	1	0.00441	0.01960	0.22	0.8221
tchexper	1	-0.00060255	0.00144	-0.42	0.6754
freelunch	1	-0.00088588	0.01819	-0.05	0.9612

The results show that *SMALL* is not linearly related to the chosen variables. The *t*-values here do not account for model heteroskedasticity. This topic is discussed in Chapter 8. Alternatives to the linear probability model are discussed in Chapter 16.

7.5 DIFFERENCES-IN-DIFFERENCES ESTIMATION

Natural experiments mimic randomized control experiments and are useful for evaluating policy changes. There is a treatment group that is affected by a policy change and a control group that is similar but which is not affected by the policy change. The situation is illustrated in the figure below. The treatment effect is the change $\overline{CD}$.

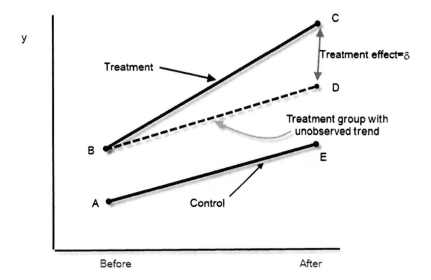

The treatment effect is estimated as

$$\hat{\delta} = \left(\hat{C} - \hat{E}\right) - \left(\hat{B} - \hat{A}\right) = \left(\overline{y}_{Treatment,After} - \overline{y}_{Control,After}\right) - \left(\overline{y}_{Treatment,Before} - \overline{y}_{Control,Before}\right)$$

Where $\overline{y}$ denotes the various sample means. The estimator is called a **differences-in-differences** (abbreviated as D-in-D, DD, or DID) estimator of the treatment effect.

The DID estimator can be conveniently calculated using a simple regression. Define y_{it} to be the observed outcome for individual i in period t. Let $AFTER_t$ be an indicator variable that equals 1 in the period after the policy change ($t = 2$) and equals 0 in the period before the policy change ($t = 1$). Let $TREAT_i$ be an indicator variable that equals 1 if individual i is in the treatment group, and equals 0 if the individual is in the control (non-treatment) group. Consider the regression model

$$y_{it} = \beta_1 + \beta_2 TREAT_i + \beta_3 AFTER_t + \delta\left(TREAT_i \times AFTER_t\right) + e_{it}$$

The example in *Principles of Econometrics, 4th Edition*, is from Card and Kruegar (1994)[1]. On April 1, 1992, New Jersey's minimum wage was increased from \$4.25 to \$5.05 per hour, while the minimum wage in Pennsylvania stayed at \$4.25 per hour. Card and Krueger collected data on 410 fast food restaurants in New Jersey (the treatment group) and eastern Pennsylvania (the control group). The "before" period is February, 1992, and the "after" period is November, 1992. Using these data they estimate the effect of the "treatment," raising the New Jersey minimum wage on employment at fast food restaurants in New Jersey.

Open *njmin3* and examine the variables.

```
options label;
data nj;
set 'njmin3';
run;
```

[1] David Card and Alan Krueger (1994) "Minimum Wages and Employment: A Case Study of the Fast Food Industry in New Jersey and Pennsylvania," *The American Economic Review*, 84, 316-361.

```
proc contents data=nj position;
title 'new jersey data';
run;
options nolabel;
```

The variables are

```
                    Variables in Creation Order

#       Variable   Type    Len     Label
1       CO_OWNED   Num      8       = 1 if company owned
2       SOUTHJ     Num      8       = 1 if in southern NJ
3       CENTRALJ   Num      8       = 1 if in central NJ
4       PA1        Num      8       = 1 if in PA, northeast suburbs of Phila
5       PA2        Num      8       = 1 if in PA, Easton etc
6       DEMP       Num      8       change in full time employment
7       nj         Num      8       = 1 if New Jersey
8       bk         Num      8       = 1 if Burger King
9       kfc        Num      8       = 1 if Kentucky Fried Chicken
10      roys       Num      8       = 1 if Roy Rodgers
11      wendys     Num      8       = 1 if Wendys
12      d          Num      8       = 1 if after NJ min wage increase
13      d_nj       Num      8       nj*d interaction
14      fte        Num      8       full time-equivalent employees
```

The mean *FTE* in the before and after periods for New Jersey and Pennsylvania data are obtained using

```
proc means data=nj;
var fte;
where d = 0 and nj = 0;
title 'summary stats: before & Pa';
run;

proc means data=nj;
var fte;
where d = 1 and nj = 0;
title 'summary stats: after & Pa';
run;

proc means data=nj;
var fte;
where d = 0 and nj =1;
title 'summary stats: before & NJ';
run;

proc means data=nj;
var fte;
where d = 1 and nj = 1;
title 'summary stats: after & NJ';
run;
```

```
              summary stats: before & Pa

              Analysis Variable : fte
```

N	Mean	Std Dev	Minimum	Maximum
77	23.3311688	11.8562831	7.5000000	70.5000000

```
              summary stats: after & Pa
```

N	Mean	Std Dev	Minimum	Maximum
77	21.1655844	8.2767320	0	43.5000000

```
              summary stats: before & NJ
```

N	Mean	Std Dev	Minimum	Maximum
321	20.4394081	9.1062391	5.0000000	85.0000000

```
              summary stats: after & NJ
```

N	Mean	Std Dev	Minimum	Maximum
319	21.0274295	9.2930238	0	60.5000000

The differences-in-differences regressions, with and without controls are:

```
proc reg data=nj;
did:model fte = nj d d_nj;
did_ctrl:model fte = nj d d_nj kfc roys wendys co_owned southj centralj
    pa1;
did_ctrl2:model fte = nj d d_nj kfc roys wendys co_owned southj centralj
    pa1;
title 'difference-in-difference regressions';
run;
```

The first set of results is

```
          difference-in-difference regressions

                    Model: did
```

Variable	DF	Parameter Estimate	Standard Error	t Value	Pr > |t|
Intercept	1	23.33117	1.07187	21.77	<.0001
nj	1	-2.89176	1.19352	-2.42	0.0156
d	1	-2.16558	1.51585	-1.43	0.1535
d_nj	1	2.75361	1.68841	1.63	0.1033

Note that the estimated coefficient of the interaction variable D_NJ matches the estimate

$$\hat{\delta} = \left(\overline{FTE}_{NJ,After} - \overline{FTE}_{PA,After} \right) - \left(\overline{FTE}_{NJ,Before} - \overline{FTE}_{PA,Before} \right)$$

$$= \left(21.0274 - 21.1656 \right) - \left(20.4394 - 23.3312 \right)$$

$$= 2.7536$$

CHAPTER **8**

Heteroskedasticity

8.1 THE NATURE OF HETEROSKEDASTICITY

The simple linear regression model is

$$y_i = \beta_1 + \beta_2 x_i + e_i$$

A key assumption in this model is that the variance of the error term is a constant,

$$\text{var}(e_i) = \sigma^2$$

for all observations $i = 1, \ldots, N$. This is called the assumption of **homoskedasticity**. If the variance of the error differs from one observation to another, so that

$$\text{var}(e_i) = \sigma_i^2$$

then the errors are said to be **heteroskedastic**. This problem is common when using cross-sectional data and panel data.

The consequences for the least squares estimator are:

1. The least squares estimator is still a linear and unbiased estimator, but it is no longer best. There is another estimator with a smaller variance, called the **generalized least squares estimator**.

2. The standard errors usually computed for the least squares estimator are incorrect. Confidence intervals and hypothesis tests that use these standard errors may be misleading. Corrected standard errors are known as **White's heteroskedasticity-consistent standard errors**, or **heteroskedasticity robust standard errors**.

8.2 PLOTTING THE LEAST SQUARES RESIDUALS

To illustrate the problem we will use the food expenditure data that was first introduced in Section 2.2 of this manual. Recall that in this example $y = FOOD\_EXP$ (food expenditure in \$) and $x = INCOME$ (income in \$100).

First, read the data set and examine its contents, and turn off the variable labels.

```
data food;
set 'food';
run;

proc contents data=food position;        * examine data set;
run;
options nolabel;                          * turn off labels;
```

```
              Variables in Creation Order
#    Variable   Type   Len   Label
1    food_exp   Num     8    household food expenditure per week
2    income     Num     8    weekly household income
```

Estimate the regression model and output the residuals (*EHAT*) and predicted values (*YHAT*) to a SAS data set called *foodout*.

```
proc reg data=food;
model food_exp = income;
output out=foodout r=ehat p=yhat;         * output resids & predicted;
title 'OLS on food expenditure data';
run;
```

The regression results are shown in Chapter 2, so we will not repeat them.

When using **PROC GPLOT** it is useful to have the labels option turned on. We create a symbol (a dot) for use in the graphs, and then plot the residuals against the explanatory variable *INCOME* and in another plot against the predicted values.

```
options label;                            * using labels for plots;
symbol1 value=dot color=blue;             * symbol for plots;

proc gplot data=foodout;                  * plot using output data;
plot ehat * income=1;                     * resid vs. x-variable;
plot ehat * yhat=1;                       * resid vs. predicted;
title 'Residual plots for food expenditure data';
run;

options nolabel;                          * turn off labels;
```

Any sign of a funnel pattern, such as the ones below, indicates a potential heteroskedasticity problem. The residuals should be plotted against **each** explanatory variable and the predicted value as a standard diagnostic step.

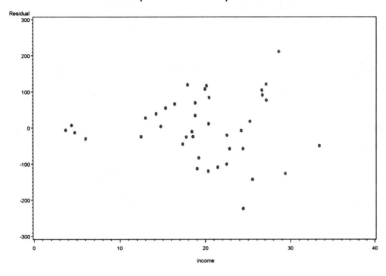

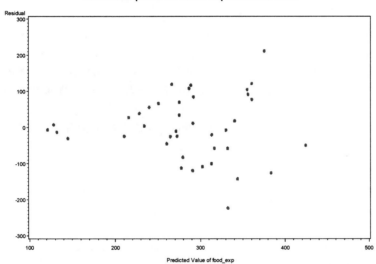

8.3 LEAST SQUARES WITH ROBUST STANDARD ERRORS

The use of heteroskedasticity robust standard errors is common in applied econometrics. When heteroskedasticity is present the usual formula for the variance of the least squares estimator,

$$\text{var}(b_2) = \frac{\sigma^2}{\displaystyle\sum_{i=1}^{N}(x_i - \overline{x})^2}$$

is incorrect. It should be

$$\text{var}(b_2) = \sum_{i=1}^{N} w_i^2 \sigma_i^2 = \frac{\sum_{i=1}^{N}\left[(x_i - \overline{x})^2 \sigma_i^2\right]}{\left[\sum_{i=1}^{N}(x_i - \overline{x})^2\right]^2}$$

where $w_i = (x_i - \overline{x})\big/\sum(x_i - \overline{x})^2$. An estimator for this variance was suggested by econometrician Hal White. The resulting standard errors (the standard error for b_2 and the standard errors for the least squares estimator of other coefficients in the multiple regression model) have become known as White's **heteroskedasticity-consistent standard errors**, or **heteroskedasticity robust**, or simply **robust, standard errors**. The term "robust" is used because they are valid when heteroskedasticity is present, and they are also valid when the errors are homoskedastic.

To obtain the White standard error for b_2 we obtain the least squares residuals $\hat{e}_i = y_i - b_1 - b_2 x_i$ and replace σ_i^2 in the formula above with the squares of the least squares residuals. The White variance estimator is given by

$$\widehat{\text{var}(b_2)} = \sum_{i=1}^{N} w_i^2 \hat{e}_i^2 = \frac{\sum_{i=1}^{N}\left[(x_i - \overline{x})^2 \hat{e}_i^2\right]}{\left[\sum_{i=1}^{N}(x_i - \overline{x})^2\right]^2}$$

The White standard error is given by the square root of this quantity. In practice a slight modification is made. The least squares fitting procedure produces squared residuals that are on average smaller than the squares of the true random errors. To correct this feature, it is common to multiply the basic White robust variance above by $N/(N-K)$, where K is the number of parameters in the model.

The corrected standard errors are obtained using **PROC REG** with a model statement option.

```
proc reg data=food;
model food_exp = income/clb hcc hccmethod=1;
title 'proc reg robust covariance';
run;
```

The first regression option **clb** is not a new one. It requests that confidence intervals be printed in the output. The option **hcc** requests heteroskedasticity consistent standard errors. This must be accompanied by a choice of methods. The standard method used in most applied work, with the inflation factor $N/(N-K)$, is obtained by specifying the option **hccmethod=1**.

The results show the usual least squares estimates and standard errors. Below these are reported as the Heteroskedasticity Consistent results, with corrected standard errors, corrected t-values and p-values. Interestingly, the interval estimates based on both correct and incorrect standard errors are displayed. Make sure you use the **correct ones**! Notice in this example that the corrected standard errors are actually smaller than the incorrect ones.

```
                    Parameter Estimates

                    Parameter       Standard
      Variable   DF   Estimate         Error    t Value    Pr > |t|

      Intercept   1   83.41600      43.41016      1.92      0.0622
      income      1   10.20964       2.09326      4.88      <.0001

                    Parameter Estimates          95% interval based on incorrect
                                                         standard errors
                 --Heteroscedasticity Consistent-
                        Standard
Variable    DF            Error    t Value    Pr > |t|    95% Confidence Limits

Intercept    1        27.46375       3.04      0.0043      -4.46328      171.29528
income       1         1.80908       5.64      <.0001       5.97205       14.44723

                    Parameter Estimates

                                Heteroscedasticity Consistent
                 Variable    DF        95% Confidence Limits

                 Intercept    1      27.81855      139.01345       95% interval based on
                 income       1       6.54736       13.87193       corrected standard errors
                    HCC Approximation Method: HC1
```

8.4 GENERALIZED LEAST SQUARES ESTIMATION

When faced with heteroskedastic errors, the best linear unbiased estimator is **generalized least squares**. The idea is to transform the data in such a way that the errors are no longer heteroskedastic, and then to apply least squares. For example, in the food expenditure example we can see that the variance of the errors is larger for larger values of *INCOME*, reflecting the greater choices in consumption enjoyed by wealthier households. If $x_i = INCOME_i$ then we might describe the variance of the error term as being proportional to *INCOME*, or

$$\text{var}(e_i) = \sigma_i^2 = \sigma^2 x_i$$

By transforming the model we can produce homoskedastic errors. To demonstrate, begin by dividing both sides of the original model $\sqrt{x_i}$

$$\frac{y_i}{\sqrt{x_i}} = \beta_1\left(\frac{1}{\sqrt{x_i}}\right) + \beta_2\left(\frac{x_i}{\sqrt{x_i}}\right) + \frac{e_i}{\sqrt{x_i}} \tag{8.1}$$

Define the following *transformed variables*

$$y_i^* = \frac{y_i}{\sqrt{x_i}} \qquad x_{i1}^* = \frac{1}{\sqrt{x_i}} \qquad x_{i2}^* = \frac{x_i}{\sqrt{x_i}} = \sqrt{x_i} \qquad e_i^* = \frac{e_i}{\sqrt{x_i}}$$

so that (8.1) can be rewritten as

$$y_i^* = \beta_1 x_{i1}^* + \beta_2 x_{i2}^* + e_i^* \tag{8.2}$$

The beauty of this transformed model is that the new transformed error term e_i^* is homoskedastic. The proof of this result is:

$$\text{var}(e_i^*) = \text{var}\left(\frac{e_i}{\sqrt{x_i}}\right) = \frac{1}{x_i}\text{var}(e_i) = \frac{1}{x_i}\sigma^2 x_i = \sigma^2$$

The best linear unbiased estimators of the parameters β_1 and β_2 are obtained by applying the usual least squares estimation procedure to the transformed model in (8.2).

8.4.1 Applying GLS using transformed data

We will first accomplish this by creating a new data set for the transformed variables. We also create a variable W that is the reciprocal of $INCOME$ for later use.

```
data gls;                               * new data set;
set food;                               * read food;
ystar = food_exp/sqrt(income);          * y variable;
x1star = 1/sqrt(income);                * transformed intercept;
x2star = income/sqrt(income);           * transformed x;
w = 1/income;                           * weight variable;
run;
```

Using the transformed data estimate the regression model using **PROC REG**. The only trick is to notice that equation (8.2) does not have a traditional intercept parameter that stands alone, so we instruct SAS not to include an intercept in the regression by adding the option **noint**. Also, we add the **clb** option for confidence intervals.

```
proc reg data=gls;                      * reg on tranformed data;
model ystar = x1star x2star/noint clb;  * suppress intercept;
title 'proc reg GLS using transformed data';
run;
```

Note first that at the top of the regression output we are warned that R^2 is redefined. As a general rule, when a model does not include an intercept the usual R^2 measure is no longer useful. Sadly, neither is the modification used by SAS. Thus we will not report or discuss it, and we urge you to do the same.

```
NOTE: No intercept in model. R-Square is redefined.
```

The parameter estimates reported are the generalized least squares estimates. This estimation procedure is more efficient than the usual least squares estimator, and we see this reflected in the fact that the standard errors are smaller than the corrected "White" standard errors, and thus the confidence intervals are narrower than those based on the robust standard errors.

Variable	DF	Parameter Estimate	Standard Error	t Value	Pr > |t|
x1star	1	78.68408	23.78872	3.31	0.0021
x2star	1	10.45101	1.38589	7.54	<.0001

Variable	DF	95% Confidence Limits	
x1star	1	30.52633	126.84183
x2star	1	7.64542	13.25660

8.4.2 Using PROC REG with a WEIGHT statement

To implement the GLS estimator we can use a **weight** statement with **PROC REG**. In the field of statistics the GLS procedure we have described is sometimes called **weighted least squares**. The weight variable we will use was created in the DATA GLS step in Section 8.4.1. If we posit that the heteroskedasticity has the form

$$\text{var}(e_i) = \sigma_i^2 = \sigma^2 x_i$$

Then for GLS we create a weight variable

$$w_i = 1/x_i$$

SAS will take the square root and multiply it by the variables to create the transformed data.

```
proc reg data=gls;
model food_exp = income/clb;          * interval estimates;
weight w;                             * using weight implies GLS;
title 'proc reg GLS using weight variable';
run;
```

The weighted least squares or GLS estimates that we obtain using this option are identical to those obtained by applying least squares to the transformed data.

Variable	DF	Parameter Estimate	Standard Error	t Value	Pr > |t|
Intercept	1	78.68408	23.78872	3.31	0.0021
INCOME	1	10.45101	1.38589	7.54	<.0001

Variable	DF	95% Confidence Limits	
Intercept	1	30.52633	126.84183
INCOME	1	7.64542	13.25660

8.5 ESTIMATING THE VARIANCE FUNCTION

You might well ask, "What happens if the wrong weight is chosen?" and "How do we know that the variance of the error term is proportional to x_i and not something else?" These are very good questions. The answer to the first is that if the wrong weight is chosen then the resulting GLS estimator is still unbiased, and consistent, but it is no longer BLUE and the standard errors will once again be calculated incorrectly. The answer to the second question is that usually we do not know *exactly* the nature of the heteroskedasticity, and for that reason we sometimes use a more general variance specification.

8.5.1 Model of multiplicative heteroskedasticity

A flexible and parsimonious model for an unknown heteroskedasticity pattern is the model of **multiplicative heteroskedasticity**. If we believe the variance is likely to depend on an explanatory variable, z_{i2}, specify the variance function as[1]

[1] The model can be extended to include more z variables

$$\sigma_i^2 = \exp(\alpha_1 + \alpha_2 z_{i2}) \tag{8.3}$$

The exponential function is convenient because it ensures we will get positive values for the variances σ_i^2 for all possible values of the parameters α_1 and α_2 and for any values of z_{i2}.

For estimation purposes, take the logarithm of both sides

$$\ln\left(\sigma_i^2\right) = \alpha_1 + \alpha_2 z_{i2}$$

Replace σ_i^2 by the squared least squares residuals, $\hat{e}_i^2$, and add an error term, to obtain

$$\ln\left(\hat{e}_i^2\right) = \alpha_1 + \alpha_2 z_{i2} + v_i \tag{8.4}$$

Estimate this model by least squares to obtain estimates $\hat{\alpha}_1$ and $\hat{\alpha}_2$. Then

$$\hat{\sigma}_i^2 = \exp(\hat{\alpha}_1 + \hat{\alpha}_2 z_{i2})$$

Weighted least squares is carried out using weight

$$w_i = \frac{1}{\hat{\sigma}_i^2}$$

8.5.2 A convenient special case

Now let $z_{i2} = \ln(x_i)$. This is a convenient trick, because the variance model becomes

$$\sigma_i^2 = \exp(\alpha_1 + \alpha_2 z_{i2}) = \exp\left(\alpha_1 + \alpha_2 \ln(x_i)\right) = \exp\left(\alpha_1 + \ln\left(x_i^{\alpha_2}\right)\right)$$
$$= \exp(\alpha_1)\exp\left(\ln\left(x_i^{\alpha_2}\right)\right) = \sigma^2 x_i^{\alpha_2}$$

We have labeled

$$\exp(\alpha_1) = \sigma^2$$

because it does not vary from observation to observation.

$$\mathrm{var}(e_i) = \sigma_i^2 = \sigma^2 x_i^{\alpha_2} \tag{8.5}$$

This is the model of proportional heteroskedasticity with the added feature that the power of x_i is the unknown α_2 that we can estimate. For the food expenditure example $z_{i2} = \ln(INCOME_i)$ so that the model we estimate is

$$\ln\left(\hat{e}_i^2\right) = \alpha_1 + \alpha_2 \ln(INCOME_i) + v_i \tag{8.6}$$

8.5.3 Two-step estimator for multiplicative heteroskedasticity

To implement the multiplicative heteroskedasticity model we carry out several steps[2]. In the first step we estimate the original regression, and save the least squares residuals. We have done this

---

[2] See Section 8.9 for use of PROC AUTOREG to estimate this model.

in Section 8.2.2. The data set *foodout* contains the least squares residuals. Now create a new data set with the log of the squared residuals and the log of *INCOME*.

```
data multhet;                      * new data set;
set foodout;                       * read FOODOUT;
lehat2 = log(ehat**2);             * ln(ehat^2);
lincome = log(income);             * ln(income);
run;
```

Estimate the regression (8.6), and save the predicted values.

```
proc reg data=multhet;
model lehat2 = lincome;            * ln(sig2) = a1+a2*lincome;
output out=fgls p=lnsig2;          * output predicted values;
title 'multiplicative model first step';
run;
```

The estimated values from this regression are

Variable	DF	Parameter Estimate	Standard Error	t Value	Pr > |t|
Intercept	1	0.93780	1.58311	0.59	0.5571
lincome	1	2.32924	0.54134	4.30	0.0001

The predicted values from this estimation are

$$\hat{p} = \hat{\alpha}_1 + \hat{\alpha}_2 \ln(INCOME)$$

The estimated values $\hat{\sigma}_i^2$ are obtained by applying the exponential function

$$\hat{\sigma}_i^2 = \exp(\hat{\alpha}_1 + \hat{\alpha}_2 \ln(INCOME_i))$$

The weight variable is the reciprocal of the estimated variance.

```
data fgls;                         * new data set;
set fgls;                          * read fgls;
sig2 = exp(lnsig2);                * sig2(i);
w = 1/sig2;                        * weight;
run;
```

The second stage regression is

```
proc reg data=fgls;
model food_exp = income;
weight w;
title 'multiplicative model second step';
run;
```

The generalized least squares estimates are

Variable	DF	Parameter Estimate	Standard Error	t Value	Pr > |t|
Intercept	1	76.05379	9.71349	7.83	<.0001
income	1	10.63349	0.97151	10.95	<.0001

8.6 LAGRANGE MULTIPLIER (LM) TEST FOR HETEROSKEDASTICITY

We hypothesize that the variance of the error term is related to some explanatory factors $z_{i2}, z_{i3}, \ldots, z_{iS}$. A general form for the variance function is

$$\text{var}(y_i) = \sigma_i^2 = E(e_i^2) = h(\alpha_1 + \alpha_2 z_{i2} + \cdots + \alpha_S z_{iS})$$

This is a *general* form because we are not specific about the function $h(.)$. One of the desirable features of the test that we develop is that it is valid for all reasonable functions $h(.)$. An example is the function used in Section 8.5, the exponential function,

$$\sigma_i^2 = h(\alpha_1 + \alpha_2 z_{i2} + \cdots + \alpha_S z_{iS}) = \exp(\alpha_1 + \alpha_2 z_{i2} + \cdots + \alpha_S z_{iS})$$

If we have a function like this, when will the errors be homoskedastic? Note that if

$$\alpha_2 = 0, \alpha_3 = 0, \ldots, \alpha_S = 0 \tag{8.7}$$

then the variance function becomes

$$\text{var}(y_i) = \sigma_i^2 = E(e_i^2) = h(\alpha_1) = \sigma^2$$

If (8.7) is true then the variance function is homoskedastic, because it does not vary from one observation to another. To carry out a test, which is often called a **Lagrange multiplier test**, of the hypothesis in (8.7) we estimate a linear regression with the squared least squares residuals on the left side, and potential explanatory variables on right side. That is, estimate the model

$$\hat{e}_i^2 = \alpha_1 + \alpha_2 z_{i2} + \cdots + \alpha_S z_{iS} + v_i \tag{8.8}$$

The test statistic for the null hypothesis is obtained by multiplying N, the number of sample observations, times the usual R^2 from the regression in (8.8). If the null hypothesis is true, then the test statistic has a chi-square distribution with $S - 1$ degrees of freedom, or

$$\chi^2 = N \times R^2 \sim \chi^2_{(S-1)}$$

If you are unfamiliar with the chi-square distribution see Appendix B.3.6. The null hypothesis of homoskedasticity is rejected if the test statistic becomes too large. Thus, for a 5% significance level, we reject H_0 and conclude that heteroskedasticity exists when $\chi^2 > \chi^2_{(.95, S-1)}$.

To implement the test we need a data set with the squared least squares residuals and some potential z variables. In the food expenditure example we will consider *INCOME* and *INCOME*^{2} as being possibly associated with the heteroskedastic pattern. Create this data set;

```
data hettest;                    * new data set;
set foodout;                     * read foodout;
ehat2 = ehat**2;                 * resid squared;
income2 = income**2;             * income squared;
run;
```

Estimate the regression (8.8) with *INCOME* on the right side.

```
proc reg data=hettest;
model ehat2 = income;
title 'LM test on income';
run;
```

The required pieces of information are given in the ANOVA table,

```
              Dependent Variable: ehat2

          Number of Observations Used        40

      Root MSE          9946.64208   R-Square    0.1846
      Dependent Mean    7612.62940   Adj R-Sq    0.1632
      Coeff Var          130.65974
```

At this point you could pull out your calculator and multiply N times R^2. Your authors prefer to have repeatable sets of commands, and to use SAS to compute both the necessary critical value and the *p*-value of the test. To do this we make use of two SAS functions:

- the CDF of a chi-square random variable V with m degrees of freedom is **probchi(v,m)**

- the 95th percentile value, the critical value for a 0.05 level test, is given by **cinv(.95,m)**

```
data test1;
s = 2;                               * number alphas;
n = 40;                              * sample size;
r2 = 0.1846;                         * r-squared;
chisq = n*r2;                        * test statistic;
pval = 1 - probchi(chisq,s-1);       * p-value;
chisq_95 = cinv(.95,s-1);            * 0.95 percentile;
run;

proc print data=test1;               * print test 1 result;
title 'LM test on income results';
run;
```

The result is a test statistic value of 7.384 which is greater than the critical value 3.84.

```
                LM test on income results

   Obs   s    n     r2     chisq       pval     chisq_95
    1    2    40   0.1846   7.384   .006580665   3.84146
```

If we use *INCOME* and *INCOME* squared in (8.8) then the code changes to

```
proc reg data=hettest;
model ehat2 = income income2;
title 'LM test adding income**2';
run;
```

Use the regression output to specify the values required for the test. These are the sample size N, the regression R^2 and the total number of parameters S in the heteroskedastic function, including the intercept.

```
data test2;
s = 3;                              * number alphas;
n = 40;                             * sample size;
r2 = 0.1889;                        * r-squared;
chisq = n*r2;                       * test statistic;
pval = 1 - probchi(chisq,s-1);     * p-value;
chisq_95 = cinv(.95,s-1);          * 0.95 percentile;
run;
proc print data=test2;             * print test 2 result;
title 'LM test result adding income**2';
run;
```

The resulting ANOVA table results are

```
                   Analysis of Variance

    Root MSE               10054    R-Square    0.1889
    Dependent Mean    7612.62933    Adj R-Sq    0.1450
    Coeff Var         132.06676
```

With the test results we again reject the null hypothesis of homoskedasticity.

```
              LM test result adding income**2

   Obs    s     n      r2     chisq     pval      chisq_95
    1     3    40    0.1889   7.556   0.022868    5.99146
```

8.7 GOLDFELD-QUANDT TEST FOR HETEROSKEDASTICITY

The Goldfeld-Quandt test is based on the ability to partition the data into two subsets with possibly different variances. The regression model is estimated using each part of the data, and the estimated variances used to construct the test statistic. That is, suppose that we divide the data into two parts consisting of N_1 and N_2 observations. Estimate the regression model,

$$y = \beta_1 + \beta_2 x_2 + \cdots + \beta_K x_K + e$$

and obtain $\hat{\sigma}_1^2$ and $\hat{\sigma}_2^2$ from the two parts. The null hypothesis is that the errors are homoskedastic, or $\sigma_1^2 = \sigma_2^2$.

If the alternative hypothesis is $\sigma_1^2 \neq \sigma_2^2$ we carry out a two tail test. The test statistic is (which estimated variance is in the numerator does not matter in this case)

$$GQ = \frac{\hat{\sigma}_2^2}{\hat{\sigma}_1^2}$$

This test statistic has an F-distribution with $(N_2 - K)$ numerator degrees of freedom and $(N_1 - K)$ denominator degrees of freedom. A two tail test at the $\alpha = 0.05$ level requires critical values $F_{(0.025, N_2-K, N_1-K)}$ and $F_{(0.975, N_2-K, N_1-K)}$. The null hypothesis of homoskedasticity is rejected if the test statistic falls in either tail of the distribution.

If you suspect a priori that the variance in part 2 of the data is larger than the variance in part 1 of the data, then a one tail test can be carried out, with alternative hypothesis $\sigma_2^2 > \sigma_1^2$. Now it matters that $\hat{\sigma}_2^2$ is in the numerator. The right-tail critical value is $F_{(0.95, N_2-K, N_1-K)}$

In the food expenditure data we suspect that the variance of the error term is larger for larger incomes. To apply the Goldfeld-Quandt test we sort the data according to the magnitude of *INCOME*. The two parts of the data will be observations 1-20 and observations 21-40. The data are sorted using **PROC SORT**.

```
proc sort data=food out=food2;       * sort food;
by income;                           * increasing income;
run;
```

Create data sets consisting of the first 20 and second 20 observations using a **SET** statement and an **IF** condition.

```
data gq1;
set food2;
if _n_ le 20;                        * first 20 obs;
run;

data gq2;
set food2;
if _n_ gt 20;                        * obs 21-40;
run;
```

Estimate the regression on part 1.

```
proc reg data=gq1;
model food_exp = income;
title 'GQ test regression 1';
run;
```

The relevant portion of the output is the estimated error variance, called by SAS the **Error Mean Square**,

```
              Analysis of Variance

                           Sum of          Mean
Source            DF      Squares        Square    F Value    Pr > F
Model              1        75194         75194      21.03    0.0002
Error             18        64346    3574.77175
```

Repeat the regression for the 2nd part of the data.

```
proc reg data=gq2;
model food_exp = income;
title 'GQ test regression 2';
run;
```

The ANOVA table is

```
                           Sum of          Mean
Source            DF      Squares        Square    F Value    Pr > F
Model              1        47688         47688       3.69    0.0707
Error             18       232595         12922
```

Note how much larger the F-statistic is for the first part of the data. Also, for the first part of the data the model $R^2 = 0.5389$, and for the second part of the data $R^2 = 0.1701$. The model fits the data much better in the first part of the data. We expect the variance to be larger in the 2nd part of the data, so we will perform a one-tail test.

Either use your calculator to divide the estimated variances, or create a data set in which the calculations are carried out.

```
data gqtest;
n1 = 20;                          * sample size part 1;
n2 = 20;                          * sample size part 2;
k = 2;                            * number parameters;
sig2_1 = 3574.77;                 * sig^2 in part 1;
sig2_2 = 12922;                   * sig^2 in part 2;
gq = sig2_2/sig2_1;               * test statistic;
fc = finv(.95,n2-k,n1-k);         * F-critical one tail test;
pval = 1 - probf(gq,n2-k,n1-k);   * p-value one tail test;
run;
proc print data=gqtest;
title 'GQ test results';
run;
```

The test statistic is 3.61, which is greater than the critical value 2.22, thus we reject the null hypothesis of homoskedasticity.

```
                         GQ test results

Obs   n1   n2   k    sig2_1   sig2_2      gq        fc         pval
 1    20   20   2   3574.77    12922   3.61478   2.21720   .004596272
```

8.8 A HETEROSKEDASTIC PARTITION

Data sometimes fall into natural groups, or partitions.[3] It is common to consider the possibility that the variances of the error term are different among groups. The model we consider in this section is called a **heteroskedastic partition**, or **grouped heteroskedasticity**. In this section our illustrative example a wage equation where earnings per hour (*WAGE*) depends on years of education (*EDUC*), years of experience (*EXPER*) and a dummy variable *METRO* that is equal to 1 for workers who live in a metropolitan area and 0 for workers who live outside a metropolitan area. We use the SAS data set *cps2*.

First open the data and examine the contents.

```
options label;                        * turn on labels;
data cps2;                            * new data set;
set 'cps2';                           * read cps2;
proc contents data=cps2 position;    * examine contents;
title 'cps2 contents';
run;
options nolabel;
```

The variables in this data set are

```
                Variables in Creation Order

    #   Variable   Type   Len   Label
    1   wage       Num    8     earnings per hour
    2   educ       Num    8     years of education
    3   exper      Num    8     experience
    4   female     Num    8     =1 if female
    5   black      Num    8     =1 if black
    6   married    Num    8     =1 if married
    7   union      Num    8     =1 if union member
    8   south      Num    8     =1 if south
    9   fulltime   Num    8     =1 if full time worker
   10   metro      Num    8     =1 if lives in metropolitan area
```

Compute summary statistics.

```
proc means data=cps2;
title 'summary stats cps2 data';
run;
```

The MEANS Procedure

Variable	N	Mean	Std Dev	Minimum	Maximum
WAGE	1000	10.2130200	6.2466405	2.0300000	60.1899986
EDUC	1000	13.2850000	2.4681708	1.0000000	18.0000000
EXPER	1000	18.7800000	11.3188213	0	52.0000000
FEMALE	1000	0.4940000	0.5002142	0	1.0000000

[3] There can be more than two groups. For an advanced treatment of the more general case see William Greene (2012) *Econometric Analysis, 7th Edition*, Prentice-Hall, 282-284.

BLACK	1000	0.0880000	0.2834367	0	1.0000000
MARRIED	1000	0.5760000	0.4944375	0	1.0000000
UNION	1000	0.1650000	0.3713663	0	1.0000000
SOUTH	1000	0.3150000	0.4647483	0	1.0000000
FULLTIME	1000	0.8730000	0.3331396	0	1.0000000
METRO	1000	0.8080000	0.3940702	0	1.0000000

Estimate a regression in which earnings per hour (*WAGE*) depends on years of education (*EDUC*), years of experience (*EXPER*) and a dummy variable *METRO* that is equal to 1 for workers who live in a metropolitan area and 0 for workers who live outside a metropolitan area.

```
proc reg data=cps2;
model wage = educ exper metro;
title 'OLS wage equation on full data set';
run;
```

Parameter Estimates

Variable	DF	Parameter Estimate	Standard Error	t Value	Pr > |t|
Intercept	1	-9.91398	1.07566	-9.22	<.0001
EDUC	1	1.23396	0.06996	17.64	<.0001
EXPER	1	0.13324	0.01523	8.75	<.0001
METRO	1	1.52410	0.43109	3.54	0.0004

The question we now ask is: How does the variance of wages in a metropolitan area compare with the variance of wages in a rural area? Are the variances likely to be the same or different? One might suspect that the greater range of different types of jobs in a metropolitan area might lead to city wages having a higher variance. Partition (split) our sample into two parts, one for the metropolitan observations (for which we use the subscript '*M*') and one for the rural observations (for which we use the subscript '*R*'). For the least squares estimator to be best linear unbiased, we require that $\text{var}(e_{Mi}) = \text{var}(e_{Ri}) = \sigma^2$; the error variance is constant for all observations. We now assume that the error variances in the metropolitan and rural regions are different. That is,

$$\text{var}(e_{Mi}) = \sigma_M^2 \qquad \text{var}(e_{Ri}) = \sigma_R^2$$

8.8.1 The Goldfeld-Quandt test

To carry out the Goldfeld-Quandt test we estimate separate regressions for the metropolitan observations (*METRO* = 1) and the rural observations (*METRO* = 0) using the **WHERE** condition with **PROC REG**.

First estimate the regression using the metropolitan data by using the condition **WHERE METRO=1** after the model statement.

```
proc reg data=cps2;
model wage = educ exper;
where metro=1;                          * condition on data;
title 'OLS wage equation metro observations';
run;
```

The resulting ANOVA table gives the estimated for the metropolitan observations, $\hat{\sigma}_M^2 = 31.824$.

```
                          Analysis of Variance

                              Sum of         Mean
Source                DF     Squares        Square    F Value   Pr > F

Model                  2    8916.17150    4458.08575   140.09   <.0001
Error                805       25618        31.82373  ←
Corrected Total      807       34534          estimated variance for metro data
```

Carry out the same steps for the rural observations,

```
proc reg data=cps2;
model wage = educ exper;
where metro=0;                       * condition on data;
title 'OLS wage equation non-metro observations';
run;
```

This yields the estimated variance for the rural observations $\hat{\sigma}_R^2 = 15.243$.

Suppose we want to test

$$H_0 : \sigma_M^2 = \sigma_R^2 \qquad \text{against} \qquad H_1 : \sigma_M^2 \neq \sigma_R^2$$

The *GQ* test statistic is the ratio of the estimated variances. For a two tail test we must find the 2.5-percentile and the 97.5 percentile of the F distribution with $N_M - K$ numerator degrees of freedom, and $N_R - K$ denominator degrees of freedom, using $N_M = 808$, $N_R = 192$ and $K = 3$. For a one sided alternative $H_1 : \sigma_M^2 > \sigma_R^2$ we compute the 95th percentile, and the *p*-value for the one tail test.

In the following data step we do these calculations. We also look ahead to the weighted least squares estimation and create a weight variable. We will return to this later.

```
data gqtest;                          * data set;
set cps2;                             * read cps2;
nm = 808;                             * number of metro observations;
nr = 192;                             * number of rural observations;
k = 3;                                * number parameters;
sig2m = 31.82373;                     * sig2 from metro;
sig2r = 15.24299;                     * sig2 from rural;
GQ = sig2m/sig2r;                     * Goldfeld-Quandt test;
f975 = finv(.975,nm-k,nr-k);          * 97.5 percentile;
f025 = finv(.025,nm-k,nr-k);          * 2.5 percentile;
f95 = finv(.95,nm-k,nr-k);            * 95 percentile;
p = 1 - probf(gq,nm-k,nr-k);          * p-value right tail test;
w = metro*(1/sig2m) + (1-metro)*(1/sig2r);
run;
```

Because we are creating the weight variable in the same data step, we have **SET** the original data set, and the data set *gqtest* has 1000 observations. To print just the results for the two tail test we need only the first observation for the relevant variables.

```
proc print data=gqtest(obs=1);
var sig2m sig2r GQ f975 f025;
title 'GQ test two tail';
run;
```

GQ test two tail

Obs	sig2m	sig2r	GQ	f975	f025
1	31.8237	15.2430	2.08776	1.26173	0.80520

Similarly, for the one tail test,

```
proc print data=gqtest(obs=1);
var sig2m sig2r GQ f95 p;
title 'GQ test right tail';
run;
```

GQ test right tail

Obs	sig2m	sig2r	GQ	f95	p
1	31.8237	15.2430	2.08776	1.21503	1.5668E-9

In both cases we reject the null hypothesis of homoskedasticity.

8.8.2 Generalized least squares estimation

To implement generalized (weighted) least squares, we use the weight variable W created in the data step in the previous section for data set *gqtest*. The statement creates the variable

$$W = \begin{cases} \dfrac{1}{\hat{\sigma}_M^2} & \text{if } METRO = 1 \\[2ex] \dfrac{1}{\hat{\sigma}_R^2} & \text{if } METRO = 0 \end{cases}$$

The estimation with weight W is accomplished using

```
proc reg data=gqtest;
model wage = educ exper metro;
weight w;
title 'GLS with weight variable';
run;
```

The resulting weighted least squares estimates are

Variable	DF	Parameter Estimate	Standard Error	t Value	Pr > |t|
Intercept	1	-9.39836	1.01967	-9.22	<.0001
EDUC	1	1.19572	0.06851	17.45	<.0001
EXPER	1	0.13221	0.01455	9.09	<.0001
METRO	1	1.53880	0.34629	4.44	<.0001

8.9 USING PROC AUTOREG FOR HETEROSKEDASTICITY

PROC AUTOREG will estimate several models of heteroskedasticity, including the model of multiplicative heteroskedasticity. Consider the two step estimation example in Section 8.5.3 of this manual. Recall that the model is

$$\sigma_i^2 = \exp\left(\alpha_1 + \alpha_2 \ln\left(INCOME\right)\right)$$
$$= \exp\left(\alpha_1\right)\exp\left(\alpha_2 \ln\left(INCOME\right)\right)$$
$$= \sigma^2 \exp\left(\alpha_2 \ln\left(INCOME\right)\right)$$

To implement that model, first read the food data and create the variable $\ln\left(INCOME\right)$.

```
data food2;
set food;
lincome = log(income);
run;
```

The specification of the model in **PROC AUTOREG** begins just like **PROC REG**.

```
proc autoreg data=food2;
model food_exp = income;
hetero lincome / link=exp test=lm;
title 'proc autoreg multiplicative hetero MLE';
run;
```

The **hetero** command specifies first (before the /) the variables to be included in the heteroskedasticity model. In the **hetero** statement the **link=exp**[4] requests the model of multiplicative heteroskedasticity; the option **test=lm** requests a Lagrange multiplier test for the presence of heteroskedasticity[5].

---

[4] Other options for LINK are LINEAR and SQUARE. See PROC AUTOREG documentation for further explanation.
[5] The test reported is slightly different than the one reported in Section 8.6.

```
              Multiplicative Heteroscedasticity Estimates

        SSE                304873.934   Observations               40
        MSE                      7622   Root MSE             87.30320
        Log Likelihood     -225.71518   Total R-Square         0.3843
        SBC                466.185887   AIC                459.430369
        MAE                68.8458133   AICC               460.51145
        MAPE               27.8524938   HQC                461.872951
        Hetero Test            9.6228   Normality Test         1.6761
        Pr > ChiSq             0.0019   Pr > ChiSq             0.4326
```

LM test for hetero

```
                        Parameter Estimates

                                  Standard                    Approx
        Variable    DF   Estimate    Error    t Value    Pr > |t|

        Intercept    1    76.0727   8.3987       9.06     <.0001
        income       1    10.6344   0.9754      10.90     <.0001
        HET0         1     1.2640   1.1410       1.11      0.2679
        HET1         1     2.7697   0.6111       4.53     <.0001
```

HET0 = σ and HET1 = α_2 MLE estimates

The **PROC AUTOREG** output has two parts. The top part reports the usual least squares estimates. Below the message "Algorithm converged" comes the second part with the multiplicative heteroskedasticity estimates. The estimated intercept and slope are very similar to those reported at the end of Section 8.5. The SAS output includes an estimate of σ (HET0) and an estimate of α_2 (HET1). By examining the t-value and p-value for this coefficient we can test the presence of heteroskedasticity very easily.

The estimation procedure in **PROC AUTOREG** is an iterative procedure, basically just repeating the two steps described in Section 8.6 over and over. The process eventually converges, with little changing from iteration to iteration, and then stops. The resulting estimates are called **maximum likelihood estimates**. See Appendix C.8 in *Principles of Econometrics, 4th Edition* for general information about maximum likelihood estimation. See Appendix 8B in this manual for details on this model estimation.

8.9.1 PROC AUTOREG for a heteroskedastic partition

The model of multiplicative heteroskedasticity implemented in **PROC AUTOREG** is also useful for grouped data as described in Section 8.8. If heteroskedasticity in the wage equation (*cps2* data) is related to *METRO* then

$$\sigma_i^2 = \exp\left(\alpha_1 + \alpha_2 METRO\right) = \exp\left(\alpha_1\right)\exp\left(\alpha_2 METRO\right) = \begin{cases} \exp\left(\alpha_1\right) = \sigma_1^2 & METRO = 0 \\ \exp\left(\alpha_1\right)\exp\left(\alpha_2\right) = \sigma_2^2 & METRO = 1 \end{cases}$$

To implement this model we use

```
proc autoreg data=cps2;
model wage = educ exper metro;
hetero metro/ link=exp test=lm;
title 'wage equation multiplicative hetero MLE';
title2 'metro as culprit variable';
run;
```

The **hetero** statement indicates that *METRO* is the variable related to heteroskedasticity.

Multiplicative Heteroscedasticity Estimates

| | | Hetero Test | 37.5550 |
| | | Pr > ChiSq | <.0001 |

Variable	DF	Estimate	Standard Error	t Value	Approx Pr > |t|
Intercept	1	-9.4015	1.1231	-8.37	<.0001
EDUC	1	1.1960	0.0677	17.66	<.0001
EXPER	1	0.1322	0.0148	8.93	<.0001
METRO	1	1.5387	0.4117	3.74	0.0002
HET0	1	3.9069	0.1574	24.82	<.0001
HET1	1	0.7324	0.0857	8.55	<.0001

The parameter estimates for the regression model parameters are very close to those in Section 8.8.2. They differ because here they are produced by an iterative process of more than two steps. Note that the estimate of α_2 (HET1) is statistically significant which indicates significant heteroskedasticity. This finding is confirmed by the **Hetero Test**.

8.9.2 An extended heteroskedasticity model

If we believe that the heteroskedasticity is related to perhaps more than one variable this can be implemented using **PROC AUTOREG**. For example, in the wage equation we may suspect heteroskedasticity related not only to *METRO* but also *EDUC*. If so, we have two variables in the **hetero** command.

```
proc autoreg data=cps2;
model wage = educ exper metro;
hetero metro educ / link=exp test=lm;
title 'wage equation multiplicative hetero MLE';
title2 'metro & educ as culprit variable';
run;
```

Now, the **Hetero Test** included in the output is a joint test of the significance of *METRO* and *EDUC* in the heteroskedasticity model. And both *METRO* (HET1) and *EDUC* (HET2) coefficients are individually significant, leading us to believe that both factors are related to the regression model's heteroskedasticity.

Multiplicative Heteroscedasticity Estimates

| | | Hetero Test | 85.5760 |
| | | Pr > ChiSq | <.0001 |

Variable	DF	Estimate	Standard Error	t Value	Approx Pr > |t|
Intercept	1	-4.8973	0.8733	-5.61	<.0001
EDUC	1	0.8587	0.0548	15.67	<.0001
EXPER	1	0.1232	0.0129	9.59	<.0001
METRO	1	1.4346	0.3740	3.84	0.0001
HET0	1	1.1298	0.1137	9.93	<.0001
HET1	1	0.6502	0.0919	7.08	<.0001
HET2	1	0.1847	0.0146	12.68	<.0001

8.10 USING SAS ODS GRAPHICS

The built in ODS graphics should be directed to a directory of your choosing, and must be "turned on" prior to using the regression procedure. We have chosen the "journal style."

```
ods listing gpath='c:\figures' style=journal;
ods graphics on;                        * must turn ODS on;
```

Carry out **PROC REG** with the **plots=(ResidualPlot)** option using the food expenditure data.

```
proc reg data=food plots=(ResidualPlot);
model food_exp = income;
title 'food expenditure with ODS graphics';
run;
```

The resulting figure (**c:\figures\ResidualPlot.png**) shows the "funnel" shape that is characteristic of heteroskedastic errors. Under homoskedasticity no such pattern should appear.

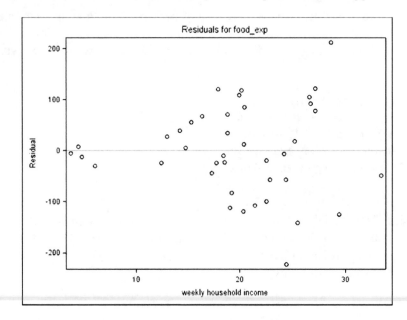

A second example, when multiple regressors are present, shows the power of ODS graphics. In this case the automatic graphics plots the residuals against each explanatory variable.

```
proc reg data=cps2 plots=(ResidualPlot);
model wage = educ exper metro;
title 'wage equation with ODS graphics';
run;
ods graphics off;                          * must turn ODS off;
```

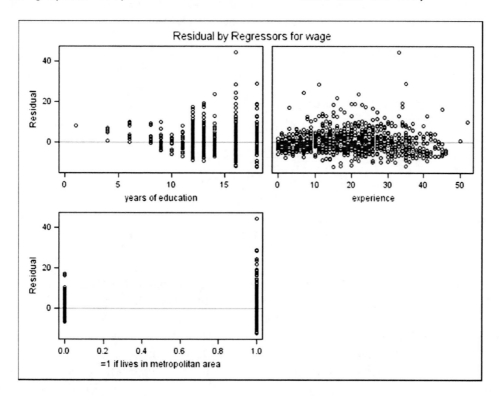

Having multiple plots reveals not only the difference in the variation of rural and metropolitan residuals, but also a pattern of increasing variance with education.

When ODS graphics are run several times all the figures are placed in **c:\figures**. If a plot name already exists SAS automatically adds a numeric extension to keep them straight.

8.11 USING PROC MODEL FOR HETEROSKEDASTIC DATA

When using **PROC MODEL** we can also allow for heteroskedastic data in several ways. First, to estimate the model by ordinary least squares with White heteroskedasticity robust standard errors, the commands for the food expenditure model add the option **hccme=1** to the **fit** statement.

```
proc model data=food;
label b1='intercept'
      b2='income';
food_exp = b1 + b2*income;
fit food_exp/hccme=1;
```

```
      title 'proc model robust covariance';
   run;
```

```
                   Approx           Approx
Parameter  Estimate  Std Err  t Value  Pr > |t|  Label
b1           83.416   27.4637     3.04    0.0043  intercept
b2         10.20964    1.8091     5.64    <.0001  income
```

Generalized least squares estimation is implemented with a **weight** statement, just as in **PROC REG**. Do not forget that the data set used must contain the weight variable *W*.

```
   proc model data=gls;
   label b1='intercept'
         b2='income';
   food_exp = b1 + b2*income;
   fit food_exp;
   weight w;
   title 'proc model weighted least squares';
   run;
```

```
                   Approx           Approx
Parameter  Estimate  Std Err  t Value  Pr > |t|  Label
b1         78.68408  23.7887     3.31    0.0021  intercept
b2         10.45101   1.3859     7.54    <.0001  income
```

PROC MODEL also includes some automatic testing commands for the tests used in Section 8.6. The $N \times R^2$ test is implemented for specified variables using the **breusch=(1 income)** option to the **fit** statement, where the "1" stands for a constant term, and then other variables associated with the potential heteroskedasticity are listed. A version of the White general specification test adds the option **white** to the fit statement. The $N \times R^2$ test is implemented for all variables, their squares and, their cross-products. In the food expenditure example this is just *INCOME* and its square.

```
   proc model data=food;
   label b1='intercept'
         b2='income';
   food_exp = b1 + b2*income;
   fit food_exp/white breusch=(1 income);  * BP test sig2 = f(1,income);
   title 'proc model heteroskedasticity tests';
   run;
```

```
                      Heteroscedasticity Test
Equation    Test           Statistic  DF Pr > ChiSq Variables
food_exp    White's Test        7.56   2    0.0229 Cross of all vars
            Breusch-Pagan       7.38   1    0.0066 1, income
```

APPENDIX 8A MONTE CARLO SIMULATIONS

8A.1 Simulating heteroskedastic data

To illustrate the properties of the ordinary and generalized least squares estimators we will carry out a simulation, or Monte Carlo experiment. In our experiment we create:

- A set of 40 x values ranging from 1/40 to 1 in increments of 1/40.
- A set of 40 random errors e_i with normal distributions, mean zero, and variances $\sigma_i^2 = .25x_i^2$. To achieve these heteroskedastic errors we multiply a $N(0,1)$ random error by $\sigma_i = .5x_i$
- A set of 40 y values are obtained as

$$y_i = \beta_1 + \beta_2 x_i + e_i = 1 + 1 \times x_i + e_i$$

The SAS commands use **streaminit** to "initialize" the random number generator **rand**. In fact the **rand** command will generate many types of random numbers. Note that we have specified a normal distribution with mean 0 and variance 1, which is then multiplied by $\sigma_i = .5x_i$ to create heteroskedastic errors, which are then added to the regression function $E(y) = 1 + x$.

We have used a **do loop**, that starts with **do** and stops with **end**, to process one observation at a time. The **output** statement writes the observation to the SAS data set *hetdata*.

```
data hetdata;                            * data set;
call streaminit(1234567);                * set random number stream;
     do n = 1 to 40;                     * do loop 40 times;
     x = n/40;                           * x variable;
     sig = .5*x;                         * std dev error;
     y = 1 + x + sig*rand('normal',0,1);     * y = 1 + 1*x + e;
     output;                             * observation to data set;
     end;                                * end do loop;
run;
```

Let us plot the data and the fitted least squares line. Create a symbol for the plot, and then use **PROC REG** to estimate the model. The **PROC REG** statement includes two additional options. First, **outest=est** creates a SAS data set containing the parameter estimates. The option **tableout** tells SAS to include in the **est** data set additional features such as standard errors, as we will see in a moment.

Additionally we add a **plot** statement following the **model** statement that will create a scatter diagram of the data and the fitted regression line.

```
symbol1 value=dot color=blue;           * symbol for scatter;
proc reg data=hetdata outest=est tableout;
model y = x;
plot y*x;
title 'regression with heteroskedastic data';
title2 'true intercept & slope = 1';
run;
```

The regression output (edited) is

```
                    regression with heteroskedastic data
                        true intercept & slope = 1

                          Analysis of Variance

                              Sum of          Mean
Source              DF       Squares        Square    F Value    Pr > F
Model                1       3.48616       3.48616      39.79    <.0001
Error               38       3.32960       0.08762
Corrected Total     39       6.81576

            Root MSE              0.29601    R-Square     0.5115
            Dependent Mean        1.49081    Adj R-Sq     0.4986
            Coeff Var            19.85562

                    Parameter      Standard
       Variable   DF   Estimate      Error    t Value    Pr > |t|

       Intercept   1    0.96653     0.09539     10.13     <.0001
       x           1    1.02299     0.16218      6.31     <.0001
```

The least squares estimates are close to the true values. The plot shows that the data are indeed heteroskedastic.

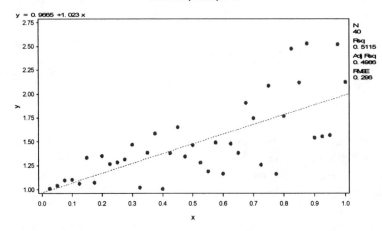

To carry out a Monte Carlo experiment we will use **PROC REG** and save the estimates from each estimation in a SAS data set *est*. Let's examine the contents

```
proc print data=est;
title 'OUTEST data from PROC REG';
run;
```

```
                    OUTEST data from PROC REG

Obs    _MODEL_    _TYPE_    _DEPVAR_    _RMSE_    Intercept       x        y
 1     MODEL1     PARMS        y        0.29601    0.9665     1.02299    -1
 2     MODEL1     STDERR       y        0.29601    0.0954     0.16218    .
 3     MODEL1     T            y        0.29601   10.1324     6.30767    .
 4     MODEL1     PVALUE       y        0.29601    0.0000     0.00000    .
 5     MODEL1     L95B         y        0.29601    0.7734     0.69467    .
 6     MODEL1     U95B         y        0.29601    1.1596     1.35131    .
```

SAS uses keywords (_TYPE_) to identify the feature saved. For example, the _TYPE_=PARMS identifies the parameter estimates. In the INTERCEPT column we find the estimated model intercept, and in the X column we find the estimated slope. The last column Y has -1 as its PARM to indicate that it is the dependent variable in the equation. We also have _TYPE_ values indicating standard errors, t-values, p-values and interval estimate upper and lower bounds.

Below, when we repeatedly use **PROC REG**, we will save these values for many samples of data, and at the end examine the estimates obtained, comparing them to what we know the true values to be. That is a Monte Carlo experiment.

8A.2 Heteroskedastic data Monte Carlo experiment

Now we replicate the data generation process described in Section 8A.1 10,000 times. For each sample of size $N = 40$ we will compute the OLS estimates and then examine their performance. What we will illustrate is that the OLS estimates behave in the way we have predicted: the OLS estimator is unbiased, will be normally distributed (since we are using normally distributed random errors in the simulation) and the variance of slope parameter estimator is 0.0309522, which we compute in Section 8A.3.

```
    title;                                  * turn off title;
    data hetmc;                             * data set;
    call streaminit(1234567);               * set random number stream;
    do sample = 1 to 10000;                 * outer loop repeat samples;
         do n = 1 to 40;                    * start inner loop;
         x = n/40;                          * x variable;
         w = 1/(x**2);                      * weight variable for gls;
         sig = .5*x;                        * error std dev;
         y = 1 + x + x*rand('normal',0,.5);     * y = 1 + 1*x + e;
         output;                            * output to data set;
         end;                               * end inner loop;
    end;                                    * end outer loop;
    run;
```

The data generation process is the same as in Section 8A.1. We do however create the weight variable W that will be used in the generalized least squares estimation.

The OLS estimator is applied to each sample. We suppress the printed output. The **outest=est** and **tableout** options cause the estimates, t-statistics, and standard errors to be printed to the data set *hetmc*, in the format shown at the end of Secton 8A.1.

```
proc reg noprint data=hetmc outest=est tableout;
model y = x;
by sample;                          * repeat for each sample;
run;
```

Examining the least squares estimates

To extract just the slope estimates we create a SAS data set with an **IF** statement identifying the _TYPE_= as PARMS. The slope estimate has the label **X** as that is what we called it in the regression model. Rename it *B2*. The **KEEP** statement tells SAS to discard all variables other than the **sample** indicator and the slope estimates.

```
data parm;                          * data set;
set est;                            * read est;
if _type_='PARMS';                  * keep if PARMS;
b2 = x;                             * rename slope;
keep sample b2;                     * keep 2 variables;
run;
```

The summary statistics, and a histogram are obtained using **PROC UNIVARIATE**.

```
proc univariate data = parm;
var b2;
histogram/normal;
title 'Sampling distribution of OLS b2';
title2 'Errors heteroskedastic';
run;
```

The summary statistics show that the average of the least squares estimates is 1.003, verifying that the least squares estimator is unbiased in the presence of heteroskedasticity. The sample variance of the 10,000 slope estimates is 0.03138, which is very close to the true value 0.03095 (computed in Section 8A.3)

```
N                    10000   Sum Weights              10000
Mean            1.00300322   Sum Observations    10030.0322
Std Deviation   0.17713537   Variance            0.03137694
```

The histogram shows that the estimates follow a bell shaped curve that is fit very well by the superimposed normal distribution.

Sampling distribution of OLS b2

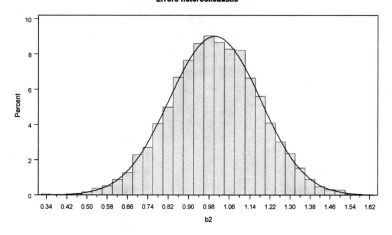

Errors heteroskedastic

Examining the usual standard error

The Monte Carlo output includes the usual (incorrect) OLS standard error. Let's examine them to verify that they are in fact incorrect. Create a data set with _TYPE_= set to STDERR. The slope estimator's standard error is labeled as **X**, so rename it and compute the implied variance of the least squares estimator by squaring the standard error.

```
data se;                            * data set;
set est;                            * read est;
if _type_='STDERR';                 * keep if STDERR;
se = x;                             * rename std error;
varb2 = se**2;                      * var(b2);
keep sample varb2 se;               * keep 3 variables;
run;
```

Compute the average value of the estimated variances and compare it to 0.0309522 which we compute in Section 8A.3.

```
proc means data=se mean;
var varb2;
title 'average value usual estimate var(b2)';
title2 'true var(b2)=  0.0309522';          * true from proc iml;
run;
```

```
           Mean
         0.0257355
```

Examining the t-tests

The average value of the incorrect estimated standard error, and variance, is too small. This will affect confidence intervals and hypothesis tests. To show this we examine the percentage of the Monte Carlo samples in which the true null hypothesis $\beta_2 = 1$ is rejected. To do this we merge the data sets containing the slope estimates (*parm*) and the incorrect standard errors (*se*). Note that we **MERGE** using the **BY SAMPLE** option. The true standard error of the OLS estimator was calculated in Section 8A.3 to be 0.17593. The variable **tstat0** uses the incorrect standard error, and **tstat** uses the true standard error. For **tstat0** we normally reject the null hypothesis if the absolute value of the *t*-statistic is greater than the 0.975 percentile of the $t_{(38)}$ distribution. For **tstat**, since its standard error is known, we use the critical value from the standard normal distribution, which is given by the **PROBIT** function. For each we record the samples in which the null hypothesis is rejected.

```
data ttest;                            * data set;
merge parm se;                         * merge statement;
by sample;                             * control merge by sample;
truese =  0.17593;                     * from proc iml code;
tstat0 = (b2 - 1)/se;                  * test with bad se;
tstat = (b2 - 1)/truese;               * test with correct se;
tc = tinv(.975,38);                    * alpha=.05 critical value;
zc = probit(.975);                     * alpha=.05 critcal z value;
reject0 = (abs(tstat0) >= tc);         * record rejection bad t;
reject1 = (abs(tstat) >= zc);          * record rejection correct t;
run;
```

Compute the percentage of rejections using **PROC MEANS.**

```
proc means data=ttest mean;              * compute only mean;
title 't-test rejection rates using incorrect and true se(b2)';
run;
```

The *t*-test with the incorrect standard error rejects the true null hypothesis 7.89% of the time, whereas the *t*-test with the true standard error rejects the true null hypothesis 5.14% of the time, which is closer to the assumed 5% rate of Type I error.

Variable	Mean
reject0	0.0789000
reject1	0.0514000

Examining the generalized least squares estimates

Repeat the same analysis for the generalized least squares estimator. It is obtained using **PROC REG** with weight variable *W*.

```
proc reg noprint data=hetmc outest=estgls tableout;
model y = x;
weight w;
by sample;                             * repeat for each sample;
run;

data parmgls;                          * data set;
set estgls;                            * read est;
if _type_='PARMS';                     * keep if PARMS;
```

```
b2 = x;                              * rename slope;
keep sample b2;                      * keep 2 variables;
run;

proc univariate data = parmgls;
var b2;
histogram/normal;
title 'Sampling distribution of gls-b2';
title2 'Errors heteroskedastic';
run;
```

The summary statistics reveal that the GLS estimator is unbiased and its variance 0.00867 is much smaller than the variance of the OLS estimator.

N	10000	Sum Weights	10000
Mean	1.00071411	Sum Observations	10007.1411
Std Deviation	0.09311496	Variance	0.0086704

The histogram reveals the expected bell shaped curve.

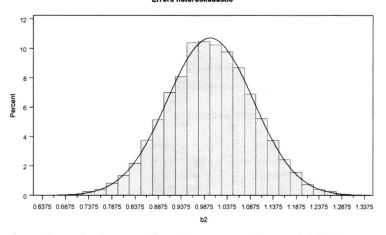

Sampling distribution of gls-b2
Errors heteroskedastic

Next, does the estimated standard error reflect the true sampling variability?

```
data segls;                          * data set;
set estgls;                          * read est;
if _type_='STDERR';                  * keep if STDERR;
se = x;                              * rename std error;
varb2 = se**2;                       * var(b2);
keep sample varb2 se;                * keep 3 variables;

proc means data=segls mean;
var varb2;
title 'average value estimated var(bls-b2)';
title2 'true var(gls-b2)=  0.0087103';
run;
```

The average value of the estimated variance of the GLS estimator is very close to the true value.

```
                Mean
            _____

             0.0086900
            _____
```

Finally, do the *t*-tests with the estimated standard errors work as they should?

```
data ttestgls;                          * data set;
merge parmgls segls;                    * merge statement;
by sample;                              * control merge by sample;
truese =  0.09333;                      * from proc iml;
tstat0 = (b2 - 1)/se;                   * test with estimated se;
tstat = (b2 - 1)/truese;                * test with true se;
tc = tinv(.975,38);                     * alpha=.05 critical value;
zc = probit(.975);                      * alpha=.05 from n(0,1);
reject0 = (abs(tstat0) >= tc);          * record rejection;
reject1 = (abs(tstat) >= zc);           * record rejection;
run;


proc means data=ttestgls mean;         * compute only mean;
title 't-test rejection rates using estimated and correct se(b2)';
run;
```

Using the estimated standard error with the *t*-distribution is just as effective as using the true standard error (from Section 8A.3) and the standard normal critical value.

```
t-test rejection rates using estimated and correct se(b2)


      Variable              Mean
      _____

      reject0            0.0480000
      reject1            0.0483000
      _____
```

8A.3 Using PROC IML to compute true variances

Regression errors are heteroskedastic when the variances of the error terms may differ from one observation to another, that is, if $var(e_i) = \sigma_i^2$. The regression model in matrix notation is introduced in Appendix 5A.4. In matrix notation denote the vector of random errors as $\mathbf{e}$ and its covariance matrix as Σ,

$$\mathbf{e} = \begin{bmatrix} e_1 \\ e_2 \\ \vdots \\ e_N \end{bmatrix} \text{ and } cov(\mathbf{e}) = \Sigma = \begin{bmatrix} \sigma_1^2 & 0 & \cdots & 0 \\ 0 & \sigma_2^2 & 0 & 0 \\ \vdots & 0 & \ddots & \vdots \\ 0 & 0 & \cdots & \sigma_N^2 \end{bmatrix} = diag\left(\sigma_1^2, \sigma_2^2, \ldots, \sigma_N^2\right)$$

where *diag* denotes a diagonal matrix. Conditional on $\mathbf{X}$ the covariance matrix of the least squares estimator when errors are heteroskedastic is

$$\text{cov}(\mathbf{b}) = (\mathbf{X'X})^{-1} \mathbf{X'\Sigma X} (\mathbf{X'X})^{-1}$$

If we allow for a factor of proportionality [which is called σ^2 for reasons that will soon be explained] in the covariance matrix of the errors as

$$\text{cov}(\mathbf{e}) = \Sigma = \sigma^2 \Omega = \sigma^2 \begin{bmatrix} w_1 & 0 & \cdots & 0 \\ 0 & w_2 & 0 & 0 \\ \vdots & 0 & \ddots & \vdots \\ 0 & 0 & \cdots & w_N \end{bmatrix}$$

In this case

$$\text{cov}(\mathbf{b}) = \sigma^2 (\mathbf{X'X})^{-1} \mathbf{X'\Omega X} (\mathbf{X'X})^{-1} \qquad (8A.1)$$

Note that the usual formula for the covariance matrix of the least squares estimator $\text{cov}(\mathbf{b}) = \sigma^2 (\mathbf{X'X})^{-1}$ is **incorrect**.

The generalized least squares estimator is the best linear unbiased estimator when the errors are heteroskedastic. Let $\mathbf{P}$ be a matrix

$$\mathbf{P} = \begin{bmatrix} \dfrac{1}{\sqrt{w_1}} & 0 & \cdots & 0 \\ 0 & \dfrac{1}{\sqrt{w_2}} & 0 & 0 \\ \vdots & 0 & \ddots & \vdots \\ 0 & 0 & \cdots & \dfrac{1}{\sqrt{w_N}} \end{bmatrix}$$

This matrix has the property that $\mathbf{P\Omega P'} = \mathbf{I}$. Using $\mathbf{P}$ to transform the regression model we have $\mathbf{Py} = \mathbf{PX\beta} + \mathbf{Pe}$. The covariance matrix of $\mathbf{Pe}$ is $\text{cov}(\mathbf{Pe}) = \sigma^2 \mathbf{P\Omega P'} = \sigma^2 \mathbf{I}$. The transformed model has homoskedastic errors, with variance σ^2 (this is the factor of proportionality). If we denote the transformed data as $\mathbf{y_*} = \mathbf{Py}$ and $\mathbf{X_*} = \mathbf{PX}$, then the generalized least squares estimator is obtained by applying "ordinary" least squares to the transformed data,

$$\hat{\beta} = (\mathbf{X_*' X_*})^{-1} \mathbf{X_*' y_*} = (\mathbf{X'\Omega^{-1}X})^{-1} \mathbf{X'\Omega^{-1}y}$$

This estimator has covariance matrix

$$\text{cov}(\hat{\beta}) = \sigma^2 (\mathbf{X_*' X_*})^{-1} = \sigma^2 (\mathbf{X'\Omega^{-1}X})^{-1}$$

For the Monte Carlo experimental design in Section 8A.1 we know that $\sigma^2 = .25$ and the variance of the error terms is $\text{var}(e_i) = \sigma^2 x_i^2 = .25 x_i^2$, or

$$\text{cov}\left(\mathbf{e}\right) = .25 \begin{bmatrix} x_1^2 & 0 & \cdots & 0 \\ 0 & x_2^2 & 0 & 0 \\ \vdots & 0 & \ddots & \vdots \\ 0 & 0 & \cdots & x_N^2 \end{bmatrix}$$

In the Monte Carlo experiment we can compute the true variances for the OLS and GLS estimators using matrix operations in **PROC IML**.

First, we begin **PROC IML** and read in data created in Section 8A.1. In addition to the data we can read in the true standard deviations, and create a vector **SIG2** that contains the true variances of the error terms. The vector **X1** is a column of ones that is our intercept variable. The scalar **N** is the number of observations and **K** is the number of parameters.

```
proc iml;                              * invoke iml;
start gls;                             * begin module;
print /,, "true gls calcuations",,;    * print message;
use hetdata;                           * open SAS dataset;
read all var{y} into y;                * read y;
read all var{x} into x2;               * read x2;
read all var{sig} into sig;            * read sig;
n = nrow(y);                           * n = number rows in y;
x1 = j(n,1,1);                         * x1 is column of ones;
x = x1||x2;                            * X is horizontal concant;
k = ncol(x);                           * define k;
sig2 = sig##2;                         * true variance;
```

We can construct the true covariance matrix of the OLS estimator using equation (8A.1). The command **DIAG** constructs a diagonal matrix from the elements of the vector **SIG2**.

```
covols = inv(x`*x)*(x`*diag(sig2)*x)*inv(x`*x);
```

From the covariance matrix we extract the variances, which are on the diagonal of the covariance matrix, using the command **DIAG**. The true standard errors are the square roots of the true variances. Create the *t*-statistics and put it all together with the horizontal concatenation operator "‖". This stacks matrices side by side.

```
varols = vecdiag(covols);              * true ols var;
seols = sqrt(varols);                  * true ols se;
b = inv(x`*x)*x`*y;                    * ols estimates;
tstat = b/seols;                       * t-statistics;
result = b||seols||tstat;              * stack results;
rname = {b1 b2};                        * row names;
cname = {est se tstat};                * column names;

print, 'OLS estimates with true standard errors',
       result[colname=cname rowname=rname format=13.5];
```

The result is

```
OLS estimates with true standard errors
                result
          EST          SE          TSTAT
B1     0.96653      0.06104      15.83515
B2     1.02299      0.17593       5.81466
```

For comparison we will compute the usual, but incorrect standard errors from $\hat{\sigma}^2 (\mathbf{X'X})^{-1}$. We call them "bad" to reinforce the fact that they are incorrect.

```
badsig2 = ssq(y-x*b)/(n-k);              * usual sig2 estimate;
badcov = badsig2*inv(x`*x);              * usual cov(b) estimate;
badse = sqrt(vecdiag(badcov));           * incorrect se;
badt = b/badse;                          * incorrect tstats;
result = b||badse||badt;                 * stack results;
rname = {b1 b2};
cname = {est se tstat};
print, 'OLS estimates with incorrect standard errors',
        ,, result[colname=cname rowname=rname format=13.5];
```

Note that the incorrect standard error for the intercept is larger than the true one, but for the slope the incorrect standard error is smaller than the true one. In general there is no way to predict whether the incorrect standard errors will be larger or smaller than the true ones.

```
OLS estimates with incorrect standard errors

                Result
          EST          SE          TSTAT
B1     0.96653      0.09539      10.13243
B2     1.02299      0.16218       6.30767
```

Now, we apply OLS to the transformed the data to implement generalized least squares. Recall the heteroskedasticity is related to the regressor (squared) which is denoted **X2** in our **PROC IML** program. The true covariance matrix for the GLS estimator is $.25(\mathbf{X_*'X_*})^{-1}$

```
ystar = y/x2;                    * transformed y's;
xstar = x/x2;                    * transformed x's;
bgls = inv(xstar`*xstar)*xstar`*ystar;  * GLS estimator;
covbgls = .25*inv(xstar`*xstar);        * covgls;
vargls = vecdiag(covbgls);              * gls variances;
print ,, 'true variance OLS', varols,,
        'true variance GLS', vargls;
```

Compare the true OLS variances to the true GLS variances. You will see that the true GLS variances are (much) smaller, reflecting the efficiency of the GLS estimator.

```
            true variance OLS
                 varols


               0.0037255
               0.0309522
```

```
                    true variance GLS
                        vargls

                       0.0001344
                       0.0087103
```

To complete the comparisons, compute the true standard errors and corresponding *t*-statistics.

```
segls = sqrt(vargls);                    * gls standard errors;
tgls = bgls/segls;                       * t-stats;
result = bgls||segls||tgls;
rname = {b1gls b2gls};                   * row names;
print ,, 'GLS estimates with true standard errors'
         ,, result[rowname=rname colname=cname format=13.5];
```

```
           GLS estimates with true standard errors
                          result
                      EST           SE          TSTAT

           B1GLS    0.99283       0.01159       85.64026
           B2GLS    0.99114       0.09333       10.61983
```

Now **finish** and **run** the module, then **quit PROC IML**.

```
finish;                                  * finish module;
run gls;                                 * run module;
quit;                                    * quit iml;
```

8A.4 White HCE Monte Carlo experiment

Several different version of the White heteroskedasticity consistent covariance matrix estimator have been suggested. In **PROC REG** the alternative methods are implemented by specifying (for example using the food expenditure data model)

```
proc reg data=food;
model food_exp = income/hcc hccmethod=1;
```

The **hccmethod** can be 0, 1, 2 or 3. These choices correspond to

$$\text{cov}(\mathbf{b}) = (\mathbf{X'X})^{-1} \mathbf{X'D_i X} (\mathbf{X'X})^{-1}$$

The choice $\mathbf{D_0}$ is a diagonal matrix using only the uncorrected squared least squares residuals on the diagonal. The other methods adjust the squared residuals in one way or another. The choice $\mathbf{D_1}$ inflates the residuals by $N/(N-K)$. The alternative $\mathbf{D_2}$ is derived on the basis of the fact that under homoskedasticity the variance of the least squares residual $\hat{e}_i$ is given by

$$\text{var}(\hat{e}_i) = \sigma^2 \left(1 - \mathbf{x_i'} (\mathbf{X'X})^{-1} \mathbf{x_i}\right)$$

where x_i is the i'th row of the $\mathbf{X}$ matrix. It divides the squared residual by the quantity in parentheses. Option $\mathbf{D}_3$ divides the squared residual by the square of the quantity in parentheses. There is strong evidence that option $\mathbf{D}_0$ should not be used, in favor of $\mathbf{D}_2$ in Monte Carlo studies. Econometrics packages tend to favor $\mathbf{D}_1$ as a default method.[6] In matrix terms these alternatives are

$$\mathbf{D}_0 = \begin{bmatrix} \hat{e}_1^2 & 0 & \cdots & 0 \\ 0 & \hat{e}_2^2 & 0 & 0 \\ \vdots & 0 & \ddots & \vdots \\ 0 & 0 & \cdots & \hat{e}_N^2 \end{bmatrix} = diag\left(\hat{e}_1^2, \hat{e}_2^2, \ldots, \hat{e}_N^2\right)$$

$$\mathbf{D}_1 = \frac{N}{N-K} diag\left(\hat{e}_1^2, \hat{e}_2^2, \ldots, \hat{e}_N^2\right)$$

$$\mathbf{D}_2 = diag\left(\ldots, \frac{\hat{e}_i^2}{1 - \mathbf{x}_i'\left(\mathbf{X'X}\right)^{-1}\mathbf{x}_i}, \ldots\right)$$

$$\mathbf{D}_3 = diag\left(\ldots, \frac{\hat{e}_i^2}{\left(1 - \mathbf{x}_i'\left(\mathbf{X'X}\right)^{-1}\mathbf{x}_i\right)^2}, \ldots\right)$$

It would be nice to explore the properties of these alternatives using the same approach used in Sections 8A.1-8A.2. Unfortunately SAS will not, it appears, output the White standard errors. As an alternative we will use PROC IML for the calculations. We will read the SAS data set *hetdata*, generated in Section 8A.1 into IML. The value of the regressor and the error variance will be held constant over the experiments. The first part of the code is the same as in Section 8A.3.

```
title;                           * clear title;
proc iml;                        * invoke iml;
start glsmc;                     * begin module;
use hetdata;                     * open SAS dataset;
read all var{x} into x2;         * read x2;
read all var{sig} into sig;      * read sig;
n = nrow(x2);                    * n = number rows in y;
x1 = j(n,1,1);                   * x1 is column of ones;
x = x1||x2;                      * X is horizontal concant;
k = ncol(x);                     * define k;
```

Define the number of Monte Carlo samples and create a matrix **STORE** in which the results from the samples will be held.

```
nsam = 10000;                    * number of mc samples;
store = j(nsam,5,0);             * storage matrix;
```

---

[6] See William Greene (2012) *Econometric Analysis, 7th edition*, pages 272-275 for further discussion.

There are several random number generators in **PROC IML**. We use **randgen** which inserts random numbers into a pre-existing vector or matrix. Call the vector of random numbers **e**.

```
e = j(n,1,0);                          * matrix for random numbers;
call randseed(1234567);                * set seed;
```

In the 10,000 iteration loops a vector of independent $N(0,1)$ random errors are multiplied by **sig** to create the heteroskedastic error. The data generation process is the same as in Section 8A.1, with intercept and slope set to 1. Compute the least squares estimates and squared residuals for each sample.

```
do iter = 1 to nsam;                   * mc loop;
call randgen(e,'normal',0,1);          * draw random sample;
e = sig#e;                             * heteroskedastic error;
y = 1 + x2 + e;                        * generate y value;
b = inv(x`*x)*x`*y;                    * ols estimates;
ehat = y - x*b;                        * residuals;
ehat2 = ehat##2;                       * residuals squared;
```

The matrices are constructed straightforwardly. The matrix $\mathbf{HAT} = \mathbf{X}(\mathbf{X'X})^{-1}\mathbf{X'}$ is used to compute the diagonal correction factor for the methods 2 and 3. The matrix is so-named since $\hat{\mathbf{y}} = \mathbf{HAT} \cdot \mathbf{y}$. Store the least squares estimate of the slope and the variance of b_2 from each method. The particular elements are extracted by specifying their positions in the matrix.

```
hce0 = inv(x`*x)*(x`*diag(ehat2)*x)*inv(x`*x);
hce1 = (n/(n-k))*hce0;
hat = vecdiag(x*inv(x`*x)*x`);
hce2 =  inv(x`*x)*(x`*diag(ehat2/(1-hat))*x)*inv(x`*x);
hce3 =  inv(x`*x)*(x`*diag(ehat2/(1-hat)##2)*x)*inv(x`*x);
store[iter,]= b[2]||hce0[2,2]||hce1[2,2]||hce2[2,2]||hce3[2,2];
end;
```

The next 4 statements output the contents of the storage matrix to a SAS data set, with variable names **varnames**.

```
varnames = {b2 hce0 hce1 hce2 hce3};
create glsest from store[colname=varnames];
append from store;
close glsest;

finish;                                * finish module;
run glsmc;                             * run module;
quit;                                  * quit iml;

proc means data=glsest mean std var min max;
var b2 hce0 hce1 hce2 hce3;
title 'variance estimator averages';
run;
```

The output shows that in this experiment the actual variance of the least squares estimator is 0.0313769. The average value of **HCE2** (method 2) is closest in this experiment, with versions 0 and 1 being too small, and version 3 being a bit too large.

```
                    The MEANS Procedure
```

Variable	Mean	Std Dev	Variance	Minimum	Maximum
B2	1.0030032	0.1771354	0.0313769	0.3240826	1.6190405
HCE0	0.0283863	0.0129338	0.000167283	0.0045009	0.1032286
HCE1	0.0298803	0.0136145	0.000185355	0.0047378	0.1086617
HCE2	0.0306162	0.0140876	0.000198461	0.0047797	0.1127338
HCE3	0.0330348	0.0153511	0.000235656	0.0050320	0.1235135

APPENDIX 8B TWO-STEP ESTIMATION

8B.1 Simulating heteroskedastic data

To illustrate the two-step estimator for the model of multiplicative heteroskedasticity we use simulated data, based on an exercise (FF3) in Peter Kennedy's (2008) *A Guide to Econometrics, 6e*, Blackwell Publishing. In our experiment we create:

- A set of 50 x values ranging from 0 to 1 following a uniform distribution.
- A set of 50 random errors e_i with normal distributions, mean zero, and variances $\sigma_i^2 = Kx_i^\alpha$. We choose $K = 0.5$ and $\alpha = 2.25$. To achieve these heteroskedastic errors we multiply a $N(0,1)$ random error by $\sigma_i = \sqrt{.5x_i^{2.25}}$
- A set of 50 y values are obtained as

$$y_i = \beta_1 + \beta_2 x_i + e_i = 1 + 1 \times x_i + e_i$$

The SAS commands use **streaminit** to "initialize" the random number generator **rand**. In fact the **rand** command will generate many types of random numbers. The first use is for the uniform distribution, which creates numbers randomly scattered between zero and one. Secondly, note that we have specified a normal distribution with mean 0 and variance 1, which is then multiplied by σ_i to create heteroskedastic errors, which are then added to the regression function $E(y) = 1 + x$.

We have used a **do-loop**, that starts with **do** and stops with **end**, to process one observation at a time. The **output** statement writes the observation to the SAS data set *hetdata*.

```
data hetdata;                        * data set;
call streaminit(1234567);            * set random number stream;
        do n = 1 to 50;              * do loop 40 times;
        x = rand('uniform');         * x variable;
        lx = log(x);                 * log(x);
```

```
                beta1 = 1;                          * intercept;
                beta2 = 1;                          * slope;
                K = .5;                             * proportionality;
                alpha = 2.25;                       * power;
                sig2 = K*(x**alpha);                * variance error;
                sig = sqrt(sig2);                   * std dev;
                y = beta1 + beta2*x + sig*rand('normal',0,1);
                one = 1;
                output;                             * output to data set;
                end;                                * end inner loop;
        run;
```

8B.2 Feasible gls in multiplicative model

The steps of the two-step estimator are outlined in Section 8.5.3.

```
        /* Estimate model by OLS and save residuals */
        proc reg data=hetdata;                  * use heteroskedastic data;
        model y = x;                            * specify model;
        output out=olsout r=ehat;               * output residuals;
        run;
```

The OLS estimates are:

Variable	DF	Parameter Estimate	Standard Error	t Value	Pr > |t|
Intercept	1	0.95144	0.10507	9.06	<.0001
x	1	1.11336	0.18180	6.12	<.0001

```
        /* Use residuals to create log(ehat^2) */
        data step2;
        set olsout;
        lehat2 = log(ehat**2);
        run;

        /* Step 2 is to estimate alpha and output predicted values */
        proc reg data=step2;
        model lehat2 = lx;
        output out=sigout p=lehat2_hat;
        run;
```

The estimates of α_1 and α_2 are

Variable	DF	Parameter Estimate	Standard Error	t Value	Pr > |t|
Intercept	1	-2.49325	0.40933	-6.09	<.0001
lx	1	1.28548	0.32792	3.92	0.0003

The estimator of α_1 is inconsistent, with the bias in large samples equaling -1.2704. A consistent estimator of α_1 is obtained by adding 1.2704, a step we take in the **PROC IML** code below. However, it is not necessary because $\sigma^2 = \exp(\alpha_1)$ is a scale factor that drops out during calculations. See Judge, et al. (1988), *Introduction to the Theory and Practice of Econometrics, 2nd Edition*, page 369.

```
/* Step 3 is to create weight variable */
data step3;
set sigout;
sig2 = exp(lehat2_hat);
wt = 1/sig2;
run;

/* Step 4 is to carry out weighted least squares */
proc reg data=step3;
model y = x;
weight wt;
run;
```

The weighted least squares, GLS estimates are

Variable	DF	Parameter Estimate	Standard Error	t Value	Pr > |t|
Intercept	1	1.00020	0.02144	46.66	<.0001
x	1	1.01275	0.09854	10.28	<.0001

8B.3 Feasible GLS in PROC IML

To examine the two-step estimator in detail, we use **PROC IML**. In the first few steps we read the data from *hetdata*, define the **X** and **Z** matrices, and constants for sample size, number of parameters (K) and number of heteroskedasticity parameters (P).

```
proc iml;                        * begin iml;
use hetdata;                     * open dataset;
read all into y var{y};          * define y;
read all into x var{x};          * define x;
read all into lx var{lx};        * define z-using log(x);
n = nrow(y);                     * define n;
one = j(n,1,1);                  * constant term;
x = one||x;                      * variables in reg;
z = one||lx;                     * variables in hetero;
k = ncol(x);                     * define k;
p = ncol(z);                     * define p;
```

The first stage of the two-step estimation is to apply OLS, compute residuals, find the logarithm of the squared residuals, and regress these on **Z**. In this case we will correct the estimated intercept to make it a consistent estimator.

```
b = inv(x`*x)*x`*y;                    * ols;
e = y-x*b;                             * ols residuals;
q = log(e##2);                         * q-vector;
ahat = inv(z`*z)*z`*q;                 * ols;
ahat[1]= ahat[1]+1.2704;               * correct alpha-1;
covahat =4.9348*inv(z`*z);             * ITPE2 eq (9.3.46);
se = sqrt(vecdiag(covahat));           * standard errors;
tstat = ahat/se;                       * t-stats for ahat;
pval = 2*(1-probt(abs(tstat),n-k));    * p-values with t-dist;
parm = {hetconst lx};                  * parameter names;
cname = {est se tstat pval};           * table column names;
result =      ahat||se||tstat||pval;   * stack results;
print /'Mutiplicative Heteroskedasticity Model',,
       '1st stage estimates ',
       result[colname=cname rowname=parm format=13.4] ;
```

The estimates are

```
        Mutiplicative Heteroskedasticity Model

                    1st stage estimates
                          result
                EST           SE          TSTAT         PVAL
HETCONST      -1.2228       0.4556       -2.6838       0.0100
LX             1.2855       0.3650        3.5216       0.0010
```

Comparing these to those obtained from Section 8B.2 we see that the intercept is now larger by 1.2704, and the standard errors, t-values and p-values are changed. In this regression we have used the correct covariance matrix for $\hat{\alpha}_1$ and $\hat{\alpha}_2$, which is $\mathrm{cov}(\hat{\boldsymbol{\alpha}}) = 4.9348(\mathbf{Z'Z})^{-1}$. Thus the t-values from this output are correct and can be used to test for heteroskedasticity. The t-statistic for $\hat{\alpha}_2$ is large, and we conclude (correctly) that $ln(x)$ affects the error variance in this data set.

Generalized least squares proceeds excluding the intercept.

```
wt = sqrt( exp(z[,2]*ahat[2]) );       * weight value ITPE2, p.369;
xstar = x/wt;                          * transform x;
ystar = y/wt;                          * transform y;
bgls = inv(xstar`*xstar)*xstar`*ystar; * feasible gls;
egls = ystar-xstar*bgls;               * transformed residuals;
sig2gls = sum(egls##2)/(n-k);          * sig2 =exp(alpha1);
cov = sig2gls*inv(xstar`*xstar);       * covariance gls;
se = sqrt(vecdiag(cov));               * se;
tstat = bgls/se;                       * t-stat;
pval = 2*(1-probt(abs(tstat),n-k));    * p-values using t-dist;
parm = {const x};                      * parameter names;
cname = {est se tstat pval};           * table column names;
result =      bgls||se||tstat||pval;   * stack results;
print /'Mutiplicative Heteroskedasticity Model',,
       '2nd step estimates ',
       result[colname=cname rowname=parm format=13.4] ;
```

```
quit;
```

The result is identical to that obtained in the previous section.

```
            Mutiplicative Heteroskedasticity Model

                     2nd step estimates
                           result
                  EST          SE        TSTAT        PVAL
     CONST     1.0002      0.0214      46.6576      0.0000
     X         1.0128      0.0985      10.2780      0.0000
```

APPENDIX 8C MULTIPLICATIVE MODEL MONTE CARLO

8C.1 Simulating heteroskedastic data

To illustrate the maximum likelihood estimator for the model of multiplicative heteroskedasticity we use simulated data, based on an exercise (FF3) in Peter Kennedy's (2008) *A Guide to Econometrics, 6e*, Blackwell Publishing. In our experiment we create:

- A set of 25 x values ranging from 0 to 1 following a uniform distribution.
- A set of 25 random errors e_i with normal distributions, mean zero, and variances $\sigma_i^2 = Kx_i^\alpha$. We choose $K = 0.5$ and $\alpha = 2.25$. To achieve these heteroskedastic errors we multiply a $N(0,1)$ random error by $\sigma_i = \sqrt{.5x_i^{2.25}}$
- A set of 25 y values are obtained as

$$y_i = \beta_1 + \beta_2 x_i + e_i = 1 + 1 \times x_i + e_i$$

The SAS commands use **streaminit** to "initialize" the random number generator **rand**. In fact the **rand** command will generate many types of random numbers. The first use is for the uniform distribution. Secondly, note that we have specified a normal distribution with mean 0 and variance 1, which is then multiplied by σ_i to create heteroskedastic errors, which are then added to the regression function $E(y) = 1 + x$.

We have used a **do loop**, that starts with **do** and stops with **end**, to process one observation at a time. The outer loop generates 10,000 samples for the Monte Carlo experiment. The **output** statement writes the observation to the SAS data set *hetmc*.

```
data hetmc;                          * data set;
call streaminit(1234567);            * set random number stream;
do sample = 1 to 10000;              * outer loop repeat samples;
     do n = 1 to 25;                 * do loop 40 times;
     x = rand('uniform');            * x variable;
     lx = log(x);                    * log(x);
     beta1 = 1;                      * intercept;
     beta2 = 1;                      * slope;
     K = .5;                         * proportionality;
```

```
            alpha = 2.25;                    * power;
            sig2 = K*(x**alpha);             * variance error;
            sig = sqrt(sig2);                * std dev;
            y = beta1 + beta2*x + sig*rand('normal',0,1);  * y = 1 + 1*x + e;
            output;                          * output to data set;
            end;                             * end inner loop;
        end;                                 * end outer loop;
    run;
```

8C.2 The least squares estimator

The steps of the Monte Carlo experiment are similar to those we have used before.

```
        /* regression with NOPRINT option */
        proc reg noprint data=hetmc outest=est tableout;
        model y = x;
        by sample;                      * repeat for each sample;
        run;


        /* create data set for slope est */
        data parm;                          * data set;
        set est;                            * read est;
        if _type_='PARMS';                  * keep if PARMS;
        b2 = x;                             * rename slope;
        keep sample b2;                     * keep 2 variables;
        run;


        /* summarize slope estimates & plot histogram */
        proc univariate data = parm;
        var b2;
        histogram/normal;
        title 'Sampling distribution of OLS b2';
        title2 'Errors heteroskedastic sig^2=.5*x^2.25';
        run;
```

The summary statistics for b_2 the least squares estimator of the slope are shown below. The average value of the slope estimates is 0.9947—the OLS estimator is unbiased. The variance of the slope estimates is 0.09507. We expect the maximum likelihood estimator to be more efficient. The plot of the coefficients [not presented] shows the distribution to be normal, as we have seen before.

```
                       The UNIVARIATE Procedure
                          Variable:  b2


N                       10000    Sum Weights              10000
Mean               0.99472966    Sum Observations    9947.29661
Std Deviation       0.3083284    Variance             0.0950664
```

8C.3 Maximum likelihood estimation

We will use **PROC AUTOREG** for the maximum likelihood estimation of the multiplicative model. The estimation results for each sample are output to a SAS data set, where we can retrieve them later. The maximum likelihood estimation algorithm used by SAS is iterative. On the **model** statement we increase the number of possible iterations from its default of 50 to 100. When trying so many samples from a complicated model, the chance of getting one that is difficult are pretty high. In the **hetero** statement we choose **LX**, the logarithm of x, to be the variable associated with the heteroskedasticity. The **link=exp** option specifies multiplicative heteroskedasticity.

```
proc autoreg noprint data=hetmc outest=estgls;
model y = x/ maxiter=100;              * change default 50 to 100;
hetero lx/ link=exp;                   * multiplicative hetero;
by sample;                             * repeat for each sample;
run;
```

The **outest** statement in **PROC AUTOREG** outputs slightly different results than **PROC REG**. Select the first sample, and print it, so that we know how to retrieve the desired results.

```
data sample;                   * new data set;
set estgls;                    * read outest;
if sample = 1;                 * keep only sample 1;
run;

proc print data=sample;
run;
```

The saved output is

Obs	_MODEL_	_TYPE_	_STATUS_	_DEPVAR_	_METHOD_	_NAME_	_MSE_
1		PARM	0 Converged	y	ML		0.15282

Obs	_SSE_	Intercept	y	x	_HET_0	_HET_1	sample
1	3.82062	1.00281	-1	0.73752	1.31647	4.07186	1

The MLE of the slope is the variable labeled "**X**" and the MLE of α_2 is called **_HET_1**.

Create a data set for the MLE of the slope, and summarize the results.

```
data parmgls;                  * data set;
set estgls;                    * read est;
if _type_='PARM';              * keep if PARM;
b2mle = x;                     * rename slope;
keep sample b2mle;             * keep 2 variables;
run;

/* summarize slope estimates & plot histogram */
proc univariate data = parmgls;
var b2mle;
histogram/normal;
title 'Sampling distribution of MLE-b2';
```

```
title2 'Errors heteroskedastic sig^2=.5*x^2.25';;
run;
```

Note that the average MLE is very nearly the true value, despite the fact that the MLE is not an unbiased estimator. Also, the variance of the 10,000 estimates is 0.03117, which is much smaller than the variance of the OLS estimates shown in Section 8C.2.

```
The UNIVARIATE Procedure
         Variable:  b2mle
```

N	10000	Sum Weights	10000
Mean	0.99821687	Sum Observations	9982.16867
Std Deviation	0.17653934	Variance	0.03116614

Summarize the ML estimates for α_2.

```
data alphagls;                        * data set;
set estgls;                           * read est;
if _type_='PARM';                     * keep if PARM;
alphahat = _HET_1;                    * rename parameter;
keep sample alphahat;                 * keep 2 variables;
run;


/* summarize alpha estimates & plot histogram */
proc univariate data = alphagls;
var alphahat;
histogram/normal;
title 'Sampling distribution of MLE-alphahat';
title2 'Errors heteroskedastic sig^2=.5*x^2.25';
run;
```

The average of the 10,000 estimates is 2.5887. The ML estimator is not unbiased. In this experiment we have used only a sample of size $N = 25$. The ML estimator is consistent, so if we were to increase the sample size the average value of the estimates would get closer to the true value of 2.25.

```
The UNIVARIATE Procedure
       Variable:  alphahat
```

N	10000	Sum Weights	10000
Mean	2.58873665	Sum Observations	25887.3665
Std Deviation	0.60528423	Variance	0.366369

The histogram of the estimates shows that their distribution is not quite normal, but again what we know about the MLE is that it is **asymptotically** normal. A sample of $N = 25$ does not come close to a "large sample."

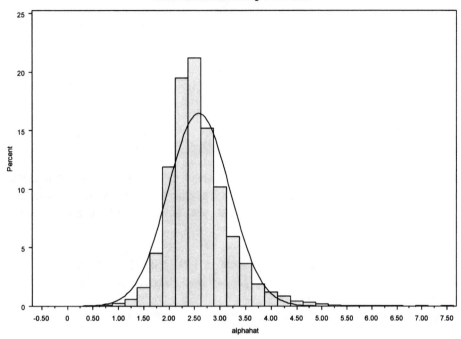

Sampling distribution of MLE-alphahat

Errors heteroskedastic sig^2=.5*x^2.25

APPENDIX 8D MULTIPLICATIVE MODEL MLE

8D.1 Using PROC AUTOREG

To illustrate maximum likelihood estimation of the multiplicative heteroskedasticity model we use the food expenditure data. This will provide a basis of comparison for our matrix language program below. In the **PROC AUTOREG** estimation, the option **covest=hessian** is used to override the SAS default. This will be explained further in Section 8D.2.

```
data food;
set 'food';
one = 1;
lincome = log(income);
run;
options nolabel;
proc autoreg data=food;
model food_exp = income/ covest=hessian;
hetero lincome / link=exp;
run;
```

The (edited) output is

```
               Multiplicative Heteroscedasticity Estimates

       Log Likelihood      -225.71519

                                    Standard              Approx
       Variable     DF    Estimate     Error   t Value   Pr > |t|

       Intercept     1     76.0725    7.3691     10.32     <.0001
       INCOME        1     10.6345    0.9149     11.62     <.0001
       HET0          1      1.2639    0.8281      1.53     0.1269
       HET1          1      2.7698    0.4482      6.18     <.0001
```

8D.2 Numerical optimization in the multiplicative model

Maximum likelihood estimation requires in most cases a numerically obtained maximum of the log-likelihood function. See Appendix C.4 in this manual for a complete introduction. For the model of multiplicative heteroskedasticity there are several fine sources discussing ML estimation.

- Judge, George G., R. Carter Hill, William E. Griffiths, Helmut Lütkepohl and Tsoung-Chao Lee (1988) *Introduction to the Theory and Practice of Econometrics, 2nd Edition*, John Wiley & Sons, Chapter 12.3.3.
- William H. Greene (2012) *Econometric Analysis, 7e*, Prentice-Hall, Chapter 14.9.2a.

The primary ingredient in maximum likelihood estimation is the log-likelihood function. If the regression errors are $e_i \sim N\left(0, \sigma_i^2 = \exp(\mathbf{z}_i'\boldsymbol{\alpha})\right)$ then, conditional on the explanatory variables

$$y_i \sim N\left(\mathbf{x}_i'\boldsymbol{\beta}, \sigma_i^2 = \exp(\mathbf{z}_i'\boldsymbol{\alpha})\right)$$

The density function of y_i is

$$f\left(y_i \mid \boldsymbol{\beta}, \boldsymbol{\alpha}\right) = \frac{1}{\sqrt{2\pi\sigma_i^2}} \exp\left\{-\frac{1}{2}\frac{\left(y_i - \mathbf{x}_i'\boldsymbol{\beta}\right)^2}{\sigma_i^2}\right\}$$

The logarithm of the density is the i'th term of the log-likelihood function.

$$L_i = \ln\left[f\left(y_i \mid \boldsymbol{\beta}, \boldsymbol{\alpha}\right)\right] = -\frac{1}{2}\ln(2\pi) - \frac{1}{2}\ln\left(\sigma_i^2\right) - \frac{1}{2}\frac{\left(y_i - \mathbf{x}_i'\boldsymbol{\beta}\right)^2}{\sigma_i^2}$$

$$= -\frac{1}{2}\ln(2\pi) - \frac{1}{2}\left(\mathbf{z}_i'\boldsymbol{\alpha}\right) - \frac{1}{2}\exp\left(-\mathbf{z}_i'\boldsymbol{\alpha}\right)\left(y_i - \mathbf{x}_i'\boldsymbol{\beta}\right)^2$$

Assuming the observations in our sample are independent, then the log-likelihood is

$$\ln L\left(\boldsymbol{\beta}, \alpha\right) = -\frac{N}{2}\ln(2\pi) - \frac{1}{2}\sum\left(\mathbf{z}_i'\boldsymbol{\alpha}\right) - \frac{1}{2}\sum\exp\left(-\mathbf{z}_i'\boldsymbol{\alpha}\right)\left(y_i - \mathbf{x}_i'\boldsymbol{\beta}\right)^2$$

Maximum likelihood estimation requires us to maximize this function with respect to $\boldsymbol{\alpha}$ and $\boldsymbol{\beta}$. For this function one option is the Newton-Raphson algorithm. Let $\boldsymbol{\theta} = \left(\boldsymbol{\alpha}'\ \boldsymbol{\beta}'\right)'$. This is a column vector that is $(K+P) \times 1$. Let the gradient (first derivative) and Hessian (second derivative)

$$g(\theta) = \frac{\partial \ln L(\theta)}{\partial \theta}, \quad H(\theta) = \frac{\partial^2 \ln L(\theta)}{\partial \theta \partial \theta'}$$

The gradient vector has the same dimension as θ and the Hessian matrix is $(K + P) \times (K + P)$.

In the j'th iteration of the iterative process, the next round estimate of θ is given by

$$\hat{\theta}_{j+1} = \hat{\theta}_j - \left[H(\hat{\theta}_j) \right]^{-1} g(\hat{\theta}_j)$$

To accomplish this estimation in SAS's **PROC IML** we must program a module for the log-likelihood function. SAS will compute the derivatives numerically and do the Newton-Raphson iterations automatically. Upon convergence, the MLE

$$\hat{\theta} \overset{a}{\sim} N\left(\theta, -\left[H(\theta) \right]^{-1} \right)$$

We can estimate the covariance matrix using numerical derivatives.

First, read in the data and define constants.

```
proc iml;                                 * begin iml;
use food;                                 * open dataset;
read all into y var{food_exp};            * define y;
read all into x var{one income};          * define x;
read all into z var{one lincome};         * define z-using log(x);
n = nrow(y);                              * define n;
k = ncol(x);                              * define k;
p = ncol(z);                              * define p;
parm = {const income hetconst lincome};   * parameter names;
```

The module for the log-likelihood must be set up a certain way so that the automatic Newton-Raphson commands will work. There must be a single input which is the parameter vector. Inside the module the parameter vector is separated, the components of the log-likelihood are computed and the single value of the log-likelihood function is produced.

```
start loglik(theta) global(y,x,z,n,k,p);
        bmle = theta[1:k];                 * beta;
        amle = theta[(k+1):(k+p)];         * alpha;
        sig2 = exp(z*amle);                * sig2;
        ehat = (y - x*bmle);               * residuals;
        ehat2 = ehat##2;                   * squared residuals;
                                           * compute LLH;
        llh = -(n/2)*log(2*3.14159) - (1/2)*sum(log(sig2))
                - (1/2)*sum(ehat2/sig2);
        return(llh);                       * return llh;
finish loglik;                             * end module;
```

The iterative process requires starting values. These will be the OLS estimates for β and the two-step estimator of α.

```
b = inv(x`*x)*x`*y;                        * ols;
e = y-x*b;                                 * ols residuals;
```

```
q = log(e##2 );                          * q-vector;
ahat = inv(z`*z)*z`*q;                   * ols;
ahat[1]= ahat[1]+1.2704;                 * correct alpha-1;
theta0=b//ahat;                          * stack;
```

The built in Newton-Raphson algorithm requires us to let it know if we are maximizing or minimizing the function. Choose **opt={1}** for maximization problems.

```
opt={1};                                 * max. problem;
```

The Newton-Raphson maximization is accomplished using **call nlpnra**. The elements must be in order, and are:

- **retcode** is a value indicating whether the maximization was successful or not. A positive value indicates convergence.
- **theta** is the value that maximizes the function.
- **"loglik"** is the name of the module for the log-likelihood function.
- **theta0** is the starting value.
- **opt** contains the options noted above.

```
call nlpnra(retcode,theta,"loglik",theta0,opt);
```

The **theta** value returned by **nlpnra** is a row, so we transpose it to create a column, and then evaluate the log-likelihood at the MLE.

```
theta = theta`;                          * create column;
llh = loglik(theta);                     * ln(1) at mle;
```

The **call nlpfdd** computes numerical derivatives. The elements must be in order and are:

- **lnl** is the value of the function.
- **g** is the gradient vector.
- **h** is the hessian matrix.
- **"loglik"** is the name of the module for the log-likelihood function.
- **theta** is the value at which the calculations are made.

```
call nlpfdd(lnl,g,h,"loglik",theta);     * numerical derivatives;
```

Having the Hessian matrix we can compute the covariance matrix of the MLE and the usual statistics.

```
cov = -inv(h);                           * covariance matrix;
se = sqrt(vecdiag(cov));                 * se;
tstat = theta/se;                        * t-stat;
pval = 2*(1-probt(abs(tstat),n-k));      * p-values using t-dist;
cname = {est se tstat pval};             * table column names;
result =     theta||se||tstat||pval;     * stack results;
print /'Mutiplicative Heteroskedasticity Model',,
```

```
'Log-likelihood value ' llh,,
'estimates ', result[colname=cname rowname=parm format=13.4] ;
```

The value of the log-likelihood we have achieved is the same as **PROC AUTOREG**. The parameter estimates and the rest are the same, except for the last digit in a couple. The reason is that we have used numerical derivatives for the Hessian and **PROC AUTOREG** does not.

```
          Mutiplicative Heteroskedasticity Model

          Log-likelihood value   -225.7152

                  EST          SE       TSTAT        PVAL
CONST         76.0729      7.3692     10.3231      0.0000
INCOME        10.6344      0.9149     11.6237      0.0000
HETCONST       0.4684      1.3097      0.3576      0.7226
LINCOME        2.7698      0.4479      6.1834      0.0000
```

8D.3 MLE based tests for heteroskedasticity

Assuming you are continuing the code from Section 8D.2, we can test for heteroskedasticity using a Lagrange multiplier test. See Judge, et al. (1988, p. 550) or Greene (2012, p. 276).

```
* Breusch-Pagan Lagrange multiplier statistic;
n = nrow(y);                        * number of obs;
sig2mle = (e`*e)/n;                 * mle of sigma^2;
q=((e##2)/sig2mle)-1;               * alternative q;
lm=(q`*z*inv(z`*z)*z`*q)/2;         * Greene 7th, p. 276;
p = ncol(z);                        * define p;
problm=1-probchi(lm,p-1);           * significance;
print,, 'Breusch-Pagan Lagrange multiplier statistic',,
     lm problm;

* Robust Lagrange multiplier statistic--Greene 7th, p.276;
u = e##2;                           * squared residuals;
ubar = e`*e/n;                      * avg squared residuals;
v = ssq(u-ubar)/n;                  * robust variance estimator;
lm = (u-ubar)`*z*inv(z`*z)*z`*(u-ubar)/v;
problm=1-probchi(lm,p-1);           * significance;
print,, 'Robust Breusch-Pagan Lagrange multiplier statistic',,
     lm problm;

quit;
```

The output is

```
        Breusch-Pagan Lagrange multiplier statistic

             lm      problm
      5.6424229   0.017531
```

```
         Robust Breusch-Pagan Lagrange multiplier statistic

                          lm     problm
                     5.6735328 0.0172227
```

8D.4 MLE using analytic derivatives

For the model of multiplicative heteroskedasticity the first and second derivatives are known and can be used along with **call nlpnra**. In the code below we have modules for the gradient and Hessian.

```
proc iml;                              * begin iml;
use food;                              * open dataset;
read all into y var{food_exp};         * define y;
read all into x var{one income};       * define x;
read all into z var{one lincome};      * define z-using log(x);
n = nrow(y);                           * define n;
k = ncol(x);                           * define k;
p = ncol(z);                           * define p;

/* module for log-likelihood function */
start loglik(theta) global(y,x,z,n,k,p); * log-likelihood module;
     bmle = theta[1:k];                * beta;
     amle = theta[(k+1):(k+p)];        * alpha;
     sig2 = exp(z*amle);               * sig2;
     ehat = (y - x*bmle);              * residuals;
     ehat2 = ehat##2;                  * squared residuals;
                                       * compute log-likelihood;
     llh = -(n/2)*log(2*3.14159) - (1/2)*sum(log(sig2))
          - (1/2)*sum(ehat2/sig2);
     return(llh);                      * return llh;
finish loglik;                         * end module;

/* module for gradient */
start grad(theta) global(y,x,z,n,k,p); * gradient module;
     bmle = theta[1:k];                * beta;
     amle = theta[(k+1):(k+p)];        * alpha;
     sig2 = exp(z*amle);               * sig2;
     ehat = (y - x*bmle);              * residuals;
     ehat2 = ehat##2;                  * e-squared;
     delb = x#(ehat/sig2);             * d(lnl)/d(beta);
     delb = delb[+,];                  * sum to form row;
     dela = -.5*z+ .5*(z#(exp(-z*amle)#ehat2));  * d(lnl)/d(alpha);
     dela = dela[+,];                  * sum to form row;
     g= delb||dela;                    * stack horizontally;
     return(g);                        * return gradient;
finish grad;                           * end module;

/* module for hessian */
start hessian(theta) global(y,x,z,n,k,p);    * Hessian module;
```

```
      bmle = theta[1:k];                    * beta;
      amle = theta[(k+1):(k+p)];            * alpha;
      sig2 = exp(z*amle);                   * multiplicative hetero;
      ehat = (y - x*bmle);                  * residuals;
      ehat2 = ehat##2;                      * resid squared;
      h11 = -(x#exp(-z*amle))`*x;           * d2(lnl)/d2(beta);
      h12 = -(x#(ehat/sig2))`*z;            * d2(lnl)/d(beta)d(alpha);
      h22= -.5*(z#(ehat2/sig2))`*z;         * del 2 lnl/del 2 alpha;
      h = (h11||h12)//((h12`)||h22);        * form symmetric matrix;
      return(h);                            * return hessian;
 finish hessian;                            * end module;


 /* starting values OLS */
 b = inv(x`*x)*x`*y;                        * ols;
 e = y-x*b;                                 * ols resisuals;
 q = log(e##2 );                            * q-vector;
 ahat = inv(z`*z)*z`*q;                     * ols;
 ahat[1]= ahat[1]+1.2704;                   * correct alpha-1;
 theta0=b//ahat;                            * stack;
 opt={1};                                   * maximize;
```

In the **call nlpnra** we add options pointing to the gradient and Hessian.

```
 call nlpnra(retcode,theta,"loglik",theta0,opt) grd="grad" hes="hessian";
 theta = theta`;                        * create column;
 llh = loglik(theta);                   * ln(1) at mle;
 h = hessian(theta);                    * evaluate hessian;
 cov = -inv(h);                         * covariance matrix;
 se = sqrt(vecdiag(cov));               * se;
 tstat = theta/se;                      * t-stat;
 pval = 2*(1-probt(abs(tstat),n-k));    * p-values using t-dist;
 parm = {const income hetconst lincome}; * parameter names;
 cname = {est se tstat pval};           * table column names;
 result =      theta||se||tstat||pval;  * stack results;
 print /'Mutiplicative Heteroskedasticity Model Analytic Derivatives',,
        'Log-likelihood value ' llh,,
        , result[colname=cname rowname=parm format=13.4] ;
        quit;
```

The output is

```
    Mutiplicative Heteroskedasticity Model Analytic Derivatives


                                         llh
                   Log-likelihood value  -225.7152


                             result
                    EST           SE        TSTAT         PVAL


        CONST    76.0729       7.3691      10.3232       0.0000
        INCOME   10.6344       0.9149      11.6238       0.0000
```

HETCONST	0.4684	1.3103	0.3575	0.7227
LINCOME	2.7698	0.4482	6.1803	0.0000

8D.5 MLE using method of scoring

In the model of multiplicative heteroskedasticity the maximum likelihood algorithm can be simplified using the Method of Scoring

$$\hat{\boldsymbol{\theta}}_{j+1} = \hat{\boldsymbol{\theta}}_j + \left[\mathbf{I}(\hat{\boldsymbol{\theta}}_j) \right]^{-1} \mathbf{g}(\hat{\boldsymbol{\theta}}_j)$$

where $\mathbf{I}(\boldsymbol{\theta})$ is the "information matrix." In this model it is given in Greene (2012, p. 555) and in Judge, et al. (1988, p. 539). Estimation reduces to a back and forth, or zig-zag, algorithm, where we have a separate updating equation for the estimates of $\boldsymbol{\beta}$ and $\boldsymbol{\alpha}$. The relevant equations are

$$\hat{\boldsymbol{\beta}}_{j+1} = \hat{\boldsymbol{\beta}}_j + \left(\mathbf{X}'\hat{\boldsymbol{\Sigma}}_j^{-1}\mathbf{X} \right)^{-1} \mathbf{X}'\hat{\boldsymbol{\Sigma}}_j^{-1}\hat{\mathbf{e}}_j$$

where $\hat{\boldsymbol{\Sigma}}_j = diag\left(..., \exp(\mathbf{z}_i'\hat{\boldsymbol{\alpha}}_j), ... \right)$ and $\hat{\mathbf{e}}_j = \mathbf{y} - \mathbf{X}\hat{\boldsymbol{\beta}}_j$. The other equation is

$$\hat{\boldsymbol{\alpha}}_{j+1} = \hat{\boldsymbol{\alpha}}_j + \left(\mathbf{Z}'\mathbf{Z} \right)^{-1} \mathbf{Z}'\mathbf{q}_j$$

where $\mathbf{q}_j$ is a vector with elements

$$q_{ij} = \exp\left(-\mathbf{z}_i'\hat{\boldsymbol{\alpha}}_j\right)\left(y_i - \mathbf{x}_i'\hat{\boldsymbol{\beta}}_j\right)^2 - 1$$

The PROC IML code follows:

```
proc iml;                              * invoke iml;
start harvey;                          * start module;
use food;                              * open dataset;
read all into y var{food_exp};         * define y;
read all into x var{one income};       * define x;
read all into z var{one lincome};      * define z-using log(x);
n = nrow(y);                           * define n;
k = ncol(x);                           * define k;
p = ncol(z);                           * define p;
one = j(n,1,1);                        * unit vector;
```

We might like to see the iteration history. Create a matrix into which results will be placed. We will not print this matrix, but you may wish to.

```
summary = j(40,3,0);                   * summary matrix;
```

Use OLS for starting values.

```
b=inv(x`*x)*x`*y;                      * regression coefficients;
e=(y-x*b);                             * residuals;
sig2=(e`*e)/(n-k);                     * error variance;
cov=sig2#inv(x`*x);                    * covariance matrix;
```

```
se= sqrt(vecdiag(cov));                  * standard errors;
tstat=b/se;                              * t-statistics;
```

So that we can perform a likelihood ratio test for heteroskedasticity, compute the log-likelihood for the OLS model. See Judge, et al. (1988, p. 223) or Greene (2012, p. 556).

```
* evaluate log likelihood;
log2pi= log(2#3.14159);                  * log of 2 * (pi);
sig2mle=(e`*e)/n;                        * m.l.e  variance;
llhols=-(n/2)*log2pi-(n/2)*log(sig2mle)
       -(1/(2*sig2mle))*(e`*e);          * ols log likelihood;
```

Initial estimate of **α** is the two-step estimator.

```
* estimate alpha;
q=log(e##2);                             * q-vector;
alpha= inv(z`*z)*z`*q;                   * itpe2, 9.3.42;
alpha[1,1]= alpha[1,1]+1.2704;           * adjust asymptotic bias;
```

The method of scoring begins by initializing the criterion function for convergence and computing the log-likelihood.

```
crit=1;                                  * convergence;
bmle=b;                                  * starting values;
amle=alpha;                              * initial estimate;
sig2 = exp(z*amle);                      * vector of variances;
ehat = (y - x*bmle);                     * residuals;
ehat2 = ehat##2;                         * squared residuals;
llh0 = -(n/2)*log2pi - (1/2)*sum(z*amle)
       - (1/2)*sum(ehat2/sig2);          * initial value of llh;
```

The actual iterations are accomplished using a **do-loop** that will do 50 iterations or until the criterion value is less than 0.0001.

```
do iter=1 to 50 while (crit > .0001);   * begin do-loop;
      sigma = diag(sig2);                * sigma matrix;

      /* beta step G7 eq(14-60) */
      delb = inv(x`*inv(sigma)*x)*x`*inv(sigma)*ehat;
```

```
/* alpha step G7 eq(14-61) */
q = inv(sigma)*ehat2 - 1;
dela = inv(z`*z)*z`*q;
bmle = bmle + delb;                 * update bmle;
amle = amle + dela;                 * update amle;
sig2 = exp(z*amle);                 * vector of variances;
ehat = (y - x*bmle);                * residuals;
ehat2 = ehat##2;                    * squared residuals;
llh = -(n/2)*log2pi - (1/2)*sum(z*amle)
        - (1/2)*sum(ehat2/sig2);    * new log-likelihood;
```

The convergence criterion is based on the changes in the estimates from iteration to iteration. Once the changes are very small, we will stop;

```
    crit = sqrt(ssq(delb//dela));    * convergence criterion;
    llh0 = llh;                      * replace old llh;
    summary[iter,]=iter||crit||llh;  * store results;
end;                                 * end do-loop;


* summary statistics;
* note print matrix summary above to see iteration history;

covaml = 2*inv(z`*z);                * cov(aml);
covbml = inv(x`*inv(sigma)*x);       * cov(bml);
sda=sqrt(vecdiag(covaml));           * std. err. of alpha;
sdb=sqrt(vecdiag(covbml));           * std. err. of bmle;
tstatb=bmle/sdb;                     * t-ratio;
theta = bmle//amle;                  * parm vector;
se = sdb//sda;                       * se vector;
tstat = theta/se;                    * tstat;
pval = 2*(1-probt(abs(tstat),n-k));  * p-values using t-dist;
parm = {const income hetconst lincome}; * parameter names;
cname = {est se tstat pval};         * table column names;
result =      theta||se||tstat||pval; * stack results;
print / 'Mutiplicative Heteroskedasticity Model Method of Scoring',,
        'Ols log-likelihood' llhols,,
      'MLE log-likelihood' llh,,
      'estimates ', result[colname=cname rowname=parm format=13.4] ;
```

The output shows that the estimates are the same as earlier versions.

```
        Mutiplicative Heteroskedasticity Model Method of Scoring


                              llhols
            Ols log-likelihood -235.5088


                              llh
            MLE log-likelihood -225.7152
```

	result			
	EST	SE	TSTAT	PVAL
CONST	76.0729	7.3670	10.3261	0.0000
INCOME	10.6344	0.9147	11.6261	0.0000
HETCONST	0.4684	1.3010	0.3600	0.7208
LINCOME	2.7698	0.4449	6.2259	0.0000

While we are here, we can compute the likelihood ratio test for heteroskedasticity. See Judge, et al. (1988, p. 545) or Greene (2012, p. 556).

```
* likelihood ratio test;
lr=2*(llh-llhols);                  * G7, page 550;
problr=1-probchi(lr,p-1);           * probability (p-1) d.f.;
print,, 'likelihood ratio statistic for'
        'multiplicative heteroskedasticity',,
        llhols llh lr problr;
```

```
likelihood ratio statistic for multiplicative heteroskedasticity

        llhols       llh        lr     problr
      -235.5088 -225.7152 19.587267 9.6108E-6
```

Compute the Wald test based on the maximum likelihood estimates. See Judge, et al (1988, p. 549) or Greene (2012, p. 556).

```
* wald test for heteroskedasticity;
zpz=inv(z`*z);
d=zpz[2:p,2:p];                     * G7, page 556;
astar=amle[2:p,1];                  * alpha-star;
lambda=(astar`*inv(d)*astar)/2;     * G7, page 556;
problam=1-probchi(lambda,p-1);      * significance;
print,, 'wald test for hetero',, lambda problam;

finish;                             * finish module;
run harvey;                         * run module;
quit;                               * quit iml;
```

```
                wald test for hetero

                lambda    problam
              38.762325 4.787E-10
```

CHAPTER **9**

Regression with Time-Series Data: Stationary Variables

9.1 TIME-SERIES DATA

Chapter 9 in *Principles of Econometrics, 4th Edition* is devoted to some of the special issues that are considered when estimating regression models with **time-series data**. Time provides a natural ordering of the data, and it leads to dynamic features in regression equations. As in *POE4*, we consider three ways in which dynamics can enter a regression relationship – through lagged values of the explanatory variable, lagged values of the dependent variable, and lagged values of the error term.

In this chapter, we maintain the assumption that the data are **stationary**. When this assumption holds, the usual econometric procedures have the proper statistical properties. Basically, stationarity requires that the means, variances and covariances of the data cannot depend on the period in which they were observed. For example, the mean and variance of GDP in the third quarter of 1973 are the same as in the fourth quarter of 2006. We discuss methods of testing for stationarity and techniques for estimating models with nonstationary variables in Chapter 12.

9.2 FINITE DISTRIBUTED LAGS

The first dynamic regression model considered in *Principles of Econometrics, 4th Edition* is a **finite distributed lag model**. Finite distributed lag models contain independent variables and their lags as regressors. It is assumed that the relationship is linear, and, after q time periods, changes in x no longer have an impact on y.

$$y_t = \alpha + \beta_0 x_t + \beta_1 x_{t-1} + \beta_2 x_{t-2} + \cdots + \beta_q x_{t-q} + e_t, \qquad t = q+1,\ldots,T \qquad (9.1)$$

As an example, we consider an economic model known as Okun's Law. In this model, the change in unemployment from one period to the next, DU_t, depends on current and lagged values of growth of output in the economy, G_t. The finite distributed lag model is written as

$$DU_t = \alpha + \beta_0 G_t + \beta_1 G_{t-1} + \beta_2 G_{t-2} + \cdots + \beta_q G_{t-q} + e_t, \qquad t = q+1,\ldots,T$$

The SAS data set *okun* contains observations on GDP growth and unemployment rate from 1985q2 to 2009q3. Before estimating the model, we examine lag and difference operators in SAS. In addition, we generate a time-series plot of the data.

9.2.1 Lag and difference operators

When working with time-series data, lagging and differencing are essential functions. The variables in our finite distributed lag model are change in quarterly employment, DU_t, and current and lagged values of quarterly GDP growth, G_t.

First, open the SAS data set *okun*, examine its contents and turn off labels.

```
data okun;                          * open data set;
set 'okun';                         * read okun;
run;
proc contents data=okun;            * examine contents;
run;
options nolabel;                    * turn off labels;
```

```
                 Alphabetic List of Variables and Attributes

# Variable Type Len Label
1 g         Num    8 percentage change in U.S. Gross Domestic
                     Product, seasonally adjusted
2 u         Num    8 U.S. Civilian Unemployment Rate (Seasonally adjusted)
```

The file contains variables for GDP growth, but instead of changes in unemployment, it contains the unemployment rate, U_t. To create the change in unemployment use the SAS difference operator **dif**. For example, **dif(u)** yields $DU_t = \Delta U_t = U_t - U_{t-1}$. To obtain a second difference we add a numerical value to the operator; **dif2(u)** yields $\Delta DU_t = DU_t - DU_{t-1}$, or the difference of the differences. To create lags, use the SAS **lag** operator with a numerical value to indicate lag length. For example, **lag(g)** yields G_{t-1}, **lag2(g)** yields G_{t-2}, and so on.

In addition to the difference and lags, we add some date variables that are useful when creating graphs for time-series data. SAS represents dates as the number of days since January 1, 1960. SAS has several different formats to represent dates; we will use the day, month, year format **'ddmonyy'd**. The 'd' following the inputted date tells SAS to convert to a numerical date rather than read 'ddmonyy' as alphanumeric data. Below we create three sample dates.

```
data dates;                         * open data set;
a='1jan59'd;
b='1feb60'd;
c='1jan61'd;
run;
```

Print these dates

```
proc print data=dates;                    * print observations;
run;
```

```
Obs        a        b        c
1       -365       31      366
```

The SAS date for January 1, 1959 is -365 because this date occurred 365 days *before* January 1, 1960. Likewise, February 1, 1960 and January 1, 1961 occurred 31 and 366 days, respectively, after the base date.

In the *okun* example, the data are quarterly and run from 1985q2 through 2009q3, 98 observations. We create three new variables *DATE*, *YEAR*, and *QTR* for each observation, which requires a few additional commands. The SAS function **intnx** increments a date (or time) by a given interval. The format is **intnx('interval',start from,increment)**. Intervals supported by SAS include **'week'**, **'month'**, **'qtr'**, and **'year'** plus several others. Since we have quarterly data, we will use **'qtr'**, starting from 1985q1 (the period before our data begins) and updating by 1 quarter (the length between successive observations). The **retain** statement tells SAS to retain the value from the previous iteration when updating. Finally, the **format** statement is used to format the *DATE* variable that we create. SAS has many formatting options. We use the format **yyqc** which gives the year followed by quarter, separated by a colon.

Finally, we create separate year and quarter variables. The *YEAR* variable is our beginning year, 1985, plus the observation number divided by 4, since we have quarterly data, rounded down to the nearest integer. Thus, for observations 1-3, *YEAR* = 1985 + 0, for observations 4-7, *YEAR* = 1985 + 1, and so forth. The variable *QTR* is created using the **mod** function which has the format **mod (value, divisor)** and returns the remainder of *value / divisor*. Thus, *QTR* = 1 + 1 for observations 1, 5, 9, ..., *QTR* = 2 + 1 for observations 2, 6, 10, ..., and so forth.

The commands to create the difference, lag, and time variables is

```
data okun;
set okun;
du = dif(u);                              * create difference;
g1 = lag(g);                              * create lags;
g2 = lag2(g);
g3 = lag3(g);
retain date '1jan85'd;                    * date variable;
date=intnx('qtr',date,1);                 * update dates;
format date yyqc.;                        * format for date;
year = 1985 + int(_n_/4);                 * year;
qtr = mod(_n_, 4) + 1;                    * quarter;
run;
```

Lagging or differencing means that we lose early observations; the number lost is equal to the number of lags or differences. SAS indicates missing observations with a '.' To see this, print the first few observations

```
proc print data=okun(obs=10);             * print first 10 obs;
run;
```

Obs	g	u	du	g1	g2	g3	date	year	qtr
1	1.4	7.3	.	.	.	.	1985:2	1985	2
2	2.0	7.2	-0.1	1.4	.	.	1985:3	1985	3
3	1.4	7.0	-0.2	2.0	1.4	.	1985:4	1985	4
4	1.5	7.0	0.0	1.4	2.0	1.4	1986:1	1986	1
5	0.9	7.2	0.2	1.5	1.4	2.0	1986:2	1986	2
6	1.5	7.0	-0.2	0.9	1.5	1.4	1986:3	1986	3
7	1.2	6.8	-0.2	1.5	0.9	1.5	1986:4	1986	4
8	1.5	6.6	-0.2	1.2	1.5	0.9	1987:1	1987	1
9	1.6	6.3	-0.3	1.5	1.2	1.5	1987:2	1987	2
10	1.7	6.0	-0.3	1.6	1.5	1.2	1987:3	1987	3

9.2.2 Time-series plots

When investigating time-series data, the first diagnostic tools used is a simple time-series plot of the data. A time-series plot will reveal potential problems with the data and suggest ways to proceed statistically. We use **PROC GPLOT** to generate time-series plots for the *DU* and *G* series, respectively. These are the series plotted in Figure 9.4 (a) in (b) in *POE4*, page 345.

```
symbol1 interpol=join value=dot color=black;* symbol for plots;
axis1 order=(-0.50 to 1.25 by 0.25);
axis2 order=(-2 to 3 by 1);
proc gplot data=okun;
plot du*date / vaxis=axis1;              * du by date;
plot g*date / vaxis=axis2;               * g by date;
title 'Time-series plots for okun data';
run;
```

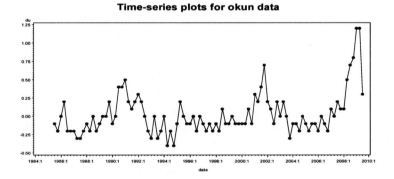

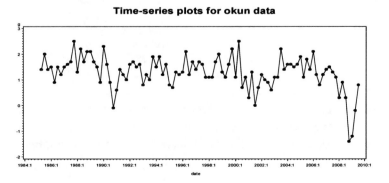

9.2.3 Model estimation

We are now ready to estimate the model. We first consider the model for $q=3$ lags:

$$DU_t = \alpha + \beta_0 G_t + \beta_1 G_{t-1} + \beta_2 G_{t-2} + \cdots + \beta_3 G_{t-3} + e_t, \qquad t = 4, \ldots, T$$

Note that for estimation purposes we begin with the 4th observation. This is due to the fact that the first three observations have missing values for G_{t-3}. This model can be estimated using **PROC REG**. However, we will use **PROC AUTOREG** since it is typically used to estimate dynamic models in SAS.

```
proc autoreg data=okun;
model du = g g1 g2 g3;
title 'proc autoreg with 3 distributed lags';
run;
```

The regression results match those in Table 9.2 of *POE4*.

The AUTOREG Procedure

Ordinary Least Squares Estimates

SSE	2.73516422	DFE				90
MSE	0.03039	Root MSE				0.17433
SBC	-44.662409	AIC				-57.431793
MAE	0.13705398	AICC				-56.757636
MAPE	73.46055	Regress R-Square				0.6524
Durbin-Watson	1.2741	Total R-Square				0.6524

Variable	DF	Estimate	Standard Error	t Value	Approx Pr > |t|
Intercept	1	0.5810	0.0539	10.78	<.0001
g	1	-0.2021	0.0330	-6.12	<.0001
g1	1	-0.1645	0.0358	-4.59	<.0001
g2	1	-0.0716	0.0353	-2.03	0.0456
g3	1	0.003303	0.0363	0.09	0.9276

Because the third lag is insignificant and takes the wrong sign, we re-estimate the model with only two lags. The resulting estimates are

Variable	DF	Estimate	Standard Error	t Value	Approx Pr > |t|
Intercept	1	0.5836	0.0472	12.36	<.0001
g	1	-0.2020	0.0324	-6.24	<.0001
g1	1	-0.1653	0.0335	-4.93	<.0001
g2	1	-0.0700	0.0331	-2.12	0.0371

You will note that we gain two degrees of freedom in the model with fewer lags; by dropping the third lag we gain one observation and are estimating one fewer parameter. You will also see that the **AIC** decreases to -60.951 and that the **SBC** decreases to -50.964 in the second model, which indicates that model with only two lags is preferable. Recall from Section 6.1.5 that SAS calculates AIC and SBC as

$$AIC = -2\ln(L) + 2k, \quad SBC = -2\ln(L) + \ln(N)k$$

See also Section 6.1.5 for code to match the calculation of the results from **PROC AUTOREG**.

The estimated coefficients can be used to produce **delay** and **interim multipliers**. The s-period **delay multiplier** is

$$\frac{\partial E(y_t)}{\partial x_{t-s}} = \beta_s$$

which is the effect of a change in x s-periods in the past on the average value of the dependent variable in the current period, when x is held constant in other periods. Setting $s = 0$ yields the **impact multiplier** β_0.

If x_t is increased by 1 unit and then maintained at its current level in subsequent periods $(t+1), (t+2), \ldots$ one can compute interim multipliers. An **interim multiplier** simply adds the immediate effect (the impact multiplier) to subsequent effects to measure the cumulative effect. The interim multiplier in period $t + 1$ is $\beta_0 + \beta_1$. In period 2, it is $\beta_0 + \beta_1 + \beta_2$, and so on. Also, an estimate of the normal growth rate that is necessary to maintain a constant unemployment rate is given by $\hat{G}_N = \hat{\alpha} / -\sum_{s=0}^{q} b_s$. Given the parameter estimates, we use SAS as a calculator to compute the interim multipliers for $s = 0, 1, 2$ as well as the normal growth rate.

```
data im;                        * new data set;
alpha = 0.5836;                 * intercept;
b0 = -0.2020;                   * coefficient lag0;
b1 = -0.1653;                   * coefficient lag1;
b2 = -0.0700;                   * coefficient lag2;
im0 = b0;                       * impact multiplier;
im1 = b0+b1;                    * interim multiplier 1;
im2 = b0+b1+b2;                 * interim multiplier 2;
ghat = alpha/-im2;              * normal growth rate;
proc print data=im;
var im0 im1 im2 ghat;           * variable list;
run;
```

The resulting output, as shown on *POE4*, page 346, is

Obs	im0	im1	im2	ghat
1	-0.202	-0.3673	-0.4373	1.33455

9.3 SERIAL CORRELATION

With time-series data, successive observations are likely to be correlated. A variable that exhibits correlation over time is said to be **autocorrelated** or **serially correlated**. Both observable time-series variables, such as DU or G, and the unobservable error, e, can be serially correlated. Serially correlated errors violate one of the assumptions of the Gauss-Markov theorem and thus have an effect on the properties of the traditional least squares estimator. Detecting autocorrelation in the least squares residuals is important because least squares may be inconsistent in this case.

To illustrate the concept of autocorrelation, we begin by examining the possibility of correlation between G_t and G_{t-1}. We then use the same methodology to examine correlation in the least squares residuals.

First, we generate a scatter plot between G_t and G_{t-1}.

```
symbol2 value=dot color=black;          * symbol for diagram;
proc gplot data=okun;
plot g1*g=2 / vaxis=axis2 haxis=axis2; * glag by g;
title 'Scatter diagram for Gt and Gt-1';
run;
```

The graph, as shown in Figure 9.5, page 348, of *POE4*, is

Scatter diagram for Gt and Gt-1

There appears to be a positive correlation between %GDP growth and its lag. Next, we will compute the numerical correlation between G_t and G_{t-1}, as well as between G_t and longer lags. The formula for this computation is

$$r_k = \frac{\sum_{t=k+1}^{T}(G_t - \bar{G})(G_{t-k} - \bar{G})}{\sum_{t=1}^{T}(G_t - \bar{G})^2} \qquad k = 1,2,\ldots \tag{9.2}$$

The sequence of correlations for $k = 1,2,\ldots$ is called a **correlogram**. A simple way to obtain a correlogram for a series is through **PROC ARIMA**. **PROC ARIMA** will be discussed further in Appendix 9A; we introduce it now in order to obtain the correlogram. The **identify** statement defines the series, G, and specifies that we want the first 12 autocorrelations.

```
ods listing gpath='c:\figures' style=journal;
ods graphics on;                        * must turn ODS on;
proc arima data=okun plots(unpack);     * initiate arima;
identify var=g nlag=12;                 * identify model;
```

```
title 'GDP growth series with ODS graphics';
run;
ods graphics off;                              * must turn ODS off;
```

The estimation output is

The ARIMA Procedure

Name of Variable = g

Mean of Working Series	1.276531
Standard Deviation	0.643619
Number of Observations	98

Autocorrelation Check for White Noise

To Lag	Chi-Square	DF	Pr > ChiSq	------------------Autocorrelations------------------					
6	49.47	6	<.0001	0.494	0.411	0.154	0.200	0.090	0.024
12	56.17	12	<.0001	-0.030	-0.082	0.044	-0.021	-0.087	-0.204

Note that SAS prints the first six autocorrelations horizontally across the first row and the next six in the second row. Thus, the autocorrelations are $r_1 = 0.494$, $r_2 = 0.411$, $r_3 = 0.154$, ..., $r_{12} = -0.204$. The column labeled **Chi-Square** contains the test statistic to jointly test whether the null hypothesis that the first 6 (and below that the first 12) autocorrelations are all zero against the alternative that at least one is nonzero. The column **Pr > Chisq** gives the p-value for this test. Thus, we conclude that at least one of the autocorrelations is significantly different from zero.

Including the ODS graphics generates a panel of four graphs. The option **Plots(unpack)** places the diagnostic graphs into separate files as opposed to placing all graphs in a single file. We are interested in the graph of the ACF, located in the file **SeriesACFPlot.png**. This graph plots the correlogram with 95% confidence intervals.

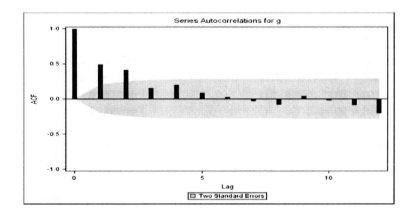

The correlogram is similar to Figure 9.6 in *POE4*, but has slightly different confidence bands. The 95% confidence bands appear in the shaded area. Autocorrelations that lie outside the bands are statistically different from zero. Approximate 95% confidence bands are computed in *POE4* using $\pm 2 / \sqrt{T} = 0.202$ (since $T = 98$). SAS uses a different method (Bartlett's) to compute the confidence bands and the results differ slightly from the simple approximation. In this example, we find that only the first two autocorrelations are significantly different from zero.

9.3.1 Residual correlogram

A residual correlogram is a graph that plots series of correlations between $\hat{e}_t$ and $\hat{e}_{t-k}$ against the time interval between the observations. To illustrate the correlogram for regression residuals, we introduce a new model which is a version of the Phillips curve, relating inflation, *INF*, to the change in unemployment, *DU*.

$$INF_t = \beta_1 + \beta_2 DU_t + e_t \tag{9.3}$$

The SAS data set *phillips_aus* contains 91 quarterly observations on inflation and unemployment rates in Australia for the period 1987q1 to 2009q3. Turn labels back on, open *phillips_aus*, examine its contents and turn off labels.

```
options label;                        * turn labels on;
data phillips;                        * open data set;
set 'phillips_aus';                   * read phillips_aus;
run;
proc contents data=phillips;          * examine contents;
run;
options nolabel;                      * turn labels off;
```

```
              Alphabetic List of Variables and Attributes

 #  Variable  Type  Len  Label

 1  inf       Num     8  Australian Inflation Rate
 2  u         Num     8  Australian Unemployment Rate  (Seasonally adjusted)
```

Next, create variables for change in unemployment, *DU*, as well as time variables.

```
data phillips;
set phillips;
du = dif(u);                          * create difference;
retain date '1oct86'd;                * date variable;
date=intnx('qtr',date,1);             * update dates;
format date yyqc.;                    * format for date;
year = 1987 + int((_n_-1)/4);         * year;
qtr = mod(_n_-1, 4) + 1;              * quarter;
run;
```

We are concerned with finding the correlogram for the least squares residuals

$$\hat{e}_t = INF_t - b_1 - b_2 DU_t \tag{9.4}$$

We estimate the model using **PROC AUTOREG**. The options **godfrey=1** and **dwprob** produce some test statistics that we will discuss in Section 9.4.

```
ods graphics on;                        * must turn ODS on;
proc autoreg data=phillips plots(unpack);
model inf = du / godfrey=1 dwprob;
output out=phillipsout r=ehat;          * save residuals;
title 'Phillips curve with ODS graphics';
run;
ods graphics off;                       * must turn ODS off;
```

The least squares results are

Variable	DF	Estimate	Standard Error	t Value	Approx Pr > |t|
Intercept	1	0.7776	0.0658	11.81	<.0001
du	1	-0.5279	0.2294	-2.30	0.0238

We use the **plots(unpack)** option to generate separate diagnostic plots. To find the residual correlogram, we look for the figure **ACFPlot**. The residual correlogram for the Phillips curve, which is similar to Figure 9.8 in *POE4*, is

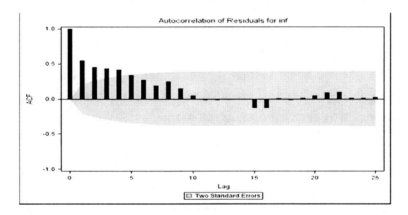

The height of each bar gives the estimated correlation between observations k periods apart and the shaded area gives the 95% confidence bounds. For this model, the first four autocorrelations are significantly different from zero. Thus, we have a strong indication of serially correlated errors. To obtain the values for the autocorrelations, use **PROC ARIMA** and the saved residuals.

```
proc arima data=phillipsout;            * initiate arima;
identify var=ehat nlag=12;              * identify model;
title 'residual autocorrelation function';
run;
```

The (edited) output is

Autocorrelation Check for White Noise

To Lag	Chi-Square	DF	Pr > ChiSq	------------------Autocorrelations------------------
6	100.87	6	<.0001	0.549 0.456 0.433 0.420 0.339 0.271
12	113.57	12	<.0001	0.191 0.251 0.153 0.050 -0.016 -0.013

Thus, the residual autocorrelations are $r_1 = 0.549$, $r_2 = 0.456$, $r_3 = 0.433$, ..., $r_{12} = -0.013$, which match the values given in *POE4*, page 353.

9.4 TESTING FOR SERIALLY CORRELATED ERRORS

The residual correlogram is one way to test for serially correlated errors. In this Section, we consider two additional tests: a Lagrange multiplier (*LM*) test and the Durbin-Watson (*DW*) test.

9.4.1 A Lagrange multipler (LM) test

A second test for serially correlated errors is based on the **Lagrange multiplier (*LM*) test** principle. The Lagrange multiplier test principle is discussed in Appendix C.8.4 of *POE4*. The test statistic is based on $T \times R^2$ from an auxiliary regression. For autocorrelation, the *LM* test is based on an auxiliary regression of least squares residuals on lagged least squares residuals and the original regressors.

For a model with serially correlated errors, $e_t = \rho e_{t-1} + v_t$, the regression model can be written as

$$y_t = \beta_1 + \beta_2 x_t + \rho e_{t-1} + v_t \qquad (9.5)$$

If e_{t-1} was observable, we could regress y_t on x_t and e_{t-1} and test the significance of the coefficient on e_{t-1}. Since e_{t-1} is unobservable, we will replace it with $\hat{e}_{t-1}$. In the context of the Phillips curve model, we estimate the regression model

$$INF_t = \beta_1 + \beta_2 DU_t + e_t$$

and save the residuals, $\hat{e}_t$. We then lag the residuals to get $\hat{e}_{t-1}$. Recall that in Section 9.3.1 we saved the residuals for this model in the dataset *phillipsout*.

Our next step is to estimate an auxiliary regression with $\hat{e}_t$ as the dependent variable and the lagged value $\hat{e}_{t-1}$ as an independent variable. Include all other independent variables from the original regression as well. In this case, the auxiliary regression is

$$\hat{e}_t = \gamma_1 + \gamma_2 DU_t + \rho \hat{e}_{t-1} + residual \qquad (9.6)$$

If the null hypothesis of no autocorrelation $H_0 : \rho = 0$ is true, then $LM = T \times R^2$ has an approximate $\chi^2(1)$ distribution where T and R^2 are the sample size and goodness-of-fit statistic, respectively, from the auxiliary regression. Rejection of the null hypothesis leads you to conclude there is significant autocorrelation.

The option **godfrey=1** included in the model statement carries out the *LM* test.

```
proc autoreg data=phillips plots(unpack);
model inf = du / godfrey=1;
output out=phillipsout r=ehat;
run;
```

In the Phillips curve example, this yields

```
Godfrey's Serial Correlation Test

Alternative              LM      Pr > LM

AR(1)                  27.5923    <.0001
```

The *LM* test statistic, 27.59, is greater than 5% critical value from a $\chi^2(1)$ distribution of 3.84 (*p*-value < .0001) and so we reject $H_0 : \rho = 0$. Note that SAS sets the first residual to zero rather than discarding it, and thus matches the alternative labeled (iv) in *POE4*, page 355.

We can also compute the *LM* test statistic by estimating the auxiliary regression ourselves. Since the lagged variable $\hat{e}_{t-1}$ appears in the regression we must either omit the first observation or set $\hat{e}_0 = 0$. The results are very similar regardless of which method you choose. We will set $\hat{e}_0 = 0$ since that is the method SAS follows. Create a new dataset with lagged residuals.

```
data actest;                          * new data set;
set phillipsout;                      * read data;
ehat1 = lag(ehat);                    * lagged residual;
if ehat1=. then ehat1=0;              * set missing to 0;
run;
```

Estimate the auxiliary regression (9.6) using **PROC AUTOREG**.

```
proc autoreg data=actest;
model ehat = du ehat1;                * auxiliary regression;
title 'LM test for serially correlated residuals';
run;
```

The required pieces of information (with $\hat{e}_0 = 0$) are given in the ANOVA table,

```
Dependent Variable        ehat

Ordinary Least Squares Estimates

SSE              23.6071112    DFE                      87
MSE                 0.27135    Root MSE            0.52091
SBC             148.464814    AIC              140.965385
MAE              0.36926306    AICC             141.244454
MAPE            129.002745    Regress R-Square     0.3066
Durbin-Watson        2.2475    Total R-Square       0.3066
```

Variable	DF	Estimate	Standard Error	t Value	Approx Pr > |t|
Intercept	1	-0.002163	0.0551	-0.04	0.9688
du	1	-0.1515	0.1937	-0.78	0.4362
ehat1	1	0.5588	0.0901	6.20	<.0001

Next use SAS as a calculator to can compute the test statistic $LM = T \times R^2$. Run the following to obtain the test statistic, the 95% critical value, and the p-value. The values for sample size (*T* = DFE + number parameters = 90) and R^2 come from the auxiliary regression output.

```
data lmtest;                        * create dataset;
q = 1;                              * number lag resids;
t = 90;                             * sample size;
r2 = 0.3066;                        * r-squared;
chisq = t*r2;                       * test statistic;
pval = 1 - probchi(chisq,q);        * p-value;
chisq_95 = cinv(.95,q);             * 0.95 percentile;
run;

proc print data=lmtest;             * print;
title 'LM test for serially correlated errors';
run;
```

The output shows that we reject the null hypothesis and conclude the errors are correlated.

```
            LM test for serially correlated errors

    Obs    q    t      r2      chisq         pval     chisq_95

     1     1    90    0.3066   27.594    .000000150    3.84146
```

9.4.2 Durbin-Watson test

A final test is the Durbin-Watson test. For a long time, the Durbin-Watson test was the standard test for $H_0 : \rho = 0$ in the AR(1) error model $e_t = \rho e_{t-1} + v_t$. It is less frequently used today because its critical values are less readily computed than those for other tests. Also, unlike the correlogram and *LM* tests, its distribution no longer holds when the equation contains a lagged dependent variable. However, the Durbin-Watson statistic is reported in most computer output.

It is assumed that the v_t are independent random errors with distribution $N(0, \sigma_v^2)$, and that the alternative hypothesis is one of positive autocorrelation. That is

$$H_0 : \rho = 0 \qquad H_1 : \rho > 0$$

The statistic used to test H_0 against H_1 is

$$d = \frac{\sum_{t=2}^{T}(\hat{e}_t - \hat{e}_{t-1})^2}{\sum_{t=1}^{T}\hat{e}_t^2} \tag{9.7}$$

where the $\hat{e}_t$ are the least squares residuals $\hat{e}_t = y_t - b_1 - b_2 x_t$. We can approximate the test statistic by

$$d \approx 2(1 - r_1) \tag{9.8}$$

where r_1 is the sample correlation between $\hat{e}_t$ and $\hat{e}_{t-1}$.

Traditionally, one would compare this value to a critical value. However, the critical value depends on the values of the explanatory variables. Fortunately, SAS is one of few softwares to produce a *p*-value for the exact *DW* test. To obtain the Durbin-Watson statistic and *p*-value we included the option **dwprob** in the model statement. This produces the following:

```
                    Durbin-Watson Statistics

     Order           DW     Pr < DW     Pr > DW

        1         0.8873     <.0001      1.0000
```

The first *p*-value (Pr < DW) is used for testing positive autocorrelation, which is the case in the Phillips curve example. Thus, we reject $H_0 : \rho = 0$ and conclude that $\rho > 0$.

9.5 ESTIMATION WITH SERIALLY CORRELATED ERRORS

A model with serially correlated errors of the form $e_t = \rho e_{t-1} + v_t$ is called a **first-order autoregressive** or **AR(1) model**. A model with q lagged errors is an AR(q) model. As long as the model does not contain lags of the dependent variable as regressors, the least squares estimator is consistent even if the errors follow an AR(q) model. However, much like with heteroskedastic errors, least squares is no longer efficient and the usual standard errors are no longer correct, leading to invalid hypothesis tests and confidence intervals. In this Section, we discuss alternative estimation strategies.

9.5.1 Least squares and HAC standard errors

Although the usual least squares standard errors are not correct, we can compute consistent standard errors for the least squares estimator just as we did in heteroskedastic models using an estimator proposed by Newey and West. The Newey-West heteroskedasticity and autocorrelation consistent (also known as HAC) standard errors are analogous to the heteroskedasticity consistent standard errors introduced in Chapter 8 of *POE4*. They are consistent in both AR(1) models and models that have higher order autocorrelated errors. Also, by using HAC standard errors, we can avoid having to specify the precise nature of the autocorrelated error model that is required for more efficient alternative estimators.

HAC standard errors are not as automatic as the robust standard error estimator in Chapter 8, however. To be robust with respect to autocorrelation one has to specify how far away in time the autocorrelation is likely to be significant. Essentially, the autocorrelated errors over the chosen time window are averaged in the computation of HAC standard errors; you have to specify how many periods over which to average and how much weight to assign each residual in that average.

The weighted average is called a **kernel** and the number of errors to average is called **bandwidth**. One can think of the kernel as the weighted average and the bandwidth as the number of terms to average. For the HAC standard errors, the Bartlett kernel ('BART') is used and the researcher selects the bandwidth.

The optimal bandwidth is generally not known, although there has been much discussion about its selection. Several methods have been proposed to compute bandwidth based on sample size. These include $B = T^{1/4}$, $B = 0.75T^{1/3}$, and $B = 4(T/100)^{2/9}$. The larger your sample size, *T*, the larger the bandwidth is. While some programs use a default method for selecting the bandwidth, SAS requires you to input a bandwidth. In addition, SAS does not have an option for requesting the HAC standard errors in **PROC REG** as it does for the heteroskedasticity consistent standard errors. To obtain the HAC standard errors you must use **PROC MODEL**.

Using the *phillips_aus* data, we run the original least squares regression but request the HAC standard errors. We request the HAC standard errors in the **fit** statement. This option is only available in SAS when GMM (Generalized Method of Moments) is chosen as the estimation procedure. However, in the linear regression model the GMM estimates are equivalent to the least squares estimates. The syntax to request the Newey-West kernel is **kernel=(bart,L+1,0)**, where *L* is the bandwidth or "lag length". In the *phillips_aus* data we have 90 observations. The three bandwidth statistics above all yield values between 3 and 4. We round this down to 3 and enter *L* + 1 = 4 in the kernel statement.

```
proc model data=phillips;
label b1='intercept'
      b2='du';
inf = b1 + b2*du;
fit inf / gmm kernel=(bart,4,0);        * fit 'inf' with HAC std errors;
title 'Phillips curve with HAC standard errors';
run;
```

The HAC standard errors produced by **PROC MODEL** match those given in *POE4*, page 358.

Parameter	Estimate	Approx Std Err	t Value	Approx Pr > |t|	Label
b1	0.777621	0.1030	7.55	<.0001	intercept
b2	-0.52786	0.3127	-1.69	0.0950	du

Note that the parameter estimates are identical to the least squares estimates in Section 9.3, but the HAC standard errors are larger. Thus, confidence intervals are wider with the HAC standard errors compared to the least squares standard errors. If we ignored the autocorrelation, we would tend to overstate the reliability of the least squares estimates.

There are a few disadvantages to using least squares estimates with HAC standard errors. First, one must specify the bandwidth for which there are several possible alternatives. More importantly, this technique does not address the issue of finding an estimator that is more efficient than ordinary least squares. We next consider using nonlinear least squares to efficiently estimate the parameters of the AR(1) model.

9.5.2 Nonlinear least squares

Continuing with the Phillips curve example, we estimate the model under the assumption that the errors follow an AR(1) model. Under this assumption, the model can be written as

$$INF_t = \beta_1 + \beta_2 DU_t + e_t \quad \text{with} \quad e_t = \rho e_{t-1} + v_t$$

As in *POE4*, we can use some algebra to obtain combine these equations as

$$INF_t = \beta_1(1-\rho) + \beta_2 DU_t + \rho INF_{t-1} - \rho\beta_2 DU_{t-1} + v_t \tag{9.9}$$

This model is nonlinear in the parameters, but has an additive white noise error. SAS has multiple options for estimating this model. First, we estimate the model using **PROC AUTOREG**, which is designed to account for autoregressive errors. Nonlinear least squares is called "unconditional least squares" in **PROC AUTOREG**, so we specify **method = uls** to obtain the nonlinear least squares estimates. The **nlag** option in the model statement is used to specify the number of lagged errors, which is 1 in the Phillips curve example.

```
ods graphics on;                        * must turn ODS on;
proc autoreg data=phillips;
model inf=du / nlag=1 method=uls;       * specify AR(1) errors;
title 'AR(1) error model with ODS graphics';
run;
ods graphics off;                       * must turn ODS off;
```

At the top of the output you will see the least squares estimates and some other preliminary estimates. We are interested in the nonlinear least squares estimates given at the bottom of the output.

Variable	DF	Estimate	Standard Error	t Value	Approx Pr > |t|
Intercept	1	0.7865	0.1244	6.32	<.0001
du	1	-0.7048	0.2480	-2.84	0.0056
AR1	1	-0.5652	0.0898	-6.29	<.0001

The parameter estimates and standard errors produced by **PROC AUTOREG** differ slightly from those reported in *POE4*, page 362. These slight differences are due to the numerical procedures used to minimize the nonlinear sum of squares function. Whereas many software packages drop the first observation, the procedures in **PROC AUTOREG** use information from all observations. In large samples, the difference between dropping the first observation or not will become very small.

$$\widehat{INF} = 0.7865 - 0.7048DU$$
$$(se) \quad (0.1244) \quad (0.2480)$$

The estimate labeled AR1 is the estimate of *negative* ρ. The way SAS specifies the autoregressive error model is $\hat{e}_t = -\rho\hat{e}_{t-1} + v_t$. The minus sign should be ignored. So the estimated AR(1) equation for the Phillips curve model is

$$\hat{e}_t = 0.5652\hat{e}_{t-1}$$
$$(0.0898)$$

Alternatively, we can estimate the parameters in equation (9.9) directly using **PROC MODEL** (or **PROC NLIN**). To do so, we first need to create lags for *INF* and *DU*.

```
data phillips;                          * open data set;
set phillips;                           * read data;
inf1 = lag(inf);                        * lag of inf;
du1 = lag(du);                          * lag of du;
run;
```

The following is **PROC MODEL** code that estimates the nonlinear equation (9.9).

```
proc model data=phillips;                    * initiate model;
label b1='intercept'
      b2='du'
      rho='AR(1)';
inf = b1*(1-rho)+rho*inf1+b2*du-rho*b2*du1; * nonlinear model;
fit inf;
title 'AR(1) error model using PROC MODEL';
run;
```

The estimates from **PROC MODEL** below are nearly identical to the results in *POE4*, page 362.

Parameter	Estimate	Approx Std Err	t Value	Approx Pr > |t|	Label
b1	0.761082	0.1245	6.11	<.0001	intercept
b2	-0.69405	0.2479	-2.80	0.0063	du
rho	0.557324	0.0902	6.18	<.0001	AR(1)

Finally, the **PROC NLIN** code below gives results that are identical to those in *POE4*. The **parms** statement specifies the model parameters as well as starting values for the iterations. Here we set the starting values to zero. If your initial starting values do not lead to convergence, trying alternative starting values may help.

```
proc nlin data=phillips method=gauss;
parms b1=0 b2=0 rho=0;                        * parameter starting values;
model inf = b1*(1-rho)+rho*inf1+b2*du-rho*b2*du1;
title 'AR(1) error model using PROC NLIN';
run;
```

While **PROC NLIN** is useful for estimating nonlinear model, it does not provide graphs such as the residual ACF that are produced by **PROC AUTOREG** and **PROC MODEL**.

9.5.3 Estimating a more general model

As on pages 362 and 363 of *POE4*, we now consider the model

$$INF_t = \delta + \theta_1 INF_{t-1} + \delta_0 DU_t + \delta_1 DU_{t-1} + v_t$$

which is a more general form of the model in equation (9.9). This model is linear in the parameters and can be estimated by least squares. This model is related to the previous model by the relationships

$$\delta = \beta_1(1-\rho) \qquad \delta_0 = \beta_2 \qquad \delta_1 = -\rho\beta_2 \qquad \theta_1 = \rho$$

The AR(1) model is a restricted version of the general model given here. This model is equivalent to the AR(1) model if $\delta_1 = -\theta_1\delta_0$.

Using the data with lagged variables *INF1* and *DU1* that we created in the previous Section, the general model can be estimated by ordinary least squares.

```
proc autoreg data=phillips;
model inf = inf1 du du1;
title 'General ARDL model using PROC AUTOREG';
run;
```

The estimates, which match those in *POE4*, page 364, are

Variable	DF	Estimate	Standard Error	t Value	Approx Pr > |t|
Intercept	1	0.3336	0.0899	3.71	0.0004
inf1	1	0.5593	0.0908	6.16	<.0001
du	1	-0.6882	0.2499	-2.75	0.0072
du1	1	0.3200	0.2575	1.24	0.2175

The estimate $\hat{\delta}_0 = -0.6882$ is similar to the least squares estimate from the original equation relating *INF* to *DU*, while the estimate $\hat{\theta}_1 = 0.5593$ is very close to the correlation obtained using least squares residuals. Examining the implied relationship between the restricted model in equation (9.9) and the general model, recall that the model in equation (9.9) imposes the restriction $\delta_1 = -\theta_1\delta_0$. We observe that $-\hat{\theta}_1\hat{\delta}_0 = -(0.5593)(-0.6882) = 0.3849$, which appears to be fairly close to the $\hat{\delta}_1 = 0.3200$.

Under the general model we can test this restriction, and thus the validity of the AR(1) model, by testing the null hypothesis $H_0 : \delta_1 = -\theta_1\delta_0$. Unfortunately, the test is complicated somewhat because the hypothesis involves an equation that is nonlinear in the parameters. The **test** statement in **PROC AUTOREG** can only be used to test linear hypotheses. To test this nonlinear hypothesis, we can use **PROC MODEL**.

```
/* test of nonlinear hypothesis using PROC MODEL */
proc model data=phillips;                 * initiate model;
label delta='intercept'
      theta1='inf1'
      delta0='du'
      delta1='du1';
inf = delta+theta1*inf1+delta0*du+delta1*du1;
fit inf;
test delta1 = -theta1*delta0;             * test HO: d1=-theta1*d0;
title 'ARDL model with test of HO:delta1=-theta1*delta0';
run;
```

The result of the chi-square (Wald) test, which matches the result on page 364 of *POE4* is

Test Results

Test	Type	Statistic	Pr > ChiSq	Label
Test0	Wald	0.11	0.7376	delta1 = -theta1*delta0

The p-value for our test statistic is 0.7376, and so we fail to reject the null hypothesis. Thus, the restricted model in Section 9.5.2 may be appropriate.

9.6 AUTOREGRESSIVE DISTRIBUTED LAG MODELS

An **autoregressive distributed lag** (ARDL) model is one that contains both lagged x's and lagged y's. A model with p lags of y and q lags of x is called ARDL(p,q) model, and has the general form

$$y_t = \delta + \delta_0 x_t + \delta_1 x_{t-1} + \cdots + \delta_q x_{t-q} + \theta_1 y_{t-1} + \cdots + \theta_p y_{t-p} + v_t \qquad (9.10)$$

The general model that we estimated in Section 9.5.3 was an ARDL(1,1) model. One advantage of an ARDL model is that by including a sufficient number of lags of y and x, we can eliminate serial correlation in the errors. In this Section, we experiment with different lag lengths in both the Phillips curve and Okun's Law equations.

9.6.1 The Phillips curve

The idea is to choose a model with an appropriate number of lags so as to eliminate serial correlation in the errors. Since theory does not necessarily help in the selection of the appropriate number of lags, we will examine the *AIC* and *SBC* statistics to find the smallest values. Note that, as shown in Section 6.1.5 of this manual, the *AIC* value that SAS uses is T times the AIC value in equation (9.54) in *POE4* plus the constant $[1 + \ln(2\pi)]$. In the ARDL model from Section 9.5.3, the coefficient for the lagged *DU* term was not significantly different from zero. Thus, we drop that term and estimate an ARDL(1,0) model.

```
proc autoreg data=phillips;
model inf = inf1 du / godfrey=5;
title 'proc autoreg ARDL(1,0) model';
run;
```

This generates the estimated regression equation given in equation (9.56), page 367, of *POE4*. The option **godfrey=5** generates the *LM* test statistics and p- values for autocorrelation of orders one to five. These match the p- values given in Table 9.3, page 368, of *POE4*.

```
                      proc autoreg ARDL(1,0) model


                          The AUTOREG Procedure
                      Dependent Variable      inf
                      Ordinary Least Squares Estimates
```

SSE	23.5905366	DFE	87
MSE	0.27116	Root MSE	0.52073
SBC	148.401602	AIC	140.902173
MAE	0.3729657	AICC	141.181243
MAPE	88.5099613	HQC	143.926384
Durbin-Watson	2.2495	Regress R-Square	0.3464
		Total R-Square	0.3464

```
            Godfrey's Serial Correlation Test

       Alternative              LM      Pr > LM

       AR(1)                 4.1301      0.0421
       AR(2)                 5.1231      0.0772
       AR(3)                 5.2208      0.1563
       AR(4)                 9.5541      0.0486
       AR(5)                12.4848      0.0287


                Parameter Estimates

                                Standard            Approx
     Variable     DF   Estimate     Error   t Value  Pr > |t|

     Intercept     1     0.3548    0.0876      4.05    0.0001
     inf1          1     0.5282    0.0851      6.21   <.0001
     du            1    -0.4909    0.1921     -2.55    0.0124
```

The *p*-values indicate there is significant serial correlation with the first, fourth, and fifth lagged residuals. After experimenting with several models, we select an ARDL(4,0) model. (Note: you will need to create several lags of both variables in order to experiment with different ARDL models.) After creating the appropriate number of lags, we can estimate the ARDL(4,0) model.

```
proc autoreg data=phillips;
model inf = inf1 inf2 inf3 inf4 du / godfrey=5;
title 'proc autoreg ARDL(4,0) model';
run;
```

The results for the ARDL(4,0) model, which match those of equation (9.57) on page 368 of *POE4*, are

```
             proc autoreg ARDL(4,0) model
                 The AUTOREG Procedure
              Dependent Variable     inf
             Ordinary Least Squares Estimates

    SSE           18.2333588   DFE                      81
    MSE              0.22510   Root MSE            0.47445
    SBC          137.739742    AIC             122.944294
    MAE           0.33041057   AICC            123.994294
    MAPE          83.6909182   HQC             128.901965
    Durbin-Watson     2.0469   Regress R-Square     0.4584
                               Total R-Square       0.4584

           Gofrey's Serial Correlation Test

       Alternative              LM      Pr > LM

       AR(1)                 0.5041      0.4777
       AR(2)                 2.5655      0.2773
       AR(3)                 2.7972      0.4240
       AR(4)                 6.7213      0.1514
       AR(5)                 6.7930      0.2365
```

```
                        Parameter Estimates

                                   Standard              Approx
        Variable    DF    Estimate     Error   t Value   Pr > |t|

        Intercept    1      0.1001    0.0983      1.02    0.3114
        inf1         1      0.2354    0.1016      2.32    0.0230
        inf2         1      0.1213    0.1038      1.17    0.2457
        inf3         1      0.1677    0.1050      1.60    0.1140
        inf4         1      0.2819    0.1014      2.78    0.0067
        du           1     -0.7902    0.1885     -4.19    <.0001
```

The *AIC* and *SBC* are considerably smaller for this model. In addition, we can reject serial correlation for the first five lagged errors.

9.6.2 Okun's Law

After experimenting with several specifications, we estimate an ARDL(1,1) model for the Okun's Law equation. Remember to create appropriate lagged variables in the data set before estimating this model.

```
proc autoreg data=okun;
model du = du1 g g1 / godfrey=5;
title 'proc autoreg ARDL(1,1) model for Okuns law';
run;
```

The (edited) results, which match those in equation (9.59) on page 370 of *POE4*, are

```
              Godfrey's Serial Correlation Test

        Alternative         LM      Pr > LM

        AR(1)           0.1697       0.6804
        AR(2)           0.2713       0.8731
        AR(3)           3.8964       0.2729
        AR(4)           6.1406       0.1889
        AR(5)           8.2256       0.1442


                   Parameter Estimates

                                   Standard              Approx
        Variable    DF    Estimate     Error   t Value   Pr > |t|

        Intercept    1      0.3780    0.0578      6.54    <.0001
        du1          1      0.3501    0.0846      4.14    <.0001
        g            1     -0.1841    0.0307     -6.00    <.0001
        g1           1     -0.0992    0.0368     -2.69    0.0084
```

We choose this specification because it has the lowest *AIC* and *SBC*, and the *LM* tests fail to reject the null hypothesis of zero autocorrelations for the first five lagged errors.

9.6.3 Autoregressive models

In this Section, we focus on estimating pure autoregressive models, which are a special case of the ARDL model with no distributed lag components. An autoregressive model of order p, denoted AR(p), is given by

$$y_t = \delta + \theta_1 y_{t-1} + \theta_2 y_{t-2} + \cdots + \theta_p y_{t-p} + v_t \tag{9.11}$$

Using the *okun* data, consider an AR(2) model for GDP growth

$$G_t = \delta + \theta_1 G_{t-1} + \theta_2 G_{t-2} + v_t$$

Estimate the model using **PROC AUTOREG**. Turning on **ODS graphics** produces many useful graphs, including the residual correlogram.

```
ods graphics on;                        * must turn ODS on;
proc autoreg data=okun;
model g = g1 g2 / godfrey=5;
title 'proc autoreg AR(2) model for Okuns law';
run;
ods graphics off;                       * must turn ODS off;
```

The (edited) results, which match those in equation (9.61) on page 371 of *POE4*, are

Godfrey's Serial Correlation Test

Alternative	LM	Pr > LM
AR(1)	1.6632	0.1972
AR(2)	2.6534	0.2654
AR(3)	3.7988	0.2840
AR(4)	4.9035	0.2973
AR(5)	5.8278	0.3233

Variable	DF	Estimate	Standard Error	t Value	Approx Pr > |t|
Intercept	1	0.4657	0.1433	3.25	0.0016
g1	1	0.3770	0.1000	3.77	0.0003
g2	1	0.2462	0.1029	2.39	0.0187

The *LM* test indicates no serial correlation for the first five lags. The residual correlogram (not shown) indicates no significant autocorrelations, except perhaps at lag 12, which is sufficiently far away so that we are not concerned with it.

9.7 FORECASTING

In this Section, we consider how to obtain forecasts for an AR model. We use SAS as a calculator to obtain short-term forecasts, typically up to 3 periods into the future. Then we examine a second forecasting procedure, exponential smoothing.

9.7.1 Forecasting with an AR model

In Section 9.6.3, we estimated an AR(2) model for GDP growth

$$G_t = 0.4657 + 0.3770G_{t-1} + 0.2462G_{t-2}$$

Suppose we now wish to forecast GDP growth for the next three quarters. Growth rates for the previous two quarters are $G_t = G_{2009Q3} = 0.8$ and $G_{t-1} = G_{2009Q2} = -0.2$. Updating the time subscripts, our model forecasts for the next three quarters are

$$\hat{G}_{t+1} = 0.4657 + 0.3770G_t + 0.2462G_{t-1} = 0.4657 + 0.3770(0.8) + 0.2462(-0.2) = 0.7181$$

$$\hat{G}_{t+2} = 0.4657 + 0.3770\hat{G}_{t+1} + 0.2462G_t = 0.4657 + 0.3770(0.7181) + 0.2462(0.8) = 0.9334$$

$$\hat{G}_{t+3} = 0.4657 + 0.3770\hat{G}_{t+2} + 0.2462\hat{G}_{t+1} = 0.4657 + 0.3770(0.9334) + 0.2462(0.7181) = 0.9944$$

In addition we can calculate the forecast errors for the next three periods in order to develop interval estimates. As shown in *POE4*, page 374, the forecast error variances are

$$\sigma_1^2 = \text{var}(u_1) = \sigma_v^2$$

$$\sigma_2^2 = \text{var}(u_2) = \sigma_v^2(1+\theta_1^2)$$

$$\sigma_3^2 = \text{var}(u_3) = \sigma_v^2((\theta_1^2+\theta_2)^2 + \theta_1^2 + 1)$$

As expected, the forecast error variance grows larger the farther we forecast into the future. Here we use SAS to calculate the forecasts, the standard error of each forecast, and a 95% confidence interval for each forecast. The **sigmav = 0.55269** is the **Root MSE** from the AR(2) model.

```
/* generate forecast */
data ar_forecast;                                    * new data set;
t = 96;                                              * number observations;
k = 3;                                               * number parameters;
gt = 0.8;
gt_1 = -0.2;
delta = 0.4657;                                      * intercept;
theta1 = 0.3770;                                     * coefficient lag1;
theta2 = 0.2462;                                     * coefficient lag2;
sigmav = 0.55269;                                    * sigma-v;
ghat1 = delta + theta1*gt + theta2*gt_1;             * 1-step ahead forecast;
ghat2 = delta + theta1*ghat1 + theta2*gt;            * 2-step ahead forecast;
ghat3 = delta + theta1*ghat2 + theta2*ghat1;         * 3-step ahead forecast;
sef1 = sigmav;                                       * se of forecast;
sef2 = sigmav*sqrt(1+theta1**2);
sef3 = sigmav*sqrt((theta1**2+theta2)**2+theta1**2+1);
lb1 = ghat1-tinv(.975,t-k)*sef1;
ub1 = ghat1+tinv(.975,t-k)*sef1;
lb2 = ghat2-tinv(.975,t-k)*sef2;
ub2 = ghat2+tinv(.975,t-k)*sef2;
lb3 = ghat3-tinv(.975,t-k)*sef3;
```

```
    ub3 = ghat3+tinv(.975,t-k)*sef3;
    proc print data=ar_forecast;
    var ghat1 sef1 lb1 ub1;
    title '1-step ahead forecast';
    proc print dara=ar_forecast;
    var ghat2 sef2 lb2 ub2;
    title '2-step ahead forecast';
    proc print data=ar_forecast;
    var ghat3 sef3 lb3 ub3;
    title '3-step ahead forecast';
    run;
```

This produces the following, which match the forecasts and intervals given in Table 9.7 on page 374 of *POE4*.

Obs	ghat1	sef1	lb1	ub1
1	0.71806	0.55269	-0.37947	1.81559

Obs	ghat2	sef2	lb2	ub2
1	0.93337	0.59066	-0.23957	2.10631

Obs	ghat3	sef3	lb3	ub3
1	0.99437	0.62845	-0.25361	2.24234

9.7.2 Exponential smoothing

Exponential smoothing is another method for forecasting one period into the future and for smoothing a data series over the sample period. Like forecasting with the AR model, exponential smoothing does not require utilizing information from any other variable. The basic idea is that the forecast for the next period is a weighted average of the forecast for the current period and the actual realized value in the current period.

$$\hat{Y}_{t+1} = \alpha Y_t + (1-\alpha)\hat{Y}_t$$

Using the series for GDP growth, a forecast from exponential smoothing is given by

$$\hat{G}_{t+1} = \alpha G_t + (1-\alpha)\hat{G}_t$$

The series $\hat{G}_t$ is the smoothed version of G_t. The degree of smoothing is controlled by the smoothing parameter, α. Smaller values of α imply greater smoothing. The value of α can reflect one's belief about the relative weight of current information or it can be estimated from historical information by minimizing the sum of squares of the **one-step forecast errors**

$$\sum_{t=2}^{T}(G_t - \hat{G}_t)^2 = \sum_{t=2}^{T}(G_t - (\alpha G_{t-1} + (1-\alpha)\hat{G}_{t-1})^2$$

Following *POE4*, page 377, we generate two smoothed series using $\alpha = 0.38$ and $\alpha = 0.8$. **PROC FORECAST** is used to obtain the exponentially smoothed forecasts. We specify **method=expo** to indicate we want to use exponential smoothing. The value of α is specified using the **weight** option. **Trend=1** indicates that we want to use single exponential smoothing (as opposed to more advanced smoothing techniques) and **lead=1** indicates that we are forecasting a single period into the future. We write the forecast values to the dataset *g_pred* while **outset** saves some summary statistics to the dataset *est*. Finally, the **var** statement indicates the series we wish to smooth and the **id** statement identifies the observations and places the appropriate forecast with each date. The code below generates to forecast for $\alpha = 0.38$

```
proc forecast data=okun interval=qtr method=expo weight=0.38 trend=1
              lead=1 out=g_pred outest=est outfull;
var g;
id date;
run;
proc print data=est;
title 'exponential smoothing with alpha=0.38';
run;
```

This output includes alpha (**weight**) and the forecast value (**S1**), as well as many other statistics that we do not show here.

Obs	_TYPE_	date	g
4	WEIGHT	2009:3	0.38
5	S1	2009:3	0.0535653

The forecast, $\hat{G}_{t+1} = 0.0536$ is given by 'S1' and matches the value in *POE4*, page 378. We can plot the actual and smoothed series using **PROC SGPLOT**.

```
proc sgplot data=g_pred;
series x=date y=g / group=_type_;
yaxis values=(-2 to 3 by 1);
xaxis values=('1apr85'd to '1jan04'd by qtr);
run;
```

This generates the following graph, which matches Figure 9.12(a) on page 377 of *POE4*. The graph will be sent to the destination specified in **ODS graphics**. Since we earlier specified the path as '**c:\figures**', we will find the figure **SGPlot.png** there.

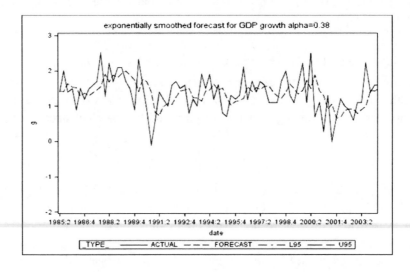

We can use the same code with **weight=0.8** to obtain the forecast $\hat{G}_{t+1} = 0.5613$, which matches the forecast in *POE4*, page 378 and generate the graph of the smoothed series in Figure 9.12(b) on page 377 of *POE4*.

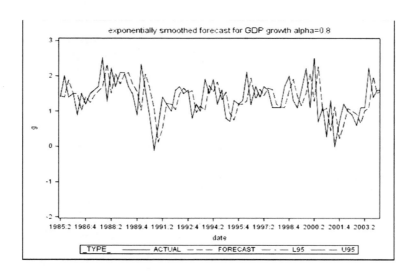

9.8 MULTIPLIER ANALYSIS

Multiplier analysis refers to the effect, and timing of the effect, of a change in one variable on the outcome of another variable. The simplest form of multiplier analysis is based on finite distributed lag model, such as that discussed in Section 9.2.3. We now turn our attention to multipliers for an ARDL model, which are similar to those for the finite distributed lag model.

$$\beta_s = \frac{\partial E(y_t)}{\partial x_{t-s}} = s \text{ period delay multiplier}$$

$$\sum_{j=0}^{s} \beta_j = s \text{ period interim multiplier}$$

$$\sum_{j=0}^{\infty} \beta_j = \text{total multiplier}$$

Adding the autoregressive terms makes the analysis a little harder. We first need to transform the ARDL model such that it is an infinite distributed lag model (which can be done for an AR model).

The ARDL(1,1) for Okun's law is

$$DU_t = \delta + \theta_1 DU_{t-1} + \delta_0 G_t + \delta_1 G_{t-1} + v_t$$

or, written with the **lag operator**, L, where $Ly_t = y_{t-1}$

$$(1 - \theta_1 L)DU_t = \delta + (\delta_0 + \delta_1 L)G_t + v_t$$

$$DU_t = (1 - \theta_1 L)^{-1}\delta + (1 - \theta_1 L)^{-1}(\delta_0 + \delta_1 L)G_t + (1 - \theta_1 L)^{-1}v_t$$

$$DU_t = \alpha + \beta_0 G_t + \beta_1 G_{t-1} + \beta_2 G_{t-2} + \beta_3 G_{t-3} + \ldots + e_t$$

This is an infinite distributed lag model. The distributed lag weights describe how the impact of a change in the growth of GDP on the rate of change in unemployment is distributed over time. The first lag weights are given in *POE4* as

$$\beta_0 = \delta_0$$
$$\beta_1 = \delta_1 + \beta_0 \theta_1$$
$$\beta_j = \beta_{j-1}\theta_1 \qquad \text{for } j \geq 2$$

Recall from Section 9.6.2 that the estimated ARDL(1,1) model is

$$DU_t = 0.3780 + 0.3501 DU_{t-1} - 0.1841 G_t - 0.0992 G_{t-1}$$

As shown on page 381 of *POE4*, the impact multiplier and the delay multipliers for the first four quarters are

$$\hat{\beta}_0 = \hat{\delta}_0 = -0.1841$$
$$\hat{\beta}_1 = \hat{\delta}_1 + \hat{\beta}_0 \hat{\theta}_1 = -0.0992 - 0.1841 \times 0.3501 = -0.1636$$
$$\hat{\beta}_2 = \hat{\beta}_1 \hat{\theta}_1 = -0.1636 \times 0.3501 = -0.0573$$
$$\hat{\beta}_3 = \hat{\beta}_2 \hat{\theta}_1 = -0.0573 \times 0.3501 = -0.0201$$
$$\hat{\beta}_4 = \hat{\beta}_3 \hat{\theta}_1 = -0.0201 \times 0.3501 = -0.0070$$

The following code uses SAS as a calculator to obtain these values.

```
/* calculate impact multipliers */
data im;                              * new data set;
delta0 = -0.1841;                     * lag0 g;
delta1 = -0.0992;                     * lag1 g;
theta1 = 0.3501;                      * lag1 du;
b0 = delta0;                          * impact mulitplier;
b1 = delta1+b0*theta1;                * interim multiplier 1;
b2 = b1*theta1;                       * interim multiplier 2;
b3 = b2*theta1;                       * interim multiplier 3;
b4 = b3*theta1;                       * interim multiplier 4;
proc print data=im;
var b0 b1 b2 b3 b4;                   * variable list;
title 'impact and first four interim mulipliers';
run;
```

This produces the following, which match the results in *POE4*.

impact and first four interim mulipliers

Obs	b0	b1	b2	b3	b4
1	-0.1841	-0.16365	-0.057295	-0.020059	-.007022656

APPENDIX 9A ESTIMATION AND FORECASTING WITH PROC ARIMA

The **ARIMA** procedure in SAS is used to estimate all types of dynamic models and to generate forecasts. We can use this procedure to estimate the models discussed in Chapter 9, as well as more complicated models that you may encounter in a course on time-series econometrics.

There are three main components when using **PROC ARIMA**. First, an **identify** statement is used to examine the time series and determine the appropriate model. The **estimate** statement is used to carry out the model estimation. Finally, the **forecast** statement can be used to produce forecasts and confidence intervals for a specified number of time periods. In this appendix, we use **PROC ARIMA** to estimate several of the models that are discussed in Chapter 9 of *POE4*.

9A.1 Finite distributed lag models in PROC ARIMA

First, consider the **finite distributed lag model** discussed in Section 9.2 of this manual. SAS and many time-series texts refer to these models as **transfer function models**. In this section, we will use **PROC ARIMA** to estimate the finite distributed lag models discussed in Section 9.2.3.

We will always turn on **ODS graphics** when using **PROC ARIMA** since it produces many useful graphs. We invoke **PROC ARIMA** and specify **data=okun**. In the identification statement, we include **var=du** to indicate that *DU* is the endogenous variable. As we saw in Section 9.3, the identification statement produces several graphs including the series ACF for the endogenous variable. Now, we also include the option **crosscorr=g** to indicate that *G* is an exogenous variable that may help explain *DU*.

```
ods graphics on;                        * must turn ODS on;
proc arima data=okun plots(unpack);     * initiate arima;
identify var=du crosscorr=g nlag=12;    * identify model;
run;
ods graphics off;                       * must turn ODS off;
```

This generates the **cross-correlation function (CCF)**. A **cross-correlogram** plots series of cross-correlations between y_t and x_{t-j} against the time interval between the observations, $j=1,2,...,m$. The **crosscorr** function in **PROC ARIMA** produces cross-correlations at both lags and leads, where the leads are specified as *negative* lags in the correlogram. Thus, we are interested in the right hand side or positive values (which represent lags) in the cross-correlogram of *DU* and *G* below

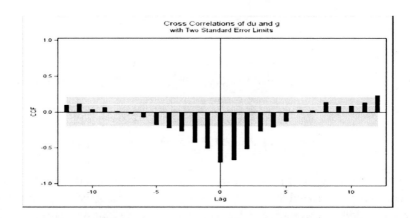

We observe that the cross-correlations at lags 1-3 lie outside the confidence bounds. Lags 4 and 12 are marginally significant, but $q=3$ seems to be an appropriate number of lagged values of G to include in the model. To estimate the distributed lag model we use

```
estimate input=((1 2 3) g) method=uls; * specify model;
run;
```

The **input** statement indicates the exogenous variable and the number of lags. **Input((1 2 3) g)** tells SAS to include 1-, 2-, and 3-period lags of the variable G. The (edited) results, which match those in Table 9.2, page 346 of *POE4* are:

The ARIMA Procedure

Unconditional Least Squares Estimation

Parameter	Estimate	Standard Error	t Value	Approx Pr > |t|	Lag	Variable	Shift
MU	0.58097	0.05389	10.78	<.0001	0	du	0
NUM1	-0.20205	0.03301	-6.12	<.0001	0	g	0
NUM1,1	0.16454	0.03582	4.59	<.0001	1	g	0
NUM1,2	0.07156	0.03530	2.03	0.0456	2	g	0
NUM1,3	-0.0033030	0.03626	-0.09	0.9276	3	g	0

Constant Estimate	0.580975
Variance Estimate	0.030391
Std Error Estimate	0.174329
AIC	-57.4318
SBC	-44.6624
Number of Residuals	95

Note that **PROC ARIMA** estimates *negative* β for the lagged exogenous variables. So remember to reverse the signs for the estimates and *t*-statistics for all lags in the distributed lag model when reporting results. In this example, the estimated model is

$$DU_t = 0.5810 - 0.2021G_t - 0.1645G_{t-1} - 0.0716G_{t-2} + 0.0033G_{t-3}$$

since we must reverse the signs for all lagged values of G.

If we run all the code, including estimation, before turning off **ODS graphics**, a number of additional graphs will be produced.

```
ods graphics on;                          * must turn ODS on;
proc arima data=okun plots(unpack);       * initiate arima;
identify var=du crosscorr=g nlag=12;      * identify model;
estimate input=((1 2 3) g) method=uls;    * specify model;
title 'finite distributed lag model using PROC ARIMA';
run;
ods graphics off;                         * must turn ODS off;
```

The file **ResidualACFPlot.png** contains the **residual correlogram**, which indicates a correlation between $\hat{e}_t$ and $\hat{e}_{t-1}$. This should always be checked since correlation between errors violates one of the assumptions of the linear regression model.

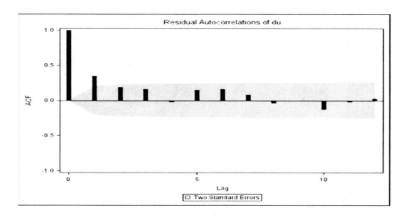

9A.2 Serially correlated error models in PROC ARIMA

PROC ARIMA can also be used to estimate models with serially correlated errors. A model with serially correlated errors of the form $e_t = \rho e_{t-1} + v_t$ is called a **first-order autoregressive** or **AR(1) model**. A model with q lagged errors is an AR(q) model. In this section, we will use **PROC ARIMA** to estimate the AR(1) model for the Phillips curve example, discussed in Section 9.5.2.

$$INF_t = \beta_1 + \beta_2 DU_t + e_t, \qquad e_t = \rho e_{t-1} + v_t$$

First, we estimate the model $INF_t = \beta_1 + \beta_2 DU_t + e_t$ using least squares and examine the autocorrelations. The code is the same as in the finite distributed lag model, except there are no lagged values of the dependent variable, DU, in this model.

```
ods graphics on;                        * must turn ODS on;
proc arima data=phillips plots(unpack); * initiate arima;
identify var=inf crosscorr=du nlag=12;  * identify model;
estimate input=du method=uls;           * specify model;
title 'OLS model for Phillips curve using PROC ARIMA';
run;
ods graphics off;                       * must turn ODS off;
```

The results, which match equation (9.22), on page 352 of *POE4* are

Unconditional Least Squares Estimation

Parameter	Estimate	Standard Error	t Value	Approx Pr > |t|	Lag	Variable	Shift
MU	0.77762	0.06582	11.81	<.0001	0	inf	0
NUM1	-0.52786	0.22940	-2.30	0.0238	0	du	0

The residual correlations, which match those given on page 353 in *POE4* are

The ARIMA Procedure

Autocorrelation Check of Residuals

Lag	Chi-Square	DF	Pr > ChiSq	--------------------Autocorrelations--------------------					
6	100.87	6	<.0001	0.549	0.456	0.433	0.420	0.339	0.271
12	113.57	12	<.0001	0.191	0.251	0.153	0.050	-0.016	-0.013
18	117.27	18	<.0001	-0.009	-0.004	-0.128	-0.128	0.009	-0.016
24	119.86	24	<.0001	0.012	0.051	0.087	0.103	0.014	0.016

The residual correlogram, which matches Figure 9.8 in *POE4* is

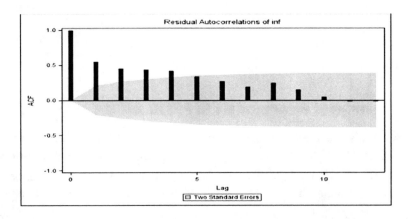

Because the first four autocorrelations lie outside the significance bounds, we conclude the errors are serially correlated. Therefore, we estimate the Phillips curve model with AR(1) errors. To estimate the model with AR(1) errors we include the option **p=1** in the **input** statement.

```
ods graphics on;                    * must turn ODS on;
proc arima data=phillips plots(unpack);* initiate arima;
identify var=inf crosscorr=du nlag=12; * identify model;
estimate p=1 input=du method=uls;    * specify model;
title 'AR(1) error model for Phillips curve using PROC ARIMA';
run;
ods graphics off;                    * must turn ODS off;
```

The results, which match the **PROC AUTOREG** results in Section 9.5.2 of this manual, are

Parameter	Estimate	Standard Error	t Value	Approx Pr > |t|	Lag	Variable	Shift
MU	0.78649	0.12435	6.32	<.0001	0	inf	0
AR1,1	0.56522	0.08984	6.29	<.0001	1	inf	0
NUM1	-0.70477	0.24798	-2.84	0.0056	0	du	0

Recall that SAS includes information from all observations and so the results are close, but not identical to, those in equation (9.45) of *POE4*.

9A.3 Autoregressive distributed lag models in PROC ARIMA

We now consider an **autoregressive** model that also contains a **finite distributed lag**. This is referred to as the **autoregressive distributed lag** (ARDL) model. The ARDL(p,q) model has the general form

$$y_t = \delta + \delta_0 x_t + \delta_1 x_{t-1} + \cdots + \delta_q x_{t-q} + \theta_1 y_{t-1} + \cdots + \theta_p y_{t-p} + v_t$$

It has p lags of the dependent variable, y_t, and q lags of the independent variable, x_t. In this section, we use **PROC ARIMA** to estimate the Phillips curve and Okun's Law equations that were discussed in Section 9.6.

The Phillips curve

The Phillips curve is a regression of inflation on its lags as well as changes in unemployment. Our starting point is the ARDL(1,0) model

$$INF_t = \delta + \theta_1 INF_{t-1} + \delta_1 DU_t + e_t$$

Following this, we will estimate an ARDL(4,0) model. Before proceeding, make sure that you have created the appropriate lagged and differenced variables for this example.

To estimate the ARDL(1,0) model, we simply include the first lag of inflation, *INF1*, along with *DU* in the **crosscorr** and **input** statements.

```
ods graphics on;                              * must turn ODS on;
proc arima data=phillips plots(unpack);       * initiate arima;
identify var=inf crosscorr=(inf1 du) nlag=12; * identify model;
estimate input=(inf1 du) method=uls;          * specify model;
title 'ARDL(1,0) model for Phillips curve using PROC ARIMA';
run;
ods graphics off;                             * must turn ODS off;
```

The results, which match those in equation (9.56), on page 367 in *POE4*, are

Parameter	Estimate	Standard Error	t Value	Approx Pr > |t|	Lag	Variable	Shift
MU	0.35480	0.08760	4.05	0.0001	0	inf	0
NUM1	0.52825	0.08508	6.21	<.0001	0	inf1	0
NUM2	-0.49086	0.19215	-2.55	0.0124	0	du	0

The residual correlogram, which matches Figure 9.9, on page 367 in *POE4*, is

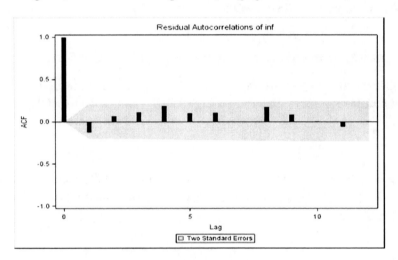

To estimate the ARDL(4,0) model, we include the first four lags of *INF* in the **crosscorr** and **input** statements.

```
ods graphics on;                          * must turn ODS on;
proc arima data=phillips plots(unpack);* initiate arima;
identify var=inf crosscorr=(inf1 inf2 inf3 inf4 du) nlag=12;
estimate input=(inf1 inf2 inf3 inf4 du) method=uls;
run;
ods graphics off;                         * must turn ODS off;
```

The results, which match those in equation (9.57), on page 368 in *POE4*, are

The ARIMA Procedure

Unconditional Least Squares Estimation

Parameter	Estimate	Standard Error	t Value	Approx Pr > |t|	Lag	Variable	Shift
MU	0.10010	0.09826	1.02	0.3114	0	inf	0
NUM1	0.23544	0.10156	2.32	0.0230	0	inf1	0
NUM2	0.12133	0.10376	1.17	0.2457	0	inf2	0
NUM3	0.16769	0.10496	1.60	0.1140	0	inf3	0
NUM4	0.28192	0.10138	2.78	0.0067	0	inf4	0
NUM5	-0.79017	0.18853	-4.19	<.0001	0	du	0

The residual correlogram indicates no serial correlation among the residuals from the ARDL(4,0) model.

Okun's Law

We now wish to estimate an ARDL(1,1) model for the Okun's Law equation.

$$DU_t = \delta + \theta_1 DU_{t-1} + \delta_1 G_t + \delta_2 G_{t-1} + e_t$$

The code to estimate this model is

```
ods graphics on;                           * must turn ODS on;
proc arima data=okun plots(unpack);        * initiate arima;
identify var=du crosscorr=(du1 g) nlag=12; * identify model;
estimate input=(du1 (1) g) method=uls;     * specify model;
title 'ARDL(1,1) model for Okuns law using PROC ARIMA';
run;
ods graphics off;                          * must turn ODS off;
```

The results, which match those in equation (9.59) on page 370 of *POE4*, are

Unconditional Least Squares Estimation

Parameter	Estimate	Standard Error	t Value	Approx Pr > |t|	Lag	Variable	Shift
MU	0.37801	0.05784	6.54	<.0001	0	du	0
NUM1	0.35012	0.08457	4.14	<.0001	0	du1	0
NUM2	-0.18408	0.03070	-6.00	<.0001	0	g	0
NUM1,1	0.09916	0.03682	2.69	0.0084	1	g	0

The residual correlogram indicates no significant autocorrelations between the residuals.

9A.4 Autoregressive models and forecasting in PROC ARIMA

The most common type of time series models are **autoregressive (AR)** models. AR models are models in which the current value of the dependent variable y_t depends on its values in the last p periods. Using the *okun* data, we examine an AR(2) model of GDP growth, discussed in Section 9.6.3.

To specify the AR(2) model, we simply specify **estimate p=2**. A very nice feature about **PROC ARIMA** is its ability to produce forecasts. Below the **estimate** statement, we include the statement **forecast lead=3**, which generates predicted values for the next 3 periods based on the estimated model.

```
ods graphics on;               * must turn ODS on;
proc arima data=okun plots(unpack);  * initiate arima;
identify var=g nlag=12;        * identify model;
estimate p=2 method=uls;       * specify model;
forecast lead=3;               * 3-pd forecast;
run;
```

```
title 'AR(2) model with 3-period forecast';
ods graphics off;                        * must turn ODS off;
```

Again, since **PROC ARIMA** uses data from all observations, the output is similar to, but not exactly the same as equation (9.61) in *POE4*.

Unconditional Least Squares Estimation

Parameter	Estimate	Standard Error	t Value	Approx Pr > |t|	Lag
MU	1.26583	0.14625	8.66	<.0001	0
AR1,1	0.37815	0.09972	3.79	0.0003	1
AR1,2	0.24940	0.10253	2.43	0.0169	2

Constant Estimate	0.47146
Variance Estimate	0.303687
Std Error Estimate	0.551078
AIC	164.6939
SBC	172.4488
Number of Residuals	98

Note that the parameter labeled **AR1,1** gives the estimated coefficient for G_{t-1} , $\hat{\theta}_1$, and **AR1,2** gives the estimated coefficient for G_{t-2}, $\hat{\theta}_2$. However, the parameter labeled **MU** is not an estimate of the intercept, δ. Rather, **MU** is the long-run average value that the series should converge to. In an AR(p) model, this long-run average is calculated as $\mu = \delta/(1 - \theta_1 - \theta_2 - \ldots - \theta_p)$. In our case, $\hat{\delta} = \hat{\mu}(1 - \hat{\theta}_1 - \hat{\theta}_2) = 0.47146$. This value is found just below the other parameters estimates and is labeled **Constant Estimate**.

The residual correlogram, which is similar to Figure 9.11 in *POE4* is

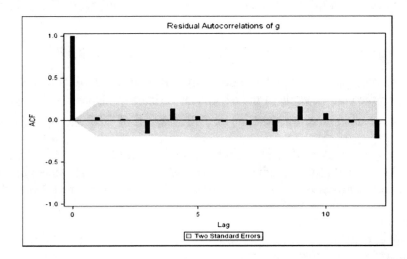

Finally, we wish to forecast future values of G_t. **PROC AUTOREG** does not compute forecasts unless values of the independent variables are provided. However, we do not know values past

time T. Time series forecasts use forecasted future values in place of the actual values. So to forecast $\hat{G}_{T+3}$, for example, we use

$$\hat{G}_{T+3} = \hat{\delta} + \hat{\theta}_1 \hat{G}_{T+2} + \hat{G}_{T+1}$$

In Section 9.7, we used SAS as a calculator to create forecasts and confidence intervals. **PROC ARIMA** computes these forecasts automatically with the **forecast** command. Since we specified **forecast lead=3**, the bottom of the output includes the following forecast:

Forecasts for variable g

Obs	Forecast	Std Error	95% Confidence Limits	
99	0.7241	0.5511	-0.3560	1.8042
100	0.9448	0.5892	-0.2099	2.0995
101	1.0093	0.6276	-0.2207	2.2394

These differ slightly from the forecasts in *POE4*, page 373, because the parameter estimates are slightly different.

APPENDIX 9B GLS ESTIMATION OF AR(1) ERROR MODEL

In Chapter 8 we discovered that the problem of heteroskedasticity could be overcome by using an estimation procedure known as generalized least squares, and that a convenient was to obtain generalized least squares estimates is to first transform the model so that it has a new uncorrelated homoscedastic error term, and to then apply least squares to the transformed model. This same kind of approach can be pursued when the errors follow an AR(1) model.

In Appendix 9C in *POE4*, it is shown that the simple regression model with AR(1) errors can be written as

$$y_t - \rho y_{t-1} = \beta_1(1-\rho) + \beta_2(x_t - x_{t-1}) + v_t$$

Thus, we can define the following transformed variables

$$y_t^* = y_t - \rho y_{t-1} \quad x_{t2}^* = x_t - x_{t-1} \quad x_{t1}^* = (1-\rho)$$

and apply least squares to the transformed model

$$y_t^* = x_{t1}^* \beta_1 + x_{t2}^* \beta_2 + v_t$$

There are two additional problems that we need to solve, however:

1. Because lagged values of y_t and x_t are needed, only $(T-1)$ observations are formed by the transformation.

2. The value of the autoregressive parameter ρ is not known.

The second problem is solved by estimating ρ from the residuals of a first-stage least squares regression. To illustrate, consider the Phillips curve model from Section 9.5.2.

$$INF_t = \beta_1 + \beta_2 DU_t + e_t, \qquad e_t = \rho e_{t-1} + v_t$$

We first regress *INF* on *DU* and save the residuals.

```
proc reg data=phillips;
model inf=du;
output out=gls r=ehat;
title 'OLS on Phillips curve data';
run;
```

Now open the *gls* data and create a lagged residual.

```
data gls;
set gls;
ehat1 = lag(ehat);
run;
```

Regress the residual on its lag to obtain an initial estimate of ρ. That is, estimate the regression $\hat{e}_t = \rho \hat{e}_{t-1} + v_t$.

```
proc reg data=gls;
model ehat = ehat1;
title 'residual regression to estimate rho';
run;
```

The regression output is

```
                          Parameter Estimates

                      Parameter      Standard
    Variable    DF    Estimate       Error      t Value   Pr > |t|

    Intercept    1    -0.00582       0.05488     -0.11     0.9157
    ehat1        1     0.54983       0.08884      6.19     <.0001
```

We can now use $\hat{\rho} = 0.54983$ to transform the data.

```
data gls;
set gls;
rho = 0.54983;
ystar = inf-rho*lag(inf);
x1star = 1-rho;
x2star = du-rho*lag(du);
run;
```

Finally, we obtain the GLS estimates by applying least squares to the transformed data.

```
proc reg data=gls;
model ystar = x1star x2star / noint clb;
title 'proc reg GLS using transformed data';
run;
```

The GLS results are

```
                        Parameter Estimates

                     Parameter      Standard
   Variable    DF     Estimate         Error    t Value    Pr > |t|

   x1star       1      0.76109       0.12171       6.25      <.0001
   x2star       1     -0.69166       0.24274      -2.85      0.0055
```

Note that these results are very close to the nonlinear least squares estimates in equation (9.45) of *POE4*. In fact, these results can be obtained iteratively. That is, we could save the residuals from the GLS estimates, re-estimate ρ, transform the data using this new estimate and obtain a second set of GLS estimates. This is the iterative procedure known as the Cochrane-Orcutt estimator. Basically, we stop when the parameter estimates are no longer changing.

There is one final problem (#1 listed above). In the transformation we have lost one observation. In large sample this is not likely to matter much, and in fact many software packages simply ignore this lost observation and use $(T-1)$ observations. On page 398-399 of *POE4* it is shown that we can improve efficiency by including a transformation of the first observation; the transformation is given in equation (9C.6) of *POE4*.

Below is **PROC IML** code to iteratively estimate the AR(1) error model using all T observations. First, read in the data.

```
/* PROC IML implementation of GLS estimation of AR(1) error model */
proc iml;                          * begin iml;
start gls;                         * start module;
use phillips2;                     * open dataset;
read all into y var{inf};          * define y;
read all into x var{du};           * define x;
t = nrow(y);                       * define n;
one = j(t,1,1);                    * constant term;
x = one||x;                        * variables in reg;
k = ncol(x);                       * define k;
df = t-k;                          * degrees of freedom;
```

We include a summary statement to store results.

```
summary = j(40,3,0);               * summary matrix;
```

Next obtain the OLS estimates and residuals.

```
/* OLS */
xtxi = inv(x`*x);                  * x transpose times x;
b = inv(x`*x)*x`*y;                * ols;
e = y - x*b;                       * ols residuals;
sse = ssq(y - x*b);                * sum of squared errors;
```

```
sig2 = sse/df;                          * variance estimate;
covb = sig2#xtxi;                       * ols cov matrix;
stderr = sqrt(vecdiag(covb));           * standard errors;
tstat = b/stderr;                       * t-statistics;
pval = 2*(1-probt(abs(tstat),df));      * p-values;
result = b||stderr||tstat||pval;        * result table;
cols = {est se tstat pval};             * result column names;
```

Use the residuals and their lags to obtain an initial estimate of ρ.

```
ehat = y-x*b;                           * residuals;
et = ehat[2:t];                         * residuals;
et_1 = ehat[1:t-1];                     * lag residuals;
rho = inv(et_1`*et_1)*et_1`*et;         * estimate of rho;
```

Next we start an a **do loop** for iterations. Note that we transform the first observation differently than the other observations. For details see equation (9C.6) in *POE4*.

```
crit = 1;                               * convergence;
do iter=1 to 40 while(crit > .0001);    * begin do-loop;
  yt = y[2:t];                          * y;
  yt_1 = y[1:t-1];                      * lag y;
  ystar = yt-rho*yt_1;                  * transform y[2:t];
  ystar1 = sqrt(1-rho**2)*y[1];         * transform y[1];
  ystar = ystar1//ystar;               * transform y;

  xt = x[2:t,];                         * x;
  xt_1 = x[1:t-1,];                     * lag x;
  xstar = xt-rho#xt_1;                  * transform x[2:t];
  xstar1 = sqrt(1-rho##2)#x[1,];        * transform x[1];
  xstar = xstar1//xstar;               * transform x;
```

Compute GLS estimates using the transformed data.

```
xtxigls = inv(xstar`*xstar);
bgls = inv(xstar`*xstar)*xstar`*ystar;* gls;
egls = ystar-xstar*bgls;                * gls residuals;
ssegls = ssq(ystar - xstar*bgls);     * sum of squared errors;
sig2gls = ssegls/df;                    * variance estimate;
covbgls = sig2gls#xtxigls;             * gls cov matrix;
stderrgls = sqrt(vecdiag(covbgls));    * standard errors;
tstatgls = bgls/stderrgls;             * t-statistics;
pvalgls = 2*(1-probt(abs(tstatgls),df));* p-values;
```

Now compute the updated estimate of ρ, based on the GLS residuals. In this step we compute the standard error, *t*- statistic and *p*- value for ρ to report in the final output.

```
ehat = y-x*bgls;                        * residuals;
et = ehat[2:t];                         * residuals;
et_1 = ehat[1:t-1];                     * lag residuals;
```

```
rhonew = inv(et_1`*et_1)*et_1`*et;    * estimate of rho;
sser = ssq(et-et_1*rhonew);           * sum of squared errors;
sig2r = sser/(t-1);                   * variance estimate;
covr = sig2r*inv(et_1`*et_1);         * cov matrix;
stdr = sqrt(vecdiag(covr));           * standard error;
tstatr = rhonew/stdr;                 * t-statistic;
pvalr = 2*(1-probt(abs(tstatr),t-1));* p-values;
```

Define the stopping criterion, when the estimate for ρ is no longer changing. Then print the final results.

```
crit = abs(rhonew-rho);               * convergence criterion;
rho = rhonew;                         * replace old rho;
resultgls = (bgls||stderrgls||tstatgls||pvalgls)//
            (rho||stdr||tstatr||pvalr);
summary[iter,]=iter||crit||rho;       * store results;
end;                                  * end do-loop;

parm = {const du rho};                * parameter names;
print / 'AR(1) error model: GLS estimates',,
        'estimates ' resultgls[colname=cols rowname=parm format=13.4];
finish;                               * finish module;
run gls;                              * run gls;
quit;                                 * quit iml;
```

The results are

                    AR(1) error model: GLS estimates

	resultgls	EST	SE	TSTAT	PVAL
estimates	CONST	0.7862	0.1218	6.4573	0.0000
	DU	-0.7024	0.2430	-2.8903	0.0048
	RHO	0.5583	0.0873	6.3932	0.0000

These results are close, but not identical, to those in equation (9.45) on page 362 of *POE4*. This is due to the fact that we are using all observations. It is noted on page 398 of *POE4* that using all observations improves efficiency; note that the standard errors obtained through the **SAS IML** program are each smaller than those in equation (9.45) of *POE4*.

CHAPTER 10

Random Regressors and Moment-Based Estimation

10.1 THE CONSEQUENCES OF RANDOM REGRESSORS

A random variable is one whose value is unknown and is not perfectly predictable until it is observed. If regression data are collected by random sampling this definition applies to all variables. If we survey randomly chosen individuals and ask about their expenditures on food last week, and ask about the size of their household, the household income, and the maximum level of education for any household member, then all of these may be treated as random variables. If $y =$ weekly food expenditure is the "dependent" variable in a regression, with $x =$ household income as the "independent" variable, then both y and x are random variables because we do not know what their values will be until the sample is obtained. In this case x is sometimes called a **random regressor** or it is said to be **stochastic**, which is another word for random. If the data are collected by random sampling, so that each (x_i, y_i) pair of values $i = 1, …, N$, comes from the same population and is independent of every other pair of values, then the least squares estimation procedure requires no modification **as long as x_i is uncorrelated with the regression error e_i**. Specify the simple regression model as

$$y_i = \beta_1 + \beta_2 x_i + e_i$$

In large samples the least squares estimator b_2 converges to $\beta_2 + \text{cov}(x,e)/\text{var}(x) \neq \beta_2$ unless $\text{cov}(x,e) = 0$. This difference between b_2 and β_2 can be called its **asymptotic bias**. If $\text{cov}(x,e) \neq 0$ the least squares estimator does not converge to the true value no matter how large the sample. The least squares estimator is said to be **inconsistent**. When there is a covariance between x and e that persists even with large samples we should consider alternatives to the least squares estimator.

How can this occur? One leading example is from labor economics. Suppose $y =$ hourly wage rate and $x =$ education level. Understanding this relationship is quite important for education policy at local, state and federal levels. The difficulty is that usually we do not know, from typical survey data, anything about the ability, intelligence, work ethic and perseverance of the individuals in the sample of data. These unobserved factors are collected into the error term e. Now the error term will be positively correlated with the explanatory variable $x =$ years of education, because more able, intelligent, industrious individuals will accumulate more years of education. Thus the least squares estimates of the return to education, β_2, will tend to be too large by "$\text{cov}(x,e)/\text{var}(x)$".

10.2 INSTRUMENTAL VARIABLES ESTIMATION

In the linear regression model $y_i = \beta_1 + \beta_2 x_i + e_i$ we usually assume that

$$E(e_i) = 0 \quad \Rightarrow \quad E(y_i - \beta_1 - \beta_2 x_i) = 0 \tag{10.1}$$

Furthermore, if x_i is fixed, or random but not correlated with e_i, then

$$E(x_i e_i) = 0 \quad \Rightarrow \quad E\big[x_i(y_i - \beta_1 - \beta_2 x_i)\big] = 0 \tag{10.2}$$

Equations (10.1) and (10.2) are moment conditions. If we replace the two population moments by the corresponding sample moments, we have two equations in two unknowns, which define the method of moments estimators for β_1 and β_2,

$$\frac{1}{N}\sum(y_i - b_1 - b_2 x_i) = 0, \qquad \frac{1}{N}\sum x_i(y_i - b_1 - b_2 x_i) = 0 \tag{10.3}$$

These two equations are equivalent to the least squares "normal" equations and their solution yields the least squares estimators.

In Section 10.1 we described the problem of correlation between x and e that makes invalid the second condition (10.2), and the second equation in (10.3). Suppose, however, that there is another variable, z, such that

1. z does not have a direct effect on y, and thus it does not belong on the right-hand side of the model as an explanatory variable.
2. z_i is not correlated with the regression error term e_i. Variables with this property are said to be **exogenous**.
3. z is strongly [or at least not weakly] correlated with x, the endogenous explanatory variable.

A variable z with these properties is called an **instrumental variable**. This terminology arises because while z does not have a direct effect on y, having it will allow us to estimate the relationship between x and y. It is a *tool*, or instrument, that we are using to achieve our objective.

If such a variable z exists, then we can use it to form the moment condition

$$E(z_i e_i) = 0 \quad \Rightarrow \quad E\big[z_i(y_i - \beta_1 - \beta_2 x_i)\big] = 0 \tag{10.4}$$

Then we can use the two equations (10.1) and (10.4) to obtain estimates of β_1 and β_2. The sample moment conditions are:

$$\frac{1}{N}\sum(y_i - \hat{\beta}_1 - \hat{\beta}_2 x_i) = 0, \qquad \frac{1}{N}\sum z_i(y_i - \hat{\beta}_1 - \hat{\beta}_2 x_i) = 0 \tag{10.5}$$

Solving these equations leads us to method of moments estimators, which are usually called the **instrumental variable (IV) estimators**,

$$\hat{\beta}_2 = \frac{\sum(z_i - \bar{z})(y_i - \bar{y})}{\sum(z_i - \bar{z})(x_i - \bar{x})} \qquad \hat{\beta}_1 = \bar{y} - \hat{\beta}_2 \bar{x} \tag{10.6}$$

These new estimators are **consistent**; that is, they converge to the true values if the instruments satisfy the conditions listed above. In large samples the instrumental variable estimators have approximate normal distributions. In the simple regression model

$$\hat{\beta}_2 \sim N\left(\beta_2, \frac{\sigma^2}{r_{zx}^2 \sum(x_i - \bar{x})^2}\right) \tag{10.7}$$

where r_{zx}^2 is the squared sample correlation between the instrument z and the random regressor x. The error variance is estimated using the estimator

$$\hat{\sigma}_{IV}^2 = \frac{\sum\left(y_i - \hat{\beta}_1 - \hat{\beta}_2 x_i\right)^2}{N - 2}$$

10.2.1 Two-stage least squares estimation

If there is more than one such instrumental variable, then the instrumental variables estimator can be modified to accommodate them. The resulting procedure is called **two-stage least squares**. If the available instruments are z_1, z_2 and z_3 then the two-steps are

1. Regress x on a constant, and z_1, z_2 and z_3. Obtain the predicted values $\hat{x}$.
2. Use $\hat{x}$ as the instrumental variable for x.

The two-stage least squares estimators are then

$$\hat{\beta}_2 = \frac{\sum(\hat{x}_i - \bar{x})(y_i - \bar{y})}{\sum(\hat{x}_i - \bar{x})(x_i - \bar{x})}, \qquad \hat{\beta}_1 = \bar{y} - \hat{\beta}_2 \bar{x} \tag{10.8}$$

These instrumental variables estimators, derived using the method of moments, are also called **two-stage least squares (2SLS) estimators**, because they can be obtained using two least squares regressions.

1. Stage 1 is the regression of x on a constant term, and z_1, z_2 and z_3. Obtain the predicted values $\hat{x}$.
2. Stage 2 is ordinary least squares estimation of the simple linear regression

$$y_i = \beta_1 + \beta_2 \hat{x}_i + error_i \tag{10.9}$$

Least squares estimation of (10.9) is numerically equivalent to obtaining the instrumental variables estimates using (10.8). Since two-stage least squares estimation and instrumental variables estimation are equivalent, we will simply refer to instrumental variables (*IV*) in all cases.

Another useful result is that the approximate, large sample, variance of $\hat{\beta}_2$ is given by the usual formula for the variance of the least squares estimator of (10.9),

$$\text{var}\left(\hat{\beta}_2\right) = \frac{\sigma^2}{\sum\left(\hat{x}_i - \overline{x}\right)^2} \tag{10.10}$$

Results for the general case are presented in Appendix 10B of this manual.

10.3 AN ILLUSTRATION USING SIMULATED DATA

A Monte Carlo simulation uses artificially created data. By creating data from a model we know, we can evaluate how alternative estimation procedures work under a variety of conditions. Specifically, let us specify a simple regression model in which the parameter values are $\beta_1 = 1$ and $\beta_2 = 1$. We want to explore the properties of the least squares estimator when x_i and e_i are correlated. Using random number generators, we create 100 pairs of x_i and e_i values, such that each has a normal distribution with mean zero and variance one. The population correlation between the x_i and e_i values is $\rho_{xe} = 0.6$.[1] We then create an artificial sample of y values by adding e to the systematic portion of the regression,

$$y = \beta_1 + \beta_2 x + e = 1 + 1 \times x + e$$

These data are contained in SAS dataset *ch10*. Open this file and examine its contents.

```
data ch10;                              * create data set;
set 'ch10';                             * read ch10.sas;
run;


proc contents data=ch10;                * explore contents;
title 'contents of ch10 sas data set';
run;


options nolabel;                        * turn off labels;
```

```
                Alphabetic List of Variables and Attributes

#    Variable   Type   Len   Label
1    X          Num    8     endogenous explanatory variable--corr(x,e)=.6
2    Y          Num    8     dependent variable = x + e with e N(0,1)
3    Z1         Num    8     instrument--corr(z1,x)=.5
4    Z2         Num    8     instrument--corr(z2,x)=.3
5    Z3         Num    8     invalid instrument--corr(z3,x)=.5 corr(z3,e)=.3
```

We have created x and y variables, and three instrumental variables z_1, z_2 and z_3. The correlation between the first instrument z_1 and x is $\rho_{xz_1} = 0.5$, and the correlation between the second instrument z_2 and x is $\rho_{xz_2} = 0.3$. The variable z_3 is correlated with x, with correlation $\rho_{xz_3} = 0.5$, but it is correlated with the error term e, with correlation $\rho_{ez_3} = 0.3$. Thus z_3 is not a valid instrument. In our sample the correlations are given by **PROC CORR**.

---

[1] Using SAS to create such data is explained in Appendix 10A.

```
proc corr data=ch10;                              * summary stats and corr;
title 'correlations using simulated data';
run;
```

Simple Statistics

Variable	N	Mean	Std Dev	Sum	Minimum	Maximum
X	100	0.23916	0.95666	23.91607	-1.64840	2.76628
Y	100	1.38629	1.83882	138.62871	-2.96671	6.72735
Z1	100	0.03421	0.89311	3.42066	-2.61576	2.09323
Z2	100	0.12057	1.02766	12.05662	-2.29936	2.10895
Z3	100	0.06219	1.10007	6.21910	-2.98265	3.14570

Pearson Correlation Coefficients, N = 100
Prob > |r| under H0: Rho=0

	X	Y	Z1	Z2	Z3
X	1.00000	0.88622	0.53315	0.22462	0.52353
		<.0001	<.0001	0.0247	<.0001
Y	0.88622	1.00000	0.33076	0.02014	0.48093
	<.0001		0.0008	0.8423	<.0001
Z1	0.53315	0.33076	1.00000	0.00467	0.05694
	<.0001	0.0008		0.9632	0.5736
Z2	0.22462	0.02014	0.00467	1.00000	-0.05753
	0.0247	0.8423	0.9632		0.5697
Z3	0.52353	0.48093	0.05694	-0.05753	1.00000
	<.0001	<.0001	0.5736	0.5697	

A first important indicator to the usefulness of the instruments is how strongly they are correlated with the explanatory variable x. In this case z_1 and z_3 are "stronger" than z_2. Based on this information we cannot detect the correlation between z_3 and the error, other than to note it is more highly correlated with y than the others.

The least squares regression of y on x reveals the problem.

```
proc reg data=ch10;
ols:model y = x;
title 'OLS using simuated data';
run;
```

Variable	DF	Parameter Estimate	Standard Error	t Value	Pr > |t|
Intercept	1	0.97889	0.08828	11.09	<.0001
X	1	1.70343	0.08995	18.94	<.0001

Because of the positive correlation between the random error term e and x the least squares estimator overestimates the true slope of the relationship, which we know to be $\beta_2 = 1$.

10.3.1 Using two-stage least squares

To implement two stage least squares we use **PROC SYSLIN**. Enter **help syslin** into the SAS command line for detailed documentation.

```
proc syslin data=ch10 2sls;        * PROC SYSLIN with 2sls;
   instruments z1;                 * specify instrument;
   endogenous x;                   * specify RHS endogenous;
   model y = x;                    * model to estimate;
   title '2sls using valid IV z1';
run;
```

In the command we specify the **2SLS** option. The instrumental variables are listed in the **instrument** statement. In the **endogenous** statement we indicate which right-hand side explanatory variables are correlated with the error term. In a multiple regression there may be some that are correlated with the error term, and some that are not. The **model** statement follows the usual SAS setup.

The output is arranged like a standard regression. Note, however, that the regression result that $SST = SSR + SSE$ does not hold up, and therefore the reported R^2 does not have its usual meaning. The overall F-statistic is however a valid test of model significance.

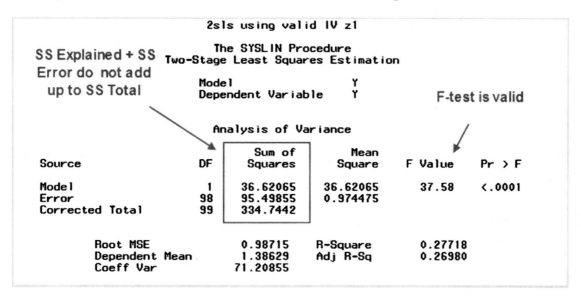

The 2SLS parameter estimates are closer to the true value than the least squares estimates.

Variable	DF	Parameter Estimate	Standard Error	t Value	Pr > |t|
Intercept	1	1.101101	0.109128	10.09	<.0001
X	1	1.192445	0.194518	6.13	<.0001

SAS reports the usual t-statistic for testing the significance of the parameter estimate. The distribution of the 2SLS estimator is only valid in large samples, and if this is taken literally the p-value should be computed using the standard normal distribution. However it is usually a better idea to be "conservative," taking into account the model's degrees of freedom. SAS (unlike some others) does this by default, computing the p-value using the t-distribution with degrees of freedom $N - K$. Also it reports the overall test of significance as an F-statistic rather than a chi-square statistic.

To implement 2SLS with the two valid instruments z_1 and z_2 use

```
proc syslin data=ch10 2sls;
instruments z1 z2;                      * corr (x,z2) = .3;
endogenous x;
model y = x;
title '2sls using valid IV z1 & z2';
run;
```

Recall that z_2 is a weaker instrument than z_1, but still valid. The estimate of the slope is closer to the true value than when only one instrument is used.

		Parameter	Standard		
Variable	DF	Estimate	Error	t Value	Pr > |t|
Intercept	1	1.137591	0.116444	9.77	<.0001
X	1	1.039872	0.194223	5.35	<.0001

For comparison purposes, consider the result of using an invalid instrument, z_3. It is invalid because it is correlated with the random error e.

```
proc syslin data=ch10 2sls;
instruments z3;                         * corr(e,z3) = .3;
endogenous x;
model y = x;
title '2sls using invalid IV z3';
run;
```

The estimated slope is just as poor as the least squares estimate. Using invalid instruments is not a good solution.

		Parameter	Standard		
Variable	DF	Estimate	Error	t Value	Pr > |t|
Intercept	1	0.963997	0.095202	10.13	<.0001
X	1	1.765715	0.172234	10.25	<.0001

10.3.2 Specification testing

When implementing 2SLS it is customary to carry out three important specification tests. We must ask:

- Are our instruments strong? If not then 2SLS will not be successful.
- Are our instruments valid? If not then 2SLS will not be successful.
- Is the variable on the right-hand side actually correlated with the error term? If not, then we do not have to use 2SLS at all.

Testing instrument strength

A standard test of instrument strength is to examine the statistical significance of the instrumental variables in the **first stage** regression, which has as its *dependent* variable x, and on the right-hand side we include all explanatory variables in the model that are not correlated with the error term (called **exogenous** variables) plus any instrumental variables. In the simple model we have been examining so far there is only one explanatory variable and it is being considered **endogenous** and correlated with the error term. Using π_0 to denote the first stage intercept and π_1 to represent the coefficient of z_1, the first stage equation is

$$x = \pi_0 + \pi_1 z_1 + v$$

The first stage equations are estimated using "ordinary" least squares (OLS).

```
proc reg data=ch10;                 * least square regression;
first_one_iv:model x = z1;          * model with one iv;
first_two_iv:model x = z1 z2;       * model with two iv;
output out=ch10out r=vhat;          * output resids for Hausman;
title 'first stage equations';
run;
```

For two-stage least squares we must have at least one valid instrument for each potentially endogenous variable. In our case there is only one endogenous regressor, so at minimum we require one valid instrument. In the first stage regressions we want to see that the instruments are strongly significant. In the case with two instruments, we should test the joint null hypothesis that both their coefficients are zero, the alternative hypothesis being that at least one [the required number of instrumental variables] of their coefficients is not zero.

The first first stage regression output shows that the instrumental variable z_1 is strongly significant. The fact that the t-value is large is important. The rule of thumb judging the strength of an instrument is that the F-test statistic value is greater than 10. For a single instrumental variable the F-statistic value is the square of the t-statistic, and in this case is the overall F-value 38.92.

Model: first_one_iv

Analysis of Variance

Source	DF	Sum of Squares	Mean Square	F Value	Pr > F
Model	1	25.75427	25.75427	38.92	<.0001
Error	98	64.84945	0.66173		
Corrected Total	99	90.60372			

Variable	DF	Parameter Estimate	Standard Error	t Value	Pr > |t|
Intercept	1	0.21963	0.08141	2.70	0.0082
Z1	1	0.57109	0.09154	6.24	<.0001

In the second first stage equation we find that the F-test of the joint significance is 24.28, which again satisfies the "rule of thumb." Note that we can examine the overall F-statistic value because there are no other variables in the first stage. If there are other exogenous variables in the first stage we will use a **test** statement to test only the instrumental variables.

Model: first_two_iv

Analysis of Variance

Source	DF	Sum of Squares	Mean Square	F Value	Pr > F
Model	2	30.22485	15.11242	24.28	<.0001
Error	97	60.37887	0.62246		
Corrected Total	99	90.60372			

Variable	DF	Parameter Estimate	Standard Error	t Value	Pr > |t|
Intercept	1	0.19473	0.07950	2.45	0.0161
Z1	1	0.56998	0.08879	6.42	<.0001
Z2	1	0.20679	0.07716	2.68	0.0087

There is more discussion of weak instrument tests in Appendix 10B of this manual and in appendix 10E of *Principles of Econometrics, 4th Edition*.

Testing the endogeneity of a regressor

When estimating the second first stage equation we included an **output** statement

```
output out=ch10out r=vhat;              * output resids for Hausman;
```

This statement writes the dataset *ch10* to the new data set *ch10out* and adds the variable *VHAT* which are the least squares residuals from the previous regression. Using these residuals we can implement the **Hausman test** for the endogeneity of *x*. One version of the Hausman test is carried out using the artificial regression

$$y = \beta_1 + \beta_2 x + \gamma \hat{v} + e$$

We have added the first stage residuals as an extra explanatory variable in the original model. If *x* is not correlated with the regression error *e* then the coefficient γ should equal zero. The Hausman test is a standard *t*-test of the null hypothesis $H_0 : \gamma = 0$ against $H_1 : \gamma \neq 0$ using the least squares estimates.

```
proc reg data=ch10out;                  * OLS reg with output data;
hausman:model y = x vhat;               * include residuals;
title 'Hausman test using IV z1 and z2';
run;
```

The estimation results show that we reject the null hypothesis $H_0 : \gamma = 0$ and thus we conclude that *x* is correlated with the error term *e* and that we should not use OLS to estimate the original equation.

Variable	DF	Parameter Estimate	Standard Error	t Value	Pr > |t|
Intercept	1	1.13759	0.07975	14.27	<.0001
X	1	1.03987	0.13301	7.82	<.0001
vhat	1	0.99573	0.16294	6.11	<.0001

Testing the validity of an instrumental variable

In the model $y = \beta_1 + \beta_2 x + e$ if x is correlated with the error e, we require at least one instrumental variable. We have determined so far that z_1 and z_2 are adequately strong instruments, thus we have a "surplus" of one instrument. In addition to being strongly (or not weakly) correlated with x, valid instruments must be uncorrelated with the error term e. This condition can only be tested for "surplus" instruments because the test is based on instrumental variables estimates, which require the minimum number of instruments to be computed. Begin by obtaining the 2SLS estimates using instruments z_1 and z_2.

```
proc syslin data=ch10 2sls out=tsls1;    * define output data set;
instruments z1 z2;                        * use two instruments;
endogenous x;                             * list endogenous;
model y = x;                              * IV with two instruments;
output r=ehat;                            * output iv/2sls resid;
title 'IV using z1 & z2 as instruments';
run;
```

We have examined these estimates earlier, so we will not repeat them here. Note two additions to the specification. First, in the **PROC SYSLIN** statement we have added the option **OUT=TSLS1**. This defines the SAS data set to which the estimated residuals will be written. Second, we have added an **OUTPUT** statement, which will write to the SAS data set *tsls1* the 2SLS/IV residuals

$$\hat{e}_{IV} = y - \hat{\beta}_1 - \hat{\beta}_2 x$$

Now, carry out a regression

$$\hat{e}_{IV} = \theta_0 + \theta_1 z_1 + \theta_2 z_2 + error$$

The test statistic for the validity of the surplus instrumental variables is NR^2 from this artificial regression. If the surplus instruments are valid then NR^2 has a large sample distribution that is chi-square with degrees of freedom equal to the number of surplus instruments. If we have K endogenous variables on the right-side of the regression, and if our number of instrumental variables is L then the degrees of freedom is $L - K$. If we have no surplus instruments then $L - K = 0$ and the test cannot be carried out.

```
proc reg data=tsls1;                  * OLS with output data;
model ehat = z1 z2;                   * 2sls resid on left side;
title 'Test validity of surplus IV = N*R2';
run;
```

The regression output shows the number of observations used and the R^2.

```
Number of Observations Used        100

Root MSE          1.05362   R-Square      0.0363
```

The value of the test statistic is $NR^2 = 100 \times 0.0363 = 3.63$. We compare this value to the critical values, either the .95 or .99 percentiles for example, from the chi-square distribution with one degree of freedom, $\chi^2_{(1)}$. These values can be found from tables, but SAS can also calculate them using the **cinv** function.

```
data chisq;
df = 1;
chi2_95 = cinv(.95,df);
chi2_99 = cinv(.99,df);
run;

proc print data=chisq;
title 'Chi-square critical values: one df';
run;
```

```
        Chi-square critical values: one df

    Obs    df    chi2_95    chi2_99
     1      1    3.84146    6.63490
```

Using the $\alpha = 0.05$ critical value, $NR^2 = 3.63 < 3.84$ and we fail to reject the validity of the surplus instrumental variable, which provides some measure of comfort.

If we include the instrument z_3 we can follow the same steps as above.

```
proc syslin data=ch10 2sls out=tsls2;   * output new data set;
instruments z1 z2 z3;                    * z3 is not valid;
endogenous x;
model y = x;
output r=ehat;
title 'IV using z1 z2 and z3--z3 is invalid';
run;

proc reg data=tsls2;
model ehat = z1 z2 z3;
title 'Test validity of surplus IV = N*R2 including z3';
run;

data chisq;
df = 2;
chi2_95 = cinv(.95,df);
chi2_99 = cinv(.99,df);
run;

proc print data=chisq;
title 'Chi-square critical values: two df';
run;
```

The value of the NR^2 test statistic is 13.11. The critical values from the $\chi^2_{(2)}$ distribution are

```
          Chi-square critical values: two df

        Obs    df    chi2_95    chi2_99
         1      2    5.99146    9.21034
```

In this case we have two surplus instruments and at the $\alpha = 0.01$ level we reject their validity, because the test statistic value 13.11 is greater than the critical value 9.21. The test does not identify which are the surplus instruments, and we do not know which are invalid. In this case we know that the test has accurately detected z_3 to be invalid.

SAS 9.2 includes an automatic test for the validity of the surplus instruments from within **PROC SYSLIN**. Add the option **OVERID** to the model statement.

```
proc syslin data=ch10 2sls;
instruments z1 z2 z3;              * z3 is not legal;
endogenous x;                      * specify endogenous;
model y = x / overid;              * automatic test;
title 'Test validity of surplus IV using automatic F-test';
run;
```

Instead of a chi-square test SAS produces a comparable test[2] based on the F-distribution. Using the test's p-value we reject the validity of the surplus instruments.

```
        Test for Overidentifying Restrictions

    Num DF      Den DF     F Value    Pr > F
      2           96         7.24     0.0012
```

10.4 A WAGE EQUATION

As a learning tool we have examined the use of instrumental variables with artificially generated data. Let us consider an important example from labor economics, the estimation of the relationship between wages, specifically ln($WAGE$), and years of education ($EDUC$). We will use the data on married women in the file *mroz* to examine this relationship, in light of issues discussed in this Chapter. Let us specify a simple model in which ln($WAGE$) depends on years of education, years of work experience, and experience squared.

$$\ln(WAGE) = \beta_1 + \beta_2 EDUC + \beta_3 EXPER + \beta_4 EXPER^2 + e$$

A person's ability (and industriousness) may affect the quality of their work and their wage. These variables are components of the error term e, since we usually have no measure for them. The problem is that not only might ability affect wages, but more able individuals may also spend more years in school, causing a correlation between the error term e and the education variable ($EDUC$). If such a correlation exists, then $EDUC$ is endogenous and the least squares estimator of the wage equation is biased and inconsistent.

---

[2] This test is attributed to Robert Basmann. It will be discussed further in Appendix 10B.

316 Chapter 10

Open the *mroz* data and examine its contents.

```
options label;                    * turn on label;
data mroz;                        * new data set;
set 'mroz';                       * read mroz;
run;
proc contents data=mroz;          * examine contents;
title 'contents of mroz data';
run;
options nolabel;                  * turn off label;
```

Alphabetic List of Variables and Attributes **(Edited)**

#	Variable	Type	Len	Label
12	EDUC	Num	3	Wife's educational attainment, in years
25	EXPER	Num	3	Actual years of wife's previous labor market experience
22	FATHEREDUC	Num	3	wife's father's education level
7	LFP	Num	3	dummy variable = 1 if woman worked in 1975, else 0
21	MOTHEREDUC	Num	3	wife's mother's education level
13	WAGE	Num	8	Wife's 1975 average hourly earnings, in 1975 dollars

The data include information on working and nonworking women. We will select only working women, who have an observed wage rate, using an **if** statement. Also we must create the ln(*WAGE*) and the square of experience.

```
data mroz2;                       * new data set;
set mroz;                         * read mroz;
if lfp = 1;                       * keep women in labor force;
exper2 = exper**2;                * experience squared;
lwage = log(wage);                * ln(wage);
run;
```

For the potentially endogenous variable *EDUC* we will consider two possible instruments: her mother's education (*MOTHEREDUC*) and her father's education (*FATHEREDUC*). Recall that a valid instrument
1. does not have a direct effect on *y*, and thus it does not belong on the right-hand side of the model as an explanatory variable. This is true for *MOTHEREDUC* and *FATHEREDUC*.
2. is not correlated with the regression error term *e*. One might wonder if a parent's education satisfies this criterion. If a child's intelligence (which is a component of *e*) is in part inherited from her parents, and if parent's education is affected by their intelligence, there is conceivable correlation between parent's education and *e*. We will want to check the validity of this assumption.
3. is strongly [or at least not weakly] correlated with *x*, the endogenous explanatory variable. While we suspect parent's education to be strongly related to a daughter's education, this too is an assumption we can check.

First, check the gross correlation between *EDUC* and the potential instruments.

```
proc corr data=mroz2;                    * pairwise correlations;
var educ mothereduc fathereduc;          * variables;
title 'Correlations between educ and potential iv';
run;
```

We see that *EDUC* is correlated with *MOTHEREDUC* and *FATHEREDUC*, and *MOTHEREDUC* is correlated with *FATHEREDUC*.

```
              Pearson Correlation Coefficients, N = 428
                    Prob > |r| under HO: Rho=0

                        EDUC        MOTHEREDUC      FATHEREDUC

     EDUC              1.00000       0.38702         0.41540
                                     <.0001          <.0001


     MOTHEREDUC        0.38702       1.00000         0.55406
                       <.0001                        <.0001


     FATHEREDUC        0.41540       0.55406         1.00000
                       <.0001        <.0001
```

Obtain the least squares estimates.

```
proc reg data=mroz2;
model lwage = educ exper exper2;
title 'OLS on ln(wage) equation';
run;
```

The estimates show an estimated rate of return to education of about 10.7% and the earnings experience profile is concave, exhibiting diminishing returns.

Variable	DF	Parameter Estimate	Standard Error	t Value	Pr > |t|
Intercept	1	-0.52204	0.19863	-2.63	0.0089
EDUC	1	0.10749	0.01415	7.60	<.0001
EXPER	1	0.04157	0.01318	3.15	0.0017
exper2	1	-0.00081119	0.00039324	-2.06	0.0397

EDUC is probably positively correlated with the unobserved ability and intelligence factors in the random error *e*, leading on average the least squares estimate to be too large. To check for this endogeneity problem we can carry out the Hausman test. First estimate the first stage and output the residuals.

```
proc reg data=mroz2;
model educ = exper exper2 mothereduc fathereduc;
test mothereduc=0,fathereduc=0;          * test joint signif;
output out=mroz2out r=vhat2;             * output residuals for Hausman;
title 'first stage with external iv mothereduc and fathereduc';
run;
```

We see that both potential instruments are individually and jointly significant. The F-value 55.40 exceeds the rule of thumb threshold of 10.

Variable	DF	Parameter Estimate	Standard Error	t Value	Pr > |t|
Intercept	1	9.10264	0.42656	21.34	<.0001
EXPER	1	0.04523	0.04025	1.12	0.2618
exper2	1	-0.00101	0.00120	-0.84	0.4022
MOTHEREDUC	1	0.15760	0.03589	4.39	<.0001
FATHEREDUC	1	0.18955	0.03376	5.62	<.0001

Test 1 Results for Dependent Variable EDUC

Source	DF	Mean Square	F Value	Pr > F
Numerator	2	230.32056	55.40	<.0001
Denominator	423	4.15739		

The Hausman test is carried out using

```
proc reg data=mroz2out;                    * reg with output data;
model lwage = educ exper exper2 vhat2; * add residuals as rhs var;
title 'Hausman test using external iv mothereduc and fathereduc';
run;
```

The t-statistic on *VHAT2* has a p-value of 0.0954, which implies that the coefficient is statistically different from zero at the 10% level, but not at the 5% level. While this is not strong statistical evidence, it is commonly believed that *EDUC* is endogenous in the wage regression.

Variable	DF	Parameter Estimate	Standard Error	t Value	Pr > |t|
Intercept	1	0.04810	0.39458	0.12	0.9030
EDUC	1	0.06140	0.03098	1.98	0.0482
EXPER	1	0.04417	0.01324	3.34	0.0009
exper2	1	-0.00089897	0.00039591	-2.27	0.0237
vhat2	1	0.05817	0.03481	1.67	0.0954

The two-stage least squares/instrumental variables estimates are obtained using **PROC SYSLIN**. In the **instruments** statement we list all the instrumental variables **and** the other exogenous variables in the regression model. To the **model** statement we add the **overid** option to test the validity of the surplus instruments.

```
proc syslin data=mroz2 2sls;              * 2sls;
instruments exper exper2 mothereduc fathereduc; * all iv/exog;
endogenous educ;                          * potentiall endog;
model lwage = educ exper exper2/overid; * test validity;
title 'IV/2sls using external iv mothereduc and fathereduc';
run;
```

The 2SLS estimates show a return to education of 6.1% rather than the 10.7% return estimated by least squares. This reduction is consistent with our expectations if *EDUC* is endogenous. The test of "overidentifying" restrictions shows that we do not reject the validity of the one surplus instrument.

Variable	DF	Parameter Estimate	Standard Error	t Value	Pr > |t|
Intercept	1	0.048100	0.400328	0.12	0.9044
EDUC	1	0.061397	0.031437	1.95	0.0515
EXPER	1	0.044170	0.013432	3.29	0.0011
exper2	1	-0.00090	0.000402	-2.24	0.0257

Test for Overidentifying Restrictions

Num DF	Den DF	F Value	Pr > F
1	423	0.37	0.5412

10.4.1 Robust specification tests

For microeconomic regressions, using cross-sections of data, it is common to anticipate heteroskedasticity. In the wage equation example, we can test for instrument relevance and endogeneity using "robust" standard errors. This topic was introduced in Section 8.3 of this manual.

Test the relevance of *MOTHEREDUC* and *FATHEREDUC* by estimating the first stage. On the **model** statement we specify the options **hcc** and **hccmethod=1** to indicate that we want a heteroskedasticity correction of the standard errors using "method 1" that is described in Section 8.3.

```
proc reg data=mroz2;
model educ = exper exper2 mothereduc fathereduc/hcc hccmethod=1;
test mothereduc=0,fathereduc=0;
output out=mrozout r=vhat2;
title 'test strength of IV using robust chi-square test';
run;
```

The first stage estimates are reported with both the usual standard errors and the robust standard errors. The two instruments *MOTHEREDUC* and *FATHEREDUC* are strongly statistically significant using the **Heteroscedasticity Consistent** standard errors.

Variable	DF	Parameter Estimate	Standard Error	t Value	Pr > |t|
Intercept	1	9.10264	0.42656	21.34	<.0001
EXPER	1	0.04523	0.04025	1.12	0.2618
exper2	1	-0.00101	0.00120	-0.84	0.4022
MOTHEREDUC	1	0.15760	0.03589	4.39	<.0001
FATHEREDUC	1	0.18955	0.03376	5.62	<.0001

		---Heteroscedasticity Consistent-- Standard		
Variable	DF	Error	t Value	Pr > |t|
Intercept	1	0.42414	21.46	<.0001
EXPER	1	0.04191	1.08	0.2812
exper2	1	0.00132	-0.76	0.4461
MOTHEREDUC	1	0.03545	4.45	<.0001
FATHEREDUC	1	0.03244	5.84	<.0001

When robust standard errors are requested, subsequent test statements produce both the usual "nonrobust" *F*-test and an asymptotically valid chi-square that is based on a heteroskedasticity corrected covariance matrix for the least squares estimator. The asymptotic chi-square test statistic can be converted to an approximate *F*-test by dividing the chi-square statistic by the test degrees of freedom, giving an approximate *F*-value of 49.525.

```
          Test 1 Results for Dependent Variable EDUC


                              Mean
     Source         DF      Square    F Value   Pr > F
     Numerator       2    230.32056    55.40    <.0001
     Denominator   423      4.15739


           Test 1 Results using Heteroscedasticity
               Consistent Covariance Estimates

              DF    Chi-Square    Pr > ChiSq
               2       99.05        <.0001
```

If heteroskedasticity is present then the Hausman test should also be carried out using robust standard errors.

```
proc reg data=mroz2out;
model lwage = educ exper exper2 vhat2/hcc hccmethod=1;
title 'Hausman test with robust variances';
run;
```

The *t*-statistic for *VHAT2* changes by only a small amount in this example.

```
                  Parameter     Standard
     Variable  DF  Estimate       Error    t Value   Pr > |t|
     Intercept  1   0.04810      0.39458     0.12     0.9030
     EDUC       1   0.06140      0.03098     1.98     0.0482
     EXPER      1   0.04417      0.01324     3.34     0.0009
     exper2     1  -0.00089897   0.00039591 -2.27     0.0237
     vhat2      1   0.05817      0.03481     1.67     0.0954


                      ---Heteroscedasticity Consistent--
                          Standard
     Variable  DF          Error    t Value   Pr > |t|
     Intercept  1         0.42210     0.11     0.9093
     EDUC       1         0.03267     1.88     0.0609
     EXPER      1         0.01512     2.92     0.0037
     exper2     1         0.00041524 -2.16     0.0310
     vhat2      1         0.03641     1.60     0.1109
```

10.5 USING PROC MODEL

10.5.1 Robust 2SLS estimation

If the data are potentially heteroskedastic then it would seem reasonable to use robust standard errors for 2SLS. While **PROC SYSLIN** does not offer this capability, **PROC MODEL** does. In **PROC MODEL** we specify the **endogenous** variables and **instruments** as we did with **PROC SYSLIN**. Rather than a **model** statement the regression specification of the model is written out (i.e., **lwage = b1 + b2*educ + b3*exper + b4*exper2;**) and the equation is estimated using a **fit** statement. The options on the **fit** statement are **2SLS** and **hccme=1**, specifying that we want two-stage least squares estimates and robust standard errors using "method = 1". The use of the **label** statement is optional, but it makes the output more readable.

```
proc model data=mroz2;
endogenous educ;
instruments mothereduc fathereduc exper exper2;
label b1 = "intercept"
      b2 = "educ"
      b3 = "exper"
      b4 = "exper2";
lwage = b1 + b2*educ + b3*exper + b4*exper2;
fit lwage/2sls hccme=1;
title 'IV/2sls with robust variances';
run;
```

The estimates are the same as those provided by **PROC SYSLIN** but the standard errors are now corrected for heteroskedasticity.

Nonlinear 2SLS Parameter Estimates

Parameter	Estimate	Approx Std Err	t Value	Approx Pr > |t|	Label
b1	0.0481	0.4298	0.11	0.9109	intercept
b2	0.061397	0.0333	1.84	0.0662	educ
b3	0.04417	0.0155	2.84	0.0047	exper
b4	-0.0009	0.000430	-2.09	0.0372	exper2

10.5.2 Using the Hausman test command

In **PROC MODEL** we can request a comparison of the estimates from two estimators using the **hausman** option.

```
proc model data=mroz2;
endogenous educ;
instruments mothereduc fathereduc exper exper2;
label b1 = "intercept"
      b2 = "educ"
      b3 = "exper"
      b4 = "exper2";
```

```
lwage = b1 + b2*educ + b3*exper + b4*exper2;
fit lwage/ols 2sls hausman;
title 'OLS & IV/2sls with automatic Hausman test';
run;
```

In the **fit** statement we request the use of two estimators, first the OLS estimator (which is the BLUE if there is no endogeneity) and then the 2SLS estimator, which is consistent if there is endogeneity. The test compares the estimates from the two estimators.

We do not advocate the use of this test. SAS reports the test degrees of freedom to be 4, which is the number of estimates being compared. However it can be shown that the correct degrees of freedom for this test is 1, the number of endogenous variables on the right-side of the equation.

```
               Hausman's Specification Test Results
      Efficient    Consistent
      under H0     under H1     DF    Statistic    Pr > ChiSq
      OLS          2SLS          4       2.70         0.6100
```

The reason for concern is that the *p*-value of the chi-square test should be calculated using 1 degree of freedom. Taking the value of the test statistic to be 2.70 as shown above, we can compute the correct *p*-value using the SAS function **probchi**, the CDF of the chi-square distribution $P(\chi^2 \leq c)$. The *p*-value for this test is in the right tail of the chi-square distribution.

```
data chisq;
df = 1;
p_val = 1 - probchi(2.70,df);
chi1_90 = cinv(.90,df);
chi1_95 = cinv(.95,df);
chi1_99 = cinv(.99,df);
run;

proc print data=chisq;
title 'Chi-square critical values: one df and Hausman p-value';
run;
```

We find that the *p*-value of the automatic Hausman test is actually about 0.10, which is borderline significant, rather than the 0.61 *p*-value reported by SAS.

```
        Chi-square critical values: one df and Hausman p-value

     Obs    df    p_val     chi1_90    chi1_95    chi1_99
      1      1    0.10035    2.70554    3.84146    6.63490
```

APPENDIX 10A SIMULATING ENDOGENOUS REGRESSORS

10A.1 Simulating the data

In Section 10.3 of this manual we use simulated data to explore the workings of OLS and 2sls estimation. To generate such data we employ **random number generators** and **Cholesky's decomposition**. In the code below we create 20000 observations on 5 variables that have certain correlations. First, create 5 independent standard normal random variables using the SAS random number generator function **RAND('NORMAL',0,1)**. The first argument specifies that the random number have a normal distribution, then the mean (0) and standard deviation (1). For more on this function enter **help rand** into the SAS command line

The 5 $N(0,1)$ variables are then combined using some coefficients that are derived using the Cholesky decomposition, which is explored further below.

```
data datagen;
nobs = 20000;                        * number of observations;
do n = 1 to nobs;                    * do loop nobs times;
        call streaminit(1234567);    * set random number stream;

        /* create 5 N(0,1) random variables */
        z1=rand('normal',0,1);
        z2=rand('normal',0,1);
        z3=rand('normal',0,1);
        z4=rand('normal',0,1);
        z5=rand('normal',0,1);

        /* apply cholesky transformation */
        dat1 = z1;
        dat2 = .6*Z1 + .8*Z2;
        dat3 = .5*Z1 - .375*z2 + .7806247*z3;
        dat4 = .3*z1 - .225*z2 - .30024*z3 + .877058*z4;
        dat5 = .5*z1 - .320256*z3 - .280659*z4 + .7540999*z5;
        output;
end;
run;
```

Check the correlations between the variables.

```
proc corr data=datagen;              * simple correlations;
var dat1 dat2 dat3 dat4 dat5;        * variables;
title 'correlations among artificial variables';
run;
```

The generated variables **dat1-dat5** have sample means near 0 and variances near 1. The correlations between **dat1** and the others are near 0.6, 0.5, 0.3 and 0.5.

Simple Statistics

Variable	N	Mean	Std Dev	Sum	Minimum	Maximum
dat1	20000	0.00169	1.00083	33.89879	-3.75313	4.06830
dat2	20000	-0.0003238	1.00082	-6.47650	-3.88269	4.89621
dat3	20000	0.00518	1.00152	103.51333	-3.70836	4.65792
dat4	20000	-0.0000625	0.99946	-1.25045	-3.70787	3.89352
dat5	20000	-0.01331	0.99856	-266.12069	-3.63964	4.24757

Pearson Correlation Coefficients, N = 20000
Prob > |r| under H0: Rho=0

	dat1	dat2	dat3	dat4	dat5
dat1	1.00000	0.59922	0.49536	0.30433	0.50254
		<.0001	<.0001	<.0001	<.0001
dat2	0.59922	1.00000	-0.01054	0.00412	0.30810
	<.0001		0.1362	0.5602	<.0001
dat3	0.49536	-0.01054	1.00000	0.00251	0.00372
	<.0001	0.1362		0.7224	0.5991
dat4	0.30433	0.00412	0.00251	1.00000	-0.00037
	<.0001	0.5602	0.7224		0.9587
dat5	0.50254	0.30810	0.00372	-0.00037	1.00000
	<.0001	<.0001	0.5991	0.9587	

Take these data observations and create a new data set, with variables x, e and three instruments z_1, z_2 and z_3. The data generation process is $y = \beta_1 + \beta_2 x + e = 1 + 1 \times x + e$. Create the "expected value of y" and add to it the random error term e to create y values. Note from the correlation matrix that the third instrument is actually invalid because **dat5** (z_3) is correlated with **dat2** (e). The other two instruments are valid and correlated to x with correlations 0.5 and 0.3. The "endogeneity" in the model is controlled by the correlation between x (**dat1**) and e (**dat2**) which is 0.6.

```
data table10;              * data set;
set datagen;               * read data;
x = dat1;                  * endogenous regressor;
e = dat2;                  * regression error;
z1 = dat3;                 * valid iv #1;
z2 = dat4;                 * valid iv #2;
z3 = dat5;                 * invalid iv #3;
ey = 1 + 1*x;              * regression function;
y = ey+e;                  * dependent variable;
run;
```

Create a data set with 100 of these 20,000 observations. Apply OLS and 2SLS estimation.

```
data n100;                 * new data set;
set table10;               * read table10;
```

```
if _n_ <= 100;                                    * keep first 100 obs;
run;


proc reg data=n100;
model y = x;
title 'ols regression with n=100';
run;
```

```
                     Parameter      Standard
Variable       DF     Estimate        Error     t Value    Pr > |t|
Intercept      1      0.87929        0.07170      12.26      <.0001
x              1      1.50515        0.07665      19.64      <.0001
```

```
    /* 2sls with 100 obs */
proc syslin data=n100 2sls;
endogenous x;
instruments z1 z2;
model y = x;
title '2sls with n=100';
run;
```

```
                     Parameter    Standard
Variable       DF     Estimate      Error     t Value    Pr > |t|
Intercept      1      0.823996    0.089186      9.24      <.0001
x              1      0.958439    0.151445      6.33      <.0001
```

Now repeat for some larger number of observations. We use $N = 10,000$. You can experiment with more or fewer observations.

```
    /* Use 10000 observations */
data n10000;
set table10;
if _n_ <= 10000;
run;


proc reg data=n10000;
model y = x;
title 'ols regression with n=10,000';
run;
```

```
                     Parameter      Standard
Variable       DF     Estimate        Error     t Value    Pr > |t|
Intercept      1      1.00208        0.00796     125.95     <.0001
x              1      1.59794        0.00801     199.41     <.0001
```

```
    proc syslin data=n10000 2sls;
endogenous x;
instruments z1 z2;
model y = x;
title '2sls with n=10,000';
run;
```

Variable	DF	Parameter Estimate	Standard Error	t Value	Pr > |t|
Intercept	1	1.010814	0.010048	100.60	<.0001
x	1	0.980291	0.017602	55.69	<.0001

The larger number of observations does not make the OLS estimate of the slope close to the true parameter value. On the other hand, the 2SLS estimate is close to the true value and has a very small standard error with this large a sample. The 2SLS least squares estimator is **consistent**, meaning that it converges to the true value as the sample size increases towards infinity.

10A.2 The Cholesky decomposition

If Σ is an $p \times p$ positive definite and symmetric matrix, then there exists an upper triangular matrix $\mathbf{U}$ such that $\mathbf{U'U} = \Sigma$. If $\mathbf{z}$ is a $p \times 1$ vector of standard random variables with mean vector 0 and covariance matrix $\mathbf{I}$ (the identity matrix), then $\mathbf{x} = \mathbf{U'z}$ has mean vector 0 and covariance matrix $\mathbf{U'IU} = \mathbf{U'U} = \Sigma$. Transposing $\mathbf{x} = \mathbf{U'z}$ we have row vector $\mathbf{x'} = (\mathbf{U'z})' = \mathbf{z'U}$. This is the result we use.

In the following **PROC IML** code we generate 20,000 observations on 5 standard normal random values. In **IML** the random number generating function is **RANDGEN** and its arguments are the storage matrix into which the random numbers will be placed (**dat**).

```
proc iml;                        * invoke iml;
title;                           * turn off titles;
start cholesky;                  * start module;
call randseed(1234567);          * set seed for random numbers;
n = 20000;                       * n = number of observations;
dat = j(n,5,0);                  * storage matrix;
call randgen(dat,'normal',0,1);  * fill dat matrix;
```

The desired covariance matrix is constructed by first creating an identity matrix and filling in covariance terms in the remaining positions.

```
cov = I(5);                      * identity matrix;
cov[1,2] = .6; cov[2,1]=.6;      * corr(x2,e);
cov[1,3] = .5; cov[3,1]=.5;      * corr(x2,z1);
cov[1,4] = .3; cov[4,1]=.3;      * corr(x2,z2);
cov[1,5] = .5; cov[5,1]=.5;      * corr(x2,z3);
cov[2,5] = .3; cov[5,2]=.3;      * corr(z3,e);
print / " cov " , cov;
```

cov

1	0.6	0.5	0.3	0.5
0.6	1	0	0	0.3
0.5	0	1	0	0
0.3	0	0	1	0
0.5	0.3	0	0	1

The Cholesky matrix is obtained using the **ROOT** function in **PROC IML**.

```
/* cholesky decomposition */
u = root(cov);                          * u`*u = cov;
print / "u " u;
```

```
      u        1      0.6       0.5       0.3       0.5
               0      0.8    -0.375    -0.225         0
               0        0 0.7806247  -0.30024 -0.320256
               0        0         0  0.877058 -0.280659
               0        0         0         0 0.7540999
```

The values in the columns are the coefficients used in forming the **dat1-dat5** variables in Section 10A.1. We can check that the decomposition works by doing a multiplication. The **FUZZ** command rounds very small values < 1E-12 to zero.

```
check = fuzz(u`*u);                     * check root function;
print / "check cholesky u" check;
```

```
check cholesky u         1      0.6      0.5      0.3      0.5
                       0.6        1        0        0      0.3
                       0.5        0        1        0        0
                       0.3        0        0        1        0
                       0.5      0.3        0        0        1
```

The matrix **dat** has 20,000 rows and 5 columns. Multiplying each row of **dat** by U creates a row of random values with 0 means and covariance matrix equal to that just above.
Check the correlations of these created values.

```
dat =  dat*u;                           * correlated data;
corrmat = corr(dat);                    * find correlations;
print / "data correlations " corrmat[format=13.4];
```

```
                    data correlations
                         corrmat

      1.0000        0.5992        0.4954        0.3043        0.5025
      0.5992        1.0000       -0.0105        0.0041        0.3081
      0.4954       -0.0105        1.0000        0.0025        0.0037
      0.3043        0.0041        0.0025        1.0000       -0.0004
      0.5025        0.3081        0.0037       -0.0004        1.0000

finish;
run cholesky;
quit;
```

Such simulated data values are those we have employed in exploring the properties of the OLS and 2SLS estimators.

APPENDIX 10B USING PROC IML FOR 2SLS

10B.1 The model, estimators and tests

The regression model in matrix notation is $\mathbf{y} = \mathbf{X\beta} + \mathbf{e}$, where $\mathbf{X}$ is $(N \times K)$. Partition the regressors into $\mathbf{X} = [\mathbf{X_1} \quad \mathbf{X_2}]$ where $\mathbf{X_1}$ contains K_1 endogenous regressors and $\mathbf{X_2}$ contains K_2 exogenous regressors. The ith observation in the regression model $y_i = \mathbf{x}_i'\mathbf{\beta} + e_i$ with $\mathbf{x}_i' = [\mathbf{x}_{i1}' \quad \mathbf{x}_{i2}']$. Endogeneity means that $E(\mathbf{x}_{i1}e_i) \neq \mathbf{0}$ while exogeneity means that $E(\mathbf{x}_{i2}e_i) = \mathbf{0}$. Assume there is an $(N \times L)$ matrix $\mathbf{Z}$ of instruments $\mathbf{Z} = [\mathbf{Z_1} \quad \mathbf{Z_2}] = [\mathbf{Z_1} \quad \mathbf{X_2}]$, where $\mathbf{Z_1}$ contains L_1 excluded or external instruments (from outside the regression specification) and $\mathbf{Z_2} = \mathbf{X_2}$ contains $L_2 = K_2$ internal instruments. If the ith row of $\mathbf{Z}$ is $\mathbf{z}_i'$, then $E(\mathbf{z}_i e_i) = \mathbf{0}$. The order condition for identification is that $L \geq K$, or equivalently that $L_1 \geq K_1$, the number of external instruments must be at least as large as the number of endogenous regressors.

Estimation

The instrumental variables, or 2SLS, estimator of $\mathbf{\beta}$ is[3]

$$\mathbf{b_{IV}} = \left[\mathbf{X'Z(Z'Z)^{-1}Z'X} \right]^{-1} \mathbf{X'Z(Z'Z)^{-1}Z'y} = [\mathbf{X'P_Z X}]^{-1} \mathbf{X'P_Z y} = \left[\mathbf{\hat{X}'\hat{X}} \right]^{-1} \mathbf{\hat{X}'y} \qquad (10\text{B}.1)$$

where $\mathbf{P_Z} = \mathbf{Z(Z'Z)^{-1}Z'}$ is a symmetric and idempotent "projection" matrix such that $\mathbf{P_Z X} = \mathbf{Z(Z'Z)^{-1}Z'X} = \mathbf{\hat{X}}$. The estimated asymptotic covariance matrix of this estimator is

$$\hat{V}(\mathbf{b_{IV}}) = \hat{\sigma}_{IV}^2 \left[\mathbf{X'Z(Z'Z)^{-1}Z'X} \right]^{-1} = \hat{\sigma}_{IV}^2 [\mathbf{X'P_Z X}]^{-1} = \hat{\sigma}_{IV}^2 \left[\mathbf{\hat{X}'\hat{X}} \right]^{-1} \qquad (10\text{B}.2)$$

with

$$\hat{\sigma}_{IV}^2 = \frac{(\mathbf{y} - \mathbf{Xb_{IV}})'(\mathbf{y} - \mathbf{Xb_{IV}})}{(N - K)} = \frac{\mathbf{\hat{e}}_{IV}'\mathbf{\hat{e}}_{IV}}{(N - K)} \qquad (10\text{B}.3)$$

Testing instrument validity

Valid instruments must satisfy the **orthogonality condition** $E(\mathbf{z}_i e_i) = \mathbf{0}$. Sargan's[4] test statistic is NR^2 from a regression of the residuals $\mathbf{\hat{e}}_{IV} = (\mathbf{y} - \mathbf{Xb_{IV}})$ on $\mathbf{Z}$,

$$SARGAN = \frac{N\left(\mathbf{\hat{e}}_{IV}'\mathbf{Z(Z'Z)^{-1}Z'\hat{e}}_{IV}\right)}{\mathbf{\hat{e}}_{IV}'\mathbf{\hat{e}}_{IV}} = \frac{N\left(\mathbf{\hat{e}}_{IV}'\mathbf{P_Z \hat{e}}_{IV}\right)}{\mathbf{\hat{e}}_{IV}'\mathbf{\hat{e}}_{IV}} \qquad (10.\text{B}.4)$$

---

[3] See William Greene (2012), pages 318-320.
[4] Wooldridge (2010), pages 134-137.

The *SARGAN* statistic has an asymptotic $\chi^2_{(L-K)}$ distribution if the orthogonality conditions hold. The test degrees of freedom $L-K$ is the number of surplus instruments, or **overidentifying restrictions**. An *F*-statistic variant suggested by Basmann corrects for degrees of freedom

$$BASMANN = \left(\frac{N-L}{L-K}\right)\frac{\left(\hat{e}'_{IV}Z(Z'Z)^{-1}Z'\hat{e}_{IV}\right)}{\hat{e}'_{IV}\hat{e}_{IV} - \hat{e}'_{IV}Z(Z'Z)^{-1}Z'\hat{e}_{IV}} = \left(\frac{N-L}{L-K}\right)\frac{\left(\hat{e}'_{IV}P_Z\hat{e}_{IV}\right)}{\hat{e}'_{IV}M_Z\hat{e}_{IV}} \qquad (10B.5)$$

Here $M_Z = I - P_Z$ and the *BASMANN* statistic has asymptotic $F_{(L-K,N-L)}$ distribution if the orthogonality conditions hold. The **overid** test option in **PROC SYSLIN** (see Section 10.3.2b) provides an alternative version of Basmann's statistic.[5]

Testing endogeneity

Sometimes we are not certain that the variables in X_1 are endogenous. Hausman's contrast test statistic is

$$H = \left(b_{IV} - b\right)'\left\{\hat{V}\left(b_{IV}\right) - \hat{V}\left(b\right)\right\}^{-1}\left(b_{IV} - b\right) \qquad (10B.6)$$

where b is the OLS estimator that is both consistent and efficient under the null hypothesis $E(x_{il}e_i) = 0$, and inconsistent under the alternative hypothesis $E(x_{il}e_i) \neq 0$. The IV/2SLS estimator b_{IV} is consistent under both the null and alternative hypotheses, but it is not efficient. Under the null hypothesis the Hausman test statistic has an asymptotic $\chi^2_{(K_1)}$ distribution. That is, the degrees of freedom are the number of potentially endogenous variables.

The default SAS test (**PROC MODEL** with **hausman** option on **fit** statement) computes the contrast using $\hat{V}(b_{IV})$ and $\hat{V}(b) = \hat{\sigma}^2(X'X)^{-1}$ with $\hat{\sigma}^2 = (y - Xb)'(y - Xb)/(N - K)$. SAS computes the degrees of freedom as the rank of the matrix $\hat{V}(b_{IV}) - \hat{V}(b)$, which is K.[6] An alternative is to compute the variance of the IV/2SLS estimator as $\hat{\sigma}^2\left[\hat{X}'\hat{X}\right]^{-1}$. Under the null hypothesis this is a consistent estimator and the Hausman test statistic simplifies to

$$H_{OLS} = \left(b_{IV} - b\right)'\left\{\hat{\sigma}^2\left[\hat{X}'\hat{X}\right]^{-1} - \hat{\sigma}^2\left(X'X\right)^{-1}\right\}^{+}\left(b_{IV} - b\right) \qquad (10B.7)$$

The matrix in braces is singular, with rank K_1, so the inverse "+" is the generalized inverse.

A regression based alternative relies upon the estimated reduced form equation. Let $X_1 = Z\Pi_1 + V_1$ denote the reduced form equation for the K_1 potentially endogenous variables. Estimate the reduced form by least squares and obtain the reduced form residuals

$$\hat{V}_1 = X_1 - Z\hat{\Pi}_1 = X_1 - Z(Z'Z)^{-1}Z'X_1 = \left(I - Z(Z'Z)^{-1}Z'\right)X_1 = M_Z X_1 \qquad (10B.8)$$

Add the reduced form residuals to the original specification

---

[5] See SAS 9.2 PROC SYSLIN documentation, page 1610.
[6] SAS computes the degrees of freedom as `df = round(trace(ginv(covbiv-covb)*(covbiv-covb)))`

$$\mathbf{y} = \mathbf{X}\boldsymbol{\beta} + \hat{\mathbf{V}}_1\boldsymbol{\gamma} + \mathbf{e} \qquad\qquad (10B.9)$$

Estimate the resulting equation by least squares and use an F-test (with K_1 and $N-K$ degrees of freedom) for the null hypotheses $H_0 : \boldsymbol{\gamma} = \mathbf{0}$, or a t-test if $K_1=1$. This test is simple, asymptotically equivalent to the contrast test, with no ambiguity about the test degrees of freedom.

10B.2 PROC IML commands

To illustrate the IML commands for 2SLS use the Mroz data, keeping observations on women in the labor force.

```
data mroz;                           * new data set;
set 'mroz';                          * read mroz;
if lfp = 1;                          * keep women in labor force;
exper2 = exper**2;                   * experience squared;
lwage = log(wage);                   * ln(wage);
one = 1;                             * intercept variable;
run;
```

First, read variables into various matrices consistent with algebraic exposition at the start of Section 10B.1.

```
proc iml;                            * invoke IML;
title;                               * turn off title;
use mroz;                            * open data set;
read all into y var{lwage};          * dependent var;
read all into x var{one educ exper exper2}; * independent var;
read all into x1 var{educ};          * endogenous var;
```

The instrument matrix includes all external and internal exogenous variables;

```
read all into z var{one exper exper2 mothereduc fathereduc}; * iv;
read all into z1 var{mothereduc fathereduc}; * external iv;
read all into z2 var{one exper exper2}; * inluded iv;
rname = {one educ exper exper2};     * names for printed results;
```

2SLS module

```
start tsls;                          * start module;
n = nrow(y);                         * number observations;
k = ncol(x);                         * number of regressors;
k1 = ncol(x1);                       * number of endogenous;
l = ncol(z);                         * number of IV;
l1 = ncol(z1);                       * number external IV;
xhat = z*inv(z`*z)*z`*x;             * X-hat;
biv = inv(xhat`*xhat)*xhat`*y;       * eq (10B.1);
ehat = y-x*biv;                      * IV residuals;
```

We use the estimator of the error variance σ^2 with the degrees of freedom correction.

```
sig2iv = ehat`*ehat/(n-k);           * eq (10.B3);
covbiv = sig2iv*inv(xhat`*xhat);     * eq (10.B2);
se = sqrt(vecdiag(covbiv));          * std error of IV;
tstat = biv/se;                      * t-stats;
pval = 2*(1-probt(abs(tstat),n-k));  * p-value;
result = biv||se||tstat||pval;       * stack results;
cname = {est se tstat pval};         * names for printed columns;

print / "2sls",, result [rowname=rname colname=cname format=13.6];
finish;                              * finish module;
run tsls;                            * run module;
```

The results match those in Section 10.4 of this manual.

2sls

result

	EST	SE	TSTAT	PVAL
ONE	0.048100	0.400328	0.120152	0.904419
EDUC	0.061397	0.031437	1.953024	0.051474
EXPER	0.044170	0.013432	3.288329	0.001092
EXPER2	-0.000899	0.000402	-2.237993	0.025740

Testing overidentifying restrictions module

Before running the following module, make sure to run the 2SLS module "**tsls**" from the previous section. The estimation equations are from Section 10B.1.2. The two tests presented are Sargan's test and an *F*-statistic version[7] The F-statistic version is slightly different than that reported by **PROC SYSLIN**.[8]

```
start overid;
num_overid = l-k;                    * number of surplus IV;
sargan = n*(ehat`*z*inv(z`*z)*z`*ehat)/(ehat`*ehat); * eq (10B.4);
chi2_crit = cinv(.95,(l-k));         * chi-sq critical value;
sargan_p = 1 - probchi(sargan,(l-k));        * sargan p-value;

print / 'Sargan chi-square test of surplus instrument validity'
      ,,sargan num_overid chi2_crit sargan_p;

den_df = n-l;                        * N - total number IV;

/* Basmann test statistic eq (10B.5)   */
basmann = ((n-l)/(l-k))*(ehat`*z*inv(z`*z)*z`*ehat)/
          (ehat`*ehat - ehat`*z*inv(z`*z)*z`*ehat);
```

---

[7] See Baum, C.F., Schaeffer, M.E., and S. Stillman (2003) "Instrumental Variables and GMM: Estimation and Testing," The Stata Journal 3(1), page 17.

[8] See Version 9.2 PROC SYSLIN documentation, page 1610.

```
    f_crit = finv(.95,l-k,n-l);                    * F critical value;
    basmann_p = 1 - probf(basmann,(l-k),(n-l));    * Basmann p-value;
    print ,, 'Basmann F-test of surplus instrument validity'
          , basmann num_overid den_df f_crit basmann_p;
    finish;
  run overid;
```

```
        Sargan chi-square test of surplus instrument validity

              sargan num_overid chi2_crit  sargan_p
            0.3780715          1 3.8414588 0.5386372


        Basmann F-test of surplus instrument validity
          basmann num_overid    den_df    f_crit basmann_p
        0.3739851          1       423 3.8635362 0.5411685
```

The degrees of freedom for the chi-square test are the number of surplus instruments, in this case one.

Hausman test for endogeneity module

Before running the following module, make sure to run the 2SLS module "**tsls**" from section 10B.2.1. The first test constructed is the Hausman contrast test given in equation (10B.6) and used by **PROC MODEL**[9]. The contrast is between the OLS estimator and the IV estimator.

```
start hausman;
/* first run tsls module */
b = inv(x`*x)*x`*y;                    * OLS estimates;
sig2ols = ssq(y-x*b)/(n-k);            * sigma-squared hat;
covb = sig2ols*inv(x`*x);              * OLS covariance;
h = (biv-b)`*inv(covbiv-covb)*(biv-b); * Contrast test eq (10B.6);
df_sas = round(trace(ginv(covbiv-covb)*(covbiv-covb)));   * SAS df;
p_sas = 1-probchi(h,df_sas);           * p value using k df;
p_correct = 1-probchi(h,k1);           * p value using k1 df;
print / "Hausman contrast test, df and pvalues", h df_sas p_sas
        p_correct;
```

The test is simplified by using the estimated error variance from OLS, equation (10B.7), to create the Durbin-Wu-Hausman chi-square test.

```
hols = (biv-b)`*ginv(inv(xhat`*xhat)-inv(x`*x))*(biv-b)/sig2ols;
pols = 1-probchi(hols,k1);
print ,, "Hausman test and p-value using OLS variance", hols pols;
```

The regression based Hausman test uses the first stage residuals which are added to the original model specification as additional regressors. Their significance is tested with an F-test.

---

[9] SAS ETS User's Guide for PROC MODEL's Hausman test, pages 1060-1061

```
v1 = x1-z*inv(z`*z)*z`*x1;          * first stage residuals;
xa = v1||x;                         * augment X-matrix;
ba = inv(xa`*xa)*xa`*y;             * OLS estimates;
sse_u = ssq(y-xa*ba);               * SSE_U for F-test;
sig2a = sse_u/(n-ncol(xa));         * estiamted error var;
sse_r = ssq(y-x*b);                 * SSE_R for F-test;
F = (sse_r-sse_u)/(k1*sig2a);       * F;
p = 1 - probf(F,k1,n-ncol(xa));     * F p-value;
print ,, "Regression based hausman test, df and p-value", F k1 p;
finish;

run hausman;                        * run Hausman;
```

The contrast test p-value with the correct degrees of freedom ($K_1 = 1$) is 0.10, and with the incorrect degrees of freedom ($K = 4$) the p-value is 0.61, changing the outcome of the test at the 10 percent level of significance. Using the contrast test with the OLS variance estimate, or the regression based test, yield, in this case, values close to the contrast test value.

```
         Hausman contrast test, df and pvalues
           h      df_sas      p_sas p_correct
     2.6956602        4   0.6099742 0.1006218


         Hausman test and p-value using OLS variance
                    hols        pols
              2.7808351   0.0953984


         Regression based hausman test, df and p-value
                    F         k1          p
              2.7925919        1   0.0954406
```

Testing for weak instruments module

It has become abundantly clear that the success of instrumental variables estimation depends upon having strong, or at least not weak, instruments. Some potentially useful tests have developed in recent years. These are neatly unified using the concept of **canonical correlation**. A basic definition and derivation is provided in Theil (1971, p. 317). It is a general correlation measure of association between two matrices, say $\mathbf{Y}$ and $\mathbf{X}$. The use of canonical correlations for analyzing the strength of instruments is nicely summarized in Baum, Schaffer and Stillman (2007, p. 485-489)[10] and the references cited therein. The theory of identification, using the notation introduced at the beginning of this appendix, requires that the $K \times L$ matrix $\mathbf{X}'\mathbf{Z}$ (asymptotically) have rank K. Equivalently, if we partial out the effect of $\mathbf{X}_2$ from the potentially endogenous variables $\mathbf{X}_1$ and the external instruments $\mathbf{Z}_1$, so that $\tilde{\mathbf{X}}_1 = \mathbf{M}_{\mathbf{X}_2}\mathbf{X}_1$ are the residuals from a least squares regression of $\mathbf{X}_1$ on $\mathbf{X}_2$ and $\tilde{\mathbf{Z}}_1 = \mathbf{M}_{\mathbf{X}_2}\mathbf{Z}_1$ are the residuals from a least squares regression of $\mathbf{Z}_1$ on $\mathbf{X}_2$, then the matrix $\tilde{\mathbf{X}}_1'\tilde{\mathbf{Z}}_1$ is $K_1 \times L_1$ and should have rank K_1. Let $r_1,...,r_{K_1}$ be the ordered canonical correlations between $\tilde{\mathbf{X}}_1$ and $\tilde{\mathbf{Z}}_1$, with r_1 being the largest and

---

[10] Enhanced Routines for Instrumental Variables / Generalized Method of Moments Estimation and Testing, The Stata Journal 7(4).

r_{K_1} being the smallest. If the smallest of these is zero, then the rank conditional fails and the equation is "not identified." In the special case of a single potentially endogenous variable and a single external instrument $(K_1 = L_1 = 1)$ then the canonical correlation is the usual correlation coefficient between the two variables. If there is a single endogenous variable, but multiple external instruments $(L_1 = 1, K_1 \geq 1)$ then the canonical correlation is the square root of the usual R^2 from the reduced form regression. In the general case the squared canonical correlations r_i^2 are the eigenvalues (characteristic roots) of

$$\left(\tilde{\mathbf{X}}_1'\tilde{\mathbf{X}}_1\right)^{-1} \tilde{\mathbf{X}}_1'\tilde{\mathbf{Z}}_1 \left(\tilde{\mathbf{Z}}_1'\tilde{\mathbf{Z}}_1\right)^{-1} \tilde{\mathbf{Z}}_1'\tilde{\mathbf{X}}_1$$

The rank condition requires that all K_1 of the canonical correlations be nonzero.

Anderson's canonical correlations test statistic $Nr_{K_1}^2$ is asymptotically $\chi^2_{(L-K+1)}$ under the null hypothesis that the rank condition holds. A similar statistic due to Cragg and Donald is $Nr_{K_1}^2 / (1 - r_{K_1}^2)$ and has as the same asymptotic $\chi^2_{(L-K+1)}$ under the null. These are tests of lack of identification. Stock and Yogo (2005) develop a test for **weak** instruments, basing their test upon the relative bias of the IV estimator to the OLS estimator, and the rejection rate when testing the coefficients of the endogenous variables of a nominal 5% test. They provide tables of critical values based on an F-statistic derived from the Cragg-Donald statistic

$$\frac{N-L}{L_1} \frac{r_{K_1}^2}{\left(1 - r_{K_1}^2\right)}$$

Abbreviated versions of the Stock and Yogo critical values tables[11] are contained in Table 10E.1 and Table 10E.2 on page 436 of *Principles of Econometrics, 4th Edition*.

A test by Anderson and Rubin is described in Greene (2012, pp. 334-336) for testing the null hypothesis $H_0 : \boldsymbol{\beta}_1 = \boldsymbol{\beta}_1^0$, with $\boldsymbol{\beta}_1$ being the coefficients of the endogenous variables in the regression $\mathbf{y} = \mathbf{X}\boldsymbol{\beta} + \mathbf{e}$. The test reduces to an F-test of the null hypothesis $H_0 : \boldsymbol{\theta}_1 = \mathbf{0}$ in the model

$$\mathbf{y} - \mathbf{X}_1\boldsymbol{\beta}_1^0 = \mathbf{Z}_1\boldsymbol{\theta}_1 + \mathbf{Z}_2\boldsymbol{\theta}_2 + error$$

The usual hypothesis is $H_0 : \boldsymbol{\beta}_1 = \mathbf{0}$. The ability of the test to reject the null hypothesis declines in the presence of weak instruments (Baum, et al. (2007, p. 491)).

The **PROC IML** code implementing these tests follows in the module **weakiv**. The two-stage least squares module **tsls** must be run prior.

```
start weakiv;
zp = z1-z2*inv(z2`*z2)*z2`*z1;          * z1 with z2 partialled out;
xp = x1-z2*inv(z2`*z2)*z2`*x1;          * x1 with z2 partialled out;
w = inv(xp`*xp)*xp`*zp*inv(zp`*zp)*zp`*xp; * matrix;
rk2 = eigval(w);                         * squared canonical corr;
rk = sqrt(rk2);                          * canonical corr;
print "canonical correlation and its square" rk rk2;
```

---

[11] More extensive tables are contained in Stock and Yogo (2005), Table 5.1 and Table 5.2, pages 100-101. "Testing for Weak Instruments in Linear IV Regression," in *Identification and Inference for Econometric Models: Essays in Honor of Thomas Rothenberg*, eds. Donald W. K. Andrews and James H. Stock, Cambridge University Press, Chapter 5.

```
anderson_lm=n*rk2;                          * N*R^2 test form;
df_lm=l1-k1+1;                              * DF = #overid + 1;
p_lm = 1-probchi(anderson_lm,df_lm);       * p-value;
print "Anderson LM test statistic for underidentification " ,,
      anderson_lm df_lm p_lm;
cd = rk2/(1-rk2);                          * cragg-donald ratio;
cragg_donald_wald = n*cd;                  * cragg_donald_wald test;
df_cd=l1-k1+1;                             * DF = #overid + 1;
p_cd = 1-probchi(cragg_donald_wald,df_cd); * p-value;
print "Cragg-Donald LM test statistic for underidentification ",,
cragg_donald_wald df_cd p_cd;

cragg_donald_F = (n-l)*cd/l1;              * cragg_donald_F test;
print "Cragg-Donald F test statistic for weakidentification ",,
cragg_donald_F,,
     "Refer to Stock Yogo Tables for critical values";

/* Anderson_Rubin test Y=x1*beta1 + x2*beta2 + error with x1 endogenous */
/* F-test of joint hypothesis beta1 = b0 */
b0=0;                                       * hypothesized values;
y0 = y-x1*b0;                              * remove x1*b0 from y;
sseu = ssq(y0 - z*inv(z`*z)*z`*y0);        * unresricted SS from full model;
sser = ssq(y0 - z2*inv(z2`*z2)*z2`*y0);    * restricted SS;
AR = (n-L)*(sser - sseu)/(l1*sseu);        * F-stat;
p_AR = 1 - probf(AR,l1,n-k);               * p-value;
print "Anderson_Rubin test " AR p_AR;

finish;
run weakiv;
quit;
```

The output is

```
                                          rk          rk2
         canonical correlation and its square 0.4555977 0.2075693

           Anderson LM test statistic for underidentification

                      anderson_lm     df_lm      p_lm
                       88.839647        2         0

         Cragg-Donald LM test statistic for underidentification

                  cragg_donald_wald      df_cd      p_cd
                       112.1103           2         0

         Cragg-Donald F test statistic for weakidentification

                         cragg_donald_F
                            55.4003
```

```
                  Refer to Stock Yogo Tables for critical values

                                        AR        p_AR
                  Anderson_Rubin test   1.9020627 0.1505318
```

It is worth noting that the canonical correlation computations can be carried out using **PROC CANCORR**.

```
    proc cancorr data=mroz;
    var educ;                              * variable set 1;
    with mothereduc fathereduc;            * variable set 2;
    partial exper exper2;                  * variables to partial out;
    run;
```

The first portion of the output is

```
The CANCORR Procedure

Canonical Correlation Analysis Based on Partial Correlations

                        Adjusted    Approximate        Squared
            Canonical   Canonical     Standard       Canonical
          Correlation Correlation        Error      Correlation

    1        0.455598    0.453976     0.038439         0.207569
```

APPENDIX 10C THE REPEATED SAMPLING PROPERTIES OF IV/2SLS

To illustrate the repeated sampling properties of the OLS and IV/2SLS estimators we use the following experimental design. In the simulation[12] we use the data generation process $y = x + e$, so that the intercept parameter is 0 and the slope parameter is 1. The first stage regression is $x = \pi z_1 + \pi z_2 + \pi z_3 + v$. Note that we have $L = 3$ instruments, each of which has an independent standard normal $N(0,1)$ distribution. The parameter π controls the instrument strength. If $\pi = 0$ the instruments are not correlated with x and instrumental variables estimation will fail. The larger π becomes the stronger the instruments become. Finally, we create the random errors e and v to have standard normal distributions with correlation ρ, which controls the endogeneity of x. If $\rho = 0$, then x is not endogenous. The larger ρ becomes the stronger the endogeneity. We create 10,000 samples of size $N = 100$ and then try out OLS and IV/2SLS under several scenarios. We let $\pi = 0.1$ (weak instruments) and $\pi = 0.5$ (strong instruments). We let $\rho = 0$ (x exogenous) and $\rho = 0.8$ (x highly endogenous).

In Appendix 10A we illustrated the use of the Cholesky decomposition. Now we seek only to simulate a pair of bivariate normal random values. Suppose that we want to obtain $y_1 \sim N(\mu_1, \sigma_1^2)$ and $y_2 \sim N(\mu_2, \sigma_2^2)$ such that y_1 and y_2 have correlation ρ. That is,

---

[12] This design is similar to that used by Jinyong Hahn and Jerry Hausman (2003) "Weak Instruments: Diagnosis and Cures in Empirical Economics," *American Economic Review*, 93(2), pp. 118-125.

$$\begin{bmatrix} y_1 \\ y_2 \end{bmatrix} \sim N(\boldsymbol{\mu}, \boldsymbol{\Sigma})$$

where

$$\boldsymbol{\mu} = \begin{pmatrix} \mu_1 \\ \mu_2 \end{pmatrix} \text{ and } \boldsymbol{\Sigma} = \begin{pmatrix} \sigma_1^2 & \rho\sigma_1\sigma_2 \\ \rho\sigma_1\sigma_2 & \sigma_2^2 \end{pmatrix} \text{ then } \mathbf{U} = \begin{pmatrix} 1 & \rho \\ 0 & \sqrt{(1-\rho^2)} \end{pmatrix}^{13}$$

That is $\mathbf{U}'\mathbf{U} = \boldsymbol{\Sigma}$. Then if z_1 and z_2 are independent standard normal random variables

$$y_1 = \mu_1 + \sigma_1 z_1 \text{ and } y_2 = \mu_2 + \rho\sigma_2 z_1 + \sqrt{\sigma_2^2(1-\rho^2)}z_2$$

In our case

$$\begin{bmatrix} e \\ v \end{bmatrix} \sim N(\boldsymbol{\mu}, \boldsymbol{\Sigma}), \ \boldsymbol{\mu} = \begin{pmatrix} 0 \\ 0 \end{pmatrix} \text{ and } \boldsymbol{\Sigma} = \begin{pmatrix} 1 & \rho \\ \rho & 1 \end{pmatrix} \text{ then } \mathbf{U} = \begin{pmatrix} \sigma_1 & \rho\sigma_2 \\ 0 & \sqrt{\sigma_2^2(1-\rho^2)} \end{pmatrix}$$

So

$$e = z_1 \text{ and } v = \rho z_1 + \sqrt{(1-\rho^2)}z_2$$

In the simulation we create 10,000 samples of size $N = 100$. For example, suppose $\pi = 0.5$ and $\rho = 0$, so that in this case there is no endogeneity and the instruments are strong. We make only brief comments in the code

```
data ch10mc;                        * data set;
nsam = 10000;
nobs=100;
pi = .5;
rho = 0;
call streaminit(1234567);           * set random number stream;
do sample = 1 to nsam;              * outer loop repeat samples;
        do n = 1 to nobs;           * start inner loop;
        z1= rand('normal',0,1);     * z1 is N(0,1);
        z2= rand('normal',0,1);     * z2 is N(0,1);
        mu_e = 0;                   * mean for y1;
        mu_v = 0;                   * mean for y2;
        sig_e = 1;                  * SD for y1;
        sig_v = 1;                  * SD for y2;
        e = mu_e + sig_e*z1;
        v = mu_v + rho*sig_v*z1+sqrt(sig_v**2-sig_v**2*rho**2)*z2;
```

Create 3 new independent normal variables as instruments.

```
        z1= rand('normal',0,1);     * z1 is N(0,1);
        z2= rand('normal',0,1);     * z2 is N(0,1);
```

---

[13] This was presented by Lingling Han (2006) "Generating Multivariate Normal Data using PROC IML," SESUG 2006: The Proceedings of the SouthEast SAS Users Group, Atlanta, GA, 2006. See http://analytics.ncsu.edu/sesug/2006/CC15_06.PDF

```
                z3= rand('normal',0,1);              * z3 is N(0,1);
                x = pi*z1 + pi*z2 + pi*z3 + v;
                y = x + e;                            * DGP;
                output;                               * output to data set;
                end;                                  * end inner loop;
        end;                                          * end outer loop;
        run;
```

Least squares regression outputting estimates and standard errors.

```
        proc reg data=ch10mc noprint outest=est outseb;
        model y = x;
        by sample;
        run;
```

Print one output data set to see its contents

```
        proc print data=est;
        where sample=1;
        title 'least squares estimation outest data';
        run;
```

```
                least squares estimation outest data


Obs    sample   _MODEL_   _TYPE_   _DEPVAR_    _RMSE_   Intercept       x        y
 1       1      MODEL1    PARMS        y       0.93744   -0.11011   0.94909    -1
 2       1      MODEL1    SEB          y       0.93744    0.09474   0.07786    -1
```

Create data sets for slope estimates and standard error.

```
        data b2; set est; if _type_='PARMS'; b2 = x; keep sample b2;
        run;
```

```
        data se2; set est; if _type_='SEB'; se2 = x; keep sample se2;
        run;
```

Estimate the first stage regression and save the residuals for the Hausman test.

```
        proc reg data=ch10mc noprint outest=ftest rsquare;
        model x = z1 z2 z3;
        output out=resids r=vhat;
        by sample;
        run;
        proc print data=ftest;
        where sample = 1;
        title 'first stage F-test outest data';
        run;
```

```
                first stage F-test outest data


Obs    sample   _MODEL_   _TYPE_   _DEPVAR_    _RMSE_   Intercept
 1       1      MODEL1    PARMS        x       0.87695   -0.092491
```

```
Obs      z1         z2        z3       x    _IN_   _P_   _EDF_   _RSQ_
 1    0.45990   0.33619   0.67946   -1     3     4      96    0.49074
```

In this case the test for weak instruments is a test of the joint significance of z_1, z_2 and z_3. The overall F-test of significance can be computed as

$$\frac{R^2/(K-1)}{(1-R^2)/(N-K)}$$

Use _RSQ_ to compute first stage F-test.

```
data ftest; set ftest; if _type_='PARMS';
f = (_RSQ_/(4-1))/((1-_RSQ_)/(100-4));
keep sample f;
run;
```

The regression based Hausman test is given by

```
proc reg data=resids noprint outest=htest tableout;
model y = x vhat;
by sample;
run;
```

```
proc print data=htest;
where sample=1;
title 'hausman test outest data';
run;
```

```
                   hausman test outest data
```

Obs	sample	_MODEL_	_TYPE_	_DEPVAR_	_RMSE_	Intercept	x	vhat	y
1	1	MODEL1	PARMS	y	0.93904	-0.09869	1.01392	-0.12729	-1
2	1	MODEL1	STDERR	y	0.93904	0.09593	0.11133	0.15601	.
3	1	MODEL1	T	y	0.93904	-1.02877	9.10724	-0.81594	.

The Hausman test statistic is the t-statistic on the variable *VHAT*.

```
data htest; set htest; if _type_='T'; hausman = vhat;
keep sample hausman;
run;
```

Obtain 2SLS estimates. **COVOUT** outputs the covariance matrix of estimates.

```
proc syslin noprint data=ch10mc outest=est2 2sls covout;
instruments z1 z2 z3;
endogenous x;
model y = x;
by sample;
run;
```

```
proc print data=est2;
where sample = 1;
title '2sls outest data';
run;
```

```
                              2sls outest data
```

Obs	sample	_TYPE_	_STATUS_	_MODEL_	_DEPVAR_	_NAME_	_SIGMA_
11	1	2SLS	0 Converged	y	y		0.94075
12	1	2SLS	0 Converged	y	y	Intercept	.
13	1	2SLS	0 Converged	y	y	x	.

Obs	Intercept	z1	z2	z3	x	y
11	-0.09869	.	.	.	1.01392	-1
12	0.00924	.	.	.	0.00219	.
13	0.00219	.	.	.	0.01244	.

```
data b2iv; set est2; if _type_='2SLS'; if _name_=' '; b2iv = x;
keep sample b2iv;
run;
```

```
data se2iv; set est2; if _type_='2SLS'; if _name_='x'; se2iv = sqrt(x);
keep sample se2iv;
run;
```

Merge all the data sets by *SAMPLE*.

```
data mc;
merge b2 se2 b2iv se2iv ftest htest;
by sample;

/* LS test beta2 = 1 */
tstat = (b2 - 1)/se2;
tc = tinv(.975,100-2);
reject = (abs(tstat) >= tc);

/* hausman test */
th = tinv(.975,100-3);
rejecth = (abs(hausman) >= th);

/* IV test beta2 = 1 */
tstativ = (b2iv - 1)/se2iv;
rejectiv = (abs(tstativ) >= tc);
run;
```

```
proc means data=mc mean std;
var f b2 se2 reject rejecth b2iv se2iv rejectiv;
title 'pi = 0.5 and rho = 0';
run;
```

```
              pi = 0.5 and rho = 0

           The MEANS Procedure

   Variable          Mean          Std Dev
   ─────────────────────────────────────────
   f              26.2654438        8.1859849
   b2              0.9994779        0.0773438
   se2             0.0763118        0.0077985
   reject          0.0506000        0.2191904
   rejecth         0.0521000        0.2222398
   b2iv            1.0003772        0.1194603
   se2iv           0.1176036        0.0193018
   rejectiv        0.0460000        0.2094956
   ─────────────────────────────────────────
```

The results for this case show that the average first-stage F is 26.27 which indicates strong instruments. The average least squares estimate is close to its true value, and the standard deviation of the estimates is close to its average standard error. The least squares t-test that the slope is 1 is rejected 5% of the time, and the Hausman test rejects endogeneity 5% of the time. These two hypotheses are true so the rejection rate is the probability of Type I error. The average of the instrumental variable estimates is close to its true value, but its sampling variability is greater than that of the least squares estimates. The instrumental variables t-test that the slope is 1 is rejected 4.6% of the time.

Repeat the experiment for alternative settings of experiment. For example if $\pi = 0.5$ and $\rho = 0.8$. The results below show the strong first stage F-test value, but now under strong endogeneity the least squares estimator is biased, and the test of the true null hypothesis that the slope is 1 is rejected 100% of the time. It should be noted that under these design settings the Hausman test performs as it should, rejecteing endogeneity 100% of the time. The IV estimator however has average value close to the true value of one, and the test that the slope is one is rejected 7% of the time, which is closer to the nominal value of 5%.

```
             pi = 0.5 and rho = 0.8

           The MEANS Procedure

   Variable          Mean          Std Dev
   ─────────────────────────────────────────
   f              26.3502521        8.1730215
   b2              1.4568211        0.0619197
   se2             0.0608310        0.0062166
   reject          1.0000000               0
   rejecth         1.0000000               0
   b2iv            1.0108313        0.1184961
   se2iv           0.1170591        0.0278608
   rejectiv        0.0702000        0.2554966
   ─────────────────────────────────────────
```

APPENDIX 10D ROBUST 2SLS AND GMM

10D.1 The model, estimators and tests

The instrumental variables, or 2SLS, estimator of $\boldsymbol{\beta}$ is from Section 10B.1 is

$$\mathbf{b}_{IV} = \left[\mathbf{X'Z(Z'Z)^{-1}Z'X} \right]^{-1} \mathbf{X'Z(Z'Z)^{-1}Z'y} = \left[\mathbf{X'P_Z X} \right]^{-1} \mathbf{X'P_Z y} = \left[\hat{\mathbf{X}}'\hat{\mathbf{X}} \right]^{-1} \hat{\mathbf{X}}'\mathbf{y} \qquad (10\text{C}.1)$$

where $\mathbf{P_Z} = \mathbf{Z(Z'Z)^{-1}Z'}$ is a symmetric and idempotent "projection" matrix such that $\mathbf{P_Z X} = \mathbf{Z(Z'Z)^{-1}Z'X} = \hat{\mathbf{X}}$. The estimated asymptotic covariance matrix of this estimator **under homoskedasticity** is

$$\hat{\mathbf{V}}\left(\mathbf{b}_{IV}\right) = \hat{\sigma}_{IV}^2 \left[\mathbf{X'Z(Z'Z)^{-1}Z'X} \right]^{-1} = \hat{\sigma}_{IV}^2 \left[\mathbf{X'P_Z X} \right]^{-1} = \hat{\sigma}_{IV}^2 \left[\hat{\mathbf{X}}'\hat{\mathbf{X}} \right]^{-1} \qquad (10\text{C}.2)$$

A covariance matrix that is robust to heteroskedasticity is

$$\breve{\mathbf{V}}\left(\mathbf{b}_{IV}\right) = \left[\hat{\mathbf{X}}'\hat{\mathbf{X}} \right]^{-1} \hat{\mathbf{X}}'\mathbf{D}\hat{\mathbf{X}} \left[\hat{\mathbf{X}}'\hat{\mathbf{X}} \right]^{-1}$$

where, using $\hat{e}_i^2$ to denote the 2SLS residuals,

$$\mathbf{D} = \frac{N}{N-K} \begin{bmatrix} \hat{e}_1^2 & & & \\ & \hat{e}_2^2 & & \\ & & \ddots & \\ & & & \hat{e}_N^2 \end{bmatrix}$$

The 2SLS estimator is not efficient in the presence of heteroskedasticity. The GMM estimator is asymptotically more efficient. If the regression $\mathbf{y} = \mathbf{X}\boldsymbol{\beta} + \mathbf{e}$ has heteroskedastic errors with covariance matrix $\text{cov}(\mathbf{e}) = \boldsymbol{\Omega} = diag\left(\sigma_1^2, \sigma_2^2, \ldots, \sigma_N^2 \right)$, then the efficient GMM estimator[14] is

$$\mathbf{b}_{GMM} = \left[\mathbf{X'Z}\hat{\mathbf{V}}^{-1}\mathbf{Z'X} \right]^{-1} \mathbf{X'Z}\hat{\mathbf{V}}^{-1}\mathbf{Z'y}$$

where $\hat{\mathbf{V}} = \mathbf{Z'DZ}$ and $\mathbf{D}$ is given above. The estimated covariance matrix of this estimator is

$$\hat{V}\left(\mathbf{b}_{GMM}\right) = \left[\mathbf{X'Z}\hat{\mathbf{V}}^{-1}\mathbf{Z'X} \right]^{-1}$$

10D.2 Using PROC MODEL and IML

To illustrate we use the Mroz data as in Appendix 10B.

```
data mroz;
set 'mroz';
if lfp = 1;
exper2 = exper**2;
```

---

[14] Greene (2012), p. 487. We have added a degrees of freedom correction.

```
lwage = log(wage);
one = 1;
run;
```

Using **PROC MODEL** for 2SLS we add **hccme=1** to the **fit** statement.

```
proc model data=mroz;
endogenous educ;
instruments exper exper2 mothereduc fathereduc;
lwage = b1 + b2*educ + b3*exper + b4*exper2;
fit lwage/ 2sls hccme=1;                    * robust option;
title '2sls with robust se';
run;
```

To obtain the GMM estimates specify **gmm** on the **fit** statement with a specific **kernel = (bart,0,)** and the option **nogengmmv** (which stands for "no" general GMM variance matrix). If these options are omitted SAS will use GMM with a more general specification of the covariance matrix.[15]

```
proc model data=mroz;
endogenous educ;
instruments exper exper2 mothereduc fathereduc;
lwage = b1 + b2*educ + b3*exper + b4*exper2;
fit lwage/ gmm kernel=(bart,0,) nogengmmv;
title 'gmm estimation of ln(wage) equation';
run;
```

For robust 2SLS the output is

```
                  2sls with robust se

               The MODEL Procedure

          Nonlinear 2SLS Summary of Residual Errors
              DF    DF                                     Adj
Equation   Model  Error     SSE     MSE  Root MSE  R-Square  R-Sq
lwage          4    424   193.0  0.4552    0.6747    0.1357  0.1296


              Nonlinear 2SLS Parameter Estimates

                               Approx              Approx
         Parameter   Estimate  Std Err  t Value   Pr > |t|
         b1            0.0481   0.4298     0.11     0.9109
         b2          0.061397   0.0333     1.84     0.0662
         b3           0.04417   0.0155     2.84     0.0047
         b4           -0.0009 0.000430    -2.09     0.0372
```

For GMM the output is

---

[15] See the SAS/ETS 9.2 Users Guide, page 997

gmm estimation of ln(wage) equation

The MODEL Procedure

Nonlinear GMM Summary of Residual Errors

Equation	DF Model	DF Error	SSE	MSE	Root MSE	R-Square	Adj R-Sq
lwage	4	424	193.1	0.4554	0.6748	0.1354	0.1293

Nonlinear GMM Parameter Estimates

Parameter	Estimate	Approx Std Err	t Value	Approx Pr > |t|
b1	0.047654	0.4298	0.11	0.9118
b2	0.061053	0.0333	1.83	0.0677
b3	0.045135	0.0155	2.92	0.0037
b4	-0.00093	0.000427	-2.18	0.0299

These results are replicated using the PROC IML code

```
proc iml;                                    * invoke IML;
use mroz;                                    * open mroz;
read all into y var{lwage};                  * dependent variable;
read all into x var{one educ exper exper2};  * regressors;
read all into z var{one exper exper2 mothereduc fathereduc}; * iv;
n = nrow(y);                                 * number of observations;
k = ncol(x);                                 * number of regressors;
l = ncol(z);                                 * number of IV;
rname = {one educ exper exper2};             * names for estimates;

/* OLS with robust se. See Wooldridge (2010) Econometric Analysis */
/* of Cross Sectional and Panel Data, Second Ed page 61, eq (4.11) */

start tsls;
ztz=z`*z;                                    * Z'Z;
ztzi = inv(ztz);                             * inv(Z'Z);
xhat = z*ztzi*z`*x;                          * X-hat;
biv = inv(xhat`*xhat)*xhat`*y;               * 2sls-Greene 7th, p.231;
ehat = y-x*biv;                              * 2sls residuals;
ehat2 = ehat##2;                             * residals squared;
bmat = xhat`*(ehat2#xhat);                   * X'*diag(e^2)*X;

/* Robust cov mat- See Wooldridge (2010), page 106            */
robust = (n/(n-k))*inv(xhat`*xhat)*bmat*inv(xhat`*xhat);
se = sqrt(vecdiag(robust));                  * robust se;
tstat = biv/se;                              * robust t;
pval = 2*(1-probt(abs(tstat),n-k));          * p-value;
result = biv||se||tstat||pval;               * stack results;
cname = {est se tstat pval};                 * column names;
print / "2sls robust hccmee=1",, result [rowname=rname colname=cname
format=13.6];
```

```
finish;
run tsls;                                       * run 2sls module;

start gmm;                                       * start module;
vhat = z`*(ehat2#z);                             * V'*diag(ehat^2)*V;

/* GMM estimator with optimal weight matrix    */
/* See Greene, 7th, page 487                   */
bgmm = inv(x`*z*inv(vhat)*z`*x)*x`*z*inv(vhat)*z`*y;

/* Covariance with df adjustment               */
covbgmm = (n/(n-k))*inv(x`*z*inv(vhat)*z`*x);
se = sqrt(vecdiag(covbgmm));                     * gmm se;
tstat = bgmm/se;                                 * tstat;
pval = 2*(1-probt(abs(tstat),n-k));              * p-value;
result = bgmm||se||tstat||pval;                  * stack result;
cname = {est se tstat pval};                     * estimate name;
print / "GMM ",, result [rowname=rname colname=cname format=13.6];
finish;                                          * finish module;
run gmm;                                         * run gmm;

quit;                                            * exit IML;
```

Yielding output

```
                        2sls robust hccmee=1

                              result
                 EST           SE          TSTAT          PVAL

ONE            0.048100     0.429798      0.111914      0.910945
EDUC           0.061397     0.033339      1.841609      0.066231
EXPER          0.044170     0.015546      2.841202      0.004711
EXPER2        -0.000899     0.000430     -2.090220      0.037193

                               GMM

                              result
                 EST           SE          TSTAT          PVAL

ONE            0.047654     0.429797      0.110875      0.911768
EDUC           0.061053     0.033335      1.831511      0.067726
EXPER          0.045135     0.015478      2.916067      0.003733
EXPER2        -0.000931     0.000427     -2.179135      0.029871
```

CHAPTER 11

Simultaneous Equations Models

11.1 SIMULTANEOUS EQUATIONS

In this chapter we consider econometric models for data that are jointly determined by two or more economic relations. Simultaneous equations models differ from econometric models we have considered so far because they consist of a *set of equations*. For example, price and quantity are determined by the interaction of two equations, one for supply and one for demand. Simultaneous equations models, which contain more than one dependent variable and more than one equation, require special statistical treatment. The least squares estimation procedure *is not* appropriate in these models and we must develop new ways to obtain reliable estimates of economic parameters.

11.1.1 Structural equations

The fundamental example is a supply and demand model that includes two structural equations, describing market demand and market supply.

$$\text{Demand:} \quad Q = \alpha_1 P + \alpha_2 X + e_d$$

$$\text{Supply:} \quad Q = \beta_1 P + e_s$$

Based on economic theory we expect the supply curve to be positively sloped, $\beta_1 > 0$, and the demand curve negatively sloped, $\alpha_1 < 0$. In this model we assume that the quantity demanded (Q) is a function of price (P) and income (X). Quantity supplied is taken to be only a function of price. We have omitted the intercepts to make the algebra easier. In practice we would include intercept terms in these models.

In this model the variables P and Q are called **endogenous** variables because their values are determined within the system we have created. The endogenous variables P and Q are *dependent* variables and both are random variables. The income variable X has a value which is determined outside this system. Such variables are said to be **exogenous**, and these variables are treated like usual "x" explanatory variables.

Random errors are added to the supply and demand equations for the usual reasons, and we assume that they have the usual properties

$$E(e_d) = 0, \quad \text{var}(e_d) = \sigma_d^2$$

$$E(e_s) = 0, \quad \text{var}(e_s) = \sigma_s^2$$

$$\text{cov}(e_d, e_s) = 0$$

Estimation of a structural equation requires that it be **identified**. In a system of M equations a necessary condition for an equation to be identified is that at least $M - 1$ system variables be omitted. In the supply and demand model above there are $M = 2$ equations including the variables Q, P, and X. The necessary condition for identification requires that at least 1 variable be omitted from each equation. The condition is met by the supply equation but not the demand equation. The supply equation parameters can be consistently estimated. The demand equation parameters cannot be consistently estimated.

11.1.2 Reduced form equations

Reduced form equations are obtained by solving the structural, simultaneous, equations for the endogenous variables. There is one reduced form equation for each endogenous variable.

$$P = \frac{\alpha_2}{(\beta_1 - \alpha_1)} X + \frac{e_d - e_s}{(\beta_1 - \alpha_1)} = \pi_1 X + v_1$$

$$Q = \beta_1 P + e_s = \frac{\beta_1 \alpha_2}{(\beta_1 - \alpha_1)} X + \frac{\beta_1 e_d - \alpha_1 e_s}{(\beta_1 - \alpha_1)} = \pi_2 X + v_2$$

On the right-hand-side of the reduced form equations are exogenous variables, parameters and random errors. These equations can be estimated by least squares. We called the reduced form equations "first stage" equations in Chapter 10.

11.1.3 Why least squares fails

The supply equation parameters can be consistently estimated, but not by the usual least squares method. In the supply equation it can be shown that the covariance between the right-hand-side variable P and the error term e_s is

$$\text{cov}(P, e_s) = E(Pe_s) = \frac{-\sigma_s^2}{\beta_1 - \alpha_1} < 0$$

It can also be shown that in large samples the least squares estimator b_1 of β_1 in the supply equation converges towards

$$b_1 \to \beta_1 + \frac{E(Pe_s)}{E(P^2)} = \beta_1 - \frac{\sigma_s^2 / (\beta_1 - \alpha_1)}{E(P^2)} < \beta_1$$

That is, the least squares estimator does not converge to β_1 in large samples. It is an inconsistent estimator. See *Principles of Econometrics, 4th Edition*, Appendix 11A for details.

11.1.4 Two-stage least squares estimation

When an equation is identified it can be estimated. There are many single equation estimation techniques. The most prominent is **two-stage least squares (2SLS)**. The least squares estimator for the supply equation fails because P is correlated with e_s. From the reduced form equation

$$P = E(P) + v_1 = \pi_1 X + v_1$$

We see that P is equals a non-random, exogenous, systematic part $E(P) = \pi_1 X$ and the random part v_1. The troublesome part of P that is correlated with e_s is v_1. The logic of 2SLS is to estimate $E(P) = \pi_1 X$ and use this in the regression model instead of P. Estimation of the supply equation by 2SLS begins with estimation of the reduced form equation for price P. The resulting fitted value $\hat{P} = \hat{\pi}_1 X$ is a second stage in which the supply equation is estimated using $\hat{P}$ as the right-hand-side explanatory variable. The resulting estimator for β_1 is consistent, asymptotically normally distributed, and has a variance formula that is valid in large samples.[1]

11.2 TRUFFLE SUPPLY AND DEMAND

Consider a supply and demand model for truffles:

$$\text{Demand:} \quad Q_i = \alpha_1 + \alpha_2 P_i + \alpha_3 PS_i + \alpha_4 DI_i + e_i^d$$

$$\text{Supply:} \quad Q_i = \beta_1 + \beta_2 P_i + \beta_3 PF_i + e_i^s$$

In the demand equation Q is the quantity of truffles traded in a particular French market place, indexed by i; P is the market price of truffles, PS is the market price of a substitute for real truffles (another fungus much less highly prized), and DI is per capita monthly disposable income of local residents. The supply equation contains the market price and quantity supplied. Also it includes PF, the price of a factor of production, which in this case is the hourly rental price of truffle-pigs used in the search process. In this model we assume that P and Q are endogenous variables. The exogenous variables are PS, DI, PF and the intercept variable. The demand equation is identified in this $M = 2$ equation system because it omits the variable PF, which appears in the supply equation. Because the demand equation omits the minimum acceptable number of variables ($M - 1 = 1$), the demand equation is said to be **just identified** or **exactly identified**. The supply equation omits PS and DI which is one more than required. It is said to be **over-identified**.

The data for this example are in the SAS data set *truffles*. Execute the usual beginning commands.

```
data truffles;                    * create data set;
set 'truffles';                   * read truffles data;
run;

proc contents data=truffles position;
title 'contents of truffle data';
run;
```

---

[1] The 2SLS estimation technique is equivalent to the **method of instrumental variables** that is explained in detail in Chapter 10 of this manual. Readers wanting a deeper understanding of 2SLS are encouraged to study Chapter 10 thoroughly.

```
options nolabel;
```

```
# Variable Type Len Label
1 P         Num   8 price of premium truffles, $ per ounce
2 Q         Num   8 quantity of truffles traded in a market period, in ounces
3 PS        Num   8 price of choice truffles (a substitute), $ per ounce
4 DI        Num   8 per capita disposable income, in units of $1000 per month
5 PF        Num   8 hourly rental price of truffle pig, $ per hour
```

Summary statistics for the data are given by **PROC MEANS.**

```
proc means data=truffles;
title 'truffles summary stats';
run;
```

Variable	N	Mean	Std Dev	Minimum	Maximum
P	30	62.7240002	18.7234619	29.6399994	105.4499969
Q	30	18.4583334	4.6130879	6.3699999	26.2700005
PS	30	22.0220001	4.0772373	15.2100000	28.9799995
DI	30	3.5269667	1.0408033	1.5250000	5.1250000
PF	30	22.7533334	5.3296536	10.5200005	34.0099983

11.2.1 The reduced form equations

The reduced form equations express each endogenous variable, P and Q, in terms of the exogenous variables PS, DI, PF and the intercept variable, plus an error term. They are:

$$Q_i = \pi_{11} + \pi_{21} PS_i + \pi_{31} DI_i + \pi_{41} PF_i + v_{i1}$$

$$P_i = \pi_{12} + \pi_{22} PS_i + \pi_{32} DI_i + \pi_{42} PF_i + v_{i2}$$

We can estimate these equations by least squares since the right-hand side variables are exogenous and uncorrelated with the random errors. The reduced form for quantity and price are obtained using **PROC REG**.

```
proc reg data=truffles;          * reduced form regression;
redform_Q:model q = ps di pf;    * quantity model;
redform_P:model p = ps di pf;    * price model;
output out=pout p=phat;          * output predict p;
test di=0,pf=0;                  * test;
title 'reduced form regressions';
run;
```

The estimates for the Quantity (Q) reduced form equation are:

```
                        Model: redform_Q

                    Parameter      Standard
        Variable    DF  Estimate       Error   t Value   Pr > |t|
        Intercept   1   7.89510      3.24342      2.43     0.0221
        PS          1   0.65640      0.14254      4.61     <.0001
        DI          1   2.16716      0.70047      3.09     0.0047
        PF          1  -0.50698      0.12126     -4.18     0.0003
```

The estimates for the Price (*P*) reduced form are:

```
                        Model: redform_P
                    Dependent Variable: P

                    Parameter      Standard
        Variable    DF  Estimate       Error   t Value   Pr > |t|
        Intercept   1  -32.51242     7.98424     -4.07     0.0004
        PS          1   1.70815      0.35088      4.87     <.0001
        DI          1   7.60249      1.72434      4.41     0.0002
        PF          1   1.35391      0.29851      4.54     0.0001
```

Identification of the demand equation

The demand equation is identified because *PF* does not appear in it. However it is not enough that it does not appear in the demand equation, since there are lots of factors that also do not appear. What is important is that *PF* is not in the demand equation and *PF* is in the supply equation. That this is true can be tested indirectly by testing the significance of *PF* in the reduced form equation for *P*. If *PF* does not appear in the supply equation then it will not appear in the reduced form equation. Indeed, modern research has shown that the effectiveness of 2SLS for the demand equation depends on the strong significance of *PF*, with a *t* statistic larger than about 3.3. We can see from the estimation results that this is true.

Identification of the supply equation

The supply equation is identified because at least one of the variables *DI* or *PS* is absent from it, and is included in the demand equation. Again we can test if this is true by testing the joint significance of *DI* and *PS* in the reduced form equation for *P*. The reasoning is that if neither *DI* nor *PS* appears in the demand equation then they will also not appear in the reduced form equation. The joint test is appropriate because for identification we require that one or the other or both appear in the demand equation. This is the reason for the inclusion of the **test di=0, ps=0** following the second reduced form equation. The result shows that these variables are jointly significant. The rule of thumb is that the *F*-value must be larger than 10 for 2SLS to be effective. More precise bounds are given by Stock-Yogo (2005) tables discussed in Chapter 10.

```
        Source          DF      Square      F Value    Pr > F

        Numerator        2    1805.81168      41.49     <.0001
        Denominator     26      43.52682
```

11.2.2 Two-stage least squares estimation

Two-stage least squares (2SLS) estimates can be obtained by replacing the endogenous variable on the right-hand side of the structural equations by the fitted value from the reduced form and then applying least squares. After the *P* reduced form equation we output the predicted value to a SAS data set. The second stage regression for the supply equation using this approach is

```
proc reg data=pout;              * regression with output data;
model q = phat pf;               * 2sls estimates;
title 'second stage regression';
run;
```

Variable	DF	Parameter Estimate	Standard Error	t Value	Pr > |t|
Intercept	1	20.03280	2.16570	9.25	<.0001
phat	1	0.33798	0.04412	7.66	<.0001
PF	1	-1.00091	0.14613	-6.85	<.0001

The second stage parameter estimates are the 2SLS parameter estimates. However the standard errors, *t*-values and *p*-values are not correct using this two least squares regressions approach. Proper estimation software, as described in the next section, should be used to avoid possibly incorrect inferences.

11.2.3 2SLS Using PROC SYSLIN

PROC SYSLIN is a powerful procedure for estimating simultaneous equations models. Enter **help syslin** in the command line and press **Enter**

Two stage least squares estimates are provided by **PROC SYSLIN** using the option **2sls.** In the specification we list the exogenous variables in an **instruments** statement. The endogenous variable(s) appearing on the right-hand side of the models is specified in the **endogenous** statement. Then we have **model** statements for the demand and supply equations

```
proc syslin data=truffles 2sls;  * proc syslin with 2sls;
instruments ps di pf;            * list instrumental variables;
endogenous p;                    * list endogenous variable;
demand:model q = p ps di;        * demand equation;
supply:model q = p pf;           * supply equation;
title '2sls estimation';
run;
```

The output for the supply equation includes the usual summary statistics, and correctly estimated standard errors, *t*-values and *p*-values.[2]

---

[2] See Appendix 10B for the algebraic details of 2SLS and SAS/IML code.

```
                    The SYSLIN Procedure
              Two-Stage Least Squares Estimation

                    Model              DEMAND
                    Dependent Variable    Q

                    Parameter    Standard
Variable      DF    Estimate      Error    t Value   Pr > |t|
Intercept      1    -4.27947    5.543885    -0.77     0.4471
P              1    -0.37446    0.164752    -2.27     0.0315
PS             1     1.296033   0.355193     3.65     0.0012
DI             1     5.013978   2.283556     2.20     0.0372


                    Model              SUPPLY
                    Dependent Variable    Q

                    Parameter    Standard
Variable      DF    Estimate      Error    t Value   Pr > |t|
Intercept      1    20.03280    1.223115    16.38     <.0001
P              1     0.337982   0.024920    13.56     <.0001
PF             1    -1.00091    0.082528   -12.13     <.0001
```

11. 3 LIMITED INFORMATION MAXIMUM LIKELIHOOD (LIML)

In recent years there has been a resurgence of interest in the **limited information maximum likelihood**, or **LIML, estimator.**[3] It belongs to a class of estimators known as the k-class, to which 2SLS also belongs. In Section 11.1.4 we described the logic of the 2SLS estimator. The least squares estimator for the supply equation fails because P is correlated with e_s. From the reduced form equation

$$P = E(P) + v_1 = \pi_1 X + v_1$$

We see that P equals a non-random, exogenous, systematic part $E(P) = \pi_1 X$ and a random part v_1. The troublesome part of P that is correlated with e_s is v_1. The logic of 2SLS is to estimate $E(P) = \pi_1 X$ and use this in the regression model instead of P. An equally valid approach is to remove the effect of the random component v_1 from P. While we do not know v_1, we can compute the least squares residuals from the estimated reduced form equation, $\hat{v}_1 = P - \hat{P} = P - \hat{\pi}_1 X$ and subtract it from P to estimate $E(P)$. The 2SLS estimates are then obtained by regressing Q on $P - \hat{v}_1$.

The k-class of estimators is a unifying framework that uses the instrumental variable $P - k\hat{v}_1$. If $k = 0$ we obtain the least squares estimator and if $k = 1$ we obtain the 2SLS estimator. The value of k for the LIML estimator is based on the data, and the exact method is discussed in Appendix 11A. To implement LIML add **liml** to the **PROC SYSLIN** statement. LIML estimates of exactly identified equations are identical to the 2SLS estimates, so we will implement it only for the supply equation, which is over-identified

---

[3] For estimation details see Greene (2012, pp. 326-329) and Appendix 11A of this chapter.

```
proc syslin data=truffles liml;        * proc syslin with liml;
instruments ps di pf;                   * list instrumental variables;
endogenous p;                           * list endogenous variable;
supply:model q = p pf;                  * supply equation;
title 'LIML estimation';
run;
```

In this example the calculated value of k for the LIML estimation is $k = 1.05$, so the LIML estimates are very similar to the 2SLS estimates.

The SYSLIN Procedure
Limited-Information Maximum Likelihood Estimation

Model   SUPPLY
Dependent Variable   Q

Variable	DF	Parameter Estimate	Standard Error	t Value	Pr > |t|
Intercept	1	20.03280	1.223197	16.38	<.0001
P	1	0.337981	0.025133	13.45	<.0001
PF	1	-1.00091	0.082952	-12.07	<.0001

NOTE: K-Class Estimation with K=1.0538610808

11.3.1 LIML modifications

The LIML estimator is not without its flaws. Improvements have been offered by Fuller (1977)[4]. These estimators are available in SAS using the **alpha=** option on the **PROC SYSLIN** statement. The usual values are **alpha = 1** and **alpha = 4**. More details are given in Appendix 11A of this manual. For example, using **alpha = 4**, we have,

```
proc syslin data=truffles liml alpha=4; * liml modified;
instruments ps di pf;                   * list instrumental variables;
endogenous p;                           * list endogenous variable;
supply:model q = p pf;                  * supply equation;
title 'Fuller k-class: alpha=4';
run;
```

Variable	DF	Parameter Estimate	Standard Error	t Value	Pr > |t|
Intercept	1	20.03280	1.222977	16.38	<.0001
p	1	0.337982	0.024559	13.76	<.0001
pf	1	-1.00091	0.081814	-12.23	<.0001

NOTE: K-Class Estimation with K=0.9057129858

---

[4] Fuller, Wayne (1977) "Some properties of a modification of the limited information estimator," *Econometrica*, 45(4), 939-953.

11.4 SYSTEM ESTIMATION METHODS

Instead of estimating each equation separately it is sometimes more efficient (smaller asymptotic standard errors) to estimate the equations of the system all at once. One case in which a system method is more efficient is when the equation error terms are correlated. In the supply in demand model this would mean that $\text{cov}(e_d, e_s) = \sigma_{ds} \neq 0$.

11.4.1 Three stage least squares (3SLS)

The three stage least squares (3SLS) estimator's first two stages are 2SLS. In the third step a generalized least squares-like estimation is applied to take into account the correlation between the error terms of the equations. Add **3sls** to the **PROC SYSLIN** statement.

```
proc syslin data=truffles 3sls;      * proc syslin with 3sls;
instruments ps di pf;                 * list instrumental variables;
endogenous p;                         * list endogenous variable;
demand:model q = p ps di;             * demand equation;
supply:model q = p pf;                * supply equation;
title '3sls estimation';
run;
```

                    Model   DEMAND
                    Dependent Variable   Q

                        Parameter   Standard
Variable	DF	Estimate	Error	t Value	Pr > |t|
Intercept	1	-4.01188	5.539203	-0.72	0.4754
P	1	-0.40042	0.163263	-2.45	0.0212
PS	1	1.263878	0.354137	3.57	0.0014
DI	1	5.600510	2.228301	2.51	0.0185

                    Model   SUPPLY
                    Dependent Variable   Q

                        Parameter   Standard
Variable	DF	Estimate	Error	t Value	Pr > |t|
Intercept	1	20.03280	1.223115	16.38	<.0001
P	1	0.337982	0.024920	13.56	<.0001
PF	1	-1.00091	0.082528	-12.13	<.0001

11.4.2 Iterated three stage least squares

The 3SLS estimator can be "iterated" by computing parameter estimates, then computing new residuals that are used in the generalized least squares-like estimation step, then new parameter estimates, new residuals, and so on, until convergence. While asymptotic theory proves that this makes no difference in large samples ("Iteration does not pay in large samples"), it does seem to improve estimator performance in smaller samples. Add **it3sls** to the **proc syslin** statement

```
proc syslin data=truffles it3sls;    * proc syslin with it3sls;
instruments ps di pf;                 * list instrumental variables;
```

```
endogenous p;                        * list endogenous variable;
demand:model q = p ps di;            * demand equation;
supply:model q = p pf;               * supply equation;
title 'iterated 3sls estimation';
run;
```

The SYSLIN Procedure
Iterative Three-Stage Least Squares Estimation

Parameter Estimates

Variable	DF	Parameter Estimate	Standard Error	t Value	Pr > |t|
Intercept	1	-3.99717	5.746507	-0.70	0.4929
p	1	-0.40184	0.169325	-2.37	0.0253
ps	1	1.262111	0.367364	3.44	0.0020
di	1	5.632739	2.309787	2.44	0.0219

Model   SUPPLY
Dependent Variable   q

Parameter Estimates

Variable	DF	Parameter Estimate	Standard Error	t Value	Pr > |t|
Intercept	1	20.03280	1.223115	16.38	<.0001
p	1	0.337982	0.024920	13.56	<.0001
pf	1	-1.00091	0.082528	-12.13	<.0001

11.4.3 Full information maximum likelihood (FIML)

While LIML is a technique designed for application to one equation at a time, **full information maximum likelihood** maximizes the likelihood function for the entire system of equations simultaneously.

```
proc syslin data=truffles fiml;     * proc syslin with fiml;
instruments ps di pf;                * list instrumental variables;
endogenous p;                        * list endogenous variable;
demand:model q = p ps di;            * demand equation;
supply:model q = p pf;               * supply equation;
title 'fiml estimation';
run;
```

The SYSLIN Procedure
Full-Information Maximum Likelihood Estimation

NOTE: Convergence criterion met at iteration 3.

Model   DEMAND
Dependent Variable   q

Variable	DF	Parameter Estimate	Standard Error	t Value	Pr > |t|
Intercept	1	-4.00275	5.345681	-0.75	0.4607
p	1	-0.40130	0.157518	-2.55	0.0171
ps	1	1.262780	0.341739	3.70	0.0010
di	1	5.620552	2.148751	2.62	0.0146

	Model	SUPPLY
	Dependent Variable	q

Variable	DF	Parameter Estimate	Standard Error	t Value	Pr > |t|
Intercept	1	20.03280	1.160349	17.26	<.0001
p	1	0.337982	0.023641	14.30	<.0001
pf	1	-1.00091	0.078293	-12.78	<.0001

11.4.4 Postscript

Estimation of systems of equations, and development of the consequences of endogeneity, put econometrics on the map and has been a topic of interest for the past 85 years. Computing has of course played a great role, since before fast computers even a multiple regression was a horrible chore. For some classic examples enter **help syslin** into the SAS command line, and go to the Examples. There you will find Klein's Model I, the training ground for a generation of economists. In the documentation of **PROC MODEL** you will find that it is capable of estimating systems of linear and nonlinear equations. A little internet searching will find you many more examples.

APPENDIX 11A ALTERNATIVES TO TWO-STAGE LEAST SQUARES

In a system of M simultaneous equations let the endogenous variables be $y_1, y_2, \ldots, y_M$. Let there be K exogenous variables, $x_1, x_2, \ldots, x_K$. Suppose the first structural equation within this system is

$$y_1 = \alpha_2 y_2 + \beta_1 x_1 + \beta_2 x_2 + e_1 \tag{11A.1}$$

The endogenous variable y_2 has reduced form $y_2 = \pi_{12} x_1 + \pi_{22} x_2 + \cdots + \pi_{K2} x_K + v_2 = E(y_2) + v_2$. The parameters of the reduced form equation are consistently estimated by least squares, so that

$$\widehat{E(y_2)} = \hat{\pi}_{12} x_1 + \hat{\pi}_{22} x_2 + \cdots + \hat{\pi}_{K2} x_K \tag{11A.2}$$

The reduced form residuals are $\hat{v}_2 = y_2 - \widehat{E(y_2)}$ so that

$$\widehat{E(y_2)} = y_2 - \hat{v}_2 \tag{11A.3}$$

The two-stage least squares estimator is an IV estimator using $\widehat{E(y_2)}$ as an instrument. Equation (11A.3) shows that the instrument used in 2SLS can be thought of as the endogenous variable y_2 "purged" of the troublesome error term v_2. A *k-class* estimator is an IV estimator using instrumental variable $y_2 - k\hat{v}_2$.

11A.1 The LIML estimator

In general equation (11A.1) can be written in **implicit form** as $\alpha_1 y_1 + \alpha_2 y_2 + \beta_1 x_1 + \beta_2 x_2 + e_1 = 0$. Let $y^* = \alpha_1 y_1 + \alpha_2 y_2$, then the equation can be written

$$y^* = -\beta_1 x_1 - \beta_2 x_2 - e_1 = \theta_1 x_1 + \theta_2 x_2 + \eta \qquad (11A.4)$$

In equation (11A.1) the exogenous variables $x_3, \ldots, x_K$ were omitted. If we had included them equation (11A.4) would be

$$y^* = \theta_1 x_1 + \cdots + \theta_K x_K + \eta \qquad (11A.5)$$

The **least variance ratio** estimator chooses α_1 and α_2, from $y^* = \alpha_1 y_1 + \alpha_2 y_2$, so that the ratio of the sum of squared residuals from (11A.4) relative to the sum of squared residuals from (11A.5) is as small as possible. Define the ratio of sum of squared residuals from the two models as

$$\ell = \frac{SSE \text{ from regression of } y^* \text{ on } x_1, x_2}{SSE \text{ from regression of } y^* \text{ on } x_1, \ldots, x_K} \geq 1 \qquad (11A.6)$$

The interesting result is that the minimum value of ℓ in (11A.6), call it $\hat{\ell}$, when used as k in the *k-class* estimator results in the *LIML* estimator. That is, use $k = \hat{\ell}$ when forming the instrument $y_2 - k\hat{v}_2$, and the resulting *IV* estimator is the *LIML* estimator.

11A.2 Fuller's modified LIML

A modification suggested by Wayne Fuller (1977)[5] uses the *k-class* value

$$k = \hat{\ell} - \frac{a}{N - K} \qquad (11A.7)$$

where K is the total number of instrumental variables (included and excluded exogenous variables) and N is the sample size. Fuller says:

> *If one desires estimates that are nearly unbiased α is set to 1. Presumably α=1 would be used when one is interested in testing hypotheses or setting approximate confidence intervals for the parameters. If one wishes to minimize the mean square error of the estimators an α of 4 is appropriate.*

The value of a is a constant. If we are estimating some parameter δ using an estimator $\hat{\delta}$, then the mean square error of estimation is

$$MSE(\hat{\delta}) = E(\hat{\delta} - \delta)^2 = \text{var}(\hat{\delta}) + \left[E(\hat{\delta}) - \delta \right]^2 = \text{var}(\hat{\delta}) + \left[bias(\hat{\delta}) \right]^2$$

Estimator *MSE* combines both variance and bias into a single measure.

---

[5] "Some Properties of a Modification of the Limited Information Estimator," *Econometrica*, 45, pp. 939-953.

11A.3 Advantages of LIML

Stock and Yogo (2005, p. 106) say "Our findings support the view that LIML is far superior to (2)SLS when the researcher has weak instruments..." when using interval estimates' coverage rate as the criterion. Also "...the Fuller-k estimator is more robust to weak instruments than (2)SLS when viewed from the perspective of bias." Some other findings are discussed by Mariano (2001)[6]

- For the 2SLS estimator the amount of bias is an increasing function of the degree of overidentification. The distributions of the 2SLS and least squares estimators tend to become similar when overidentification is large. LIML has the advantage over 2SLS when there are a large number of instruments.

- The LIML estimator converges to normality faster than the 2SLS estimator and is generally more symmetric.

11A.4 Stock-Yogo weak IV tests for LIML

Tables 11B.1 and 11B.2[7] in *Principles of Econometrics, 4th Edition* contain Stock-Yogo critical values for testing weak instruments. Table 11B.1 contains the critical values using the criterion of maximum LIML test size for a 5% test. Note that for $L > 1$ LIML critical values are lower than the *2SLS* critical values in *POE4* Table 10E.1. This means that the Cragg-Donald F-test statistic does not have to be as large for us to reject the null hypothesis that the instruments are weak when using LIML instead of 2SLS. Table 11B.2 contains the critical values for the test of weak instruments using the relative bias criterion for the Fuller modification of *LIML*, using $a = 1$. There is no similar table for *LIML* because the *LIML* estimator does not have a finite expected value and thus the concept of bias breaks down.

11A.5 LIML and k-class algebra

The regression model in matrix notation is $\mathbf{y} = \mathbf{X}\boldsymbol{\beta} + \mathbf{e}$, where $\mathbf{X}$ is $(N \times K)$. Partition the regressors into $\mathbf{X} = [\mathbf{X}_1 \quad \mathbf{X}_2]$ where $\mathbf{X}_1$ contains K_1 endogenous regressors and $\mathbf{X}_2$ contains K_2 exogenous regressors. The ith observation in the regression model $y_i = \mathbf{x}_i'\boldsymbol{\beta} + e_i$ with $\mathbf{x}_i' = [\mathbf{x}_{i1}' \quad \mathbf{x}_{i2}']$. Endogeneity means that $E(\mathbf{x}_{i1}e_i) \neq \mathbf{0}$ while exogeneity means that $E(\mathbf{x}_{i2}e_i) = \mathbf{0}$. Assume there is an $(N \times L)$ matrix $\mathbf{Z}$ of instruments $\mathbf{Z} = [\mathbf{Z}_1 \quad \mathbf{Z}_2] = [\mathbf{Z}_1 \quad \mathbf{X}_2]$, where $\mathbf{Z}_1$ contains L_1 excluded or external instruments (from outside the regression specification) and $\mathbf{Z}_2 = \mathbf{X}_2$ contains $L_2 = K_2$ internal instruments. If the ith row of $\mathbf{Z}$ is $\mathbf{z}_i'$, then $E(\mathbf{z}_i e_i) = \mathbf{0}$. The order condition for identification is that $L \geq K$, or equivalently that $L_1 \geq K_1$, the number of external instruments must be at least as large as the number of endogenous regressors.

A convenient expression for the k-class estimator is[8]

$$\hat{\boldsymbol{\beta}}(k) = [\mathbf{X}'(\mathbf{I} - k\mathbf{M}_Z)\mathbf{X}]^{-1} \mathbf{X}'(\mathbf{I} - k\mathbf{M}_Z)\mathbf{y}$$

---

[6] R. S. Mariano (2001) "Simultaneous Equation Model Estimators," in *The Companion to Theoretical Econometrics*, edited by Badi Baltagi, Blackwell Publishing, pp. 139-142.

[7] These are portions of, respectively, Table 5.4, page 103, and Table 5.3, page 102 in Stock and Yogo (2005).

[8] Baum, et al. (2007), page 479. This formula is not recommended for computations with a large sample size. Our purpose is to illustrate, not provide computationally efficient algorithms.

where $\mathbf{M}_Z = \mathbf{I} - \mathbf{Z}(\mathbf{Z}'\mathbf{Z})^{-1}\mathbf{Z}'$. The estimator of the error variance is

$$\hat{\sigma}^2(k) = \left(\mathbf{y} - \mathbf{X}\hat{\boldsymbol{\beta}}(k)\right)'\left(\mathbf{y} - \mathbf{X}\hat{\boldsymbol{\beta}}(k)\right)/\left(N - K\right)$$

The estimated covariance matrix is then

$$\widehat{\text{cov}}\left(\hat{\boldsymbol{\beta}}(k)\right) = \hat{\sigma}^2(k)\left[\mathbf{X}'(\mathbf{I} - k\mathbf{M}_Z)\mathbf{X}\right]^{-1}$$

The value of k leading to the LIML estimator is the smallest characteristic root of the matrix $\left(\mathbf{W}_1\right)^{-1}\mathbf{W}_0$ where

$$\mathbf{W}_0 = \left(\mathbf{I} - \mathbf{Z}_2\left(\mathbf{Z}_2'\mathbf{Z}_2\right)^{-1}\mathbf{Z}_2'\right)\mathbf{Y}_0 \text{ and } \mathbf{W}_1 = \left(\mathbf{I} - \mathbf{Z}\left(\mathbf{Z}'\mathbf{Z}\right)^{-1}\mathbf{Z}'\right)\mathbf{Y}_0$$

The matrix $\mathbf{Y}_0$ contains all the endogenous variables in the equation $\mathbf{Y}_0 = \begin{bmatrix} \mathbf{y} & \mathbf{X}_1 \end{bmatrix}$. Greene (2012, p. 328) suggests finding the roots of the symmetric matrix $\mathbf{W}_1^{-1/2}\mathbf{W}_0\mathbf{W}_1^{-1/2}$. The advantage of this is that the symmetric matrix has real roots. Equivalently we let $\mathbf{C}$ be the Cholesky decomposition of $\mathbf{W}_1$ and find the minimum root of $\mathbf{C}\mathbf{W}_0\mathbf{C}'$. This is no real problem for SAS which can find the roots of $\left(\mathbf{W}_1\right)^{-1}\mathbf{W}_0$. We did not take this approach because the roots are returned in complex number format, with the real part in the first column and the complex part, which is zero in this case, in the second column. Extracting minimum of the first column (the real part) achieves the same thing. It is less messy using our approach.

11A.6 PROC IML for LIML and k-class

For illustration we use the Mroz data set. This illustration was introduced in Chapter 10 Appendix E, Section 10E.2.1. With the Mroz data we estimate the *HOURS* supply equation

$$HOURS = \beta_1 + \beta_2 MTR + \beta_3 EDUC + \beta_4 KIDSL6 + \beta_5 NWIFEINC + e \qquad (11B.8)$$

The model treats as endogenous *MTR* and *EDUC* with external instruments *MOTHEREDUC*, *FATHEREDUC* and *EXPER*. This is Model 3 in *POE4*, page 471.

```
title;
data mroz;
set 'mroz';
if lfp=1;
lwage = log(wage);
nwifeinc = (faminc-wage*hours)/1000;
one=1;
run;

proc syslin data=mroz liml;
instruments kidsl6 nwifeinc exper mothereduc fathereduc;
endogenous mtr educ;
model hours = mtr educ kidsl6 nwifeinc;
run;
```

The LIML estimates of this model are

Variable	DF	Parameter Estimate	Standard Error	t Value	Pr > |t|
Intercept	1	18587.91	3683.605	5.05	<.0001
MTR	1	-19196.5	4003.682	-4.79	<.0001
EDUC	1	-197.259	64.62124	-3.05	0.0024
KIDSL6	1	207.5531	163.2521	1.27	0.2043
nwifeinc	1	-104.942	20.68667	-5.07	<.0001

NOTE: K-Class Estimation with K=1.0028826564

```
proc syslin data=mroz liml alpha=1;
instruments kidsl6 nwifeinc exper mothereduc fathereduc;
endogenous mtr educ;
model hours = mtr educ kidsl6 nwifeinc;
title 'Fuller k-class alpha=1 for hours equation';
run;
```

Variable	DF	Parameter Estimate	Standard Error	t Value	Pr > |t|
Intercept	1	18157.76	3560.406	5.10	<.0001
MTR	1	-18731.2	3871.255	-4.84	<.0001
EDUC	1	-191.139	62.74365	-3.05	0.0025
KIDSL6	1	193.2619	159.1505	1.21	0.2253
nwifeinc	1	-102.634	20.03425	-5.12	<.0001

NOTE: K-Class Estimation with K=1.0005185902

```
proc syslin data=mroz liml alpha=4;
instruments kidsl6 nwifeinc exper mothereduc fathereduc;
endogenous mtr educ;
model hours = mtr educ kidsl6 nwifeinc;
title 'Fuller k-class alpha=4 for hours equation';
run;
```

Variable	DF	Parameter Estimate	Standard Error	t Value	Pr > |t|
Intercept	1	17047.29	3251.505	5.24	<.0001
MTR	1	-17528.9	3539.288	-4.95	<.0001
EDUC	1	-175.414	58.04409	-3.02	0.0027
KIDSL6	1	156.4060	148.9998	1.05	0.2945
nwifeinc	1	-96.6664	18.40140	-5.25	<.0001

NOTE: K-Class Estimation with K=0.9934263916

In the PROC IML code below the choice of **alpha = 0** yields LIML estimates. Fuller *k*-class esetimates are obtained by specifying **alpha = 1** or **alpha = 4**. These choices are made after the modules have been put in memory.

```
proc iml;
title;

start liml;
use mroz;
```

```
read all into y0 var{hours mtr educ};            * all endogenous;
read all into z1 var{exper mothereduc fathereduc};   * external iv;
read all into z2 var{one kidsl6 nwifeinc};           * included iv;
read all into z var{one kidsl6 nwifeinc exper mothereduc fathereduc};
read all into x1 var{mtr educ};          * right-hand side endogenous;
read all into x var{one mtr educ kidsl6 nwifeinc};
read all into y var{hours};
rname = {one mtr educ kidsl6 nwifeinc};
n = nrow(y);                             * observations;
k = ncol(x);                             * number of regressors;
l = ncol(z);                             * number of IV;
k1 = ncol(x1);                           * number rhs endogenous;
l1 = ncol(z1);                           * number external IV;

/* endogenous with x1 partialled out */
e0=y0-z2*inv(z2`*z2)*z2`*y0;             * G7, eq (10-52);
w0 = e0`*e0;                             * cross product matrix;

/* G7, p. 328, middle */
e1=y0-z*inv(z`*z)*z`*y0;        * endog with z partialled out;
w1 = e1`*e1;                    * G7, eq (10-54 );
w1inv=inv(w1);
c=root(w1inv);                  * (w1)^-1/2, G7, below eq (10-54);
a = c*w0*c`;                    * G7, D matrix, below eq (10-54);
lam = min(eigval(a));          * characteristic roots;
kclass = lam - alpha/(n-1);    * Fuller k-class adjustment;
```

This estimator formulation not best for large *N*.

```
mz = i(n)-z*inv(z`*z)*z`;                 * residual maker, G7, eq (3-14);
covliml = inv(x`*(i(n)-kclass*mz)*x);   * k-class cov without sig2;
bliml = covliml*x`*(i(n)-kclass*mz)*y;  * k-class estimator;
ehat = y - x*bliml;
sig2_liml = ssq(y-x*bliml)/(n-k);        * error variance;
covliml=sig2_liml*covliml;               * k-class cov matrix;
se_liml = sqrt(vecdiag(covliml));        * std error;
tstat = bliml/se_liml;                   * t-stats;
pval = 2*(1-probt(abs(tstat),n-k));      * p-value;
result = bliml||se_liml||tstat||pval;
cname = {est se tstat pval};             * names for printed columns;

if alpha ^= 0 then do;
print "Fuller k-class alpha ",, alpha ,,
      "LIML minimum eigenvalue " ,, lam ,,
      "Fuller k for k-class estimation " ,, kclass;
print  "Fuller k-class estimates",,
       result [rowname=rname colname=cname format=13.7];
end;

if alpha = 0 then do;
```

```
print "LIML minimum eigenvalue " ,, lam ,,
        ,,"LIML estimates",,
        result [rowname=rname colname=cname format=13.7];
end;

finish;

start weakiv;
zp = z1-z2*inv(z2`*z2)*z2`*z1;        * z1 with z2 partialled out;
xp = x1-z2*inv(z2`*z2)*z2`*x1;        * x1 with z2 partialled out;
w = inv(xp`*xp)*xp`*zp*inv(zp`*zp)*zp`*xp; * matrix;
eigvalues = eigval(w);                * w nonsymmetic eigenval complex;
eigvalues = eigvalues[,1];            * extract real part;
rk2 = min(eigvalues);      * minimum eigenvalue squared canon corr;
rk = sqrt(rk2);                       * canonical corr;
print / "canonical correlation and its square" ,, rk rk2;


anderson_lm=n*rk2;                    * N*R^2 test form;
df_lm=l1-k1+1;                        * DF = #overid + 1;
p_lm = 1-probchi(anderson_lm,df_lm);  * p-value;
print "Anderson LM test statistic for underidentification " ,,
        anderson_lm df_lm p_lm;
cd = rk2/(1-rk2);                     * ratio;
cragg_donald_wald = n*cd;             * cragg_donald_wald test;
df_cd=l1-k1+1;                        * DF = #overid + 1;
p_cd = 1-probchi(cragg_donald_wald,df_cd); * p-value;
print "Cragg-Donald LM test statistic for underidentification ",,
        cragg_donald_wald df_cd p_cd;


cragg_donald_F = (n-1)*cd/l1;         * cragg_donald_F test;
print "Cragg-Donald F test statistic for weakidentification ",,
        cragg_donald_F,,
        "Refer to Stock Yogo Tables for critical values";
```

The Anderson_Rubin F-test is discussed in Greene (2012), pages 335-336.

```
b0=0;                                 * hypothesized values;
y0 = y-x1*b0;                         * remove x1*b0 from y;
sseu = ssq(y0 - z*inv(z`*z)*z`*y0);   * unresricted SS from full model;
sser = ssq(y0 - z2*inv(z2`*z2)*z2`*y0); * restricted SS;
AR = (n-L)*(sser - sseu)/(l1*sseu);   * F-stat;
p_AR = 1 - probf(AR,l1,n-k);          * p-value;
print "Anderson_Rubin F test " AR p_AR;
finish;
```

Before running the module **overid** run the **liml** or **tsls** module. The Sargan test is NR^2 from a regression of 2SLS or LIML residuals on all IV. See Wooldridge (2010) Econometric Analysis of CS & TS Data, 2nd Ed., pages 134-137.

```
start overid;                         * start module;
```

```
num_overid = 1-k;                          * number of surplus IV;
sargan = n*(ehat`*z*inv(z`*z)*z`*ehat)/(ehat`*ehat); * eq (10B.4);
chi2_crit = cinv(.95,(1-k));               * chi-sq critical value;
sargan_p = 1 - probchi(sargan,(1-k));    * sargan p-value;

print / 'Sargan chi-square test of surplus instrument validity'
       ,,sargan num_overid chi2_crit sargan_p;
```

SAS uses a modified version of Sargan test due to Basmann. The test statistic has an F(l-k, n-l) distribution. See Version 9.2 PROC SYSLIN documentation, page 1610 .

```
den_df = n-l;                                * N - total number IV;
basmann = ((n-l)/(1-k))*(ehat`*z*inv(z`*z)*z`*ehat)/
          (ehat`*ehat - ehat`*z*inv(z`*z)*z`*ehat);  * eq (10B.5);
f_crit = finv(.95,1-k,n-l);                  * F critical value;
basmann_p = 1 - probf(basmann,(1-k),(n-l));  * Basmann p-value;
print ,, 'Basmann F-test of surplus instrument validity'
      , basmann num_overid den_df f_crit basmann_p;
finish;
```

Now choose **alpha** and run the modules.

```
alpha = 0;                                  * alpha = 0 gives liml;

run liml;
run weakiv;
run overid;
quit;
```

The resulting LIML estimates are

```
                    LIML minimum eigenvalue
                         1.0028827


                       LIML estimates

                          result
                EST           SE         TSTAT         PVAL
ONE       18587.9059805  3683.6053435   5.0461177   0.0000007
MTR      -19196.516698   4003.6815532  -4.7947162   0.0000023
EDUC       -197.2591080    64.6212402  -3.0525429   0.0024122
KIDSL6      207.5531296   163.2521060   1.2713657   0.2042972
NWIFEINC   -104.9415449    20.6866675  -5.0729072   0.0000006
```

The **weakiv** module produces

```
            canonical correlation and its square


                   rk        rk2
             0.2400494 0.0576237
```

```
           Anderson LM test statistic for underidentification

              anderson_lm      df_lm       p_lm
               24.662951          2 4.4107E-6

        Cragg-Donald LM test statistic for underidentification

            cragg_donald_wald      df_cd        p_cd
                   26.171022          2 2.0751E-6

        Cragg-Donald F test statistic for weakidentification

                      cragg_donald_F
                        8.6013795

            Refer to Stock Yogo Tables for critical values

                                           AR       p_AR
              Anderson_Rubin F test   11.008498 5.6642E-7
```

The module **overid** produces

```
           Sargan chi-square test of surplus instrument validity

              sargan num_overid chi2_crit  sargan_p
             1.2302306         1 3.8414588 0.2673622

           Basmann F-test of surplus instrument validity

            basmann num_overid   den_df   f_crit basmann_p
            1.216481          1      422 3.8635887 0.2706809
```

APPENDIX 11B MONTE CARLO SIMULATION

In Appendix 10C of this manual we carried out a Monte Carlo simulation to explore the properties of the IV/2SLS estimators. It was based on Chapter 10F.2 in *Principles of Econometrics, 4th Edition*. Here we employ the same experiment, adding aspects of the new estimators we have introduced in this appendix. The data generation process is the same as used in Appendix 10C of this manual.

```
data ch11mc;                          * data set;
nsam = 10000;
nobs=100;
pi = .5;
rho = .8;
call streaminit(1234567);             * set random number stream;
do sample = 1 to nsam;                * outer loop repeat samples;
    do n = 1 to nobs;                 * start inner loop;
      r1= rand('normal',0,1);         * r1 is N(0,1);
      r2= rand('normal',0,1);         * r2 is N(0,1);
      mu_e = 0;                       * mean for y1;
```

```
        mu_v = 0;                        * mean for y2;
        sig_e = 1;                       * SD for y1;
        sig_v = 1;                       * SD for y2;
        e = mu_e + sig_e*r1;
        v = mu_v + rho*sig_v*r1+sqrt(sig_v**2-sig_v**2*rho**2)*r2;

        z1= rand('normal',0,1);          * z1 is N(0,1);
        z2= rand('normal',0,1);          * z2 is N(0,1);
        z3= rand('normal',0,1);          * z3 is N(0,1);
        x = pi*z1 + pi*z2 + pi*z3 + v;
        y = x + e;                       * DGP;
        output;                          * output to data set;
        end;                             * end inner loop;
    end;                                 * end outer loop;
run;
```

First calculate the first stage F-test for the significance of the instruments in the reduced form.

```
    proc reg data=ch11mc noprint outest=ftest rsquare;
    model x = z1 z2 z3;
    by sample;
    run;
    data ftest; set ftest; if _type_='PARMS';
    f = (_RSQ_/(4-1))/((1-_RSQ_)/(100-4));
    keep sample f;
    run;
```

Then compute for comparison the same 2SLS estimates from the previous Monte Carlo experiment.

```
    proc syslin noprint data=ch11mc outest=est2 2sls covout;
    instruments z1 z2 z3;
    endogenous x;
    model y = x;
    by sample;
    run;

    proc print data=est2;
    where sample = 1;
    title '2sls outest data';
    run;

    data b2iv; set est2; if _type_='2SLS'; if _name_=' '; b2iv = x;
    keep sample b2iv;
    run;

    data se2iv; set est2; if _type_='2SLS'; if _name_='x'; se2iv = sqrt(x);
    keep sample se2iv;
    run;
```

Next, compute the LIML estimates and store them similarly.

```
proc syslin noprint data=ch11mc outest=est3 liml covout;
instruments z1 z2 z3;
endogenous x;
model y = x;
by sample;
run;

proc print data=est3;
where sample = 1;
title 'liml outest data';
run;

data b2liml; set est3; if _type_='LIML'; if _NAME_=' '; b2liml = x;
keep sample b2liml;
run;

data se2liml; set est3; if _type_='LIML'; if _NAME_='x';
se2liml = sqrt(x);
keep sample se2liml;
run;
```

The Fuller k-class estimates for $\alpha = 1$ and $\alpha = 4$ are done the same way.

```
proc syslin noprint data=ch11mc outest=est4 liml alpha=1;
instruments z1 z2 z3;
endogenous x;
model y = x;
by sample;
run;

proc print data=est4;
where sample = 1;
title 'LIML alpha=1 outest data';
run;

data b2f1; set est4; if _type_='LIML'; if _name_=' '; b2f1 = x;
keep sample b2f1;
run;

proc syslin noprint data=ch11mc outest=est5 liml alpha=4;
instruments z1 z2 z3;
endogenous x;
model y = x;
by sample;
run;

proc print data=est5;
where sample = 1;
```

```
title 'LIML alpha=4 outest data';
run;

data b2f4; set est5; if _type_='LIML'; if _name_=' '; b2f4 = x;
keep sample b2f4;
run;
```

Now merge the data sets and make some calculations.

```
data mc;
merge b2iv se2iv ftest b2liml se2liml b2f1 b2f4;
by sample;
tc = tinv(.975,100-2);
```

Use a two-tail test at the 5% level of significance for the true null hypothesis that $\beta_2 = 1$ using both the IV estimator and the LIML estimator: the values of **rejectiv** and **rejectliml** are 1 if the hypothesis is rejected and 0 otherwise.

```
tstativ = (b2iv - 1)/se2iv;
rejectiv = (abs(tstativ) >= tc);
tliml = (b2liml-1)/se2liml;
rejectliml = (abs(tliml) >= tc);
```

We also compare the squared error of the IV estimator and the Fuller k-class estimator with $\alpha = 4$

```
mseb2iv= (b2iv-1)**2;
mseb2f4 = (b2f4-1)**2;
run;
```

Summarize the results using PROC MEANS.

```
proc means data=mc mean std;
var f b2iv rejectiv rejectliml b2f1 mseb2iv mseb2f4;;
title 'rho = .8 and pi = 0.5';
run;
```

```
                    rho = .8 and pi = 0.5

                     The MEANS Procedure
```

Variable	Mean	Std Dev
f	26.3502521	8.1730215
b2iv	1.0108313	0.1184961
rejectiv	0.0702000	0.2554966
rejectliml	0.0543000	0.2266200
b2f1	1.0003014	0.1197970
mseb2iv	0.0141572	0.0227075
mseb2f4	0.0128470	0.0180708

First, examine the percentage rejections of the true null hypothesis $\beta_2 = 1$ using a two-tail test at the 5% level of significance. The Monte Carlo rejection rate for the *IV/2SLS* estimator is 7% and for the *LIML* estimator it is 5.4%. This finding is consistent with Stock and Yogo's conclusion about coverage rates of the two interval estimation approaches.

In these experiments there is little difference between the averages of the two-stage least squares estimates and the Fuller modified *k*-class estimator with $\alpha = 1$. A greater contrast shows up when comparing how close the estimates are to the true parameter value using the mean square error criterion. The empirical mean square error for the IV/2SLS estimator is 0.01415 and for the Fuller modification of LIML with $\alpha = 4$ it is 0.01285. Recall that the mean square error measures how close the estimates are to the true parameter value. For the *IV/2SLS* estimator the empirical mean square error is

$$\text{mse}\left(\hat{\beta}_2\right) = \sum_{m=1}^{10000} \left(\hat{\beta}_{2m} - \beta_2\right)^2 \Big/ 10000$$

The Fuller modified LIML has lower mean square error than the IV/2SLS estimator

In the above Monte Carlo experiment the instruments were strong. Make the instruments weak by changing to $\pi = 0.1$ and rerun the experiment.

rho = .8 and pi = 0.1

The MEANS Procedure

Variable	Mean	Std Dev
f	2.0357697	1.5138886
b2iv	1.3298330	0.5487132
rejectiv	0.2805000	0.4492660
rejectliml	0.1334000	0.3400235
b2f1	1.3289620	0.3876812
mseb2iv	0.4098459	2.2724678
mseb2f4	0.3224628	0.2406258

Now we see substantial differences between the test rejection rate using the LIML estimator and the IV. The 5% test is rejected 28% of the time for the IV estimator but "only" 13.3% for LIML. The Fuller modified estimator with $\alpha = 1$ suffers about the same amount of bias as the IV estimator in this very weak instrument setting. The MSE of the Fuller modified estimator with $\alpha = 4$ is considerably lower than that for the IV estimator. It should be noted that in a few samples with this setting the estimates could not be obtained because of extreme collinearity.

CHAPTER **12**

Regression with Time-Series Data: Nonstationary Variables

12.1 STATIONARY AND NONSTATIONARY VARIABLES

Chapter 12 in *Principles of Econometrics, 4th Edition* describes how to estimate regression models with **time-series data** that is **nonstationary**. We already worked with time-series data in Chapter 9 of this manual. We saw how including lagged values of the dependent variable or explanatory variables as regressors, or considering lags in the errors, can be used to model dynamic relationships. We used **PROC AUTOREG** and **PROC ARIMA** to estimate these dynamic models, and showed how autoregressive models can be used in forecasting.

An important assumption maintained throughout Chapter 9 was that the data are **stationary**. A time series y_t is stationary if its mean and variance are constant over time and the covariance between two values in the series depends only on the length of time between the two values and not the times at which they are observed. For example, the mean and variance of GDP in the third quarter of 1973 are the same as in the fourth quarter of 2006.

Formally, the time series y_t is stationary if for all values, and every time period, it is true that

$$E(y_t) = \mu \qquad \text{[constant mean]} \qquad (12.1a)$$

$$\text{var}(y_t) = \sigma^2 \qquad \text{[constant variance]} \qquad (12.1b)$$

$$\text{cov}(y_t, y_{t+s}) = \text{cov}(y_t, y_{t-s}) = \gamma_s \qquad \text{[covariance depends on } s\text{, not } t\text{]} \qquad (12.1c)$$

The aim of this chapter is to describe how to estimate models involving nonstationary variables. First, we examine ways to distinguish whether a time series is stationary or nonstationary. One of the first diagnostic tools for examining whether or not a variable is stationary is a simple time series plot of the data.

To illustrate, we use the SAS dataset *usa*, which contains observations for some key economic variables for the U.S. economy 1984q1 to 2009q4. The variables are real gross domestic product (*GDP*), inflation rate (*INF*), Federal funds rate (*F*), and the three-year bond rate (*B*). To begin, open the dataset, examine its contents and turn off labels.

```
data usa;                              * open data set;
set 'usa';                             * read usa;
run;
proc contents data=usa;                * examine contents;
run;
options nolabel;                       * turn off labels;
```

```
              Variables in Creation Order

   #   Variable    Type    Len    Label

   1   gdp         Num      8     real US gross domestic product
   2   inf         Num      8     annual inflation rate
   3   f           Num      8     federal funds rate
   4   b           Num      8     3-year Bond rate
```

The first thing to do is plot each series as well as the change in each variable $\Delta y_t = y_t - y_{t-1}$, also known as the **first difference**, against time. To begin we create date variables which are useful when plotting the data and creating partitions across time. Section 9.2.1 of this manual discusses SAS lag and difference operators as well as date representations.

```
data usa;                              * open data set;
set usa;                               * read data;
dgdp = dif(gdp);                       * first differences;
dinf = dif(inf);
df = dif(f);
db = dif(b);
retain date '1oct83'd;                 * date variable;
date=intnx('qtr',date,1);              * update dates;
format date yyqc.;                     * format for date;
year = 1984 + int((_n_-1)/4);          * year;
qtr = mod(_n_-1, 4) + 1;               * quarter;
run;
```

We print the first few observations to check that we have created the variables correctly.

```
proc print data=usa (obs=5);
run;
```

You will note that we lose an observation for the differenced variables.

Obs	gdp	inf	f	b	dgdp	dinf	df	db	date	year	qtr
1	3807.4	9.47	9.69	11.19	.	.	.	.	1984:1	1984	1
2	3906.3	10.03	10.56	12.64	98.9	0.56	0.87	1.45	1984:2	1984	2
3	3976.0	10.83	11.39	12.64	69.7	0.80	0.83	0.00	1984:3	1984	3
4	4034.0	11.51	9.27	11.10	58.0	0.68	-2.12	-1.54	1984:4	1984	4
5	4117.2	10.51	8.48	10.68	83.2	-1.00	-0.79	-0.42	1985:1	1985	1

Now we are ready to plot the time series. Plot the level and first difference for each series. For the first differences we include a reference line a zero so that we can easily observe positive and negative changes. We specify **value=point** and **interpol=join** in order to obtain a smooth line. First, plot GDP and change in GDP.

```
symbol1 value=point interpol=join;      * symbol for diagram;
proc gplot data=usa;
plot gdp*date = 1 / hminor=1;
title 'Real gross domestic product (GDP)';
run;
proc gplot data=usa;
plot dgdp*date = 1 / hminor=1 vref=0;
title 'Change in GDP';
run;
```

This generates the following, which match Figure 12.1, panels (a) and (b) in *POE4*

Real gross domestic product (GDP)

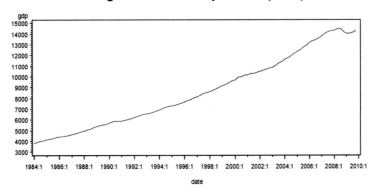

Change in GDP

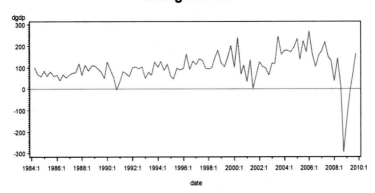

Real GDP does not appear to be stationary since it is trending upward over time and thus does not have a constant mean. Change in GDP fluctuates up and down around an upward trend until dropping sharply in the financial crisis. We can generate graphs for the other plots in a similar manner. The plots for inflation rate and change in inflation rate are

Inflation rate

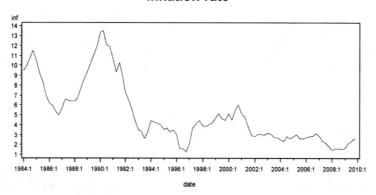

Change in the inflation rate

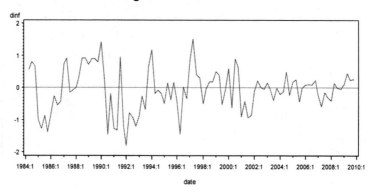

The inflation rate fluctuates up and down, but overall appears to be drifting downward and so it may not be stationary. However, changes in the interest rate appear to fluctuate around a constant value, zero. The plots for the Fed funds rate, the three-year bond rate, and their changes are given below.

Federal funds rate

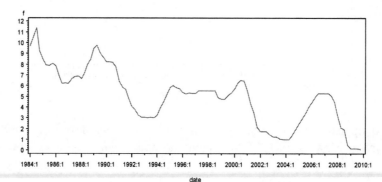

Change in the Federal funds rate

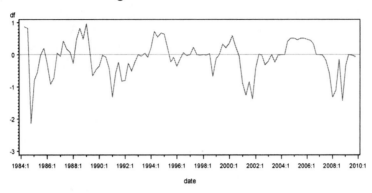

Three-year bond rate

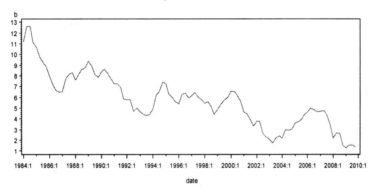

Change in the bond rate

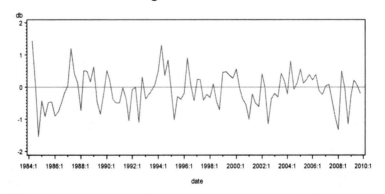

As with interest rates, the Fed funds and bond rates fluctuate up and down, but appear to drift down slightly over the sample period. The changes in the Fed funds and bond rates appear to fluctuate around a constant value indicating that they may be stationary.

The next thing to do is to examine summary statistics. We split the data into two sample periods, 1984q2 to 1996q4 and 1997q1 to 2009q4. Note that the first period consists of 51 observations while the second period consists of 52 observations. This is because we do not observe the differenced variables for 1984q1. Compute summary statistics for each subsample to see whether there are changes in the sample means and standard deviations over time.

```
proc means data=usa;               * summary statistics;
var gdp inf f b dgdp dinf df db;   * variable list;
where dgdp ne . and year <= 1996; * sample period 1;
title 'summary statistics 1984q2 to 1996q4';
run;
```

The summary statistics for sample period 1, which match Table 12.1, page 477, of *POE4* are

summary statistics 1984q2 to 1996q4
The MEANS Procedure

Variable	N	Mean	Std Dev	Minimum	Maximum
gdp	51	5813.02	1204.60	3906.30	8023.00
inf	51	6.9037255	3.3378106	1.2800000	13.5500000
f	51	6.4172549	2.1305390	2.9900000	11.3900000
b	51	7.3431373	1.9397747	4.3200000	12.6400000
dgdp	51	82.6588235	29.3334770	-4.6000000	161.8000000
dinf	51	-0.1605882	0.8320058	-1.8000000	1.4300000
df	51	-0.0864706	0.5860711	-2.1200000	0.9700000
db	51	-0.1029412	0.6312822	-1.5400000	1.4500000

Similarly, for period 2, we use

```
proc means data=usa;               * summary statistics;
var gdp inf f b dgdp dinf df db;   * variable list;
where year > 1996;                 * sample period 2;
title 'summary statistics 1997q1 to 2009q4';
run;
```

and obtain the following summary statistics.

summary statistics 1997q1 to 2009q4
The MEANS Procedure

Variable	N	Mean	Std Dev	Minimum	Maximum
gdp	52	11458.19	2052.13	8137.00	14484.90
inf	52	3.2194231	1.1166185	1.4500000	6.0400000
f	52	3.4875000	2.0252687	0.1200000	6.5200000
b	52	3.9771154	1.5643220	1.2700000	6.5600000
dgdp	52	120.2750000	92.9198661	-293.7000000	267.9000000
dinf	52	0.0251923	0.4617422	-0.9300000	1.5200000
df	52	-0.0992308	0.5142893	-1.4300000	0.5900000
db	52	-0.0875000	0.4788502	-1.3300000	0.8100000

The summary statistics support the hypothesis that the first differences for inflation, Federal Funds rate, and Bond rate are stationary while the other variables are not. However, this does not constitute a hypothesis test. We carry out formal tests for stationarity in Section 12.3.

12.1.1 The first-order autoregressive model

The first-order autoregressive model, the AR(1) model, is a useful univariate time-series model for explaining the difference between stationary and nonstationary series. It is given by

$$y_t = \rho y_{t-1} + v_t, \quad |\rho| < 1 \tag{12.2}$$

where the errors v_t are independent, with zero mean and constant variance σ_v^2, and may be normally distributed. In the context of time-series models the errors are sometimes known as "shocks" or "innovations." The assumption $|\rho| < 1$ implies that shocks dissipate over time. It can be shown that the series is stationary in this case.

12.1.2 Random walk models

Consider the special case of $\rho = 1$ in equation (12.2)

$$y_t = y_{t-1} + v_t \tag{12.3a}$$

This model is known as a **random walk** model. Each realization of the random variable y_t contains last period's value y_{t-1} plus a random error v_t. These series wander upward or downward with no real pattern. In these models, shocks are permanent.

Adding a constant term to this model yields

$$y_t = \alpha + y_{t-1} + v_t \tag{12.3b}$$

This model is known as a **random walk with drift**. In this case, the random variable y_t increases by the amount α each period. Thus, the series drifts upwards (or downwards if $\alpha < 0$).

Finally, if we add a time trend to the model we obtain

$$y_t = \alpha + \delta t + y_{t-1} + v_t \tag{12.3c}$$

This model is known as a **random walk with drift and trend**. The time trend term has the effect of strengthening the trend behavior. In Section 12.3 we introduce a formal test for stationarity. We test the null hypothesis of a random walk against the alternative of a stationary process. The critical values for the test statistic depend on which of the three random walk models we suspect.

12.2 SPURIOUS REGRESSIONS

The main reason it is important to test whether a series is stationary or not before estimating a regression is to avoid the problem of **spurious regressions**. In time-series data it is common to find a statistically significant relationship even when none exists if the series are nonstationary. Such regressions are said to be spurious.

To illustrate we use the data set *spurious*. The data consist of 700 observations on two series, *RW1* and *RW2*, which were generated as independent random walks.

$$rw_1 : y_t = y_{t-1} + v_{t1}$$

$$rw_2 : y_t = y_{t-2} + v_{t2}$$

The errors are independent $N(0,1)$ random errors. The series were generated independently and have no actual relationship with one another. We wish to explore the empirical relationship between these unrelated series. To begin, open the data file and use **PROC MEANS** to obtain summary statistics.

```
data spurious;                        * open data set;
set 'spurious';                       * read spurious;
run;
proc means data=spurious;             * summary statistics;
title 'means of two random walks: rw1 and rw2';
run;
```

```
               means of two random walks: rw1 and rw2
                         The MEANS Procedure
```

Variable	N	Mean	Std Dev	Minimum	Maximum
rw1	700	39.4416283	15.7424228	4.8056350	64.4510565
rw2	700	25.6799646	15.6969533	-4.9565003	49.2034719

We begin by plotting each series against time. Since the data are artificial and do not have an actual date, we create a time index using the observation number.

```
data spurious;                        * open data set;
set spurious;                         * read data;
time = _n_;                           * time variable;
run;
```

Next, we create a time series plot of the two series. SAS allows 46 different line types as well as different colors and symbols to help identify different series in a graph. We specify **width=3** and **line=20** for the plot of *RW2* in order to differentiate the two lines.

```
goptions reset=all;
legend1 label=none
        position=(top center inside)
        mode=share;                   * create legend;
symbol1 value=none interpol=join color=blue;
symbol2 value=none interpol=join color=black width=3 line=20;
symbol3 value=dot color=black;
```

```
proc gplot data=spurious;
plot rw1*time=1 rw2*time=2 / overlay legend=legend1;
title 'plot of rw1 and rw2 over time';
run;
```

The time series plot, which matches Figure 12.3, panel (a) in *POE4* is

plot of rw1 and rw2 over time

Even though there is no relationship between them the series appear to move together.
Next, we generate a scatter plot of *RW1* against *RW2*.

```
plot rw1*rw2=3;
title 'scatter diagram of rw1 and rw2';
run;
```

The scatter plot, which matches Figure 12.3, panel (b) in *POE4*, reveals a potentially spurious relationship between the two variables.

scatter diagram of rw1 and rw2

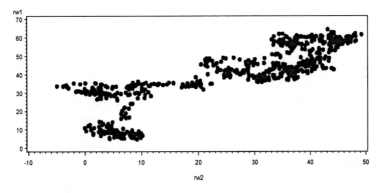

A linear regression of *RW1* on *RW2* confirms the appearance of a linear relationship. We estimate the regression using **PROC AUTOREG** and include the option **godfrey=1** to carry out the *LM* test.

```
proc autoreg data=spurious;
model rw1 = rw2 / godfrey=1;
title 'regression with LM test for serial correlation';
run;
```

The regression results, which match those on page 482 of *POE4*, are

Ordinary Least Squares Estimates

SSE	51112.3314	DFE	698
MSE	73.22684	Root MSE	8.55727
SBC	5003.10662	AIC	4994.00446
MAE	7.11662344	AICC	4994.02168
MAPE	37.4260241	Regress R-Square	0.7049
Durbin-Watson	0.0221	Total R-Square	0.7049

Godfrey's Serial Correlation Test

Alternative	LM	Pr > LM
AR(1)	682.9579	<.0001

Variable	DF	Estimate	Standard Error	t Value	Approx Pr > |t|
Intercept	1	17.8180	0.6205	28.72	<.0001
rw2	1	0.8420	0.0206	40.84	<.0001

The $R^2 = 0.70$ and the estimated slope is positive (0.842) and significant ($t = 40.84$). However, the results are completely meaningless or spurious. The variables are unrelated. The cause of the spurious result is the nonstationarity of the variables. You should always check for stationarity when working with time series data. When the data are nonstationary, the least squares estimator and least squares predictor do not have their usual properties and *t*-statistics are unreliable. The *LM* test indicates that the residuals are highly correlated, a sign that there is a problem with the regression.

12.3 UNIT ROOT TESTS FOR STATIONARITY

The most popular test for determining whether or not a series is stationary is the (augmented) **Dickey-Fuller test**. Consider the AR(1) model $y_t = \rho y_{t-1} + v_t$. The process is stationary when $|\rho| < 1$, but when $\rho = 1$, it becomes the nonstationary random walk process $y_t = y_{t-1} + v_t$. Thus, one way to test for stationarity is to test $H_0 : \rho = 1$ against the alternative $H_1 : \rho < 1$. Since we are testing the null hypothesis $\rho = 1$ the test is known as a **unit root test for stationarity**.

The test is generally carried out by subtracting y_{t-1} from both sides of the equation to obtain

$$y_t - y_{t-1} = \rho y_{t-1} - y_{t-1} + v_t$$

$$\Delta y_t = (\rho - 1) y_{t-1} + v_t \qquad (12.4)$$

$$= \gamma y_{t-1} + v_t$$

where $\gamma = \rho - 1$ and $\Delta y_t = y_t - y_{t-1}$. Now we test the null hypothesis $H_0 : \gamma = 0$ (nonstationary) against $H_1 : \gamma < 0$ (stationary).

There are three versions of the test, depending on whether the series contains no constant and no trend, a constant but no trend, or both a constant and trend. Therefore, to perform this test, a few decisions have to be made regarding the time series. Sometimes these choices can be made based on visual inspection of the time series plots. By inspecting the plots you try to determine whether the time series have a nonzero mean or if they have a linear or quadratic trend. If the trend in the series is quadratic then the differenced version of the series will have a linear trend in them.

For example, in the GDP series the differenced time series has a nonzero mean and a slight upward drift so you would choose an **Augmented Dickey-Fuller** (ADF) test that includes a constant and a time trend. The differenced time series for the Federal Funds and three-year bond rates have a nonzero mean, but appear to wander around a constant amount. Thus, we would choose an ADF test with a constant but no time trend for these series.

The three versions of the Dickey-Fuller regression are

Series Characteristics	Regression Model
No Constant and No Trend	$\Delta y_t = \gamma y_{t-1} + v_t$
Constant, but No Trend	$\Delta y_t = \alpha + \gamma y_{t-1} + v_t$
Constant and Trend	$\Delta y_t = \alpha + \gamma y_{t-1} + \lambda t + v_t$

In each case, the null and alternative hypotheses are $H_0 : \gamma = 0$ and $H_1 : \gamma < 0$. You estimate the appropriate regression, compute the t-ratio for γ and compare it to the critical value in your text or to the one provided by SAS. Since y_t is nonstationary when the null hypothesis is true, the usual t-statistic and p-values do not apply. For this reason, the test statistic is often called a τ (*tau*) **statistic**, and its value must be compared to specially generated critical values. The critical values for the Dickey-Fuller test are given in Table 12.2, page 486, of *POE4*. These critical values are different than the standard critical values used in most hypothesis tests.

The augmented version of the Dickey-Fuller test adds lagged differences of y_t to the model. For example, the augmented model with a constant but no trend is

$$\Delta y_t = \alpha + \gamma y_{t-1} + \sum_{s=1}^{m} a_s \Delta y_{t-s} + v_t \qquad (12.5)$$

where $\Delta y_{t-1} = (y_{t-1} - y_{t-2})$, $\Delta y_{t-2} = (y_{t-2} - y_{t-3}), \ldots$. You need to choose the number of lagged differences to include. Put in just enough to ensure that the residuals, v_t, are uncorrelated. You can do this by examining the **autocorrelation function** (ACF) of the residuals. The hypotheses for stationarity and nonstationarity are expressed in terms of γ in the same way and the test values are the same as those for the Dickey-Fuller test.

12.3.1 The Dickey-Fuller tests: an example

As an example, consider the Federal Funds rate, F, and the 3-year bond rate, B, from the *usa* data. The time series plots show that both series appear to drift downward over time, indicating they may be nonstationary. Both series fluctuate around a nonzero mean, so we include a constant but no trend. Finally, one lagged difference term is enough to eliminate autocorrelation in the residuals for both series. Therefore, we estimate the regressions

$$\Delta F_t = \alpha + \gamma F_{t-1} + a_1 \Delta F_{t-1} + v_t$$

$$\Delta B_t = \alpha + \gamma B_{t-1} + a_1 \Delta B_{t-1} + v_t$$

In Section 12.1 we created the first differences of each series and plotted these over time. We now create a lag of value the value and the difference of each series in order to estimate the regressions.

```
data usa;                          * open data set;
set usa;                           * read data;
f1 = lag(f);                       * lag f;
df1 = lag(df);                     * lag df;
b1 = lag(b);                       * lag b;
db1 = lag(db);                     * lag db;
run;
```

Run the regression for the Federal Funds series

```
proc autoreg data=usa;
model df = f1 df1;
title 'augmented Dickey-Fuller test for federal funds rate';
run;
```

The regression results, which match those on page 487 of *POE4*, are

Variable	DF	Estimate	Standard Error	t Value	Approx Pr > |t|
Intercept	1	0.1725	0.1002	1.72	0.0883
f1	1	-0.0446	0.0178	-2.50	0.0139
df1	1	0.5611	0.0810	6.93	<.0001

The τ statistic for the Federal Funds rate is -2.50. Table 12.2 of *POE4* gives the 5% critical value of -2.86. Since $-2.50 > -2.86$, we fail to reject the null hypothesis that the series is nonstationary.

SAS provides another option for carrying out the Dickey-Fuller test. The **%DFTEST** macro carries out the regression and gives the τ statistic and *p*-value. The format is **%DFTEST(SAS-dataset, variable <,OPTIONS>)**. To test for a unit root in the Federal Funds series type

```
%dftest(usa,f,ar=1,outstat=dfout);    * Dickey-Fuller test;
proc print data=dfout;                 * print results;
title 'Dickey-Fuller test for federal funds rate';
run;
```

We choose **ar=1** since we only want to include one lagged difference (the default is **ar=3**). The **outstat=dataset** option writes the results to the SAS dataset *dfout*. The results are

Dickey-Fuller test for federal funds rate

Obs	_TYPE_	_STATUS_	_DEPVAR_	_NAME_	_MSE_	Intercept	AR_V
1	PARM	0 Converged	AR_V		0.19834	0.17252	-1
2	COV	0 Converged	AR_V	Intercept	0.19834	0.01005	.
3	COV	0 Converged	AR_V	DLAG_V	0.19834	-0.00160	.
4	COV	0 Converged	AR_V	AR_V1	0.19834	0.00146	.

Obs	DLAG_V	AR_V1	_NOBS_	_TAU_	_TREND_	_DLAG_	_PVALUE_
1	-0.044621	0.56106	102	-2.50482	1	1	0.11730
2	-0.001598	0.00146	102	-2.50482	1	1	0.11730
3	0.000317	-0.00017	102	-2.50482	1	1	0.11730
4	-0.000169	0.00656	102	-2.50482	1	1	0.11730

The parameter estimates are given in the top row, labeled **PARM**, and match those from **PROC AUTOREG**. The covariance matrix is provided in the lines below the coefficients. The τ statistic is -2.50482 and the *p*-value = $0.1173 > 0.05$, so we fail to reject the null hypothesis of nonstationarity.

Finally, **PROC AUTOREG** has a **stationarity** option in the model statement that carries out an alternative unit root test, the **Phillips-Perron test**[1]. To carry out we specify the dependent variable with no regressors in the model statement.

```
proc autoreg data=usa;
model f = / stationarity=(phillips);   * Phillips-Perron test;
title 'Phillips-Perron test for federal funds rate';
run;
```

The Phillips-Perron test is automatically carried out for all three models: no constant and no trend (**Zero Mean**), constant and no trend (**Single Mean**), and both constant and trend (**Trend**). SAS computes two alternative test statistics, **Rho** and **Tau**, and their *p*-values. The Phillips-Perron test statistics have the same asymptotic distributions as the corresponding ADF tests. The results for the Federal Funds series are

Phillips-Perron Unit Root Test

Type	Lags	Rho	Pr < Rho	Tau	Pr < Tau
Zero Mean	2	-2.4090	0.2850	-1.7804	0.0720
Single Mean	2	-4.4283	0.4860	-1.4650	0.5480
Trend	2	-10.5791	0.3780	-2.2891	0.4360

For all cases, the test statistics are greater than the corresponding critical values at the 5% level of significance.

---

[1] The test statistic is a modification of the Dickey-Fuller test statistic. The Phillips-Perron statistic is computationally intensive, but has the same asymptotic distribution as the Dickey-Fuller statistic. For details see William Greene (2012) *Econometric Analysis, 7th Edition*, Prentice Hall, 752-753.

Now run the regression for the 3-year bond rate.

```
proc autoreg data=usa;
model db = b1 db1;
title 'augmented Dickey-Fuller test for 3 year bond rate';
run;
```

The regression results, which match those on page 487 of *POE4*, are

Variable	DF	Estimate	Standard Error	t Value	Approx Pr > |t|
Intercept	1	0.2369	0.1292	1.83	0.0697
b1	1	-0.0562	0.0208	-2.70	0.0081
db1	1	0.2903	0.0896	3.24	0.0016

The τ statistic for the 3-year bond rate of $-2.70 > -2.86$, so we to reject the null hypothesis that the 3-year bond rate series is nonstationary. To obtain the *p*-value for the Dickey-Fuller test, run the **%DFTEST** macro.

```
%dftest(usa,b,ar=1,outstat=dbout);    * Dickey-Fuller test;
proc print data=dbout;                * print results;
title 'Dickey-Fuller test for 3 year bond rate';
run;
```

This yields a *p*-value of 0.0772, and so we fail to reject the null hypothesis of nonstationarity at the 5% level of significance. Finally, we can use the **stationarity=(phillips)** option in **PROC AUTOREG** to obtain the Phillips-Perron τ statistics.

```
proc autoreg data=usa;
model b = / stationarity=(phillips);   * Phillips-Perron test;
title 'Phillips-Perron test for 3 year bond rate';
run;
```

Since we assume a constant but no trend for this series, the relevant test output is

Phillips-Perron Unit Root Test

Type	Lags	Rho	Pr < Rho	Tau	Pr < Tau
Single Mean	2	-4.5093	0.4780	-1.6995	0.4290

The Phillips-Perron test also fails to reject that the 3-year bond series is nonstationary.

12.3.2 Order of integration

So far, we have considered only whether a series is stationary or nonstationary. It is possible that the first difference of a nonstationary process is stationary. This concept is called "order of intergration." A series, y_t, that can be made stationary by taking the first difference is said to be **integrated or order 1**, denoted as **I(1)**.

Consider the nonstationary random walk process $y_t = y_{t-1} + v_t$. Taking the first difference of y_t yields $\Delta y_t = y_t - y_{t-1} = v_t$. The first difference, $\Delta y_t = v_t$, is stationary since v_t, being an independent $(0, \sigma_v^2)$ random variable, is stationary. To test whether a series, y_t, is stationary we regress Δy_t on y_{t-1} and possibly a constant, a trend, and some lagged differences. Therefore, to test whether the first difference, Δy_t, is stationary we regress $\Delta(\Delta y_t)$ on Δy_{t-1} and possibly some other variables.

In Section 12.3.1, we could not reject that the Federal Funds rate and the 3-year bond rate series were nonstationary. However, the plots of the first differences of these series seem to indicate that the first differences, ΔF_t and ΔB_t, are stationary. These series appear to wander around a zero mean, so we will use the version of the Dickey-Fuller test with no constant and no trend.

In each case, we regress the difference of the first difference on the lagged first difference. The first difference a series, $\Delta F_t = F_t - F_{t-1}$, is easily obtained in SAS using function **dif(f)**. To obtain the difference of the first difference, $\Delta(\Delta F_t) = \Delta F_t - \Delta F_{t-1}$, we use the function **dif(df)**. For the *usa* data, we have already created the first differences, *DF* and *DB*, and their lags, *DF1* and *DB1*, in Section 12.3.1. Below we create the difference of the differences, *DDF* and *DDB*.

```
data usa;              * open data set;
set usa;               * read data;
ddf = dif(df);         * difference of df;
ddb = dif(db);         * difference of db;
run;
```

To see what these data look like, print the first few observations for F and B as well as the differences and lags we have created.

```
proc print data=usa (obs=10);
var f df df1 ddf b db db1 ddb;
run;
```

The data are

Obs	f	df	df1	ddf	b	db	db1	ddb
1	9.69	.	.	.	11.19	.	.	.
2	10.56	0.87	.	.	12.64	1.45	.	.
3	11.39	0.83	0.87	-0.04	12.64	0.00	1.45	-1.45
4	9.27	-2.12	0.83	-2.95	11.10	-1.54	0.00	-1.54
5	8.48	-0.79	-2.12	1.33	10.68	-0.42	-1.54	1.12
6	7.92	-0.56	-0.79	0.23	9.76	-0.92	-0.42	-0.50
7	7.90	-0.02	-0.56	0.54	9.29	-0.47	-0.92	0.45
8	8.10	0.20	-0.02	0.22	8.84	-0.45	-0.47	0.02
9	7.83	-0.27	0.20	-0.47	7.94	-0.90	-0.45	-0.45
10	6.92	-0.91	-0.27	-0.64	7.18	-0.76	-0.90	0.14

Note that we lose one observation when taking differences. Taking lags or differences of the difference causes us to lose an additional observation. Now we estimate the regression to test whether the first difference of the Federal Funds rate is stationary. Since the first difference appears to wander around a zero mean, we specify the **noint** option in our **model** statement.

```
proc autoreg data=usa;
model ddf = df1 / noint;              * specify no intercept;
title 'Dickey-Fuller test for differenced federal funds series';
run;
```

The regression results, which match those on page 488 of *POE4*, are

Variable	DF	Estimate	Standard Error	t Value	Approx Pr > |t|
df1	1	-0.4470	0.0815	-5.49	<.0001

The τ statistic for the first difference of the Federal Funds rate is -5.49. This is less than the 5% critical value of -1.94 for the model with no constant and no intercept, which is given in Table 12.2 of *POE4*. Thus, we reject the null hypothesis and conclude the first difference of the Fed Funds rate is a stationary series.

Next, we use the **%DFTEST** option to obtain the *p*-value. We modify the code from Section 12.3.1 to indicate that we are testing for stationarity of the first difference. We include the option **ar=0** since we do not have any additional lags of the first differences. The option **trend=0** indicates that we do not wish to include a constant or a trend.

```
%dftest(usa,df,ar=0,trend=0,outstat=ddfout);* Dickey-Fuller test;
proc print data=ddfout;                      * print results;
title 'Dickey-Fuller test for differenced fed funds series';
run;
```

This yields the same parameter estimates and τ statistic as **PROC AUTOREG**, and gives a *p*-value of 0.0000035. Finally, we can use **PROC AUTOREG** to obtain the Phillips-Perron τ statistic. Specify the differenced value ΔF_t (df) as the dependent variable with no regressors and include the **stationarity=(phillips)** option.

```
proc autoreg data=usa;
model df = / stationarity=(phillips);  * Phillips-Perron test;
title 'Phillips-Perron test for differenced fed funds series';
run;
```

This yields

Phillips-Perron Unit Root Test

Type	Lags	Rho	Pr < Rho	Tau	Pr < Tau
Zero Mean	2	-46.6819	0.0010	-5.5314	0.0010
Single Mean	2	-48.4380	0.0010	-5.6564	0.0010
Trend	2	-48.3618	0.0010	-5.6275	0.0010

Since we did not include an intercept or trend, the row labeled **Zero Mean** is of primary interest.

Regardless of the model however, the Phillips-Perron test strongly rejects the null hypothesis of nonstationarity, which leads us to conclude that the Federal Funds series is stationary in its first difference.

Now estimate the regression for the first difference of the 3-year bond rate

```
proc autoreg data=usa;
model ddb = db1 / noint;                 * specify no intercept;
title 'Dickey-Fuller test for differenced 3 year bond rate series';
run;
```

The regression results, which match those on page 488 of *POE4*, are

Variable	DF	Estimate	Standard Error	t Value	Approx Pr > |t|
db1	1	-0.7018	0.0916	-7.66	<.0001

The τ statistic for the first difference of the 3-year bond rate is $-7.66 < -1.94$, so we reject the null hypothesis and conclude the first difference of the 3-year bond rate is a stationary series.

Next, run the **%DFTEST** to obtain the *p*-value, the use **PROC AUTOREG** to run the Phillips-Perron test.

```
%dftest(usa,db,ar=0,trend=0,outstat=ddbout);* Dickey-Fuller test;
proc print data=ddbout;                      * print results;
title 'Dickey-Fuller test for differenced 3 year bond rate series';
run;
```

```
proc autoreg data=usa;
model db = / stationarity=(phillips);  * Phillips-Perron test;
title 'Phillips-Perron test for differenced 3 year bond rate series';
run;
```

The *p*-value for the Dickey-Fuller test is 0.0000035. The relevant output for the Phillips-Perron test is

Phillips-Perron Unit Root Test

Type	Lags	Rho	Pr < Rho	Tau	Pr < Tau
Zero Mean	2	-72.6416	0.0010	-7.6824	0.0010

The Phillips-Perron test supports the result that the first difference of the 3-year bond rate is stationary.

12.4 COINTEGRATION

Two nonstationary time series are **cointegrated** if they tend to move together through time. For example, the Dickey-Fuller tests have led us to conclude that the Federal Funds rate and the 3-

year bond rate series are both nonstationary. However, the plots of these series indicate that they tend to follow a similar path over time.

If y_t and x_t are nonstationary I(1) variables, but there is a linear combination of these variables that is a stationary I(0) process the two series are cointegrated. A natural linear combination to examine is the error $e_t = y_t - \beta_1 - \beta_2 x_t$. Since we cannot observe the error, we test the stationarity of the least squares residuals $\hat{e}_t = y_t - b_1 - b_2 x_t$.

Testing for cointegration involves regressing one I(1) variable on another using least squares. Test the residuals for stationarity using the augmented Dickey-Fuller (ADF) test. The null hypothesis is that the residuals are nonstationary. Rejection of this leads to the conclusion that the residuals follow a stationary I(0) process and the series are cointegrated. The test for stationarity is based on the equation

$$\Delta\hat{e}_t = \gamma\hat{e}_{t-1} + v_t \tag{12.6}$$

Again, there are three sets of critical values depending on whether the residuals are derived from a regression equation with no constant term, a constant and no trend, or a constant and a trend. The critical values for the cointegration test are slightly different because the test is based upon estimated values. These critical values are given in Table 12.4, page 489, of *POE4*. This cointegration test is often referred to as the Engle-Granger test.

12.4.1 An example of a cointegration test

As an example, consider the Federal Funds rate, F, and the 3-year bond rate, B, from the *usa* data. Based upon the tests in 12.3.1 and 12.3.2, we conclude that both series are I(1) since both were found to be nonstationary, but their first differences are stationary. The first step is to regress one variable on the other. We will estimate the regression $B_t = \beta_1 + \beta_2 F_t + e_t$. We save the residuals for use in an augmented Dickey-Fuller regression.

```
proc autoreg data=usa;
model b = f;                          * model;
output out=usaout r=ehat;            * save residuals;
title 'save residuals to test for cointegration';
run;
```

The least squares regression results, which match those in equation (12.9) of *POE4*, are

Ordinary Least Squares Estimates

SSE	66.9519745	DFE			102
MSE	0.65639	Root MSE			0.81018
SBC	258.624802	AIC			253.33602
MAE	0.64178174	AICC			253.454832
MAPE	12.5937543	Regress R-Square			0.8946
Durbin-Watson	0.3193	Total R-Square			0.8946

Variable	DF	Estimate	Standard Error	t Value	Approx Pr > |t|
Intercept	1	1.1398	0.1741	6.55	<.0001
f	1	0.9144	0.0311	29.42	<.0001

Next we test for stationarity in the residuals. Estimate the model $\Delta\hat{e}_t = \gamma\hat{e}_{t-1} + a_1\Delta\hat{e}_{t-1} + v_t$, which is the augmented Dickey-Fuller regression with one lagged term to correct for autocorrelation. Open the data set *usaout* and create the necessary lagged and differenced residuals.

```
data usaout;                          * open data set;
set usaout;                           * read data;
dehat = dif(ehat);                    * first difference;
ehat1 = lag(ehat);                    * lag of ehat;
dehat1 = lag(dehat);                  * lag of first difference;
run;
```

Now we estimate the augmented Dickey-Fuller regression. Since the residuals have a mean of zero, we specify the **noint** option.

```
proc autoreg data=usaout;
model dehat = ehat1 dehat1 / noint;    * ADF regression;
title 'test for cointegration';
run;
```

The results, which match those on page 489 of *POE4*, are

Variable	DF	Estimate	Standard Error	t Value	Approx Pr > |t|
ehat1	1	-0.2245	0.0535	-4.20	<.0001
dehat1	1	0.2540	0.0937	2.71	0.0079

Note that this is the augmented Dickey-Fuller version of the test with one lagged term, $\Delta\hat{e}_{t-1}$, to correct for autocorrelation. The null hypothesis is that the residuals are nonstationary and thus the series are not cointegrated. The alternative hypothesis is the residuals are stationary and hence the series are cointegrated. In this example, the τ statistic is -4.20. Since there is a constant term in the cointegration regression, $B_t = \beta_1 + \beta_2 F_t + e_t$, we use the 5% critical value from Table 12.4 of *POE4*, which is -3.37. In this example, $-4.20 < -3.37$ so we reject the null hypothesis and conclude the Federal Funds rate and 3-year bond rate are cointegrated.

When testing for cointegration, you do not want to use the **%DFTEST** macro because the *p*-value will be wrong. It does not take into account that the regressors are estimated so the critical values the macro uses are invalid.

However, we can test for cointegration with **PROC AUTOREG**. Recall that in a model with no regressors, the option **stationarity=(phillips)** is used to carry out the Phillips-Perron unit root test. If we specify this option in a model with regressors, **PROC AUTOREG** computes the **Phillips-Ouliaris**[2] cointegration test statistic.

```
proc autoreg data=usa;
model b = f / stationarity=(phillips);   * PO cointegration test;
title 'Phillips-Ouliaris cointegration test';
run;
```

---

[2] The Phillips-Ouliaris (1990) test is similar to the augmented Dickey-Fuller test but with an adjustment to the DF test statistic. See William Greene (2012), *Econometric Analysis*, *7th Edition*, Prentice Hall, 752-753 for details on computation.

The output is

```
                       Phillips-Ouliaris
                      Cointegration Test


              Lags            Rho              Tau

                2          -21.0600          -3.4486

                                    Standard              Approx
       Variable      DF     Estimate       Error    t Value    Pr > |t|

       Intercept      1       1.1398      0.1741       6.55     <.0001
       f              1       0.9144      0.0311      29.42     <.0001
```

The Phillips-Ouliaris cointegration test statistic has the same asymptotic distribution as the Engle-Granger test statistic. In this example, τ statistic is $-3.4486 < -3.37$ so we reject the null hypothesis and conclude that the Federal Funds rate and the 3-year bond rate are cointegrated.

12.4.2 The error correction model

Cointegration is a relationship between two nonstationary, I(1), variables. These variables tend to move together such that the residuals are I(0). In this section, we examine a dynamic relationship between I(0) variables, which embeds a cointegrating relationship, known as the short-run **error correction model**.

As an example, start with an autoregressive distributed lag (ARDL) model, introduced in Chapter 9. Consider an ARDL(1,1) model, where 3-year bond rate is regressed on its first lag as well as the Fed Funds rate and its first lag

$$B_t = \delta + \theta_1 B_{t-1} + \delta_0 F_t + \delta_1 F_{t-1} + v_t \tag{12.7}$$

After some manipulation (see *POE4*, page 491) this can be written as

$$\Delta B_t = (\theta_1 - 1)(B_{t-1} - \beta_1 - \beta_2 F_{t-1}) + \delta_0 \Delta F_t + v_t \tag{12.8}$$

where the term in parentheses is called an error correction equation since it shows the deviation of B_{t-1} from its long-run value, $\beta_1 + \beta_2 F_{t-1}$. In this example, we use nonlinear least squares to estimate the regression

$$\Delta B_t = \alpha(B_{t-1} - \beta_1 - \beta_2 F_{t-1}) + \delta_0 \Delta F_t + \delta_1 \Delta F_{t-1} + v_t$$

where $\alpha = \theta_1 - 1$. We include the additional lag, ΔF_{t-1}, to ensure that the residuals are purged of all serial correlation effects. Since the model is nonlinear, we estimate the parameters using **PROC NLIN**.

```
proc nlin data=usa method=gauss;
parms alpha=0 beta1=0 beta2=0 delta0=0 delta1=0; * starting values;
model db = alpha*(b1+beta1+beta2*f1)+delta0*df+delta1*df1;
title 'error correction model using PROC NLIN';
run;
```

The output, which matches the results on page 491 of *POE4*, is

```
                        The NLIN Procedure

                        Approx
   Parameter   Estimate   Std Error   Approximate 95% Confidence Limits

     alpha     -0.1419     0.0497       -0.2404      -0.0433
     beta1     -1.4292     0.6246       -2.6689      -0.1895
     beta2     -0.7766     0.1225       -1.0196      -0.5335
     delta0     0.8425     0.0897        0.6643       1.0206
     delta1    -0.3268     0.0848       -0.4951      -0.1586
```

Next, we use SAS to generate the estimated residuals: $\hat{e}_t = (B_t - 1.4292 - 0.7766 F_t)$ and its lag, first difference, and lagged difference.

```
data usa;                           * open data set;
set usa;                            * read data;
resid = b1-1.4292-0.7766*f1;        * estimated residual;
resid1 = lag(resid);                * lagged residual;
dresid = dif(resid);                * first difference;
dresid1 = lag(dresid);              * lagged difference;
run;
```

Finally, estimate the augmented Dickey-Fuller regression, $\Delta\hat{e}_t = \gamma\hat{e}_{t-1} + a_1\Delta\hat{e}_{t-1} + v_t$, to test for a cointegrating relationship.

```
proc autoreg data=usa;
model dresid = resid1 dresid1 / noint; * ADF regression;
title 'test for cointegrating relationship';
run;
```

The results, which match those on page 492 of *POE4*, except for some slight differences due to rounding, are

Variable	DF	Estimate	Standard Error	t Value	Approx Pr > |t|
resid1	1	-0.1686	0.0431	-3.91	0.0002
dresid1	1	0.1802	0.0929	1.94	0.0552

The τ statistic is $-3.91 < -3.37$ so we reject the null hypothesis and conclude that the Federal Funds rate and the 3-year bond rate are cointegrated.

CHAPTER 13

Vector Error Correction and Vector Autoregressive Models

13.1 VEC AND VAR MODELS

In Section 12.4, we examine cointegrating relationships between pairs of nonstationary variables. We assumed that one variable was the dependent variable, y_t, and the other was the independent variable, x_t. However, in many cases the two variables are simultaneously determined.

The **vector autoregressive (VAR)** model is a general framework used to describe the dynamic interrelationship among stationary variables. The first step in time-series analysis should be determining whether the levels of the data are stationary. If the levels are not stationary, then check to see if the first differences are.

Consider two time-series variables, y_t and x_t. Generalizing the discussion about dynamic relationships in Chapter 9 of *Principles of Econometrics, 4th Edition* yields a system of equations.

$$
\begin{aligned}
y_t &= \beta_{10} + \beta_{11} y_{t-1} + \beta_{12} x_{t-1} + v_t^y \\
x_t &= \beta_{20} + \beta_{21} y_{t-1} + \beta_{22} x_{t-1} + v_t^x
\end{aligned}
\tag{13.1}
$$

The equations in (13.1) describe a system in which each variable is a function of its own lag, and the lag of the other variable in the system. In this example, since the maximum lag is of order 1, we have a VAR(1). If y_t and x_t are stationary I(0) variables, the above system can be estimated using least squares applied to each equation.

If, however, y_t and x_t are not stationary in their levels, but are stationary in differences (i.e. they are I(1)), then we work with the first differences. In this case, the VAR(1) model is

$$
\begin{aligned}
\Delta y_t &= \beta_{11} \Delta y_{t-1} + \beta_{12} \Delta x_{t-1} + v_t^{\Delta y} \\
\Delta x_t &= \beta_{21} \Delta y_{t-1} + \beta_{22} \Delta x_{t-1} + v_t^{\Delta x}
\end{aligned}
\tag{13.2}
$$

The differenced variables are all I(0), so the above system can be estimated using least squares applied to each equation.

Finally, if y_t and x_t are I(1) variables, but are cointegrated, the system of equations can be modified to allow for a cointegrating relationship between them. The **vector error correction (VEC)** model is a special form of the VAR for I(1) variables that are cointegrated. The VEC model is

$$\Delta y_t = \alpha_{10} + \alpha_{11}(y_{t-1} - \beta_0 - \beta_1 x_{t-1}) + v_t^y$$

(13.3)

$$\Delta x_t = \alpha_{20} + \alpha_{21}(y_{t-1} - \beta_0 - \beta_1 x_{t-1}) + v_t^x$$

We can estimate the parameters of the VEC model using nonlinear least squares. Alternatively, we can use a two-step least squares procedure. First, obtain least squares estimates for the model $y_t = \beta_0 + \beta_1 x_t + e_t$. In the second step, replace $y_{t-1} - \beta_0 - \beta_1 x_t$ in equation (13.3) with the least squares residuals, $\hat{e}_{t-1} = y_{t-1} - b_0 - b_1 x_t$.

$$\Delta y_t = \alpha_{10} + \alpha_{11}\hat{e}_{t-1} + v_t^y$$

$$\Delta x_t = \alpha_{20} + \alpha_{21}\hat{e}_{t-1} + v_t^x$$

Note that both the first differences and the cointegration residuals are stationary I(0) variables. Thus, the above system can be estimated by least squares applied to each equation.

13.2 ESTIMATING A VECTOR ERROR CORRECTION MODEL

In this example, we use data on quarterly real GDP of Australia and the United States to estimate a VEC model. We use the VEC model when the data are (1) nonstationary in levels but are stationary in differences and (2) the variables are cointegrated. The first step is to look at plots of the data and the second step is to run tests for stationarity, in both levels and differences, and to test for cointegration. The SAS data set *gdp* contains quarterly observations for Australian and U.S. real GDP for the sample period 1970q1 to 2000q4. The data have been scaled so that both economies show a real GDP value of 100 in 2000.

First, open *gdp*, examine its contents and turn off labels.

```
data gdp;                        * open data set;
set 'gdp';                       * read gdp;
run;
proc contents data=gdp;          * examine contents;
run;
options nolabel;                 * turn off labels;
```

```
        Alphabetic List of Variables and Attributes

    #    Variable    Type    Len    Label
    2    aus         Num     8      real GDP of Australia
    1    usa         Num     8      real GDP of USA
```

Next, open the data set and create the first difference of each series and a date variable in order to plot the data over time. See Section 9.2.1 for a discussion of SAS lag and difference operators and the creation of date variables.

```
data gdp;                           * open data set;
set gdp;                            * read data;
dusa = dif(usa);                    * first differences;
daus = dif(aus);
retain date '1oct69'd;              * date variable;
date=intnx('qtr',date,1);          * update dates;
format date yyqc.;                  * format for date;
year = 1970 + int((_n_-1)/4);       * year;
qtr = mod(_n_-1, 4) + 1;            * quarter;
run;
```

It is always a good idea to print a few observations to ensure that variables have been created correctly.

```
proc print data=gdp (obs=5);            * summary statistics;
title 'first 5 observations for GDP data';
run;
```

You will note that we lose an observation for the differenced series. The data should look like this.

```
                first 5 observations for GDP data


Obs      usa       aus       dusa      daus      date      year     qtr

 1     38.3011   38.2355       .          .      1970:1    1970      1
 2     38.3734   38.7551    0.0723     0.5196    1970:2    1970      2
 3     38.7137   38.7706    0.3403     0.0155    1970:3    1970      3
 4     38.2991   38.8948   -0.4146     0.1242    1970:4    1970      4
 5     39.3615   39.5621    1.0624     0.6673    1971:1    1971      1
```

Now we plot the levels of the two GDP series. We specify **line=20** to obtain a dashed line for the *AUS* series.

```
legend1 label=none
        position=(top center inside)
        mode=share;                     * create legend;
symbol1 value=none interpol=join color=blue width=3;
symbol2 value=none interpol=join color=black width=3 line=20;
proc gplot data=gdp;
plot usa*date=1 aus*date=2 / hminor=1 overlay legend=legend1;
title 'Real gross domestic products(GDP=100 in 2000)';
run;
```

This generates the following plot, which matches Figure 13.1, page 502, in *POE4*.

Real gross domestic products(GDP=100 in 2000)

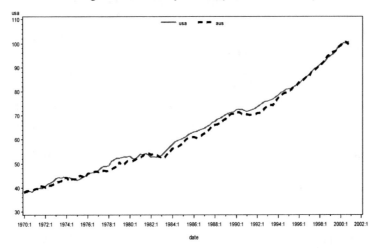

The plot suggests that the levels are nonstationary since both series are trending upward. They appear to have a common trend, an indication that they may be cointegrated. Next we plot the differences of the two GDP series.

```
proc gplot data=gdp;
plot dusa*date=1 daus*date=2 / hminor=1 vref=0 overlay legend=legend1;
title 'Change in real gross domestic products';
run;
```

The plot for the first differences is

Change in real gross domestic products

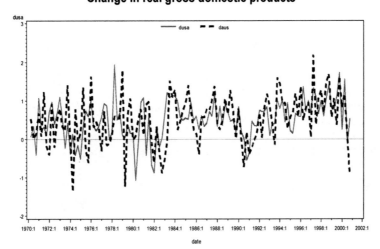

The first differences for both series appear to be stationary around a nonzero mean. We next carry out unit root tests for stationarity and cointegration.

Unit root tests are performed using the procedures discussed in Chapter 12. Augmented Dickey-Fuller regressions require some judgment about specification. The user must decide whether to include a constant, a trend or drift, and the lag lengths for the differences that augment the regular Dickey-Fuller regressions. The plots give some clues about specification.

We use the **%dftest** macro to carry out the ADF tests (see Section 12.3.1). Looking at the plots, it appears that the Dickey-Fuller regressions for the levels should have a constant and a time trend. Thus, we specify **trend=2** in the macro. Lag lengths can be chosen by model selection rules or by selecting a maximum lag length, say 4, and eliminating lags until the coefficient for the last lag is significantly different from zero at the 10% significance level. Through the process of elimination, we included 2 lags in the U.S. equation and 4 lags in the Australia equation.

```
%dftest(gdp,usa,ar=2,trend=2,outstat=dfusa);     * Dickey-Fuller test;
proc print data=dfusa;
title 'ADF test for real GDP: U.S.';
run;

%dftest(gdp,aus,ar=4,trend=2,outstat=dfaus);     * Dickey-Fuller test;
proc print data=dfaus;
title 'ADF test for real GDP: Australia';
run;
```

The output of the augmented Dickey-Fuller test for U.S. GDP is

```
                        ADF test for real GDP: U.S.

Obs _TYPE_  _STATUS_    _DEPVAR_  _NAME_      _MSE_   Intercept AR_V        time

 1  PARM  0 Converged   AR_V                0.22840   0.61599  -1  0.009504057
 2  COV   0 Converged   AR_V     Intercept  0.22840   0.30737   .  0.004195451
 3  COV   0 Converged   AR_V     time       0.22840   0.00420   .  0.000063166
 4  COV   0 Converged   AR_V     DLAG_V     0.22840  -0.00908   . -.000130005
 5  COV   0 Converged   AR_V     AR_V1      0.22840   0.00654   .  0.000085233
 6  COV   0 Converged   AR_V     AR_V2      0.22840   0.01239   .  0.000160265


  Obs  DLAG_V    AR_V1     AR_V2    _NOBS_    _TAU_   _TREND_ _DLAG_  _PVALUE_

   1  -0.014265  0.20246   0.20494   121    -0.85911    2      1     0.95650
   2  -0.009076  0.00654   0.01239   121    -0.85911    2      1     0.95650
   3  -0.000130  0.00009   0.00016   121    -0.85911    2      1     0.95650
   4   0.000276 -0.00024  -0.00041   121    -0.85911    2      1     0.95650
   5  -0.000242  0.00849  -0.00152   121    -0.85911    2      1     0.95650
   6  -0.000413 -0.00152   0.00914   121    -0.85911    2      1     0.95650
```

The first row, **_TYPE_=PARM**, lists the parameter estimates. The rows below give the covariance matrix. The −1 under **AR_V** indicates that it is the dependent variable. The estimated ADF regression is

$$\hat{U}_t = 0.6160 + 0.0095t - 0.0143U_{t-1} + 0.2025\Delta U_{t-1} + 0.2049\Delta U_{t-2}$$
$$(0.5544)\ (0.0079)\ (0.0166)\qquad (0.0921)\qquad\quad (0.0956)$$

The ADF regression with two lags for the U.S. yields a τ statistic of -0.859 with p-value 0.9565. Thus, we fail to reject the null hypothesis that the data are nonstationary. You will note that the constant and trend terms are insignificant. However, running the ADF test without these terms (i.e. specifying **trend=0**) still leads us to conclude that the data are nonstationary.

Similarly, the ADF regression with four lags for Australia yields a τ statistic of -0.612 with p-value 0.9763, so we again fail to reject the null hypothesis that the data are nonstationary.

Next, we repeat these tests for the differenced series. We again use the strategy of eliminating lags to arrive at one and two lags for the differenced U.S. and Australia series, respectively. For the differenced series, we include a constant but not a trend, so we specify **trend=1** in the **%dftest** macro.

```
%dftest(gdp,dusa,ar=1,trend=1,outstat=dfdusa);   * Dickey-Fuller test;
proc print data=dfdusa;
title 'ADF test for differenced real GDP: U.S.';
run;

%dftest(gdp,daus,ar=2,trend=1,outstat=dfdaus);   * Dickey-Fuller test;
proc print data=dfdaus;
title 'ADF test for difference real GDP: Australia';
run;
```

The output of the augmented Dickey-Fuller test for differenced U.S. GDP is

ADF test for differenced real GDP: U.S.

Obs	_TYPE_	_STATUS_	_DEPVAR_	_NAME_	_MSE_	Intercept	AR_V
1	PARM	0 Converged	AR_V		0.23398	0.27265	-1
2	COV	0 Converged	AR_V	Intercept	0.23398	0.00484	.
3	COV	0 Converged	AR_V	DLAG_V	0.23398	-0.00569	.
4	COV	0 Converged	AR_V	AR_V1	0.23398	0.00286	.

Obs	DLAG_V	AR_V1	_NOBS_	_TAU_	_TREND_	_DLAG_	_PVALUE_
1	-0.53138	-0.23536	121	-5.04076	1	1	.000103126
2	-0.00569	0.00286	121	-5.04076	1	1	.000103126
3	0.01111	-0.00558	121	-5.04076	1	1	.000103126
4	-0.00558	0.00807	121	-5.04076	1	1	.000103126

The ADF regression with one lag for the differenced U.S. series yields a τ statistic of -5.041 with p-value 0.0001. The ADF regression with two lags for the differenced Australia series yields a τ statistic of -4.438 with p-value 0.00048. Thus, in both cases we conclude that the differenced series is stationary and the U.S. and Australian real GDP are I(1) variables.

Finally, we check for cointegration in the two GDP series. In this example, we regress Australian GDP on U.S. GDP since it makes sense to think of GDP in the smaller economy responding to GDP in the larger economy. We do not include a constant since there does not appear to be any systematic difference between the two series. Run the regression and save the residuals in order to test for a cointegrating relationship.

```
proc autoreg data=gdp;
model aus = usa / noint;
output out=gdpout r=ehat;              * output residuals;
title 'regress Australian GDP on U.S. GDP';
run;
```

The regression results, which match equation (13.7), page 502 of *POE4*, are

Variable	DF	Estimate	Standard Error	t Value	Approx Pr > |t|
USA	1	0.9853	0.001657	594.79	<.0001

To test for cointegration, we perform a Dickey-Fuller test using the saved residuals as described in Section 12.4.1. Create the first difference and the first lag of the residuals.

```
data gdpout;                          * open data set;
set gdpout;                           * read data;
dehat = dif(ehat);                    * first difference;
ehat1 = lag(ehat);                    * lag of ehat;
run;
```

To carry out the unit root test we apply the Dickey-Fuller test to the residuals. Recall from Section 12.4.1 that if the residuals are stationary then the two I(1) series, *AUS* and *USA*, are cointegrated. We carry out the regression with the differenced residual as the dependent variable and the lagged residual as the explanatory variable.

```
proc autoreg data=gdpout;
model dehat = ehat1 / noint;          * ADF regression;
title 'test for cointegration';
run;
```

The regression results, which match equation (13.8), page 502 of *POE4*, are

Variable	DF	Estimate	Standard Error	t Value	Approx Pr > |t|
ehat_1	1	-0.1279	0.0443	-2.89	0.0046

The τ statistic is -2.89. Since the cointegrating relationship does not include an intercept term, the 5% critical value, from Table 12.4 in *POE4*, is -2.76. Therefore, we reject the null hypothesis of no cointegration and conclude that the two real GDP series are cointegrated, so the VEC model is appropriate.

To measure the one quarter response of GDP to economic shocks we regress the first difference of each series on a constant and the lagged residuals from the cointegrating relationship. This gives us estimates of the α's for the VEC model in equation (13.3).

```
proc autoreg data=gdpout;
model daus = ehat1;
run;
```

```
proc autoreg data=gdpout;
model dusa = ehat1;
run;
```

The VEC model results for { A_t, U_t }, which match equation (13.9) in *POE4* are

```
                    Dependent Variable    daus

                                Standard            Approx
   Variable      DF    Estimate    Error    t Value   Pr > |t|

   Intercept      1     0.4917    0.0579      8.49    <.0001
   ehat_1         1    -0.0987    0.0475     -2.08    0.0399


                    Dependent Variable    dusa

                                Standard            Approx
   Variable      DF    Estimate    Error    t Value   Pr > |t|

   Intercept      1     0.5099    0.0467     10.92    <.0001
   ehat_1         1     0.0303    0.0383      0.79    0.4312
```

The results indicate that Australian GDP responds to disequilibrium between the two economies. Thus, if $\hat{e}_{t-1} = A_t - 0.985U_t > 0$, Australian GDP tends to fall back toward the equilibrium level. In the U.S. equation, the t-ratio indicates that $\hat{e}_{t-1}$ is insignificant. This is consistent with the hypothesis that the Australian economy reacts to economic conditions in the U.S., but not vice versa.

13.3 ESTIMATING A VAR MODEL

The **vector autoregressive** (VAR) model is somewhat simpler to estimate than the VEC model. The VAR model is used when there is no cointegrating relationship between the series. If the series are stationary in levels then we estimate the model in equation (13.1). If the data are not stationary in levels, take first differences and estimate the model in equation (13.2).

As an example, consider macroeconomic data on the log of real personal disposable income, Y_t, and the log of real personal consumption expenditure, C_t. The data are in the SAS data set *fred*, and include quarterly observations for the sample period 1960q1 to 2009q4. As in the previous example, the first step is to determine whether the variables are stationary. If they are stationary, then we can estimate a VAR model. If they are not, then difference them and check to make sure the differences are stationary, and check for cointegration in the levels. If they are cointegrated, estimate the VEC model. If not, estimate a VAR model[1].

Turn labels back on, open *fred*, examine its contents, and turn labels back off.

```
data fred;                              * open data set;
```

---

[1] For a more advanced discussion of VEC and VAR models see William Greene (2012), *Econometric Analysis, 7th Edition*, Prentice Hall, 756-768. Also Walter Enders (2010), *Applied Econometric Time Series, 3rd Edition*, Wiley, Chapters 5-6; Enders is an excellent reference for all of the time-series topics discussed in this manual.

```
set 'fred';                        * read gdp;
run;
proc contents data=fred;           * examine contents;
run;
options nolabel;                   * turn labels off;
```

Alphabetic List of Variables and Attributes

```
#   Variable   Type   Len   Label

1    c          Num     8    log of real consumption expenditure
2    y          Num     8    log of real disposable income
```

Next, open the data set and create the first difference of each series and a date variable in order to plot the data over time.

```
data fred;                         * open data set;
set fred;                          * read data;
dc = dif(c);                       * first differences;
dy = dif(y);
retain date '1oct59'd;             * date variable;
date=intnx('qtr',date,1);          * update dates;
format date yyqc.;                 * format for date;
year = 1960 + int((_n_-1)/4);      * year;
qtr = mod(_n_-1, 4) + 1;           * quarter;
run;
```

Now we plot the levels of the two series in order to identify whether constants or trends should be included in the unit root tests. Note that we are using the same **legend** and **symbol** that we specified for the graphs in Section 13.2.

```
proc gplot data=fred;
plot y*date=1 c*date=2 / hminor=1 overlay legend=legend1;
title 'Real personal disposable income and consumption expenditure';
run;
```

This generates the following plot, which matches Figure 13.3, page 504, in *POE4*.

Real personal disposable income and consumption expenditure

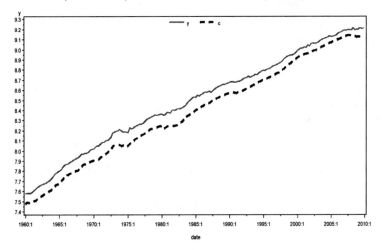

The plot suggests that both series are nonstationary in levels since both series are trending upward. They appear to have a common trend, an indication that they may be cointegrated. Next we plot the series in differences.

```
proc gplot data=fred;
plot dy*date=1 dc*date=2 / hminor=1 vref=0 overlay legend=legend1;
title 'Differences in real income and consumption expenditure';
run;
```

The plot for the first differences is

Differences in real income and consumption expenditure

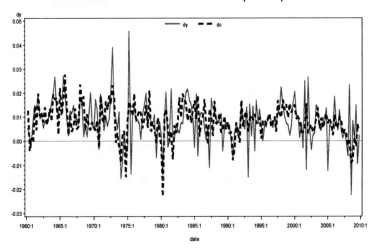

The first differences for both series appear to be stationary around a nonzero mean. We next carry out unit root tests for stationarity and cointegration.

Both series appear to be nonstationary in levels. The graphs indicate that the levels have a nonzero mean so we include a constant term in the ADF regressions (and perhaps a trend). The other decision that needs to be made is the number of lags to include in the augmented Dickey-Fuller regressions. Following *POE4*, page 503, we estimate the ADF regressions with an intercept only and augment the regression with three lagged differences for real personal consumption, C, and zero lagged differences for real personal disposable income, Y.

```
%dftest(fred,c,ar=3,trend=1,outstat=dfc);   * Dickey-Fuller test;
proc print data=dfc;
title 'ADF test for consumption with 3 lags';
run;


%dftest(fred,y,ar=0,trend=1,outstat=dfy);   * Dickey-Fuller test;
proc print data=dfy;
title 'ADF test for disposable income with 0 lags';
run;
```

The ADF regression with three lags for real personal consumption yields a τ statistic of -1.995, which matches the result on page 503 in *POE4*; the *p*-value is 0.2884. The ADF regression with zero lags for real personal disposable income yields a τ statistic of -2.741 with *p*-value 0.0694. Thus, for both series, we fail to reject the null hypothesis of nonstationarity at the 5% level of significance.

The differenced series appear to be stationary around a nonzero mean. Therefore, we include a constant but no trend in the ADF regressions. We include three lags in each ADF regression.

```
%dftest(fred,dc,ar=3,trend=1,outstat=dfdc); * Dickey-Fuller test;
proc print data=dfdc;
title 'ADF test for differenced consumption with 3 lags';
run;


%dftest(fred,dy,ar=3,trend=1,outstat=dfdy); * Dickey-Fuller test;
proc print data=dfdy;
title 'ADF test for differenced disposable income with 3 lags';
run;
```

The ADF regression with three lags for differenced real personal consumption yields a τ statistic of -5.046 with *p*-value 0.0001. The ADF regression with three lags for differenced real personal disposable income yields a τ statistic of -5.951 with *p*-value 0.0001. In both cases we reject the null hypothesis of nonstationarity. Hence, we conclude that both series are nonstationary in levels but are stationary in differences (i.e., they are I(1)). The next step is to test for cointegration.

We consider the cointegrating relationship, $C_t = \beta_1 + \beta_2 Y_t + e_t$, which is estimated using least squares. Estimate the regression and save the residuals.

```
proc autoreg data=fred;
model c = y;
output out=fredout r=ehat;
title 'estimate cointegrating relationship: C = B1+B2Y+e';
run;
```

The regression results, which match equation (13.10) on page 503 of *POE4*, are

Variable	DF	Estimate	Standard Error	t Value	Approx Pr > |t|
Intercept	1	-0.4042	0.0251	-16.13	<.0001
y	1	1.0353	0.002947	351.30	<.0001

To test for cointegration, we regress the differenced residuals on the lagged residuals and include one lagged differenced residual to augment the regression. First, create the appropriate lags and differences of the residuals.

```
data fredout;              * open data set;
set fredout;               * read data;
dehat = dif(ehat);         * first difference;
ehat1 = lag(ehat);         * lag of ehat;
dehat1 = lag(dehat);       * lagged difference;
run;
```

Now estimate the augmented Dickey-Fuller regression model $\Delta \hat{e}_t = \gamma \hat{e}_{t-1} + \delta \Delta \hat{e}_{t-1} + v_t$.

```
proc autoreg data=fredout;
model dehat = ehat1 dehat1 / noint;   * ADF regression;
title 'Engle-Granger test for cointegration';
run;
```

The results of the ADF regression, which match equation (13.10) on page 503 of *POE4*, are

Variable	DF	Estimate	Standard Error	t Value	Approx Pr > |t|
ehat1	1	-0.0876	0.0305	-2.87	0.0045
dehat1	1	-0.2994	0.0672	-4.46	<.0001

Since the potential cointegrating relationship contains an intercept, the 5% critical value for the cointegration test, given in Table 12.4 of *POE4*, is -3.37. The τ statistic is $-2.87 > -3.37$, so we conclude that the errors are nonstationary. That is, we reject the null hypothesis and conclude there is no cointegrating relationship between C and Y. We conclude that the perceived relationship between the series is spurious. Therefore, we should apply the VAR model using first differences, as given by equation (13.2), rather than the VEC model.

To estimate the VAR model, we regress the difference of each variable, ΔC_t and ΔY_t, on its own past value as well as the past value of the other variable in the system of equations. In this example, we include only one past lag of each variable and estimate a VAR(1) model. In practice, one should test for significance of lag terms greater than one.

First, open the data set and create lags for each differenced series.

```
data fredout;              * open data set;
set fredout;               * read data;
dc1 = lag(dc);             * lag first difference;
dy1 = lag(dy);
run;
```

Since the differences are stationary we estimate each equation using least squares.

```
proc autoreg data=fredout;
model dc = dc1 dy1;
title 'VAR regression for personal consumption expenditure';
run;

proc autoreg data=fredout;
model dy = dc1 dy1;
title 'VAR regression for real personal disposable income';
run;
```

The VAR results, which match equations (13.11a) and (13.11b) on page 504 of *POE4* are

VAR regression for personal consumption expenditure

The AUTOREG Procedure
Dependent Variable   dc
Parameter Estimates

Variable	DF	Estimate	Standard Error	t Value	Approx Pr > |t|
Intercept	1	0.005278	0.000757	6.97	<.0001
dc1	1	0.2156	0.0747	2.88	0.0044
dy1	1	0.1494	0.0577	2.59	0.0104

VAR regression for real personal disposable income

The AUTOREG Procedure
Dependent Variable   dy
Parameter Estimates

Variable	DF	Estimate	Standard Error	t Value	Approx Pr > |t|
Intercept	1	0.006037	0.000986	6.12	<.0001
dc1	1	0.4754	0.0973	4.88	<.0001
dy1	1	-0.2172	0.0752	-2.89	0.0043

The results indicate that quarterly growth in consumption (ΔC_t) is significantly related to its own past value (ΔC_{t-1}) and also significantly related to the quarterly growth in the last period's income (ΔY_{t-1}). Quarterly growth in income is significantly negatively related to its own past value and significantly positively related to the last period's change in consumption.

In practice, it is a good idea to test the residuals of the VAR for autocorrelation. Include enough lags so that the residuals are uncorrelated.

13.4 IMPULSE RESPONSES AND VARIANCE DECOMPOSITIONS

Impulse response functions show the effects of shocks on the adjustment path of the variables. Forecast error variance decompositions measure the contribution of each type of shock to the forecast error variance. Both computations are useful is assessing how shocks to economic variables work their way through a system.

The SAS procedure **PROC VARMAX** can be used to estimate VAR (or VEC) models and can generate graphs of impulse response functions. We illustrate how to use **PROC VARMAX** to estimate the VAR(1) model using the income and consumption data in *fred* and obtain a graph of the simple impulse response function.

First, turn on **ODS graphics** so that the impulse response plot can be generated. To request this output specify **plot=impulse** in the **PROC VARMAX** statement line. In the **model** statement we specify the dependent variables in the system, ΔC and ΔY, and that we with to include one lag (**p=1**). Finally, we specify **lead=6** in the output line to request a 6-period ahead forecast.

```
ods listing gpath='c:\figures' style=journal;
ods graphics on;                          * must turn ODS on;
proc varmax data=fredout plot=impulse;
model dc dy / p=1;
output lead=6;
title 'estimate VAR model and generate impulse response';
run;
ods graphics off;                         * must turn ODS off;
```

The VAR estimates, which match those in equations (13.11a) and (13.11b) in *POE4* are

Model Parameter Estimates

Equation	Parameter	Estimate	Standard Error	t Value	Pr > |t|	Variable
dc	CONST1	0.00528	0.00076	6.97	0.0001	1
	AR1_1_1	0.21561	0.07475	2.88	0.0044	dc(t-1)
	AR1_1_2	0.14938	0.05773	2.59	0.0104	dy(t-1)
dy	CONST2	0.00604	0.00099	6.12	0.0001	1
	AR1_2_1	0.47543	0.09733	4.88	0.0001	dc(t-1)
	AR1_2_2	-0.21717	0.07517	-2.89	0.0043	dy(t-1)

The impulse response responses of ΔC and ΔY to a shock in ΔY are

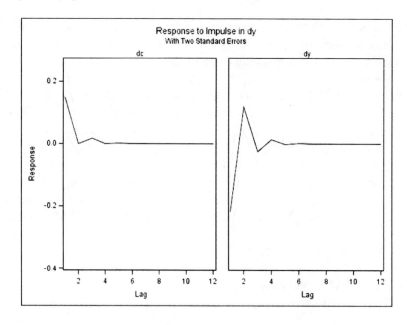

The impulse response responses of ΔC and ΔY to a shock in ΔC are

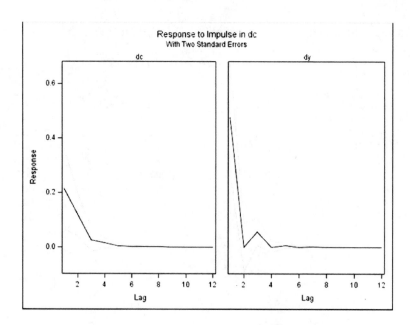

For details on the impulse responses see pages 506-507 in *POE4*.

The forecasts produced by **PROC VARMAX** are

```
                            Forecasts

                              Standard
    Variable    Obs    Forecast    Error       95% Confidence Limits

    dc          200    0.00650    0.00658    -0.00639      0.01938
                201    0.00778    0.00696    -0.00586      0.02143
                202    0.00808    0.00701    -0.00565      0.02181
                203    0.00823    0.00701    -0.00551      0.02197
                204    0.00826    0.00701    -0.00548      0.02201
                205    0.00828    0.00701    -0.00546      0.02203
    dy          200    0.00741    0.00856    -0.00938      0.02419
                201    0.00752    0.00902    -0.01016      0.02519
                202    0.00811    0.00908    -0.00968      0.02589
                203    0.00812    0.00908    -0.00968      0.02592
                204    0.00819    0.00908    -0.00962      0.02599
                205    0.00819    0.00908    -0.00961      0.02599
```

PROC VARMAX gives summary statistics that show $\sigma_{\Delta C} = 0.00696$ and $\sigma_{\Delta Y} = 0.00902$. As shown in *POE4*, pages 508-509, the one-step ahead forecasts have standard errors equal to these values. The two-step ahead forecast has slightly larger variance, which is a combination of the variances of both variables in the system (see *POE4* for details). The variances do not grow beyond this point since we estimated a model with just one lag in this example.

POE4 discusses the interpretation of impulse responses and variance decomposition for the special case where the shocks are uncorrelated. This is not usually the case. Contemporaneous interactions and correlated errors complicate the identification of shocks. This topic is discussed in greater detail in textbooks devoted to time-series analysis[2].

---

[2] Two references you might consider are Lütkepohl, H. (2005) *Introduction to Multiple Time Series Analysis*, Springer, Chapter 9, and Walter Enders (2010) *Applied Econometric Time Series, 3rd Edition*, Wiley, Chapter 5.

CHAPTER **14**

Time-VaryingVolatility and ARCH Models

14.1 TIME-VARYING VOLATILITY

In this chapter we examine models in which the **variance changes over time**. The model we focus on is called the **autoregressive conditional heteroskedastic (ARCH)** model. In this chapter we are concerned with stationary series, but with conditional variances that change over time.

First, we illustrate the problem graphically using data on stock returns. The SAS data set *returns* contains monthly returns to a number of stock price indices: the U.S. Nasdaq (*NASDAQ*), the Australian All Ordinaries (*ALLORDS*), the U.K. FTSE (*FTSE*), and the Japanese Nikkei (*NIKKEI*). The data are from the sample period 1988m1 to 2010m7.

To begin, open *returns*, examine its contents, and turn off labels.

```
data returns;                        * open data set;
set 'returns';                       * read returns;
run;
proc contents data=returns position; * examine contents;
run;
options nolabel;                     * turn off labels;
```

Variables in Creation Order

#	Variable	Type	Len	Label
1	nasdaq	Num	8	NASDAQ stock Index (USA)
2	allords	Num	8	All Ordinaries Stock Index (Australia)
3	ftse	Num	8	FTSE Stock Index (UK)
4	nikkei	Num	8	NIkkei Stock Index (Japan)

We first us **PROC MEANS** to obtain summary statistics.

```
proc means data=returns;
title 'summary statistics for stock returns data';
run;
```

We see that average monthly returns for the sample period are slightly positive for all indices except the Japanese Nikkei. In addition, the relatively large standard deviations and ranges indicate that returns are volatile.

The MEANS Procedure

Variable	N	Mean	Std Dev	Minimum	Maximum
nasdaq	271	0.7085482	6.8083178	-26.0087972	19.8653007
allords	271	0.4531693	4.0215329	-15.0877625	12.3850075
ftse	271	0.4139039	4.3244101	-13.9535768	13.4917694
nikkei	271	-0.3010387	6.3957161	-27.2162319	18.2845628

The next step is to plot each series and examine their distributions. First, we create a date variable in order to plot the data over time. See Section 9.2.1 for a discussion of SAS date variables. In this example, we modify the code slightly since we are using monthly (rather than quarterly) data.

```
options nolabel;                        * turn off labels;
data returns;                           * open data set;
set returns;                            * read data;
retain date '1dec87'd;                  * date variable;
date=intnx('mon',date,1);               * update dates;
format date yymmc.;                     * format for date;
year = 1988 + int((_n_-1)/12);          * year;
month = mod(_n_-1, 12) + 1;             * month;
run;
```

Print a few observations to check that dates have been created correctly.

```
proc print data=returns (obs=6);
title 'returns data with date variables';
run;
```

returns data with date variables

Obs	nasdaq	allords	ftse	nikkei	date	year	month
1	4.20678	-4.8824	4.45914	9.11532	1988:01	1988	1
2	6.26874	-0.5104	-1.23611	6.63704	1988:02	1988	2
3	2.04969	12.3850	-1.49805	3.94980	1988:03	1988	3
4	1.22050	2.8963	3.36873	4.37363	1988:04	1988	4
5	-2.37503	7.2582	-0.99259	-0.06199	1988:05	1988	5
6	6.38125	-0.7688	4.02031	1.27570	1988:06	1988	6

Now generate the plots for the levels of the series.

```
symbol1 value=point interpol=join;       * symbol for diagram;
proc gplot data=returns;
plot nasdaq*date=1 / hminor=1;
title 'United States: Nasdaq';
run;
plot allords*date=1 / hminor=1;
title 'Australia: All Ordinaries';
run;
plot ftse*date=1 / hminor=1;
title 'United Kingdom: FTSE';
run;
plot nikkei*date=1 / hminor=1;
title 'Japan: Nikkei';
run;
```

This generates the following plots, which match those in Figure 14.1, page 520, of *POE4*.

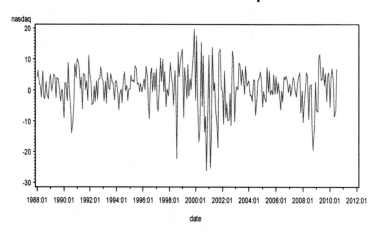

United States: Nasdaq

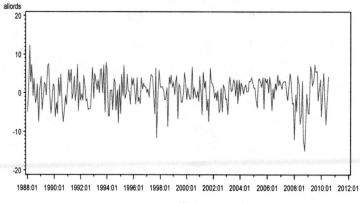

Australia: All Ordinaries

United Kingdom: FTSE

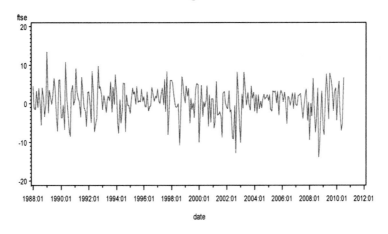

Japan: Nikkei

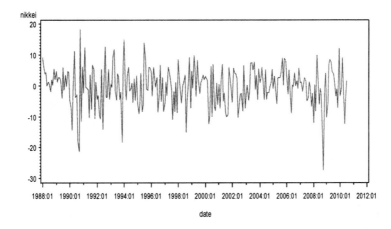

The series are characterized by random, rapid changes and are said to be **volatile**. Notice that the volatility changes over time as well. Large changes tend to be followed by large changes, and small changes tend to be followed by small changes. For example, the U.S. NASDAQ index experienced a period of relatively small changes from 1992 to 1996, but became more volatile from 1996 until early 2004. This is called **time-varying volatility**. The other indices exhibit similar periods of varying volatility.

The **histogram** command is used to generate graphs of the empirical distribution of returns. Using **PROC UNIVARIATE**, we generate histograms for the monthly returns of the stock indices. The **normal** option overlays the normal distribution (using the respective sample means and variances) on top of these histograms. The following generates the histogram for the U.S. Nasdaq index. Plots for the other indices are generated by changing the series name in the **var** statements; we also change the **endpoints** to match the graphs in Figure 14.2(a)-(d) of *POE4*.

```
proc univariate data=returns;
var nasdaq;
histogram / normal endpoints=-30 to 30 by 2.5;
title 'United States: Nasdaq';
run;
```

This generates the following histograms, which match those in Figure 14.2, page 521, of *POE4*.

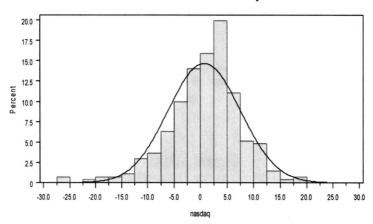

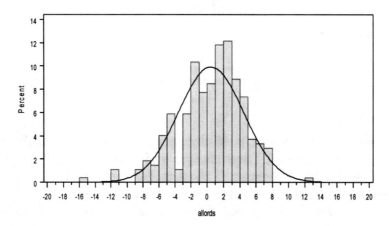

United Kingdom: FTSE

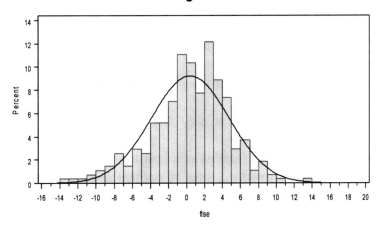

Japan: Nikkei

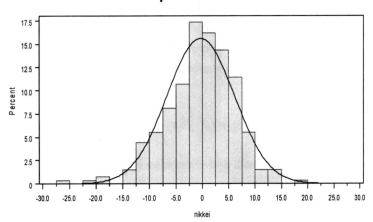

Note that there are more observations around the mean and in the tails than in the normal distribution. Distributions with these properties – more peaked around the mean and relatively fat tails – are said to be **leptokurtic**.

14.2 TESTING, ESTIMATING, AND FORECASTING

The basic ARCH model consists of two equations. The **mean equation** describes the behavior of the mean of the series; it is a linear regression function that contains a constant and possibly some other variables. In the examples below, the regression function contains only an intercept.

$$y_t = \beta + e_t \tag{14.1a}$$

In this case we expect the time series to vary randomly about its mean, β. If the mean of the time series drifts over time or is explained by other variables, these would be added to the regression equation. The error term is **conditionally normal** with variance that depends on information available in the previous period, $t-1$.

$$e_t \mid I_{t-1} \sim N(0, h_t) \tag{14.1b}$$

Finally, the **variance equation** describes how the error variance, h_t, behaves.

$$h_t = \alpha_0 + \alpha_1 e_{t-1}^2, \quad \alpha_0 > 0, \quad 0 \le \alpha_1 < 1 \tag{14.1c}$$

The variance in the current period is a function of a constant term and the lagged squared error. The parameters in the equation, α_0 and α_1, must be positive to ensure a positive variance. The coefficient α_1 must be less than 1, or h_t will continue to increase over time, eventually exploding. This is an ARCH(1) model since there is only one lagged squared error term.

14.2.1 Testing for ARCH effects

A Lagrange multiplier (*LM*) test can be used to test for the presence of ARCH effects (i.e. $\alpha_1 > 0$). Since we do not know that actual error values, the test is performed using the residuals from least squares estimation of the mean equation. First, estimate the mean equation then save the estimated residuals $\hat{e}_t$ and obtain their squares $\hat{e}_t^2$. Regress the squared residuals on a constant and the lagged squared residuals:

$$\hat{e}_t^2 = \gamma_0 + \gamma_1 \hat{e}_{t-1}^2 + v_t \tag{14.2}$$

where v_t is a random error term. The null and alternative hypotheses are:

$$H_0 : \gamma_1 = 0$$

$$H_1 : \gamma_1 \ne 0$$

If there are no ARCH effects, then $\gamma_1 = 0$ and the fit for the auxiliary regression will be poor. The test statistic is $(T-q)R^2$, where T is the sample size, q is the number of $\hat{e}_{t-j}^2$ terms on the right-hand side of (14.2), and R^2 is coefficient of determination. If the null hypothesis is true, then the test statistic $(T-q)R^2$ is distributed (in large samples) as $\chi^2(q)$. For the ARCH(1) model, the test statistic $(T-1)R^2$ is distributed as $\chi^2(1)$ if the null hypothesis is true.

As an example, consider stock returns for a hypothetical company Brighten Your Day (BYD) Lighting. The data are in the SAS data set *byd*, and include observations on monthly returns, r_t, for 500 months.

The first thing to do is to plot the time series. Since the data contains a single undated time series, we add a time variable that is equal to the observation number.

```
data byd;                              * open data set;
set 'byd';                             * read byd;
time = _n_;                            * time variable;
run;
```

We first obtain summary statistics using **PROC MODEL**.

```
proc means data=byd;
title 'summary statistics for BYD data';
run;
```

We see that the average return is 1.0783%.

summary statistics for BYD data

The MEANS Procedure

Variable	N	Mean	Std Dev	Minimum	Maximum
r	500	1.0782942	1.1850245	-2.7685660	7.0088740
time	500	250.5000000	144.4818328	1.0000000	500.0000000

The first thing to do is plot the time series.

```
symbol1 value=point interpol=join;    * symbol for diagram;
proc gplot data=byd;
plot r*time=1 / hminor=1;
title 'BYD returns';
run;
```

This generates the plot below, which matches the top panel of Figure 14.5, page 524, of *POE4*.

BYD returns

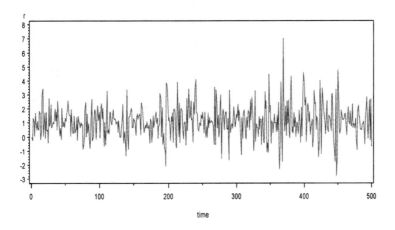

There is visual evidence of time-varying volatility. Towards the end of the series, returns for BYD appear to become more volatile. An ARCH(1) model is proposed and the ARCH(1) model is tested against the null hypothesis of no ARCH effects using the *LM* test described above. To perform the test for ARCH effects, perform a regression for returns using only an intercept, and save the residuals.

```
proc autoreg data=byd;
model r = ;
output out=bydout r=ehat;
title 'estimate mean of byd returns and save residuals';
run;
```

To test for ARCH effects we estimate the auxiliary regression $\hat{e}_t^2 = \gamma_0 + \gamma_1 \hat{e}_{t-1}^2 + v_t$. Open the SAS data set *bydout* and create the squared residual and its lag.

```
data bydout;                          * open data set;
set bydout;                           * read data;
ehatsq = ehat**2;                     * squared residuals;
ehatsq1 = lag(ehatsq);                * lagged squared residuals;
run;
```

Now estimate the auxiliary regression.

```
proc autoreg data=bydout;
model ehatsq = ehatsq1;               * auxiliary regression;
title 'test for ARCH effects in byd data';
run;
```

The regression results, which match those on page 523 of *POE4*, are:

```
                    test for ARCH effects in byd data


                         The AUTOREG Procedure
                    Dependent Variable      ehatsq
                    Ordinary Least Squares Estimates
```

SSE	2983.28626	DFE		497
MSE	6.00259	Root MSE		2.45002
SBC	2320.82502	AIC		2312.39981
MAE	1.37314066	AICC		2312.424
MAPE	2175618.42	Regress R-Square		0.1246
Durbin-Watson	2.0670	Total R-Square		0.1246

Variable	DF	Standard Estimate	Approx Error	t Value	Pr > |t|
Intercept	1	0.9083	0.1244	7.30	<.0001
ehatsq1	1	0.3531	0.0420	8.41	<.0001

The coefficient of determination is 0.1246. The *t*-statistic indicates that the first-order coefficient is significant. The *LM* test statistic is $(T-q)R^2 = (500-1) \times 0.1246 = 62.175$, which is greater than the 5% critical value for the $\chi^2_{(1)}$ distribution of 3.84. Thus, we reject the null hypothesis and conclude that ARCH(1) effects are present. (The *LM* statistic in *POE4* is calculated as $499 \times 0.124 = 61.876$.)

We can also use SAS as a calculator to print the LM test results for ARCH effects.

```
data archtest;
t = 500;                          * sample size;
q = 1;                            * # ARCH effects;
rsq = 0.1246;                     * Regression R-sq;
lm = (t-q)*rsq;                   * LM test statistic;
chic_95 = cinv(.95,q);           * 95% critical value;
chic_99 = cinv(.99,q);           * 99% critical value;
pval = 1 - probchi(lm,1);        * p-value;
run;
proc print data=archtest;        * print;
var t rsq lm chic_95 chic_99 pval;   * variable list;
title 'LM test for ARCH effects';
run;
```

The *LM* test results are

```
                  LM test for ARCH effects

Obs    t      rsq       lm      chic_95    chic_99      pval

 1    500    0.1246   62.1754   3.84146    6.63490    3.1086E-15
```

14.2.2 Estimating an ARCH model

ARCH models are estimated by the maximum likelihood method (see Appendix C.8 in *POE4*). In SAS, ARCH models can be estimated using **PROC AUTOREG** or **PROC MODEL**. In **PROC AUTOREG**, we specify maximum likelihood estimation with the option **method = ml**. The **archtest** options carries out the LM test for ARCH effects. Finally, the option **garch = (q=1)** is used to specify the ARCH(1) model. The **generalized ARCH** (or **GARCH**) model is discussed in Section 14.3.1. In SAS, we specify an ARCH(*q*) model by the option **garch = (q=number of lags)**.

```
proc autoreg data=bydout;
model r = / method=ml archtest
          garch=(q=1);               * ARCH(1) errors;
output out=bydout r=ehat_arch ht=harch;* forecast volatility;
title 'estimate ARCH(1) model and forecast volatility';
run;
```

The (edited) results, which match those in equations (14.4a) and (14.4b), page 524, of *POE4*, are

Q and LM Tests for ARCH Disturbances

Order	Q	Pr > Q	LM	Pr > LM
1	62.6104	<.0001	62.2819	<.0001
2	84.4581	<.0001	66.2737	<.0001
3	97.7368	<.0001	68.5130	<.0001
4	100.3119	<.0001	68.7221	<.0001
5	105.0300	<.0001	70.4004	<.0001
6	106.0590	<.0001	70.5316	<.0001
7	106.4676	<.0001	72.2938	<.0001
8	107.6972	<.0001	73.0515	<.0001
9	109.6069	<.0001	73.3493	<.0001
10	111.5931	<.0001	73.5252	<.0001
11	111.7335	<.0001	73.9982	<.0001
12	111.9903	<.0001	75.1742	<.0001

The AUTOREG Procedure

Variable	DF	Estimate	Standard Error	t Value	Approx Pr > |t|
Intercept	1	1.0639	0.0394	26.97	<.0001
ARCH0	1	0.6421	0.0632	10.16	<.0001
ARCH1	1	0.5693	0.1028	5.54	<.0001

PROC AUTOREG automatically produces *LM* tests (as well as another test called the *Q* test) up to 12 lags. Both strongly suggest the presence of ARCH effects at all lag lengths. The *LM* test statistic for ARCH(1) effects is 62.282 (this value is differs slightly from the value, 62.175, we calculated using the 2-step approach).

The parameter estimates include the intercept from the mean equation, and the intercept (ARCH0) and first-order coefficient (ARCH1) from the variance equation, $h_t = \alpha_0 + \alpha_1 e_{t-1}^2$. Note that the estimated coefficients, $\hat{\alpha}_0$ and $\hat{\alpha}_1$, satisfy the conditions for positive variance, and that the *t*-statistic of the first-order coefficient indicates a significant ARCH(1) effect.

Alternatively, the model can be estimated using **PROC MODEL**. To do this, specify the mean equation (which includes an intercept only in this example) and the variance equation (a constant plus the lagged squared residual). The function **resid.r** computes the residuals of the mean equation. The **fiml** option is used to specify **full information maximum likelihood** estimation. The **mse.r** is used by SAS to specify lagged values in estimation. Finally, the **bounds** statement is used to ensure that the parameters in the variance equation are positive.

```
proc model data=bydout;                      * initiate model;
r = intercept;                               * mean equation;
h.r = arch0+arch1*xlag(resid.r**2, mse.r);   * variance equation;
fit r / fiml method=marquardt;
bounds arch0 arch1 >= 0;                      * restrict arch parameters;
title 'ARCH(1) estimates using PROC MODEL';
run;
```

The results obtained using **PROC MODEL** are:

Nonlinear FIML Parameter Estimates

Parameter	Estimate	Approx Std Err	t Value	Approx Pr > |t|
intercept	1.063664	0.0399	26.63	<.0001
arch0	0.642503	0.0649	9.90	<.0001
arch1	0.569355	0.0913	6.23	<.0001

The estimates from **PROC MODEL** are very close, but not quite identical to the estimates obtained from **PROC AUTOREG**[1].

14.2.3 Forecasting volatility

Once we have estimated the ARCH model, we can use it to forecast next period's return r_{t+1} and the conditional volatility h_{t+1}. In this example, the forecasted return is just a constant since we did not include any explanatory variables in the mean equation of the ARCH model.

$$\hat{r}_{t+1} = \hat{\beta}_0 = 1.063$$

Since $\hat{e}_t = r_t - \hat{r}_t = r_t - \hat{\beta}_0$ in this example, the forecasted error variance is

$$\hat{h}_{t+1} = \hat{\alpha}_0 + \hat{\alpha}_1 \left(r_t - \hat{\beta}_0 \right)^2 = 0.642 + 0.569 \left(r_t - 1.063 \right)^2$$

Note that the forecasted error variance is larger when the actual return is farther from the expected return, and smaller when the actual return is near the mean. **PROC AUTOREG** allows you to save the estimated conditional variance. We saved these conditional variances with the variable name *HARCH* by including the option **ht = harch** in the **output** statement of **PROC AUTOREG**. We now plot the conditional variances, $\hat{h}_t$, over time.

```
proc gplot data=bydout;
plot harch*time=1 / hminor=10;
title 'plot of conditional variance: ARCH(1) model';
run;
```

---

[1] The likelihood functions that are maximized by **PROC AUTOREG** and **PROC MODEL** differ slightly.

This yields the following time series plot, which matches Figure 14.6, page 525, of *POE4*.

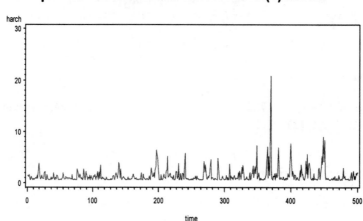

plot of conditional variance: ARCH(1) model

14.3 EXTENSIONS

The ARCH(1) model can be extended in a number of ways[2]. One obvious extension is to allow for more lags. The ARCH(q) model is given by

$$h_t = \alpha_0 + \alpha_1 e_{t-1}^2 + \alpha_2 e_{t-2}^2 \ldots + \alpha_q e_{t-q}^2 \qquad (14.3)$$

In this case, the variance or volatility in a given period depends on the magnitudes of the squared error in the past q periods. Testing, estimating, and forecasting, are natural extensions of the case with one lag. To estimate the ARCH(q) model using **PROC AUTOREG**, we simply use the option **GARCH=(q=XX)**, where XX is the number of included lags.

14.3.1 The GARCH model – generalized ARCH

Another extension is the **Generalized ARCH** model, or **GARCH**. The GARCH model adds lags of the conditional variance to the standard ARCH model. For example, a GARCH(1,1) model is given by

$$h_t = \alpha_0 + \alpha_1 e_{t-1}^2 + \beta_1 h_{t-1} \qquad (14.4)$$

The GARCH model allows us to capture long lagged effects with few parameters. The GARCH(p,q) model includes p lags of h_t and q lags of e_t^2 in the model.

To illustrate the GARCH model, we estimate a GARCH(1,1) model using the *byd* data. In **PROC AUTOREG** we simply use the option **GARCH=(p=1,q=1)** in the model statement.

---

[2] See Walter Enders (2010) *Applied Econometric Time Series*, Wiley, Chapter 3 for a more advanced discussion of ARCH processes and extensions to the ARCH model.

```
proc autoreg data=bydout;
model r = / method=ml archtest
               garch=(p=1,q=1);                    * GARCH(1,1) errors;
output out=bydout r=ehat_garch ht=hgarch11;* forecast volatility;
title 'estimate GARCH(1,1) model and forecast volatility';
run;
```

The GARCH(1,1) parameter estimates and standard errors produced by **PROC AUTOREG** are:

estimate GARCH(1,1) model and forecast volatility
The AUTOREG Procedure

Variable	DF	Standard Estimate	Approx Error	t Value	Pr > |t|
Intercept	1	1.0499	0.0405	25.95	<.0001
ARCH0	1	0.4011	0.0899	4.46	<.0001
ARCH1	1	0.4909	0.1015	4.83	<.0001
GARCH1	1	0.2380	0.1115	2.13	0.0328

The Intercept estimate is the predicted mean return, **ARCH0** is the estimated intercept of the conditional variance, **ARCH1** is the estimated coefficient for the lagged squared residuals, $\hat{e}_{t-1}^2$, and **GARCH1** is the estimated coefficient for the lagged variance, $\hat{h}_{t-1}$. Thus, the estimated model can be written as

$$\hat{r}_t = 1.050$$
$$\hat{h}_t = 0.401 + 0.491\hat{e}_{t-1}^2 + 0.238\hat{h}_{t-1}$$
$$(t) \qquad (4.83) \qquad (2.13)$$

These results are very close to the results on page 526 of *POE4*. The significance of the **GARCH1** term suggests that the GARCH(1,1) model is better than the ARCH(1) results.

We again plot the predicted conditional variances that we saved in the **output** statement.

```
proc gplot data=bydout;
plot hgarch11*time=1 / hminor=10;
title 'plot of conditional variance: GARCH(1,1) model';
run;
```

This yields the following time series plot, which matches Figure 14.7(b), page 527, of *POE4*.

plot of conditional variance: GARCH(1,1) model

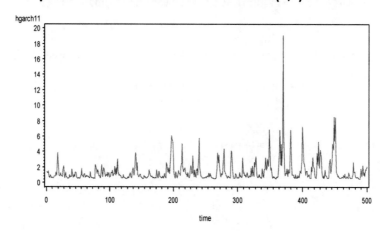

To estimate the GARCH(1,1) model using **PROC MODEL**, we simply add the lagged variance term to our variance equation. The **parms** statement is used to specify positive starting values for the parameters; if initially, **PROC MODEL** does not converge, adding or changing starting values may help.

```
proc model data=bydout;                  * initiate model;
parms arch0 .1 arch1 .1 garch .1;        * starting values;
r = intercept;                           * mean equation;
h.r = arch0+arch1*xlag(resid.r**2, mse.r)+garch1*xlag(h.r, mse.r);
fit r / fiml method=marquardt;
bounds arch0 arch1 garch1 >= 0;          * restrict arch parameters;
title 'GARCH(1,1) estimates using PROC MODEL';
run;
```

The results from **PROC MODEL** are:

Nonlinear FIML Parameter Estimates

Parameter	Estimate	Approx Std Err	t Value	Approx Pr > |t|
intercept	1.049593	0.0395	26.57	<.0001
arch0	0.401573	0.0846	4.75	<.0001
arch1	0.491345	0.0860	5.71	<.0001
garch1	0.237792	0.0905	2.63	0.0089

One advantage to using **full information maximum likelihood (FIML)** in **PROC MODEL** is that it is efficient and often results in smaller standard errors.

14.3.2 Allowing for an asymmetric effect - threshold GARCH

The **threshold GARCH** model, or **T-GARCH**, is a model in which positive and negative shocks are treated asymmetrically. For example, financial markets tend to be more volatile in response to negative news than to positive news. The T-GARCH(1,1) model is given by

$$h_t = \delta + \alpha_1 e_{t-1}^2 + \gamma d_{t-1} e_{t-1}^2 + \beta_1 h_{t-1}$$

$$d_t = \begin{cases} 1 & e_t < 0 \text{ (bad news)} \\ 0 & e_t \geq 0 \text{ (good news)} \end{cases}$$

(14.5)

where γ is known as the asymmetry or leverage term. We obtain the standard GARCH model when $\gamma = 0$. Otherwise, when the shock is positive (i.e. good news) the effect on volatility is α_1, but when the shock is negative (i.e. bad news) the effect on volatility is $\alpha_1 + \gamma$. Hence, if γ is significant and positive, negative shocks have a larger effect on conditional variance, h_t, than positive shocks.

The **hetero** statement in **PROC AUTOREG** allows us to specify variables that are related to the heteroskedasticity of the residuals. In this case, we wish to create the 'bad news' term $d_{t-1}\hat{e}_{t-1}^2$.

```
data bydout;                      * open data set;
set bydout;                       * read data;
dt = (ehat_garch<0);              * bad news indicator;
dt1 = lag(dt);                    * lag;
ehat_gsq = (ehat_garch**2);       * squared residual;
ehat_gsq1 = lag(ehat_gsq);        * lag;
desq1 = dt1*(ehat_gsq1);          * variable for TGARCH;
run;
```

Print a few observations

```
proc print data=bydout (obs=5);
title 'byd data with bad news indicator';
run;
```

The edited output (we have saved each set of residuals - ehat, ehat_arch, ehat_garch - to *bydout* but only report the garch residuals here) is.

byd data with bad news indicator

Obs	ehat_garch	hgarch11	r	time	dt	dt1	ehat_gsq	ehat_gsq1	desq1
1	-1.04988	1.43097	0.00000	1	1	.	1.10224	.	.
2	-1.27707	1.28270	-0.22719	2	1	1	1.63091	1.10224	1.10224
3	0.30097	1.50694	1.35084	3	0	1	0.09058	1.63091	1.63091
4	0.05568	0.80416	1.10556	4	0	0	0.00310	0.09058	0.00000
5	-0.98438	0.59397	0.06550	5	1	0	0.96900	0.00310	0.00000

We see, for example, that observations 1, 2, and 5 had negative residuals and thus $d_t = 1$ for those observations.

To specify a T-GARCH(1,1) model in **PROC AUTOREG**, we includes the additional term in equation (14.4). To obtain the T-GARCH model estimates, we use the **hetero** statement to add the term $d_{t-1}e_{t-1}^2$.

```
proc autoreg data=bydout;
model r = / method=ml archtest
            garch=(p=1,q=1);          * GARCH(1,1) errors;
output out=bydout ht=htgarch;         * forecast volatility;
hetero desq1;                         * bad news term;
title 'estimate T-GARCH(1,1) model and forecast volatility';
run;
```

The T-GARCH(1,1) parameter estimates from **PROC AUTOREG** are:

```
              estimate T-GARCH(1,1) model and forecast volatility
                          The AUTOREG Procedure
```

Variable	DF	Estimate	Standard Error	t Value	Approx Pr > |t|
Intercept	1	0.9948	0.0440	22.59	<.0001
ARCH0	1	0.3478	0.0917	3.79	0.0001
ARCH1	1	0.2641	0.0803	3.29	0.0010
GARCH1	1	0.2902	0.1159	2.50	0.0123
HET1	1	0.4530	0.1776	2.55	0.0108

The coefficient names are the same as in Section 14.3.1, but with the additional term **HET1**, which is the estimated coefficient for $d_{t-1}\hat{e}_{t-1}^2$. Thus, the estimated model is

$$\hat{r}_t = 0.995$$

$$\hat{h}_t = 0.348 + 0.264\hat{e}_{t-1}^2 + 0.453d_{t-1}\hat{e}_{t-1}^2 + 0.290\hat{h}_{t-1}$$

$$(t) \qquad (3.29) \qquad (2.55) \qquad (2.50)$$

These results are fairly close, but not identical, to the results on page 528 of *POE4*. The results indicate that good news increases volatility by a factor of 0.2641. Bad news increases volatility by a factor (0.2641 + 0.4530). The bad news coefficient (**HET1**) is significanct, indicating that bad news does lead to greater volatility in financial markets. We again save and plot the predicted conditional variances.

```
proc gplot data=bydout;
plot htgarch*time / hminor=10;
title 'plot of conditional variance: T-GARCH(1,1) model';
run;
```

This yields the following time series plot, which matches Figure 14.7(d), page 527, of *POE4*.

plot of conditional variance: T-GARCH(1,1) model

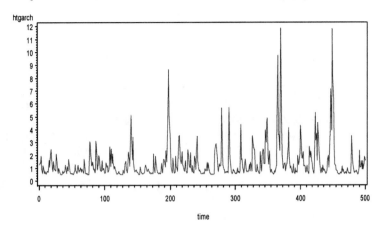

We obtain results somewhat closer to those in *POE4* using **PROC MODEL**. The labels are optional, but help when reading output. To specify the T-GARCH(1,1) model using **PROC MODEL** we include the term **gamma*xlag(-resid.r<0,mse.r)*xlag(resid.r**2,mse.r)**. The confusing part of this if you're referring to *POE4* is the negative sign in the indicator term. **PROC MODEL** defines the indicator function opposite to how it is defined in *POE4*; the code below works to estimate the correct model.

```
proc model data=bydout;                    * initiate model;
label intercept='mean'
      arch0='var intercept'
      arch1='et_1_sq'
      gamma='dt_1*et_1_sq'
      garch1='ht_1';
parms arch0 .1 arch1 .1 garch .1 delta .1;
r = intercept;                             * mean equation;
h.r = arch0+arch1*xlag(resid.r**2,mse.r)+garch1*xlag(h.r,mse.r)
      +gamma*xlag(-resid.r<0,mse.r)*xlag(resid.r**2,mse.r);
fit r / fiml method=marquardt;
bounds arch0 arch1 garch1 >= 0;            * restrict arch parameters;
title 'T-GARCH(1,1) estimates using PROC MODEL';
run;
```

The results from **PROC MODEL** are:

T-GARCH(1,1) estimates using PROC MODEL

Nonlinear FIML Parameter Estimates

Parameter	Estimate	Approx Std Err	t Value	Approx Pr > |t|	Label
intercept	0.996215	0.0424	23.47	<.0001	mean
arch0	0.357289	0.0782	4.57	<.0001	var intercept
arch1	0.263986	0.0765	3.45	0.0006	et_1_sq
gamma	0.48489	0.1647	2.94	0.0034	dt_1*et_1_sq
garch1	0.285937	0.0893	3.20	0.0014	ht_1

The parameter estimates using **PROC MODEL** are nearly identical to those in *POE4*. The estimated equations are:

$$\hat{r}_t = 0.996$$

$$\hat{h}_t = 0.357 + 0.264\hat{e}_{t-1}^2 + 0.485d_{t-1}\hat{e}_{t-1}^2 + 0.286\hat{h}_{t-1}$$

$$(t) \qquad (4.57) \qquad (2.94) \qquad (3.20)$$

The main difference we observe with **PROC MODEL** is that the standard errors are smaller.

14.3.3 GARCH-in-mean and time-varying risk premium

Another variation of the GARCH model is the GARCH-in-mean (GARCH-M) model. In this model, the mean return increases with risk. Thus, the volatility, h_t, is included in the return equation.

$$y_t = \beta_0 + \theta h_t + e_t$$

If the parameter, θ, is positive then higher risk leads to higher mean returns. To add the GARCH-in-mean term to the regression, specify **mean=linear** in the GARCH statement. (SAS also supports MEAN=LOG, which estimates $y_t = \beta_0 + \theta \ln(h_t) + e_t$, and MEAN=SQRT, which estimates $y_t = \beta_0 + \theta\sqrt{h_t} + e_t$.)

Use *bydout* to estimate a GARCH-M model with asymmetric volatility.

```
proc autoreg data=bydout;
model r = / method=ml archtest
           garch=(p=1,q=1,mean=linear);* GARCH-M(1,1) errors;
hetero desq1;                          * bad news term;
output out=bydout ht=hgarchm p=preturn;* forecast volatility;
title 'GARCH-M model and forecast volatility';
run;
```

The results, which are similar to those at the bottom of page 528 in *POE4*, are

GARCH-M model

The AUTOREG Procedure

Variable	DF	Standard Estimate	Approx Error	t Value	Pr > |t|
Intercept	1	0.7960	0.0752	10.59	<.0001
ARCH0	1	0.3283	0.0850	3.86	0.0001
ARCH1	1	0.3052	0.0895	3.41	0.0007
GARCH1	1	0.3138	0.1078	2.91	0.0036
DELTA	1	0.2186	0.0693	3.16	0.0016
HET1	1	0.3147	0.1589	1.98	0.0476

The GARCH-in-mean term (portion of mean return to compensate for risk) is given by the **DELTA** variable. Thus, the estimated model is

$$\hat{r}_t = 0.796 + 0.219 h_t$$

$$(t) \qquad (3.16)$$

$$\hat{h}_t = 0.328 + 0.305\hat{e}_{t-1}^2 + 0.315 d_{t-1}\hat{e}_{t-1}^2 + 0.314\hat{h}_{t-1}$$

$$(t) \qquad (3.41) \qquad (1.98) \qquad (2.91)$$

We again save and plot the predicted conditional variances.

```
proc gplot data=bydout;
plot hgarchm*time=1 / hminor=10;
title 'plot of conditional variance: GARCH-M';
run;
```

The plotted predicted error variances, which are similar to Figure 14.7(f), page 527, in *POE4* are

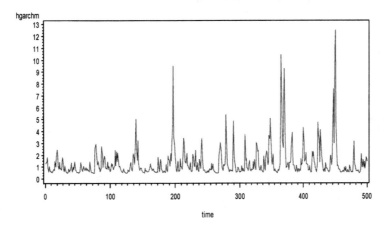

plot of conditional variance: GARCH-M

The predicted mean return is no longer constant. In addition to the error variances, we output the predicted return, *PRETURN*, and generate a plot.

```
proc gplot data=bydout;
plot preturn*time=1 / hminor=10;
title 'plot of predicted returns: GARCH-M';
run;
```

The plot of predicted returns is

plot of predicted returns: GARCH-M

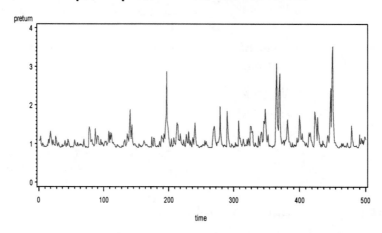

Note that the expected returns are higher when the conditional variances are higher.

We obtain results much closer to those in *POE4* using **PROC MODEL**. To estimate the asymmetric GARCH-M model using **PROC MODEL**, we run the code from the T-GARCH model with a few changes. First, we include an additional term **theta*h** in the mean equation. Second, we must change the order of the equation: **h** comes first, then **r**, and finally we specify **h.r=h** below the return equation.

```
proc model data=bydout;                    * initiate model;
label intercept='mean'
      theta='h_t (return due to risk)'
      arch0='var intercept'
      arch1='et_1_sq'
      gamma='dt_1*et_1_sq'
      garch1='ht_1';
parms arch0 .1 arch1 .1 garch .1 delta .1 theta .1;
h = arch0+arch1*xlag(resid.r**2,mse.r)+garch1*xlag(h.r,mse.r)
    +gamma*xlag(-resid.r<0,mse.r)*xlag(resid.r**2,mse.r);
r = intercept+theta*h;                     * mean equation;
h.r = h;
fit r / fiml method=marquardt;
bounds arch0 arch1 garch1 >= 0;            * restrict arch parameters;
title 'GARCH-M estimates using PROC MODEL';
run;
```

The results from **PROC MODEL** are:

```
GARCH-M estimates using PROC MODEL

The MODEL Procedure
Nonlinear FIML Parameter Estimates

                     Approx              Approx
Parameter  Estimate  Std Err  t Value  Pr > |t|  Label

theta      0.195287  0.0632    3.09     0.0021   h_t (return
                                                 due to risk)
arch0      0.370893  0.0703    5.27    <.0001    var intercept
arch1      0.298192  0.0792    3.77     0.0002   et_1_sq
intercept  0.820216  0.0684   11.99    <.0001    mean
gamma      0.31426   0.1409    2.23     0.0262   dt_1*et_1_sq
garch1     0.27738   0.0753    3.68     0.0003   ht_1
```

The trick is sorting the parameters out (which is helped considerably by use of **labels**). The estimated equations are:

$$\hat{r}_t = 0.820 + 0.195 h_t$$
$$(t) \qquad \quad (3.09)$$

$$\hat{h}_t = 0.371 + 0.298\hat{e}_{t-1}^2 + 0.314 d_{t-1}\hat{e}_{t-1}^2 + 0.277\hat{h}_{t-1}$$
$$(t) \qquad \qquad (3.77) \qquad \quad (2.23) \qquad \qquad (3.68)$$

The parameter estimates using **PROC MODEL** are nearly identical to those on page 528 of *POE4*. Once again, the standard errors obtained using **PROC MODEL** are smaller.

CHAPTER **15**

Panel Data Models

15.1 A MICROECONOMETRIC PANEL

The data file *nls_panel* contains a panel of data for 716 women for 5 years. Open the data file and examine the contents on key variables.

```
data nls;
set 'nls_panel';
keep id year lwage educ exper tenure black south union;
run;

proc contents data=nls position;
title 'NLS data variables';
run;
options nolabel;
```

                         Variables in Creation Order

#	Variable	Type	Len	Label
1	id	Num	8	identifier for panel individual; 716 total
2	year	Num	8	year interviewed (1982, 1983, 1985, 1987, 1988)
3	lwage	Num	8	ln(wage/GNP deflator)
4	educ	Num	8	current grade completed
5	south	Num	8	= 1 if south
6	black	Num	8	= 1 if black; 0 if white
7	union	Num	8	= 1 if union member
8	exper	Num	8	= total work experience
9	tenure	Num	8	= job tenure, in years

To take advantage of the cross section and time series nature of the data we must use the variables identifying the individual and time, *ID* and *YEAR*. The data are strongly balanced, which means that for each individual we have the same number of time series observations, here 5, though the years, 1982, 1983, 1985, 1987 and 1988 are not evenly spaced. This is called a "balanced panel" and it was created by the authors from a larger data set, *nls*, which is not balanced. Most panel data sets have large numbers of missing observations. This one does not have missing values for the key variables. If we print the first few observations we can see how they are stacked by individual.

```
proc print data=nls (obs=10);
title 'NLS observations';
run;
```

NLS observations

Obs	id	year	lwage	educ	south	black	union	exper	tenure
1	1	82	1.80829	12	0	1	1	7.6667	7.66667
2	1	83	1.86342	12	0	1	1	8.5833	8.58333
3	1	85	1.78937	12	0	1	1	10.1795	1.83333
4	1	87	1.84653	12	0	1	1	12.1795	3.75000
5	1	88	1.85645	12	0	1	1	13.6218	5.25000
6	2	82	1.28093	17	0	0	0	7.5769	2.41667
7	2	83	1.51586	17	0	0	0	8.3846	3.41667
8	2	85	1.93017	17	0	0	0	10.3846	5.41667
9	2	87	1.91903	17	0	0	1	12.0385	0.33333
10	2	88	2.20097	17	0	0	1	13.2115	1.75000

We will fit models with quadratic terms. Create those variables.

```
data nls;
set nls;
exper2 = exper**2;
tenure2 = tenure**2;
run;
```

15.2 A POOLED MODEL

A pooled model is one where individuals are simply pooled together with no provision for individual or time differences.

$$y_{it} = \beta_1 + \beta_2 x_{2it} + \beta_3 x_{3it} + e_{it}$$

A basic regression specification is estimated using **PROC REG**.

```
proc reg data=nls;
model lwage = educ exper exper2 tenure tenure2 black south union;
title 'NLS pooled OLS regression';
run;
```

Analysis of Variance

Source	DF	Sum of Squares	Mean Square	F Value	Pr > F
Model	8	251.53504	31.44188	215.50	<.0001
Error	3571	521.02619	0.14590		
Corrected Total	3579	772.56123			

Root MSE	0.38197	R-Square	0.3256	
Dependent Mean	1.91824	Adj R-Sq	0.3241	
Coeff Var	19.91280			

Parameter Estimates

Variable	DF	Parameter Estimate	Standard Error	t Value	Pr > |t|
Intercept	1	0.47660	0.05616	8.49	<.0001
educ	1	0.07145	0.00269	26.57	<.0001
exper	1	0.05569	0.00861	6.47	<.0001
exper2	1	-0.00115	0.00036129	-3.18	0.0015
tenure	1	0.01496	0.00441	3.39	0.0007
tenure2	1	-0.00048604	0.00025770	-1.89	0.0594
black	1	-0.11671	0.01572	-7.43	<.0001
south	1	-0.10600	0.01420	-7.46	<.0001
union	1	0.13224	0.01496	8.84	<.0001

15.2.1 Cluster-robust standard errors

Panel data has several observations per individual. The individual's error term may have some common components that are present for each time period. For example, if we are estimating a wage equation, the unobserved characteristics of any individual, such as ability, are present in each time period. The error terms for each individual may show an intercorrelation within the "cluster" of observations specific to the individual. To relax the usual assumption of zero error correlation over time for the same individual we write

$$\text{cov}\left(e_{it}, e_{is}\right) = \psi_{its}$$

Notice that this alternative assumption also relaxes the assumption of homoskedasticity because, when $t = s$, we have

$$\text{cov}\left(e_{it}, e_{it}\right) = \text{var}\left(e_{it}\right) = \psi_{itt}$$

The error variance can be different in different time periods, but is constant over individuals. To avoid confusion with different σ^2's that will be used later, we have introduced another Greek letter "psi" (ψ) to denote the variances and covariances.

Under these assumptions the least squares estimator is unbiased and consistent, but the usual least squares estimator variance formulas no longer hold. It is much the same as in Chapters 8 and 9, where we used a "robust" covariance matrix for the least squares estimator. Similarly, in this case, we have "robust-cluster" standard errors. The concept and procedures are explained in *Principles of Econometrics, 4th Edition*, Appendix 15A on pages 581-583. SAS implements robust standard errors with a simple option in **PROC PANEL**. To learn more about **PROC PANEL** enter **help panel** into the SAS command line.

Before using this procedure, we must sort the data by *ID* and *YEAR*.

```
proc sort data=nls;
by id year;
run;
```

```
proc panel data=nls;
id id year;
model lwage = educ exper exper2 tenure tenure2 black south
      union / pooled hccme=4;
title 'proc panel: NLS pooled OLS cluster corrected standard errors';
title2 'No DF correction';
run;
```

The **id** statement is required to identify the variables indexing the cross-section and time-series observations. The option **pooled** indicates that we are estimating a pooled least squares regression. The option **hccme = 4** requests cluster corrected standard errors.

```
Dependent Variable: lwage
```

Model Description

Estimation Method	Pooled
Number of Cross Sections	716
Time Series Length	5
Hetero. Corr. Cov. Matrix Estimator	4

Fit Statistics

SSE	521.0262	DFE	3571
MSE	0.1459	Root MSE	0.3820
R-Square	0.3256		

Variable	DF	Estimate	Standard Error	t Value	Pr > |t|	Label
Intercept	1	0.4766	0.0844	5.65	<.0001	Intercept
educ	1	0.071449	0.00549	13.02	<.0001	
exper	1	0.055685	0.0113	4.93	<.0001	
exper2	1	-0.00115	0.000492	-2.33	0.0196	
tenure	1	0.01496	0.00711	2.10	0.0354	
tenure2	1	-0.00049	0.000409	-1.19	0.2353	
black	1	-0.11671	0.0281	-4.16	<.0001	
south	1	-0.106	0.0270	-3.92	<.0001	
union	1	0.132243	0.0270	4.89	<.0001	

Note that the output now shows **Hetero. Corr. Cov. Matrix Estimator**, and a message that the identifies the number of cross-section and time-series observations. Compared to the incorrect standard errors provided using **PROC REG** with no correction, these robust standard errors are slightly larger.

The robust covariance matrix used by **PROC PANEL** does not incorporate any finite sample degrees of freedom correction factor. The meaning of this is discussed in Appendix 15B in *Principles of Econometrics, 4th Edition* and in Appendix 15A of this manual. For the present we note that one correction factor is $(N/(N-1)) \times ((NT-1)/(NT-K))$. In this case, with $K = 9$, the correction factor is small, 1.00364.

An alternative procedure in SAS is **PROC SURVEYREG**. Enter **help surveyreg** into the SAS command line for a discussion. As its name indicates there are many specialized features in this procedure for dealing with survey data. Cluster corrected standard errors are obtained using

```
proc surveyreg data=nls;
   cluster id;
   model lwage = educ exper exper2 tenure tenure2 black south union;
   title 'proc surveyreg: NLS pooled OLS cluster corrected standard errors';
   title2 'DF correction';
run;
```

Here the cluster correction is automatic upon entering **cluster id**, which identifies the cross-section variable. The output is in a bit different format.

Estimated Regression Coefficients

Parameter	Estimate	Standard Error	t Value	Pr > |t|
Intercept	0.4766001	0.08456293	5.64	<.0001
educ	0.0714488	0.00549950	12.99	<.0001
exper	0.0556850	0.01131014	4.92	<.0001
exper2	-0.0011475	0.00049247	-2.33	0.0201
tenure	0.0149600	0.00712317	2.10	0.0361
tenure2	-0.0004860	0.00041023	-1.18	0.2365
black	-0.1167139	0.02813417	-4.15	<.0001
south	-0.1060026	0.02706156	-3.92	<.0001
union	0.1322432	0.02707467	4.88	<.0001

The estimates are identical, but note that the standard errors are just a little bit larger. Multiplying the **PROC PANEL** standard errors by $\sqrt{1.00364} = 1.00182$ yields the corrected standard errors used by **PROC SURVEYREG**.

15.3 THE FIXED EFFECTS MODEL

The fixed effects model allows for differences in the intercept parameter for each individual. The model is

$$y_{it} = \beta_{1i} + \beta_2 x_{2it} + \beta_3 x_{3it} + e_{it}, \quad i = 1, \ldots, N$$

Note that the intercept now includes a subscript i which means that it is individual specific. We have in effect introduced N new parameters, one intercept parameter for each individual. To accomplish this we can create N indicator variables such as

$$D_{1i} = \begin{cases} 1 & i = 1 \\ 0 & \text{otherwise} \end{cases} \qquad D_{2i} = \begin{cases} 1 & i = 2 \\ 0 & \text{otherwise} \end{cases} \qquad D_{3i} = \begin{cases} 1 & i = 3 \\ 0 & \text{otherwise} \end{cases}$$

If N is not too large then these indicator variables can be added to the regression model as additional variables. This is called the least squares dummy variable model.

$$y_{it} = \beta_{11}D_{1i} + \beta_{12}D_{2i} + \cdots + \beta_{1,10}D_{10i} + \beta_2 x_{2it} + \beta_3 x_{3it} + e_{it}$$

To illustrate, create a smaller version of *nls_panel* with only 10 individuals. Create a dummy variable for each person.

```
data nls10;
set nls;
if id < 11;
d1=(id=1); d2=(id=2); d3=(id=3); d4=(id=4); d5=(id=5);
d6=(id=6); d7=(id=7); d8=(id=8); d9=(id=9); d10=(id=10);
run;
```

Examine the summary statistics for key variables.

```
proc means data=nls10;
var lwage educ exper exper2 tenure tenure2 black south union;
title 'summary stats for NLS10';
run;
```

summary stats for NLS10

The MEANS Procedure

Variable	N	Mean	Std Dev	Minimum	Maximum
lwage	50	2.1976656	0.3770917	1.2809330	3.5791290
educ	50	14.2000000	1.6781914	12.0000000	17.0000000
exper	50	12.5092298	2.8275516	7.5769230	19.0448700
exper2	50	164.3159764	73.0560290	57.4097621	362.7070733
tenure	50	6.4983335	5.3571825	0	19.0000000
tenure2	50	70.3537542	96.2006985	0	361.0000000
black	50	0.1000000	0.3030458	0	1.0000000
south	50	0	0	0	0
union	50	0.4400000	0.5014265	0	1.0000000

Note that among these 10 individuals none lived in the south, so that variable *SOUTH* will be omitted from the analysis in this section.

The least squares dummy variable model, including all the dummy variables and suppressing the constant is then estimated using

```
proc reg data=nls10;
model lwage = d1-d10 exper exper2 tenure tenure2 union / noint;
test d1=d2=d3=d4=d5=d6=d7=d8=d9=d10;
title 'NLS10 dummy variable regression';
run;
```

We suppress the automatic constant term as its inclusion would create exact collinearity.

Variable	DF	Parameter Estimate	Standard Error	t Value	Pr > |t|
d1	1	0.15192	1.09674	0.14	0.8906
d2	1	0.18691	1.07148	0.17	0.8625
d3	1	-0.06303	1.35091	-0.05	0.9631
d4	1	0.18564	1.34349	0.14	0.8909
d5	1	0.93900	1.09778	0.86	0.3982
d6	1	0.79450	1.11177	0.71	0.4796
d7	1	0.58121	1.23591	0.47	0.6411
d8	1	0.53794	1.09750	0.49	0.6271
d9	1	0.41835	1.08405	0.39	0.7019
d10	1	0.61457	1.09017	0.56	0.5765
exper	1	0.23800	0.18776	1.27	0.2133
exper2	1	-0.00819	0.00790	-1.04	0.3074
tenure	1	-0.01235	0.03414	-0.36	0.7197
tenure2	1	0.00230	0.00269	0.85	0.3989
union	1	0.11354	0.15086	0.75	0.4567

The analysis of variance table includes the usual information and shows that we have estimated 15 parameters.

To test the equality of the intercepts form the null and alternative hypotheses.

$$H_0 : \beta_{11} = \beta_{12} = \cdots = \beta_{1N}$$

$$H_1 : \text{the } \beta_{1i} \text{ are not all equal}$$

Use SAS's **test** statement with 9 pairs of equalities. The test result is

Test 1 Results for Dependent Variable lwage

Source	DF	Mean Square	F Value	Pr > F
Numerator	9	0.31503	4.13	0.0011
Denominator	35	0.07621		

We reject the null hypothesis that the intercepts are equal.

Alternatively we can estimate the model using only 9 dummy variables and keeping the intercept. We do this now for later comparison to the fixed effects estimator. Note that the test statement now tests that the coefficients of the dummy variables are zero, but that the result is the same.

```
proc reg data=nls10;
model lwage = d1-d9 exper exper2 tenure tenure2 union;
test d1=d2=d3=d4=d5=d6=d7=d8=d9=0;
title 'NLS10 regression omitting one DV';
run;
```

Variable	DF	Parameter Estimate	Standard Error	t Value	Pr > |t|
Intercept	1	0.61457	1.09017	0.56	0.5765
d1	1	-0.46265	0.28384	-1.63	0.1121
d2	1	-0.42766	0.20573	-2.08	0.0450
d3	1	-0.67760	0.43318	-1.56	0.1268
d4	1	-0.42893	0.48357	-0.89	0.3811
d5	1	0.32443	0.18505	1.75	0.0883
d6	1	0.17993	0.25580	0.70	0.4865
d7	1	-0.03336	0.30308	-0.11	0.9130
d8	1	-0.07663	0.19411	-0.39	0.6954
d9	1	-0.19622	0.20077	-0.98	0.3351
exper	1	0.23800	0.18776	1.27	0.2133
exper2	1	-0.00819	0.00790	-1.04	0.3074
tenure	1	-0.01235	0.03414	-0.36	0.7197
tenure2	1	0.00230	0.00269	0.85	0.3989
union	1	0.11354	0.15086	0.75	0.4567

Test 1 Results for Dependent Variable lwage

Source	DF	Mean Square	F Value	Pr > F
Numerator	9	0.31503	4.13	0.0011
Denominator	35	0.07621		

15.3.1 The fixed effects estimator

The above approach works for small N. If we have thousands of individuals it is inconvenient to introduce indicator variables for each. Fixed effects estimation can be carried out using a single command that we will discuss below. First, however, we will consider an alternative approach using data that is in deviations from the mean form. To proceed, first find individual averages of the regression data for each individual.

$$\bar{y}_i = \frac{1}{T}\sum_{t=1}^{T} y_{it} = \beta_{1i} + \beta_2 \frac{1}{T}\sum_{t=1}^{T} x_{2it} + \beta_3 \frac{1}{T}\sum_{t=1}^{T} x_{3it} + \frac{1}{T}\sum_{t=1}^{T} e_{it}$$

$$= \beta_{1i} + \beta_2 \bar{x}_{2i} + \beta_3 \bar{x}_{3i} + \bar{e}_i$$

The "bar" notation $\bar{y}_i$ indicates that we have averaged the values of y_{it} over time. Then, subtract this averaged equation from

$$y_{it} = \beta_{1i} + \beta_2 x_{2it} + \beta_3 x_{3it} + e_{it} \quad t = 1, \ldots, T$$

to obtain

$$y_{it} = \beta_{1i} + \beta_2 x_{2it} + \beta_3 x_{3it} + e_{it}$$

$$- \quad (\bar{y}_i = \beta_{1i} + \beta_2 \bar{x}_{2i} + \beta_3 \bar{x}_{3i} + \bar{e}_i)$$

$$\overline{}$$

$$y_{it} - \bar{y}_i = \beta_2 (x_{2it} - \bar{x}_{2i}) + \beta_3 (x_{3it} - \bar{x}_{3i}) + (e_{it} - \bar{e}_i)$$

Least squares applied to this equation will produce the fixed effects estimates. While a bit tedious, we will demonstrate this result, just to convince the doubting reader.

First, create the summary statistics by **id**, and print a few.

```
proc means data=nls10 mean;          * summary stats;
by id;                                * for each id;
var lwage educ exper exper2 tenure tenure2 black union;
output out=nlsout;                    * output id means;
title 'NLS10 sample means by id';
run;

proc print data=nlsout (obs=5);       * print several obs;
title 'NLS10 sample means by id';
run;
```

NLS10 sample means by id

O b s	i d	_ T Y P E _	_ F R E Q _	_ S T A T _	l w a g e	e d u c	e x p e r	e x p e r 2	t e n u r e	t e n u r e 2	b l a c k	u n i o n
1	1	0	5	N	5.00000	5	5.0000	5.000	5.00000	5.0000	5	5
2	1	0	5	MIN	1.78937	12	7.6667	58.778	1.83333	3.3611	1	1
3	1	0	5	MAX	1.86342	12	13.6218	185.553	8.58333	73.6736	1	1
4	1	0	5	MEAN	1.83281	12	10.4462	113.993	5.41667	35.4875	1	1
5	1	0	5	STD	0.03230	0	2.4676	52.637	2.77201	29.8101	0	0

Save only the sample mean for each variable and create deviations about the mean. Then print a few of these observations.

```
data means;                           * data set for means;
set nlsout;                           * read nlsout;
if _STAT_='MEAN';                     * keep only means;
lwage_m = lwage;
exper_m = exper;
exper2_m = exper2;
tenure_m = tenure;
tenure2_m = tenure2;
union_m = union;
keep id year lwage_m exper_m exper2_m tenure_m tenure2_m union_m;
run;

/* deviations about means */
data nlsdot;                          * data set for deviations;
merge nls10 means;                    * merge nls and means;
by id;                                * match means to data lines;
lwage_dot = lwage - lwage_m;
```

```
exper_dot = exper - exper_m;
exper2_dot = exper2 - exper2_m;
tenure_dot = tenure - tenure_m;
tenure2_dot = tenure2 - tenure2_m;
union_dot = union - union_m;
run;

proc print data=nlsdot (obs=10);          * print some lines;
var id year lwage lwage_m lwage_dot exper exper_m exper_dot;
title 'NLS10 deviations about the mean';
run;
```

NLS10 deviations about the mean

Obs	id	year	lwage	lwage_m	lwage_dot	exper	exper_m	exper_dot
1	1	82	1.80829	1.83281	-0.02452	7.6667	10.4462	-2.77949
2	1	83	1.86342	1.83281	0.03061	8.5833	10.4462	-1.86282
3	1	85	1.78937	1.83281	-0.04344	10.1795	10.4462	-0.26666
4	1	87	1.84653	1.83281	0.01372	12.1795	10.4462	1.73334
5	1	88	1.85645	1.83281	0.02364	13.6218	10.4462	3.17564
6	2	82	1.28093	1.76939	-0.48846	7.5769	10.3192	-2.74231
7	2	83	1.51586	1.76939	-0.25354	8.3846	10.3192	-1.93461
8	2	85	1.93017	1.76939	0.16078	10.3846	10.3192	0.06538
9	2	87	1.91903	1.76939	0.14964	12.0385	10.3192	1.71923
10	2	88	2.20097	1.76939	0.43158	13.2115	10.3192	2.89231

Apply least squares estimation to the data in deviation from mean form.

```
proc reg data=nlsdot;
model lwage_dot = exper_dot exper2_dot tenure_dot tenure2_dot
      union_dot/noint;
title 'NLS10 fixed effects regression using PROC REG: SE incorrect';
run;
```

Variable	DF	Parameter Estimate	Standard Error	t Value	Pr > |t|
exper_dot	1	0.23800	0.16559	1.44	0.1575
exper2_dot	1	-0.00819	0.00697	-1.17	0.2464
tenure_dot	1	-0.01235	0.03011	-0.41	0.6836
tenure2_dot	1	0.00230	0.00237	0.97	0.3380
union_dot	1	0.11354	0.13305	0.85	0.3980

The standard errors from this least squares regression are not correct. This is because the estimate of the error variance used by the least squares software is $\hat{\sigma}_{e*}^2 = SSE/(NT-5)$, which neglects the fact that we have used N individual means to center the data. The centering process uses up a degree of freedom for each individual. Then what is required is $\hat{\sigma}_e^2 = SSE/(NT-N-5)$. It is better to use the automatic software for fixed effects, so this calculation will be done correctly.

15.3.2 The fixed effects estimator using PROC PANEL

Fixed effects estimation is accomplished using **PROC PANEL** command with the option **fixone**, which is short for "one way fixed effects," the one-way indicating we allow intercept differences across individuals.

```
proc panel data=nls10;
id id year;
model lwage = exper exper2 tenure tenure2 union / fixone;
title 'NLS10 fixed effects regression using PROC PANEL';
run;
```

The first part of the output identifies the model and reports an abbreviated ANOVA.

```
                        The PANEL Procedure
                      Fixed One Way Estimates

Dependent Variable: lwage


                        Model Description

            Estimation Method           FixOne
            Number of Cross Sections        10
            Time Series Length               5


                         Fit Statistics

        SSE            2.6672   DFE                  35
        MSE            0.0762   Root MSE         0.2761
        R-Square       0.6172
```

The test for the significance of the fixed effects is reported next.

```
              F Test for No Fixed Effects
        Num DF      Den DF     F Value    Pr > F
           9          35         4.13     0.0011
```

SAS reports the dummy variable regression results, omitting the last dummy variable and including an intercept.

Variable	DF	Estimate	Standard Error	t Value	Pr > |t|	Label
CS1	1	-0.46265	0.2838	-1.63	0.1121	Cross Sectional Effect 1
CS2	1	-0.42766	0.2057	-2.08	0.0450	Cross Sectional Effect 2
CS3	1	-0.6776	0.4332	-1.56	0.1268	Cross Sectional Effect 3
CS4	1	-0.42893	0.4836	-0.89	0.3811	Cross Sectional Effect 4
CS5	1	0.324429	0.1850	1.75	0.0883	Cross Sectional Effect 5
CS6	1	0.179928	0.2558	0.70	0.4865	Cross Sectional Effect 6
CS7	1	-0.03336	0.3031	-0.11	0.9130	Cross Sectional Effect 7
CS8	1	-0.07663	0.1941	-0.39	0.6954	Cross Sectional Effect 8
CS9	1	-0.19622	0.2008	-0.98	0.3351	Cross Sectional Effect 9
Intercept	1	0.614569	1.0902	0.56	0.5765	Intercept
exper	1	0.237997	0.1878	1.27	0.2133	
exper2	1	-0.00819	0.00790	-1.04	0.3074	
tenure	1	-0.01235	0.0341	-0.36	0.7197	
tenure2	1	0.002296	0.00269	0.85	0.3989	
union	1	0.113544	0.1509	0.75	0.4567	

The reporting of the "cross-section" effects generates lots of output for larger panels.

15.3.3 Fixed effects using the complete panel

Now we use the complete panel data set to estimate the wage equation.

```
proc panel data=nls;
id id year;
model lwage = exper exper2 tenure tenure2 south union / fixone;
title 'NLS fixed effects regression using PROC PANEL';
run;
```

The overall *F*-test for 715 individual differences shows that there are significant differences between at least some individuals.

```
            The PANEL Procedure
          Fixed One Way Estimates
             Model Description

       Estimation Method          FixOne
       Number of Cross Sections      716
       Time Series Length              5
```

```
                      Fit Statistics

      SSE            108.7985    DFE              2858
      MSE              0.0381    Root MSE       0.1951
      R-Square         0.8592
```

```
                  F Test for No Fixed Effects

          Num DF       Den DF     F Value    Pr > F
             715         2858       19.66    <.0001
```

The parameter estimates appear after all the cross-section effects. Note that we do not include the variables *BLACK* or *EDUC* since they do not vary across individual.

```
                    The PANEL Procedure
                  Fixed One Way Estimates
```

Dependent Variable: lwage

```
                         Standard
Variable    DF  Estimate    Error  t Value  Pr > |t|  Label
Intercept    1  0.899436   0.1019     8.82    <.0001  Intercept
exper        1  0.041083   0.00662    6.21    <.0001
exper2       1  -0.00041   0.000273  -1.50    0.1346
tenure       1  0.013909   0.00328    4.24    <.0001
tenure2      1   -0.0009   0.000206  -4.35    <.0001
south        1  -0.01632   0.0361    -0.45    0.6516
union        1  0.063697   0.0143     4.47    <.0001
```

15.4 RANDOM EFFECTS ESTIMATION

The random effects model treats the heterogeneity across individuals as a random component. The model is

$$y_{it} = \bar{\beta}_1 + \beta_2 x_{2it} + \beta_3 x_{3it} + (e_{it} + u_i)$$

$$= \bar{\beta}_1 + \beta_2 x_{2it} + \beta_3 x_{3it} + v_{it}$$

where the combined error is

$$v_{it} = u_i + e_{it}$$

The key properties of this new error term is that it is homoskedastic

$$\sigma_v^2 = \text{var}(v_{it}) = \text{var}(u_i + e_{it}) = \sigma_u^2 + \sigma_e^2$$

but serially correlated in a special way. For individual i

$$\text{cov}(v_{it}, v_{is}) = \sigma_u^2$$

The correlation of these observations is

$$\rho = \mathrm{corr}(v_{it}, v_{is}) = \frac{\mathrm{cov}(v_{it}, v_{is})}{\sqrt{\mathrm{var}(v_{it})\,\mathrm{var}(v_{is})}} = \frac{\sigma_u^2}{\sigma_u^2 + \sigma_e^2}$$

This intra-individual correlation is very important. For two individuals i and j

$$\mathrm{cov}\left(v_{it}, v_{js}\right) = 0$$

The model's parameters are estimated by (feasible) generalized least squares. This estimation is implemented by **PROC PANEL** in the same way fixed effects estimation is carried out. Random effects estimation is accomplished by simply changing the **fixone** option to **ranone**. We continue with the data file *nls_panel* used in the previous section.

```
proc panel data=nls;
id id year;
model lwage = educ exper exper2 tenure tenure2 black south
        union / ranone bp;
title 'NLS random effects with Breusch-Pagan test';
run;
```

The option **bp** is present to have SAS print the Breush-Pagan test for the presence of random effects. The first part of the output identifies the procedure and recognizes Wayne Fuller and George Battese, the developers of the estimator.

```
                 The PANEL Procedure
        Fuller and Battese Variance Components (RanOne)
```

The "variance components" are reported as

```
              Variance Component Estimates

    Variance Component for Cross Sections   0.111498
    Variance Component for Error            0.038068
```

These are $\hat{\sigma}_u^2 = 0.111498$ and $\hat{\sigma}_e^2 = 0.038068$. These values are slightly different than those reported in *POE4* on page 557. Statisticians have studied this model intensively over the years, and many alternative estimators exist. The estimator used by SAS is that of Fuller and Battese. The ones reported in *POE4* are those of Swamy and Arora. The details of this estimator are given in Appendix 15B of this manual and in Appendix 15B of *POE4*.

Next, the Hausman test is a comparison between the fixed effects estimator and the random effects estimator. Because the random effects estimator includes EDUC and BLACK, which are not included in the fixed effects model, SAS does not report the contrast test. More about this below.

```
              Hausman Test for
              Random Effects

        DF    m Value    Pr > m
         0       .          .
```

The Breush-Pagan test statistic is for the presence of random effects. The null hypothesis is that $\sigma_u^2 = 0$. More about this test below.

```
          Breusch Pagan Test for Random
                 Effects (One Way)

          DF    m Value    Pr > m
          1     3859.28    <.0001
```

The parameter estimates are

Variable	DF	Estimate	Standard Error	t Value	Pr > |t|
Intercept	1	0.533959	0.0806	6.63	<.0001
educ	1	0.073274	0.00539	13.60	<.0001
exper	1	0.043557	0.00635	6.86	<.0001
exper2	1	-0.00056	0.000262	-2.13	0.0335
tenure	1	0.01415	0.00316	4.48	<.0001
tenure2	1	-0.00076	0.000194	-3.90	<.0001
black	1	-0.11691	0.0305	-3.83	0.0001
south	1	-0.08118	0.0225	-3.60	0.0003
union	1	0.079889	0.0132	6.05	<.0001

Despite the fact that SAS uses slightly different estimators for the variance components than in *POE4*, these estimates are very close to those in Table 15.9 of *POE4*, page 556.

15.4.1 The Breusch-Pagan test

To test for the presence of random effects we use the Breusch-Pagan test statistic

$$BP = \frac{NT}{2(T-1)}\left\{\frac{\sum_{i=1}^{N}\left(\sum_{t=1}^{T}\hat{e}_{it}\right)^2}{\sum_{i=1}^{N}\sum_{t=1}^{T}\hat{e}_{it}^2} - 1\right\}^2$$

The original *LM* test due to Breusch and Pagan uses the distribution under H_0 as $\chi^2_{(1)}$. Subsequent authors pointed out that the alternative hypothesis for using *BP* is $H_1:\sigma_u^2 \neq 0$, and that we can do better by using *LM* as a one-sided test with alternative hypothesis $H_1:\sigma_u^2 > 0$. The adjustment for a chi-square test at significance α is to use the $100(1-2\alpha)$ percentile of the χ^2-distribution. This critical value for an $\alpha = 0.05$ test is 2.706. The reported value by SAS is 3859, which is far greater than the critical value, indicating that random effects are present.

15.4.2 The Hausman test

To check for any correlation between the error component u_i and the regressors in a random effects model we can use a Hausman test. The test compares the coefficient estimates from the random effects model to those from the fixed effects model. The idea underlying Hausman's test is that both the random effects and fixed effects estimators are consistent if there is no correlation between u_i and the explanatory variables x_{kit}. If both estimators are consistent then they should converge to the true parameter values β_k in large samples. That is, in large samples the random effects and fixed effects estimates should be similar. On the other hand, if u_i is correlated with any x_{kit} the random effects estimator is inconsistent, while the fixed effects estimator remains consistent. Thus in large samples the fixed effects estimator converges to the true parameter values, but the random effects estimator converges to some other value that is not the value of the true parameters. In this case, we expect to see differences between the fixed and random effects estimates.

To implement the test estimate the random effects model including only variables that also vary across time for each individual.

```
proc panel data=nls;
id id year;
model lwage = exper exper2 tenure tenure2 south union / ranone;
title 'NLS random effects with Hausman test';
run;
```

The Hausman test is reported as

Hausman Test for
Random Effects

DF	m Value	Pr > m
6	27.75	0.0001

The chi-square statistic comparing all 6 coefficients, which has a small p-value again leading us to reject the hypothesis that the coefficient estimates are equal to one another. This difference suggests that the random effects estimator is inconsistent. It may be the result of an endogenous variable, such as education, or some other misspecification

Variable	DF	Estimate	Standard Error	t Value	Pr > |t|
Intercept	1	1.46636	0.0399	36.73	<.0001
exper	1	0.044945	0.00635	7.08	<.0001
exper2	1	-0.00059	0.000262	-2.27	0.0235
tenure	1	0.013833	0.00316	4.38	<.0001
tenure2	1	-0.00076	0.000195	-3.92	<.0001
south	1	-0.12276	0.0240	-5.12	<.0001
union	1	0.07316	0.0133	5.49	<.0001

Using the estimates of the coefficient of *SOUTH* from the fixed effects and random effects model, as in equation (15.37) in *POE4*, we have

$$t = \frac{b_{FE,k} - b_{RE,k}}{\left[\text{se}\left(b_{FE,k}\right)^2 - \text{se}\left(b_{RE,k}\right)^2\right]^{1/2}} = \frac{-0.01632 - (-0.12276)}{\left[(0.0361)^2 - (0.0240)^2\right]^{1/2}} = \frac{0.10644}{0.02697} = 3.947$$

This test statistic is asymptotically normal when the null hypothesis is true, and the critical value 1.96 is exceeded by the test statistic value, thus we reject the equality of the two coefficients.

Using these test variations we reject the null hypothesis that the random effect is uncorrelated with the regressors, casting doubt on random effects estimation.

15.5 SETS OF REGRESSION EQUATIONS

In this section we will examine investment data from two firms, General Electric (GE) and Westinghouse (WE). These are two firms among 10 in Grunfeld's classic data. To begin, issue the usual initial commands. Open the data file *grunfeld2*. Read in the data and examine its contents.

```
options label;
data grunfeld2;
set 'grunfeld2';
run;

proc contents data=grunfeld2 position;
title 'Grunfeld data on GE & Westinghouse';
run;

options nolabel;
```

```
                    Variables in Creation Order

# Variable Type Len Label
1 inv       Num   8 gross investment in plant and equipment, millions of $1947
2 v         Num   8 value of common and preferred stock, millions of $1947
3 k         Num   8 stock of capital, millions of $1947
4 firm      Num   8 firm id
5 year      Num   8 year
```

For each of the firms in the data there are 20 time series observations. The data file *grunfeld2* omits all the data on firms other than GE or WE and the data are in a panel data format, with $FIRM = 1$ denoting GE and $FIRM = 2$ denoting Westinghouse.

The equations we consider first are two investment models. If the models have the same parameters we can estimate a pooled regression model using all 40 observations

$$INV_{GE,t} = \beta_1 + \beta_2 V_{GE,t} + \beta_3 K_{GE,t} + e_{GE,t} \quad t = 1,\ldots,20$$

$$INV_{WE,t} = \beta_1 + \beta_2 V_{WE,t} + \beta_3 K_{WE,t} + e_{WE,t} \quad t = 1,\ldots,20$$

To obtain pooled regression estimates with **PROC REG** use

```
proc reg data=grunfeld2;
model inv = v k;
title 'pooled least squares';
run;
```

```
                       Analysis of Variance

                                 Sum of           Mean
Source                 DF        Squares         Square    F Value   Pr > F
Model                   2         70506          35253      78.75    <.0001
Error                  37         16563      447.64874
Corrected Total        39         87069

               Root MSE              21.15771    R-Square    0.8098
               Dependent Mean        72.59075    Adj R-Sq    0.7995
               Coeff Var             29.14657

                         Parameter      Standard
         Variable   DF    Estimate        Error    t Value    Pr > |t|
         Intercept   1    17.87200      7.02408       2.54      0.0153
         v           1     0.01519      0.00620       2.45      0.0191
         k           1     0.14358      0.01860       7.72      <.0001
```

If the firm parameters are not identical the models will be

$$INV_{GE,t} = \beta_{1,GE} + \beta_{2,GE}V_{GE,t} + \beta_{3,GE}K_{GE,t} + e_{GE,t} \quad t = 1,\dots,20$$

$$INV_{WE,t} = \beta_{1,WE} + \beta_{2,WE}V_{WE,t} + \beta_{3,WE}K_{WE,t} + e_{WE,t} \quad t = 1,\dots,20$$

To test whether we should pool the data or not, estimate a dummy variable model

$$INV_{it} = \beta_{1,GE} + \delta_1 D_i + \beta_{2,GE}V_{it} + \delta_2 D_i \times V_{it} + \beta_{3,GE}K_{it} + \delta_3 D_i \times K_{it} + e_{it}$$

where $D = 1$ for Westinghouse observations. Create this dummy variable and its interactions

```
data grunfeld2;
set grunfeld2;
d = 0;
if firm=2 then d=1;
dv = d*v;
dk = d*k;
run;
```

Use regress to estimate the model with dummy variables, using GE as the base when the indicator variables are zero.

```
proc reg data=grunfeld2;
model inv = d v dv k dk;
test d = dv = dk = 0;
title 'fully interacted DV model';
run;
```

Variable	DF	Parameter Estimate	Standard Error	t Value	Pr > |t|
Intercept	1	-9.95631	23.62636	-0.42	0.6761
d	1	9.44692	28.80535	0.33	0.7450
v	1	0.02655	0.01172	2.27	0.0300
dv	1	0.02634	0.03435	0.77	0.4485
k	1	0.15169	0.01936	7.84	<.0001
dk	1	-0.05929	0.11695	-0.51	0.6155

Test the significance of the coefficients of the indicator and slope-indicator variables.

Test 1 Results for Dependent Variable inv

Source	DF	Mean Square	F Value	Pr > F
Numerator	3	524.39389	1.19	0.3284
Denominator	34	440.87711		

There is no strong evidence that the coefficients are different in these two regressions. However, we should also test for differences in variances. Use the Goldfeld-Quandt test discussed in Chapter 8. We estimate two separate regressions using **PROC REG** with the **by** qualifier.

```
proc reg data=grunfeld2;
by firm;
model inv = v k;
title 'separate regressions';
run;
```

The ANOVA tables are

```
-------------------------------- firm=1 --------------------------------
```

Source	DF	Sum of Squares	Mean Square	F Value	Pr > F
Model	2	31632	15816	20.34	<.0001
Error	17	13217	777.44634		
Corrected Total	19	44849			

```
-------------------------------- firm=2 --------------------------------
```

Source	DF	Sum of Squares	Mean Square	F Value	Pr > F
Model	2	5165.55292	2582.77646	24.76	<.0001
Error	17	1773.23393	104.30788		
Corrected Total	19	6938.78686			

The Goldfeld-Quandt test statistic is 7.45, which is greater than the 5% critical value 2.27, so we reject the null hypothesis of homoskedasticity. We have strong evidence that the error variances of the two equations are different.

15.5.1 Seemingly unrelated regressions

Seemingly unrelated regressions (SUR) permits equation coefficients and variances to differ, and also allows for contemporaneous correlation between the errors,

$$\text{cov}\left(e_{GE,t}, e_{WE,t}\right) = \sigma_{GE,WE}$$

The SUR estimator is a generalized least squares estimator, and because the data are stacked, one firm atop the other, we must rearrange it into a wide format prior to obtaining SUR estimates.

```
data ge;
set grunfeld2; if firm=1;
inv_ge = inv; v_ge = v; k_ge = k;
keep year inv_ge v_ge k_ge;
run;

data we;
set grunfeld2; if firm=2;
inv_we = inv; v_we = v; k_we = k;
keep year inv_we v_we k_we;
run;

data grunfeld;
merge ge we;
by year;
run;
```

Estimate the separate regressions and output the residuals.

```
proc reg data=grunfeld;                 * general electric;
model inv_ge = v_ge k_ge;
output out=geout r=ehat_ge;             * output residuals;
title 'GE regression by least squares';
run;

proc reg data=grunfeld;                 * westinghouse;
model inv_we = v_we k_we;
output out=weout r=ehat_we;             * output residuals;
title 'WE regression by least squares';
run;
```

Check the residual correlation.

```
data all;                               * new dataset;
merge geout weout;                      * merge residuals;
run;
proc corr;                              * correlations;
var ehat_ge ehat_we;                    * residuals;
title 'residual correlation';
run;
```

```
               Pearson Correlation Coefficients, N = 20
                   Prob > |r| under HO: Rho=0


                           ehat_ge           ehat_we
            ehat_ge        1.00000           0.72896
                                             0.0003


            ehat_we        0.72896           1.00000
                           0.0003
```

We find substantial correlation between the residuals of the two firms.

With the data in wide form SUR estimation uses **PROC SYSLIN**. The command is

```
proc syslin data=grunfeld sur;              * syslin with sur;
ge: model inv_ge = v_ge k_ge;               * ge;
we: model inv_we = v_we k_we;               * westinghouse;
title 'SUR estimation';
run;
```

```
                    Model                   GE


                     Parameter    Standard
     Variable    DF  Estimate     Error     t Value   Pr > |t|
     Intercept   1   -27.7193     29.32122  -0.95     0.3577
     v_ge        1   0.038310     0.014415   2.66     0.0166
     k_ge        1   0.139036     0.024986   5.56     <.0001

                    Model                   WE


                     Parameter    Standard
     Variable    DF  Estimate     Error     t Value   Pr > |t|
     Intercept   1   -1.25199     7.545217  -0.17     0.8702
     v_we        1   0.057630     0.014546   3.96     0.0010
     k_we        1   0.063978     0.053041   1.21     0.2443
```

Using **PROC SYSLIN** we can test hypotheses about the parameters in one equation or hypotheses cross-equation. For example,

```
proc syslin data=grunfeld sur;
ge: model inv_ge = v_ge k_ge;
test_1: test v_ge=k_ge;                            * test an equation;
we: model inv_we = v_we k_we;
stest_1: stest ge.v_ge = we.v_we;                  * test across equations;
stest_2: stest ge.intercept = we.intercept,
             ge.v_ge = we.v_we,ge.k_ge = we.k_we;
title 'SUR with tests';
run;
```

The first test, **test_1**, tests for the GE equation whether the coefficients of V and K are equal.

```
                        Test Results

    Num DF      Den DF    F Value    Pr > F    Label
        1          34       11.44    0.0018    TEST_1
```

The second test, **stest_1**, is a **system** test of whether the coefficient of *V* is the same for the GE and WE equations. Note that the test command is **stest** and that the variable names are preceded by their equation labels, **ge.v_ge**, so that the equations are properly identified.

```
                        Test Results

    Num DF      Den DF    F Value    Pr > F    Label
        1          34        2.80    0.1033    STEST_1
```

The third test, **stest_2**, tests if all the coefficients of the GE equation are equal to all the coefficients of the WE equation. The results are

```
                        Test Results

    Num DF      Den DF    F Value    Pr > F    Label
        3          34        3.01    0.0437    STEST_2
```

15.5.2 Using PROC MODEL for SUR

The usual estimates, those provided by **PROC SYSLIN**, are obtained using

```
proc model data=grunfeld;
inv_ge = b1_ge + b2_ge*v_ge + b3_ge*k_ge;
inv_we = b1_we + b2_we*v_we + b3_we*k_we;
fit inv_ge inv_we/sur covs corrs;
test b2_ge=b2_we;
title 'SUR with proc model';
run;
```

```
               Nonlinear SUR Parameter Estimates

                             Approx               Approx
    Parameter    Estimate    Std Err    t Value   Pr > |t|
    b1_ge        -27.7193    29.3212      -0.95    0.3577
    b2_ge         0.03831     0.0144       2.66    0.0166
    b3_ge        0.139036     0.0250       5.56    <.0001
    b1_we        -1.25199     7.5452      -0.17    0.8702
    b2_we         0.05763     0.0145       3.96    0.0010
    b3_we        0.063978     0.0530       1.21    0.2443

                        Test Results
    Test        Type     Statistic   Pr > ChiSq   Label
    Test0       Wald         2.72        0.0989    b2_ge=b2_we
```

There is an investment equation specified for each firm. The **fit** statement lists both dependent variables and has the options **sur covs corrs**. The first requests SUR estimation, and the second and third request that the covariance and correlation of the residuals be reported. Note that the reported test is a Wald chi-square test rather than the *F*-test reported by **PROC SYSLIN**.

Secondly, both **PROC MODEL** and **PROC SYSLIN** will carry out **iterative SUR**. Here the estimated covariance matrices of residuals are continually updated until convergence.

```
proc model data=grunfeld;
inv_ge = b1_ge + b2_ge*v_ge + b3_ge*k_ge;
inv_we = b1_we + b2_we*v_we + b3_we*k_we;
fit inv_ge inv_we/itsur;
title 'iterative SUR with proc model';
run;
```

Note the option **itsur** on the **fit** statement. After six iterations we obtain

```
            Nonlinear ITSUR Summary of Residual Errors
```

Equation	DF Model	DF Error	SSE	MSE	Root MSE	R-Square	Adj R-Sq
inv_ge	3	17	14041.9	826.0	28.7401	0.6869	0.6501
inv_we	3	17	1818.9	107.0	10.3437	0.7379	0.7070

```
            Nonlinear ITSUR Parameter Estimates
```

Parameter	Estimate	Approx Std Err	t Value	Approx Pr > |t|
b1_ge	-30.7185	29.6591	-1.04	0.3148
b2_ge	0.040489	0.0145	2.78	0.0127
b3_ge	0.135961	0.0255	5.32	<.0001
b1_we	-1.69715	7.5148	-0.23	0.8240
b2_we	0.059335	0.0144	4.11	0.0007
b3_we	0.055814	0.0529	1.06	0.3060

The conventional wisdom is that iteration pays in finite samples, which is certainly the case here.

Thirdly, with **PROC MODEL** we can obtain robust SUR estimates. Enter **help model** into the SAS command line, then select the **PROC MODEL** documentation from the key word search. Then find **Heteroskedasticity** and below it find **Seemingly Unrelated Regression HCCME**

```
proc model data=grunfeld;
inv_ge = b1_ge + b2_ge*v_ge + b3_ge*k_ge;
inv_we = b1_we + b2_we*v_we + b3_we*k_we;
fit inv_ge inv_we/sur hccme=1;
test b2_ge=b2_we;
title 'SUR with robust covariance';
run;
```

Note the option **hccme=1** on the **fit** statement.

```
                    Nonlinear SUR Parameter Estimates

                                  Approx                Approx
            Parameter   Estimate  Std Err    t Value   Pr > |t|

             b1_ge      -27.7193   23.1313     -1.20     0.2472
             b2_ge        0.03831   0.0130      2.95     0.0089
             b3_ge       0.139036   0.0192      7.22    <.0001
             b1_we       -1.25199   8.1511     -0.15     0.8797
             b2_we        0.05763   0.0156      3.70     0.0018
             b3_we       0.063978   0.0536      1.19     0.2487

                              Test Results

   Test        Type       Statistic   Pr > ChiSq   Label
   Test0       Wald            2.71       0.1000    b2_ge=b2_we
```

Compare the standard errors and test result to previous estimates.

APPENDIX 15A POOLED OLS ROBUST COVARIANCE MATRIX

Let the regression equation for the i'th cross section be denoted

$$\mathbf{y}_i = \mathbf{X}_i\boldsymbol{\beta} + \mathbf{e}_i$$

where

$$\mathbf{y}_i = \begin{bmatrix} y_{i1} \\ y_{i2} \\ \vdots \\ y_{iT} \end{bmatrix} \quad \mathbf{X}_i = \begin{bmatrix} 1 & x_{i12} & \cdots & x_{i1K} \\ 1 & x_{i22} & \cdots & x_{i2K} \\ \vdots & \vdots & & \vdots \\ 1 & x_{iT2} & \cdots & x_{iTK} \end{bmatrix}_{T \times K} \quad \boldsymbol{\beta} = \begin{bmatrix} \beta_1 \\ \beta_2 \\ \vdots \\ \beta_K \end{bmatrix} \quad \mathbf{e}_i = \begin{bmatrix} e_{i1} \\ e_{i2} \\ \vdots \\ e_{iT} \end{bmatrix}$$

Here we consider the assumptions that

$$E(\mathbf{e}_i) = \mathbf{0} \quad E(\mathbf{e}_i\mathbf{e}_i') = \boldsymbol{\Omega}_i \quad E(\mathbf{e}_i\mathbf{e}_j') = \mathbf{0}$$

That is, while the errors for different cross-section units are uncorrelated, the $T \times T$ covariance matrix for the errors of the i'th cross-section may exhibit heteroskedasticity and/or serial correlation of unknown form.[1] The pooled regression model is written in stacked format as $\mathbf{y} = \mathbf{X}\boldsymbol{\beta} + \mathbf{e}$ where

---

[1] See William Greene, *Econometric Analysis*, 7th Edition, Pearson/Prentice-Hall, 2012, page 351. Also Jeffrey Wooldridge, *Econometric Analysis of Cross Section and Panel Data*, 2nd Edition, 2010, MIT Press, page 172.

$$\mathbf{y} = \begin{bmatrix} \mathbf{y}_1 \\ \mathbf{y}_2 \\ \vdots \\ \mathbf{y}_N \end{bmatrix} \quad \mathbf{X} = \begin{bmatrix} \mathbf{X}_1 \\ \mathbf{X}_2 \\ \vdots \\ \mathbf{X}_N \end{bmatrix}_{NT \times K} \quad \mathbf{e} = \begin{bmatrix} \mathbf{e}_1 \\ \mathbf{e}_2 \\ \vdots \\ \mathbf{e}_N \end{bmatrix}$$

The pooled OLS estimator is $\mathbf{b} = (\mathbf{X'X})^{-1}\mathbf{X'y}$. Denote the least squares residual vector for the i'th cross-section be $\hat{\mathbf{e}}_i = \mathbf{y}_i - \mathbf{X}_i\mathbf{b}$. An estimator of the covariance matrix of $\mathbf{b}$ that is robust to "clustering" is

$$\text{cov}(\mathbf{b}) = (\mathbf{X'X})^{-1}\left[\sum_{i=1}^{N}\mathbf{X}_i'\hat{\mathbf{e}}_i\hat{\mathbf{e}}_i'\mathbf{X}_i\right](\mathbf{X'X})^{-1}$$

This estimator is used by **PROC PANEL**. If we add a degrees of freedom correction we have the estimator used by **PROC SURVEYREG**.

$$\text{cov}(\mathbf{b}) = \frac{N}{N-1}\frac{NT-1}{NT-K}(\mathbf{X'X})^{-1}\left[\sum_{i=1}^{N}\mathbf{X}_i'\hat{\mathbf{e}}_i\hat{\mathbf{e}}_i'\mathbf{X}_i\right](\mathbf{X'X})^{-1}$$

15A.1 NLS examples

Read the *nls* data and apply **PROC PANEL**.

```
data nls;
set 'nls_panel';
run;

proc panel data=nls;
id id year;
model lwage = educ exper exper2 tenure tenure2 black south
      union / pooled hccme=4;
run;
```

Variable	DF	Estimate	Standard Error	t Value	Pr > |t|
Intercept	1	0.4766	0.0844	5.65	<.0001
educ	1	0.071449	0.00549	13.02	<.0001
exper	1	0.055685	0.0113	4.93	<.0001
exper2	1	-0.00115	0.000492	-2.33	0.0196
tenure	1	0.01496	0.00711	2.10	0.0354
tenure2	1	-0.00049	0.000409	-1.19	0.2353
black	1	-0.11671	0.0281	-4.16	<.0001
south	1	-0.106	0.0270	-3.92	<.0001
union	1	0.132243	0.0270	4.89	<.0001

Using PROC SURVEYREG we have

```
proc surveyreg data=nls;
cluster id;
```

```
model lwage = educ exper exper2 tenure tenure2 black south union;
run;
```

Estimated Regression Coefficients

| | | Standard | | |
Parameter	Estimate	Error	t Value	Pr > |t|
Intercept	0.4766001	0.08456293	5.64	<.0001
educ	0.0714488	0.00549950	12.99	<.0001
exper	0.0556850	0.01131014	4.92	<.0001
exper2	-0.0011475	0.00049247	-2.33	0.0201
tenure	0.0149600	0.00712317	2.10	0.0361
tenure2	-0.0004860	0.00041023	-1.18	0.2365
black	-0.1167139	0.02813417	-4.15	<.0001
south	-0.1060026	0.02706156	-3.92	<.0001
union	0.1322432	0.02707467	4.88	<.0001

15A.2 Using PROC IML

Continue the example from the previous section. The **SAS/IML** code reveals that we obtain the clustering portion of the covariance matrix of **b** by looping across cross-section units.

```
proc iml;
title;
start robust_ols;
use nls;

/* read data */
read all into y var{lwage};
read all into xs var{educ exper exper2 tenure
           tenure2 black south union};

/* define matrices */
t=5;
n=716;
x = j(n*t,1,1)||xs;
k = ncol(x);
olsdf = n*t-k;

/* OLS and residuals */
b = inv(x`*x)*x`*y;
ehat = y-x*b;

/* loop for cluster */
bmat=0;
do ind = 1 to n;
       i1 = 1 + t*(ind-1);
       i2 = t + t*(ind-1);
       xi = x[i1:i2,];
       yi = y[i1:i2,];
       ei = ehat[i1:i2,];
```

```
        bmat = bmat + xi`*ei*ei`*xi;
end;

/* robust covariance matrix and results */
robust = inv(x`*x)*bmat*inv(x`*x);
se = sqrt(vecdiag(robust));
tstat = b/se;

cf = (n/(n-1))*(n*t-1)/(n*t-k);
se_c = sqrt(cf)*se;
tstat_c = b/se_c;
result = b||se||tstat||se_c||tstat_c;
rname = {one educ exper exper2 tenure
            tenure2 black south union};
cname = {est se tstat se_c tstat_c};

print / "OLS with fully robust se",,
        result [rowname=rname colname=cname format=13.6];
finish;

run robust_ols;
quit;
```

The **SAS/IML** results match **PROC PANEL** (SE & TSTAT) and **PROC SURVEYREG** (SE_C & TSTAT_C).

```
                   OLS with fully robust se

                              result
              EST         SE        TSTAT        SE_C       TSTAT_C

ONE        0.476600    0.084409    5.646294    0.084563    5.636040
EDUC       0.071449    0.005490   13.015501    0.005500   12.991864
EXPER      0.055685    0.011290    4.932424    0.011310    4.923467
EXPER2    -0.001148    0.000492   -2.334399    0.000492   -2.330160
TENURE     0.014960    0.007110    2.104011    0.007123    2.100190
TENURE2   -0.000486    0.000409   -1.186969    0.000410   -1.184814
BLACK     -0.116714    0.028083   -4.156021    0.028134   -4.148473
SOUTH     -0.106003    0.027012   -3.924217    0.027062   -3.917091
UNION      0.132243    0.027026    4.893274    0.027075    4.884388
```

APPENDIX 15B PANEL DATA ESTIMATION DETAILS

15B.1 Estimating variance components

The random effects model for $K = 3$ is

$$y_{it} = \overline{\beta}_1 + \beta_2 x_{2it} + \beta_3 x_{3it} + (u_i + e_{it})$$

where u_i is the individual specific error and e_{it} is the usual regression error. We will discuss the case for a balanced panel, with T time series observations for each of N individuals. To implement generalized least squares estimation we need to consistently estimate σ_u^2, the variance of the individual specific error component, and σ_e^2, the variance of the regression error.

The regression error variance σ_e^2 comes from the fixed effects estimator. The panel data regression in "deviation about the individual mean" form is

$$y_{it} - \bar{y}_i = \beta_2(x_{2it} - \bar{x}_{2i}) + \beta_3(x_{3it} - \bar{x}_{3i}) + (e_{it} - \bar{e}_i) \tag{15B.1}$$

The least squares estimator of this equation yields the same estimates and sum of squared residuals (denoted here by SSE_{DV}) as least squares applied to a model that includes a dummy variable for each individual in the sample. A consistent estimator of σ_e^2 is obtained by dividing SSE_{DV} by the appropriate degrees of freedom, which is $NT - N - K_{slopes}$, where K_{slopes} is the number of parameters that are present in the transformed model (15B.1)

$$\hat{\sigma}_e^2 = \frac{SSE_{DV}}{NT - N - K_{slopes}}$$

The estimator of σ_u^2 requires a bit more work. We begin with the time averaged observations

$$\bar{y}_i = \bar{\beta}_1 + \beta_2 \bar{x}_{2i} + \beta_3 \bar{x}_{3i} + u_i + \bar{e}_i \quad i = 1, \dots, N$$

The least squares estimator of this equation is called the **between estimator**, as it uses variation between individuals as a basis for estimating the regression parameters. This estimator is unbiased and consistent. The error term in this model is $u_i + \bar{e}_i$; it is uncorrelated across individuals, and has homoskedastic variance

$$\text{var}(u_i + \bar{e}_i) = \text{var}(u_i) + \text{var}(\bar{e}_i) = \text{var}(u_i) + \text{var}\left(\sum_{t=1}^{T} e_{it} \Big/ T\right)$$

$$= \sigma_u^2 + \frac{1}{T^2} \text{var}\left(\sum_{t=1}^{T} e_{it}\right) = \sigma_u^2 + \frac{T\sigma_e^2}{T^2} = \sigma_u^2 + \frac{\sigma_e^2}{T}$$

We can estimate this variance by estimating the between regression, and dividing the sum of squared residuals, SSE_{BE}, by the degrees of freedom $N - K_{BE}$, where K_{BE} is the total number of parameters in the between regression, including the intercept parameter. Then

$$\widehat{\sigma_u^2 + \frac{\sigma_e^2}{T}} = \frac{SSE_{BE}}{N - K_{BE}}$$

With this estimate in hand we can estimate σ_u^2 as

$$\hat{\sigma}_u^2 = \widehat{\sigma_u^2 + \frac{\sigma_e^2}{T}} - \frac{\hat{\sigma}_e^2}{T} = \frac{SSE_{BE}}{N - K_{BE}} - \frac{SSE_{DV}}{T(NT - N - K_{slopes})}$$

We have obtained the estimates of σ_u^2 and σ_e^2 using what is called the Swamy-Arora method.

15B.2 Using PROC PANEL

To illustrate we use the *nls* data. First, read and sort.

```
data nls;
set 'nls_panel';
run;

proc sort data=nls;
by id year;
run;
```

The fixed effects estimator is

```
proc panel data=nls;
id id year;
model lwage = exper exper2 tenure tenure2 south union / fixone;
title 'NLS fixed effects regression using PROC PANEL';
run;
```

The estimates are reported earlier. The one component we should focus on in this appendix is

```
                 Fit Statistics

     SSE        108.7985   DFE            2858
     MSE          0.0381   Root MSE     0.1951
```

The MSE in this output (under "Fit Statistics") is

$$\hat{\sigma}_e^2 = \frac{SSE_{DV}}{NT - N - K_{slopes}} = 0.0381$$

The between estimator is obtained using the option **btwng** (or "between group").

```
proc panel data=nls;
id id year;
model lwage = exper exper2 tenure tenure2 south union / btwng;
title 'NLS between groups regression using PROC PANEL';
run;
```

```
              The PANEL Procedure
            Between Groups Estimates
```

Dependent Variable: lwage

```
              Model Description

     Estimation Method         BtwGrps
     Number of Cross Sections      716
     Time Series Length              5
```

```
                         Fit Statistics

         SSE             106.0397   DFE               709
         MSE               0.1496   Root MSE        0.3867
         R-Square          0.1788
```

```
                       Parameter Estimates
                          Standard
Variable      DF  Estimate   Error  t Value  Pr > |t|  Label
Intercept      1  1.122034  0.1416    7.92   <.0001    Intercept
exper          1  0.106411  0.0264    4.03   <.0001
exper2         1  -0.00317  0.00112  -2.82   0.0050
tenure         1  0.012474  0.0139    0.90   0.3684
tenure2        1  -0.00016  0.000798 -0.20   0.8442
south          1  -0.20082  0.0302   -6.64   <.0001
union          1  0.121197  0.0394    3.08   0.0022
```

The MSE from this model is

$$\widehat{\sigma_u^2 + \frac{\sigma_e^2}{T}} = \frac{SSE_{BE}}{N - K_{BE}} = 0.1496$$

The random effects estimates are obtained using the option **ranone**.

```
proc panel data=nls;
id id year;
model lwage = exper exper2 tenure tenure2 south union / ranone;
title 'NLS random effects using PROC PANEL';
run;
```

The reported estimates are

```
                    Fit Statistics
        SSE         132.2510   DFE             3573
        MSE           0.0370   Root MSE      0.1924
```

```
             Variance Component Estimates

Variance Component for Cross Sections    0.173595
Variance Component for Error             0.038068
```

```
                          Standard
    Variable     DF   Estimate    Error   t Value   Pr > |t|
    Intercept     1    1.46636   0.0399    36.73     <.0001
    exper         1   0.044945   0.00635    7.08     <.0001
    exper2        1   -0.00059   0.000262  -2.27     0.0235
    tenure        1   0.013833   0.00316    4.38     <.0001
    tenure2       1   -0.00076   0.000195  -3.92     <.0001
    south         1   -0.12276   0.0240    -5.12     <.0001
    union         1    0.07316   0.0133     5.49     <.0001
```

Note that SAS reports the variance components estimates for "Error" as 0.038068, which is the MSE from the fixed effects estimation. The variance component for "Cross-Sections" is an estimate of σ_u^2 using the method of Fuller and Battese. We will not explain this method. See the SAS documentation.

15B.3 Using PROC IML

To compute these estimates in **PROC IML**, first read in the data.

```
proc iml;
title;
start re;
use nls;
read all into y var{lwage};
read all into xs var{exper exper2 tenure tenure2 south union};

n = 716;
t = 5;

/* names for re & between estimator parameters */
parmname = {intercept exper exper2 tenure tenure2 south union};

/* names for fe estimator parameters */
parmfe = {exper exper2 tenure tenure2 south union};
```

For the between estimator we must create time averaged data. We take the simple approach of looping through the data *N* times, and find the averages of the *T* observations per individual.

```
ks = ncol(xs);                          * number of slopes;
ybar = j(n,1,0);                        * y-bar storage vector;
jt = j(t,1,1);                          * column of ones;
xbars = j(n,ks,0);                      * x-bar storage vector;
do ind = 1 to n;                        * loop through firm data;
      first = (ind - 1)*t + 1;          * firm obs # 1;
      last = ind*t;                     * firm obs # T;
      ybar[ind,] = jt`*y[first:last,]/t;      * y-bar;
      xbars[ind,] = jt`*xs[first:last,]/t;    * x-bar;
end;                                    * end loop;
```

Add an intercept variable and apply least squares.

```
xbar = j(n,1,1)||xbars;                 * add intercept;
kb = ncol(xbar);                        * between model regressors;
bstar = inv(xbar`*xbar)*xbar`*ybar;     * least squares;
v = ybar - xbar*bstar;                  * residuals;
sig2b = ssq(v)/(n-kb);                  * between model variance;
covbet = sig2b*inv(xbar`*xbar);         * between estimator cov;
sebet = sqrt(vecdiag(covbet));          * between est. std. err;
tstat = bstar/sebet;                    * between est. t-values;
result = bstar||sebet||tstat;           * between est. results;
cname = {est se tstat};                 * column names;
```

```
print / "between group model"
        ,, result [rowname=parmname colname=cname format=13.5];
```

                    between group model

                           result
	EST	SE	TSTAT
INTERCEPT	1.12203	0.14158	7.92499
EXPER	0.10641	0.02638	4.03434
EXPER2	-0.00317	0.00112	-2.81601
TENURE	0.01247	0.01386	0.90012
TENURE2	-0.00016	0.00080	-0.19655
SOUTH	-0.20082	0.03024	-6.64077
UNION	0.12120	0.03936	3.07916

Compute the fixed effects estimates.

```
xdot = xs - xbars@jt;                * deviations about mean;
ydot = y - ybar@jt;                  * deviations;
bfe = inv(xdot`*xdot)*xdot`*ydot;    * LS = fixed effects est;
ehat = ydot - xdot*bfe;              * residuals;
sig2e = ssq(ehat)/(n*t-n-ks);        * estimate variance;
covb = sig2e*inv(xdot`*xdot);        * covariance matrix;
seb = sqrt(vecdiag(covb));           * standard errors;
tstat = bfe/seb;                     * t-statistics;
result = bfe||seb||tstat;            * results;

print / "fixed effects model" ,,
        result [rowname=parmfe colname=cname format=13.5];
```

                     fixed effects model

                           result
	EST	SE	TSTAT
EXPER	0.04108	0.00662	6.20590
EXPER2	-0.00041	0.00027	-1.49653
TENURE	0.01391	0.00328	4.24332
TENURE2	-0.00090	0.00021	-4.35357
SOUTH	-0.01632	0.03615	-0.45153
UNION	0.06370	0.01425	4.46879

Our estimate of the "cross-section" variance component is

$$\hat{\sigma}_u^2 = \overbrace{\sigma_u^2 + \frac{\sigma_e^2}{T}} - \frac{\hat{\sigma}_e^2}{T} = \frac{SSE_{BE}}{N - K_{BE}} - \frac{SSE_{DV}}{T\left(NT - N - K_{slopes}\right)}$$

Compute this value.

```
sig2u = sig2b - sig2e/t;             * Estimator of sigma_u squared;
print / "variances used in calculations",, sig2e sig2b sig2u;
sigu = sqrt(sig2u);
sige = sqrt(sig2e);
```

```
rho = sig2u/(sig2u+sig2e);
print ,, "standard deviation individual error " ,, sigu;
print ,, "standard deviation overall error " ,, sige;
print ,, "error correlation      " ,,rho;
```

```
                 variances used in calculations

                  sig2e      sig2b      sig2u
               0.0380681  0.1495624  0.1419488


            standard deviation individual error

                         sigu
                      0.3767609


             standard deviation overall error

                         sige
                      0.1951104


                   error correlation

                         rho
                      0.7885305
```

Using the estimated variance components we create the differencing fraction

$$\theta = 1 - \frac{\sigma_e}{\sqrt{T\sigma_u^2 + \sigma_e^2}}$$

```
theta = 1 - sqrt(sig2e/(t*sig2u+sig2e));    * differencing fraction;

print ,, "fractional difference factor" ,, theta;
```

```
                fractional difference factor

                         theta
                      0.7743766
```

With this value we create partial differences and obtain the generalized least squares estimates.

```
ystar = y - theta*(ybar@jt);              * fractional differences;

x = j(n*t,1,1)||xs;                       * X matrix;
xbar = j(n,1,1)||xbars;                   * X means;
xstar = x - theta*(xbar@jt);              * fractional differences;

bhat = inv(xstar`*xstar)*xstar`*ystar;    * GLS = random effects est;
ehat = ystar - xstar*bhat;                * residuals;
sig2 = ssq(ehat)/(n*t-(ks+1));            * estimate variance;
covb = sig2*inv(xstar`*xstar);            * covariance matrix;
seb = sqrt(vecdiag(covb));                * standard errors;
tstat = bhat/seb;                         * t-statistics;
```

```
result = bhat||seb||tstat;                    * results;

print / "random effects model" ,,
       result [rowname=parmname colname=cname format=13.5];
finish;                                       * finish module;
run re;                                        * run module;
quit;                                          * quit iml;
```

```
                    random effects model

                         result
                  EST          SE         TSTAT
INTERCEPT       1.46480     0.03974      36.85582
EXPER           0.04570     0.00642       7.11366
EXPER2         -0.00063     0.00027      -2.37025
TENURE          0.01380     0.00320       4.31403
TENURE2        -0.00074     0.00020      -3.76160
SOUTH          -0.13164     0.02311      -5.69610
UNION           0.07465     0.01343       5.56006
```

These are slightly different from those obtained using PROC PANEL because we estimated the cross-section error variance using an alternative method.

APPENDIX 15C ROBUST FIXED EFFECTS ESTIMATION

In fixed effects estimation we demean the data prior to estimating the regression coefficients by least squares. Denote the demeaned values of the dependent variable as $\ddot{y}_{it} = y_{it} - \overline{y}_i$ where $\overline{y}_i = \sum_{t=1}^{T} y_{it}/T$. Similarly $\ddot{\mathbf{x}}_{it} = \mathbf{x}_{it} - \overline{\mathbf{x}}_i$ and $\overline{\mathbf{x}}_i = \sum_{t=1}^{T} \mathbf{x}_{it}/T$. Stack all NT observations into matrices $\ddot{\mathbf{y}}$ and $\ddot{\mathbf{X}}$. The fixed effects estimator is $\mathbf{b}_{FE} = \left(\ddot{\mathbf{X}}'\ddot{\mathbf{X}}\right)^{-1}\ddot{\mathbf{X}}'\ddot{\mathbf{y}}$. The usual covariance matrix for the fixed effects estimator is $\text{cov}\left(\mathbf{b}_{FE}\right) = \hat{\sigma}_e^2\left(\ddot{\mathbf{X}}'\ddot{\mathbf{X}}\right)^{-1}$ where $\hat{\sigma}_e^2 = SSE_{FE}/\left(NT - N - K_{slopes}\right)$ and SSE_{FE} is the sum of squared residuals $\ddot{e}_{it} = \ddot{y}_{it} - \ddot{\mathbf{x}}_{it}'\mathbf{b}_{FE}$. If we denote by $\ddot{\mathbf{e}}_i$ and $\ddot{\mathbf{X}}_i$ the fixed effects residuals and the demeaned explanatory variables for the i'th cross-sectional unit, then the robust covariance matrix estimator for $\mathbf{b}_{FE}$ is [Wooldridge (2010, p. 311)]

$$\text{cov}(\mathbf{b}_{FE}) = \left(\ddot{\mathbf{X}}'\ddot{\mathbf{X}}\right)^{-1}\left[\sum_{i=1}^{N} \ddot{\mathbf{X}}_i'\ddot{\mathbf{e}}_i\ddot{\mathbf{e}}_i'\ddot{\mathbf{X}}_i\right]\left(\ddot{\mathbf{X}}'\ddot{\mathbf{X}}\right)^{-1}$$

We also report the robust covariance matrix with a degrees of freedom correction.

$$\text{cov}(\mathbf{b}_{FE}) = \frac{N}{N-1}\frac{NT}{NT - K_{slopes}}\left(\ddot{\mathbf{X}}'\ddot{\mathbf{X}}\right)^{-1}\left[\sum_{i=1}^{N} \ddot{\mathbf{X}}_i'\ddot{\mathbf{e}}_i\ddot{\mathbf{e}}_i'\ddot{\mathbf{X}}_i\right]\left(\ddot{\mathbf{X}}'\ddot{\mathbf{X}}\right)^{-1}$$

The SAS/IML code follows, assuming the data *nls* is in memory.

```
proc iml;
title;
start robust_fe;
use nls;
read all into y var{lwage};
read all into xs var{exper exper2 tenure tenure2 south union};
t=5;
n=716;
ks = ncol(xs);
parmname = {exper exper2 tenure tenure2 south union};

/* indivdual means */
ybar = j(n,1,0);
jt = j(t,1,1);
xbar = j(n,ks,0);
do ind = 1 to n;
      i1 = 1 + t*(ind-1);
      i2 = t + t*(ind-1);
      ybar[ind,] = jt`*y[i1:i2,]/t;
      xbar[ind,] = jt`*xs[i1:i2,]/t;
end;

/* deviations about means */
ydot = y - ybar@jt;
xdot = xs - xbar@jt;

/* fixed effects estimation */
bfe = inv(xdot`*xdot)*xdot`*ydot;
edot = ydot - xdot*bfe;
sig2e = edot`*edot/(n*t-n-ks);

/* standard FE covariance matrix */
cov = sig2e*inv(xdot`*xdot);
se = sqrt(vecdiag(cov));
tstat = bfe/se;
pval =2*(1-probt(abs(tstat),n*t-n-ks));
tc = tinv(.975,n*t-n-ks);
result = bfe||se||tstat||pval;
cname = {est se tstat pval};
print / "Fixed Effects with traditional standard errors",,
        result [rowname=parmname colname=cname format=13.7];

/* loop for cluster correction */
bmat=0;
do ind=1 to n;
      i1 = 1 + t*(ind-1);
      i2 = t + t*(ind-1);
      xi = xdot[i1:i2,];
      ei = edot[i1:i2,];
      bmat = bmat + xi`*ei*ei`*xi;
```

```
end;

/* robust with no df correction */
robust0 = inv(xdot`*xdot)*bmat*inv(xdot`*xdot);

/* robust with DF correction for cluster covariance matrix */
robust1 = (n/(n-1))*((n*t)/(n*t-ks))
        *inv(xdot`*xdot)*bmat*inv(xdot`*xdot);

se = sqrt(vecdiag(robust0));
tstat = bfe/se;
pval =2*(1-probt(abs(tstat),n*t-n-ks));
result = bfe||se||tstat||pval;
cname = {est se tstat pval};
print / "Fixed Effects with robust se-No DF correction",,
        result [rowname=parmname colname=cname format=13.7];
se = sqrt(vecdiag(robust1));
tstat = bfe/se;
pval =2*(1-probt(abs(tstat),n*t-n-ks));
result = bfe||se||tstat||pval;
cname = {est se tstat pval};
print / "Fixed Effects with robust se-DF correction",,
        result [rowname=parmname colname=cname format=13.7];
finish;
run robust_fe;
quit;
```

[fixed effects with usual standard errors omitted]

Fixed Effects with robust se-No DF correction

	result			
	EST	SE	TSTAT	PVAL
EXPER	0.0410832	0.0082278	4.9932446	0.0000006
EXPER2	-0.0004091	0.0003294	-1.2417730	0.2144222
TENURE	0.0139089	0.0042089	3.3046160	0.0009628
TENURE2	-0.0008962	0.0002491	-3.5973602	0.0003269
SOUTH	-0.0163224	0.0583902	-0.2795402	0.7798505
UNION	0.0636972	0.0168346	3.7837043	0.0001577

Fixed Effects with robust se-DF correction

	result			
	EST	SE	TSTAT	PVAL
EXPER	0.0410832	0.0082404	4.9855733	0.0000007
EXPER2	-0.0004091	0.0003299	-1.2398652	0.2151270
TENURE	0.0139089	0.0042154	3.2995391	0.0009803
TENURE2	-0.0008962	0.0002495	-3.5918335	0.0003339
SOUTH	-0.0163224	0.0584800	-0.2791108	0.7801800
UNION	0.0636972	0.0168605	3.7778913	0.0001614

APPENDIX 15D THE HAUSMAN-TAYLOR ESTIMATOR

The **Hausman-Taylor estimator** is an instrumental variables estimator applied to the random effects model, to overcome the problem of inconsistency caused by correlation between the random effects and some of the explanatory variables. This model is discussed in *Principles of Econometrics, 4th Edition*, Chapter 15.6. To explain how it works consider the regression model

$$y_{it} = \beta_1 + \beta_2 x_{it,exog} + \beta_3 x_{it,endog} + \beta_3 w_{i,exog} + \beta_4 w_{i,endog} + u_i + e_{it}$$

We have divided the explanatory variables into 4 categories:

$x_{it,exog}$: exogenous variables that vary over time and individuals

$x_{it,endog}$: endogenous variables that vary over time and individuals

$w_{i,exog}$: time-invariant exogenous variables

$w_{i,endog}$: time-invariant endogenous variables

The model equation is written as if there is one variable of each type, but in practice there could be more than one. For the Hausman-Taylor estimator to work the number of exogenous time-varying variables $(x_{it,exog})$ must be at least as great as the number of endogenous time-invariant variables $(w_{i,endog})$.

For the wage equation we will make the following assumptions

$$x_{it,exog} = \{EXPER, EXPER2, TENURE, TENURE2, UNION\}$$
$$x_{it,endog} = \{SOUTH\}$$
$$w_{i,exog} = \{BLACK\}$$
$$w_{i,endog} = \{EDUC\}$$

Following Chapter 10, we need instruments for $x_{it,endog}$ and $w_{i,endog}$. Since the fixed effects transformation $\tilde{x}_{it,endog} = x_{it,endog} - \overline{x}_{i,endog}$ eliminates correlation with u_i, we have $\tilde{x}_{it,endog}$ as a suitable instrument for $x_{it,endog}$. Also, the variables $\overline{x}_{i,exog}$ are suitable instruments for $w_{i,endog}$. The exogenous variables can be viewed as instruments for themselves, making the complete instrument set $x_{it,exog}$, $\tilde{x}_{it,endog}$, $w_{i,exog}$, $\overline{x}_{i,exog}$. Hausman and Taylor modify this set slightly using $\tilde{x}_{it,exog}$, $\tilde{x}_{it,endog}$, $w_{i,exog}$, $\overline{x}_{i,exog}$ which can be shown to yield the same results. Their estimator is applied to the partially demeaned data used for the random effects, generalized least squares, model

$$y_{it}^* = \beta_1 + \beta_2 x_{it,exog}^* + \beta_3 x_{it,endog}^* + \beta_3 w_{i,exog}^* + \beta_4 w_{i,endog}^* + v_{it}^*$$

where, for example, $y_{it}^* = y_{it} - \hat{\alpha}\overline{y}_i$, and $\hat{\alpha} = 1 - \hat{\sigma}_e / \sqrt{T\hat{\sigma}_u^2 + \hat{\sigma}_e^2}$. The estimate $\hat{\sigma}_e^2$ is obtained from fixed-effects residuals; an auxiliary instrumental variables regression[2] is needed to find $\hat{\sigma}_u^2$.

To illustrate we use the data *nls*.

[2] Details can be found in Greene (2012, pp. 394-398). Our steps follow documentation for XTHTAYLOR in Stata 11.

```
proc iml;
start xthtaylor;
use nls;
t = 5;                              * t = number of years;
n = 716;                            * n = number of individuals;
```

Form the various data matrices.

```
read all into y var{lwage};

/* time varying (TV) exogenous */
read all into x1 var{exper exper2 tenure tenure2 union};

/* time varying (TV) endogenous */
read all into x2 var{south};

/* time invariant (TI) exogenous */
read all into z1 var{black};

/* time invariant (TI) endogenous */
read all into z2 var{educ};
```

The estimates names are in the order: TV exog, TV endog, TI exogenous, const, TI endog. Note that the constant term is a time-invariant exogenous variable.

```
htname ={exper exper2 tenure tenure2 union south const black educ };
```

Below this point the code is automatic. Define some constants.

```
k1 = ncol(x1);
k2 = ncol(x2);
z1 = j(n*t,1,1)||z1;                * add constant;
g1 = ncol(z1);
g2 = ncol(z2);
```

Create time averages.

```
ybar = j(n,1,0);                    * y-bar storage vector;
jt = j(t,1,1);                      * column of ones;
x1bar = j(n,k1,0);                  * x1-bar storage vector;
x2bar = j(n,k2,0);                  * x2-bar storage vector;
z1bar = j(n,g1,0);                  * z1-bar storage vector;
z2bar = j(n,g2,0);                  * z2-bar storage vector;

do ind = 1 to n;                    * loop through firm data;
      first = (ind - 1)*t + 1;           * firm obs # 1;
      last = ind*t;                      * firm obs # T;
      ybar[ind,] = jt`*y[first:last,]/t;      * y-bar;
      x1bar[ind,] = jt`*x1[first:last,]/t;    * x1-bar;
```

```
              x2bar[ind,] = jt`*x2[first:last,]/t;    * x2-bar;
              z1bar[ind,] = jt`*z1[first:last,]/t;    * z1-bar;
              z2bar[ind,] = jt`*z2[first:last,]/t;    * z2-bar;
        end;                                          * end loop;
```

Obtain the within (fixed effects estimates). This is Greene (2012, p. 396) step 1.

```
        ytilde = y - ybar@jt;                  * fractional differences;
        x1tilde = x1 - x1bar@jt;
        x2tilde = x2 - x2bar@jt;
        xtilde = x1tilde||x2tilde;
        bfe = inv(xtilde`*xtilde)*xtilde`*ytilde;* FE estimator;
        etilde = ytilde - xtilde*bfe;          * FE residuals;
        sig2e = (etilde`*etilde)/(n*t-n);      * var(eit) no df correction;
```

Step 2 in Greene (2012, p. 396) is also described in Stata 11 XTHTAYLOR documentation.

```
        xbar = (x1bar@jt)||(x2bar@jt);         * X-bar with nt rows;
        dit = (ybar@jt)-xbar*bfe;              * residuals;
        z = z1||z2;                            * time invariant;
        w = x1||z1;                            * instruments;
        zhat = w*inv(w`*w)*w`*z;               * first stage;
        dhat = inv(zhat`*zhat)*zhat`*dit;      * second stage;
        x = x1||x2;                            * time varying;
        eit = y - x*bfe -z*dhat;               * eit p. 176;

        /* time average these residuals */
        ebar = j(n,1,0);
        do ind = 1 to n;                       * loop through individual data;
                first = (ind - 1)*t + 1;       * obs # 1;
                last = ind*t;                  * obs # T;
                ebar[ind,] = jt`*eit[first:last,]/t;    * e-bar;
        end;
```

Step 3 in Greene (2012, p. 396) is to obtain the variance components. See Stata 11 XTHTAYLOR documentation pp. 176-177.

```
        s2 = (t/n)*sum(ebar##2);               * s^2 p. 176;
        sigmu2 = (s2-sig2e)/t;                 * sig_mu^2 p. 177;
        theta = 1 - (sig2e/(sig2e+t*sigmu2))##.5;    * theta p. 177;
        sige = sqrt(sig2e);
        sigmu = sqrt(sigmu2);
```

Create fractional differences and instruments.

```
        ystar = y - theta*(ybar@jt);
        x1star = x1 - theta*(x1bar@jt);
        x2star = x2 - theta*(x2bar@jt);
        z1star = z1 - theta*(z1bar@jt);
        z2star = z2 - theta*(z2bar@jt);
```

```
      xstar = x1star||x2star;
      zstar = z1star||z2star;
      z = xstar||zstar;                         * transformed regressors;
      w = xtilde||(x1bar@jt)||z1;               * HT instruments;
```

Carry out IV estimation.

```
      zhat = w*inv(w`*w)*w`*z;                  * first stage;
      bht = inv(zhat`*zhat)*zhat`*ystar;        * second stage;
      eiv = ystar - z*bht;                      * 2sls resid;
      sig2iv = (eiv`*eiv)/(n*t-ncol(z));        * 2sls sig^2;
      covbiv = sig2iv*inv(zhat`*zhat);          * cov(biv);
      sebiv = sqrt(vecdiag(covbiv));            * standard errors;
      tval = bht/sebiv;
      pval = 2*(1-probt(abs(tval),n*t-ncol(z)));

      result = bht||sebiv||tval||pval;
      cname = {est se tstat pval};

      print / "Hausman Taylor Model Estimates" ,,
            result [rowname=htname colname=cname format=13.5];

      print ,, "Variance components and theta", sige sigmu theta;

      finish;                                   * finish module;
  run xthtaylor;                                * run module;
  quit;                                         * quit iml;
```

```
             Hausman Taylor Model Estimates

                          result
                  EST          SE        TSTAT         PVAL
   EXPER       0.03991     0.00647      6.16382      0.00000
   EXPER2     -0.00039     0.00027     -1.46222      0.14377
   TENURE      0.01433     0.00316      4.53388      0.00001
   TENURE2    -0.00085     0.00020     -4.31885      0.00002
   UNION       0.07197     0.01345      5.34910      0.00000
   SOUTH      -0.03171     0.03485     -0.91003      0.36287
   CONST      -0.75077     0.58624     -1.28066      0.20040
   BLACK      -0.03591     0.06007     -0.59788      0.54996
   EDUC        0.17051     0.04446      3.83485      0.00013

              Variance components and theta
                  sige      sigmu       theta
              0.1949059   0.44987   0.8097825
```

CHAPTER 16

Qualitative and Limited Dependent Variable Models

16.1 MODELS WITH BINARY DEPENDENT VARIABLES

In a binary choice model a decision-maker chooses between two mutually exclusive outcomes. We will illustrate **binary choice models** using an important problem from transportation economics. How can we explain an individual's choice between driving (private transportation) and taking the bus (public transportation) when commuting to work, assuming, for simplicity, that these are the only two alternatives? We represent an individual's choice by the dummy variable

$$y = \begin{cases} 1 & \text{individual drives to work} \\ 0 & \text{individual takes bus to work} \end{cases}$$

If we collect a random sample of workers who commute to work, then the outcome y will be unknown to us until the sample is drawn. Thus, y is a random variable. If the probability that an individual drives to work is p, then $P[y=1]=p$. It follows that the probability that a person uses public transportation is $P[y=0]=1-p$. The probability function for such a binary random variable is

$$f(y) = p^y (1-p)^{1-y}, \quad y = 0,1$$

where p is the probability that y takes the value 1. This discrete random variable has expected value $E(y) = p$ and variance $\text{var}(y) = p(1-p)$.

What factors might affect the probability that an individual chooses one transportation mode over the other? One factor will certainly be how long it takes to get to work one way or the other. Define the explanatory variable

$$x = \text{(commuting time by bus – commuting time by car)}$$

There are other factors that affect the decision, but let us focus on this single explanatory variable. *A priori* we expect that as x increases, and commuting time by bus increases relative to commuting time by car, an individual would be more inclined to drive. That is, we expect a positive relationship between x and p, the probability that an individual will drive to work.

16.1.1 The linear probability model

The linear regression model for explaining the choice variable y, is called the **linear probability model**. It is given by

$$y = E(y) + e = \beta_1 + \beta_2 x + e$$

One problem with the linear probability model is that the error term is heteroskedastic; the variance of the error term e varies from one observation to another. The variance of the error term e is

$$\text{var}(e) = (\beta_1 + \beta_2 x)(1 - \beta_1 - \beta_2 x)$$

If we adopt the linear probability model we should use generalized least squares estimation. This is generally done by first estimating the linear probability model by least squares, then the estimated variance of the error term is

$$\hat{\sigma}_i^2 = \widehat{\text{var}(e_i)} = (b_1 + b_2 x_i)(1 - b_1 - b_2 x_i)$$

Using this estimated variance the data can be transformed as $y_i^* = y_i/\hat{\sigma}_i$ and $x_i^* = x_i/\hat{\sigma}_i$, then the model $y_i^* = \beta_1 \hat{\sigma}_i^{-1} + \beta_2 x_i^* + e_i^*$ is estimated by least squares, to produce the **feasible generalized least squares** estimates. Both least squares and feasible generalized least squares are consistent estimators of the regression parameters.

In practice certain difficulties may arise with the implementation of this procedure. They are related to another problem with the linear probability model – that of obtaining probability values that are less than 0 or greater than 1. Values like these do not make sense as probabilities, and we are left in a difficult situation. It also means that some of the estimated variances may be negative. The standard fix-up is to set negative predicted values to a small value like .001, and values greater than one to .999. Making these changes will not hurt in large samples.

To implement these ideas in SAS we first read in the data, examine the contents and means.

```
data transport;                          * read transport data;
set 'transport';
run;


proc contents;                           * examine contents;
title 'contents of transport data';
run;
```

```
              Alphabetic List of Variables and Attributes

#    Variable    Type    Len    Label

4    auto        Num     8      = 1 if auto chosen
1    autotime    Num     8      commute time via auto, minutes
2    bustime     Num     8      commute time via bus, minutes
3    dtime       Num     8      = (bus time - auto time)/10, 10 minute units
```

```
options nolabel;
proc means;                                   * summary statistics;
title 'summary stats transport data';
run;
```

```
                    summary stats transport data

                        The MEANS Procedure

Variable    N        Mean        Std Dev       Minimum       Maximum
─────────────────────────────────────────────────────────────────────
autotime    21    49.3476190    32.4349136    0.2000000    99.1000000
bustime     21    48.1238095    34.6308230    1.6000000    91.5000000
dtime       21    -0.1223810     5.6910367   -9.0700000     9.1000000
auto        21     0.4761905     0.5117663            0     1.0000000
─────────────────────────────────────────────────────────────────────
```

Least squares estimation of the linear probability model uses **PROC REG** with robust standard errors. Predicted values are output for following generalized least squares estimation. Note in this case that the robust standard error is smaller than the usual standard error.

```
proc reg data=transport;
model auto=dtime/clb hcc hccmethod=1;   * using robust se;
title 'linear probability model with robust se';
output out=lpmout p=p;                  * output predicted prob;
run;
```

```
                    Parameter      Standard
Variable     DF     Estimate         Error     t Value    Pr > |t|
Intercept     1      0.48480        0.07145       6.79      <.0001
dtime         1      0.07031        0.01286       5.47      <.0001
```

```
              --Heteroscedasticity Consistent-
                    Standard
Variable    DF       Error    t Value    Pr > |t|    95% Confidence Limits
Intercept    1      0.07120     6.81      <.0001      0.33525      0.63434
dtime        1      0.00851     8.26      <.0001      0.04339      0.09723
```

```
                           Heteroscedasticity Consistent
            Variable    DF       95% Confidence Limits
            Intercept    1      0.33576      0.63383
            dtime        1      0.05250      0.08812
```

To implement generalized least squares, first, note that some predictions are outside the feasible range.

```
proc print data=lpmout;                 * print predicted;
title 'predictions linear probability model';
run;
```

The output for selected observations is

```
Obs    autotime    bustime    dtime    auto       p
 3        4.1        86.9       8.28      1    1.06696
 6        0.2        91.2       9.10      1    1.12462
 8       89.9         2.2      -8.77      0   -0.13182
11       99.1         8.4      -9.07      0   -0.15292
20       95.1        22.2      -7.29      0   -0.02776
```

Prior to the GLS transformation we "adjust" the infeasible values. The estimated variance in equation (16.6) is computed and the weighting variable is its reciprocal.

```
data gls;                                * read predicted values;
set lpmout;
if p<0 then p=.001;                      * set negative to .001;
if p>1 then p=.999;                      * set > 1 to .999;
sig2 = p*(1-p);                          * var(phat);
w = 1/sig2;                              * weight is variance reciprocal;
run;
```

Such a fix-up results in a small estimated variance and a large weight in the GLS estimation relative to other observations.

```
proc print data=gls;                     * print transformed data;
title 'cleaned GLS data';
run;
```

```
                         cleaned GLS data

Obs    autotime    bustime    dtime    auto       p         sig2         w
 3        4.1        86.9       8.28      1    0.99900     0.00100    1001.00
 6        0.2        91.2       9.10      1    0.99900     0.00100    1001.00
 8       89.9         2.2      -8.77      0    0.00100     0.00100    1001.00
11       99.1         8.4      -9.07      0    0.00100     0.00100    1001.00
20       95.1        22.2      -7.29      0    0.00100     0.00100    1001.00
```

```
proc reg data=gls;
model auto=dtime/clb;
weight w;
title 'GLS for linear probability model';
run;
```

Compare these point and interval estimates to the least squares estimates.

Variable	DF	Parameter Estimate	Standard Error	t Value	Pr > |t|
Intercept	1	0.49091	0.01442	34.04	<.0001
dtime	1	0.05845	0.00170	34.29	<.0001

Variable	DF	95% Confidence Limits	
Intercept	1	0.46072	0.52109
dtime	1	0.05488	0.06202

16.1.2 The probit model

To keep the choice probability p within the interval $[0,1]$ a nonlinear S-shaped relationship between x and p can be used. The *slope* of this curve gives the change in probability given a unit change in x. The probit statistical model expresses the probability p that y takes the value 1 to be

$$p = P[Z \leq \beta_1 + \beta_2 x] = \Phi(\beta_1 + \beta_2 x)$$

where $\Phi(z)$ is cumulative distribution function of the standard normal random variable. Because this model is nonlinear in the parameters maximum likelihood estimation is used. The properties of maximum likelihood estimators are discussed in book Appendix C, and details related to the probit model are given in Appendix 16A of this chapter. In this model we can examine the effect of a one unit change in x on the probability that $y = 1$, which is known as the **marginal effect** of x, using the derivative,

$$\frac{dp}{dx} = \phi(\beta_1 + \beta_2 x)\beta_2$$

where $\phi(\beta_1 + \beta_2 x)$ is the standard normal probability density function evaluated at $\beta_1 + \beta_2 x$. In order to predict the probability that an individual chooses the alternative $y = 1$ we can estimate the probability p to be

$$\hat{p} = \Phi(\tilde{\beta}_1 + \tilde{\beta}_2 x)$$

where we have replaced the unknown parameters by their estimated values. By comparing to a threshold value, like 0.5, we can predict choice using the rule

$$\hat{y} = \begin{cases} 1 & \hat{p} > 0.5 \\ 0 & \hat{p} \leq 0.5 \end{cases}$$

The probit model is estimated in SAS using **PROC QLIM**, where "QLIM" stands for "Qualitative" and "Limited" dependent variable models. To see all the wonderful models this procedure can estimate enter "**help qlim**" in the SAS command line

Read the "Overview" section. To estimate a probit model we add the option **discrete** to the model statement.

```
proc qlim data=transport;            * proc qlim;
model auto=dtime/discrete;           * discrete for probit;
output out=probitout xbeta marginal; * output;
title 'probit';
run;
```

The output contains several sections. The first summarizes the outcome variable and items related to the maximization of the log-likelihood function. These will not mean much to you now, but details of the estimation are given in an appendix to this chapter.

```
               The QLIM Procedure
          Discrete Response Profile of auto
                                      Total
       Index        Value        Frequency
         1            0              11
         2            1              10
```

```
                    Model Fit Summary

    Number of Endogenous Variables          1
    Endogenous Variable                  auto
    Number of Observations                 21
    Log Likelihood                   -6.16516
    Maximum Absolute Gradient      9.85945E-7
    Number of Iterations                    9
    Optimization Method         Quasi-Newton
    AIC                              16.33032
    Schwarz Criterion                18.41936
```

The second section provides various "R^2-like" measures. They do not have the same interpretation as R^2 in a regression model and we advise in general that they not be reported. For more on their calculation enter **help qlim** into the SAS command line, then select **Details: QLIM Procedure > Ordinal Discrete Choice Modeling > Goodness-of-Fit Measures.** Perhaps the most useful of these numbers is the value of the **Likelihood Ratio (R)** which is the value of the likelihood ratio test of overall model significance, somewhat analogous to the overall F-test statistic in a regression model. It is a test that all the variable coefficients are zero, except the intercept.

```
                 Goodness-of-Fit Measures

Measure                   Value    Formula
Likelihood Ratio (R)     16.734    2 * (LogL - LogL0)
Upper Bound of R (U)     29.065    - 2 * LogL0
Aldrich-Nelson           0.4435    R / (R+N)
Cragg-Uhler 1            0.5493    1 - exp(-R/N)
Cragg-Uhler 2            0.7329    (1-exp(-R/N)) / (1-exp(-U/N))
Estrella                 0.6948    1 - (1-R/U)^(U/N)
Adjusted Estrella        0.5497    1 - ((LogL-K)/LogL0)^(-2/N*LogL0)
McFadden's LRI           0.5758    R / U
Veall-Zimmermann         0.7639    (R * (U+N)) / (U * (R+N))
McKelvey-Zavoina         0.7352
```

The parameter estimates themselves are reported in the usual way. The standard error is derived from the asymptotic variance formula for maximum likelihood estimators. See Appendix 16A.1 for explicit formulas.

```
                                  Standard              Approx
Parameter    DF    Estimate         Error    t Value   Pr > |t|
Intercept     1   -0.064434      0.399244     -0.16     0.8718
dtime         1    0.299990      0.102869      2.92     0.0035
```

The output statement **output out=probitout xbeta marginal;** writes to the SAS dataset *probitout* the data and three additional quantities. Print a few observations.

```
proc print data=probitout (obs=5);
title 'probit output';
run;
```

probit output

Obs	autotime	bustime	dtime	auto	Xbeta_ auto	Meff_P1_ dtime	Meff_P2_ dtime
1	52.9	4.4	-4.85	0	-1.51938	-0.037733	0.037733
2	4.1	28.5	2.44	0	0.66754	-0.095775	0.095775
3	4.1	86.9	8.28	1	2.41948	-0.006410	0.006410
4	56.2	31.6	-2.46	0	-0.80241	-0.086737	0.086737
5	51.8	20.2	-3.16	0	-1.01240	-0.071689	0.071689

The option **xbeta** produces the output item *XBETA_AUTO*. It is $\tilde{\beta}_1 + \tilde{\beta}_2 x$ for each observation, where $\tilde{\beta}_1 = -0.064434$ is the estimated intercept parameter and $\tilde{\beta}_2 = 0.29999$. This quantity can be used to estimate the predicted probability for each observation. The variables *MEFF_P1_DTIME* and *MEFF_P2_DTIME* result from the option **marginal** and are discussed below.

Using the variable *XBETA_AUTO* we can compute the predicted probability that $y = 1$ (person drives) and plot these values against *DTIME*. This probability is $\hat{p} = \Phi(\tilde{\beta}_1 + \tilde{\beta}_2 x)$. The cdf of the standard normal random variable is computed by SAS using the function **probnorm**.

```
data transport2;
set probitout;
p_auto = probnorm(xbeta_auto);        * evaluate estimated prob;
phat = (p_auto >= .5);                * phat = 1 if p >= .5;
run;
```

Sort the data by *DTIME* and print the predicted values.

```
proc sort data=transport2;
by dtime;
run;

proc print data=transport2;
title 'probit predictions';
run;
```

probit predictions

Obs	autotime	bustime	dtime	auto	Xbeta_ auto	Meff_P1_ dtime	Meff_P2_ dtime	p_auto	phat
1	99.1	8.4	-9.07	0	-2.78534	-0.00247	0.00247	0.00267	0
2	89.9	2.2	-8.77	0	-2.69534	-0.00317	0.00317	0.00352	0
3	95.1	22.2	-7.29	0	-2.25136	-0.00949	0.00949	0.01218	0
19	18.5	84.0	6.55	1	1.90050	-0.01967	0.01967	0.97132	1
20	4.1	86.9	8.28	1	2.41948	-0.00641	0.00641	0.99223	1
21	0.2	91.2	9.10	1	2.66547	-0.00343	0.00343	0.99616	1

Note that none of the predicted probabilities *P_AUTO* is outside the unit interval. Now plot the predicted probabilities against *DTIME*.

```
symbol1 value=dot color=blue interpol=join;
proc gplot data=transport2;
plot p_auto * dtime=1;
title 'probit predictions';
run;
```

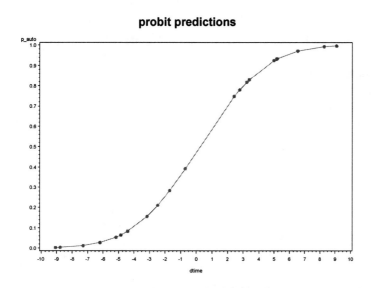

As the magnitude of the variable *DTIME* increases, the probability of a person driving increases from zero to one. The slope of this curve is the increase in probability given a 1-minute increase in *DTIME*. It is called the **marginal effect** of *DTIME* and changes at every point. It can be calculated at a representative value or it can be calculated for each value in the sample and averaged. The output variables *MEFF_P1_DTIME* and *MEFF_P2_DTIME* are, respectively, for each observation the change in probability that $y = 0$ and $y = 1$. Use **PROC MEANS** to compute the average and standard deviation.

```
proc means data=transport2;
var meff_p1_dtime meff_p2_dtime;
title 'average probit marginal effects';
run;
```

average probit marginal effects

The MEANS Procedure

Variable	N	Mean	Std Dev	Minimum	Maximum
Meff_P1_dtime	21	-0.0484069	0.0364573	-0.1152559	-0.0024738
Meff_P2_dtime	21	0.0484069	0.0364573	0.0024738	0.1152559

Across the sample the "average" marginal effect of one additional minute of travel time via bus increases the probability of auto travel by 0.0484 with standard deviation 0.0365.

16.1.3 The logit model

An alternative to the probit model is called **logit**. In the logit model the probability p that the observed value y takes the value 1 is

$$p = P[L \leq \beta_1 + \beta_2 x] = \Lambda(\beta_1 + \beta_2 x) = \frac{1}{1 + e^{-(\beta_1 + \beta_2 x)}}$$

This probability formulation is somewhat simpler to work with because there is no integral as in the probit formulation. The logit model adds the qualifier **(d=logit)** to the **discrete** model option.

```
proc qlim data=transport;
model auto=dtime/discrete(d=logit);
output out=logitout marginal;
title 'logit estimates';
run;
```

The parameter estimates are different from the probit estimates.

Parameter	DF	Estimate	Standard Error	t Value	Approx Pr > |t|
Intercept	1	-0.237575	0.750477	-0.32	0.7516
dtime	1	0.531098	0.206425	2.57	0.0101

However, the marginal effects are very similar for probit and logit.

```
proc means data=logitout;
var meff_p1_dtime meff_p2_dtime;
title 'logit average marginal effects';
run;
```

```
                logit average marginal effects

                     The MEANS Procedure
```

Variable	N	Mean	Std Dev	Minimum	Maximum
Meff_P1_dtime	21	-0.0461540	0.0371525	-0.1211742	-0.0033454
Meff_P2_dtime	21	0.0461540	0.0371525	0.0033454	0.1211742

16.1.4 A labor force participation model

An example that illustrates the use of probit is based on Thomas Mroz's (1987) study of married women's labor force participation and wages. The data are in the SAS data set *mroz* and consist of 753 observations on married women. Of these 325 did not work outside the home, and thus had no hours worked and no reported wages. Can we explain the choice to participate in the labor force? Open the data set, examine the contents and summary statistics.

```
options label;
data mroz;                              * mroz data;
set 'mroz';
run;
proc contents data=mroz position;      * contents;
title 'mroz data contents';
run;

options nolabel;
proc means data=mroz;                   * summary stats;
var lfp educ exper age kidsl6 kids618;
title 'mroz summary stats';
run;
```

mroz summary stats

The MEANS Procedure

Variable	N	Mean	Std Dev	Minimum	Maximum
LFP	753	0.5683931	0.4956295	0	1.0000000
EDUC	753	12.2868526	2.2802458	5.0000000	17.0000000
EXPER	753	10.6308101	8.0691299	0	45.0000000
AGE	753	42.5378486	8.0725740	30.0000000	60.0000000
KIDSL6	753	0.2377158	0.5239590	0	3.0000000
KIDS618	753	1.3532537	1.3198739	0	8.0000000

Estimate a probit model explaining the labor force choice using the woman's years of education, experience, age, and two dummy variables: one for children at home who are less than 6 years old, and one for children who are between 6-18 years of age. Using a **test** statement we can test whether the presence of children is a significant factor in the choice. The option "/ **LR**" requests a likelihood ratio test. Twice the difference between the log-likelihood function values from the full and restricted models (with *KIDSL6* and *KIDS618* omitted) has a chi-square distribution with 2 degrees of freedom (the number of hypotheses) if the null hypothesis is true.

```
proc qlim data=mroz;
model lfp = educ exper age kidsl6 kids618/discrete;
kids: test kidsl6=0,kids618=0/ LR;
output out=lfpout marginal;
title 'probit model for labor force participation';
run;
```

Parameter	DF	Estimate	Standard Error	t Value	Approx Pr > |t|
Intercept	1	0.703693	0.492194	1.43	0.1528
EDUC	1	0.113243	0.023496	4.82	<.0001
EXPER	1	0.073850	0.007431	9.94	<.0001
AGE	1	-0.058856	0.008222	-7.16	<.0001
KIDSL6	1	-0.867717	0.116483	-7.45	<.0001
KIDS618	1	0.029130	0.042937	0.68	0.4975

```
                          Test Results

Test              Type         Statistic   Pr > ChiSq   Label
KIDS              L.R.           65.01       <.0001      kids16   =   0 ,
                                                         kids618  =   0
```

The parameter estimates show that education and experience have significant positive effects on the decision to join the labor force. Age and children less than 6 have a negative and significant effect. The presence of older children is not significant in this model. The joint hypothesis test shows that the two variables indicating children presence are jointly significant.

The marginal effects are relevant for continuous variables.

```
proc means data=lfpout;
var meff_p2_educ meff_p2_exper meff_p2_age;
title 'probit average marginal effects';
run;
```

                    probit average marginal effects

                         The MEANS Procedure

Variable	N	Mean	Std Dev	Minimum	Maximum
Meff_P2_EDUC	753	0.0348235	0.0102581	0.0033155	0.0451769
Meff_P2_EXPER	753	0.0227096	0.0066897	0.0021621	0.0294614
Meff_P2_AGE	753	-0.0180990	0.0053315	-0.0234800	-0.0017232

We estimate that, on average, another year of education increases the probability of a woman working by 0.035, holding other factors constant.

Because the number of children is a discrete variable, the probability effect of another child must be computed as a discrete change in probability. Compute, for example, the probability of a woman working who has 12 years of education, 10 years of experience, is 35 years of age, has 1 child less than 6, and has 1 child between 6 and 18. Subtract the probability of the same woman working if she has 2 children less than 6.

```
data kids;
educ = 12;
exper = 10;
age = 35;
kids16 = 1;
kids618 = 1;
dp = probnorm(0.703693+0.113243*educ+0.073850
        *exper-0.058856*age-0.867717*kids16+0.029130*kids618)
- probnorm(0.703693+0.113243*educ+0.073850
        *exper-0.058856*age-0.867717*(kids16+1)+0.029130*kids618);
run;
proc print data=kids;
var dp;
title 'effect of additional small child on labor force participation';
run;
```

We find that the difference in the probability, of having one small child at home rather than two, is 0.29396.

16.2 PROBIT FOR CONSUMER CHOICE

We use the choice between Coke and Pepsi as an example to illustrate more about the linear probability model and probit model for binary choice. Open the data file *coke*, create an *ID* variable and examine its contents.

```
options label;
data coke;
set 'coke';
run;

proc contents data=coke position;
title 'coke data contents';
run;
options nolabel;
```

```
                  Variables in Creation Order

# Variable   Type Len Label
1 coke       Num    8 =1 if coke chosen, =0 if pepsi chosen
2 pr_pepsi   Num    8 price of 2 liter bottle of pepsi
3 pr_coke    Num    8 price of 2 liter bottle of coke
4 disp_      Num    8 = 1 if pepsi is displayed at time
  pepsi               of purchase, otherwise = 0
5 disp_coke  Num    8 = 1 if coke is displayed at time
                      of purchase, otherwise = 0
6 pratio     Num    8 price coke relative to price pepsi
```

The variable *COKE*

$$COKE = \begin{cases} 1 & \text{if Coke is chosen} \\ 0 & \text{if Pepsi is chosen} \end{cases}$$

The expected value of this variable is $E(COKE) = P(COKE = 1) = p_{COKE}$ probability that Coke is chosen. As explanatory variables we use the relative price of Coke to Pepsi (*PRATIO*), as well as *DISP_COKE* and *DISP_PEPSI*, which are indicator variables taking the value 1 if the respective store display is present and 0 if it is not present. We expect that the presence of a Coke display will increase the probability of a Coke purchase, and the presence of a Pepsi display will decrease the probability of a Coke purchase.

The cumulative distribution function for a logistic random variable is

$$\Lambda(l) = P[L \le l] = \frac{1}{1 + e^{-l}}$$

In the logit model the probability p that the observed value y takes the value 1 is

$$p = P\left[L \le \beta_1 + \beta_2 x\right] = \Lambda\left(\beta_1 + \beta_2 x\right) = \frac{1}{1 + e^{-(\beta_1 + \beta_2 x)}}$$

The probit and logit models for the choice are the same except for the cumulative distribution function. The two models are

$$p_{COKE} = E\left(COKE\right) = \Phi\left(\beta_1 + \beta_2 PRATIO + \beta_3 DISP\_COKE + \beta_4 DISP\_PEPSI\right)$$

$$p_{COKE} = E\left(COKE\right) = \Lambda\left(\gamma_1 + \gamma_2 PRATIO + \gamma_3 DISP\_COKE + \gamma_4 DISP\_PEPSI\right)$$

Let us examine the alternative models and model results obtained using logit, probit, and the linear probability model. Begin with the linear probability model. Use **PROC REG** with robust standard errors. Save the estimates for later and obtain the linear predictions.

```
proc reg data=coke;
model coke = pratio disp_coke disp_pepsi / hcc hccmethod=1;
title 'linear probability model for coke choice';
run;
```

Variable	DF	Parameter Estimate	Standard Error	t Value	Pr > |t|
Intercept	1	0.89022	0.06548	13.59	<.0001
pratio	1	-0.40086	0.06135	-6.53	<.0001
disp_coke	1	0.07717	0.03439	2.24	0.0250
disp_pepsi	1	-0.16566	0.03560	-4.65	<.0001

Variable	DF	---Heteroscedasticity Consistent-- Standard Error	t Value	Pr > |t|
Intercept	1	0.06530	13.63	<.0001
pratio	1	0.06037	-6.64	<.0001
disp_coke	1	0.03393	2.27	0.0231
disp_pepsi	1	0.03436	-4.82	<.0001

Obtain the probit estimates and output the marginal effects and predicted values of the outcome variable.

```
proc qlim data=coke;
model coke = pratio disp_coke disp_pepsi / discrete;
output out=probitout marginal predicted;
title 'probit estimates for coke choice';
run;
```

The (**edited**) output is

```
                    Model Fit Summary
            Number of Observations              1140
            Log Likelihood               -710.94858
```

Parameter	DF	Estimate	Standard Error	t Value	Approx Pr > |t|
Intercept	1	1.108060	0.189959	5.83	<.0001
pratio	1	-1.145963	0.180883	-6.34	<.0001
disp_coke	1	0.217187	0.096608	2.25	0.0246
disp_pepsi	1	-0.447297	0.101403	-4.41	<.0001

The marginal effects are

```
proc means data=probitout;
var meff_p1_pratio meff_p2_pratio;
title 'probit average marginal effects';
run;
```

                    probit average marginal effects

                        The MEANS Procedure

Variable	N	Mean	Std Dev	Minimum	Maximum
Meff_P1_pratio	1140	0.4096951	0.0667242	0.0614731	0.4569719
Meff_P2_pratio	1140	-0.4096951	0.0667242	-0.4569719	-0.0614731

The consequence of the output option **predicted** is a variable *P_coke* that is 1 or 0 depending on whether the predicted probability is less than, or greater than, 0.5. We define a success when we predict that a person chose coke when that was actually true, or that they chose pepsi when they did choose pepsi. We have a success when *P_coke = COKE*.

```
data predict;
set probitout;
success = (P_coke = coke);
run;

proc sort data=predict;
by coke;
run;

proc means data=predict n sum mean;
var success;
by coke;
title 'coke predictive success';
run;
```

                        coke predictive success
-------------------------------- coke=0 ----------------------------------
                        Analysis Variable : success

N	Sum	Mean
630	507.0000000	0.8047619

```
-------------------------------- coke=1 -----------------------------------
                    Analysis Variable : success

                N               Sum                Mean
             --------------------------------------------------
               510        247.0000000           0.4843137
             --------------------------------------------------
```

In this sample, 630 people chose pepsi and we correctly predicted 507 of their choices. Of the coke drinkers we correctly predicted 247 of them.

16.2.1 Wald tests

Hypothesis tests concerning individual coefficients in probit and logit models are carried out in the usual way based on an "asymptotic-t" test. If the null hypothesis is $H_0 : \beta_k = c$, then the test statistic using the probit model is

$$t = \frac{\tilde{\beta}_k - c}{\text{se}(\tilde{\beta}_k)} \overset{a}{\sim} t_{(N-K)}$$

where $\tilde{\beta}_k$ is the parameter estimator, N is the sample size, and K is the number of parameters estimated. The test is asymptotically justified, and if N is large the critical values from the $t_{(N-K)}$ distribution will be very close to those from the standard normal distribution. In smaller samples, however, the use of the t-distribution critical values can make minor differences and is the more "conservative" choice. The t-test is based on the **Wald principle**. This testing principle is discussed in *Principles of Econometrics, 4th Edition*, Appendix C.8.4b.

SAS **PROC QLIM** has a "built in" test statement that is convenient to use. The Wald test is obtained using the option **wald.** To illustrate, using the probit model, consider the two hypotheses

Hypothesis (1) $H_0 : \beta_3 = -\beta_4, \quad H_1 : \beta_3 \neq -\beta_4$

Hypothesis (2) $H_0 : \beta_3 = 0, \beta_4 = 0, \quad H_1 :$ either β_3 or β_4 is not zero

Hypothesis (1) is that the coefficients on the display variables are equal in magnitude but opposite in sign, or that the effect of the Coke and Pepsi displays are equal but opposite effect on the probability of choosing Coke. The Wald test statistic generated by SAS will be a $\chi^2_{(1)}$ statistic because one hypothesis is being tested. It will be the square of the t-statistic. Hypothesis (2) is a joint test that neither the Coke nor Pepsi display affects the probability of choosing Coke. Here we are testing 2 hypotheses, so that the Wald test statistic has an asymptotic $\chi^2_{(2)}$ distribution.

```
proc qlim data=coke;
model coke = pratio disp_coke disp_pepsi / discrete;
test 'HO: 1' disp_coke+disp_pepsi=0 / wald;
test 'HO: 2' disp_coke=0, disp_pepsi=0 / wald;
title 'probit tests for coke choice';
run;
```

```
                          Test Results

Test            Type          Statistic   Pr > ChiSq   Label
'HO: 1'         Wald               5.40       0.0201    disp_coke +
                                                        disp_pepsi = 0

'HO: 2'         Wald              19.46       <.0001    disp_coke = 0 ,
                                                        disp_pepsi = 0
```

Hypothesis (1) yields the Wald statistic 5.40, with p-value 0.0201 generated from the $\chi^2_{(1)}$ distribution. Hypothesis (2) yields the Wald statistic 19.46 with p-value < 0.0001 generated from the $\chi^2_{(2)}$ distribution. We reject both hypotheses at the 5% level.

16.2.2 Likelihood ratio tests

When using maximum likelihood estimators, such as probit and logit, tests based on the likelihood ratio principle are generally preferred. Appendix C.8.4a in *POE4* contains a discussion of this methodology. One test component is the log-likelihood function value in the unrestricted, full model (call it $\ln L_U$) evaluated at the maximum likelihood estimates. The second ingredient is the log-likelihood function value from the model that is "restricted" by imposing the condition that the null hypothesis is true (call it $\ln L_R$). The likelihood ratio test statistic is $LR = 2(\ln L_U - \ln L_R)$. If the null hypothesis is true, the statistic has an asymptotic chi-square distribution with degrees of freedom equal to the number of hypotheses being tested. The null hypothesis is rejected if the value LR is larger than the chi-square distribution critical value.

To illustrate, first the overall test of model significance. Under the null hypothesis the restricted model is $P(COKE = 1) = \Phi(\beta_1)$. SAS automatically reports this test value.

```
                  Goodness-of-Fit Measures

Measure                   Value    Formula
Likelihood Ratio (R)     145.82    2 * (LogL - LogL0)
```

We can test other hypotheses using this principle. Hypothesis (1) on the previous page is tested by first imposing the hypothesis as a restriction on the model. If this hypothesis is true then

$$P(COKE = 1) = \Phi(\beta_1 + \beta_2 PRATIO + \beta_4 (DISP\_PEPSI - DISP\_COKE))$$

Create a variable equal to the difference of displays, and estimate the resulting "restricted model.

```
data coke2;
set coke;
disp_diff = disp_pepsi-disp_coke;
run;

proc qlim data=coke2;
model:model coke = pratio disp_diff / discrete;
title 'probit restricted model for coke choice';
title2 'hypothesis 1';
run;
```

```
                         Model Fit Summary
               Log Likelihood                -713.65949
```

The test statistic is $LR = 2\left(\ln L_U - \ln L_R\right) = 2\left(-710.94858 - \left(-713.65949\right)\right) = 5.42$

To test Hypothesis (2) that the display variables are not significant, we estimate the restricted model $P\left(COKE = 1\right) = \Phi\left(\beta_1 + \beta_2 PRATIO\right)$ and repeat.

```
     proc qlim data=coke;
     model:model coke = pratio / discrete;
     title 'probit restricted model for coke choice';
     title2 'hypothesis 2';
     run;
```

```
                         Model Fit Summary
               Log Likelihood                -720.72431
```

The test statistic is $LR = 2\left(\ln L_U - \ln L_R\right) = 2\left(-710.94858 - \left(-720.72431\right)\right) = 19.55$

SAS's automatic *LR* test is obtain in **PROC QLIM** using a **test** statement with option **lr**.

```
     proc qlim data=coke;
     model coke = pratio disp_coke disp_pepsi / discrete;
     test 'HO: 1' disp_coke+disp_pepsi=0 / lr;
     test 'HO: 2' disp_coke=0, disp_pepsi=0 / lr;
     title 'probit tests for coke choice';
     run;
```

```
                         Test Results

Test        Type        Statistic   Pr > ChiSq   Label
'HO: 1'     L.R.             5.42       0.0199     disp_coke +
                                                   disp_pepsi  = 0
'HO: 2'     L.R.            19.55      <.0001      disp_coke   = 0 ,
                                                   disp_pepsi  = 0
```

16.3 MULTINOMIAL LOGIT

Multinomial logit is a choice model when there are more than two alternatives. It is specifically adapted for situations when the explanatory variables are constant across alternatives, and generally are choice-maker characteristics. Let us consider a problem with $J = 3$ alternatives. An example might be the choice facing a high school graduate. Shall I attend a 2-year college, a 4-year college, or not go to college? The factors affecting this choice might include household income, the student's high school grades, family size, race, the student's gender, and the parent's education. As in the logit and probit models, we will try to explain the probability that the ith person will choose alternative j,

$$p_{ij} = P\left[\text{individual } i \text{ chooses alternative } j\right]$$

In our example there are $J = 3$ alternatives, denoted by $j = 1, 2,$ or 3. These numerical values have no meaning because the alternatives in general have no particular ordering, and are assigned arbitrarily.

If we assume a single explanatory factor x_i that does not vary across alternatives, then the multinomial logit probabilities of individual i choosing alternatives $j = 1, 2, 3$ are:

$$p_{i1} = \frac{1}{1 + \exp(\beta_{12} + \beta_{22}x_i) + \exp(\beta_{13} + \beta_{23}x_i)} \, , \quad j = 1$$

$$p_{i2} = \frac{\exp(\beta_{12} + \beta_{22}x_i)}{1 + \exp(\beta_{12} + \beta_{22}x_i) + \exp(\beta_{13} + \beta_{23}x_i)} \, , \quad j = 2$$

$$p_{i3} = \frac{\exp(\beta_{13} + \beta_{23}x_i)}{1 + \exp(\beta_{12} + \beta_{22}x_i) + \exp(\beta_{13} + \beta_{23}x_i)} \, , \quad j = 3$$

The parameters β_{12} and β_{22} are specific to the 2nd alternative, and β_{13} and β_{23} are specific to the 3rd alternative. The parameters specific to the first alternative are set to zero to solve an **identification problem**, and to make the probabilities sum to one. Setting $\beta_{11} = \beta_{21} = 0$ leads to the "1" in the numerator of p_{i1} and the "1" in the denominator of each probability.

The model is estimated by maximum likelihood methods in SAS using PROC MDC (Multinomial Discrete Choice). To locate full documentation enter into the command line

```
✓ help mdc                    ▼
```

As in probit models for binary choice, we can use the estimated model to estimate the choice probabilities. To predict the actual choice we might choose the alternative with the maximum probability. We can also compute, for a single continuous explanatory variable x, a marginal effect for alternative m as

$$\left.\frac{\Delta p_{im}}{\Delta x_i}\right|_{\text{all else constant}} = \frac{\partial p_{im}}{\partial x_i} = p_{im}\left[\beta_{2m} - \sum_{j=1}^{3}\beta_{2j}p_{ij}\right]$$

16.3.1 Example: post-secondary education choice

In the SAS data set *nels_small* we have 1000 observations on students who chose, upon graduating from high school, either no college (*PSECHOICE*=1), a 2-year college (*PSECHOICE*=2), or a 4-year college (*PSECHOICE*=3). For illustration purposes we focus on the explanatory variable *GRADES*, which is an index ranging from 1.0 (highest level, A+ grade) to 13.0 (lowest level, F grade) and represents combined performance in English, Math and Social Studies.

Of the 1000 students 22.2% selected to not attend a college upon graduation, 25.1% selected to attend a 2-year college, and 52.7% attended a 4-year college. The average value of *GRADES* is 6.53, with highest grade a 1.74 and lowest grade a 12.33.

Read the data, creating a individual identifier *ID* using the automatic variable _N_.

```
data nels_small;
set 'nels_small';
id=_n_;                              * create person id;
```

```
label id='person id';
run;
```

Examine contents, summary statistics and a few observations.

```
proc contents data=nels_small position;
title 'nels_small contents';
run;
options nolabel;
proc means data=nels_small;
title 'nels_small summary stats';
run;
proc print data=nels_small(obs=5);
title 'nels_small observations';
run;
```

```
                      nels_small observations
```

Obs	PSECHOICE	HSCATH	GRADES	FAMINC	FAMSIZ	PARCOLL	FEMALE	BLACK	id
1	2	0	9.08	62.5	5	0	0	0	1
2	2	0	8.31	42.5	4	0	1	0	2
3	3	0	7.42	62.5	4	0	1	0	3
4	3	0	7.42	62.5	4	0	1	0	4
5	3	0	7.42	62.5	4	0	1	0	5

The data shows one observation per individual. **PROC MDC** requires a quite different data format. For each individual there must be 3 rows of data, corresponding to the 3 options each person has. A binary variable *CHOICE* indicates which alternative is chosen. We also create dummy variables for the 3 alternatives named *NOCOLL*, *YRS2* and *YRS4*.

```
data new;
set nels_small;
choice = (psechoice=1); nocoll = 1; yrs2 = 0; yrs4 = 0; output;
choice = (psechoice=2); nocoll = 0; yrs2 = 1; yrs4 = 0; output;
choice = (psechoice=3); nocoll = 0; yrs2 = 0; yrs4 = 1; output;
run;
proc print data=new(obs=6);
var id choice nocoll yrs2 yrs4 grades;
title 'nels_small stacked data';
run;
```

The observations on selected variables for the first two individuals are

Obs	id	choice	nocoll	yrs2	yrs4	GRADES
1	1	0	1	0	0	9.08
2	1	1	0	1	0	9.08
3	1	0	0	0	1	9.08
4	2	0	1	0	0	8.31
5	2	1	0	1	0	8.31
6	2	0	0	0	1	8.31

So that we can estimate the effect of grades on each outcome we create interaction variables between *GRADES* and choices *YRS2* and *YRS4*. The interaction between *GRADES* and *NOCOLL* is not used because its coefficient is normalized to zero.

```
data nels2;
set new;
grades_yrs2=yrs2*grades;
grades_yrs4=yrs4*grades;
run;
```

The **PROC MDC** command for estimation is

```
proc mdc data=nels2;
model choice = yrs2 grades_yrs2 yrs4 grades_yrs4/ type=clogit nchoice=3;
id id;
output out=nelsout p=p;
title 'multinomial logit education choice';
run;
```

In the model statement we include the dummy variables *YRS2* and *YRS4* that are attached to "intercept" parameters β_{12} and β_{13}. The two interaction variables are attached to parameters β_{22} and β_{23}. The option **type=clogit** indicates that we are using a Conditional Logit model[1] software and **nchoice=3** indicates the number of alternatives facing each person. The **id** statement specifying the person indicator (here **id**) is required. We output the predicted probabilities for later use.

The output from **PROC MDC** is extensive. The first part tells us that our maximum likelihood estimation algorithm converged (which is good) and some summary measures.

```
                    The MDC Procedure

                Conditional Logit Estimates

Algorithm converged.

                    Model Fit Summary
         Dependent Variable                    choice
         Number of Observations                  1000
         Number of Cases                         3000
         Log Likelihood                    -875.31309
         Log Likelihood Null (LogL(0))          -1099
         Maximum Absolute Gradient         1.36764E-9
         Number of Iterations                       5
         Optimization Method        Newton-Raphson
         AIC                                     1759
         Schwarz Criterion                       1778
```

A second portion gives us the percentage of choices in the original data.

---

[1] It is a common trick to use conditional logit software to estimate multinomial choice models. The conditional logit model is discussed in the next section.

```
                    Discrete Response Profile
         Index   CHOICE      Frequency      Percent
           0        1            222         22.20
           1        2            251         25.10
           2        3            527         52.70
```

A third portion gives various R^2-like measures.

```
                  Goodness-of-Fit Measures

   Measure                    Value    Formula
   Likelihood Ratio (R)       446.6    2 * (LogL - LogL0)
   Upper Bound of R (U)       2197.2   - 2 * LogL0
   Aldrich-Nelson             0.3087   R / (R+N)
   Cragg-Uhler 1              0.3602   1 - exp(-R/N)
   Cragg-Uhler 2              0.4052   (1-exp(-R/N)) / (1-exp(-U/N))
   Estrella                   0.393    1 - (1-R/U)^(U/N)
   Adjusted Estrella          0.3869   1 - ((LogL-K)/LogL0)^(-2/N*LogL0)
   McFadden's LRI             0.2033   R / U
   Veall-Zimmermann           0.4492   (R * (U+N)) / (U * (R+N))

   N = # of observations, K = # of regressors
```

Finally the estimates themselves are reported in the usual way. The order of the parameters being estimated are β_{12}, β_{22}, then β_{13}, β_{23}. The standard errors are based on a formula for the asymptotic covariance of maximum likelihood estimators.

```
                  Conditional Logit Estimates

                                  Standard             Approx
   Parameter      DF   Estimate      Error   t Value   Pr > |t|
   yrs2            1     2.5064      0.4184      5.99   <.0001
   grades_yrs2     1    -0.3088      0.0523     -5.91   <.0001
   yrs4            1     5.7699      0.4043     14.27   <.0001
   grades_yrs4     1    -0.7062      0.0529    -13.34   <.0001
```

We see that each of the estimated coefficients is significantly different from zero. Further interpretation will require some work. For further analysis we create a data set with the probabilities for each person in a single row. To that end we create a new variable *ALT* that takes the values 1, 2, and 3, indicating the alternative number. First, create an alternative identifier and examine the output data set.

```
        data nelsout2;
        set nelsout;
        alt = 1 + mod(_n_-1,3);
        run;
        proc print data=nelsout2(obs=6);
        var id alt choice nocoll yrs2 yrs4 grades p;
        title 'predicted probabilities';
        run;
```

```
                       predicted probabilities

   Obs    id    alt    choice    nocoll    yrs2    yrs4    GRADES      p
    1     1      1        0         1        0       0       9.08    0.44076
    2     1      2        1         0        1       0       9.08    0.32738
    3     1      3        0         0        0       1       9.08    0.23186
    4     2      1        0         1        0       0       8.31    0.35110
    5     2      2        1         0        1       0       8.31    0.33078
    6     2      3        0         0        0       1       8.31    0.31812
```

Using *ALT*, separate the output data set into 3 separate data sets containing only the probabilities of each alternative, *P1*, *P2* and *P3*. Merge these into a single data set. Each row has the probabilities of the 3 choices for an individual.

```
data alt1; set nelsout2; if alt=1; p1 = p; keep p1;
data alt2; set nelsout2; if alt=2; p2 = p; keep p2;
data alt3; set nelsout2; if alt=3; p3 = p; keep p3;
data alt;
merge alt1-alt3;
run;
proc print data=alt(obs=5);
title 'predicted probabilities for each alternative';
run;
```

```
           predicted probabilities for each alternative

           Obs       p1         p2         p3
            1      0.44076    0.32738    0.23186
            2      0.35110    0.33078    0.31812
            3      0.25388    0.31484    0.43128
            4      0.25388    0.31484    0.43128
            5      0.25388    0.31484    0.43128
```

The predicted probabilities for individuals 3-5 are the same because they had the same *GRADES*, which is the only predictor in our model.

Now we use the equation for the marginal effect, and use the fact that $\beta_{21} = 0$ as a result of the normalization rule for multinomial logit

$$\frac{\partial p_{im}}{\partial x_i} = p_{im} \left[\beta_{2m} - \sum_{j=1}^{3} \beta_{2j} p_{ij} \right]$$

$$= p_{im} \left[\beta_{2m} - \left(\beta_{21} p_{i1} + \beta_{22} p_{i2} + \beta_{23} p_{i3} \right) \right]$$

$$= p_{im} \left[\beta_{2m} - \left(\beta_{22} p_{i2} + \beta_{23} p_{i3} \right) \right]$$

Applying this formula very simply for each alternative for each observation we have

```
data marginals;
set alt;
b22 = -0.3088;
```

```
b23 = -0.7062;
der1 = p1*(0-b22*p2-b23*p3);
der2 = p2*(b22-b22*p2-b23*p3);
der3 = p3*(b23-b22*p2-b23*p3);
keep p1-p3 der1-der3;
run;
proc means data=marginals;
title 'multinomial logit average marginal effects';
run;
```

multinomial logit average marginal effects

Variable	N	Mean	Std Dev	Minimum	Maximum
p1	1000	0.2220000	0.1739746	0.0098080	0.7545629
p2	1000	0.2510000	0.0784017	0.0702686	0.3314252
p3	1000	0.5270000	0.2388916	0.0399892	0.9199234
der1	1000	0.0743747	0.0368409	0.0065846	0.1170336
der2	1000	0.0256336	0.0285765	-0.0456746	0.0536615
der3	1000	-0.1000083	0.0289869	-0.1316845	-0.0245741

Note that the average of the predicted probabilities for each alternative matches the proportion of the original sample that was chosen. This is a property of conditional logit models. Also we see that, averaging across all 1000 individuals, increasing the value of grades by one (meaning worse marks) increases the probability of choosing *NOCOLL* by 0.07, increases the probability of choosing a 2-year college by 0.026. The probability of choosing a 4-year college declines by 0.10.

Rather than computing the marginal effects for each observation we can compute them at a specified value of *GRADES*, such as the median, 6.64.

```
data mef;
x = 6.64;
b12 = 2.5064;
b13 = 5.7699;
b22 = -0.3088;
b23 = -0.7062;
```

The predicted probabilities are calculated using

```
den = 1 + exp(b12+b22*x) + exp(b13+b23*x);
p1 = 1/den;
p2 = exp(b12+b22*x)/den;
p3 = exp(b13+b23*x)/den;
```

The marginal effects are

```
der1 = p1*(0-b22*p2-b23*p3);
der2 = p2*(b22-b22*p2-b23*p3);
der3 = p3*(b23-b22*p2-b23*p3);
run;
```

Print these values.

```
proc print data=mef;
var p1-p3 der1-der3;
title 'marginal effects on probabilities at median';
run;
```

marginal effects on probabilities at median

Obs	p1	p2	p3	der1	der2	der3
1	0.18101	0.28558	0.53341	0.084148	0.044574	-0.12872

The estimated probability of a student with median grades attending a 4-year collage is 0.53. If *GRADES* increase (worse marks) we estimate that the probability of attending a 4-year college decreases by 0.129, given that *GRADES* was initially at its median value.

16.4 CONDITIONAL LOGIT

In the previous section we examined the multinomial logit model for choice. The single explanatory variable did not change across the choice alternatives. In this section we consider a similar model called **conditional logit**. In this model the explanatory variable takes different values across both individuals and alternatives. To illustrate we consider a marketing model of choice among $J = 3$ alternative soda types, Pepsi ($j = 1$), 7-Up ($j = 2$) and Coke Classic ($j = 3$). Scanner data[2] from supermarket checkouts records purchases and prices. Customers shopping at different locations on different days face different shelf prices for these products. We wish to model the probability that an individual i will choose alternative j, $p_{ij} = P[\text{individual } i \text{ chooses alternative } j]$. The conditional logit model specifies these probabilities as

$$p_{ij} = \frac{\exp(\beta_{1j} + \beta_2 PRICE_{ij})}{\exp(\beta_{11} + \beta_2 PRICE_{i1}) + \exp(\beta_{12} + \beta_2 PRICE_{i2}) + \exp(\beta_{13} + \beta_2 PRICE_{i3})}$$

The parameter β_2 determines the effect of the price upon the probability of selection and β_{11} and β_{12} are "alternative specific constants." The parameter β_{13} is set to zero to identify the model. Estimation of the unknown parameters is by maximum likelihood.

Post-estimation analysis includes examining the estimated probabilities of selection and calculation of marginal effects. In the marketing model we are interested in the "own price" effect, the change in the probability of selecting alternative j when the price of alternative j changes, other factors held constant. The "cross-price" effect measures the change in probability of selecting alternative j given a change in the price of alternative k. In this example these can be shown to be

---

[2] Original data from A.C. Nielsen is now publically available at http://research.chicagogsb.edu/marketing/databases/index.aspx

$$\frac{\partial p_{ij}}{\partial PRICE_{ij}} = p_{ij}\left(1 - p_{ij}\right)\beta_2 \text{ [own price effect]}$$

$$\frac{\partial p_{ij}}{\partial PRICE_{ik}} = -p_{ij}p_{ik}\beta_2 \text{ [cross-price effect]}$$

Open the SAS data set *cola* and examine its contents.

```
options label;
data cola;
set 'cola';
run;
proc contents data=cola position;
title 'cola contents';
run;
options nolabel;
```

```
                    Variables in Creation Order

  #   Variable     Type     Len    Label
  1   ID           Num       4     customer id
  2   CHOICE       Num       3     = 1 if brand chosen
  3   PRICE        Num       8     price of 2 liter soda
  4   FEATURE      Num       3     = 1 featured item at the time of purchase
  5   DISPLAY      Num       3     = 1 if displayed at time of purchase
```

Print a few observations.

```
proc print data=cola(obs=6);
title 'cola observations';
run;
```

```
                    cola observations

      Obs    ID    CHOICE    PRICE    FEATURE    DISPLAY
        1     1       0       1.79       0          0
        2     1       0       1.79       0          0
        3     1       1       1.79       0          0
        4     2       0       1.79       0          0
        5     2       0       1.79       0          0
        6     2       1       0.89       1          1
```

Because there are $J = 3$ alternatives, each customer *ID* has 3 lines of information for Pepsi, 7-Up and Coke, respectively. *CHOICE* indicates which of the 3 alternatives were selected. *PRICE* is the price of each alternative at the time of purchase. *FEATURE* and *DISPLAY* are indicator variables signaling that the product was featured at the time, or if there was a special store display.

Examine the summary statistics.

```
proc means data=cola;
title 'cola summary stats';
run;
```

cola summary stats

The MEANS Procedure

Variable	N	Mean	Std Dev	Minimum	Maximum
ID	5466	911.5000000	526.0141351	1.0000000	1822.00
CHOICE	5466	0.3333333	0.4714476	0	1.0000000
PRICE	5466	1.1851336	0.3059794	0.1600000	2.9900000
FEATURE	5466	0.5087816	0.4999686	0	1.0000000
DISPLAY	5466	0.3635199	0.4810567	0	1.0000000

Data include 1822 purchases, the average price paid being $1.185.

We will "trick" SAS into computing some additional probabilities by adding two more observations to the data with *CHOICE* that is missing. In the pseudo-data the price of Pepsi is $1.00, the price of 7-Up is $1.25 and price of Coke is $1.10 and $1.25

```
data more;
input id choice price feature display;
datalines;
9998 . 1.00 0 0
9998 . 1.25 0 0
9998 . 1.10 0 0

9999 . 1.00 0 0
9999 . 1.25 0 0
9999 . 1.25 0 0
;

data cola;
set cola more;
run;
```

We must also create the alternative specific indicators.

```
data cola;
set cola;
alt = 1 + mod(_n_-1,3);
pepsi = (alt=1);
sevenup = (alt=2);
coke = (alt=3);
run;

proc print data=cola(obs=6);
title 'cola observations';
run;
```

The data now includes these additional variables.

```
                        cola observations

 Obs   ID   CHOICE   PRICE   FEATURE   DISPLAY   alt   pepsi   sevenup   coke
   1    1      0      1.79      0         0        1     1        0        0
   2    1      0      1.79      0         0        2     0        1        0
   3    1      1      1.79      0         0        3     0        0        1
   4    2      0      1.79      0         0        1     1        0        0
   5    2      0      1.79      0         0        2     0        1        0
   6    2      1      0.89      1         1        3     0        0        1
```

Maximum likelihood estimation of the conditional logit model is carried out using **PROC MDC**. The option **outest=est** writes parameter estimates to a SAS dataset. The **model** statement relates choice to *PRICE* and indicator variables for *PEPSI* and *SEVENUP*. The indicator for *COKE* is omitted and defines the base category. The options **type=clogit** indicates estimation model and **nchoice=3** indicates that there are 3 alternatives. The **id** statement indicating the customer number (*ID*) is required. The predicted values *PHAT* are output to a SAS dataset.

```
proc mdc data=cola outest=est;
model choice = price pepsi sevenup/ type=clogit nchoice=3;
id id;
output out=colaout p=phat;
title 'cola conditional logit';
run;
```

The output is extensive. The first section indicates that the maximization algorithm converged, and gives us some summary statistics. These are explained in detail in Appendix C.4. We see that among the 1822 customers 34.58% chose Pepsi, 37.43% chose 7-Up and 27.99% chose Coke.

```
                   The MDC Procedure
                Conditional Logit Estimates

Algorithm converged.

                   Model Fit Summary

         Dependent Variable                    CHOICE
         Number of Observations                 1822
         Number of Cases                        5466
         Log Likelihood                         -1825
         Log Likelihood Null (LogL(0))          -2002
         Maximum Absolute Gradient          7.5088E-11
         Number of Iterations                      4
         Optimization Method         Newton-Raphson
         AIC                                    3655
         Schwarz Criterion                      3672
```

```
           Discrete Response Profile
    Index   CHOICE   Frequency   Percent
      0        1        630       34.58
      1        2        682       37.43
      2        3        510       27.99
```

Various Goodness-of-Fit measures are given, with the most useful being the Likelihood Ratio (R) which tests the overall model significance. In this case the null hypothesis is that the 3 model parameters are zero. The null hypothesis is rejected, comparing the value 354.22 to the 99th percentile of the $\chi^2_{(3)}$ critical value 11.345.

```
                    Goodness-of-Fit Measures
Measure                    Value    Formula
Likelihood Ratio (R)       354.22   2 * (LogL - LogL0)
Upper Bound of R (U)       4003.3   - 2 * LogL0
Aldrich-Nelson             0.1628   R / (R+N)
Cragg-Uhler 1              0.1767   1 - exp(-R/N)
Cragg-Uhler 2              0.1988   (1-exp(-R/N)) / (1-exp(-U/N))
Estrella                   0.1842   1 - (1-R/U)^(U/N)
Adjusted Estrella          0.1812   1 - ((LogL-K)/LogL0)^(-2/N*LogL0)
McFadden's LRI             0.0885   R / U
Veall-Zimmermann           0.2368   (R * (U+N)) / (U * (R+N))


N = # of observations, K = # of regressors
```

The parameter estimates are reported in the usual way, with standard errors based on the asymptotic distribution of the maximum likelihood estimator.

```
                    Conditional Logit Estimates

                                  Standard              Approx
Parameter   DF    Estimate         Error     t Value    Pr > |t|
PRICE        1     -2.2964         0.1377     -16.68     <.0001
pepsi        1      0.2832         0.0624       4.54     <.0001
sevenup      1      0.1038         0.0625       1.66     0.0965
```

Based on the negative sign of the *PRICE* coefficient, which is statistically different from zero, we can conclude that the own price effect is negative, and the cross price effect is positive. The Pepsi brand "intercept" is positive and significant while that for 7-Up is positive but insignificant. This implies that if the prices of the alternatives were equal, Pepsi would have the highest estimated probability of selection. Recall that the intercept parameter for Coke is set to zero.

A simple post-estimation analysis is provided by the predicted probabilities for our pseudo-observations.

```
proc print data=colaout;
where id >= 9998;
var id phat price alt;
title 'predicted probabilities';
run;
```

```
               predicted probabilities

       Obs      ID      phat     PRICE     alt
       5467    9998    0.48319    1.00      1
       5468    9998    0.22746    1.25      2
       5469    9998    0.28934    1.10      3
       5470    9999    0.52768    1.00      1
       5471    9999    0.24841    1.25      2
       5472    9999    0.22391    1.25      3
```

The 15-cent higher price for Coke in the second set of prices causes the estimated probability of choosing Coke to fall from 0.289 to 0.224, while the probabilities of the other brands being selected increase.

16.4.1 Marginal effects

Calculation of marginal effects is accomplished by first writing the "stacked" form of the output data into a "wide" version, with a single line for each customer *ID*, and then applying the marginal effect formulas.

The SAS **array** statement creates 3 new variables (*PHAT1-PHAT3*) from the single variable *PHAT*. The **do-end** loop cycles through the data, reading first the data line for Pepsi, then the data line for 7-Up and then the data line for Coke. The new variable *PHAT1* contains the estimated probability for Pepsi, and so on.

```
data marginals;
array predict(3) phat1-phat3;
do i=1 to 3 until(last.id);
        set colaout;
        by id;
        predict(i)=phat;
end;
if id >= 9998 then delete;
beta2 = -2.29637;
d11 = phat1*(1-phat1)*beta2;
d22 = phat2*(1-phat2)*beta2;
d33 = phat3*(1-phat3)*beta2;
d12 = -phat1*phat2*beta2;
d13 = -phat1*phat3*beta2;
d23 = -phat2*phat3*beta2;
keep id phat1-phat3 d11 d22 d33 d23 d12 d13 d23;
run;
```

Print a few observations for some of the variables created.

```
proc print data=marginals(obs=10);
var id phat1 d11 d12 d13;
title 'marginal effects data';
run;
```

```
                    marginal effects data

        Obs    ID    phat1      d11       d12       d13
         1     1    0.38622   -0.54436   0.28630   0.25806
         2     2    0.12842   -0.25703   0.03165   0.22538
         3     3    0.15195   -0.29591   0.16407   0.13185
         4     4    0.24985   -0.43039   0.11981   0.31058
         5     5    0.38622   -0.54436   0.28630   0.25806
         6     6    0.79800   -0.37016   0.19468   0.17548
         7     7    0.86750   -0.26395   0.13882   0.12513
         8     8    0.32397   -0.50294   0.43979   0.06314
         9     9    0.15230   -0.29648   0.04452   0.25196
        10    10    0.23748   -0.41583   0.10825   0.30759
```

For each customer we see the estimated probability of a Pepsi purchase, and the Pepsi own and cross price effects.

Find the average marginal effects using **PROC MEANS**.

```
proc means data=marginals;
var phat1-phat3 d11 d22 d33 d23 d12 d13 d23;
title 'average marginal effects';
run;
```

```
                    average marginal effects
```

Variable	N	Mean	Std Dev	Minimum	Maximum
phat1	1822	0.3457739	0.1357092	0.0265940	0.8861610
phat2	1822	0.3743139	0.1533277	0.0074994	0.9526731
phat3	1822	0.2799122	0.1347828	0.0192187	0.8030879
d11	1822	-0.4772028	0.1002913	-0.5740902	-0.0594455
d22	1822	-0.4838602	0.0949637	-0.5740925	-0.0170923
d33	1822	-0.4211656	0.1148581	-0.5739809	-0.0432851
d23	1822	0.2139115	0.0846018	0.0018313	0.4819168
d12	1822	0.2699487	0.0958705	0.0152610	0.5017614
d13	1822	0.2072541	0.0928804	0.0012604	0.4733329

When interpreting these, recall that *PRICE* is measured in dollars, so a 1-unit change is unrealistically large. The marginal effect for a 10-cent change is obtained by multiplying the marginal effect by 0.10. Also note that the average estimated probabilities equal the proportions in the sample, which is a property of the conditional logit model.

16.4.2 Testing the IIA assumption

In both conditional and multinomial logit a strong implicit assumption is the "Independence of Irrelevant Alternatives," or IIA. The meaning of this assumption can be shown by forming the odds ratio of two choices. In the conditional logit model

$$\frac{p_{ij}}{p_{ik}} = \frac{\exp\left(\beta_{1j} + \beta_2 PRICE_{ij}\right)}{\exp\left(\beta_{1k} + \beta_2 PRICE_{ik}\right)} = \exp\left[\left(\beta_{1j} - \beta_{1k}\right) + \beta_2\left(PRICE_{ij} - PRICE_{ik}\right)\right]$$

The odds ratio of alternative j to alternative k does not depend on how many other alternatives there might be, or what they are.

The Hausman specification test compares two estimators. The first estimator will come from the conditional logit model with a full set of alternatives, and the second estimator is based on a reduced, subset, of alternatives. If IIA holds both estimators are consistent, but the estimator based on the reduced subset of alternatives should be less efficient than the estimator based on the full set of alternatives. If IIA does not hold then the estimator based on the reduced set will be inconsistent. The Hausman test statistic[3] is

$$H = \left(\tilde{\beta}_s - \tilde{\beta}_f\right)' \left(\hat{V}_s - \hat{V}_f\right)^{-1} \left(\tilde{\beta}_s - \tilde{\beta}_f\right)' \overset{a}{\sim} \chi^2_{(K)}$$

where

- $\tilde{\beta}_f$ conditional logit maximum likelihood estimator based on a full set of choices

- $\hat{V}_f$ estimated asymptotic covariance matrix using full set of choices

- $\tilde{\beta}_s$ conditional logit maximum likelihood estimator based on a subset of choices

- $\hat{V}_s$ estimated asymptotic covariance matrix using a subset of choices

- K is the number of parameters in the contrast.

The full set and the corresponding subsets can be formed in many ways. For example, if there are $J = 3$ alternatives, there are 3 subsets containing only 2 alternatives. However the subset is formed the null hypothesis that IIA holds should not be rejected.

There are some practical difficulties when carrying out the test. The deletion of an alternative requires us to delete from the sample all individuals who selected that alternative. Thus the full set of choices model is based on a larger sample than the model for the reduced subset of choices. The second "problem" is that the difference of the two estimated covariance matrices, $\hat{V}_s - \hat{V}_f$, is often not positive definite, leading to a negative value for the chi-square statistic, which is not feasible.

In the following code we first estimate the full ($J = 3$) choice model. The **PROC MDC** statement includes the option **outest=colaparm covout**. Not only are parameter estimates saved but also the estimated variances and covariances, that is $\hat{V}_f$.

```
proc mdc data=cola outest=colaparm covout;
model choice = price display feature pepsi sevenup/
      type=clogit nchoice=3;
id id;
title 'conditional logit estimates';
run;
```

Print the data set *colaparm*.

```
proc print data=colaparm;
title 'cola outest data';
run;
```

---

[3] Greene (2012, pp. 767-768)

In the contrast test we will use only the common model coefficients of *PRICE, DISPLAY* and *FEATURE*. The coefficient covariance matrix is indicated by the box.

```
                              cola outest data

Obs  _MODEL_  _TYPE_  _STATUS_      _DEPVAR_  _METHOD_  _NAME_    _LIKLHD_

 1            PARMS   0 Converged   CHOICE    ML                 -1811.35
 2            COV     0 Converged   CHOICE    ML        PRICE     -1811.35
 3            COV     0 Converged   CHOICE    ML        DISPLAY   -1811.35
 4            COV     0 Converged   CHOICE    ML        FEATURE   -1811.35
 5            COV     0 Converged   CHOICE    ML        pepsi     -1811.35
 6            COV     0 Converged   CHOICE    ML        sevenup   -1811.35        Vf

Obs  _STDERR_     PRICE      DISPLAY      FEATURE        pepsi       sevenup

 1      .        -1.84919    0.47266     -0.040855      0.28409      0.090663
 2   0.18866      0.03559    0.00624      0.007459     -0.00087      0.002400
 3   0.09354      0.00624    0.00875     -0.002030      0.00007     -0.000414
 4   0.08308      0.00746   -0.00203      0.006901     -0.00013      0.001046
 5   0.06256     -0.00087    0.00007     -0.000127      0.00391      0.002079
 6   0.06397      0.00240   -0.00041      0.001046      0.00208      0.004092
```

If we consider the reduced subset that deletes Coke as an alternative, we must locate all the Coke drinkers in the sample and delete them, and keep only Pepsi and 7-Up as alternatives. First, from the stacked data set, create a data set with one row per *ID* indicating choices.

```
data choices;
array choices(3) choice1-choice3;
do i=1 to 3 until(last.id);
        set cola;
        by id;
        choices(i)=choice;
end;
keep id choice1-choice3;
run;
```

Find the *ID*s of Coke drinkers.

```
data cokeid;
set choices;
if choice3=1;
run;
```

Merge with the *cola* dataset, then delete those who chose Coke, and further delete the Coke alternative.

```
data nocoke;
merge cola cokeid;
by id;
if choice3=1 then delete;
drop choice1-choice3 coke;
if alt < 3;
run;
```

Estimate the conditional logit model using this reduced dataset.

```
proc mdc data=nocoke outest=nocokeparm covout;
model choice = price display feature sevenup/ type=clogit nchoice=2;
id id;
title 'conditional logit with no coke';
run;
```

Using PROC IML we will construct the Hausman statistic.

```
proc iml;
title;
start hausman;
* extract estimates & cov from full model;
use colaparm;
read all into cola var{price display feature};
bf = cola[1,];
covf = cola[2:4,];
* extract estimates & cov from subset model;
use nocokeparm;
read all into nocoke var{price display feature};
bs = nocoke[1,];
covs = nocoke[2:4,];
* test statistic, critical value & p-value;
H = (bs-bf)*inv(covs-covf)*(bs-bf)`;
chi95 = cinv(.95,3);
pval = 1 - probchi(H,3);
print,, "Hausman test IIA",, H chi95 pval;
finish;
run hausman;
quit;
```

```
                      Hausman test IIA

                   H        chi95        pval
              13.949063 7.8147279 0.0029753
```

The result shows that we reject the validity of the IIA assumption of the conditional logit model is violated. This is a problem. A variety of models have been proposed that do not make the IIA assumption. These included **nested logit**, **heteroskedastic extreme value model, multinomial probit** and **mixed (random parameter) logit**[4]. Such models are beyond the scope of this work, however it should be noted that SAS 9.2 **PROC MDC will estimate** such specifications. In the command line enter **help mdc** then examine the Overview of the MDC procedure.

---

[4] See Greene (2012), Sections 18.25 and 18.2.7 for descriptions of these models.

16.5 ORDERED CHOICE MODELS

The choice options in multinomial and conditional logit models have no natural ordering or arrangement. However, in some cases choices are ordered in a specific way. Examples include:

1. Results of opinion surveys in which responses can be strongly disagree, disagree, neutral, agree or strongly agree.
2. Assignment of grades or work performance ratings. Students receive grades A, B, C, D, F which are ordered on the basis of a teacher's evaluation of their performance. Employees are often given evaluations on scales such as Outstanding, Very Good, Good, Fair and Poor which are similar in spirit.

When considering the problem of choosing what type of college to attend after graduating from high school we might rank the possibilities as

$$y = \begin{cases} 3 & \text{4-year college (the full college experience)} \\ 2 & \text{2-year college (a partial college experience)} \\ 1 & \text{no college} \end{cases}$$

The usual linear regression model is not appropriate for such data, because in regression we would treat the y values as having some numerical meaning when they do not.

Denote our unobservable sentiment towards the ranked alternatives by y_i^*. For simplicity, let us focus on the single college choice explanatory variable *GRADES*. The model is then

$$y_i^* = \beta GRADES_i + e_i$$

Because there are $M = 3$ alternatives there are $M - 1 = 2$ thresholds μ_1 and μ_2, with $\mu_1 < \mu_2$[5]. The observed choice is determined by

$$y = \begin{cases} 3 \text{ (4-year college)} & \text{if} \quad y_i^* > \mu_2 \\ 2 \text{ (2-year college)} & \text{if} \quad \mu_1 < y_i^* \le \mu_2 \\ 1 \text{ (no college)} & \text{if} \quad y_i^* \le \mu_1 \end{cases}$$

The **ordered probit model** assumes that the errors have the standard normal distribution. Then, for example, the probability of choosing no college is:

$$P[y = 1] = P\left[y_i^* \le \mu_1\right] = P\left[\beta GRADES_i + e_i \le \mu_1\right]$$

$$= P\left[e_i \le \mu_1 - \beta GRADES_i\right]$$

$$= \Phi\left(\mu_1 - \beta GRADES_i\right)$$

Estimation, as with previous choice models, is by maximum likelihood. If we treat *GRADES* as a continuous variable, what is the marginal effect on the probability of each outcome, given a 1-unit change in *GRADES*? For example,

---

[5] The index model does not contain an intercept because it would be exactly collinear with the threshold variables.

$$\frac{\partial P[y=1]}{\partial GRADES} = -\phi(\mu_1 - \beta GRADES) \times \beta$$

where $\phi(\cdot)$ denotes the probability density function of a standard normal distribution.[6]

We will use the previously encountered NELS data to illustrate. The variable *PSECHOICE* takes the values 1, 2 and 3 indicating student choice.

```
data nels_small;
set 'nels_small';
keep psechoice grades;
run;
proc print data=nels_small (obs=5);
title 'nels_small observations';
run;
```

```
                nels_small observations

        Obs     PSECHOICE     GRADES
         1          2          9.08
         2          2          8.31
         3          3          7.42
         4          3          7.42
         5          3          7.42
```

Supplement the data with two additional incomplete observations on students with *GRADES* = 6.64 and *GRADES* = 2.635.

```
data more;
input psechoice grades;
datalines;
. 6.64
. 2.635
;
run;
data pse;
set nels_small more;
run;
```

Ordered probit (and logit) models can be estimated using **PROC QLIM**. The nomenclature is the same as binary probit with the addition of the model option **limit1=varying**. This tells SAS not to include an intercept in the model and to estimate the two thresholds μ_1 and μ_2.

```
proc qlim data=pse;
model psechoice = grades / discrete(d=normal) limit1=varying;
output out=pseout proball marginal;
title 'ordered probit';
run;
```

---

[6] For more details enter **help qlim** in the command line, and examine **Details: QLIM procedure, Ordinal Discrete Modeling**. See also William Greene (2012) *Econometric Analysis, 7th Edition* Chapter 18.3.

The **output** statement requests predicted probabilities of each choice and marginal effects. The printed output includes a summary of choices made in the sample, and the usual fit statistics, which we have deleted.

Index	Value	Total Frequency
1	1	222
2	2	251
3	3	527

Print the predicted probabilities and marginal effects for the two supplementary data points.

```
proc print data=pseout;
where psechoice = .;
title 'ordered probit outest';
run;
```

```
                      ordered probit outest
```

Obs	PSECHOICE	GRADES	Meff_P1_ GRADES	Meff_P2_ GRADES	Meff_P3_ GRADES	Prob1_ PSECHOICE	Prob2_ PSECHOICE	Prob3_ PSECHOICE
1001	.	6.640	0.080882	0.041265	-0.12215	0.18151	0.29695	0.52153
1002	.	2.635	0.012453	0.041326	-0.05378	0.01627	0.08364	0.90008

We see that for a student with median grades ($GRADES = 6.64$) the probability of choosing a four-year college is 0.52153, a two-year college 0.29695, and so on. The marginal effects are evaluated for each observation. Average these over the entire sample.

```
proc means data=pseout;
var meff_p1_grades meff_p2_grades meff_p3_grades;
where psechoice ne .;
title 'average marginal effects'; run;
                  average marginal effects

            The MEANS Procedure
```

Variable	N	Mean	Std Dev	Minimum	Maximum
Meff_P1_GRADES	1000	0.0751867	0.0373397	0.0066701	0.1223257
Meff_P2_GRADES	1000	0.0239209	0.0351007	-0.0597587	0.0597697
Meff_P3_GRADES	1000	-0.0991076	0.0230250	-0.1223257	-0.0292963

The average effect of increasing *GRADES* by one-unit (a worsening of grades) is different for each possible choice. It increases the probability of choosing no-college or a two-year college and reduces the probability of choosing a 4-year college.

16.6 MODELS FOR COUNT DATA

When the dependent variable in a regression model is a count of the number of occurrences of an event, the outcome variable is $y = 0, 1, 2, 3, \ldots$ Examples include:

- The number of trips to a physician a person makes during a year.
- The number of fishing trips taken by a person during the previous year.
- The number of alcoholic drinks a college student takes in a week.

While we are again interested in explaining and predicting probabilities, such as the probability that an individual will take two or more trips to the doctor during a year, the probability distribution we use as a foundation is the Poisson, not the normal or the logistic. If Y is a Poisson random variable, then its probability function is

$$f(y) = P(Y = y) = \frac{e^{-\lambda}\lambda^y}{y!}, \quad y = 0, 1, 2, \ldots$$

The factorial (!) term $y! = y \times (y-1) \times (y-2) \times \cdots \times 1$. This probability function has one parameter, λ, which is the mean (and variance) of Y. That is, $E(Y) = \mathrm{var}(Y) = \lambda$. In a regression model we try to explain the behavior of $E(Y)$ as a function of some explanatory variables. We do the same here, keeping the value of $E(Y) \geq 0$ by defining

$$E(Y) = \lambda = \exp(\beta_1 + \beta_2 x)$$

This choice defines the **Poisson regression model** for count data.

Model parameters are estimated by maximum likelihood. As in other modeling situations we would like to use the estimated model to predict outcomes, determine the marginal effect of a change in an explanatory variable on the mean of the dependent variable, and test the significance of coefficients. Prediction of the conditional mean of y is straightforward. Given the maximum likelihood estimates $\tilde{\beta}_1$ and $\tilde{\beta}_2$, and given a value of the explanatory variable x_0, then

$$\widehat{E(y_0)} = \tilde{\lambda}_0 = \exp\left(\tilde{\beta}_1 + \tilde{\beta}_2 x_0\right)$$

This value is an estimate of the expected number of occurrences observed, if x takes the value x_0. The probability of a particular number of occurrences can be estimated by inserting the estimated conditional mean into the probability function, as

$$\widehat{\Pr(Y = y)} = \frac{\exp\left(-\tilde{\lambda}_0\right)\tilde{\lambda}_0^y}{y!}, \quad y = 0, 1, 2, \ldots$$

The marginal effect of a change in a continuous variable x in the Poisson regression model is not simply given by the parameter, because the conditional mean model is a nonlinear function of the parameters. Using our specification that the conditional mean is given by $E(y_i) = \lambda_i = \exp(\beta_1 + \beta_2 x_i)$, and using rules for derivatives of exponential functions, we obtain the marginal effect

$$\frac{\partial E(y_i)}{\partial x_i} = \lambda_i \beta_2$$

To estimate this marginal effect, replace the parameters by their maximum likelihood estimates, and select a value for *x*.

Andrew Bernard and Meghan Busse[7] examined the effect of a country's economic resources on the number of medals, a count variable, won. The data are in the SAS data set *olympics*. Open the data set and examine its contents.

```
options label;
data olympics;
set 'olympics';
run;
proc contents data=olympics position;
title 'olympics contents';
run;
options nolabel;
```

                    Variables in Creation Order

#	Variable	Type	Len	Label
1	COUNTRY	Num	4	country code
2	YEAR	Num	3	olympics year
3	GDP	Num	8	gross domestic product, 1995 dollars
4	POP	Num	8	population
5	GOLD	Num	3	number of gold medals won
6	SILVER	Num	3	number of silver medals won
7	BRONZE	Num	3	number of bronze medals won
8	MEDALTOT	Num	4	total number of medals won
9	HOST	Num	3	= 1 if host country
10	PLANNED	Num	3	= 1 if non-soviet planned
11	SOVIET	Num	3	= 1 if soviet

Using the data from 1988, we estimate a Poisson regression explaining the number of medals won (*MEDALTOT*) as a function of the logarithms of population and gross domestic product (1995 $). Create these variables and reduced data file, deleting lines with missing observations.

```
data olympics2;
set olympics;
lnpop = log(pop);
lngdp = log(gdp);
label lnpop='log(pop)' lngdp='log(gdp)';
if year=88;
if medaltot ne .;
if pop ne .;
keep medaltot lnpop lngdp;
run;
```

---

[7] "Who Wins the Olympic Games: Economic Resources and Medal Totals," *The Review of Economics and Statistics*, 2004, 86(1), 413-417.

```
proc means data=olympics2;
title 'olympics summary stats';
run;
```

```
                   olympics summary stats

                    The MEANS Procedure

Variable    N        Mean      Std Dev      Minimum      Maximum
```

Variable	N	Mean	Std Dev	Minimum	Maximum
MEDALTOT	151	4.8874172	16.6267026	0	132.0000000
lnpop	151	15.3888992	2.1648771	9.9034876	20.8185760
lngdp	151	23.1265873	2.4248134	17.9048426	29.4343797

Add two observations with median population, first with median GDP (5.51e+09) then raising GDP to the 75th percentile (5.18e+10).

```
data more;
input medaltot pop gdp;
lnpop = log(pop);
lngdp = log(gdp);
keep medaltot lnpop lngdp;
datalines;
. 5921270 5.51E09
. 5921270 5.18E10
;

data medals;
set olympics2 more;
run;
```

The SAS procedure **PROC COUNTREG** estimates the Poisson model using maximum likelihood. The option **dist=poisson** specifies the Poisson model. The **output** statement creates **xbeta** which is $\tilde{\beta}_1 + \tilde{\beta}_2 x_i$ for each observation, and **pred=phat** gives the predicted mean outcome.

```
proc countreg data=medals;
model medaltot = lnpop lngdp / dist=poisson;
output out=out88 xbeta=xbeta pred=phat;
title 'poisson regression';
run;
```

The estimation output includes some fit summary values and the usual parameter estimates.

```
                  The COUNTREG Procedure

                    Model Fit Summary
```

Dependent Variable	MEDALTOT
Number of Observations	151
Missing Values	2

```
Data Set                    WORK.MEDALS
Model                         Poisson
Log Likelihood               -722.33650
Maximum Absolute Gradient    3.03072E-9
Number of Iterations                  6
Optimization Method      Newton-Raphson
AIC                                1451
SBC                                1460
```

Algorithm converged.

```
                           Standard             Approx
Parameter   DF   Estimate     Error   t Value  Pr > |t|
Intercept    1  -15.887459   0.511805  -31.04   <.0001
lnpop        1    0.180038   0.032280    5.58   <.0001
lngdp        1    0.576603   0.024722   23.32   <.0001
```

Print the output data:

```
proc print data=out88;
var xbeta phat;
where medaltot = .;
title 'poisson model predictions';
run;
```

```
            poisson model predictions

         Obs     xbeta      phat
         152   -0.14683   0.86344
         153    1.14524   3.14320
```

For a country with median population and GDP the predicted mean number of medals is 0.86. If the country's GDP rises to the 75th percentile the prediction increases to 3.14.

The Poisson assumptions imply that $E(y) = \text{var}(y)$. This assumption is often violated by economic data. A model that relaxes this assumption is based on the **negative binomial** distribution. Several variations of this model are estimated by PROC COUNTREG. Enter **help countreg** into the command window and see **Negative Binomial Regression**. Another frequent problem is that of "excess zeros." If you are asked "How many times did you go fishing last year?" You might answer zero. In this case "zero" has two potential meanings. It might mean you have never gone fishing in your life and therefore did not go last year, or it may mean you do go fishing but just not last year. In such situations there are **zero inflated** versions of the Poisson model and negative binomial models. Enter **help countreg** again and read about these models.[8]

16.7 LIMITED DEPENDENT VARIABLE MODELS

In the usual "normal" regression model the dependent variable is continuous and if normally distributed can range from minus to plus infinity. Many other models have dependent variables

---

[8] The negative binomial and zero inflated models are advanced. In addition to the SAS documentation see William Greene (2012) *Econometric Analysis, 7th Edition*, pages 805-815 and 821-826.

that are not unlimited, but that are limited in some way. Discrete dependent variables models could fall into this category since the outcome is limited to an observation that is 0 or 1. In this section we consider two more such models.

16.7.1 Censored variable models

A censored dependent variable has a substantial fraction of the observations that take some limiting value. An example that illustrates the situation is based on Thomas Mroz's (1987) study of married women's labor force participation and wages. The data are in the SAS data set *mroz* and consist of 753 observations on married women. Of these 325 did not work outside the home, and thus had no hours worked. Open the data, creating the log of wage and defining a dummy variable that equals 1 if a woman has children and 0 otherwise.

```
options label;
data mroz;
set 'mroz';
if wage>0 then lwage = log(wage); else lwage=0;
kids = (kidsl6+kids618>0);
label lwage='log(wage)' kids='kids';
keep lwage kids hours educ exper age kidsl6 mtr lfp;
run;

proc contents data=mroz position;
title 'mroz data contents';
run;
options nolabel;
```

```
                    Variables in Creation Order

# Variable Type Len Label
1 LFP       Num   3 dummy variable = 1 if woman worked in 1975, else 0
2 HOURS     Num   4 Wife's hours of work in 1975
3 KIDSL6    Num   3 Number of children less than 6 years old in household
4 AGE       Num   3 Wife's age
5 EDUC      Num   3 Wife's educational attainment, in years
6 MTR       Num   8 marginal tax rate facing the wife, includes Soc Sec taxes
7 EXPER     Num   3 Actual years of wife's previous labor market experience
8 lwage     Num   8 log(wage)
9 kids      Num   8 kids
```

Create a **histogram** using **PROC SGPLOT**. The option **scale=count** produces a count on the vertical axis rather than a percent.

```
proc sgplot data=mroz;
title "Wife's hours of work 1975";
histogram hours / scale=count;
run;
```

Output is listed in the **Results** window

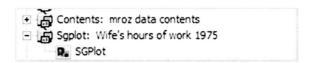

The histogram shows that many of the observed values of *HOURS* are zero.

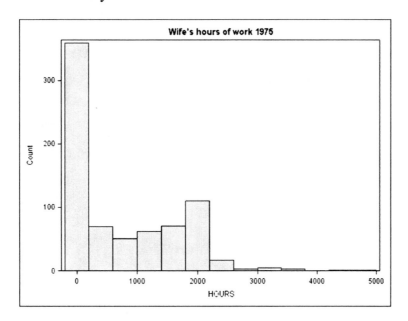

For censored data like these the usual regression function the regression function is no longer given by $E(y|x) = \beta_1 + \beta_2 x$. Instead $E(y|x)$ is a complicated nonlinear function of the regression parameters β_1 and β_2, the error variance σ^2, and x. The least squares estimators of the regression parameters obtained by running a regression of y on x are biased and inconsistent—least squares estimation fails. If having all the limit observations present is the cause of the problem, then why not drop them out? This does not work either. The regression function becomes the expected value of y, conditional on the y values being positive, or $E(y|x, y > 0)$. Once again it can be shown that this regression function is nonlinear

The observed sample is obtained within the framework of an **index** or **latent variable model** Let the latent variable be

$$y_i^* = \beta_1 + \beta_2 x_i + e_i$$

with the error term assumed to have a normal distribution, $e_i \sim N(0, \sigma^2)$. The observable outcome y_i takes the value zero if $y_i^* \le 0$, but $y_i = y_i^*$ if $y_i^* > 0$. In this case we can apply an alternative estimation procedure, which is called **Tobit** in honor of James Tobin, winner of the 1981 Nobel Prize in Economics, who first studied this model. Tobit is a maximum likelihood procedure that recognizes that we have data of two sorts, the limit observations $(y = 0)$ and the nonlimit observations $(y > 0)$.

For comparison purpose estimate a regression model for hours using least squares on all observations.

```
proc reg data=mroz;
model hours = educ exper age kidsl6;
title 'hours equation using all data';
run;
```

The estimates based on 753 observations are:

Variable	DF	Parameter Estimate	Standard Error	t Value	Pr > |t|
Intercept	1	1335.30603	235.64870	5.67	<.0001
EDUC	1	27.08568	12.23989	2.21	0.0272
EXPER	1	48.03981	3.64180	13.19	<.0001
AGE	1	-31.30782	3.96099	-7.90	<.0001
KIDSL6	1	-447.85469	58.41252	-7.67	<.0001

Use only the 428 observations with positive hours.

```
proc reg data=mroz;
model hours = educ exper age kidsl6;
where hours>0;
title 'hours equation using censored data';
run;
```

Variable	DF	Parameter Estimate	Standard Error	t Value	Pr > |t|
Intercept	1	1829.74590	292.53559	6.25	<.0001
EDUC	1	-16.46211	15.58083	-1.06	0.2913
EXPER	1	33.93637	5.00919	6.77	<.0001
AGE	1	-17.10821	5.45767	-3.13	0.0018
KIDSL6	1	-305.30898	96.44904	-3.17	0.0017

Tobit models are estimated in SAS using **PROC QLIM**[9]. The **endogenous** statement specifies hours to be censored (note the tilde "~") with a lower bound at zero, **lb=0**.

In the Tobit model the parameters β_1 and β_2 are the intercept and slope of the latent variable model. In practice we are interested in the marginal effect of a change in x on either the regression function of the observed data $E(y|x)$ or on the regression function conditional on $y > 0$, $E(y|x, y>0)$. The slope of $E(y|x)$ has a relatively simple form, being a scale factor times the parameter value, and is

$$\frac{\partial E(y|x)}{\partial x} = \beta_2 \Phi\left(\frac{\beta_1 + \beta_2 x}{\sigma}\right)$$

where Φ is the cumulative distribution function (cdf) of the standard normal random variable that is evaluated at the estimates and a particular x-value. SAS will compute these values for each sample observation. The **output** statement option **marginal** leads to calculation of these values.

---

[9] PROC QLIM is very powerful, estimating the basic Tobit model, as well as other variations, and bivariate models. Enter **help qlim** into the command line and see **Overview: QLIM Procedure** and **Limited Dependent Variable Models**.

```
proc qlim data=mroz;
model hours = educ exper age kidsl6;
endogenous hours ~ censored(lb=0);
output out=tobit marginal;
title 'tobit';
run;
```

The output shows some sample statistics including the number of limit observations.

```
                  The QLIM Procedure

          Summary Statistics of Continuous Responses
```

						N Obs	N Obs
		Standard		Lower	Upper	Lower	Upper
Variable	Mean	Error	Type	Bound	Bound	Bound	Bound
HOURS	740.5764	871.314216	Censored	0		325	

The **Model Fit Summary** (edited) includes the value of log-likelihood function, and because the maximum likelihood estimation is uses numerical optimization, the number of iterations is shown and the happy message **Algorithm converged**.

```
                  Model Fit Summary
          Number of Endogenous Variables          1
          Endogenous Variable                 HOURS
          Number of Observations                753
          Log Likelihood                      -3827
```

Algorithm converged.

The estimates themselves show that *EDUC* has a larger coefficient estimate. In Tobit the standard deviation of the error distribution σ is estimated jointly with the other parameters, and is reported.

Parameter	DF	Estimate	Standard Error	t Value	Approx Pr > |t|
Intercept	1	1349.839626	386.299070	3.49	0.0005
EDUC	1	73.292361	20.474593	3.58	0.0003
EXPER	1	80.535195	6.287792	12.81	<.0001
AGE	1	-60.767342	6.888151	-8.82	<.0001
KIDSL6	1	-918.915313	111.660436	-8.23	<.0001
_Sigma	1	1133.697183	42.062527	26.95	<.0001

The average marginal effects are

```
proc means data=tobit;
title 'tobit average marginal effects';
run;
```

```
                      tobit average marginal effects

                         The MEANS Procedure


Variable        N        Mean       Std Dev      Minimum      Maximum
───────────────────────────────────────────────────────────────────────
Meff_EDUC      753    43.0799159   17.0057571    1.3104850   71.1017088
Meff_EXPER     753    47.3371222   18.6862853    1.4399886   78.1280604
Meff_AGE       753   -35.7179376   14.0996229  -58.9510528   -1.0865346
Meff_KIDSL6    753  -540.1216979  213.2125418  -891.4496429  -16.4304262
───────────────────────────────────────────────────────────────────────
```

16.7.2 Sample selection model

The econometric model describing the situation is composed of two equations. The first, is the **selection equation** that determines whether the variable of interest is observed. The sample consists of N observations, however the variable of interest is observed only for $n < N$ of these. The selection equation is expressed in terms of a latent variable z_i^* which depends on one or more explanatory variables w_i, and is given by

$$z_i^* = \gamma_1 + \gamma_2 w_i + u_i \quad i = 1, \ldots, N$$

For simplicity we will include only one explanatory variable in the selection equation. The latent variable is not observed, but we do observe the binary variable

$$z_i = \begin{cases} 1 & z_i^* > 0 \\ 0 & \text{otherwise} \end{cases}$$

The second equation is the linear model of interest. It is

$$y_i = \beta_1 + \beta_2 x_i + e_i \quad i = 1, \ldots, n \quad N > n$$

A **selectivity problem** arises when y_i is observed only when $z_i = 1$, and if the errors of the two equations are correlated. In such a situation the usual least squares estimators of β_1 and β_2 are biased and inconsistent.

Consistent estimators are based on the conditional regression function[10]

$$E\left[y_i \mid z_i^* > 0 \right] = \beta_1 + \beta_2 x_i + \beta_\lambda \lambda_i \quad i = 1, \ldots, n$$

where the additional variable λ_i is "Inverse Mills Ratio." It is equal to

$$\lambda_i = \frac{\phi(\gamma_1 + \gamma_2 w_i)}{\Phi(\gamma_1 + \gamma_2 w_i)}$$

where, as usual, $\phi(\cdot)$ denotes the standard normal probability density function, and $\Phi(\cdot)$ denotes the cumulative distribution function for a standard normal random variable. While the value of λ_i

---

[10] Further explanation of this material requires understanding the truncated normal distribution, which is beyond the scope of this book. See William Greene (2012) *Econometric Analysis, 7th Edition*, Prentice-Hall, Chapter 19.5.

is not known, the parameters γ_1 and γ_2 can be estimated using a probit model, based on the observed binary outcome z_i. Then the estimated IMR,

$$\tilde{\lambda}_i = \frac{\phi(\tilde{\gamma}_1 + \tilde{\gamma}_2 w_i)}{\Phi(\tilde{\gamma}_1 + \tilde{\gamma}_2 w_i)}$$

is inserted into the regression equation as an extra explanatory variable, yielding the estimating equation

$$y_i = \beta_1 + \beta_2 x_i + \beta_\lambda \tilde{\lambda}_i + v_i \quad i = 1, \ldots, n$$

Least squares estimation of this equation yields consistent estimators of β_1 and β_2. A word of caution, however, as the least squares estimator is inefficient relative to the maximum likelihood estimator, and the usual standard errors and t-statistics produced after estimation of the augmented equation are incorrect.

As an example we will reconsider the analysis of wages earned by married women using the Mroz (1987) data. In the sample of 753 married women, 428 have market employment and nonzero earnings. First, let us estimate a simple wage equation, explaining ln(*WAGE*) as a function of the woman's education, *EDUC*, and years of market work experience (*EXPER*), using the 428 women who have positive wages.

```
proc reg data=mroz;
model lwage = educ exper;
where lfp=1;
title 'least squares on censored data';
run;
```

The estimates are:

Variable	DF	Parameter Estimate	Standard Error	t Value	Pr > |t|
Intercept	1	-0.40017	0.19037	-2.10	0.0361
EDUC	1	0.10949	0.01417	7.73	<.0001
EXPER	1	0.01567	0.00402	3.90	0.0001

To employ the two-step Heckit method we first estimate a probit model for labor force participation, saving $\tilde{\gamma}_1 + \tilde{\gamma}_2 w_i$ using an **output** statement with the option **xbeta**. The **output** option **mills** saves the inverse mills ratio.

```
proc qlim data=mroz;
model lfp = age educ kids mtr / discrete(d=normal);
output out=probitout xbeta mills;
title 'probit selection equation';
run;
```

Using the probit estimates create the numerator $\phi(\tilde{\gamma}_1 + \tilde{\gamma}_2 w_i)$ and denominator $\Phi(\tilde{\gamma}_1 + \tilde{\gamma}_2 w_i)$ using the **pdf** function and **probnorm** for the normal CDF. The inverse mills ratio *IMR* is the ratio of these two values.

```
data probitout;
set probitout;
pdf = pdf('normal',xbeta_lfp);
cdf = probnorm(xbeta_lfp);
IMR = pdf/cdf;
run;
```

Include the *IMR* into the regression equation using observations with positive wages. **The standard errors reported by this equation are not correct.**[11]

```
proc reg data=probitout;
model lwage = educ exper IMR;
where lfp=1;
title 'least squares with IMR';
run;
```

Variable	DF	Parameter Estimate	Standard Error	t Value	Pr > |t|
Intercept	1	0.81054	0.49447	1.64	0.1019
EDUC	1	0.05846	0.02385	2.45	0.0146
EXPER	1	0.01632	0.00400	4.08	<.0001
IMR	1	-0.86644	0.32699	-2.65	0.0084

You may verify that using the automatically created *IMR* leads to the same results.

```
proc reg data=probitout;
model lwage = educ exper mills_lfp;
where lfp=1;
title 'least squares with automatic IMR';
run;
```

The more efficient maximum likelihood estimation procedure should usually be employed. It is available in PROC QLIM[12]. The probit selection equation is specified, followed by a **model** for the equation of interest. The option **select(lfp=1)** indicates the Heckit model.

```
proc qlim data=mroz;
model lfp = age educ kids mtr / discrete(d=normal);
model lwage = educ exper / select(lfp=1);
title 'Heckit MLE';
run;
```

The output includes the breakdown of the observations into observed and unobserved.

---

[11] SAS/IML code for the two step Heckit estimator including corrected standard errors (heckit.sas) can be found at the book website.
[12] Enter **help qlim** into the command line, then see **Selection Models**.

```
          Discrete Response Profile of LFP
                                    Total
          Index        Value      Frequency
            1            0           325
            2            1           428
```

The usual **Model Fit Statistics** are given and the **Parameter Estimates**. The estimates are for the "lwage" and "lfp" equations are estimated jointly in the maximum likelihood method. The value _Rho is the estimated correlation between the error in the selection equation and the error in the equation of interest. It should be less than 1 in absolute value. If it is 0 there is no "selection bias" present. In this case we reject the hypothesis that rho is zero.

```
                                        Standard                Approx
Parameter          DF      Estimate        Error    t Value    Pr > |t|
lwage.Intercept     1      0.668586      0.234985      2.85     0.0044
lwage.EDUC          1      0.065816      0.016634      3.96    <.0001
lwage.EXPER         1      0.011767      0.004093      2.87     0.0040
_Sigma.lwage        1      0.849442      0.042480     20.00    <.0001
LFP.Intercept       1      1.595958      0.623695      2.56     0.0105
LFP.AGE             1     -0.013262      0.005938     -2.23     0.0255
LFP.EDUC            1      0.063931      0.021745      2.94     0.0033
LFP.kids            1     -0.152592      0.099580     -1.53     0.1254
LFP.MTR             1     -2.291885      0.537563     -4.26    <.0001
_Rho                1     -0.839469      0.034897    -24.06    <.0001
```

APPENDIX 16A PROBIT MAXIMUM LIKELIHOOD ESTIMATION

16A.1 Probit estimation

Let y take the values 1 and 0 to indicate one of two possible outcomes, and suppose $\mathbf{x}_i$ is a $K \times 1$ vector of observations on explanatory variables, including an intercept. In the probit model $P(y_i = 1) = \Phi(\mathbf{x}_i'\boldsymbol{\beta})$ where $\Phi(\cdot)$ is the cumulative distribution function of the standard normal distribution. Given a sample of N independent observations, the likelihood function is

$$L(\boldsymbol{\beta}) = \prod_{i=1}^{N} \left[\Phi(\mathbf{x}_i'\boldsymbol{\beta}) \right]^{y_i} \times \left[1 - \Phi(\mathbf{x}_i'\boldsymbol{\beta}) \right]^{1-y_i}$$

The log-likelihood function is

$$\ln L(\boldsymbol{\beta}) = \sum_{i=1}^{N} y_i \ln \Phi(\mathbf{x}_i'\boldsymbol{\beta}) + \sum_{i=1}^{N} (1 - y_i) \ln \left[1 - \Phi(\mathbf{x}_i'\boldsymbol{\beta}) \right]$$

For the numerical optimization we need first and second derivatives[13]. For convenience, define $z_i = \mathbf{x}_i'\boldsymbol{\beta}$. The vector of first derivative values (or gradient) is

---

[13] Greene (2012), Chapter 17.3 provides these same equations in somewhat condensed notation.

$$\frac{\partial \ln L(\boldsymbol{\beta})}{\partial \boldsymbol{\beta}} = \sum_{i=1}^{N} y_i \frac{\phi(z_i)}{\Phi(z_i)} \mathbf{x_i} - \sum_{i=1}^{N} (1-y_i) \frac{\phi(z_i)}{1-\Phi(z_i)} \mathbf{x_i}$$

$$= \sum_{i=1}^{N} \left[y_i \frac{\phi(z_i)}{\Phi(z_i)} - (1-y_i) \frac{\phi(z_i)}{1-\Phi(z_i)} \right] \mathbf{x_i}$$

The matrix of second derivatives (or Hessian) is

$$\frac{\partial^2 \ln L(\boldsymbol{\beta})}{\partial \boldsymbol{\beta} \partial \boldsymbol{\beta}'} = -\sum_{i=1}^{N} \phi(z_i) \left\{ y_i \frac{\phi(z_i)+z_i\Phi(z_i)}{\left[\Phi(z_i)\right]^2} + (1-y_i) \frac{\phi(z_i)-z_i\left[1-\Phi(z_i)\right]}{\left[1-\Phi(z_i)\right]^2} \right\} \mathbf{x_i x_i'}$$

$$= \mathbf{X'DX}$$

where

$$\mathbf{D} = diag\left[-\phi(z_i) \left\{ y_i \frac{\phi(z_i)+z_i\Phi(z_i)}{\left[\Phi(z_i)\right]^2} + (1-y_i) \frac{\phi(z_i)-z_i\left[1-\Phi(z_i)\right]}{\left[1-\Phi(z_i)\right]^2} \right\} \right]$$

is a diagonal matrix. In the Newton-Raphson[14] iterative estimation process, the updating equation is

$$\boldsymbol{\beta}_{j+1} = \boldsymbol{\beta}_j - \left[\frac{\partial^2 \ln L(\boldsymbol{\beta})}{\partial \boldsymbol{\beta} \partial \boldsymbol{\beta}'} \bigg|_{\boldsymbol{\beta}_j} \right]^{-1} \frac{\partial \ln L(\boldsymbol{\beta})}{\partial \boldsymbol{\beta}} \bigg|_{\boldsymbol{\beta}_j}$$

16A.2 Predicted probabilities

In the probit model the predicted probability when $\mathbf{x} = \mathbf{x}_0$ is $\hat{P} = \Phi\left(\mathbf{x}_0'\hat{\boldsymbol{\beta}}\right)$ where $\hat{\boldsymbol{\beta}}$ is the vector of maximum likelihood estimates. Using the delta method

$$\text{var}\left(\hat{P}\right) = \left[\frac{\partial \Phi(\mathbf{x}_0'\boldsymbol{\beta})}{\partial \boldsymbol{\beta}} \bigg|_{\hat{\boldsymbol{\beta}}} \right]' \text{var}\left(\hat{\boldsymbol{\beta}}\right) \left[\frac{\partial \Phi(\mathbf{x}_0'\boldsymbol{\beta})}{\partial \boldsymbol{\beta}} \bigg|_{\hat{\boldsymbol{\beta}}} \right]$$

Let $z = \mathbf{x}'\boldsymbol{\beta}$. Then, using the chain rule, and that the derivative of a cdf is a pdf, we have

$$\frac{\partial \Phi(z)}{\partial \boldsymbol{\beta}} = \frac{d\Phi(z)}{dz} \times \frac{\partial z}{\partial \boldsymbol{\beta}} = \phi(z)\mathbf{x}$$

The estimated variance of the predicted probability is

$$\widehat{\text{var}}\left(\hat{P}\right) = \left[\phi\left(\mathbf{x}_0'\hat{\boldsymbol{\beta}}\right) \right]^2 \mathbf{x}_0' \, \text{var}\left(\hat{\boldsymbol{\beta}}\right) \mathbf{x}_0$$

---

[14] See Appendix C.4 for more details on numerical optimization in SAS.

This is useful as a basis for constructing interval predictions $\hat{P} \pm t_c se(\hat{P})$ where the standard error of the prediction $se(\hat{P}) = \left[\widehat{var}(\hat{P}) \right]^{1/2}$. Also, if $\mathbf{x}_0$ and $\mathbf{x}_1$ are vectors of predictors then the estimated difference in the probability that $y = 1$ is

$$\Delta \hat{P} = \Phi\left(\mathbf{x}_1'\hat{\boldsymbol{\beta}}\right) - \Phi\left(\mathbf{x}_0'\hat{\boldsymbol{\beta}}\right)$$

This finite difference approach is useful when one or more of the explanatory variables is discrete. The variance of this quantity is

$$\widehat{var}\left(\Delta \hat{P}\right) = \left[\phi\left(\mathbf{x}_1'\hat{\boldsymbol{\beta}}\right)\mathbf{x}_1 - \phi\left(\mathbf{x}_0'\hat{\boldsymbol{\beta}}\right)\mathbf{x}_0 \right]' var\left(\hat{\boldsymbol{\beta}}\right) \left[\phi\left(\mathbf{x}_1'\hat{\boldsymbol{\beta}}\right)\mathbf{x}_1 - \phi\left(\mathbf{x}_0'\hat{\boldsymbol{\beta}}\right)\mathbf{x}_0 \right]$$

An asymptotic t-test of the significance of the difference is based on

$$t = \frac{\Delta \hat{P}}{se\left(\Delta \hat{P}\right)} = \frac{\Phi\left(\mathbf{x}_1'\hat{\boldsymbol{\beta}}\right) - \Phi\left(\mathbf{x}_0'\hat{\boldsymbol{\beta}}\right)}{\left[\widehat{var}\left(\Delta \hat{P}\right) \right]^{1/2}}$$

16A.3 Marginal effects

Assuming that the explanatory variables are continuous, the marginal effect on the probability that $y = 1$ is a derivative. If $\mathbf{x} = \mathbf{x}_0$ is vector of interesting values, then $\hat{P} = \Phi\left(\mathbf{x}_0'\hat{\boldsymbol{\beta}}\right)$, where $\hat{\boldsymbol{\beta}}$ is the vector of maximum likelihood estimates. The estimated marginal effect of a change in $\mathbf{x}$ is

$$\mathbf{me}\left(\hat{\boldsymbol{\beta}}\right) = \frac{\widehat{\partial P}}{\partial \mathbf{x}} = \left. \frac{\partial \Phi\left(\mathbf{x}'\boldsymbol{\beta}\right)}{\partial \mathbf{x}} \right|_{\hat{\boldsymbol{\beta}}} = \phi\left(\mathbf{x}'\hat{\boldsymbol{\beta}}\right)\hat{\boldsymbol{\beta}}$$

To obtain the covariance matrix of this vector we must use the delta method, in conjunction with the "product rule" for derivatives.

$$var\left[\mathbf{me}\left(\hat{\boldsymbol{\beta}}\right) \right] = \left[\frac{\partial \mathbf{me}\left(\boldsymbol{\beta}\right)}{\partial \boldsymbol{\beta}'} \right]_{\hat{\boldsymbol{\beta}}} \times var\left(\hat{\boldsymbol{\beta}}\right) \times \left[\frac{\partial \mathbf{me}\left(\boldsymbol{\beta}\right)}{\partial \boldsymbol{\beta}'} \right]_{\hat{\boldsymbol{\beta}}}'$$

$$\frac{\partial \mathbf{me}\left(\boldsymbol{\beta}\right)}{\partial \boldsymbol{\beta}'} = \frac{\partial \phi\left(\mathbf{x}'\boldsymbol{\beta}\right)\boldsymbol{\beta}}{\partial \boldsymbol{\beta}'} = \phi\left(\mathbf{x}'\boldsymbol{\beta}\right)\mathbf{I}_K + \boldsymbol{\beta}\frac{d\phi(z)}{dz}\frac{\partial z}{\partial \boldsymbol{\beta}'}$$

A property of the normal density function is that $d\phi(z)/dz = -z\phi(z)$. Then, the estimated asymptotic variance of the marginal effects is

$$\widehat{var}\left[\mathbf{me}\left(\hat{\boldsymbol{\beta}}\right) \right] = \left[\phi\left(\mathbf{x}_0'\hat{\boldsymbol{\beta}}\right) \right]^2 \left[\mathbf{I}_K - \left(\mathbf{x}_0'\hat{\boldsymbol{\beta}}\right)\hat{\boldsymbol{\beta}}\mathbf{x}' \right] var\left(\hat{\boldsymbol{\beta}}\right) \left[\mathbf{I}_K - \left(\mathbf{x}_0'\hat{\boldsymbol{\beta}}\right)\hat{\boldsymbol{\beta}}\mathbf{x}' \right]'$$

16A.4 SAS/IML code for probit

The fundamentals of numerical optimization using SAS are discussed in Appendix C. As an illustration we will use Mroz's data on labor force participation, and estimate a model explaining a woman's labor force participation *LFP* as a function of age (*AGE*), years of education (*EDUC*) and the number of children less than 6 years old (*KIDSL6*). In addition to the probit estimates we will predict the probability of her participation for a woman with average age and education with no small children at home, compute the marginal effects of the continuous variables, and the effect on the probability of participation of an increase in *KIDSL6* from 0 to 1. First read the data and use PROC QLIM to estimate the model.

```
options nolabel;
data mroz;
set 'mroz';
run;

proc qlim data=mroz;
model lfp = age educ kidsl6 / discrete;
title 'probit estimates for labor force participation';
run;
```

The (edited) output is

The QLIM Procedure
Discrete Response Profile of LFP

Index	Value	Total Frequency
1	0	325
2	1	428

Model Fit Summary

Log Likelihood   -466.07734

Goodness-of-Fit Measures

Measure	Value	Formula
Likelihood Ratio (R)	97.592	2 * (LogL - LogL0)

Parameter	DF	Estimate	Standard Error	t Value	Approx Pr > |t|
Intercept	1	0.320661	0.411167	0.78	0.4355
AGE	1	-0.033876	0.006713	-5.05	<.0001
EDUC	1	0.122922	0.022081	5.57	<.0001
KIDSL6	1	-0.867276	0.111209	-7.80	<.0001

The IML code follows. References to "G7" are Greene (2012).

```
proc iml;                             * invoke IML;
title;
start probit;                         * start module;
use mroz;                             * open dataset;
read all into x var{age educ kidsl6}; * read X;
read all into y var{lfp};             * read y;
bname ={const,age, educ, kidsl6};     * variable names;

n = nrow(y);                          * number of obs;
```

```
x = j(n,1,1)||x;                        * add const to X;
k = ncol(x);                            * columns X;

/* evaluate derivatives at x0 */
/* discrete change x0 to x1    */
x0 = x[:,];                             * x0 data means;
x0[4]=0;                                * kids16=0;
x1 = x0;                                * x1 data means;
x1[4]=1;                                * kids16=1;

/*  Define Log likelihood function for probit */
start lnl(bmle) global(y,x);
   cdf = probnorm(x*bmle`);
   logl = sum(y#log(cdf) + (1-y)#log(1-cdf)); * G7, p.691, eq.17-16;
   return(logl);
finish lnl;

/* standard normal pdf   */
start pdf(z);
   pdf = exp(-z#z/2)/sqrt(8*atan(1));
   return(pdf);
finish pdf;

/*  Calculate gradient */
start grad(bmle) global(y,x);
   z = x*bmle`;
   pdf = pdf(z);
   cdf = probnorm(z);
   del = (y#(pdf/cdf) - (1-y)#(pdf/(1-cdf)))#x; * G7, p.691;
   del = del[+,];
   return(del);
finish GRAD;

/*  Calculate Hessian       */
start hess(bmle) global(y,x);
   z = x*bmle`;
   pdf = pdf(z);
   cdf = probnorm(z);
   d = y#((pdf+z#cdf)/cdf##2) + (1-y)#((pdf - z#(1-cdf))/(1-cdf)##2);
   d = pdf#d;
   H = -x`*(d#x);
   return(H);
finish hess;

/* begin estimation       */
bmle0 = inv(x`*x)*x`*y;                       * OLS starting values;
bmle0 = bmle0`;

/* MLE estimation   */
opt = {1 0};
```

```
call nlpnra(retcode,bmle,"lnL",bmle0,opt) grd="GRAD" hes="hess";

/* summary stats  */
n1 = sum(y);
lnr =  n1*log(n1/n) + (n-n1)*log((n-n1)/n);   * G7, p.704, eq.17-29;
lnu = lnl(bmle);
lrstat = 2*(lnu - lnr);
pval = 1 - probchi(lrstat,(k-1));
print "LR test of overall significance",, lnr lnu lrstat pval;

h = hess(bmle);
v = -inv(h);
se = sqrt(vecdiag(v));
bmle = bmle`;
tstat = bmle/se;
pval = 2*(1-probt(abs(tstat),(n-k)));
result = bmle||se||tstat||pval;
cname = {est se tstat pval};

print "probit results",, result[colname=cname rowname=bname];

/* Marginal Effects for continuous variables  */

z0 = x0*bmle;
f0 = pdf(z0);
mfx = f0*bmle;
vmfx = (f0##2)*(I(k)-z0*bmle*x0)*v*(I(k)-z0*bmle*x0)`;
semfx = sqrt(vecdiag(vmfx));
tstat = mfx/semfx;
pval = 2*(1-probt(abs(tstat),(n-k)));
result = mfx||semfx||tstat||pval||(x0`);
cname = {mfx se_mfx tstat pval x0};
print "x0 vector " x0[colname=bname],,
      "x1 vector " x1[colname=bname];

print "probit Marginal Effects at x0",,
       result[colname=cname rowname=bname];

/* Predicted probability       */
phat0 = probnorm(z0);
vphat0 = (f0##2)*x0*v*x0`;
sephat0 = sqrt(vphat0);
print "prediction at x0",, phat0 sephat0;

/* Effect of a dummy variable */
z1 = x1*bmle;
f1 = pdf(z1);
phat1 = probnorm(z1);
dp = phat1 - phat0;
vdp = (f1*x1-f0*x0)*v*(f1*x1-f0*x0)`;
```

```
sedp = sqrt(vdp);
tstat = dp/sedp;
pval = 2*(1-probt(abs(tstat),(n-k)));
print "ME of discrete change x0 to x1",, dp sedp tstat pval;

finish;
run probit;
quit;
```

The output is

```
                LR test of overall significance

                lnr        lnu      lrstat       pval
           -514.8732  -466.0773   97.591737          0


                     probit results

                         result
                        EST          SE        TSTAT          PVAL
        CONST     0.320661   0.4111641    0.7798857     0.4357045
        AGE      -0.033876   0.0067131   -5.046187      5.662E-7
        EDUC     0.1229217   0.0220801    5.5670911     3.6103E-8
        KIDSL6   -0.867276   0.1112115   -7.798439      2.109E-14


                         x0
                     CONST        AGE        EDUC      KIDSL6
        x0 vector        1  42.537849  12.286853           0



                         x1
                     CONST        AGE        EDUC      KIDSL6
        x1 vector        1  42.537849  12.286853           1

                probit Marginal Effects at x0

                            result
                  MFX      SE_MFX      TSTAT        PVAL         X0

        CONST   0.1185579  0.1514169  0.7829902   0.4338804          1
        AGE    -0.012525   0.0024289  -5.15663    3.2212E-7  42.537849
        EDUC    0.0454478  0.0081319  5.5888314   3.2022E-8  12.286853
        KIDSL6 -0.320658   0.0383042  -8.37136    2.22E-16           0

                     prediction at x0

                       phat0      sephat0
                     0.6517265  0.0202074


                ME of discrete change x0 to x1

                    dp        sedp       tstat        pval
              -0.335149   0.039957   -8.387745    2.22E-16
```

APPENDIX A

Math Functions

A.1 SAS MATH AND LOGICAL OPERATORS

The basic arithmetic, comparison and logical operators are

Arithmetic Operator	Function	Priority
**	Exponentiation	1
-	Negation	2
*	Multiplication	3
/	Division	3
+	Addition	4
-	Subtraction	4

Comparison Operator	Definition
= or EQ	Equal to
^= or NE	Not equal to
< or LT	Less than
> or GT	Greater than
>= or GE	Greater than or equal to
<= or LE	Less than or equal to

Logical operators return a 1 if a statement is true and returns a 0 if the statement is false.

```
x = (a=b);        x = 1 if a=b, x = 0 if a≠b
```

The logical operator **AND** returns a 1 if two statements linked together are both true and returns a 0 if either statement is false.

```
x = (a=b and c=d);
```

In this case,

```
x = 1 if a=b and c=d, x = 0 if a≠b or c≠d
```

The logical operator **OR** returns a 1 if two statements linked together are both true and returns a 0 if either statement is false.

```
x = (a=b or c=d);
```

Now

```
x = 1 if a=b or c=d, x = 0 if a≠b and c≠d
```

For more, enter **help arithmetic operators**, or **help logical operators,** into the SAS command line and then select

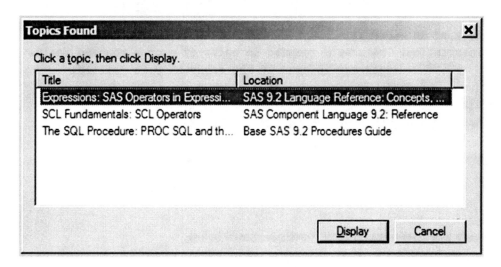

A.2 MATH FUNCTIONS

Below is a summary of common math functions in SAS.

```
abs(x)
    Description:  returns the absolute value of x.

ceil(x)
    Description:  returns the unique integer n such that n - 1 < x < n.

exp(x)
    Description:  returns the exponential function of e^x.  This function
                  is the inverse of ln(x).

floor(x)
    Description:  returns the unique integer n such that n < x < n + 1.
```

```
int(x)
    Description:  returns the integer obtained by truncating x toward 0;

lagN(x)
    Description:  returns the N'th lag of x.

log(x)
    Description:  returns the natural logarithm x.

max(x1,x2,...,xn)
    Description:  returns the maximum value of x1, x2, ..., xn.

min(x1,x2,...,xn)
    Description:  returns the minimum value of x1, x2, ..., xn.

round(x,y) or round(x)
    Description:  returns x rounded in units of y or x rounded to the
                  nearest integer if the argument y is omitted.

sqrt(x)
    Description:  returns the square root of x.
```

For a complete listing of SAS functions, select **HELP** on the SAS menu

then navigate to **Functions and Call Routines** shown below.

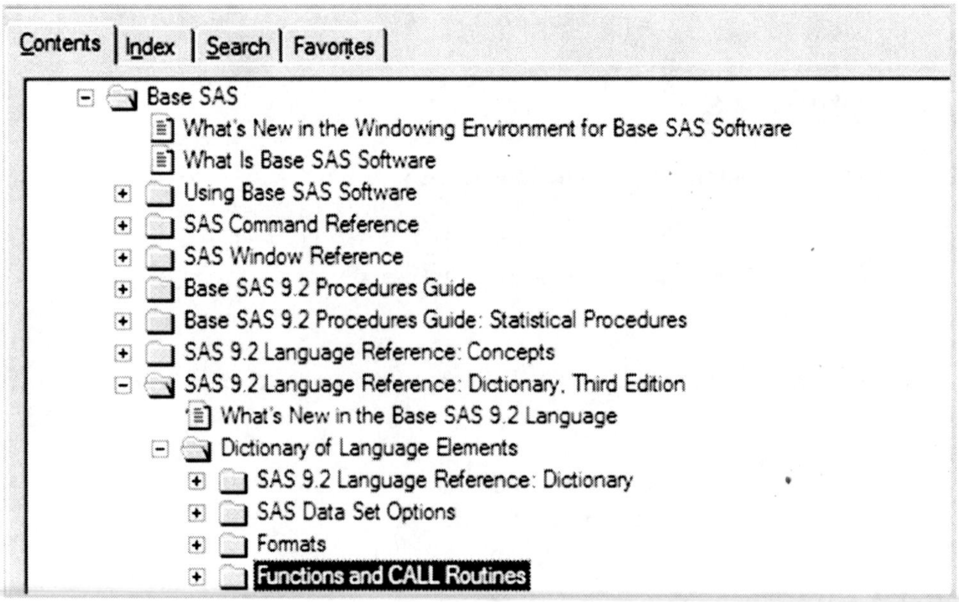

![Screenshot of SAS Help Contents navigation tree]

Contents | Index | Search | Favorites

- Base SAS
  - What's New in the Windowing Environment for Base SAS Software
  - What Is Base SAS Software
  - Using Base SAS Software
  - SAS Command Reference
  - SAS Window Reference
  - Base SAS 9.2 Procedures Guide
  - Base SAS 9.2 Procedures Guide: Statistical Procedures
  - SAS 9.2 Language Reference: Concepts
  - SAS 9.2 Language Reference: Dictionary, Third Edition
    - What's New in the Base SAS 9.2 Language
    - Dictionary of Language Elements
      - SAS 9.2 Language Reference: Dictionary
      - SAS Data Set Options
      - Formats
      - Functions and CALL Routines

A.3 MATRIX MANIPULATION

Within SAS/IML (see Appendix 5A) the basic math operators include:

```
+       addition
-       subtraction
#       scalar or elementwise multiplication
/       scalar or elementwise division
`       transpose
*       matrix multiplication
||      horizontal concatenation; a||b = {a b}
```

$$// \quad \text{vertical concatenation; } a//b = \begin{Bmatrix} a \\ b \end{Bmatrix}$$

```
##      element power; raises each element in the matrix to a power
**      matrix power
@       Kronecker or direct product
[ ]     subscript
<       less than
<=      less than or equal to
>       greater than
>=      greater than or equal to
```

The following can be used within the subscript operator:

```
+       addition; let y = {3, 4, 6}, then y[+]=3+4+6=13
#       multiplication; y[#]=3*4*6=72
:       mean; y[:]=(3+4+6)/n=13/3
##      sum of squares. y[##]=9+16+36=61
```

Scalar functions in SAS/IML:

abs(x)
    Description: returns the absolute value of x.

exp(x)
    Description: returns the exponential function of e^x.

log(x)
    Description: returns the natural logarithm x.

sqrt(x)
    Description: returns the square root of x.

block(A,B)
    Description: creates a new block diagonal matrix from the specified

$$\text{matrices.} \quad \text{Block (A,B)} = \begin{Bmatrix} A & 0 \\ 0 & B \end{Bmatrix}$$

det(X)
    Description: returns the determinant of x.

diag(X)
    Description: creates a diagonal matrix with elements of x on the
                      diagonal.

call eigen(L,P,X)
    Description: returns the eigenvalues and vectors of X.

eigval(X)
    Description: returns the eigenvalues of X;

i(n)
    Description: returns an (n x n) identity matrix.

j(r,c,n)
    Description: returns an (r x c) matrix of identical values (n). For
                      Example, j(n,1,1) returns an (n x 1) vector of ones.

max(X)
    Description: returns the maximum matrix element.

min(X)
    Description: returns the minimum matrix element.

ncol(X)
    Description: returns the number of columns in matrix X.

nrow(X)
    Description: returns the number of rows in matrix X.

root(X)
    Description: Cholesky decomposition.

ssq(X)
    Description: returns the sum of squares of matrix elements.

sum(X)
    Description: returns the sum of matrix elements.

trace(X)
    Description: returns the trace of X (sum of diagonal elements).

vecdiag(X)
    Description: returns a vector of the diagonal elements in matrix X.

For more SAS/IML functions click **HELP** on the SAS menu

Then follow the path shown below to SAS/IML documentation

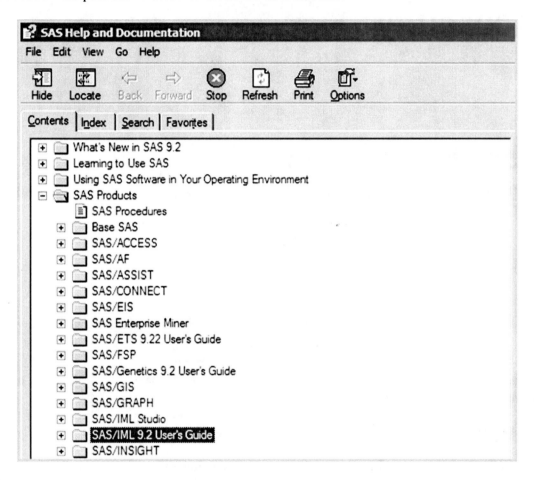

Then

APPENDIX B

Probability

B.1 PROBABILITY CALCULATIONS

Let X be a random variable with cumulative distribution function (*cdf*) $F(x)$. Then the probability that X is less than or equal to any value $X = c$ is

$$P(X \leq c) = F(c)$$

For probabilities "greater than"

$$P(X > c) = 1 - F(c)$$

SAS provides the *cdf*s for many random variables. In the command window enter **help cdf**.

Because this list of functions is so important, we list them on the next page. The syntax of the commands for computing cumulative probabilities is

cdf('distribution name',value,parameter, parameter)

The distribution names are given in the table below. The **value** is $X = c$, the **parameters** control the location and shape of the distributions. The examples we will consider are for the normal, *t*-, *F*-, and chi-square distributions. For these distributions the relevant parameters are:

- normal: mean and standard deviation
- *t*: degrees of freedom
- *F*: numerator degrees of freedom, denominator degrees of freedom
- chi-square: degrees of freedom

CDF Functions

To illustrate the calculations let $X = 2$. The normal distribution with mean μ and variance σ^2 is abbreviated $N(\mu, \sigma^2)$. For the normal *cdf* function in SAS the second parameter is the **standard deviation** σ. Values we obtain are:

$$\mathbf{n1} = P\left[N(\mu = 1, \sigma^2 = 1^2) \le 2 \right] = 0.84134$$

$$\mathbf{n2} = P\left[N(\mu = 2, \sigma^2 = 1^2) \le 2 \right] = 0.5$$

$$\mathbf{n3} = P\left[N(\mu = 3, \sigma^2 = 1^2) > 2 \right] = 0.84134$$

For the *t*-distribution with m degrees of freedom the usual abbreviation is $t_{(m)}$. The calculations we illustrate are:

$$\mathbf{t1} = P\left[t_{(4)} \le 2 \right] = 0.94194$$

$$\mathbf{t2} = P\left[t_{(10)} > 2 \right] = 0.036694$$

The chi-square distribution with m degrees of freedom is abbreviated as $\chi^2_{(m)}$. We compute

$$\mathbf{c1} = P\left[\chi^2_{(4)} \le 2 \right] = 0.26424$$

$$\mathbf{c2} = P\left[\chi^2_{(10)} > 2\right] = 0.99634$$

The F-distribution has two parameters, v_1 the numerator degrees of freedom and v_2 the denominator degrees of freedom, abbreviated as $F_{(v_1, v_2)}$. We illustrate

$$\mathbf{f1} = P\left[F_{(4,30)} \leq 2\right] = 0.88007$$
$$\mathbf{f2} = P\left[F_{(10,30)} > 2\right] = 0.069614$$

The code and output for these calculations is

```
data prob;
x = 2;                              * x value;
n1 =  cdf('normal',x,1,1);          * prob[N(1,1)<=x];
n2 =  cdf('normal',x,2,1);          * prob[N(2,1)<=x];
n3 =  1-cdf('normal',x,3,1);        * prob[N(3,1)>x];
t1 =  cdf('T',x,4);                 * prob[T(4)<=x];
t2 =  1-cdf('T',x,10);              * prob[T(10)>x];
c1 =  cdf('chisquare',x,4);         * prob[chisq(4)<=x];
c2 =  1-cdf('chisquare',x,10);      * prob[chisq(10)>x];
f1 =  cdf('F',x,4,30);              * prob[F(4,30)<=x];
f2 =  1-cdf('F',x,10,30);           * prob[F(10,30)>x];
run;

proc print data=prob;
var n1 n2 n3;
title 'normal probability computations';
run;

proc print data=prob;
var t1 t2;
title 't-distribution probability computations';
run;

proc print data=prob;
var c1 c2;
title 'chi-square distribution probability computations';
run;

proc print data=prob;
var f1 f2;
title 'F-distribution probability computations';
run;
```

```
            normal probability computations
         Obs       n1       n2       n3
          1     0.84134      0.5   0.84134

         t-distribution probability computations
              Obs        t1       t2
               1      0.94194   0.036694

     chi-square distribution probability computations
              Obs        c1       c2
               1      0.26424   0.99634

         F-distribution probability computations
              Obs        f1       f2
               1      0.88007   0.069614
```

B.2 QUANTILES

To find a value that defines a certain **percentile** use SAS **quantile functions.**

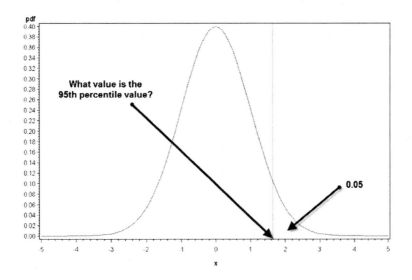

Enter **help quantile** into the command line

The syntax for the command is QUANTILE(dist, probability, parm1,parm2) where **dist** is one of the names of the **probability** distributions listed under **CDF Functions** in the previous section. The probability is a value between 0 and 1, and **parm1, parm2** are parameters of the particular distribution of interest, in the same manner as the **cdf** functions.

```
data quant;
p = 0.95;                            * probability value;
nc =  quantile('normal',p,1,1);      * prob[N(1,1)<=nc]=.95;
tc =  quantile('T',p,4);             * prob[T(4)<=tc]=.95;
```

```
chic =  quantile('chisquare',p,4);        * prob[chisq(4)<=chic]=.95;
fc =  quantile('F',p,4,30);               * prob[F(4,30)<=fc]=.95;
run;

proc print data=quant;
var nc;
title '95th percentile for N(1,1) distribution';
run;

proc print data=quant;
var tc;
title '95th percentile for t(4) distribution';
run;

proc print data=quant;
var chic;
title '95th percentile for chi-square(4) distribution';
run;

proc print data=quant;
var fc;
title '95th percentile for F(4,30) distribution';
run;
```

```
            95th percentile for N(1,1) distribution
                    Obs         nc
                     1       2.64485

            95th percentile for t(4) distribution
                    Obs         tc
                     1       2.13185

          95th percentile for chi-square(4) distribution
                    Obs        chic
                     1       9.48773

            95th percentile for F(4,30) distribution
                    Obs         fc
                     1       2.68963
```

B.3 PLOTTING PROBABILITY DENSITY FUNCTIONS

Becoming familiar with the shapes of the basic probability density functions is very useful. In this section we plot various normal, t, chi-square, and F-densities. SAS has functions parallel to the *cdf* functions that generate probability density values. Enter **help pdf** into the command line.

✓ help pdf ▼

B.3.1 Normal distribution

The syntax is the same as the **cdf** function. Let's generate data from several normal density functions with different means and variances. In the following loop we compute 101 values at increments of 0.1 from −5 to 5.

```
data normal;
     do n = 1 to 101;                            * do loop 101 times;
             x = -5 + (n-1)/10;                  * x = -5 to 5;
             n01 = pdf('normal',x,0,1);          * N(0,1);
             n11 = pdf('normal',x,1,1);          * N(1,1);
             n21 = pdf('normal',x,2,1);          * N(2,1);
             n04 = pdf('normal',x,0,2);          * N(0,4);
             n09 = pdf('normal',x,0,3);          * N(0,9);
             output;                             * observation to data set;
     end;                                        * end do loop;
run;
```

For the graphs we will specify symbols for each curve, and labels for the x and y axes.

```
symbol1 interpol=join value=none color=blue;
symbol2 interpol=join value=dot color=green   height=.5;
symbol3 interpol=join value=square color=red   height=.5;
axis1 label=("x");
axis2 label=("pdf");
```

For each graph we will have a **legend** identifying information about the plots.

```
legend1 label=(justify=c "Distribution"
               justify=c "Parameters")
value=(tick=1  justify=c "N(0,1)"
       tick=2  justify=c "N(1,1)"
       tick=3  justify=c "N(2,1)");
```

The first plot will be for normal density functions with standard deviation 1 and differing means. For complete documentation for **PROC GPLOT** enter **help gplot** into the command window. It has many, many options. The examples below will illustrate some basics.

```
proc gplot data=normal;
plot n01*x=1 n11*x=2 n21*x=3 / overlay
                               haxis=axis1 vaxis=axis2
                               legend=legend1;
title1 "Normal density functions";
title2 "Changing mean";
run;
```

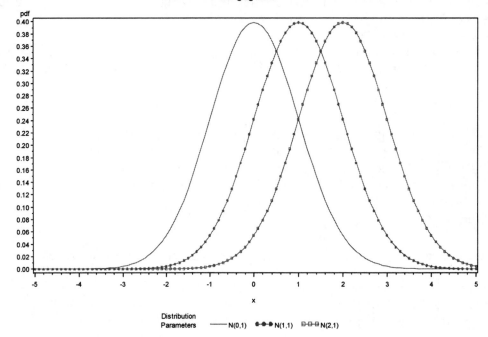

Change the legend and **gplot** statement for the plot of normal densities with mean 0 and differing standard deviations.

```
legend2 label=(justify=c "Distribution"
               justify=c "Parameters")
value=(tick=1  justify=c "N(0,1)"
       tick=2  justify=c "N(0,4)"
       tick=3  justify=c "N(0,9)");

proc gplot data=normal;
plot n01*x=1 n04*x=2 n09*x=3 / overlay
                               haxis=axis1 vaxis=axis2
                               legend=legend2;
title1 "Normal density functions";
title2 "Changing variance";
run;
```

Normal density functions
Changing variance

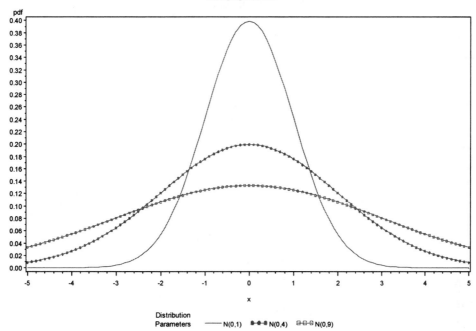

B.3.2 t-distribution

The range of a *t*-random variable is $-\infty$ to $+\infty$. A $t_{(m)}$ random variable has expected value $E\left[t_{(m)}\right]=0$ and variance $\operatorname{var}\left[t_{(m)}\right]=m/(m-2)$. It has a symmetric *pdf* that approaches the *pdf* of the standard normal $N(0,1)$ as $m \to \infty$.

We generate values and implement plots as above.

```
data tdist;
     do n = 1 to 101;           * do loop 101 times;
     x = -5 + (n-1)/10;         * x = -5 to 5;
     t4 = pdf('T',x,4);         * df=4;
     t10 = pdf('T',x,10);       * df=10;
     t30 = pdf('T',x,30);       * df=30;
     output;                    * observation to data set;
     end;                       * end do loop;
run;

legend3 label=(justify=c "Distribution"
               justify=c "Parameters")
value=(tick=1  justify=c "df=4"
       tick=2  justify=c "df=10"
       tick=3  justify=c "df=30");
```

```
proc gplot data=tdist;
plot t4*x=1 t10*x=2 t30*x=3 / overlay
                              haxis=axis1 vaxis=axis2
                              legend=legend3;
title1 "t-distribution density functions";
title2 "Changing degrees of freedom";
run;
```

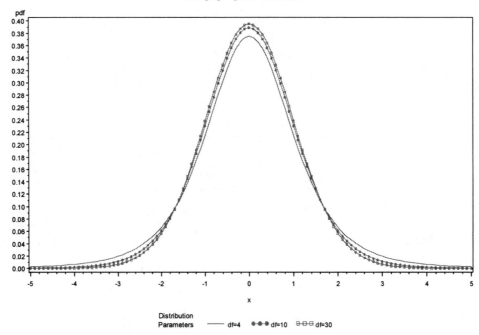

t-distribution density functions
Changing degrees of freedom

B.3.3 Chi-square distribution

If $V \sim \chi^2_{(m)}$ the its values $v \geq 0$. It has mean $E(V) = m$ and variance $\text{var}(V) = 2m$. Chi-square random variables take values greater than, or equal to, 0. The density is skewed, with long tail to the right, but as $m \to \infty$ the density becomes more symmetric.

```
data chisquare;
     do n = 1 to 101;                * do loop 101 times;
     x = (n-1)/2;                    * x = 0 to 50;
     chisq4 = pdf('chisquare',x,4);  * df=4;
     chisq10 = pdf('chisquare',x,10); * df=10;
     chisq30 = pdf('chisquare',x,30); * df=30;
     output;                         * observation to data set;
     end;                            * end do loop;
run;
```

```
legend4 label=(justify=c "Distribution"
               justify=c "Parameters")
value=(tick=1  justify=c "df=4"
       tick=2  justify=c "df=10"
       tick=3  justify=c "df=30");

proc gplot data=chisquare;
plot chisq4*x=1 chisq10*x=2 chisq30*x=3 / overlay
                             haxis=axis1 vaxis=axis2
                             legend=legend4;
title1 "Chi-square density functions";
title2 "Changing degrees of freedom";
run;
```

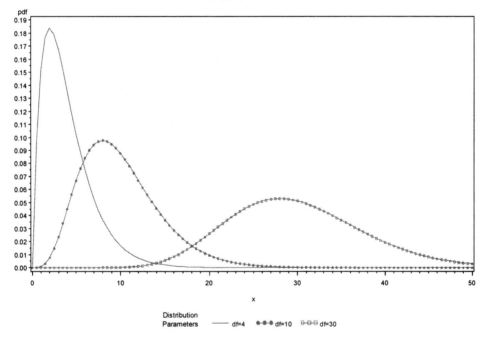

B.3.4 F-distribution

An *F*-random variable must take non-negative values. Its mean and variance are complicated and will not be given here.

```
data fdist;
    do n = 1 to 101;               * do loop 101 times;
    x = (n-1)/25;                  * x = 0 to 4;
    f4 = pdf('F',x,4,30);          * df1=4;
    f10 = pdf('F',x,10,30);        * df1=10;
    f30 = pdf('F',x,30,30);        * df1=30;
    output;                        * observation to data set;
```

```
        end;                                           * end do loop;
    run;

    legend5 label=(justify=c "Distribution"
                   justify=c "Parameters")
    value=(tick=1   justify=c "df1=4"
           tick=2   justify=c "df1=10"
           tick=3   justify=c "df1=30");

    proc gplot data=fdist;
    plot f4*x=1 f10*x=2 f30*x=3 / overlay
                                  haxis=axis1 vaxis=axis2
                                  legend=legend5;
    title1 "F density functions";
    title2 "Changing numerator degrees of freedom";
    title3 "Denominator df=30";
    run;
```

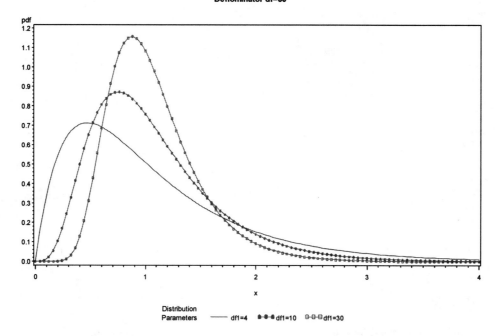

B.4 RANDOM NUMBERS

Modern econometrics and economics use simulation. The basis for simulations is the ability to create random numbers from various distributions. Enter **help rand** into the command window. SAS provides a list of functions from which random numbers can be generated. The syntax is very similar to the **cdf** and **pdf** functions. Computer software gives us the option of creating reproducible strings of random numbers. The **streaminit** function below creates a string based upon the starting value in parentheses.

Below we provide code to simulate values from a normal, chi-square and uniform distributions. The uniform distribution has values between 0 and 1, with intervals of equal length having equal probability of occurring. The value "123" we use to initialize the stream is arbitrary.

```
data random;
call streaminit(123);                  * initialize stream;
do i=1 to 1000;                        * create 1000 values;
      n14=rand('normal',1,2);          * N(1,4);
      chisq4=rand('chisquare',4);      * chi-square df=4;
      u=rand('uniform');               * uniform on 0,1 interval;
      output;
end;
run;
```

Histograms of the values suggest the shape of the *pdf*s. We will use **PROC SGPLOT**. For each histogram we superimpose a normal density (using **density**) and a "free-form" nonparametric version (using **density** with **kernel** option).

```
proc sgplot data=random;
histogram n14;
title1 "Normal N(1,4) histogram";
density n14;                           * fit normal density;
density n14 / type=kernel;             * fit curve;
keylegend / location=inside position=topright;
run;
```

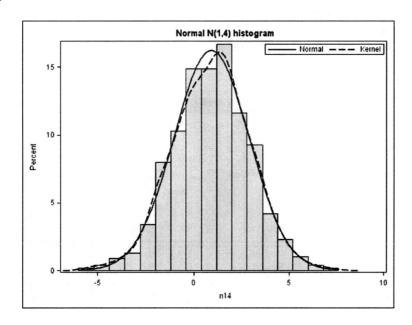

```
proc sgplot data=random;
histogram chisq4;
title1 "Chisquare df=4 histogram";
```

```
density chisq4;
density chisq4 / type=kernel;
keylegend / location=inside position=topright;
run;
```

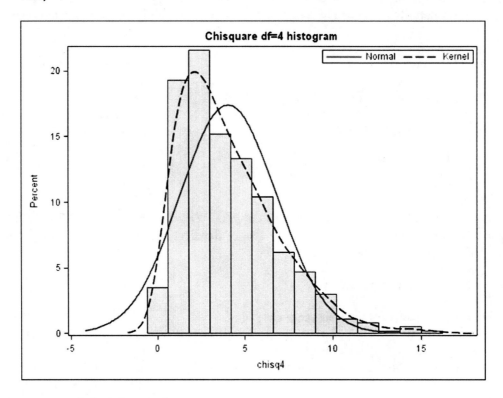

```
proc sgplot data=random;
histogram u;
title1 "Uniform distribution histogram";
run;
```

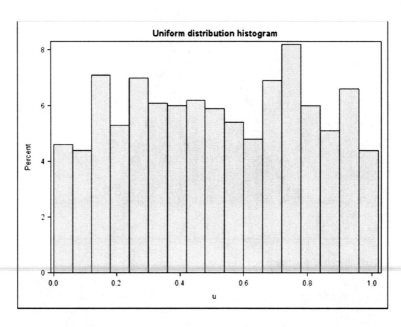

APPENDIX C

Review of Statistical Inference

C.1 HISTOGRAM

Consider the hip width of 50 randomly selected adults contained in the SAS data set *hip*. Open the data.

```
data hip;
set 'hip';
run;

proc contents;
title 'hip data contents';
run;
```

```
        Alphabetic List of Variables and Attributes

    #    Variable    Type    Len    Label
    1    y           Num       8    hip width, inches
```

Construct a (percentage) histogram using **PROC SGPLOT**. The **type=kernel** will fit a nonparametric curve that is useful for visualizing the distribution shape.

```
proc sgplot data=hip;
histogram y;
density y / type=kernel;
title "Hip data histogram";
run;
```

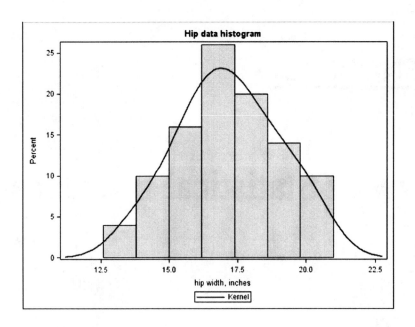

C.2 SUMMARY STATISTICS

Summary statistics are obtained using **PROC MEANS**.

```
proc means data=hip;
title "proc means basic output";
run;
```

```
                    proc means basic output

                    The MEANS Procedure

          Analysis Variable : y hip width, inches
```

N	Mean	Std Dev	Minimum	Maximum
50	17.1582000	1.8070132	13.5300000	20.4000000

For the 50 hip data sample values $y_1, \ldots, y_N$ the sample mean, which is an estimate of the population mean μ, is

$$\bar{y} = \sum_{i=1}^{N} y_i / N = 17.1582$$

The sample variance is an estimate of the population variance σ^2 and is given by

$$\hat{\sigma}^2 = \frac{\sum (y_i - \bar{y})^2}{N-1}$$

The quantity reported by SAS is the standard deviation, $\hat{\sigma} = 1.8070132$. The default version of **PROC MEANS** also reports the number of sample observations N and the minimum and maximum values in the data.

PROC MEANS will compute many other statistics[1]. In the command line enter **help means**, and locate the link describing the **PROC MEANS** statement. Scroll down to find a list of keywords describing a list of statistics that can be computed.

Descriptive statistic keywords

CLM	NMISS
CSS	RANGE
CV	SKEWNESS|SKEW
KURTOSIS|KURT	STDDEV|STD
LCLM	STDERR
MAX	SUM
MEAN	SUMWGT
MIN	UCLM
MODE	USS
N	VAR

Quantile statistic keywords

MEDIAN|P50	Q3|P75
P1	P90
P5	P95
P10	P99
Q1|P25	QRANGE

Hypothesis testing keywords

PROBT|PRT	T

For example, compute the sample mean and variance, as well as the standard error of the mean

$$\operatorname{se}\left(\bar{y}\right) = \hat{\sigma}^2 / N$$

Also, output these values and the sample size for future use.

```
proc means data=hip mean var stderr;
output out=hip1 n=n mean=mean stderr=se;
title "proc means selected output";
run;
```

---

[1] **PROC UNIVARIATE** computes a wide array of detailed summary statistics.

```
                    proc means selected output

                       The MEANS Procedure

               Analysis Variable : y hip width, inches

            Mean            Variance          Std Error
     ─────────────────────────────────────────────────────
          17.1582000        3.2652967        0.2555503
     ─────────────────────────────────────────────────────
```

C.2.1 Estimating higher moments

When computing the sample variance $\hat{\sigma}^2$ uses the degrees of freedom corrected sample size $N-1$ as divisor.

Central moments are expected values, $\mu_r = E\left[(Y-\mu)^r\right]$, and thus they are averages in the population. In statistics the **Law of Large Numbers** says that sample means converge to population averages (expected values) as the sample size $N \to \infty$. We can estimate the higher moments by finding the sample analog, and replacing the population mean μ by its estimator $\bar{Y}$, so that

$$\tilde{\mu}_2 = \sum\left(Y_i - \bar{Y}\right)^2 \Big/ N = \tilde{\sigma}^2$$

$$\tilde{\mu}_3 = \sum\left(Y_i - \bar{Y}\right)^3 \Big/ N$$

$$\tilde{\mu}_4 = \sum\left(Y_i - \bar{Y}\right)^4 \Big/ N$$

Note that in these calculations we divide by N and not $N-1$, since we are using the Law of Large Numbers (i.e., large samples) as justification, and in large samples the correction has little effect. Using these sample estimates of the central moments we can obtain estimates of the skewness coefficient (S) and kurtosis coefficient (K) as

$$\widehat{skewness} = S = \frac{\tilde{\mu}_3}{\tilde{\sigma}^3}$$

$$\widehat{kurtosis} = K = \frac{\tilde{\mu}_4}{\tilde{\sigma}^4}$$

In **PROC MEANS** specify the option **vardef=n** to force higher moments to be computed as above. Also, SAS reports kurtosis as $K-3$, which is the actually "excess kurtosis" relative to the kurtosis of the normal distribution. We output these results for further use.

```
proc means data=hip vardef=n var std kurt skew;
output out=hip2 n=n skew=skew kurt=kurt;
title "proc means vardef=n for higher moments";
run;
```

```
proc means vardef=n for higher moments

            The MEANS Procedure

    Analysis Variable : y hip width, inches
```

Variance	Std Dev	Kurtosis	Skewness
3.1999908	1.7888518	-0.6684658	-0.0138250

C.2.2 Jarque-Bera normality test

The normal distribution is symmetric, and has a bell-shape with a peakedness and tail-thickness leading to a kurtosis of 3. Thus we can test for departures from normality[2] by checking the skewness and kurtosis from a sample of data. If skewness is not close to zero, and if kurtosis is not close to 3, then we would reject the normality of the population.

The **Jarque-Bera** test statistic allows a joint test of these two characteristics,

$$JB = \frac{N}{6}\left(S^2 + \frac{(K-3)^2}{4} \right)$$

If the true distribution is symmetric and has kurtosis 3, which includes the normal distribution, then the JB test statistic has a chi-square distribution with 2 degrees of freedom if the sample size is sufficiently large. If $\alpha = .05$ then the critical value of the $\chi^2_{(2)}$ distribution is 5.99. We reject the null hypothesis and conclude that the data are non-normal if $JB \geq 5.99$. If we reject the null hypothesis then we know the data have non-normal characteristics, but we do not know what distribution the population might have.

Using the output data set *hip2*

```
data normaltest;
set hip2;
jb = (n/6)*(skew**2 + (kurt**2)/4);
pvalue = 1 - cdf('chisquare',jb,2);
run;

proc print data=normaltest;
var jb pvalue;
title "Jarque-Bera test for normality";
run;
```

```
            Jarque-Bera test for normality

            Obs       jb       pvalue
             1      0.93252    0.62734
```

---

[2] PROC UNIVARIATE provides other tests for normality.

C.3 CONFIDENCE INTERVAL FOR THE MEAN

The standardized random variable

$$t = \frac{\bar{Y} - \mu}{\hat{\sigma}/\sqrt{N}} \sim t_{(N-1)}$$

The notation $t_{(N-1)}$ denotes a t-distribution with $N-1$ "degrees of freedom." Let the critical value t_c be the $100(1-\alpha/2)$-percentile value $t_{(1-\alpha/2, N-1)}$. This critical value has the property that $P\left[t_{(N-1)} \leq t_{(1-\alpha/2, N-1)}\right] = 1 - \alpha/2$. The $100(1-\alpha)\%$ interval estimator for μ is $\bar{Y} \pm t_c \hat{\sigma}/\sqrt{N}$ or $\bar{Y} \pm t_c \operatorname{se}(\bar{Y})$

Using the data from the output data set *hip1*,

```
data hip1;
set hip1;
tc = quantile('T',.975,n-1);
lb = mean-tc*se;
ub = mean+tc*se;
run;

proc print data=hip1;
var mean se tc lb ub;
title "interval estimate of population mean hip width";
run;
```

```
        interval estimate of population mean hip width

Obs      mean        se         tc        lb        ub
 1      17.1582    0.25555    2.00958    16.6447   17.6717
```

C.4 TESTING THE POPULATION MEAN

Consider the null hypothesis $H_0 : \mu = c$. If the sample data come from a normal population with mean μ and variance σ^2, then

$$t = \frac{\bar{Y} - \mu}{\hat{\sigma}/\sqrt{N}} \sim t_{(N-1)}$$

If the null hypothesis $H_0 : \mu = c$ is true, then

$$t = \frac{\bar{Y} - c}{\hat{\sigma}/\sqrt{N}} \sim t_{(N-1)}$$

If the null hypothesis is not true, then the t-statistic does not have the usual t-distribution.

C.4.1 A right-tail test

If the alternative hypothesis $H_1 : \mu > c$ is true, then the value of the t-statistic tends to become larger than usual for the t-distribution. Let the critical value t_c be the $100(1-\alpha)$-percentile $t_{(1-\alpha, N-1)}$ from a t-distribution with $N-1$ degrees of freedom. If the t-statistic is greater than or equal to t_c then we reject $H_0 : \mu = c$ and accept the alternative $H_1 : \mu > c$.

Let's test the null hypothesis that the mean population hip width is 16.5 inches or less, against the alternative that hip width is greater than 16.5.

```
data hiptest;
set hip1;
h0=16.5;
tstat = (mean-h0)/se;
tc = quantile('T',.95,n-1);
pvalue = 1-cdf('T',tstat,n-1);
run;

proc print data=hiptest;
var mean se h0 tstat tc pvalue;
title "One tail test: true mean > 16.5";
run;
```

```
                     One tail test: true mean > 16.5

    Obs     mean       se       h0      tstat        tc        pvalue
     1     17.1582   0.25555   16.5    2.57562    1.67655    .006536945
```

C.4.2 A two-tail test

Consider the alternative hypothesis $H_1 : \mu \neq c$. If the alternative hypothesis $H_1 : \mu \neq c$ is true, then values of the test statistic may be unusually "large" or unusually "small." The rejection region consists of the two "tails" of the t-distribution, and this is called a two-tail test. The upper critical value is the $100(1 - \alpha/2)$-percentile from a t-distribution with $N-1$ degrees of freedom, $t_c = t_{(1-\alpha/2, N-1)}$, so that $P[t \geq t_c] = P[t \leq -t_c] = \alpha/2$. Use the output data set *hip1* to test the null hypothesis that the population mean hip width is 17 inches, against the alternative that it is not.

```
data hiptest;
set hip1;
h0=17;
tstat = (mean-h0)/se;
tc_025 = quantile('T',.025,n-1);
tc_975 = quantile('T',.975,n-1);
pvalue = 2*(1-cdf('T',abs(tstat),n-1));
run;
```

The above command for the **pvalue** uses the absolute value of the t-statistic so that the command will be correct whether the t-value is positive or negative.

```
proc print data=hiptest;
var mean se h0 tstat tc_025 tc_975 pvalue;
title "Two tail test: true mean = 17";
run;
```

Two tail test: true mean = 17

Obs	mean	se	h0	tstat	tc_025	tc_975	pvalue
1	17.1582	0.25555	17	0.61906	-2.00958	2.00958	0.53875

C.4.3 Automatic tests using PROC TTEST

It will not surprise you that SAS has a procedure for testing hypotheses about population means. Enter **help ttest** into the command line to see all its options. Here we provide the commands and output to replicate the one- and two-tail tests in the sections above. As you will see there is lots of output. Find the relevant bits.

```
proc ttest data=hip h0=16.5 sides=u alpha=0.05;
var y;
title "Automatic one tail test: true mean=16.5";
run;
```

Automatic one tail test: true mean=16.5

The TTEST Procedure

Variable: y (hip width, inches)

N	Mean	Std Dev	Std Err	Minimum	Maximum
50	17.1582	1.8070	0.2556	13.5300	20.4000

Mean	95% CL Mean		Std Dev	95% CL Std Dev	
17.1582	16.7298	Infty	1.8070	1.5095	2.2518

DF	t Value	Pr > t
49	2.58	0.0065

```
proc ttest data=hip h0=17 sides=2 alpha=0.05;
var y;
title "Automatic two tail test: true mean=17";
run;
```

Automatic two tail test: true mean=17

The TTEST Procedure

Variable: y (hip width, inches)

N	Mean	Std Dev	Std Err	Minimum	Maximum
50	17.1582	1.8070	0.2556	13.5300	20.4000

```
    Mean        95% CL Mean         Std Dev      95% CL Std Dev
  17.1582    16.6447  17.6717        1.8070      1.5095   2.2518

                  DF    t Value     Pr > |t|
                  49       0.62       0.5387
```

C.5 MAXIMUM LIKELIHOOD ESTIMATION: ONE PARAMETER

Many complex models can be estimated using the **maximum likelihood** principle. The method requires us to obtain the values of the parameters that maximize, with respect to the unknown parameters, the joint probability density function of the observed data.

C.5.1 A coin flip example

To illustrate consider an experiment in which we flip a coin, which may or may not be "fair," 3 times, and observe the outcome to be a head, on one side of the coin, or a tail, on the other side of the coin. Define the observed outcome as

$$X = \begin{cases} 1 & HEAD \\ 0 & TAIL \end{cases}$$

Let the probability that $X = 1$ be p, and the probability that $X = 0$ be $1 - p$. The probability function for this Bernouilli random variable is

$$P(X = x) = f(x \mid p) = p^x (1-p)^{1-x}, \quad x = 0,1$$

Suppose in the 3 flips of the coin we observe 2 heads and 1 tail, or $x_1 = 1$, $x_2 = 1$, and $x_3 = 0$. Assuming these are independent flips, the joint probability function is

$$f(x_1, x_2, x_3 \mid p) = f(x_1 \mid p) f(x_2 \mid p) f(x_3 \mid p)$$

$$= p \times p \times (1-p) = p^2 - p^3$$

$$= L(p \mid x_1 = 1, x_2 = 1, x_3 = 0)$$

The maximum likelihood estimate of p is that value, $\tilde{p}$, that maximizes this **likelihood function**, $L(p)$. You see that the joint probability function $f(x_1, x_2, x_3)$ and the likelihood function $L(p)$ are the same, but with the joint probability function interpreted as a function of the x_i given the value of the parameter p, and the likelihood function interpreted as a function of the unknown parameter and given the observed data $x_1 = 1$, $x_2 = 1$, and $x_3 = 0$. A picture of this likelihood function for values of p between 0 and 1 is shown in Figure C.1a [Note, when $p = 1$ $L(p) = 0$].

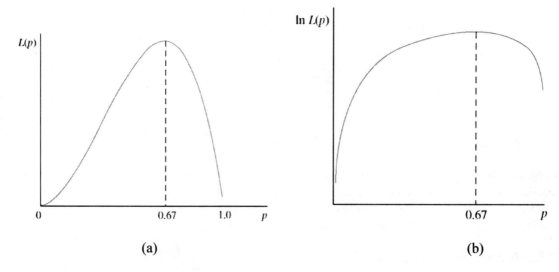

(a)   (b)

Figure C.1 (a) A likelihood function (b) The log-likelihood function

Mathematically it is easier to maximize the logarithm of the likelihood function.

$$\ln L(p) = \ln\left(p \times p \times (1-p)\right)$$

$$= \ln(p) + \ln(p) + \ln(1-p) = 2\ln(p) + \ln(1-p)$$

The two functions, $L(p)$ and $\ln L(p)$ reach their maximum values at the same value of p and the maximum likelihood estimate of p, given the 3 data points $x_1 = 1$, $x_2 = 1$, and $x_3 = 0$ is $\tilde{p} = 2/3 = 0.67$. This numeric value was obtained using calculus. At the maximum of a function the slope must be zero and the second derivative must be negative. The slope of the log-likelihood function is

$$\frac{d\ln L(p)}{dp} = \frac{d\left[2\ln(p) + \ln(1-p)\right]}{dp} = \frac{2}{p} - \frac{1}{1-p} = g(p)$$

Here $g(p)$ is shorthand notation for "the gradient evaluated at p", where gradient is the slope at a point. Setting this value to zero and solving yields $\tilde{p} = 2/3$. The second derivative is

$$\frac{d^2 \ln L(p)}{dp^2} = \frac{d\left[\dfrac{2}{p} - \dfrac{1}{1-p}\right]}{dp} = \frac{-2}{p^2} - \frac{1}{(1-p)^2} = H(p)$$

The second derivative, known as the "Hessian" $H(p)$, is negative for all values of p between 0 and 1, so that $\tilde{p} = 2/3$ is the maximum likelihood estimate of p, given this sample of values.

If we were not able to solve for the maximum likelihood estimate using calculus, what would we do? **Numerical optimization** describes the approach we will take, which uses iterative algorithms to locate the maximizing value of a function. For the function $L(p)$, which is a function of a single parameter p, the Newton-Raphson algorithm is

$$p_{n+1} = p_n - \left[\frac{d^2 \ln L(p)}{dp^2}\bigg|_{p=p_n}\right]^{-1} \frac{d \ln L(p)}{dp}\bigg|_{p=p_n} = p_n - \left[H(p)\big|_{p=p_n}\right]^{-1} g(p)\big|_{p=p_n}$$

Given an initial estimate, p_1, the steps taken by this algorithm lead to a **local** maximum or minimum.

For this one parameter problem the calculations can be done in the SAS/Data step:

```
data mle;                                   * create data set;
phat = 1/4;                                 * starting value;
      do n = 1 to 7;                        * do-loop 7 iterations;
      loglike = 2*log(phat)+log(1-phat);    * log-likelihood function;
      g = 2/phat - 1/(1-phat);              * gradient;
      h = -2/phat**2 - 1/(1-phat)**2;       * hessian;
      phat = phat - (h**-1)*g;              * Newton Raphson step;
      output;                               * write to sas data set;
      end;                                  * end do-loop;
run;
proc print data=mle;
var n phat loglike g h;
title 'MLE for coin flip example';
run;
```

```
              MLE for coin flip example

Obs   n     phat      loglike       g          h
 1    1    0.44737   -3.06027    6.66667    -33.7778
 2    2    0.64794   -2.20181    2.66106    -13.2675
 3    3    0.66713   -1.91187    0.24629    -12.8319
 4    4    0.66667   -1.90954   -0.00630    -13.5189
 5    5    0.66667   -1.90954   -0.00000    -13.5000
 6    6    0.66667   -1.90954   -0.00000    -13.5000
 7    7    0.66667   -1.90954    0.00000    -13.5000
```

The parameter estimate, which we have called *PHAT* converges from the starting value of ¼ (which is a poor guess) to the maximum likelihood estimate in 5 steps. How do we know when the iterative algorithm has done its work? When the estimates have stopped changing, or more properly when the gradient, first derivative, reaches zero. Note that at the maximizing value the value of the log-likelihood function is -1.90954, and the value of the Hessian (second derivative) is -13.50, ensuring that $\hat{p} = 2/3$ is a local maximum. In this problem there is only one solution because the Hessian is negative for all values of p between 0 and 1, so the log-likelihood is function is "globally concave."

C.5.2 Statistical inference

If we use maximum likelihood estimation, how do we perform hypothesis tests and construct confidence intervals? The answers to these questions are found in some remarkable properties of estimators obtained using maximum likelihood methods. Let us consider a general problem. Let X be a random variable (either discrete or continuous) with a probability density function $f(x|\theta)$, where θ is an unknown parameter. The log-likelihood function, based on a random sample $x_1, \ldots, x_N$ of size N, is

$$\ln L(\theta) = \sum_{i=1}^{N} \ln f(x_i \mid \theta)$$

If the probability density function of the random variable involved is relatively smooth, and if certain other technical conditions hold, then in large samples the maximum likelihood estimator $\hat{\theta}$ of a parameter θ has a probability distribution that is approximately normal, with expected value θ and a variance $V = \mathrm{var}(\hat{\theta})$ that we will discuss in a moment. That is, we can say

$$\hat{\theta} \overset{a}{\sim} N(\theta, V)$$

where the symbol $\overset{a}{\sim}$ denotes "asymptotically distributed." The word "asymptotic" refers to estimator properties when the sample size N becomes large, or as $N \to \infty$. To say that an estimator is asymptotically normal means that its probability distribution, that may be unknown when samples are small, becomes approximately normal in large samples.

Based on the normality result we can immediately construct a t-statistic, and obtain both a confidence interval and a test statistic from it. Specifically, if we wish to test the null hypothesis $H_0 : \theta = c$ against a one-tail or two-tail alternative hypothesis then we can use the test statistic

$$t = \frac{\hat{\theta} - c}{\mathrm{se}(\hat{\theta})} \overset{a}{\sim} t_{(N-1)}$$

If the null hypothesis is true, then this t-statistic has a distribution that can be approximated by a t-distribution with $N-1$ degrees of freedom in large samples.

If t_c denotes the $100(1-\alpha/2)$ percentile $t_{(1-\alpha/2, N-1)}$, then a $100(1-\alpha)\%$ confidence interval for θ is

$$\hat{\theta} \pm t_c \mathrm{se}(\hat{\theta})$$

A key ingredient in both the test statistic and confidence interval expressions is the standard error $\mathrm{se}(\hat{\theta})$. Where does this come from? Standard errors are square roots of estimated variances. The part we have delayed discussing is how we find the variance of the maximum likelihood estimator, $V = \mathrm{var}(\hat{\theta})$. The variance V is given by the inverse of the negative expectation of the second derivative of the log-likelihood function,

$$V = \mathrm{var}(\hat{\theta}) = \left[-E\left(\frac{d^2 \ln L(\theta)}{d\theta^2} \right) \right]^{-1}$$

The quantity

$$I(\theta) = -E\left(\frac{d^2 \ln L(\theta)}{d\theta^2} \right)$$

is an **information** measure that involves an expected value operation. This expectation can be difficult, but it can be consistently estimated by

$$-\left(\frac{d^2 \ln L(\theta)}{d\theta^2}\right) = -H(\theta)$$

C.5.3 Inference in the coin flip example

If we flip the coin N times we observe N sample values $x_1, x_2, \ldots, x_N$. Assuming that the flips are independent, we can form the joint probability function

$$f(x_1, \ldots, x_N \mid p) = f(x_1 \mid p) \times \cdots \times f(x_N \mid p) = p^{\sum x_i}(1-p)^{N-\sum x_i} = L(p \mid x_1, \ldots, x_N)$$

For the general problem we are considering the log-likelihood function is

$$\ln L(p) = \sum_{i=1}^{N} \ln f(x_i \mid p) = \left(\sum_{i=1}^{N} x_i\right) \ln(p) + \left(N - \sum_{i=1}^{N} x_i\right) \ln(1-p)$$

The first derivative is

$$\frac{d \ln L(p)}{dp} = \frac{\sum x_i}{p} - \frac{N - \sum x_i}{1-p}$$

Setting this to zero, and replacing p by $\hat{p}$ to denote the value that maximizes $\ln L(p)$, yields the maximum likelihood estimator

$$\hat{p} = \frac{\sum x_i}{N} = \overline{x}$$

This is the sample proportion of 1s in N flips. In Section C.5.1 we used $N = 3$ flips and found by numerical optimization that the maximum likelihood estimate was 2/3. This shows that in some cases the maximum likelihood estimator can be derived analytically.

The second derivative of the log-likelihood function is

$$\frac{d^2 \ln L(p)}{dp^2} = -\frac{\sum x_i}{p^2} - \frac{N - \sum x_i}{(1-p)^2}$$

To calculate the variance of the maximum likelihood estimator we need the "expected value" of the second derivative. In the expectation we treat the x_i values as random because these values vary from sample to sample.

$$E(x_i) = 1 \times P(x_i = 1) + 0 \times P(x_i = 0) = 1 \times p + 0 \times (1-p) = p$$

Then, we find the expected value of the second derivative as

$$E\left(\frac{d^2 \ln L(p)}{dp^2}\right) = -\frac{N}{p(1-p)}$$

The variance of the sample proportion, which is the maximum likelihood estimator of p, is then

$$V = \text{var}(\hat{p}) = \left[-E\left(\frac{d^2 \ln L(p)}{dp^2} \right) \right]^{-1} = \frac{p(1-p)}{N}$$

The asymptotic distribution of the sample proportion, that is valid in large samples, is

$$\hat{p} \overset{a}{\sim} N\left(p, \frac{p(1-p)}{N} \right)$$

To estimate the variance V we must replace the true population proportion by its estimate,

$$\hat{V} = \frac{\hat{p}(1-\hat{p})}{N}$$

The standard error that we need for hypothesis testing and interval estimation is

$$\text{se}(\hat{p}) = \sqrt{\hat{V}} = \sqrt{\frac{\hat{p}(1-\hat{p})}{N}}$$

In the example we used to motivate maximum likelihood estimation, we used $N = 3$ observations and obtained $\hat{p} = 2/3$. The requirements for inference are **large samples**. The asymptotic normal distribution of the maximum likelihood estimator is an approximation that works well in large samples, but with small samples the approximate normal distribution is not valid. "What is a large sample?" This is a frequently asked question and there is no one simple rule or number that can be provided as an answer. It depends in part on the complexity of the problem. For the sample proportion 50 observations may be enough to ensure approximate normality. Pollsters often take $N = 1000$ ensuring a ±0.03 margin of error.

C.6 MAXIMUM LIKELIHOOD ESTIMATION

Some notation must be developed for the general K parameter case. Let y be an observable random variable with density function $f(y|\theta)$ where θ is a $K \times 1$ vector with elements $(\theta_1, \theta_2, \ldots, \theta_K)$. Based on N observations $\mathbf{y}' = (y_1, y_2, \ldots, y_N)$ the log-likelihood function is

$$\ln L(\theta|\mathbf{y}) = \sum_{i=1}^{N} \ln f(y_i|\theta) = \ln L(\theta)$$

Denote the vector of first derivatives (also known as the **score vector** and **gradient vector**) as

$$\mathbf{g} = \frac{\partial \ln L(\theta|\mathbf{y})}{\partial \theta} = \sum_{i=1}^{N} \frac{\partial \ln f(y_i|\theta)}{\partial \theta} = \sum_{i=1}^{N} \mathbf{g}_i$$

The matrix of second derivatives, or Hessian, is

$$\mathbf{H} = \frac{\partial^2 \ln L(\theta|\mathbf{y})}{\partial \theta \partial \theta'} = \sum_{i=1}^{N} \frac{\partial^2 \ln f(y_i|\theta)}{\partial \theta \partial \theta'} = \sum_{i=1}^{N} \mathbf{H}_i$$

Under standard assumptions[3] The maximum likelihood estimator $\hat{\theta}$ has an asymptotic normal distribution,

$$\hat{\theta} \overset{a}{\sim} N\left(\theta, \left[\mathbf{I}(\theta)\right]^{-1}\right)$$

The information matrix $\mathbf{I}(\theta)$ is

$$\mathbf{I}(\theta) = -E\left\{\frac{\partial^2 \ln L(\theta \mid \mathbf{y})}{\partial \theta \partial \theta'}\right\}$$

For inference we evaluate the information matrix at the maximum likelihood estimates, so that the asymptotic covariance matrix is estimated as

$$\widehat{\text{cov}}(\hat{\theta}) = \left[\mathbf{I}(\hat{\theta})\right]^{-1} = \hat{\mathbf{V}}_1$$

In many cases the information matrix is consistently estimated using the negative of the Hessian.

$$\widehat{\text{cov}}(\hat{\theta}) = \left[-\frac{\partial^2 \ln L(\theta \mid \mathbf{y})}{\partial \theta \partial \theta'}\bigg|_{\hat{\theta}}\right]^{-1} = \left[-\mathbf{H}(\hat{\theta})\right]^{-1} = \hat{\mathbf{V}}_2$$

A third possibility is the estimator of Berndt, Hall, Hall and Hausman (**BHHH**), or **outer product of gradients (OPG)**. Let

$$\hat{\mathbf{g}}_i = \frac{\partial \ln f(y_i \mid \theta)}{\partial \theta}\bigg|_{\hat{\theta}}$$

Stacking these $K \times 1$ vectors into the rows of a $N \times K$ matrix we have

$$\hat{\mathbf{G}} = \begin{bmatrix} \hat{\mathbf{g}}_1' \\ \hat{\mathbf{g}}_2' \\ \vdots \\ \hat{\mathbf{g}}_N' \end{bmatrix}$$

Then

$$\widehat{\text{cov}}(\hat{\theta}) = \left[\sum_{i=1}^{N} \hat{\mathbf{g}}_i \hat{\mathbf{g}}_i'\right]^{-1} = \left[\hat{\mathbf{G}}'\hat{\mathbf{G}}\right]^{-1} = \hat{\mathbf{V}}_3$$

These three estimators of the covariance matrix are asymptotically equivalent but the differences may be quite large in finite samples.

To maximize the log-likelihood function we must in general uses numerical methods because the first order conditions for the maximization problem cannot be solved analytically. The iterative algorithm called Newton's method[4] is

$$\hat{\theta}_{t+1} = \hat{\theta}_t - \mathbf{H}_t^{-1}\mathbf{g}_t$$

---

[3] See William Greene, *Econometric Analysis*, 7*th* *Edition*, 2012, p. 517. We omit many technical conditions and details in this brief presentation.

[4] Greene (2012), p. 1098.

where $\mathbf{H}_t$ is the Hessian matrix evaluated at the t'th round estimate $\hat{\boldsymbol{\theta}}_t$, and $\mathbf{g}_t$ is the gradient vector evaluated at $\hat{\boldsymbol{\theta}}_t$. Because of the asymptotic equivalence of the alternative covariance matrices to variants of Newton's method are the **method of scoring**

$$\hat{\boldsymbol{\theta}}_{t+1} = \hat{\boldsymbol{\theta}}_t + \left[\mathbf{I}\left(\hat{\boldsymbol{\theta}}_t\right) \right]^{-1} \mathbf{g}_t$$

and the BHHH algorithm

$$\hat{\boldsymbol{\theta}}_{t+1} = \hat{\boldsymbol{\theta}}_t + \left[\hat{\mathbf{G}}'_t \hat{\mathbf{G}}_t \right]^{-1} \mathbf{g}_t$$

C.6.1 Exponential distribution example

William Greene (2012, p. 522) has an example using an exponential distribution that illustrates many points concerning maximum likelihood estimation and inference. He was kind enough to let us use his example here. The data, shown below, are artificially generated.

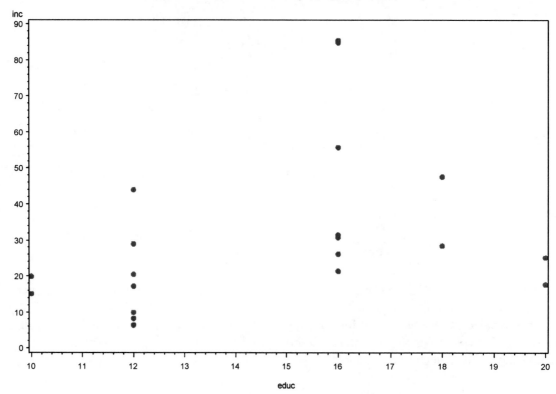

Education and Income Data
William Greene, Econometric Analysis, 7e, 2012, Table FC.1

The model he proposes is embodied in the exponential density function

$$f\left(y_i = INCOME_i \mid x_i = EDUCATION, \beta\right) = \frac{1}{\beta + x_i} e^{-y_i/(\beta + x_i)}$$

This is an example of an exponential distribution, where

$$f(y) = \lambda e^{-\lambda y} \text{ for } y \geq 0, \lambda > 0$$

with $E(y) = 1/\lambda$ and $\text{var}(y) = 1/\lambda^2$.

In the *INCOME-EDUCATION* example $E(y_i) = 1/\lambda_i = \beta + x_i$. The likelihood function for the exponential model is

$$L(\beta \mid \mathbf{y}, \mathbf{x}) = \prod_{i=1}^{N} \frac{1}{\beta + x_i} e^{-y_i/(\beta + x_i)}$$

The log-likelihood and first and second derivatives are

$$\ln L(\beta) = -\sum_{i=1}^{N} \ln(\beta + x_i) - \sum_{i=1}^{N} \frac{y_i}{\beta + x_i}$$

$$\frac{d \ln L(\beta)}{d\beta} = \sum_{i=1}^{N} \left[\frac{-1}{\beta + x_i} + \frac{y_i}{(\beta + x_i)^2} \right] = \sum_{i=1}^{N} g_i = g$$

$$\frac{d^2 \ln L(\beta)}{d\beta^2} = \sum_{i=1}^{N} \frac{1}{(\beta + x_i)^2} - 2\sum_{i=1}^{N} \frac{y_i}{(\beta + x_i)^3}$$

Using the fact that $E(y_i) = \beta + x_i$,

$$E\left(\frac{d^2 \ln L(\beta)}{d\beta^2} \right) = \sum_{i=1}^{N} \frac{1}{(\beta + x_i)^2} - 2\sum_{i=1}^{N} \frac{E(y_i)}{(\beta + x_i)^3} = -\sum_{i=1}^{N} \frac{1}{(\beta + x_i)^2} = H(\beta)$$

Consequently

$$\mathbf{I}(\beta) = -E\left(\frac{d^2 \ln L(\beta)}{d\beta^2} \right) = \sum_{i=1}^{N} \frac{1}{(\beta + x_i)^2}$$

The three covariance matrix estimators are

$$\hat{\mathbf{V}}_1 = \left[\mathbf{I}(\hat{\beta}) \right]^{-1} = \left[\sum_{i=1}^{N} \frac{1}{(\hat{\beta} + x_i)^2} \right]^{-1}$$

$$\hat{\mathbf{V}}_2 = \left[-H(\hat{\beta}) \right]^{-1}$$

$$\hat{\mathbf{V}}_3 = \left[\sum_{i=1}^{N} \hat{g}_i^2 \right]^{-1}$$

C.6.2 Gamma distribution example

The exponential distribution is a special case of the gamma distribution, which turns out to be quite important in this illustration. The gamma distribution[5] is

$$f(y) = \frac{\lambda^\rho}{\Gamma(\rho)} e^{-\lambda y} y^{\rho-1} \text{ for } y \geq 0, \lambda > 0, \rho > 0$$

If y has this gamma distribution $E(y) = \rho/\lambda$ and $\text{var}(y) = \rho/\lambda^2$. If $\rho = 1$, then the gamma distribution simplifies to the exponential distribution. For the *INCOME-EDUCATION* example the proposed probability model is

$$f(y_i \mid x_i, \beta, \rho) = \frac{(\beta + x_i)^{-\rho}}{\Gamma(\rho)} y_i^{\rho-1} e^{-y_i/(\beta + x_i)}$$

The log-likelihood is then

$$\ln L(\beta, \rho) = \sum_{i=1}^N \ln \left[\frac{(\beta + x_i)^{-\rho}}{\Gamma(\rho)} y_i^{\rho-1} e^{-y_i/(\beta + x_i)} \right]$$

$$= -\rho \sum_{i=1}^N \ln(\beta + x_i) - \sum_{i=1}^N \ln\Gamma(\rho) + (\rho - 1)\sum_{i=1}^N \ln y_i - \sum_{i=1}^N \frac{y_i}{\beta + x_i}$$

Define $\theta = [\beta \ \ \rho]'$, then the gradient vector is

$$\mathbf{g}(\theta) = \begin{bmatrix} \dfrac{\partial \ln L(\beta, \rho)}{\partial \beta} \\[2ex] \dfrac{\partial \ln L(\beta, \rho)}{\partial \rho} \end{bmatrix} = \begin{bmatrix} -\rho \displaystyle\sum_{i=1}^N \frac{1}{\beta + x_i} + \sum_{i=1}^N \frac{y_i}{(\beta + x_i)^2} \\[2ex] -\displaystyle\sum_{i=1}^N \ln(\beta + x_i) - N\frac{\partial \ln\Gamma(\rho)}{\partial \rho} + \sum_{i=1}^N \ln y_i \end{bmatrix}$$

The derivative of the log gamma function $\ln\Gamma(\rho)$ is actually a special mathematical function of its own called the "digamma" function.

$$\frac{\partial \ln\Gamma(\rho)}{\partial \rho} = \frac{\Gamma'(\rho)}{\Gamma(\rho)} = \Psi = \text{ digamma function}$$

The Hessian is

$$\mathbf{H} = \begin{bmatrix} \dfrac{\partial^2 \ln L(\beta, \rho)}{\partial \beta^2} & \dfrac{\partial \ln L(\beta, \rho)}{\partial \beta \partial \rho} \\[2ex] \dfrac{\partial \ln L(\beta, \rho)}{\partial \beta \partial \rho} & \dfrac{\partial^2 \ln L(\beta, \rho)}{\partial \rho^2} \end{bmatrix} = \begin{bmatrix} \rho \displaystyle\sum_{i=1}^N \frac{1}{(\beta + x_i)^2} - 2\sum_{i=1}^N \frac{y_i}{(\beta + x_i)^3} & -\displaystyle\sum_{i=1}^N \frac{1}{\beta + x_i} \\[2ex] -\displaystyle\sum_{i=1}^N \frac{1}{\beta + x_i} & -N\frac{\partial^2 \ln\Gamma(\rho)}{\partial \rho^2} \end{bmatrix}$$

The second derivative of $\ln\Gamma(\rho)$ is called the "trigamma" function

---

[5] Greene (2012), p. 1024

$$\frac{\partial^2 \ln L(\beta,\rho)}{\partial \rho^2} = -N \frac{\partial^2 \ln \Gamma(\rho)}{\partial \rho^2} = -N\Psi', \quad \Psi' = \text{trigamma function}$$

The information matrix uses the fact that $\lambda = 1/(\beta + x_i)$ and $E(y_i) = \rho/\lambda = \rho(\beta + x_i)$

$$\mathbf{I}(\theta) = -E(\mathbf{H}) = -E \begin{bmatrix} \dfrac{\partial^2 \ln L(\beta,\rho)}{\partial \beta^2} & \dfrac{\partial \ln L(\beta,\rho)}{\partial \beta \partial \rho} \\[3mm] \dfrac{\partial \ln L(\beta,\rho)}{\partial \beta \partial \rho} & \dfrac{\partial^2 \ln L(\beta,\rho)}{\partial \rho^2} \end{bmatrix} = \begin{bmatrix} -\rho \displaystyle\sum_{i=1}^{N} \dfrac{1}{(\beta + x_i)^2} & -\displaystyle\sum_{i=1}^{N} \dfrac{1}{\beta + x_i} \\[3mm] -\displaystyle\sum_{i=1}^{N} \dfrac{1}{\beta + x_i} & -N \dfrac{\partial^2 \ln \Gamma(\rho)}{\partial \rho^2} \end{bmatrix}$$

C.6.3 Testing the gamma distribution

In the gamma distribution probability model a hypothesis of interest is $H_0 : \rho = 1$ against $H_1 : \rho \neq 1$. If the null hypothesis is true then the model reduces to the exponential model. There are three fundamental hypothesis testing methods we can use: the likelihood ratio (LR) test, the Wald test, and the Lagrange Multiplier (LM) test.

The likelihood ratio test uses the test statistic

$$LR = 2\left(\ln L\left(\hat{\theta}_U\right) - \ln L\left(\hat{\theta}_R\right)\right) \overset{a}{\sim} \chi^2_{(J)}$$

where $\ln L\left(\hat{\theta}_U\right)$ is the log-likelihood function evaluated at the "unrestricted" maximum likelihood estimates, from the gamma probability model, $\hat{\theta}_U = \begin{bmatrix} \hat{\beta} & \hat{\rho} \end{bmatrix}'$; the term $\ln L\left(\hat{\theta}_R\right)$ is the log-likelihood function for the gamma probability model evaluated at the "restricted" maximum likelihood estimates, assuming that the null hypothesis is true. In this case $\hat{\theta}_R = \begin{bmatrix} \hat{\beta}_R & 1 \end{bmatrix}'$ where $\hat{\beta}_R$ is the estimate of β from the exponential model. In fact, $\ln L\left(\hat{\theta}_R\right)$ is the value of the log-likelihood function from the exponential model, which is the restricted model in this case. If the null hypothesis is true the *LR* test statistic is asymptotically chi-square with degrees of freedom J = number of hypotheses = 1.

The Wald test for the J linear hypotheses $\mathbf{R\theta} = \mathbf{r}$ is

$$W = \left(\mathbf{R\hat{\theta} - r}\right)'\left[\mathbf{RVR'}\right]^{-1}\left(\mathbf{R\hat{\theta} - r}\right)$$

where $\hat{\theta}$ comes from the unrestricted maximum likelihood estimation, and $\mathbf{V}$ is one of the three asymptotic covariance matrices for the maximum likelihood estimator. It has the same asymptotic distribution as the likelihood ratio *LR* test statistic if the null hypothesis is true. In the gamma probability model example $\mathbf{R} = \begin{bmatrix} 0 & 1 \end{bmatrix}$ and $\mathbf{r} = 1$, so the Wald statistic reduces to

$$W = (\hat{\rho} - 1)\mathbf{V}_{22}^{-1}(\hat{\rho} - 1) = \left[\frac{(\hat{\rho} - 1)}{\text{se}(\hat{\rho})}\right]^2$$

where $\mathbf{V}_{22}$ is the (2,2) element of $\mathbf{V}$, the variance of $\hat{\rho}$. In the case of one hypothesis the Wald test is the *t*-test statistic squared.

The Lagrange Multiplier statistic is given by

$$LM = \left[\frac{\partial \ln L(\theta)}{\partial \theta}\right]'_{\hat{\theta}_R} \mathbf{V}_R \left[\frac{\partial \ln L(\theta)}{\partial \theta}\right]_{\hat{\theta}_R}$$

This is the gradient of the log-likelihood function for the unrestricted model evaluated at the restricted maximum likelihood estimates. The middle term $\mathbf{V}_R$ is an estimate of the asymptotic covariance matrix evaluated at the restricted maximum likelihood estimates. Usually the test is formulated using the information matrix

$$LM = \left[\frac{\partial \ln L(\theta)}{\partial \theta}\right]'_{\hat{\theta}_R} \left[\mathbf{I}\left(\hat{\theta}_R\right)\right]^{-1} \left[\frac{\partial \ln L(\theta)}{\partial \theta}\right]_{\hat{\theta}_R}$$

It is convenient in some cases to use the outer product of the gradient (**OPG**) form of this test statistic,

$$LM = \left[\frac{\partial \ln L(\theta)}{\partial \theta}\right]'_{\hat{\theta}_R} \left[\hat{\mathbf{G}}'_R \hat{\mathbf{G}}_R\right]^{-1} \left[\frac{\partial \ln L(\theta)}{\partial \theta}\right]_{\hat{\theta}_R}$$

C.7 EXPONENTIAL MODEL USING SAS/IML

Using SAS/IML we can maximize the log-likelihood using the Method of Newton. First, create the data set *expmle.*

```
data expmle;
input obs inc educ;
datalines;
1          20.5      12
2          31.5      16
3          47.7      18
4          26.2      16
5          44.0      12
6          8.28      12
7          30.8      16
8          17.2      12
9          19.9      10
10         9.96      12
11         55.8      16
12         25.2      20
13         29.0      12
14         85.5      16
15         15.1      10
16         28.5      18
17         21.4      16
18         17.7      20
19         6.42      12
```

```
20        84.9       16
;

symbol1 interpol=none value=dot color=blue;
axis1 label=("educ");
axis2 label=("inc");

proc gplot data=expmle;
plot inc*educ=1 / haxis=axis1 vaxis=axis2;
title1 "Education and Income Data";
title2 "William Greene, Econometric Analysis, 7e, 2012, Table FC.1";
run;
```

C.7.1 Direct Maximization

In the following IML code we use a starting value of $\beta = 10$, and use as the convergence criterion that the change in the estimate differ by less than 1E-10. The variance estimate is obtained from the information measure.

```
proc iml;                             * invoke IML;
title;                                * turn off title;
start mle;                            * MLE module;
use expmle;                           * open data set;
read all into x var{educ};           * read x;
read all into y var{inc};            * read y;
beta = 10;                            * starting value;
crit = 1;                             * initialize convergence crit;
n = nrow(x);                          * number of obs;
result = j(10,5,0);                   * storage matrix;

/* loops to compute newton-raphson steps */

do iter = 1 to 10 while (crit > 1.0e-10);     * start do;
     logl = -log(beta+x) - y/(beta+x);        * log-l vector;
     logl = sum(logl);                        * log-l scalar;
     g = sum (-1/(beta+x) + y/((beta + x)##2));         * gradient;
     h = sum ((1/(beta+x)##2) - 2*y/((beta+x)##3));     * hessian;
     betanew = beta - inv(h)*g;                         * method of newton;
     crit = sqrt(ssq(betanew - beta));        * evaluate converge;
     result[iter,] = iter||g||beta||crit||logL;   * store iteration;
     beta = betanew;                              * update beta;
end;                                      * end do loop;

info = sum(1/(beta+x)##2);                * information;
cov = inv(info);                          * variance mle;
cnames = {iter,g,beta,crit,logl};         * names for matrix;
print ,result [colname=cnames];           * iteration history;
pnames = {beta};                          * parameter name;
```

```
print , "The Maximum Likelihood Estimates Exponential Model",
        beta [rowname=pnames];
print , "Asymptotic Variance-From Information",
        cov [rowname=pnames colname=pnames];

finish;                                          * end module;
run mle;
quit;
```

The printed output is

```
                          result
          ITER         G      BETA       CRIT       LOGL
             1 0.1837115        10  3.8313981  -88.88332
             2 0.0433387 13.831398  1.5736249  -88.47311
             3 0.0043397 15.405023  0.1951163  -88.43669
             4 0.0000561 15.600139  0.0025873  -88.43626
             5 9.6641E-9 15.602727  4.4613E-7  -88.43626
             6 1.509E-16 15.602727  7.105E-15  -88.43626
             0         0         0          0          0
             0         0         0          0          0
             0         0         0          0          0
             0         0         0          0          0


        The Maximum Likelihood Estimates Exponential Model
                           beta

                    BETA 15.602727


          Asymptotic Variance-From Information
                        cov
                           BETA

                    BETA 44.254604
```

C.7.2 Using SAS optimizers

Rather than programming the Method of Newton ourselves, it is preferable to use SAS's powerful built in optimization routines. In the command line enter **help iml**, click **Overview**, and then **Optimization Subroutines.**

Visit http://support.sas.com/documentation/onlinedoc/iml/index.html and click on **SAS/IML 9.2 User's Guide (PDF) version.** In this 1057 page document you will find a complete guide to numerical optimization in Chapter 11, "Nonlinear Optimization Examples."

The essential idea is that we write a **module** to compute the log-likelihood. This module has one input which is the parameter value and one output which is the log-likelihood function value. The **opt** = {1 1} specifies that we want to **maximize** the function (first argument) and want some printed output (second argument). The optimization routine is **NLPNRA**. Its arguments are **retcode** (positive value implies success), **beta** (the name of the solution, or optimizing value)the name of the module for the log-likelihood (in quotes), **beta0** (the starting value), and **opt** (controlling the process). The actual names of the arguments are not important, but their position in the **CALL** is important. With no further options the Method of Newton (modified with various improvements like step-size selection) uses numerical derivatives for the gradient and hessian. The analytic forms can be used if modules are written for them. The remainder of the code takes the maximum likelihood estimates and computes the three versions of the asymptotic variance.

```
proc iml;                                    * invoke iml;
start expmle;                                * start module;
use expmle;                                  * open data set;
read all into x var{educ};                   * read x;
read all into y var{inc};                    * read y;
beta0 = 10;                                   * starting value;

/* module to compute log-likelhood */
start lnl(beta) global(y,x);                 * log-likelihood;
     logl = -log(beta+x) - y/(beta+x);       * log-l vector;
     logl = sum(logl);                       * log-l scalar;
     return(logl);                           * value returned;
finish lnl;                                   * end module;

opt = {1 1};                                  * options;

/* use Newton-Raphson algorithm */
call nlpnra(retcode,beta,"lnl",beta0,opt);
print / "The Maximum Likelihood Estimates Exponential Model",beta;

/* Information matrix module */
start info(beta) global(y,x);                * information matrix;
     info = sum(1/(beta+x)##2);              * information;
     return(info);                           * value returned;
finish info;                                  * end module;

/* compute information matrix and its inverse */
info = info(beta);                              * compute information;
covmle = inv(info);                    * cov from Information matrix;
print "Asymptotic Variance-From Information measure", covmle;
/* gradient first derivative module */
start grad(beta) global(y,x);
     g = sum (-1/(beta+x) + y/((beta + x)##2));
     return(g);
finish grad;

/* Hessian module */
start hess(beta) global(y,x);
     h = sum ((1/(beta+x)##2) - 2*y/((beta+x)##3));
     return(h);
finish hess;

H = hess(beta);
cov = -inv(H);                               * cov from Hessian;
print  "Asymptotic Variance-From Hessian", cov;
```

```
start bhhh(beta) global(y,x);
        g = (-1/(beta+x) + y/((beta + x)##2));
        bhhh = g`*g;
        return(bhhh);
finish bhhh;


bhhh = bhhh(beta);
covbh3 = inv(bhhh);                        * cov from BHHH;
print  "Asymptotic Variance-From BHHH", covbh3;
finish;
run expmle;
```

The first part of the output is from the **CALL NLPNRA** command, and it shows the essential output.

```
          Newton-Raphson Optimization with Line Search

                  Without Parameter Scaling
            Gradient Computed by Finite Differences
          CRP Jacobian Computed by Finite Differences

             Parameter Estimates            1      At starting values
                    Optimization Start

 Active Constraints              0   Objective Function      -88.88332019
   Max Abs Gradient Element  0.1837114854
```

| | | | | | | Max Abs | | Slope |
| | Rest | Func | Act | Objective | Obj Fun | Gradient | Step | Search |
Iter	arts	Calls	Con	Function	Change	Element	Size	Direc
1	0	3	0	-88.47311	0.4102	0.0433	1.000	-0.704
2	0	4	0	-88.43669	0.0364	0.00434	1.000	-0.0682
3	0	5	0	-88.43626	0.000426	0.000056	1.000	-0.0008
4	0	6	0	-88.43626	7.302E-8	5.744E-8	1.000	-146E-9

```
                    Optimization Results

   Iterations                   4   Function Calls                    7
   Hessian Calls                5   Active Constraints                0
   Objective Function  -88.43626288   Max Abs Gradient Element  5.7440827E-8
   Slope of Search Direction -1.459703E-7   Ridge                    0

   GCONV convergence criterion satisfied. ◄— convergence
```

Value of objective function at convergence

The maximum likelihood estimate and variance from information measure are as before.

```
        The Maximum Likelihood Estimates Exponential Model
                            beta


                         15.602726

        Asymptotic Variance-From Information measure
                          covmle


                         44.254601
```

The asymptotic variance from the Hessian (2nd derivative) is close to result from information measure. However the variance estimate from BHHH is far from these values.

```
Asymptotic Variance-From Hessian
                cov

              46.16336

Asymptotic Variance-From BHHH
              covbh3

            100.51157
```

C.7.3 Maximum likelihood estimation of gamma model

To estimate the gamma probability model we define the parameter vector $\theta' = \begin{bmatrix} \beta & \rho \end{bmatrix}$. The structure of this code is similar to that for the exponential model, but the modules are a bit more more complex because this is a two parameter problem. We use some specialized functions from SAS **lgamma, digamma** and **trigamma** which are the log of the gamma function, and its first and second derivatives, respectively.

```
start gammamle;
use expmle;
read all into x var{educ};
read all into y var{inc};
theta0 = {-4  4};                    * starting values;
pnames = {beta,rho};                 * names for parameters;

/* module for log-likelihood                          */
/* LGAMMA returns the natural log of the gamma function */
start lnl(theta) global(y,x);
      beta = theta[1];
      rho = theta[2];
      logl = -rho*log(beta+x) - lgamma(rho) - y/(beta+x)
           + (rho-1)*log(y);
      logl = sum(logl);
      return(logl);
finish lnl;

/* module for the gradient */
/* DIGAMMA returns ratio of derivative of gamma function over
         gamma function */
start grad(theta) global(y,x);
      g = j(1,2,0);
      beta = theta[1];
      rho = theta[2];
      g[1] = sum (-rho/(beta+x) + y/((beta + x)##2));
      g[2] = sum (-log(beta+x) - diGamma(rho) + log(y) );
      return(g);
finish grad;

/* module for hessian */
/* TRIGAMMA returns derivative of the DIGAMMA function */
```

```
start hess(theta) global(y,x);
      n = nrow(y);
      beta = theta[1];
      rho = theta[2];
      h11 = sum ((rho/(beta+x)##2) - 2*y/((beta+x)##3));
      h22 = -n * triGamma(rho);
      h12 = -sum (1/(beta+x));
      h = (h11||h12)//(h12`||h22);
      return(h);
finish hess;

/* module for information matrix */
start info(theta) global(y,x);
      n = nrow(y);
      beta = theta[1];
      rho = theta[2];
      h22 = -n * triGamma(rho);
      h12 = -sum (1/(beta+x));
      i11 = -rho*sum(1/(beta+x)##2);
      info = - ((i11||h12)//(h12||h22));
      return(info);
finish info;

/* module for BHHH  */
start bhhh(theta) global(y,x);
      beta = theta[1];
      rho = theta[2];
      g1 = (-rho/(beta+x) + y/((beta + x)##2));
      g2 = (-log(beta+x) - diGamma(rho) + log(y) );
      gmat = g1||g2;
      bhhh = gmat`*gmat;
      return(bhhh);
finish bhhh;

opt = {1 0};
call nlpnra(retcode,theta,"lnl",theta0,opt);
loglu = lnl(theta);                      * save for future use;

/* compute hessian, information matrix & BHHH */
H = hess(theta);
info = info(theta);
bhhh = bhhh(theta);

/* alternative covariance matrices */
cov = -inv(H);                           * cov from Hessian;
covmle = inv(info);                      * cov from Information matrix;
covbh3 = inv(bhhh);                      * cov from BHHH;

print / "The Maximum Likelihood Estimates-Gamma Model",
        theta[colname=pnames];
```

```
print ,, "Asymptotic Covariance Matrix-From Hessian",
        cov[rowname=pnames colname=pnames];
print ,, "Asymptotic Covariance Matrix-From Information Matrix",
        covmle[rowname=pnames colname=pnames];
print ,, "Asymptotic Covariance Matrix-From bhhh",
        covbh3[rowname=pnames colname=pnames];

finish gammamle;
run gammamle;
```

The maximum likelihood estimates and the 3 versions of the asymptotic covariance matrix are:

```
The Maximum Likelihood Estimates-Gamma Model
                    theta
                 BETA        RHO


               -4.718504 3.1508962


     Asymptotic Covariance Matrix-From Hessian
                     cov
                 BETA        RHO


        BETA 5.4991445  -1.65285
        RHO   -1.65285 0.6308518

  Asymptotic Covariance Matrix-From Information Matrix
                    covmle
                 BETA        RHO


        BETA 4.9003183 -1.472864
        RHO  -1.472864 0.5767542

     Asymptotic Covariance Matrix-From bhhh
                    covbh3
                 BETA        RHO


        BETA 13.372205 -4.321744
        RHO  -4.321744 1.5372233
```

C.7.4 Testing the gamma model

Continuing after the **gammamle module** we can implement the various tests of the null hypothesis $\rho = 1$. In the **waldtest** module we perform the Wald test using each of the three versions of the asymptotic covariance matrix.

```
start waldtest;
rho = theta[2];                         * parameter of interest;

/* Wald test using variance from -inv(H) */
wald = (rho-1)*inv(cov[2,2])*(rho-1);
pval = 1 - probchi(wald,1);
critval = cinv(.95,1);
```

```
/* Wald test using variance from inv(info) */
waldmle = (rho-1)*inv(covmle[2,2])*(rho-1);
pvalmle = 1 - probchi(waldmle,1);

/* Wald test using variance from inv(bhhh) */
waldbh3 = (rho-1)*inv(covbh3[2,2])*(rho-1);
pvalbh3 = 1 - probchi(waldbh3,1);

print / "Wald tests of rho=1" ,,
        "Wald test using -inv(Hessian) for covariance matrix"
         ,, wald critval pval;

print "Wald test using inv(Info) for covariance matrix"
        ,, waldmle critval pvalmle;

print "Wald test using inv(bhhh) for covariance matrix"
        ,, waldbh3 critval pvalbh3;
finish waldtest;
run waldtest;


                   Wald tests of rho=1

       Wald test using -inv(Hessian) for covariance matrix

               wald     critval       pval

          7.3335048 3.8414588 0.0067681

       Wald test using inv(Info) for covariance matrix

               waldmle    critval    pvalmle

           8.021362 3.8414588 0.0046229

       Wald test using inv(bhhh) for covariance matrix

               waldbh3    critval    pvalbh3

          3.0095526 3.8414588 0.0827751
```

Using the BHHH covariance matrix we fail to reject the null hypothesis at the 5% level of significance.

For the likelihood ratio test we must quickly obtain the restricted estimates from the exponential model.

```
start rmle;                              * start module;
use expmle;                              * open data set;
read all into x var{educ};               * read x;
read all into y var{inc};                * read y;
beta0 = 10;                              * starting value;
```

```
/* module to compute log-likelhood */
start lnlr(beta) global(y,x);               * log-likelihood;
      logl = -log(beta+x) - y/(beta+x);     * log-l vector;
      logl = sum(logl);                     * log-l scalar;
      return(logl);                         * value returned;
finish lnlr;                                * end module;

opt = {1 0};                                * options;
call nlpnra(retcode,betar,"lnlr",beta0,opt);
finish rmle;                                * end RMLE module;
run rmle;
```

For the test, recall that we computed the value of the log-likelihood function at the unrestricted maximum likelihood estimates in the module **gammamle**. The value is called **loglu**.

```
start lrtest;
rho = 1;                            * hypothesized value;
thetar = betar//rho;               * restricted estimate theta;
loglr = lnl(thetar);               * restricted log-L;
lr = -2*(loglr-loglu);             * Likelihood Ratio test;
pval = 1 - probchi(LR,1);
critval = cinv(.95,1);
print / "Likelihood ratio test rho=1" ,,
        "unrestricted log-likelihood = " loglu ,,
        "restricted Log-likelihood   = " loglr ,,
        "Results of LR test",, LR critval pval;
finish lrtest;
run lrtest;
```

```
                Likelihood ratio test rho=1

                                          loglu
        unrestricted log-likelihood =  -82.91605

                                          loglr
        restricted Log-likelihood   =  -88.43626

                   Results of LR test

                   lr    critval      pval
            11.040429 3.8414588 0.0008915
```

Finally, the LM test module.

```
start lmtest;

/* calculations for LM test using Hessian */;
g = grad(thetar);                  * gradient at rmle;
g = g`;                            * g transpose;
h = hess(thetar);                  * hessian at restricted mle;
lm = g`*(-inv(h))*g;               * LM test;
```

```
critval = cinv(.95,1);                  * critical value;
pval = 1 - probchi(LM,1);               * pvalue;
print / "Lagrange multiplier tests of rho=1" ,,
        "Results of LM test using Hessian",, lm critval pval;

/* calcuations for LM using information matrix */
info = info(thetar);                    * info at restricted mle;
covmle = inv(info);                     * covariance matrix;
lmmle = g`*covmle*g;                    * LM test using info mat;
pvalmle = 1 - probchi(lmmle,1);
print "Results of LM test using Information matrix",,
        lmmle critval pvalmle;

/* calcuations for LM using BHHH matrix */
bhhh = bhhh(thetar);                    * outer product gradient;
covbh3 = inv(bhhh);                     * cov from BHHH;
lmbh3 = g`*covbh3*g;                    * LM test;
pvalbh3 = 1 - probchi(lmbh3,1);
print "Results of LM test using BHHH",, lmbh3 critval pvalbh3;
finish lmtest;
run lmtest;

quit;
```

```
              Lagrange multiplier tests of rho=1

              Results of LM test using Hessian

                    lm     critval        pval
              5.1161604 3.8414588   0.023704


          Results of LM test using Information matrix

                  lmmle    critval     pvalmle
              4.782547 3.8414588   0.0287496

              Results of LM test using BHHH

                  lmbh3    critval     pvalbh3
              15.686792 3.8414588   0.0000747
```

INDEX